BEHAVIOR AND MEDICINE

Dedicated to
my sons Joshua and Jeremiah,
who have given direction,
meaning and purpose to my life.
– DW

To my father, Roscoe V. Stuber, MD,
who taught me what it means to be a physician.
– MS

Cover art:
Death and Life by Gustav Klimt (1910/15)
Oil on canvas, 180.5 × 200.5 cm. Leopold Museum, Vienna, Austria. Used by permission.

Gustav Klimt was one of the most remarkable artists of the 20th century. This particular *fin de siècle* painting, one of the editors' favorites, was awarded first prize in a world exhibition held in Rome in 1911. It is allegorical and depicts the human condition in a direct and dramatic way. One sees all the major facets of life clustered on the right side of the canvas – most notably birth, love, sex, sorrow, and suffering – and Klimt uses the left side of the canvas to remind us that death is always waiting at the end of the ride. The viewer is reminded of William James' poignant comment, "Life is a banquet, but there is always a skeleton staring in at the window." Most physicians will deal with many of the themes represented in Klimt's painting during their personal and professional lives.

BEHAVIOR AND MEDICINE

FIFTH EDITION

Editors

DANNY WEDDING, PhD, MPH
Associate Dean and Professor of Psychology
California School of Professional Psychology
Alliant International University
San Francisco, CA

MARGARET L. STUBER, MD
Jane and Marc Nathanson Professor of Psychiatry
Semel Institute for Neuroscience and Human Behavior
David Geffen School of Medicine
University of California – Los Angeles
Los Angeles, CA

HOGREFE

Library of Congress Cataloguing-in-Publication Data

is available via the Library of Congress Marc Database
under the LC Control Number 2010924865

Canadian Cataloguing in Publication Data

Behavior and medicine / editors, Danny Wedding, Margaret L. Stuber. — 5th ed.

Includes bibliographical references and index.
ISBN 978-0-88937-375-4.

1. Medicine and psychology—Textbooks.   2. Sick—Psychology—Textbooks.
3. Health behavior—Textbooks.
I. Stuber, Margaret L., 1953–   II. Wedding, Danny

R726.5.B45   2010   155.9'16   C2010-901964-4

© 2010 by Hogrefe Publishing

PUBLISHING OFFICES
USA: Hogrefe Publishing, 875 Massachusetts Avenue, 7th Floor, Cambridge, MA 02139,
               Tel. 866 823-4726, Fax 617 354-6875, E-mail customerservice@hogrefe-publishing.com
Europe: Hogrefe Publishing, Rohnsweg 25, 37085 Göttingen, Germany
               Tel. +49 551 49609-0, Fax +49 551 49609-88, E-mail publishing@hogrefe.com

SALES AND DISTRIBUTION
USA: Hogrefe Publishing, Customer Services Department, 30 Amberwood Parkway, Ashland, OH 44805
               Tel. 800 228-3749, Fax 419 281-6883, E-mail customerservice@hogrefe.com
Europe: Hogrefe Publishing, Rohnsweg 25, 37085 Göttingen, Germany
               Tel. +49 551 49609-0, Fax +49 551 49609-88, E-mail publishing@hogrefe.com

OTHER OFFICES
Canada: Hogrefe Publishing, 660 Eglinton Ave. East, Suite 119–514, Toronto, Ontario M4G 2K2
Switzerland: Hogrefe Publishing, Länggass-Strasse 76, CH-3000 Bern 9

Hogrefe Publishing
Incorporated and registered in the Commonwealth of Massachusetts, USA, and in Göttingen, Lower Saxony, Germany

The Editors have undertaken every effort to identify those holding rights in the literary and art works cited in this volume and to obtain their permission for this use. If you should be aware of any additional rights not covered by the credits given, please contact the publisher at one of the addresses given on this page.

Printed and bound in the USA
ISBN 978-0-88937-375-4

Cover design: Daniel Kleimenhagen, Designer AGD

Foreword

In medical education we spend a disproportionate amount of time teaching the biomedical model at the expense of other important areas – areas that contribute to both the art and science of medicine. There is no specialty in medicine that is untouched by the behavioral and social sciences, dimensions that regularly challenge our way of thinking about medicine and disease. While it is attractive, and in some ways comforting, to many students to be able to reduce disease to a series of biomedical events, this is not currently possible and it may never be possible. In fact, health care without the richness of the behavioral perspective is not medicine at all.

Once a cancer, a mental illness, or even diabetes has been diagnosed, the power of our treatments to alter the outcome is influenced by a mélange of behavioral and social factors. A disease, or more accurately an illness, in one culture, place, and time may be perceived as completely normal in a different setting. People suffer "illnesses" that are life events, while doctors diagnose and treat "diseases" that are pathological events. **Illnesses** are experiences filtered through a myriad of social, economic, cultural, and educational lenses that each impact normal function. **Diseases** are pathological abnormalities of the normal function and structure of organs and cells. Biomedical science places a large emphasis on disease, while medicine is the blending of treating both illness and disease – requiring mastery of both art and science.

The practice of medicine involves far more than an understanding of scientific information and facts. It is also about culture – not only the culture of our patients but the culture of our profession: "the culture of medicine." Medicine is certainly its own culture with a requisite body of knowledge shared by a large group, a common set of beliefs and values that are accepted with great thought and passed along from generation to generation: special symbols, rituals, meanings, hierarchies, roles, special possessions, unique aspects of language, and behaviors derived from social learning. The culture of modern medicine influences how we think about essential human experiences including race, gender identity, conception, human development, sickness and disease, social responsibility, aging, dying, and spirituality. At times our medical thinking does not mesh with that of our patients. Conditions like menopause, Asperger's syndrome, AIDS, and suicide can have profoundly different cultural meanings. Medicine is reductionistic. To many these diseases are understood as disorders of hormones, neurochemicals, and viral agents, while others understand them as disorders of spiritual influences, behaviors, and complex interplays between biology, environment, and culture.

While humans share many biological similarities, health care is an area in which understanding human differences is essential. We often do not understand why some groups have a disproportionate burden of illness, but it is likely that genetics, environment, and behavior interact to create this havoc. Add to this social stigma, physical disability, access to health care, and economic deprivation, and you can partially explain the large disparities in US health care. Only with an understanding of these social and behavioral issues can we provide appropriate medical care.

These are not easy times to practice medicine or to learn medicine. There are some who brag that America has the best health care system in the world. I think the data argue otherwise. A quick look at any newspaper reminds us that far too many of us have no access to health care, much of the health care we do provide is not evidence-based and of poor quality, the rate of medical errors is unacceptably high, and the chance of surviving, say, a cancer depends as much on your skin color and ethnicity as it does on your health insurance. Despite spending more per person on health care than any other nation on the planet we are ranked in the middle of all nations in terms of major indicators of health status (longevity, infant mortality, immunization rates, etc.). There are regions such as South Central Los Angeles, Oakland, Detroit, and the Bronx, where men have shorter life expectancies than those in Hanoi or Cape Town. A baby born in Sacramento is now less likely to survive than one born in Beijing or Havana. Access to our system of health care is not fair—in 2010 we still had 45 million uninsured and 23 million underinsured, and most of these people were working Americans. All this might be fine if Americans were satisfied with the quality and access to their health care, but we are not – at least not compared to people living in the United Kingdom, Japan, France, or Germany. So there is an urgent need for change that will address these aspects of heath and will alter both the practice of medicine and medical education itself.

Biomedicine, behavior, and social factors (social, cultural, political, and economic forces) are inextricably linked to health outcomes. *Behavior & Medicine* does a wonderful job of introducing the health sciences student to this complex interface. It is only through understanding these critical interplays that we can open our minds and design interventions for patients that are achievable and acceptable and truly act in our patients' best interest. According to Piaget we learn through two processes, namely, assimilation (importing new information into an existing belief system) and accommodation (changing our belief system based on new information). For many, this book offers the chance to understand a more complete picture of the art and science of medicine and to develop a more inclusive belief system that will lead to a more meaningful practice of medicine and permit better patient care.

Students will likely be frustrated that in much of clinical care there is no easy answer. When a person presents with a complex illness linked to a dysfunctional family, deep-rooted cultural beliefs, destructive behaviors, and limited access to health care, there are often no MRI scans or lab tests that offer a quick diagnosis. Diagnosis requires a good fund of knowledge, careful listening (both for what is spoken and also for what is not spoken), and a health-care team that works well together. To properly care for patients there will need to be an understanding of culture, religion, economics, power, education, the human spirit, psychology, and biomedicine. *Behavior & Medicine* begins the process of helping us to understand these important linkages between behavior and disease.

Michael Wilkes, MD, PhD
Professor of Medicine
University of California, Davis
Sacramento, CA

Foreword

Behavior, a living organism's actions in response to stimuli, is the cause, the goal, and the reason for everything. Our DNA, RNA, proteins, cells, organs, systems, memories, and experiences, in the context of our surroundings, cause our actions that sustain and reproduce ourselves, help sustain our fellow humans and—if we humans behave especially well—other species. When our brains (the organs of our behaviors) die, we are said to die, even while our hearts beat and machines breathe for us.

Our behaviors determine whether we are good doctors. Our professional behaviors are responses to the behaviors of our patients, fellow professionals, and others with whom we work. Our behaviors extend and shorten our lives—sometimes dramatically. Our symptoms and often our signs of illness are expressed by behaviors. Our personalities and our individuality are reflected as behaviors. The objectives and competencies of our medical educations are themselves behaviors. In its 2004 report, *Improving Medical Education: Enhancing the Behavioral and Social Science Content of Medical School Curricula,* the Institute of Medicine (IOM) of the National Academy of Sciences states unequivocally that "approximately half of all causes of morbidity and mortality in the United States are linked to behavioral and social factors."

So behavior is pretty important. And everyone who practices medicine must know a ton about it; be competent in it; and even be "sort of" expert in it. Personally, behavior is the only thing that interests me, and every doctor, medical student, and smart person I have ever met is interested in it.

So it is always a joy when a splendid book on behavior is published, in this instance the fifth edition of Danny Wedding and Margi Stuber's *Behavior and Medicine.* The chapters in the book are a response to the IOM and the Accreditation Council of Graduate Medical Education (ACGME) recommendation that "medical students should be provided with an integrated curriculum in the behavioral and social sciences throughout the 4 years of medical school" and the recommendation that medical students demonstrate competency in the following domains:
- Mind-body interactions in health and disease
- Patient behavior
- Physician role and behavior
- Physician-patient interactions
- Social and cultural issues in health care, and
- Health policy and economics

The IOM and ACGME also recommends that the U.S. Medical Licensing Examination (USMLE) should include increased behavioral and social science content on its certifying examinations.

Like its predecessors, this edition is written crystal clearly, and is a very enjoyable, up-to-date "read" filled with wise and crucial information. Each of its chapters is theoretically sound, clinically precious, and unusually helpful in preparing for clinical practice and USMLE Step 1 and Step 2 examinations. As in the previous editions, the literary quotes and artwork give the book a unique texture. All the authors are experts and fine writers.

Frederick S. Sierles, MD
Professor and Director of Medical Student Education
in Psychiatry and Behavioral Sciences
and inaugural member, Master Teacher's Guild,
Rosalind Franklin University of Medicine and Science
North Chicago, IL

Preface

We were pleased and gratified with the enthusiastic reception of the last edition of *Behavior and Medicine*. The book has now been read by tens of thousands of medical students, and most of these former students are now practicing medicine. One likes to think that the clinical practice of these students will be influenced by the book, and that patient care will be a little more humane, a little more gentle, and perhaps a little more effective because some of the ideas in *Behavior and Medicine* took root.

The two editors share a passion for convincing medical students that understanding human behavior is absolutely critical to their future practice, and we have been happy and congenial collaborators.

Hogrefe publishes both in the U.S. and internationally, and they are able to market *Behavior and Medicine* to relevant groups of students around the world. Many medical schools in non-English speaking countries use English language texts, and *all* physicians need to be conversant with the basic principles of behavioral science covered in *Behavior and Medicine*. We're proud that *Behavior and Medicine* has been used to educate medical students in Canada, Great Britain, Australia, New Zealand, South Africa, Thailand, Scandinavia, and dozens of other countries as well as the original target group—medical students preparing to take the United States Medical Licensing Examination.

We have been pleased with the warm reception *Behavior and Medicine* has received in a number of health professions outside of medicine. Although the book clearly targets medical students and has the avowed aim of helping these students pass the behavioral science portion of the USMLE, professors in training programs in nursing, dentistry, public health, social work, and psychology have adopted the book and found its content germane to their students. In addition, a number of physician assistant training programs have used *Behavior and Medicine* as a core text.

All of the sample questions at the end of the book, designed to help students prepare for the Behavioral Science questions on the National Boards, have been updated and revised to reflect the current USMLE format. Dr. Stuber has spent hundreds of hours preparing these questions, and we believe they offer a useful preview of the kind of behavioral science questions that will be encountered on the USMLE. The student who reads the book and reviews the sample questions should have little trouble with the Behavioral Science section of the USMLE examination; in fact, one of our most gratifying personal rewards as editors and medical educators has been the numerous students who have reported that they "aced" the Behavioral Science section of the USMLE after studying *Behavior and Medicine*.

We have highlighted all **key words, names,** and **phrases** by putting them in bold type, and we have emphasized all the *key concepts* that we think are likely to show up on the USMLE by putting them in italics. Thus, a student who does not have time to read each chapter (and, regrettably, this may include all too many medical students) can still prepare for class examinations and the Behavioral Science portions of the USMLE by reviewing the bold and italicized text. This is not an ideal situation, but we have taught medical students long enough to realize it is both pragmatic and necessary.

We have worked hard to make this new edition *clinically relevant*, and almost all chapters include a Case Study illustrating the application of the principles being discussed. Every case draws on the clinical experience of the authors and illustrates how the principles of the chapter can be applied in a clinical setting.

Multiple interlocking themes link each chapter in the fifth edition. One theme is the simultaneous *poignancy and beauty of the transitions of life*. As children we were filled with awe and fascination; later we worked through the turmoil of adolescence; still later we each trembled at the touch of a lover. Some of us will be fortunate enough to grow old with someone we care about deeply. All of us will die. Those students who take time to appreciate the majesty of this unfolding will be better physicians and more effective healers.

A second theme of the book is the *salience of the sense of self*. Every cell in the body changes with age and time, but a continuing awareness of self, a continuity of personal identity, significantly shapes and influences our behavior.

A third theme is reflected in the title of *Behavior and Medicine*. Morbidity and mortality are profoundly affected by how we behave; what we eat, drink, and smoke; whom we choose as our sexual partners; how often we exercise; and whether we take medicines as prescribed. Most people are aware of the factors affecting their health and yet continue to engage in maladaptive and harmful behavior. Only the most naive health-care provider sees his or her job as simply telling patients how they *should* behave.

A fourth theme, reflected especially in the section of the book dealing with health care policy, is that *the U. S. health-care system is inefficient, inequitable, and inadequate*. As practitioners, we have witnessed first hand how the corporatization of health care and the rise of for-profit medicine has changed the way health care is delivered and financed in the United States. I am ashamed to live in a wealthy country that stands alone among developed nations in not providing health care for all of her citizens; however, we are encouraged that as this book goes to press, the United States appears to be on the cusp of genuine health care reform.

A final theme of the book is the *brevity of life and the certainty of death*. The art and poems that illustrate every chapter in the book often portray scenes or descriptions of death. Paradoxically, awareness and acceptance of death can make life richer, fuller, and more meaningful.

It has been profoundly rewarding for us to have a role in the education of several thousand medical students. We hope we have affected their lives; they have clearly shaped ours.

Danny Wedding   **Margaret L. Stuber**
San Francisco, CA   Los Angeles, CA

ACKNOWLEDGMENTS

One of the pleasures in editing a book is the brief opportunity to thank the many people who contribute to it.

We especially appreciate the chapter authors who were patient with our frequent queries and multiple revisions of their work. Every contributor is a seasoned medical educator, and all are prominent authorities in their respective fields.

The book continues to reflect the values and priorities set by the book's original advisory board. The members of the advisory board and their original university affiliations were John E. Carr, PhD (University of Washington), Ivan N. Mensh, PhD (University of California at Los Angeles), Sidney A. Orgel, PhD (SUNY, Health Sciences Center at Syracuse), Edward P. Sheridan, PhD (Northwestern University), James M. Turnbull, MD (East Tennessee University), and Stuart C. Yudofsky, MD (University of Chicago).

We benefited tremendously from comments made by our colleagues in the Association of Directors of Medical School Education in Psychiatry (ADMSEP), the Association of Psychologists in Academic Health Centers (APAHC), and the Association for the Behavioral Sciences and Medical Education (ABSAME). Many of these individuals use *Behavior and Medicine* as a text, and a significant number are chapter authors in the current edition. These colleagues made dozens of helpful suggestions that have been incorporated in this new edition.

Rob Dimbleby, our editor at Hogrefe Publishing, has become a wonderful friend and valued collaborator. We truly appreciate his support, good judgment, clear thinking, and consistent good humor.

Vicki Eichhorn did more than anyone else to help with the fifth edition. She is an extraordinary assistant, and Danny Wedding would not be half as productive without her. We especially appreciate the extra efforts she took to ensure that we met the production deadlines set by Hogrefe. Vicki lead a small army of support staff at the Missouri Institute of Mental Health (MIMH) who cheerfully pitched in with the numerous administrative tasks associated with publication of the new edition. We also gratefully acknowledge the cheerful and meticulous contributions of Marleen Castaneda and Debra Seacord in the preparation of the final version of this edition, without whom Margaret Stuber would be hopelessly disorganized.

Danny Wedding   **Margaret Stuber**
dwedding@alliant.edu   mstuber@mednet.ucla.edu

Contributors

Adam Aréchiga, PsyD, DrPH, CHES, CNS
Assistant Professor
Department of Psychology
Loma Linda University
Loma Linda, CA

Debra Bendell Estroff, PhD
Professor
Fielding Graduate University
Clinical Professor
David Geffen School of Medicine at UCLA
Los Angeles, CA

Jonathan Bergman, MD
Department of Urology
David Geffen School of Medicine at UCLA
Los Angeles, CA

Pilar Bernal, MD
Child and Adolescent Psychiatrist
Kaiser Permanente
Adjunct Clinical Associate Professor
Department of Psychiatry
Stanford University
Palo Alto, CA

Sarah J. Breier, PhD, RN
Associate Director
MU Center for Health Ethics
Adjunct Assistant Professor of Nursing
University of Missouri
Columbia, MO

Howard Brody, MD, PhD
John P. McGovern Centennial Chair in Family Medicine
Director, Institute for the Medical Humanities
University of Texas Medical Branch
Galveston, TX

George R. Brown, MD
Professor of Psychiatry, Chief of Psychiatry
James H. Quillen VA Medical Center
Professor and Associate Chairman
Department of Psychiatry
East Tennessee State University
Johnson City, TN

Brenda Bursch, PhD
Professor of Clinical Psychiatry & Biobehavioral
Sciences, and Pediatrics
Clinical Director, Pediatric Psychiatry Consultation-
Liaison Service
Semel Institute for Neuroscience and Human Behavior
David Geffen School of Medicine at UCLA
Los Angeles, CA

Salvador Ceniceros, MD
Private practice
Plymouth, IN

Steven Cody, PhD
Professor
Department of Psychiatry & Behavioral Medicine
Joan C. Edwards School of Medicine
Marshall University
Huntington, WV

Randall Espinoza, MD, MPH
Clinical Professor
Department of Psychiatry and Biobehavioral Sciences
David Geffen School of Medicine at UCLA
Director, Geriatric Psychiatry Fellowship Training Program
Medical Director, ECT Program
Associate Director, UCLA Center on Aging
Los Angeles, CA

Beverly J. Field, PhD
Assistant Professor
Departments of Anesthesiology and Psychiatry
Washington University School of Medicine
Division of Pain Management
St. Louis, MO

Timothy W. Fong, MD
Assistant Clinical Professor of Psychiatry
Co-Director, UCLA Gambling Studies Program
Director, UCLA Addiction Psychiatry Fellowship and
Clinic
Semel Institute for Neuroscience and Human Behavior
at UCLA
Los Angeles, CA

Kenneth E. Freedland, PhD
Professor of Psychiatry
School of Medicine
Washington University
Saint Louis, MO

Mary L. Hardy, MD
Medical Director
Simms/Mann-UCLA Center for Integrative Oncology
Jonsson Comprehensive Cancer Center
David Geffen School of Medicine at UCLA
Los Angeles, CA

Donald M. Hilty, MD
Director, Rural Program in Medical Education
Professor and Vice-Chair of Faculty Development
Department of Psychiatry and Behavioral Sciences
University of California, Davis
Sacramento, CA

Ka-Kit Hui, MD, FACP
Professor and Director
UCLA Center for East-West Medicine
Department of Medicine
David Geffen School of Medicine at UCLA
Los Angeles, CA

Peter Kunstadter, PhD
Senior Research Associate
Program for HIV Prevention and Treatment (PHPT)
Chiang Mai, Thailand

Joseph D. LaBarbera, PhD
Associate Professor
Department of Psychiatry
Vanderbilt University
School of Medicine
Nashville, TN

Russell F. Lim, MD
Clinical Professor
Director of Diversity Education and Training
Department of Psychiatry and Behavioral Sciences
University of California, Davis
School of Medicine
Davis, CA

John C. Linton, PhD, ABPP
Professor and Vice-Chair
Department of Behavioral Medicine
West Virginia University School of Medicine
Charleston, WV

William R. Lovallo, PhD
Professor of Psychiatry and Behavioral Sciences
University of Oklahoma Health Sciences Center
Director, Behavioral Sciences Laboratories
VA Medical Center
Oklahoma City, OK

Francis G. Lu, MD
Luke & Grace Kim Endowed Professor in Cultural Psychiatry
Director of Cultural Psychiatry
Associate Director of Residency Training
Department of Psychiatry & Behavioral Sciences
UC Davis Health System
Sacramento, CA

Gregory Makoul, PhD
Chief Academic Officer
Senior Vice President for Innovation and Quality Integration
Saint Francis Hospital and Medical Center
Professor of Medicine
University of Connecticut School of Medicine
Farmington, CT

James Randy Mervis, MD
Clinical Professor of Psychiatry and Biobehavioral Sciences
David Geffen School of Medicine at UCLA
Chief, Geropsychiatry Consultation Services
Greater Los Angeles Veterans Affairs Health System, Sepulveda Campus
Sepulveda, CA

Todd E. Peters, MD
Fellow in Child and Adolescent Psychiatry
Alpert Medical School of Brown University
Bradley Hospital
East Providence, RI

Jeannine Rahimian, MD, MBA
Assistant Clinical Professor
Department of Obstetrics and Gynecology
David Geffen School of Medicine at UCLA
Los Angeles, CA

John E. Ruark, MD, FACP
Adjunct Clinical Associate Professor of Psychiatry
Stanford University School of Medicine
Stanford, CA

Steven C. Schlozman, MD
Co-Director, Medical Student Education in Psychiatry,
Harvard Medical School
Associate Director, Child and Adolescent Psychiatry Residency, MGH/McLean Program in Child Psychiatry
Staff Child Psychiatrist, Massachusetts General Hospital
Assistant Professor of Psychiatry, Harvard Medical School
Lecturer in Education, Harvard Graduate School of
Education
Cambridge, MA

Adit V. Shah
Research Assistant
Mindsight Institute
Los Angeles, CA

Daniel J. Siegel, MD
Clinical Professor
UCLA School of Medicine
Co-Director, Mindful Awareness Research Center
Psychiatry and Biobehavioral Sciences
Semel Institute for Neuroscience and Human Behavior
Los Angeles, CA

Madeleine W. Siegel
Research Assistant
Mindsight Institute
Los Angeles, CA

David M. Snyder, MD, FAAP
Medical Director, Assessment Center for Children
Exceptional Parents Unlimited, Fresno, CA
Associate Clinical Professor, Department of Pediatrics
UCSF School of Medicine
Fresno, CA

Denise Stephens, MA, LMFT
Rater Manager
CNS Network, Inc.
Garden Grove, CA

Carl D. Stevens, MD, MPH
Clinical Professor of Medicine
Director of Curriculum Development
Office of the Dean, Division of Educational
Development and Research
David Geffen School of Medicine at UCLA
Los Angeles, CA

Margaret L. Stuber, MD
Jane and Marc Nathanson Professor of Psychiatry
Semel Institute for Neuroscience and Human Behavior
David Geffen School of Medicine at UCLA
Los Angeles, CA

Robert A. Swarm, MD
Chief, Division of Pain Management
Professor of Anesthesiology
Washington University School of Medicine
St. Louis, MO

Harsh K. Trivedi, MD
Executive Medical Director and Chief-of-Staff
Vanderbilt Psychiatric Hospital
Associate Professor of Psychiatry
Vanderbilt Medical School
Nashville, TN

Danny Wedding, PhD, MPH
Associate Dean and Professor of Psychology
California School of Professional Psychology
Alliant International University
San Francisco, CA

Peter B. Zeldow
Private practice
Chicago, IL

Poetry Credits

The following poems are reproduced with permission of the respective rights holders.

Chapter	Poem	Permission
Chapter 1 (p. 19)	*Seizure* by Jeanne Murray Walker	From *Poetry* (1986). Used with permission.
Chapter 3 (p. 33)	*Only Stars* by Duncan Darbishire	Used with permission.
Chapter 3 (p. 40)	*Emily Drowned* by Duncan Darbishire	Used with permission.
Chapter 4 (p. 51)	*The Discovery of Sex* by Debra Spencer	From *Pomegranate.* © Hummingbird Press. Reprinted by permission.
Chapter 5 (p. 64)	*The Pleasures of Old Age* by Michael Blumenthal	From *Against Romance* by Michael Blumenthal, copyright © 1987 by Michael Blumenthal. Used by permission of Viking Penguin, a division of Penguin Group (USA) Inc.
Chapter 7 (p. 96)	*The Knitted Glove* by Jack Coulehan	Used with permission.
Chapter 9 (p. 126)	*Two Suffering Men* by Eugene Hirsch	Used with permission.
Chapter 12 (p. 157)	*Unrequited Love* by Elizabeth Bartlett	Used with permission.
Part 3 (p. 166)	*Doctor's Row* by Conrad Aiken	From *Collected Poems,* Oxford University Press, copyright © 1970 by Conrad Aiken. Reprinted by permission of Brandt and Hochman Literary Agents, Inc.
Chapter 14 (p. 181)	*Peau d'Orange* by Marcia Lynch	Used with permission.
Chapter 15 (p. 193)	*Patients* by U. A. Fanthorpe	Used with permission.
Chapter 16 (p. 201)	*But Her Eyes Spoke Another Language* by Duncan Darbishire	Used with permission.
Chapter 21 (p. 260)	*Rock of Ages* by Jack Coulehan	Used with permission.
Part 5 (p. 266)	*The Hands* by John Stone	From *Renaming the Streets* © 1985, Louisiana State University. Reprinted by permission.

Contents

PART 1: MIND-BODY INTERACTIONS IN HEALTH AND DISEASE

PART 2: PATIENT BEHAVIOR

PART 3: THE PHYSICIAN'S ROLE

PART 4: PHYSICIAN-PATIENT INTERACTIONS

PART 5: SOCIAL AND CULTURAL ISSUES IN HEALTH CARE

PART 6: APPENDICES

Mind-Body Interactions in Health and Disease

1 Brain, Mind, and Behavior

Daniel J. Siegel, Madeleine W. Siegel, & Adit V. Shah

To speak, to walk, to seize something by the hand! . . .
To be this incredible God I am! . . .
O amazement of things, even the last particle!
O spirituality of things!
I too carol the Sun, usher'd or at noon, or as now, setting;
I too throb to the brain and beauty of the earth . . .

  WALT WHITMAN
  Song at Sunset
  Leaves of Grass

What does a professional in the art of healing need to know about the science of the brain and the nature of the mind? How does knowledge about the brain and its influence on behavior enrich clinical practice? Why should a practitioner who works to help alleviate the suffering of others invest the time and energy into understanding the brain and behavior when there are so many other details to learn about illness and treatment? The simple answer to each of these questions is that in order to understand how to treat people, we need to understand how patients experience their illness, how they perceive their encounter with you, and their behaviors that may support a path toward healing. At the heart of a person's inner experience and outer behavior is the mind.

One dictionary definition states that the mind is "considered as a subjectively perceived, functional entity, based ultimately upon physical processes but with complex processes of its own: it governs the total organism and its interaction with the environment." The mind is often viewed as synonymous with the psyche, the soul, the spirit, and the intellect. From this perspective, the mind is not distinguished from the "heart," and thoughts are not separated from feelings. In this chapter we will explore the ways in which we can view the mind as the core of a person's evolving identity. The ways in which that person responds in an interview, a diagnostic test, or a discussion about potential illnesses, and his or her specific attitude and approach to treatment are each a function of that person's mind.

One aspect of the mind is a process that regulates the flow of energy and information. Your mind is taking in the information of these words at the moment you read them. You are investing energy in the reading of this sentence, and the layers of information processing beneath your awareness are making linkages to ideas and facts you've thought of in the past. In fact, most of the flow of energy and information—the essence of our minds—is beneath our awareness. Mental activity, such as feeling and thinking, can enter conscious awareness and subsequently be shared within our own conscious mind and with other people. When the important feelings and thoughts in our nonconscious mental lives remain out of the spotlight of conscious attention, they can still influence our decisions, reactions, and behaviors. This is true whether we are professionals or patients.

In this chapter we'll be offering you a way to think about the mind at the center of human experience. The benefit for you in reading through this chapter will be that you'll gain a new perspective into the minds of others, and perhaps even your own. This skill can be called "mindsight" and permits us to see and shape the internal world. Research has now clearly shown that knowing your own mind can help you in many important ways in your work as a clinician. Because of the necessary brevity of this discussion, only major concepts will be highlighted. If you are interested in further reading you may find the works cited in the Suggested Readings to be an excellent way to learn more about this fascinating topic.

The separation of psychology from the premises of biology is purely artificial, because the human psyche lives in indissoluble union with the body.

  C.G. JUNG

BRAIN AND MIND

You can see from the definition given above that the mind has the interesting quality of being "based ultimately upon physical processes" but that it also has "complex processes of its own." The mind is a subjective entity, meaning that we each experience within us the process of mind that may not be wholly available to objective, and especially quantitative, analysis. The reason we need to pay attention to subjective mental life is that objective research shows us that physical health is directly related to mental well-being. The subjective nature of the mind and the mind's well-being are, in fact, some of the most important contributors to physiological well-being. For example, studies have quantitatively proven that how patients focus their attention during a medical treatment, such as "light therapy" for psoriasis, has a profound impact on the outcome of medical interventions. People who practice a form of attending to the present moment, called **mindful awareness**, have been shown to have improved immune function. Physicians trained in mindful awareness also have diminished stress from their intense medical practices. The focus of attention literally means how you regulate the flow of information—i.e., how you regulate your mind. Our mental life directly affects medical states—such as those of the heart, immune system, and lungs.

You may be wondering how a "subjective entity" such as the mind can affect the physical processes of the cardiovascular system or the activity of the immune system. One way to explore this relationship between mental function and physiology is to take a look at the connection between the information and energy flow of the mind and the physical activity of the brain.

Many disciplines of science are concerned with understanding the mind. One of those fields is the fascinating area of neuroscience, the study of the structure and function of the nervous system. Branches of this field study specific aspects of neural functioning, such as how the activity of the brain is associated with thinking, emotion, attention, social relationships, memory, and even moral decision-making. Taken as a whole, the field of neuroscience has been exploding with new insights into the correlation between the brain's function and internal mental processes affecting the outward expression of behaviors. The numerous and expanding insights into brain-mind correlations have direct relevance for the clinical practitioner.

> Future generations, paying tribute to the medical advances of our time, will say: "Strange that they never seemed to realize that the real causes of ill-health were to be found largely in the mind."
>
> LORD PLATT
> Professor of Medicine, Manchester, UK
> *British Medical Journal*

Neural Activity Correlates with Specific Mental Processes

While science demonstrates correlations between activity in the brain and the subjective experience of the mind we can only say at this point that these are associational findings. In other words, *neural activity in one area of the brain at one point in time correlates directly with mental activity of a certain type.* Here's one example: When you look at a picture of, say, the Golden Gate Bridge, we know that the posterior part of your brain, in the occipital lobe of the neocortex, will become active. You may already know that this back part of your brain has been called the **visual cortex** because of this association. We even know that if you *remember* the visual scene of the Golden Gate Bridge, that same area of the cortex will be activated. In fact, remembering anything you've seen will activate that posterior region.

But here's a new finding that puts a slight twist on what we should call that area. It's been known for some time that blind people use the occipital cortex to process what they feel with their fingers, including the raised letters of Braille. Recently a study examined the brain function of people who volunteered to be blindfolded for five days and use only their fingers to feel their way around the controlled environment in which they lived during that period of time. Without the input of their optic nerves during that sightless period, the input from their fingers became dominant in influencing the activity of their occipital lobes, and their occipital lobes were activated whenever they touched something with their fingers.

What does this mean? This study proves that *the brain is an ever-changing, dynamic organ that is extremely responsive to experience.* Also, as this study reveals, the precious information-processing real estate of the brain is open to "the most competitive bidder." In the study just described, the now dominant input from the fingers to sense the spatial world came to be "processed" in the occipital lobe. In fact, some researchers have suggested that the visual cortex be renamed the "spatial cortex." For us, the important issue is that our five senses and where we focus our attention directly shape the neural architecture and function of the brain.

The overly simplistic view that the mind is "just the activity of the brain" can mislead us into reductionistic thinking and unhelpful conclusions. In the example given, our minds can be understood to harness any neural machinery necessary to create a three-dimensional perspective and image of the spatial world. In fact, a range of studies has demonstrated that how we harness the flow of energy and information—how our mind functions with the focus of attention—can directly shape the connections in the brain. Some people even believe that the mind "uses the brain" to create whatever it needs. In this chapter, we embrace this open dimension of the associational and bi-directional influence of mind-brain relationships.

Mental Experience Occurs As Neurons Become Active

Mental processes occur when neurons fire. Whenever you think of "experience," try translating that into the idea of "neural firing in the brain." That is to say, every time you have an experience, there is specific activity occurring in your brain where only certain clusters of neurons are becoming active. The benefit of this thinking is that it helps you understand aspects of how the mind works. The firing of neurons can lead to a cascade of associated firings because the brain is an intricate, interwoven set of web-like neural circuits. Specific regions in the brain are devoted to specific forms of mental processing, such as spatial perception for the occipital regions, as we discussed earlier. Knowing a bit about brain anatomy can therefore inform us about the architecture of our mental lives. The more we can understand the underlying structure and function of our internal, mental lives the more we can understand ourselves and patients. In fact, studies of the doctor-patient relationship reveal that such an understanding of others' minds, called **empathy**, is one of the more important factors in determining the extent to which clinicians can help others with their difficulties.

To understand the mind in a deeper way, we are turning toward the brain for scientifically based insights that can build our capacities to be empathically sensitive to the subjective lives of others. Here we are starting with the principle that mental processes emerge as neurons fire in specific areas of the brain. What does **"neural firing"** really mean? Recall that the basic cell of the nervous system is the neuron. This long, spindly cell reaches out to other neurons to connect at a space called the **synapse**. Synaptic junctions are generally at the receiving neurons' **cell body** or its **dendrite**. The electrical current, known as an **action potential**, passing down the length of the neuron, leads to the release of neurotransmitters from the pre-synaptic neuron to influence the firing of the post-synaptic neuron. Ultimately the summation of the excitatory versus inhibitory transmitters at the synaptic cleft will determine if the downstream (post-synaptic) neuron will in turn send an action potential down its membrane to influence further neural firing.

Here are the numbers that illuminate the fascinating complexity of the whole process: *The average neuron in your brain is connected directly to about ten thousand other neurons, and the estimated twenty to one hundred billion neurons in your brain allow for trillions of connections in a spider-web of soft neural tissue in your skull.* When we add to this the trillions of supportive cells, called glia, that have

Head Stripped From Top to Show Ventricles and Cranial Nerves *J. Dryander (1537). Courtesy of the National Library of Medicine. Brain size and cranial capacity have not been demonstrated to be meaningfully related to intelligence in humans.*

uncertain but likely contributions to information flow in the brain, then we can see how complex the neural processes are that influence our mental lives.

Neurons That Fire Together, Wire Together

Before this seems too overwhelming, remember that there are several principles that make this intricate anatomy actually quite understandable, interesting, and relevant for clinical practice. One of these is our third general principle: *neurons that fire together, wire together.*

Described long ago, this underlying property of the nervous system has now been explored in great detail. The "linkages" among neurons, the synaptic connections interweaving numerous neurons to one another, is what we mean by the saying that "neurons wire together." The first part of the principle, "Neurons that fire together," means that when we have an experience the brain becomes activated in various regions. When neurons are activated at a given time, the connections among those simultaneously active neurons are strengthened. This is why if you've had an experience (remember, "neural firing patterns activated") say, of hearing a certain song when you've felt very happy, in the future you are likely to have the same feeling (neural firing of joy) when you hear that same song (neural firing in response to the sounds of the music). This is how learning and memory work. Neurons that fire together at one time are more likely to fire together in the future because the synaptic connections that link them together have become strengthened due to the experience.

In fact, it is these synaptic connections that shape the architecture of the brain, making each of us unique. Even identical twins will have subtle differences between their brains that are created by the unique experiences that shape the synaptic connections that directly influence how the mind emerges from the activity of the brain. Our inner mental life—a life of thoughts, feelings, and memories—is directly shaped by how our neurons connect with one another—which in turn has been directly shaped by our own experiences. In addition, our external behavior is directly shaped by the synaptic connections within our skulls. In short, the brain shapes both our minds and our behavior.

The Mind Can Shape the Connections in the Brain

The fascinating relationship between brain and mind goes even deeper than the one-way street of the brain leading to mental activity and behavioral output. A fourth principle reveals the bi-directionality of mental process and neural firing: *the mind shapes the connections in the brain*. Recall that an important aspect of the mind is the regulation of energy and information flow. Also consider the fact that the mind has "processes of its own," beyond the physical processes of the brain from which it emerges. Researchers have clearly established the mind's power to shape neural firing patterns.

Try this out: think of what you had for dinner last night. Now try to imagine, using visual imagery, what you'll have for dinner tonight. In this simple exercise, you have chosen (with a little suggestion from these words, but ultimately of your own volition) to use your mind in ways that involve aspects of memory and visualization in your occipital region. Now consider this question: did your mind cause your brain to become active in these areas, or did your brain activate first followed by your mind? The force of mental power to activate the brain gives us a profoundly important insight into how our minds can directly shape the physical state of our bodies. In this exercise, the information flowing from these printed words to your eyes directly influenced your mind—the flow of energy and information within you.

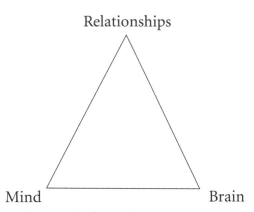

FIGURE 1.1 A "triangle of well-being" that reveals how energy and information flow is shared in empathic relationships, regulated by a coherent mind, and flows through the neural connections of an integrated brain and its extensive interconnections throughout the embodied nervous system.

It is helpful in life and in clinical work to realize that a person's "mental will" and "intention" are both mental processes that can shape how neurons fire. In turn, how neurons fire shapes how they alter their connections with each other. As those neural connections change, the patterns of the mind—ways of thinking, feeling, and behaving—can change. In other words, the mind directly shapes the physical properties of the brain which in turn alter how our bodies, including the brain, function. These somatic and neural changes in turn can directly influence how our minds function, and how we feel and how we interact with others. As we'll see, the mind and the brain are profoundly social.

One way of envisioning the connections among mind, brain, and interpersonal relationships is to view them within a triangle of energy and information flow. The mind is the regulation of that flow, the brain is the mechanism shaping that flow, and relationships are how we share energy and information flow with one another.

Consciousness Permits Choice and Change

This raises the fifth and final principle for this section: *With consciousness comes the possibility of choice and change.* Neural connections in the brain allow for certain patterns of thinking, feeling, and behaving to be enacted. In the course of normal living, these mental activities are often on "automatic pilot," and are likely shaped largely by the neural connections that then directly influence mental processes. With conscious awareness, however, something new appears to enter this otherwise automatic self-fulfilling brain prophecy. With focal attention–the focusing of awareness onto a process–the power of the mind can be engaged to

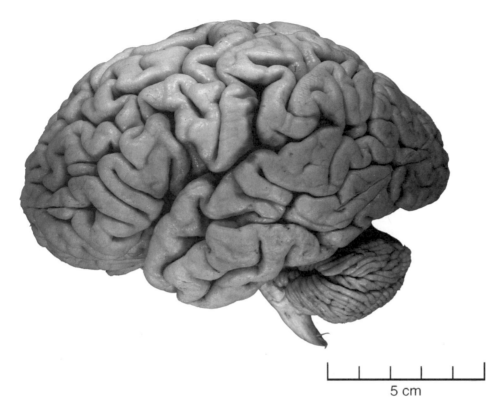

FIGURE 1.2 The Human Brain. Courtesy of the University of Wisconsin-Madison Brain Collection (see also www.brainmuseum.org). *Few of us pause to reflect on the majesty of the human brain, or the extent to which it is an integral part of what we call the self.*

5 cm

actually alter old habits of behaving, emotionally responding and thinking. With consciousness there is the possibility to "wake up" and change old patterns. Studies reveal how carefully paying attention may even lead to the secretion of neurochemicals that actually promote neuroplasticity—how the brain changes in response to experience. With practice in living *intentionally,* these new mentally activated neural firings can create the changed neural wiring that will make these new patterns of mind more likely to occur, even automatically. In other words, what initially required deliberate conscious attention to change old patterns can become a new and less energy-consuming set of behaviors in the future. This is the essence of new learning and how it becomes embedded in new synaptic linkages in the brain itself.

EXPERIENCE AND GENES SHAPE THE BRAIN: RELATIONSHIPS, CULTURE AND LIFELONG DEVELOPMENT

As you've seen in our earlier discussion, experience not only involves neural firing, but it also shapes neural connections. This may come as a surprise to many who thought that genes solely dictate the structure of the brain. The fact is that both genes and experience shape the brain's structural properties—the ways that neurons are synaptically connected to each other. About one third of our genes di-

rectly determine neural connections, and another one sixth indirectly influence synaptic connections. That's one half of our genome influencing neural architecture. In the womb, genes play a major role in shaping the basic foundation of the brain. Even after birth, genes continue to influence how our neurons link up to one another. However, both the environment in the womb and our experiences after birth influence the synaptic linkages within our brains. When a baby is born, the distinct neural patterns emerging from these pre-birth influences contribute to what is called our innate **temperament**. These constitutional patterns of responding and perceiving can make some of us shy and others outgoing. Some may be quite sensitive to stimuli and become overwhelmed easily, while others thrive with intense sounds and sights.

As we grow our temperamental features interact with our experiences in shaping the person that we become—what some call our **personality**. One of the earliest types of experiences that shape us is our relationship with our caregivers. Known as **attachment**, these early child-caregiver experiences are thought to directly shape the circuitry of the brain responsible for how a child comes to regulate his emotions, govern his thoughts, and engage with other people. But while early attachment is extremely important, *the brain proves to be open to change throughout the lifespan.* Understanding the impact of early life experiences on how you grew up has scientifically been proven to be an important aspect of how the mind can "wake up" and *not* repeat unhelpful learned patterns from the past. These attachment studies resulted in two important findings: (1)

It is never too late to make sense of one's early life experiences and become the person one may truly want to be and (2) without such understanding, individuals often live on "automatic pilot" and repeat sub-optimal ways of relating to others within their personal and professional lives.

Given that the brain continues to make new connections and possibly even grow new neurons throughout its lifespan, *each of us can use the power of our mind to alter the connections in our brains*. The experiences we continue to have within the specific culture in which we live can continue to shape how our brains are changing in response to experience. Becoming aware of the impact of these cultural and personal experiences on our continually changing brains can help us understand the ways in which our external environment shapes our internal world.

Becoming aware of ourselves and waking up means becoming conscious of the power of the mind to make choices that may have previously been considered impossible. Neither our genes nor our early life experiences permanently restrict our minds. The key for clinicians is learning how to teach patients scientifically grounded facts about how central the mind is in shaping its own pathway.

CENTRAL ORGANIZING PRINCIPLES

Self-Regulation

These are powerful ideas that are not easily taken in and understood by either professionals or patients. Fortunately there are a few central principles that can help organize these ideas about brain, mind, behavior, experience, and physiology. One of these principles has to do with *self-regulation*. In physiology we learn about the process of **homeostasis**, how the body maintains its various systems in balance for optimal functioning. Whether it is the renal system, the cardiovascular system, or the respiratory system, we can examine how homeostasis is maintained to achieve a state of health and well-being. Whenever a system is stressed, homeostasis is challenged. Some stressors lead to high-energy processes that strive to regain homeostasis; other stressors can lead to overwhelming imbalance and devastation that can cause a massive shutting down of normal functioning and even death without intensive intervention.

The brain also functions as a self-regulatory system that achieves balance by using a number of domains of functioning. In the simplest terms, the brain moves toward neural homeostasis by alternately using internal and external factors. Internal components of the nervous system would include the synaptic connections in the brain itself, or the level of firing in particular regions. External factors of the nervous system would involve input from the environment, such as altering the signals being received from other people. For example, a newborn who is overwhelmed with stimuli from the external environment will fall asleep in order to maintain balance. In other words, the mind can utilize its different internal and interpersonal capacities to alter its functioning in order to maintain equilibrium in the long-run. Homeostasis of the body parallels equilibrium of the mind. The concept of **self-regulation** implies that this equilibrium is achieved by altering internal elements, such as how you think or feel, and external interpersonal elements, such as the people you communicate with during a stressful period. Self-regulation in our lives entails modifying both individual and relational elements to achieve equilibrium in mind, brain, and relationships.

Out of the Balanced Flow: Chaos or Rigidity

Our brain achieves balance by directing the flow of energy and information within its neural firing patterns to optimize functioning. One way to describe this neural equilibrium is to use the metaphor of a river. Each bank represents the extreme poles of brain balance: one bank is a state of chaos, the other bank is a state of rigidity. Down the middle between rigidity and chaos flows the river of well-being which can be defined as harmony. In this harmonious state, one is flexible, adaptive, coherent, energized, and stable. Using the acronym **FACES** can be used to remember these five qualities of neural equilibrium and mental well-being.

The neurons encased in the skull achieve equilibrium through a process called **neural integration**. Integration means the linking together of differentiated components into a functional whole. Neural integration is what the brain naturally strives to do. When a brain is integrated, it is able to achieve the most flexible, adaptive, and stable states of functioning, the "FACES" flow of the mind and brain that occurs when information and energy are flowing in a harmonious manner. When the brain cannot achieve such integration, a person can experience states of either chaos or rigidity. The brain may become inflexible, maladaptive, incoherent, depleted of energy, and unstable. You may notice such a stressed neural or mental system in yourself or others by observing how internal mental processes, such as thoughts or feelings, or external behaviors, such as reactions to others, occur in response to the extremes of rigidity or of chaos.

As a general starting point, this central organizing principle of self-regulation emerging from the brain's natural drive toward integration helps us see when the everyday challenges of life become overwhelming and when stress has produced a mental pathway that is rigid or chaotic. As a professional, the river metaphor can help you understand how you, your colleagues, or your patients may be adapting to life's daily challenges to neural homeostasis and mental well-being.

THE BRAIN IN THE PALM OF YOUR HAND

We've now seen that behavior emanates from the neural firing patterns of the brain and other areas of the nervous system in creating the mind. Mental processes emerge from the firing patterns of particular clusters of neurons. Knowing a bit about these neural regions can be helpful in getting a sense of the relationships between brain and behavior. We've explored the notion that mental well-being and neural equilibrium flow like a harmonious, coherent river with rigidity and chaos on either side. In this flow, however, there are twists and turns as the body attempts to integrate its differentiated components to achieve these pathways. As we explore the different regions of the brain, keep in mind that this neural integration involves how differentiated, specialized areas are brought together as a functional whole. This is what neural integration is—the ways that the brain links disparate areas together as a functional whole. When integration is achieved, equilibrium is possible and that state of a coherent and harmonious mind can occur. When integration is impaired, the mind moves into rigid or chaotic states that are not adaptive.

The Logical Left and Nonverbal Right Hemisphere

One way that we can see the nature of how the overall mental system functions is through examining the emotional state of a person. Emotions involve subjective internal feelings, physiological changes in the body, and often, but not always, nonverbal communication. Nonverbal expressions include eye contact, facial expressions, tone of voice, gestures, posture, timing, and intensity of responses. You can remember these seven nonverbal signals by pointing to your eyes, circling your face, pointing to your voice box, gesturing with your hands, pointing to your body, and then pointing to your watch. Interestingly, *these nonverbal expressions are both sent and received by the nonverbal right hemisphere of your brain.* In contrast, words are most often sent and received by your left hemisphere, the seat of logic and linear thinking. The right hemisphere, however, appears to be more closely linked to our emotional limbic areas that register autobiographical memory and receive an integrated map of the body, including input from the heart and intestines.

The Subcortical Brainstem and Limbic Regions

In addition to having two halves of the brain that are separated in the cortex and the limbic areas but are connected via the corpus callosum, we also have other regions worthy of knowing a bit about. If you put your thumb in the middle of your palm and fold your fingers over the top, you'll have a pretty handy model of the brain and a useful way to visualize some major brain regions. Your wrist is the representation of the spinal cord coming up your back and connecting to the brain at the base of the skull. The first of three major areas we'll be examining in this model is the brainstem, located in the middle of the palm of your hand. The brainstem carries out basic physiological regulation functions, such as heart rhythms and sleep-wake cycles. The brainstem is also responsible for the survival reflexes of fight, flight or freeze in reaction to threat. The next major region is represented by your thumb and is the limbic area. (Ideally we'd have two thumbs, a left and right limbic area). In this region are the areas of the brain responsible for generating emotion, motivation, the appraisal of the meaning of experiences, and attachment relationships. Evolved in our mammalian heritage, these limbic areas include the **amygdala**, responsible for the fear response, and the **hippocampus**, which is involved in certain forms of memory.

The Cortex

If you fold your fingers over the limbic thumb area, you'll find the location of the **cortex**, which also developed during our journey into mammalian life. This "outer bark" of the brain is in general responsible for complex representations, such as perception and thinking. In general, the posterior lobes of the cortex carry out perception. The frontal lobes, located from the second-to-last knuckles to your fingertips, represent the regions responsible for motor action and planning as well as more complex thinking and reasoning. The front most part of this area is represented from your last knuckles down to your fingernails and is called the prefrontal cortex. As you'll see, the prefrontal cortex is important for many functions relevant for understanding the connections among mind, brain, and behavior.

The Prefrontal Cortex

The prefrontal cortex can be divided into two areas: a side part and a middle part. Naturally the whole brain could be divided ultimately into at least one hundred billion parts, the neurons in the brain. But the brain's numerous neurons are clustered into groupings that work together as differentiated regions that carry out specialized functions. As we've seen, the brain strives toward integration of these differentiated areas. The prefrontal regions' anatomic location actually makes them quite important in connecting separate areas to each other. The side part, called the **dorsal lateral**

prefrontal cortex, is important in creating working memory. Acting like the "chalkboard of the mind," this side region links its activity with other activated areas to create the experience of conscious awareness. When we say "put [something] in the front of your mind," we are inviting the dorsal lateral prefrontal cortex to link its activity with whatever that something is, whether an abstract thought to a bodily sensation.

The middle part of the prefrontal cortex is also in a unique position to integrate widely separated areas into a functional whole. Take a look at where the middle two fingernail regions rest in your hand-model of the brain. Notice how this middle prefrontal cortex area "touches everything" just as this area of the brain links the brainstem, limbic areas, and cortex into a functional whole. As we'll see below, this area also links the input of the body and the input from the social world, binding together somatic, cerebral and social functions into an integrated process.

The middle part of the prefrontal cortex consists of the regions called the **orbitofrontal cortex**, located just behind the eyes, the **anterior cingulate**, just behind it, and the **ventrolateral** and **medial prefrontal cortex** behind the fore-

head to the side and front. Together, these four regions carry out very important integrative functions. Here is a list of nine functions mediated by the middle prefrontal regions extracted from the research literature on the human brain:

1. *Bodily Regulation:* This area regulates the two branches of the autonomic nervous system, and it keeps the sympathetic ("accelerator") and parasympathetic ("brakes") branches in balance.
2. *Attuned Communication:* When we lock eyes with someone and align our own state of mind with another person, this resonant state involves the activation of the middle prefrontal cortex.
3. *Emotional Balance:* The lower limbic areas generating emotion are able to achieve enough arousal for creating meaning in life but are kept from becoming excessively aroused and disabling a person's information processing. This is achieved by the inhibitory action of the fibers from the middle prefrontal regions that extend to the limbic areas such as the amygdala.
4. *Response Flexibility:* Our ability to take in multiple channels of stimuli and pause before acting long enough to

---

CASE EXAMPLE: Neurobiology and Personality

Accounts of a documented brain injury suffered by one Phineas Gage in 1848 when an iron pole was accidentally blasted through his head, irrevocably damaging his prefrontal and orbitofrontal cortex, revealed how the prefrontal regions of the brain play a crucial role in mediating our personality (he miraculously survived this massive injury, but his personality altered). This middle prefrontal region, as we've seen above, also plays an essential role in facilitating our healthy relationships with others—and even with ourselves—as the following case reveals.

Barbara was a forty-year old mother of three who sustained substantial trauma to the area just behind her forehead when her car was hit head-on by a drunk driver; the lesions followed the upper curve of her car's steering wheel. This area is a profoundly integrative region of the brain, linking widely disparate brain regions to each other. The important functions of the middle prefrontal area discussed above—from attuning to others and balancing emotions, having insight and acting morally—were compromised following the accident, subsequent brain surgery, and rehabilitation.

Cortical activity creates neural firing patterns that enable us to form representations—or "maps"—of various aspects of our world. Maps serve to create an image in our minds. For example, when we take in the light reflected from a bird sitting in a tree, our eyes send signals back to our occipital cortex, and the neurons there fire in certain patterns that permit us to have the visual picture of the bird.

The prefrontal cortex, the most damaged part of the frontal lobe of Barbara's brain, makes complex representations that permit us to create concepts in the present, think of experiences in the past, and plan and make images about the future. The prefrontal cortex is also responsible for the neural representations that enable us to make im-

ages of the subjective mental life of others and of ourselves. These representations of our mental world can be called "mindsight maps."

After Barbara emerged from her coma, her impairments seemed to result in a new personality. Some of her habits, like what she liked to eat and how she would brush her teeth, remained the same. There was nothing significantly changed in how her brain mapped out these basic behavioral functions. But the ways in which she thought, felt, behaved, and interacted with others were profoundly altered. Like Phineas Gage, Barbara's personality was changed forever.

Above all, Barbara seemed to have lost the very map-making ability that would enable her to honor the reality and importance of her own or others' subjective inner lives. Her mindsight maps were no longer forming amidst the now jumbled middle prefrontal circuitry upon which they depended for their creation. This middle prefrontal trauma had also disrupted communication between Barbara and her family—she could neither send nor receive the connecting signals enabling her to join minds with the people she had loved most. Barbara had lost the vital capacity for mindsight that would allow her family members to "feel felt" by her, to feel that their minds were inside of Barbara's own mind. While she could still see the objective, outside world well, the inner world of the mind had disappeared from her sense of what existed.

These prefrontal areas damaged after Barbara's accident play a vital role in integrating the various regions of the brain. This important function of neural integration brings together the processing of emotional, social, and bodily inputs in the creation of patterns of perception, thinking, and behavior that we call personality. Neural integration is also what enables us to see one another's minds—and to connect with one another in empathic, caring relationships.

choose from a range of adaptive responses is mediated by this region.

5. *Extinction of Fear:* Recent studies have revealed that the middle prefrontal region sends **GABA** (the inhibitory neurotransmitter **gamma amino butyric acid**) fibers downward to the fear-generating amygdala to inhibit the amygdala generated fear response.

6. *Empathy:* Putting yourself in the mental perspective of another person, seeing through another's eyes, involves middle prefrontal activity.

7. *Insight:* Having the capacity to reflect on your past, link it to the present, and anticipate and plan for the future are middle prefrontal activities.

8. *Morality:* Studies of individuals with damage to the middle prefrontal region reveal that moral reasoning appears to be processed via the integrative circuitry of this region. When the prefrontal cortex is damaged, people may become amoral, no longer able to consider the larger good for others when thinking through a problem.

9. *Intuition:* The input of our body's organs, such as the physiological state of the intestines and heart, find their way to the middle prefrontal regions. These organs appear to have neural processors surrounding them that act as a kind of "peripheral brain" in which our gut and heart's responses actually process information about the social and personal worlds. Intuition may involve paying attention to these important nonverbal sources of knowledge.

How Attunement Promotes Neural Integration and Well-Being

The nine functions carried out via the integrative fibers of the middle prefrontal regions reveal that our brains are involved in linking together bodily, social, and mental processes into one set of integrated functions. Research suggests that secure parent-child relationships early in life may promote at least the first eight of these listed middle prefrontal functions. Mindful awareness practices, such as mindfulness meditation, also promote many of these same integrative functions. What might loving relationships between parent and child and mindful awareness share in common? With mindful awareness what is created is a state of attending to moment-by-moment experience without being swept up by judgments and reactivity. This is a form of "internal attunement." With empathic relationships, a parallel kind of acceptance but this time directed toward another person, just as he or she is, is part of the "interpersonal attunement" at the heart of secure attachment and healthy relationships in general. A range of research suggests that these inner and interpersonal forms of attunement promote the growth of the integrative fibers of the

> **BOX 1.1** The Importance of Self-Care for Primary-Care Physicians
>
> A recent study demonstrated the benefits of mindfulness for primary care physicians. A continuing medical education course was provided for clinicians to improve well-being and decrease burnout. During a period of two months, practicing physicians met once a week to learn mindfulness meditation, reflective communication, and self-awareness skills. During these sessions, the practicing doctors met in small groups to discuss their thoughts and feelings regarding patient care and to reflect on the value of being a clinician. After a 10-month follow-up phase, the clinicians experienced improved attitudes toward their patients and an enhanced sense of well-being.
>
> Learning the skills of mindful awareness and the importance of reflection can save clinicians from disabling stress and emotional burnout. Remembering the personal meaning of your clinical profession can also help you maintain a sense of purpose and value in your work. Before caring for others, one must first learn to care for oneself. This study demonstrates the importance of internal attunement, self-awareness, and self-care for the health of practicing physicians.

brain—especially in the prefrontal region. When working with patients, empathy and compassion will help promote this integrative sense of harmony and well-being. And, when relating to yourself as a physician, learning to be mindful has been shown to help prevent burnout, reduce stress, and increase empathy for patients, and self-compassion. Practicing mindfulness techniques can help keep your self-regulating and integrating prefrontal circuits well functioning.

Repairing Ruptures: The High Road and the Low Road

As the case of Barbara above reveals, neurological damage to the middle prefrontal region may result in impairment of a range of the functions. In addition, it appears that under conditions of emotional stress many people may be at risk of moving from this integrated, "higher mode" or high road of functioning in which these nine processes are intact to a nonintegrated, "lower mode" or low road of functioning in which some or all of these processes may be temporarily impaired. You can picture this movement from the high road to the low road in your hand model by taking your hand-brain and lifting up your cortical fingers to expose the thumb-limbic areas. With intense emotion it may be possible to flood the middle prefrontal cortex and temporarily disable the integrative fibers of this region from performing their important functions. In such a lower mode of processing, the brain produces a rigid or chaotic state of mind. This temporary "flipping your lid" can in-

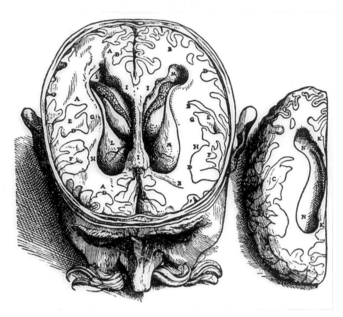

Horizontal View of the Brain Exposing the Lateral Ventricles Woodcut from Andres Vesalius' anatomy text *De humani corporis fabrica* (1543) . Courtesy of the National Library of Medicine.

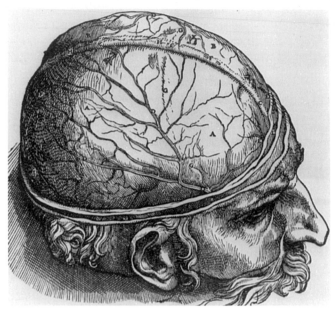

Head With Scalp Exposed to Show Dura Mater and Middle Cerebral Artery Woodcut from Andres Vesalius' anatomy text *De humani corporis fabrica* (1543). Courtesy of the National Library of Medicine.

volve any or all of the following: loss of regulation of bodily functions, disconnection from others, emotional imbalance causing rigid shutting down or chaotic flooding, inflexible knee-jerk reflexes instead of adaptive thoughtful responses, loss of empathy for others, lack of insight, return of deep fears, being out of touch with intuition, and amoral behavior.

Temporarily losing our coherent minds when our brains become nonintegrated can be both confusing and frightening to ourselves and to those around us. This can be seen in how we "flip our lids" under conditions of stress and lose the integrative balance and coordination of our middle prefrontal region. Understanding the emotional triggers that activate such low road states can be an important step in making sense of such sudden shifts in an otherwise well-functioning individual. Whether it happens in yourself, your colleagues, or your patients, seeing the human aspect of such common lower mode activities can be an important step in bringing compassion to the experience. Each of us can lose our minds; what is important is to make the repair with others that is necessary to reestablish an open, trusting connection. Such repair is one of the key ingredients to healthy relationships of all sorts, from friendships or child-parent attachments to the relationship between patient and doctor.

In addition to repairing relationships that may have been affected by low road experiences, it is also important to try to understand the triggers that may have caused them in the first place. Examining the experiences of the person in the hours and days before the event may be important to establish a background state of mind of the person. Trying to determine the trigger is akin to finding the "straw that broke the camel's back," the final piece of an emotional puzzle that destroyed the middle prefrontal area's ability to cope. Often, triggers are related to the context of what was occurring in a person's life and relationships. Feeling frustrated, misunderstood, helpless, threatened or ignored are common emotional states that may trigger low road states. When we are reactive, we may move rapidly into a fight-flight-freeze mode mediated by our brainstem's survival reflexes. Even as physicians we may be prone to entering such states under stress. Sometimes these emotional states are related to things from the past stored in various forms of memory. We'll turn now to learning about how the brain remembers to understand more about brain-behavior relationships.

THE NATURE OF MEMORY

The Brain is an Association Organ

Memory is the way in which an experience changes the probability of how our brains function in the future. There are many layers of memory that are important for a health-care professional to understand in order to help patients with their present difficulties. Memory will not only shape how a patient comes to you with their current problems but it will also influence how they take what you offer them and use it in the future. In many ways, memory links a person's past, present, and future together into one integrated process. Your role as a health care provider will be more effective if you understand how to help your patients integrate these three dimensions of their lives into one process that will offer them the best chance of living a healthy lifestyle, accepting clinical recommendations and following through with interventions that positively influence their well-being.

Each time we have an experience, neurons fire. When neurons become active, the synaptic connections among those that are firing can be strengthened. New synapses can form, or old ones can be made stronger. Other aspects of synaptic change can include alterations in the amount of neurotransmitters released and changes in the number of post-synaptic receptors. These changes are the ways in which experiences alter the structure and function of the brain.

We now are also learning that the brain throughout the lifespan appears to be able to grow new neurons in response to new experiences. Studied primarily in the hippocampus, these new neurons are created by the continual division of stem cells in the brain. This cellular growth is called **neurogenesis**, and it is another way in which experience alters brain structure and function. Yet another way of changing the functional connectivity among neurons is to grow the **myelin** sheath along the long axonal lengths, increasing conduction speed by one hundred times and diminishing the refractory period between firings by thirty times. Myelin increases the functional connection among synaptically linked neurons.

Overall, the process through which experience alters brain structure is called **neuroplasticity**. When the action potential flows down the axonal membrane leading to release of neurotransmitters at the synaptic junction that links that neuron to another neurons' dendrites and cell bodies, genetic material in the nucleus of the pre-synaptic neuron is sometimes activated. With the unraveling of DNA, the transcription into RNA, and finally the translation into protein at the ribosomes, new protein building blocks for cellular growth can be formed. Proteins are an essential component of long-term changes in neuronal connections.

Memory is all about how new associations among neurons are made based on earlier firing patterns. This area of study enables us to deepen our understanding of how past experiences can positively change the way a person behaves in the future. Understanding some of what we know now about neuroplasticity can help you as a professional optimize the nature of your interaction with a patient by helping them remember your clinical recommendations.

Short and Long Term Memory

When we are aware of something in the moment we can link that current information to the side part of our prefrontal cortex and have the mental experience of something being in "our mind's eye" or on the "chalkboard of our mind." In this moment of awareness we can have short-term memory for the things upon which we are focusing our attention. This **short-term memory** may last less than a minute without further rehearsal and does not involve DNA transcription, RNA translation or protein synthesis. Such short-term memory appears to involve a temporary functional associational enhancement, likely via neurotransmitter release and neural firing processes. With this moment-to-moment awareness we pay attention to sensory, bodily, and mental activity that can be recalled seconds or even minutes later. We can be aware of our senses bringing in information from the outside world or our **interoception** bringing in data from our body. We can also become aware of our self-reflection enabling us to focus on our minds' thoughts, feelings, or memories.

Short-term memory is also-called immediate memory or working memory; it enables us to deal with a limited number of items. When elements on our chalkboard of working or immediate memory are sorted through and categorized and chunked together, they then can be stored in a more long-term form that does require translation, transcription, and protein synthesis. However, if a patient is in a state of high arousal and distress, elements in working memory may not be processed into long-term storage. Excessive anxiety and fear can hinder the integration of short term working memory into the long-term memory.

Long-term memory always involves gene activation and protein production which alter the structural connections among neurons. As the healthy brain is open to change across the lifespan, memory can continue to occur in a long-term manner if the mind of the person continues to take on new experiences that promote neuroplasticity. Optimal levels of arousal are needed to convert this new information into long-term memory. Too little arousal, such as boredom and other instances of under-stimulation, can lead to impaired memory integration into long-term storage. Excessive arousal, such as in instances of distress and shock, can also impair long-term processing. This provides a way of understanding the familiar clinical situation in which a patient does not process what the doctor says. A state of distress may directly impair the patient's capacity to hold on to details of the diagnosis and/or treatment because the DNA, RNA and protein synthesis processes were hindered by the release of the stress hormone **cortisol**.

Being open to creating new connections, keeping neuroplasticity alive and engaging in new experiences are important for all of us as we age. New approaches to keeping the mind young involve mental exercises that stimulate the brain in new ways. Aerobic exercise, novelty, and the careful focus of attention all promote neuroplasticity. The neurobiology of this makes sense: our brains are designed to change their neural connections if they are challenged with new stimulation. We can decide to take on these new challenges with our minds that purposefully stimulate our brains to grow new connections over the lifespan. Novel experiences should be engaging and lead to optimal arousal: they should not be too stressful, but not boring either. In many ways this flow toward optimal arousal is the same as that which we've discussed for mental well-being. Under-stimulation is similar to the state of rigidity; excess stimulation is akin to the state of chaos.

Encoding, Storage, and Retrieval

As with optimal learning, short-term memory transitions into long-term encoding and storage with the gene activation and protein synthesis that enables neuronal connections to change. **Encoding** is the initial firing of neurons and the stimulation of new connections. **Storage** is the way in which new neuronal linkages create the potential for new firing patterns through the activation of newly associated groups of neurons in the future. *Storage is a probability function, not a photo-copy machine.* The conditions at the time of recall will shape the nature of *retrieval*, which is the re-activation of associations of neuronal groups similar—but never identical—to the groups associated with the encoding process.

Imagine telling a patient that they potentially have a serious, life threatening illness. The way in which this interaction transpires will have a large impact on how the patient remembers the discussion. If, for example, the patient is noticeably anxious from the outset and your demeanor is austere and not emotionally tuned in to his or her anxiety, the patient's state of emotional flooding is likely to increase. This may lead to either a difficulty remembering what you said in the long-term or to the association of excessive fear and a sense of being left alone with the potential diagnosis. This feeling of being alone at a time of great stress is itself stress-increasing. On the other hand, if a patient feels understood by you, it will greatly reduce his or her anxiety and will help elicit the physiological mechanisms of memory necessary to enable encoding and storage of the important things you have to say at that time. *It is up to you as a medical professional to become sensitive to the internal state of your patient to best help him or her remember the important communications between the two of you about crucial medical issues.*

Making an effort to view the interaction from the patient's perspective will help optimize the clinical experience for your patient. Being aware of a patient's internal state and being concerned about his or her diagnosis is essential if your patient is going to feel understood and comforted by you. This is how you can use empathy to maximize your medical intervention. Once that connection is established and the patient feels safe and understood, discussions about the technical issues involved in the medical work-up can occur without hyperarousal.

Implicit and Explicit Memory

Memory can be divided into two types—implicit and explicit—both of which dramatically influence the way information is perceived and processed in the brain. **Implicit memory** is available throughout the lifespan and perhaps even prenatally. Implicit memory includes the domains of emotion, perception, motor response, and likely also bodily sensation. In addition, implicit memory includes the generalizations the brain creates as summations of repeated experiences, called mental models, or **schema**. **Priming**, the way the mind is readied to respond to future events in a certain fashion, is also a product of implicit processing. Implicit memory differs greatly from common preconceptions of "memory" in that it does not create a feeling of something being recalled from the past. Interestingly, implicit memory does not require conscious, focal attention to be encoded. Implicit memory is encoded whenever these specific domains of neural firing, from perceptions to motor action, are activated. This initial implicit encoding causes new synapses to be formed that will guide subsequent responses to a similar input. Therefore, these subsequent responses are influenced by the implicit memory formed after the initial encoding without the individual's awareness that something from the past is influencing his behavior. For example, you know not to touch fire because you know that it will burn you—even if you can't remember a specific time when you were burned by fire. This implicit "knowing" is probably due to an experience you had as a young child when you touched a fire and experienced pain or were told not to touch the fire. The pain was immediately perceived and processed in your brain, creating an implicit association between fire and pain to protect you from a similar experience in the future. Implicit memories do not require the hippocampus to be activated, so patients with damage to the medial temporal lobes which house the hippocampus will still be able to both encode and retrieve implicit memories.

Explicit memory becomes available in the second year of life as the hippocampus is thought to mature after that time. Explicit memory includes two domains: **factual (semantic) memory** and **episodic (autobiographical) memory**. When you recall an explicit fact or a sense of the self in the past, you have the internal sensation that a memory is being recalled. Explicit memory requires conscious and focused attention to be encoded. Explicit memories are formed by the creation of new synapses after a conscious experience is processed via the hippocampus. For short and long-term explicit memory retrieval, the hippocampus also must be activated for recollection to occur. Neither short nor long-term memories are in and of themselves permanent. However, these long-term memories have the potential to become permanent through **consol-**

idation. While long-term memory requires the focused attention of the hippocampus for retrieval, consolidated (permanent) memory does not. Thus, consolidated memories, such as your name or date of birth, can be recalled even if the hippocampus is damaged or removed.

Impaired explicit memory encoding can often occur from trauma suffered in certain regions of the brain. An example of this is amnesia, which is a result of damage to the medial temporal regions (including the hippocampus). There are two types of amnesia—retrograde and anterograde. **Retrograde amnesia** refers to the inability to recall explicit memories encoded prior to the damage. **Anterograde amnesia** is the inability to form new explicit memories following the damage.

This overall discussion of memory and the importance of attuning to the patient's experience highlights the need for medical professionals to appreciate their essential role in paying attention to the internal mental state of their patients. One word we commonly use for this internal state is **emotion**. Though emotion has many definitions in science, for medical practice we can say that the patients' emotional states will directly influence how they recall their interactions with you. The emotional states that directly shape neuroplasticity can be understood and then approached in ways that optimize learning and memory. We'll turn now to emotion and interpersonal relationships to deepen our insights into this important dimension of brain and behavior.

WHAT IS EMOTION?

Emotion as a Form of Integration

Emotion is a profoundly important part of human life. The science of emotion can involve a range of academic disciplines that explore the ways different cultures promote the communication of internal states to one another, how an individual develops within social relationships across his or her lifespan, or how the brain integrates its functioning with the bodily and social processes that are fundamental to its organization. Whether the scientist is from anthropology, psychology, or neurobiology, it is fascinating that each of them studying emotion uses the concept of integration. Though specific definitions of "emotion" may differ, each field of science examining this sometimes elusive process of emotion highlights the fundamentally integrative role emotion plays in the developmental, social, mental, or somatic life of the person.

Recall that integration means the linking together of separate elements of a system into a functional whole. In this way we can say that emotion may be a way of describing how a system is becoming integrated. When we are emotionally close to others, our minds are integrated with

them. When we feel emotionally understood, others see our minds in a clear and authentic fashion. When we feel emotionally whole, often many pieces of our life are "falling in to place" or becoming a coherent, integrated whole. Emotional well-being often emerges when we integrate the various dimensions of our lives, including our social, somatic, and mental aspects of our experiences across our life's path.

Categorical Emotion

There are two practical ways we describe emotion. One common way is using what Charles Darwin called **categorical emotions**. These are the universally perceived categories of sadness, anger, fear, disgust, surprise, happiness, and shame. Other categories have later been described with a huge variety of these internal states that become integrated to the point that they can be expressed externally as classic facial expressions. Most cultures have names for these categories, and hence they are called "universal." We are also learning that each of these categories of emotion has a physiological finger print, a characteristic profile of cardiovascular activity that correlates with specific patterns of nonverbal expressions.

Primary Emotion

Another important dimension of emotion can be seen before the person is aroused to the level of having a categorical emotion communicated on the face or through tone of voice as one of the universal expressions. The aspect of emotion that occurs before categories of emotion arise can be called *primary emotion*. Primary emotion is the way that the internal state of our brains and bodies are organizing their functioning to shape some very important aspects of our internal worlds.

Here is one way to describe this fundamental nature of the subjective quality of our ongoing internal mental state. First we orient our attention to a particular internal or external stimulus. This **initial orientation** directs the energy and information flow of our minds, and thus is a first step in creating mental life. Next we appraise the object of our attention as either good or bad. Should we get closer to it if it is good or move away from it if it is bad? This is called **appraisal** and is exactly what our limbic, emotion-generating brain areas are designed to do. After initial orientation and appraisal there is a rapid **elaboration of arousal** that continues to govern the flow of energy and information processing. As arousal is elaborated it channels neuronal firing in specific directions and thus shapes the nature of our internal mental state.

Primary emotion occurs all the time. We orient our attention, appraise the meaning of events, and respond depending on those appraisals. Orientation, appraisal, and arousal are the primary elements of the internal "emotional state" that continually shapes our subjective mental state of mind. We become aware of others' primary emotional states by their focus of attention and by their nonverbal expressions. Those nonverbal expressions we've discussed earlier reveal the internal, primary emotions of the individual. *As a medical professional, being aware of the importance of these nonverbal signals such as eye contact, facial expression and tone of voice can enable you to "tune in" to the primary emotional state of your patient.* It is this moment-to-moment "attunement" to your patients' states that will enable you to get a glimpse into their internal world. In turn, when your patients realize that you are attuned to their internal mental life, they will feel comforted and secure by their connection with you as their physician. Studies have even demonstrated that patients with a common cold will have improved immune function and faster recovery when they have a visit with a more empathic doctor.

Why is being aware of another's primary or categorical emotional states so important? Relationships between clinician and patient (or between spouses, friends, or children and their parents) that involve a respectful attitude and sensitivity to the internal subject emotional state of the other person are those that promote well-being in both individuals. This respect begins with a sense that the internal subjective experience of another person is important. People feel cared about and respected. The subjective mental life of another person is different from yours, but it is worthy of being understood and embraced for its uniqueness and importance. *Being sensitive to the internal state of another means focusing your mind on the nonverbal signals of the other person and thinking about what these may mean.* An excessive state of arousal and an appraisal of some communication from you as being negative can greatly impair memory and how a patient will respond to your suggestions. Being aware of these internal reactions in the patient can help you tune in to their concerns in a sensitive and respectful manner. You may be pleasantly surprised at how direct and helpful an awareness of emotional communication can be.

LEFT MEETS RIGHT

To enhance the patient-physician relationship, it is important to understand how brain, mind, and behavior work together. We've seen how the internal state of activation of the brain shapes the subjective experience of mind. How you pay respect and attention to this internal mental state can make a crucial difference in the outcome of the

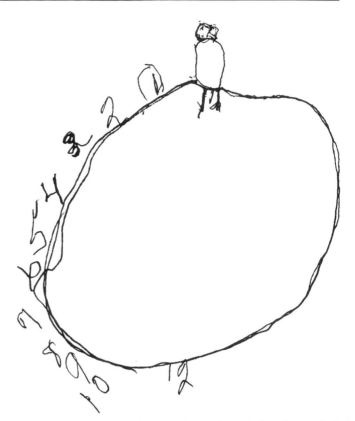

FIGURE 1.3 An example of hemineglect. When asked to draw a clock, this patient ignored the right half of space.

doctor-patient relationship. Your mental state and the mental state of your patient are shaped by the location of activations in each of your brains. One very general way to describe these locations of neuronal firings is in the separation of the two halves of the brain. Though some writers have taken the science beyond reasonable boundaries and dichotomized whole societies as either "right-brained" or "left-brained," it is nevertheless a biological reality over millions of years of evolution that our nervous systems are asymmetric, and left is different from right. Knowing these neurobiological asymmetries can greatly aid your understanding of your own and your patients' mental life. As you'll see in this brief overview, knowing distinctive regions of the brain can help you be more sensitive to your patients' and your own internal mental states.

During in-utero development, the lower brainstem structures give rise to asymmetric limbic regions. After birth, these subcortical asymmetries in turn influence the development of the right and left cortex in very different ways. The right hemisphere develops earlier than the left, being more active in both its growth and neural firing during the first two to three years of life. After that time, the child goes through cyclical alternating periods of dominance in growth and activity of the left and the right hemisphere of the brain.

The Right Mode of Processing

The right and left hemispheres have somewhat different anatomical connections. *The right hemisphere appears to have cortical columns that are more horizontally integrated with each other, meaning that there is more cross-modal integration.* The cortex is divided into vertically arranged columns of roughly six cell layers in thickness. These columns specialize in processing certain "modes" of mental activities, such as vision or hearing. With more horizontal integration across these vertical columns, there is a cross-modality integration that creates a different kind of wholeness to the way the right hemisphere processes information. This integrated state results in processing across various forms of perceptual input, enabling the right hemisphere to create holistic, visuospatial representations. The right hemisphere also specializes in having an integrated map of the whole body, the capacity to send and receive nonverbal signals, and it stores representations of autobiographical memory. Because of the right cortex's more direct neural connections to the limbic areas, the right hemisphere also specializes in more direct, intense, and raw affective or emotional experience.

For this reason it also appears that the right hemisphere specializes in the process of *emotional resonance* in which our internal affective and physiological states are directly influenced by what we see in another person. These important nonverbal emotional processes make the right hemisphere an important component of the experience of **empathy** or putting ourselves in the mental experience of another person. It is likely our right modes that enable us to "feel felt" by another person. Some neurologists are now referring to the right side of our brains as the seat of our social and emotional selves.

The Left Mode of Processing

The left hemisphere in contrast seems to have cortical columns that are more vertically integrated. This lends the left hemisphere a specialization in what is called "digital processing" (compared to the "analogical processing" of the right side) in which information is handled in a very vertically refined, yes-no, on-off, manner. *Language, linear processing, logic,* and *literal thinking* are the four-L's of the Left hemisphere. We use linguistic language to both understand with our left hemispheres and to communicate with others. The left loves linearity and predictability, and your left hemisphere is currently highly active as you read this long, linear, linguistic sentence. One word follows the next and then the next. The logic of the left is called **syllogistic reasoning,** and is the way we (our left hemispheres) search for cause-effect relationships in the world around us, and within us.

When we encounter others, both our hemispheres are important in becoming active in the communication that will occur. No one mode or side is better than the other. However, the two modes are quite different. Sometimes we may move toward over-use of one and that exclusion of the other at times of stress, or just out of habit. For example, if we become overwhelmed with a patient's serious diagnosis, our left hemisphere may attempt to take over communication and shut down our empathy for the patient's pain. Brief adaptations like "leaning to the left" may be quite natural and temporarily helpful to reduce overwhelming emotional reactions. However, prolonged exclusion of the right hemisphere from interactions with our patients, our friends, or even ourselves, can lead to serious problems in those professional and personal relationships. Our own sense of vitality and well-being can become seriously compromised if we do not find a way to integrate the two sides of our experience.

To appreciate the limits of your personal control of your behavior, try the following experiment:
1. While sitting at your desk, lift your right foot off the floor and make clockwise circles with it.
2. Now, while doing this, draw the number "6" in the air with your right hand. Your foot will change direction.

The Importance of Integrating Right and Left

Bringing the right and the left hemispheres of our brains together is an important first step. Patients may also become overly dominant in one side or another in response to what you may say to them. For example, someone who is just flooded with fear may be processing mainly with the right side of his brain. He may need to use self-talk and logic to help him after he feels that you are open and trying to understand him. But bringing in his left hemisphere is not done for the purpose of shutting off his emotions. Rather, it is to bring him into an integrated state of balance, so that he can be aware of his emotions and help regulate them in a more helpful manner. As studies have shown, naming an internal affective state helps the whole system come into balance.

At other times patients may be so terrified that they shut off their right hemisphere's functioning, or at least their awareness of the input of the right mode of processing. In this condition you may sense that a patient is quite distant from his or her autobiographical recollections and is "living" in a very logical, linear, linguistic, and literal internal mental world. In this state, the patient may seem disconnected and defended. It is important not to flood the patient with right hemisphere activation, but your awareness of their defended state should be noted in your own mind and gentle support should be offered to ease the patient's reconnection with the emotions being processed in a nonverbal way in the right hemisphere.

In many ways we use our left hemisphere's language to communicate with the left hemisphere of another person. We use the nonverbal language of our right cortices to relate to the right hemisphere of someone else. Feeling connected to our doctors involves both what they say to us in words and how they reveal their connection to our own internal states by way of their nonverbal signals. *Your facial expressions, eye contact, tone of voice, gestures, posture, and timing and intensity of your responses are the direct route to connecting your right hemisphere to that of your patient.* When these nonverbal signals from you reflect openness and caring about the internal, often right hemisphere, states of your patient, he or she will feel secure and comforted. A new discovery has illuminated some of the basic mechanisms of this compassionate and empathic connection we can make with each other.

NEURONS THAT MIRROR OTHER MINDS

The Mirror Neuron System

In the mid-1990s a system of neurons was discovered, first in monkeys and later established in humans, called the **mirror neuron system**. These neurons reveal how our brains are profoundly social and focus on the internal mental state of another individual. In many ways the doctor-patient relationship may be shaped by the automatic processes that the mirror neuron system creates.

The first discovery of mirror neurons occurred serendipitously when a researcher studying single-neuron's activity found that that neuron being studied became active in response to both eating a peanut and observing another person eating a peanut. No, these are not peanut neurons, but they are a system of neurons that showed us a number of profound aspects of our brain's functional neuroanatomy. First of all, this study revealed that *motor action and perception are integrated processes.* In the cortex, the posterior perceptual regions are indeed linked by axonal fibers that connect the perceptual columns to the frontal motor regions of the cortex. But these motor-perceptual neural systems did not just fire off at any perception: mirror neurons only became active with the observation of an act with intention.

If a woman lifted her hand in front of you to her mouth, you'd have no idea what she was about to do. You couldn't detect her intention and you would not be able to anticipate the outcome of her action. However, if she held a cup of water in her hand, you'd be able to detect what the likely goal of her action of lifting was, and you'd anticipate she'd drink from the cup. Mirror neurons reveal a summation and learning process in the brain that detects intentional acts. In this way the mirror neuron system reveals how the brain makes maps of the internal intentional state of another person's mind.

Detecting Intention and Creating Emotional Resonance

The profound implication of this finding is that beyond just encoding neural maps of perceptions or motor actions, *the brain appears to create maps of others' minds.* Some researchers have taken this extremely exciting and revolutionary finding and explored how the mirror neuron system is involved in emotional resonance and empathy.

Our mirror neurons enable us to observe an intentional act in someone else and then prime or ready or brains to carry out that same act. When others' yawn or drink a cup of water, we yawn or get thirsty. In addition to priming our brains for action, mirror neurons also prime our brains for emotional resonance and empathy. We drive the mirror neuron data downward through a set of connections that can be called the "resonance circuits." We observe another's nonverbal expressions of her internal state and our own internal state is directly shaped by what we perceive. If you see sadness on another person's face your brain will activate circuitry that creates a sad affective texture in your brain, and the somatic responses in your heart, lungs, intestines, and musculature will reflect that sadness. In other words, your feelings and your bodily state will be shaped directly by what you sense in another person. This is called **emotional resonance**.

Resonance as the Gateway of Empathy

The next step in the unfolding story comes when we use the prefrontal part of our neocortex—the topmost part of our "resonance circuitry"—the part behind our eyes and forehead, to create the mechanisms of compassion and empathy. *Empathy means imagining the internal mental state of another person.* This is a form of mindsight map that enables us to picture the internal mental state of others. When the middle prefrontal cortex creates the step of "looking inward" at its own limbic and somatic states, we call this **interoception**. Next the prefrontal region *interprets* interoceptive data to surmise what the self is experiencing in that moment. Am I feeling sad? Am I frightened? Do I feel relieved? These are all the types of questions your prefrontal cortex may mediate before it takes the next step of *attribution* in which it attributes these internal states to the person you are observing.

The benefit of this capacity to have emotional resonance, and then the interoception, interpretation, and attribution of empathy, is that emotional resonance allows us to understand both ourselves and others. With such insight and empathy, life can make sense, relationships can feel profoundly rewarding, and people can be helped to heal.

As a clinical professional, though, these mirror neuron and resonance mechanisms reveal how there is a risk to emotional resonance. Without awareness it is possible that the automatic emotional resonance process may create in you the same affective states of distress of your patients, and this experience can become overwhelming. One term used to describe this process is **secondary traumatization.** Fortunately with consciousness of this important healing process, the healer can also be helped, as we've seen in the earlier discussion of mindful awareness practices and the reduction of burnout and stress. By putting these internal states of your affective feelings and your body's responses "out in the open," you can successfully deal with your internal responses in a way that is helpful to you and also supports your efforts to have a healthy doctor-patient relationship. This way of reducing stress while maintaining empathy for your patients is a form of mindful awareness, a part of developing your mindsight skills to see and shape the internal world.

Knowing that your internal state will be shaped by your patient's enables you to take steps to 1) make your emotional resonance a part of your awareness—becoming mindful of how you feel and what your body is sensing; and 2) to examine how this interoceptive data can be consciously interpreted and then used in a positive way to understand your patients. *At first this may be a laborious process, but soon, as with any learned skill, this empathic intelligence of mindsight will become more automatic.* The exciting news is that the more you come to be open to these often nonverbal internal processes, the more you'll come to understand your self. In addition you'll find that your work with patients becomes more rewarding and that their relationship with you will become more deeply healing.

THE ROLE OF SUBJECTIVE EXPERIENCE IN CLINICAL PRACTICE

The Stories of Our Lives

Ultimately the movement toward well-being involves helping patients adapt by integrating the wholeness of their social, mental, and somatic selves. Linking the two halves of the brain is one step in bringing this integrated state of

SEIZURE

I gave you what I could when you were born,
salt water to rock you,
your half of nine month's meat,
miles of finished veins,
and all the blood I had to spare.

And then I said, this is the last time
I divide myself in half, the last time
I lie down in danger and rise bereft,
the last time I give up half my blood.

Fifteen months later, when I walked into your
room
your mobile of the sun, moon,
and stars was tilting
while your lips twisted,
while you arched your back.

Your fingers groped for something in the air.
Your arms and legs flailed like broken wings.
Your breath was a load too heavy
for your throat to heave into your lungs.
You beat yourself into a daze against your crib.

We slapped your feet,
we flared the lights,
we doused you in a tub of lukewarm water.
But your black eyes rolled.
You had gone somewhere
and left behind a shape of bluish skin,
a counterfeit of you.

It was then,
before the red wail of the police car,
before the IV's, before the medicine
dropped into you like angels, before you woke
to a clear brow, to your own funny rising voice,

it was then that I would have struck the bargain,
all my blood
for your small shaking.
I would have called us even.

JEANNE MURRAY WALKER

wellness into being. Often we must first start with ourselves in learning what this integrated left-right connection feels like. One way to feel that sense of wholeness is in helping the stories of our lives become coherent—i.e., making sense of our life experiences.

As the left side of our brains has a drive to use language to tell the linear story of the events of our lives, many authors see the left hemisphere as the narrative drive for our species to tell stories. But when we realize that the autobiographical details of our lives are stored in the right hemisphere along with the affective meaning and texture of our internal and interpersonal lives, then it becomes clear that to tell a coherent and meaningful story of our lives we must come to integrate the left and the right sides of the brain. This is how we deepen our self-understanding.

In your own life it may be helpful to reflect to yourself, in a journal, or with close friends, on how the events of your own life have brought you to where you are now in your life's journey. When you come to understand yourself in this open and coherent way, you may find that nonverbal memories in the form of pictures and sensations in your mind become activated and then sorted through by the linguistic, logical, linear processing of your left hemisphere. As you come to put words to the previously word-less images in your head, you may find, as many studies have shown, that there is a deep sense of harmony that emerges in your mind. Research has also shown that telling your life story can improve your immune function and physiological well-being.

Making sense of your own mind and creating a coherent story of your life enables you to have an openness to the events of your life that promote a sense of well-being. In addition, such a receptive state of awareness in your own mind creates an openness to others' experiences that promotes well-being within relationships. As you find your way to helping patients deal with their suffering and the challenges in their life, such openness will enable them to feel deeply comforted and to have the strength to face their difficulties with you as their care provider.

Mental coherence will also create an openness in you that will help you be attuned to your own mental and somatic state of being. You'll be able to remain compassionate to your own needs for rest and relaxation in the exciting and challenging work of helping others in need. By taking care of yourself and being attuned to your own needs you can serve as a model for how your patients can come to learn to take care of their own needs as well.

SUMMARY

In this chapter we've been exploring how to integrate the objective findings of science into a deeper understanding of the subjective nature of mental life. By turning to the brain, we've been able to understand different aspects of how neural functioning creates memory, learning, emotion, and the nature of our communication with others.

One of the important principles from this perspective is that the subjective essence of the mind is objectively the most important dimension of how we communicate with one another. Also, because the brain is a profoundly social organ of the body, *interpersonal relationships and the communication patterns that shape them directly influence neural functioning*. When the brain functions optimally and relationships are empathic, the mind becomes coherent and the body-proper can adapt to stress in a more effective manner. In this way the doctor-patient relationship that places the subjective experience of the patient at the top of the priority list of "things to pay attention to" will be the most likely to be optimally supportive and helpful to the patient.

We now have objective, scientifically established data that the subjective nature of our lives is one of the most essential dimensions of health and healing. This is a tremendously exciting time, and one in which we can integrate this scientific importance of subjectivity into our daily lives with our patients—and with our selves.

CASE STUDY

Ms. Smith is a 30-year old business school student who comes to the university medical clinic with a complaint of pain in her arm and jaw. She has finished her first semester of graduate school and is now embarking with four other students on a new business venture involving novel approaches to selling software on the internet. You perform a physical exam that appears normal as does her EKG and chest X-Ray. Her vital signs and basic lab work are normal, and there is no family history of early cardiac disease or psychiatric illness such as panic disorder.

After further questioning, you find that Ms. Smith has recently felt quite anxious. She has had difficulty falling asleep and awakens frequently during the night. In the office she denies other symptoms of depression, such as loss of appetite or energy, negative mood or preoccupations with feelings of guilt or sadness. Ms. Smith also reveals that she "is afraid of falling flat on [her] face" if she tries something new. There is insufficient evidence to suggest cardiac disease, but something about this patient's statement feels important.

You ask Ms. Smith to say what comes to her mind about "falling on her face," and she immediately begins to experience an intensification of pain in her arm. She then grasps her jaw and tells you she feels pain there as well. You ask her to say more about this pain, noting that she does not appear to be in acute cardiac distress, and she tells you that she feels as if she has fallen down. On further questioning you find that when Ms. Smith was in preschool learning to ride a tricycle, she had hit a rock and fallen on her face, fracturing her arm and breaking two of her front teeth. Knowing about the nature of trauma and implicit memory, you realize that this may be an example of blocked integration of this implicit form of somatosensory memory with Ms. Smith's larger narrative of her life. With overwhelming events, the hippocampus may be blocked from integrating the basic elements of implicit memory into its explicit autobiographical form.

When implicit memory is not integrated into the higher forms of factual and autobiographical explicit memory, it is often reactivated without an individual being aware that something is being accessed from the past. The "meaning" of that early traumatic event is not only that this patient feels pain implicitly without recognizing its origins in the past, but also that there is a general "theme" that is extracted from that event—i.e., trying anything new is fraught with danger. In reflecting on this issue and later writing in her journal about the tricycle accident and her fear of attempting anything new, Ms. Smith's anxiety and sleep disturbances are abated. She is now able to place within her conscious awareness a narrative reflection on how an earlier frightening event led her to fear exploring new experiences in her life. Nine months later she reports that she remains symptom free and that her business venture was a success.

SUGGESTED READINGS

Beer, J.S., Shimamura, A.P., & Knight, R.T. (2004). Frontal lobe contributions to executive control of cognitive and social behavior. In M.S. Gazzaniga (Ed.), *The cognitive neurosciences III* (pp. 1091–1104). Cambridge, MA: MIT Press.
A very helpful chapter that provides an overview of how our frontal lobes help to create the fundamental thinking and interpersonal nature of our human lives.

Cozolino, L. (2010). *The neuroscience of psychotherapy: Healing the social brain* (2nd edition). New York: Norton.
This book bridges the gap between psychotherapy and neurobiology by elegantly synthesizing the science behind brain function with real life experiences and clinical practice.

Damasio, A. (1994). *Descartes' error: Emotion, reason, and the human brain.* New York: Grosset/Putnam.
A classic text creatively integrating the history of Phineas Gage with modern neurology in exploring how damage to the prefrontal cortex alters personality.

Davidson, R.J. (2004). The neurobiology of personality and personality disorders. In D.S. Charney & E.J. Nester (Eds.), *Neurobiology of mental illness* (2nd ed., pp. 1062–1075). Oxford: Oxford University Press.
This textbook chapter describes the neural underpinnings of personality and is embedded in an overall resource book that is on the cutting edge of the neurobiology of psychiatric disorders.

Doidge, N. (2007). *The brain that changes itself: Stories of personal triumph from the frontiers of brain science.* New York: Penguin.
This book explores how the brain can be strengthened and rewired, just like a muscle in the body, even after it has suffered substantial trauma. Using case studies and interviews with leading researchers, this book looks at the exciting possibilities in this new field of psychotherapy.

Krasner, M.S., R.M. Epstein, & H. Beckman et al. (2009). Association of an educational program in mindful communication with burnout, empathy, and attitudes among primary care physicians. *Journal of the American Medical Association, 302*(12), 1284–1293.
This study revealed how an educational program for physicians that focused on mindful communication and self-awareness could help improve the clinicians' psychological well being, their chances of decreasing "burnout," and their ability to relate to patients in their roles as primary care physicians.

Macrae, C.N., Heatherton, T.F., & Kelley, W.M. (2004). A self less ordinary: The medial prefrontal cortex and you. In M.S. Gazzaniga (Ed.), *The cognitive neurosciences III* (pp. 1067–1076). Cambridge, MA: MIT Press.
This chapter offers an exciting view of the middle aspect of the prefrontal cortex that appears to play a central role in the organization of personality. The chapter is a part of a huge volume exploring a wide range of topics within the large field of cognitive neuroscience with excellent chapters summarizing the latest in research in this important area.

Rakel, D.P., Hoeft, T.J., Barrett, B.P., Chewning, B.A., Craig, B.M., & Niu, M. (2009). Practitioner empathy and the duration of the common cold. *Family Medicine, 41,* 494–501.

Siegel, D.J. (2007). *The mindful brain: Reflection and attunement in the cultivation of well-being.* New York: WW Norton.
This book reviews the science behind mindful awareness and the neural mechanisms that may underlie the way being aware of present moment experiences with curiosity, acceptance, and openness may promote neural integration.

Siegel, D.J. (2010). *Mindsight: The new science of personal transformation.* New York: Bantam Random House.
This book explores the interpersonal and neurobiological nature of insight and empathy, focusing on how individuals can promote both in their own lives to foster well-being in themselves and those with whom they interact.

Families, Relationships, and Health

Margaret L. Stuber

Happy families are all alike; every unhappy family is unhappy in its own way.

LEO TOLSTOY
Anna Karenina

Much of the focus of medical student education is on the patient or the doctor-patient interaction. However, treatment of medical illness requires that physicians look beyond the individual patient to the social context in which patients exist. The social context will determine aspects of health behavior, including how a patient expresses symptoms, who comes to the office or hospital with the patient, and how decisions are made about treatment. It is the social network that helps patients cope with illness, and which supplies the instrumental assistance that determines whether or not a patient can function at home or on the job. The social network in turn is influenced by a patient's medical diagnosis, treatment decisions, and the way the patient responds to illness and treatment.

This chapter will explore the impact of a social support network on the doctor-patient interaction, the patient's health, and treatment decisions, as well as the impact of illness on the family and social network. Discussion and case examples will illustrate how physicians can use this knowledge to plan treatment and increase patient adherence.

WHAT IS A SOCIAL NETWORK?

A social network is the community of people upon whom one can rely for emotional and physical (instrumental) support. Traditional sources of a social network include the nuclear and extended family, the school or work community, the religious community, and the neighborhood. Each of these groups shares some common beliefs, values, and experiences that lead them to help one another. Examples of community support would include helping a neighbor "raise" a barn, bringing food when a member of your religious community is sick, or giving a classmate a school assignment from a day they missed school. Within this type of community everyone knows everyone else, sometimes more than a member may have wished. This is the kind of village that could be counted on to raise a child.

Changes in the family and community in the United States over the past 50 years have altered many aspects of the social network. The two-parent family with an at-home mother is no longer the norm. Extended families living in the same house—or even in the same town—are increasingly uncommon. Family size in the United States has decreased to an average of just over two children per household. People are less likely to stay in one job for the duration of their career, making it less usual for families to raise their children entirely in one neighborhood. All of these changes reduce the stability, size, and availability of social networks.

CASE EXAMPLE

A 22-year-old college student volunteered to serve as a living-related donor to his sister for a partial liver transplant. During his interview with the doctor to determine his eligibility to donate, one of his brothers asked to come into the office. The brother addressed the prospective donor, saying that this was not his decision to make. Given that the proposed procedure would endanger his life to save that of his sister, the family felt that this was a family decision, and needed to be discussed as such. The doctor explained that according to U.S. law, this was a decision the young man could make independently. However, she encouraged the young man to discuss the decision with his family before finalizing the donation.

Despite these changes, social networks continue to exist and have a strong impact on individuals. This is particularly true for people who move to the United States from other countries. Although the size of their social network is diminished with much of the extended family far away, family and community remain important, and their role may be enhanced because of the family's isolation from its cultural base. Conflicts between the expectations of the country of origin and the adopted country are common, and often difficult to communicate.

HOW FAMILIES AND FRIENDS ALTER DIAGNOSIS AND TREATMENT DECISIONS

Patients make decisions within a social network. These decisions can include how patients respond to preventative care, and whether or not their symptoms are serious enough to justify a visit to a doctor. For example, the difficulty involved in following a low fat, low salt or low carbohydrate diet will differ tremendously depending on whether or not the family usually eats a lot of cheese, highly flavored food, or a rice-based diet. If the physician makes recommendations to the patient, but not to the person who is preparing the meals, it is unlikely the physician's advice will be followed. Similarly, even if the person who needs the diet is the person cooking, that does not necessarily mean that he or she is the person who determines what the family eats. It is difficult for a family to have multiple different meals for the family. Thus, if one person is to really follow a prescribed diet, it is often necessary for the rest of the family to adhere to the same diet.

Seeking care for symptoms may seem like a personal decision. However, if the patient is the primary wage-earner, or does not usually have access to the family car, or is responsible for care of multiple children, symptoms may be ignored for the sake of the family. For example, *a clinic to treat women with HIV found that the best way to get women to come in was to offer medical care for their children* at the same clinic. The mothers were much more likely to seek medical care for their children than to seek out care for their own problems.

Unfortunately, medical treatment is often complex and expensive. It requires organization to make and keep appointments, fill prescriptions, and cope with insurance and bills. Children and the elderly generally must rely on other family members to perform these tasks, but illness can make it difficult for even normally independent adults to take care of the dozens of details associated with health care. Chaotic or multiproblem families are less likely to successfully carry out these tasks. As one pediatric nurse noted, *you know a family is in trouble if having a child diagnosed with cancer is not the worst thing that ever happened to the family.*

Migrant Mother (Florence Owens Thompson), *photograph by Dorothea Lange (1936).* Courtesy of the Library of Congress, Washington, D.C., Prints and Photographs Division, FSA/OWI Collection, LC-USF34-9097-C. *Poverty is a significant stressor for families.*

HOW FAMILIES AND FRIENDS HELP PATIENTS COPE

Social support has repeatedly been found to be a significant, independent predictor of emotional well-being in adults and children with chronic or acute illness or injury. These studies have looked at a range of illnesses including adolescents with severe burns, children with cancer, and adults with heart disease. The evidence is clear: *People who have extended and available social support networks, consisting of friends and/or family members, are less anxious, and are less likely to become depressed or develop posttraumatic stress disorder.* One very large study of psychiatric symptoms in response to highly stressful events found that individuals with more support from friends had less psychiatric morbidity after death or serious illness in the family at a 3-year follow-up. Another study showed that the emotional outcome of adolescents with significant burns was more significantly correlated with their social support network than with the size or location of the burn.

HOW FAMILIES AND FRIENDS HELP PATIENTS RECOVER FROM ILLNESS

A famous study of women with metastatic breast cancer was a model for a series of investigations into the utility of social support in decreasing both psychiatric and medical morbidity and mortality. This Stanford study found that *women who participated in a structured support group lived longer than matched comparisons.* Replications have sought to explain the mechanism and identify the "active ingredient" of the intervention; however, these studies have produced mixed results. One explanation for the effect of group therapy on longevity is that the groups reduced isolation and helplessness, which in turn reduced the physical stress response, which facilitated healing and/or immune response. Other investigators have seen an improved immune response in cancer patients who were involved in psychoeducational support groups. However, not all support groups are equally effective in benefiting participants.

This variability may result because the type of interactions between the patient and the social support network influence the usefulness of the network. Studies of individuals with schizophrenia, depression, and bipolar affective disorder, for example, have found that patients with these serious mental illnesses can be harmed if the social network is very emotionally involved with the patient but is not supportive. *Patients living with family members who were deeply involved but were highly critical of the patient suffered more* *relapses and required more medication than patients whose family members were less involved and less critical.*

At the simplest level, social support can make it easier or harder to follow treatment recommendations, which in turn greatly influences morbidity and mortality. Adolescents are a classic example, as this is an age when any treatment that alters one's appearance is extremely poorly tolerated because of social pressure. A teenager may really mean it when she says she would rather die than lose all her hair. Likewise, young children may be humiliated if they need to go to the nurse for medications during the day at school, as it sets them apart from the other students. Women may delay seeking care for obvious breast masses because of the social (or marital) pressure to keep the discovery of a lump private or to ensure that their breasts remain intact. Although few patients actually say they would rather die than lose a breast, this sadly occurs all too often.

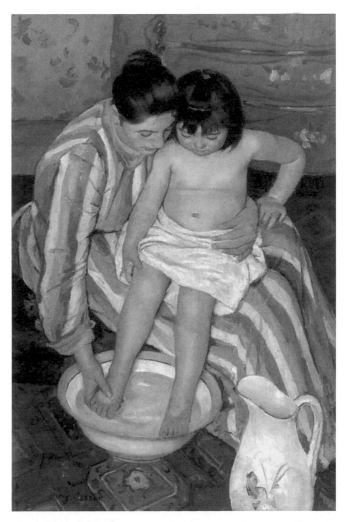

The Child's Bath (1893) *Mary Cassatt, American, 1844–1926.* Oil on canvas, 100 × 66 cm. Robert A. Waller Fund, 1910.2. © The Art Institute of Chicago. *Even well-intentioned parents often fail to follow treatment recommendations for their children.*

HOW FAMILIES AND FRIENDS ARE AFFECTED BY ILLNESS

Lengths of stay in hospitals have shortened dramatically over the past 10 to 20 years. Although this is partially a result of improved medications and the awareness that long convalescent periods are not always desirable, it is also based on the sometimes mistaken belief that uncomplicated recovery can occur safely at home. Given the tremendous expense of each day spent in a hospital, patients are frequently sent home within 24 hours of an uncomplicated delivery, a cardiac catheterization, and even a mastectomy. The assumption behind such discharges is that the patient will have someone who can drive them home, help them with activities of daily living, and be alert for any complications that might arise. However, this is not always the case. Elderly patients may have a spouse at home who is willing, but who is equally old and in frail health, and simply unable to help the patient get to the toilet or bath. Adults who live alone may not have any friends or family who can take off work to care for them. Their adult children may have families of their own and already be stressed coping with school, work, and childcare. In each of these cases, one or two crises can generally be handled. However, when care becomes a chronic need, the financial and emotional toll can be overwhelming to all concerned.

A recent study of adolescents living with parents who had AIDS and a study of the emotional well-being of teens whose parents had died provided insight into the impact of chronic illness on family members. Both of these studies revealed that *adolescents were more emotionally distressed during the period of chronic illness than they were after the death of the parent.* The teens reported much more uncertainty and instability in their living situation during the time of illness than after the parental death. Similar findings have been reported for children who lost a parent to cancer—the disruption of school, living situations, and activities was even more distressing than the grief related to the death of a parent.

For parents of a child who is seriously injured or has a life-threatening illness, a sense of helplessness and horror can lead to both acute and long-term symptoms of traumatic stress. Acute symptoms include nightmares, hypervigilance, and numbing or avoidance of reminders. All of these can be understood as normal or even adaptive responses to a terrible event. However, these symptoms also can become chronic, and lead to clinical distress or reduced function. This is more likely when the parent is anxious even before the event, when the event is perceived by the parent as likely to result in the death of the child, or when the treatment is perceived by the parent as very stressful. It is important to remember that *symptoms are dependent on the perception of the individual,* and not on what is seen by the physician as the "objective" threat. For example, studies have found no significant correlation between the perceptions of pa-

The Family *Egon Schiele (1918).* Österreichische Galerie Belvedere, Vienna. *Psychoanalysts believe that the fundamental structure of personality is established in the first few years of life.*

tients and physicians as to the life-threat or treatment intensity for childhood cancer. The correlation between the perception of life-threat between parents and physicians is statistically significant, but low enough to suggest they are not actually assessing the same variable.

The **resilience** (ability to recover from or adjust easily to misfortune or change) of families is another critically important variable affecting health. For example, one study of resilient mothers with spinal cord injuries compared with healthy mothers found no difference in the individual adjustment, attitudes toward their parents, self-esteem, gender roles, or family functioning. Even patients and caregivers who experience a medical diagnosis and treatment as traumatic may report that there were some positive consequences as a result of the experience. *Studies over the past 20 years have found that patients with HIV, childhood cancer survivors, and caregivers of Alzheimer's patients have reported changes in how they look at what is important in their lives, and an increased appreciation for interpersonal relationships.* This has resulted in the study of what is called "posttraumatic growth," which is further described below.

THE ROLE OF THE RELIGIOUS COMMUNITY AND SPIRITUAL BELIEF IN HEALTH

Most of the population of the United States reports a belief in a higher power or God, and the power of religion and spiritual belief has been a topic of growing interest in the medical community. As research has become more sophisticated, it has become clear that there are at least two separate factors that mediate the impact of religion or spirituality on health. One is the religious or spiritual community. The other is personal faith or spirituality. Each is considered below.

A **religious or spiritual community** is a group of people who are joined by a common set of beliefs. This can be a formal church, temple, or mosque, with written expectations of the faithful, or a less formal group such as a prayer group, or practitioners of a form of meditation. This may be a group one is born into, or a group that one joins. *The power of the group results from providing a sense of community and a meeting place for whatever rituals are special to that community*. Membership in the community provides a clear sense of one's role and often instructs members in how to properly deal with difficult issues. For example, many religious groups provide guidelines and rituals to help deal with death and grief, and support one another through these difficult transitions. For those who are comfortable with the expectations of their religious community, these traditions are reassuring and provide social support at difficult times. However, for those who are estranged from their communities, or who straddle two communities (such as second-generation Americans or those who marry outside their own community of believers), the community can add stress to an already difficult situation.

The strength of support from the religious community is generally measured with questions such as

- Are you a member of an organized religion or spiritual group?
- Do you go to religious or spiritual gatherings or services? How often?
- Do you get emotional support from your religious or spiritual organization?
- Do you get physical support from your religious or spiritual organization, such as food, transportation, or money?

Many religious communities provides support similar to that of an extended family. One example is The Church of the Latter Day Saints, or Mormon Church, which is well-known for the support they provide for members who are seriously ill. Food, lodging, and visitors can be arranged for family members who are caring for a patient, even when care is provided at a hospital far from the patient's home.

Personal faith or spirituality may be shared with others, but is essentially a private sense of meaning or purpose. Personal faith may be consistent with an established doctrine or dogma, but it is perceived as being individually experienced. *The strength of personal faith or spirituality is independent of the degree of participation in a religious community*, although some people with personal faith will also attend religious services. The support it provides is not physical or instrumental, but entirely emotional or spiritual.

The language of inquiry about faith can be tricky. When asked if they are "religious," many people assume the question has to do with an organized or formal religious set of beliefs. They may say they are spiritual, but not religious, or that they are religious, but not observant. Similarly, people may say they are religious, and really be referring to a set of beliefs with which they were raised, but which are no longer of personal importance.

Personal faith or spirituality is generally measured by questions such as

- How important is your faith or spirituality in your daily life?
- Do you get strength or support from your faith?
- Is prayer or a spiritual practice a part of your daily life?

Some individuals experience illness as a test of their faith, and believe they became ill because their faith was insufficient. This may take the form of a belief that faith will heal them, or that failure to recover is evidence of insufficient faith. This viewpoint is classically represented in the **Church of Christ, Scientist**, where traditional medication and physicians are seen as unnecessary to those of faith. However, some variation on this idea is present in many other belief systems. Another challenging belief for physicians is that illness is sent as a trial or punishment that must be endured. Physicians then must balance their desire to help the patient with respect for the patient's personal values and beliefs.

Traumatic events can sometimes reveal or even create a stronger sense of personal faith. **Posttraumatic growth** refers to an increased sense of meaning or purpose after a traumatic event. People sometimes report that the traumatic event they experienced resulted in the destruction of their usual assumptions about how the world worked, and that out of the ashes, a new and stronger faith was born. This may include a change in their formal religious faith, or a reorganizing of their values and priorities. The term is generally used for relatively permanent changes. Posttraumatic growth has been reported by patients, spouses, parents, and adult children who have dealt with a variety of medical issues, including childhood cancer, HIV, prostate cancer, Alzheimer's disease, and heart disease.

CASE EXAMPLE

A woman was distraught over her son's diagnosis of cancer. It was not until one of the medical team was able to talk with her alone that it became clear that the woman was overcome with guilt. She believed that God was taking her son away from her as punishment for a sexual affair that occurred early in her marriage. She could not share this with anyone in her family or her church, effectively removing all social support from her at a time of crisis in her life.

HOW TO WORK WITH FAMILIES AND COMMUNITIES

Pediatricians learn early that they are never only working with one patient. Since the child is not the decision-maker, at least one parent is always involved. *A wise pediatrician involves both parents whenever possible, and is always aware of which parent makes which decisions.* Obviously when parents are divorced, a determination must be made as to which parent makes medical decisions. However, even in cases in which the parents are happily married to each other, one parent often takes on primary responsibility for getting the child to a clinic or staying with them at the hospital. Relying on that parent to communicate everything for the other parent is a tremendous burden for the first parent, and excludes the other parent from a full understanding of the medical situation.

Similarly, geriatricians are usually careful to assess the support network of their patients as part of the assessment of activities of daily living. The participation of the patient's spouse, adult children, siblings, or even neighbors or grandchildren may be necessary for decision-making and ensuring adherence with complex regimens of medication and other treatment. The best strategy is to determine who the key players are, and keep them informed and involved by including them in clinic visits and telephoning them about new developments. This is somewhat more complex with adults than with minors, as any such communication can only be done with the permission of the patient, unless the patient is not competent to make medical decisions. It can be time-consuming to determine who else should be involved, and to communicate with them. However, the cost in time and success of treatment can be significant if this is not done. *The stress of visiting a doctor makes it difficult for even organized patients to keep track of their own questions, as well as the doctor's answers and instructions.* A friend or relative can help the patient remember what has been said. Possibly more important, involvement of the friend or relative reduces the likelihood that they will sabotage the treatment plan through disagreeing with treatment recommendations or unwittingly supporting the patient's resistance.

Young and middle-aged adults generally handle most of their medical care by themselves. However, *the importance of the immediate and extended family and social support system can be enormous.* The spouse may be the true decision-maker in some families, or the patient may feel unable to make decisions that would affect the family without first discussing the decision with the family. Some families may even prefer that all medical information be conveyed to someone other than the patient. This is only legally permissible if the patient requests that information be handled in this way, and this situation is usually very difficult for the physician. It is important to recognize that shielding pa-

La Vie (1903) *Pablo Picasso, Spanish, 1881–1973. Oil on canvas, 196.5 × 129.2 cm. The Cleveland Museum of Art, 2003. Gift of the Hanna Fund, 1945.24. © 2010 Estate of Pablo Picasso / Artists Rights Society (ARS), New York. Picasso's* La Vie *is one of his most enigmatic paintings. The standing male originally was a self-portrait; Picasso later changed the picture to portray his friend Carlos Casagemas who had committed suicide in 1901. The embracing couple in the top painting appears to pay homage to Gauguin, the crouching figure in the lower painting is reminiscent of Van Gogh's Sorrow, a lithograph of the unhappy prostitute he lived with in Amsterdam. The painting is allegorical and leaves the viewer thinking about the life cycle, sexuality, the complexity of relationships, and human suffering. All four of these themes are reflected in* Behavior and Medicine, *and physicians must deal with all of these problems in their daily practice.*

tients from information is usually done out of a belief that too much information will compromise the health of the patient by removing hope or causing anxiety. Physicians generally feel more comfortable with this approach when it involves pediatric patients rather than adults. However, the same principals apply in either case. This approach reduces open communication within the family, and it creates dependency in the patient. In families in which this is the norm, this may be well tolerated. In others, this can lead to isolation and anxiety for the patient, who can tell others are upset, but are not discussing why.

In situations in which communication occurs with a family member rather than directly with a patient, the physician must carefully choose which family members to involve. This must not be done without the permission of the patients except in extreme circumstances. The classic situation that arises in pediatrics is with adolescents. Although parents may be the medical decision-makers, vital information may be missed if the entire history and exam is done with the parent in the room. *Adolescents should not be expected to be comfortable asking questions or giving personal information in front of their parents, particularly when the discussion deals with sex or drugs.* On the other hand, parents *do* need to give permission for medical treatment. How much parents need to be involved in decisions about treatment related to sexuality and drugs varies from state to state. Some states have parental notification laws regarding abortion, for example. All states require reporting of sexual abuse or physical abuse of minors. Although these laws require reporting a suspicion of child abuse to the police, the nonoffending parent would usually also have to be informed.

> Family likeness has often a deep sadness in it. Nature, that great tragic dramatist, knits us together by bone and muscle, and divides us by the subtler web of our brains; blends yearning and repulsion; and ties us by our heart-strings to the beings that jar us at every movement.
>
> GEORGE ELIOT
> *Adam Bede*

SUMMARY

Physicians never treat patients in isolation from their families and community. Understanding how a social network influences the patient's perspective, and how the network can be used to support health and healing, is extremely useful. A wise doctor works with the beliefs and social supports to provide the best medical care possible.

CASE STUDY

A 7-year-old girl is diagnosed with acute lymphoblastic leukemia. She is the only child of her parents, who are observant Roman Catholics. The girl is very anxious, and wants her mother with her for all procedures. However, the mother is very difficult for the staff to manage, arguing with them about who she will allow to perform procedures on her daughter. A private conversation with the mother reveals that she feels very angry with God about this illness. She had miscarried twins 2 years earlier, and now is beginning to feel that she is cursed. Her husband is coping with their daughter's illness by working long hours, and spending all of his free time at Mass and prayer meetings. Their marriage is deteriorating, as her whole life is dedicated to dealing with her daughter and the doctors, and her faith is shattered.

Some 7 years later, the now 14-year-old daughter comes in with her mother for a check-up. She has successfully navigated 2 years of treatment, a later relapse, and a bone marrow transplant. Her parents are divorced, and her father has remarried and has two other children. When the adolescent is seen alone she says her primary goal is to have some other focus in her life than cancer. She begs the doctor to get her mother off her back, so she can be a "normal" teenager. A separate meeting with the mother reveals that she also sees the cancer episode as finally over. However, she finds she does not know what to do with her life now. She has put all of her energy into fighting for her daughter's life. She has left the church, has no hobbies, works at a boring job, and has no friends. She eventually accepts a referral to a psychiatrist, who helps her focus on creating a life for herself, which includes, but is not dependent on, her daughter.

SUGGESTED READINGS

Barskova, T., & Oesterreich, R. (2009). Post-traumatic growth in people living with a serious medical condition and its relations to physical and mental health: A systematic review. *Disability and Rehabilitation, 3,* 1–25.

This review examines published studies of posttraumatic growth after the diagnosis of cancer, HIV/AIDS, cardiac disease, multiple sclerosis, and rheumatoid arthritis. Results indicate that the quality of social support, the patients' coping strategies, and several indicators of mental and physical health were consistently associated with posttraumatic growth. This suggests there is a potential adaptive significance to posttraumatic growth after a serious medical diagnosis.

Curlin, F.A., Lawrence, R.E., Odell, S., Chin, M.H., Lantos, J.D., Koenig, H.G., & Meador, K.G. (2007). Religion, spirituality, and medicine: Psychiatrists' and other physicians' differing observations, interpretations, and clinical approaches. *American Journal of Psychiatry, 164,* 1825–1831.

This study analyzes surveys from 1,144 physicians about how they interpret the relationship between religion/spirituality and health, and how they address religion/spirituality issues with patients. The majority of nonpsychiatric physicians reported that they felt it was usually or always appropriate to inquire about religion/spirituality, and 74% reported that their patients sometimes or often mention religion/spirituality issues. Psychiatrists were much more likely to address religious and spiritual issues with their patients (92%), but were also more likely than other physicians to see religion and spirituality as having potential for causing suffering.

Schaefer, K.G., & Block, S.D. (2009). Physician communication with families in the ICU: Evidence-based strategies for improvement. *Current
Opinion in Critical Care, 15*(6), 569–577.
This paper reviews the current evidence that effective physician communication about prognosis with families of intensive care unit patients can improve family satisfaction, reduce length of stay in the
ICU, and reduce adverse family bereavement outcomes.

Schor, E.L. (2003). American Academy of Pediatrics Task Force on the
Family. *Pediatrics, 6*, 1541–1571.
This report summarizes the essential role of the family in the practice
of pediatrics and provides guidelines on how best a pediatrician can
work with families .

3 Birth, Childhood and Adolescence

Harsh K. Trivedi & Todd E. Peters

The life of a child from birth through adolescence is marked by enormous personal and interpersonal growth. The many "firsts" which occur, such as saying "mama" for the first time or taking the first few steps, mark the achievement of numerous developmental milestones. However, the fascinating interplay between a child's genes and his or her environment can create significant variability in the rate and extent of development. For example, a child with a genetic trajectory for normal motor ability may not sit up until 11 months of age when raised in a neglectful environment with poor nutrition. More commonly, the findings are less dramatic and parents will ask questions such as, "Our older daughter started talking at 10 months, but our son is nearly a year old and only says a few words. Is that normal?" It is critical to understand normal child development as a foundation upon which to better appreciate areas of potential concern.

Beyond the inherent variability of development across different children, there is the additional complexity of development occurring along multiple lines within each child. Studying a group of first graders, one quickly notices that there are significant differences in motor development as seen in the way they hold their pencils and work on fine motor tasks. In addition, if you study one particular child from the group, he or she may be developmentally on schedule for motor development, but may have mild cognitive delays. This creates the need for a structured method by which to study development.

Children can be studied from the perspective of gross motor, fine motor, language, cognitive, social, or a myriad of other developmental lines. At any given time, a clinical snapshot can be taken of a child to study where he or she stands along different developmental lines. Children can often be at different levels of development depending upon which line is being assessed. A clinically important factor to keep in mind is that many children may appear at age level on most developmental tasks and initially only exhibit a delay along one particular line of development. If left untreated, this delay has the potential to affect development along other lines over time. For example, consider the child with age-appropriate cognitive and visual-motor development, but who has motor speech delay. If this motor articulation problem is not addressed in the child with speech delay, the development of language and socialization skills may be hindered.

It is also important to consider how the same developmental delay may manifest differently based upon the child's age and developmental stage. The child with speech delay may express poor frustration tolerance as a toddler, may be quite shy and anxious during latency, and may become irritable and withdrawn during adolescence. This complexity of variable presentations during development combined with the intertwining of progress among the different developmental lines makes systematic study of the child even more important.

As you take clinical snapshots of different children, it is important to understand normal development for various age groups in order to distinguish what is clinically significant. For example, ask yourself this question: What should a child entering elementary school be able to do? The linking of important periods of life with developmental milestones will make it easier to remember what most children are able to do at a particular age.

When potentially troublesome areas are found, early intervention is critical, as a delay in treatment may further hamper other lines of development. Also, children can be remarkably resilient in making developmental gains once their individual problems are addressed, but it is important to act before children are so delayed that their global functioning is affected. Finding out that a child in the seventh

TABLE 3.1 Overview of development across structural theories and developmental lines.

Structural Theories	Birth–6mo	6mo–1yo	1yo–2yo	2yo–3yo	3yo–4yo	4yo–5yo	5yo–7yo	7yo–11yo	11yo–18yo
Piaget's Cognitive Stages	Sensorimotor			Pre-Operational			Concrete		Formal
Erikson's Psychosocial Stages	Trust v. Mistrust		Autonomy v. Shame & Doubt		Initiative v. Guilt		Industry v. Inferiority		Ego Identity v. Role Diffusion
Freud's Psychosexual Stages	Oral		Anal		Phallic		Latency		Adolescence
Developmental Lines*									
Gross Motor	Head Steady, Roll Over	Sit No Support, Stands	Walks, Jumps	Balance on 1 Foot, Hops	Heel to Toe Walk, Balance on each Foot 6 Sec.				
Fine Motor	Follow to Midline, Grasps Rattle	Pass Cube, Pincer Grasp	Tower 2 Cubes, Vertical Line	Copy a Circle, Copy a Cross	Copy a Square				
Speech and Language	Coos, Laughs	Turn to Voice, "Mama/Dada"	1-3 words, Body Parts - 6	Speech All Understandable, Name 4 Colors	Define 7 words				
Social	Regards Hand, Social Smile	Wave Bye-Bye, Imitate Activities	Use Utensil, Wash Hands	Put on Shirt, Dress Without Help					

Birth 6mo 1yo 2yo 3yo 4yo 5yo 7yo 11yo 18yo

* Adapted from the Denver II, DA Form 5694, 1988. Copyright W.K. Frankenburg and J.B. Dodds, 1990.

grade has oppositional behavior and school refusal because he has an undiagnosed learning disorder and is tormented about being "stupid" by classmates is a grave disservice to that child. Even when the learning disorder issues are addressed, the damage to the child's self-esteem and long history of poor social interactions with peers may result in lasting problems that are harder to correct.

Lastly, just as children can present with different symptomatology based upon their developmental stage, it is important to remember that the intervention must be developmentally appropriate to be most effective. When planning treatment for a child with speech delay, the intervention will be different for a 2-year-old, a 6-year-old, or an adolescent.

OVERVIEW OF DEVELOPMENT

When studying development, it is important to keep an eye on the development of the entire child and to extrapolate how one particular delay may be affecting multiple areas of a child's functioning. Table 3.1 presents an overview of development and lists major developmental theories and milestones from birth to 18 years of age to provide the "big picture" as you explore this topic in greater

depth. Rather than memorizing which stage comes after Erikson's stage of **Autonomy vs. Shame and Doubt**, it is more helpful to be able to put the information in context and to understand how the successful resolution of that stage can help guide further development. Specifically, it is important to keep interrelating the various developmental lines and structural theories to decipher how these different aspects of development intertwine to allow a particular child to reach age-appropriate developmental milestones.

Developmental Lines

Development can be studied from the perspective of tracking a particular domain over time. For example, how does gross motor function develop from birth through adolescence? By following the attainment of successive milestones across many children, a population-based standard distribution is created which plots the range of variability in the development of each milestone. Based upon this data, the concept of "normal" refers to those children who fall within two standard deviations of the mean. Domains commonly studied include gross motor, fine motor, language, and social abilities.

ONLY STARS

This evening there are only stars—
Roland is born and I delivered him.
One hour ago my apprehensive hands
slid his body down onto a towel,
cut his cord and wrapped him in a sheet.
For one quick moment I held my child
and he blended with my half-crooked arm
as if he had been held that way forever.
This evening there are only stars.

This evening there are only stars
and one small human is made half from me
and half from his adoring mother.
He is of the morning dew and unaware
that I am of the afternoon and see into the night.
We all come from the same drumming darkness,
take the light of one brief life
and then return into the blackness whence we came.
But, though we are ephemeral, we have
a galaxy which fires us from within—
this evening there are only stars.

DUNCAN DARBISHIRE

Structural Theories of Development

Development can also be studied by examining how the attainment of certain skills allows for the progressive learning of new ones. The structural theories introduce the concept that there is some formation or reorganization of the mind that allows further progression of development.

Many different theories have been formulated to explain development. The major theories that will be covered in this chapter include Freud's Theory of Psychosexual Development, Erikson's Theory of Psychosocial Development, Piaget's Theory of Cognitive Development, Mahler's Theory of Separation-Individuation, and Bowlby's Attachment Theory. Each theory adopts different labels for stages that occur at different age ranges. For this chapter, children will be described using developmental snapshots at specific age groups. The goal is to understand the child by incorporating the multiple developmental lines and structural theories in order to gain a more complete view of the child from multiple perspectives. Each structural theory will be further detailed in age-specific "Developmental Snapshots" later in this chapter.

You may give them your love but not your thoughts.
For they have their own thoughts.
You may house their bodies but not their souls,
For their souls dwell in the house of tomorrow, which you cannot
visit, not even in your dreams.

KHALIL GIBRAN
The Prophet

Sigmund Freud's Phases of Psychosexual Development

Freud developed the **psychoanalytic theory**, a body of hypotheses concerning mental functioning and personality development. One of Freud's most important contributions was the concept of the **unconscious**, which refers to thoughts and motives existing outside a person's awareness that have the capacity to influence thoughts and actions. Freud's psychoanalytic treatment used the process of **free association** (in which a patient says everything that comes to mind) to bring unconscious material into conscious awareness.

Freud's theory of the mind was broken up into three divisions: the **id, ego**, and **superego**. The id is unconscious and serves as the root of impulses and primitive, pleasure-based needs. The ego is a conscious mediator of the id and controls behaviors and thoughts. The third division is the superego, which is part of the unconscious and regulates the ego. The superego formed through the internalization of standards learned from society and authority figures, such as parents, and serves as the focus of aspiration and personal goals. Freud also introduced the concept of **drives**, instinctual urges that produce a state of psychic excitation or tension, that impel the individual to activity. The two major drives, sexual and aggressive, are each associated with psychic energy. The psychic energy associated with the sexual drive is termed **libido**. The source of these drives is the id, which is attempted to be regulated by the rational part of the mind, which is the ego. Initially, the ego cedes power to the id, but over time the ego attempts to control the id in effort to offer personal gratification.

TABLE 3.2 Phases of Freud's theory of psychosexual development

Phase	Age (Years)
Oral	Birth to 1
Anal	1 to 3
Phallic	3 to 5
Latency	5 to 11
Genital	11 and above

Freud's theory of psychosexual development describes the sequential manifestations of the sexual drive from infancy onward. He postulated that developmental stages progressed as the child's focus of **libidinal energy** changed to different erotic areas (Table 3.2). The child's goal during each stage is to experience the pleasure that comes from that area while attempting to lessen pain. Resolution of conflict involved in each of these stages allows the individual to move toward achieving normal adult functioning. Through this theory, Freud stressed the importance that development in childhood, including infancy, has on the grown adult.

Freud published his *Three Essays on the Theory of Sexuality* in 1915; in this work, he described the mouth, anus, and genitalia as foci for *libidinal energy*. He also added a period of decreased sexual interest, termed *latency*, which continues until the onset of puberty. Despite more recent work that has shown significant psychosexual activity during the latency phase, Freud's theory of psychosexual phases is a helpful tool in understanding development.

Erik Erikson's Stages of Psychosocial Development

Erikson focused more on the interplay between biology and society as it influences psychosocial development. In contrast to Freud, he stressed the importance of childhood events and experiences during adulthood. Furthermore, Erikson focused primarily on the ego (rather than the id drives of Freud) and its association with social underpinnings. He presented the **epigenetic principle** which states that development occurs sequentially through eight stages over the course of a lifetime. Each stage has two possible outcomes, one positive (healthy) and the other negative (unhealthy), and builds upon the progress made in the previous stage. If a stage is not satisfactorily resolved, then the person is unable to achieve a new and higher level of functioning (Table 3.3). In addition, if stressors or disruptions occur, regression may occur to an earlier stage of development.

TABLE 3.3 Stages of Erikson's Theory of Psychosocial Development

Stage	Age (Years)
Basic Trust versus Mistrust	Birth to 1
Autonomy versus Shame and Doubt	1 to 3
Initiative versus Guilt	3 to 5
Industry versus Inferiority	5 to 11
Ego Identity versus Role Diffusion	11 to 21
Intimacy versus Isolation	21 to 40
Generativity versus Stagnation	40 to 60
Ego Integrity versus Despair	60 to death

As our society changes, the relative age spans for each of the stages may shift as well. For example, as people live longer and retire later in life, the generativity versus stagnation stage may become prolonged and the ego integrity versus despair stage may be delayed.

> The adolescent mind is essentially a mind of the moratorium, a psychosocial stage between childhood and adulthood, and between the morality learned by the child and the ethics developed by the adult.
>
> ERIK ERIKSON
> *Childhood and Society*

Jean Piaget's Stages of Cognitive Development

Piaget studied children's thoughts and behavior to derive his theory of cognitive development. He theorized that intellectual functions formed the core of personality and provided for the coordinated progression of development along all spheres. Like Freud and Erikson, he believed that future stages depended on properly negotiated previous stages. However, although the stages occur sequentially, they rely on the maturation of the nervous system and on life experiences to determine their rate of progress (Table 3.4).

Piaget focused on equilibration, which is the pattern of knowledge formulation when a child addresses a novel situation. Vital to equilibration are the concepts of **assimilation** and **accommodation**, which are necessary tools for cognitive development. *Assimilation is defined as the ability to fit an experience with an existing cognitive structure.* Consider a child who turns on a switch at home and understands that by turning the switch, he caused the lights to turn on. By assimilation, he can then correlate that turning on a switch at his grandparents' home may also cause the lights to turn on. *Accommodation, however, is the process of adapting the existing cognitive structure to new experiences.* For example, when faced with an object placed out of reach, a child uses accommodation to figure out that the baseball bat he usually uses to hit balls can also be used as an implement to reach distant objects. Cognition grows through these novel experiences, using prior learned behavior to

TABLE 3.4 Stages of Piaget's Theory of Cognitive Development

Stage	Age (Years)
Sensorimotor	Birth to 2
Preoperational Thought	3 to 6
Concrete Operations	7 to 10
Formal Operations	11 and above

foster new growth. However, if the new task differs too much from the previous learned experience, frustration or fear can grow secondary to this gap. These intense emotions can prevent a new equilibrium from being reached, limiting further growth.

> Mother is the name for God in the lips and hearts of little children . . .
>
> WILLIAM THACKERAY
> *Vanity Fair*

TABLE 3.5 Stages of Bowlby's Attachment Theory

Stage	Age
Preattachment	Birth to 8–10 weeks
Attachment in the Making	8–10 weeks to 6 months
Clear-Cut Attachment	6 months to end of life

John Bowlby's Attachment Theory

Bowlby's **attachment theory** incorporated his psychoanalytic understanding of child development with evolutionary theory to postulate a genetic basis for infant attachment to caregivers. He described attachment as "a warm, intimate and continuous relationship with the mother in which both find satisfaction and enjoyment." Attachment is contrasted by **bonding**, which is a set of feelings that parents have toward their child distinct from the child's feelings toward his or her parents. Bowlby theorized that attachment behaviors promote nearness to the attachment figure so that dangers can be avoided. Early attachment behaviors include crying, smiling, and cooing. Later attachment behaviors include verbalizing and nonverbal signaling; these behaviors persist throughout life. Bowlby described three stages of attachment (Table 3.5). During the **preattachment** stage (birth to 8–10 weeks), the baby orients to the caregiver, follows her with his eyes over a 180 degree range, and turns toward her voice; however, the infant does not discriminate among caregivers. In the second stage, the **attachment in the making** stage (8–10 weeks to 6 months), the infant becomes attached to one or more figures in his or her environment. In these first two stages, as long as the infant's needs are being satisfied, separation from a particular person does not induce distress. In the **clear cut attachment** stage (6 months to end of life), the infant is distressed by separation from the caregiver and stops crying and clings upon her return.

Margaret Mahler's Theory of Separation-Individuation

Mahler studied the separation-individuation process between mother and child from birth to 3 years of age (Table 3.6). The **normal autistic phase** (birth to 4 weeks) refers to a state of half-sleep, half-wake during which the major task is to achieve homeostatic equilibrium with the environ-

ment. In the **normal symbiotic phase** (3–4 weeks to 4–5 months), the infant has a vague awareness of the mother, but still functions as if he and the caretaker are in a state of undifferentiation or fusion. Mahler identified four subphases of separation-individuation. The first subphase, **differentiation** (5 to 10 months), describes the process of "hatching from the autistic shell" as the infant develops a more alert sensorium. "Stranger anxiety" develops at this time, and is most prominent around 8 months. The second subphase, **practicing** (10 to 16 months), is marked by upright locomotion and using mother as "home base." Separation anxiety typically develops around this time. During the third subphase, **rapprochement** (16 to 24 months), the infant becomes more aware of himself as separate from the mother, and a sense of identity is consolidated. Two characteristic patterns of behavior emerge: shadowing of the mother and running from her. These *rapprochement crises* are ultimately resolved as the child experiences gratification from doing things for himself. The fourth subphase of separation-individuation is termed **consolidation and object constancy**, and refers to the child's internalization of the mother as stable and reliable. This allows the child to tolerate separations from mother because he knows she will return.

TABLE 3.6 Mahler's Phases of Separation-Individuation

Stage	Age
Normal Autistic Phase	Birth to 4 weeks
Normal Symbiotic Phase	3–4 weeks to 4–5 months
Differentiation	5 months to 10 months
Practicing	10 months to 16 months
Rapprochement	16 months to 24 months
Consolidation and Object Constancy	24 months to 36 months

DEVELOPMENTAL SNAPSHOTS

Infancy (Birth to 18 Months)

The average newborn weighs between 7 and 7.5 pounds, and measures 19–21 inches in length. Growth occurs at a faster rate during the first year of life than at any subsequent period until the onset of puberty. An infant will normally grow between 10 and 12 inches within the first year of life, and height at age 2 will be about 50% of mature adult height. Weight gain is approximately an ounce a day for the first few months of life. Birth weight is doubled by 4 months of age, tripled by the end of the first year, and quadrupled by age 2. The average infant gains 14 pounds in the first year of life.

A newborn child is born in a state of complete dependency for survival and must rely on parents and caretakers for all aspects of basic care. The child has poor sensory organ function, only minimal control over limb movements, and is unable to communicate other than by crying. Due to the child's inability to self-soothe and the need for immediate responses from caregivers, control over eye gaze, head turning, and sucking are used to indicate needs and desires.

The major developmental tasks in these first months of life involve the formation of a secure attachment, regulation of the sleep wake cycle, and creation of a feeding pattern. The ability of the child and parents to resolve these issues is often dependent upon the child's temperament. **Temperament** refers to a set of inborn traits that shape the child's approach to the world. The child's personality will be determined by the interaction of these individual differences in behavioral style with the environment. Chess and Thomas identified nine temperamental traits of infants (Table 3.7) that correlate with labels like "easy," "difficult," and "slow to warm up." The concept of temperament is helpful as it incorporates the role of the child in these early interactions and stresses the concept of "goodness of fit" between child and caregiver. It stresses that there needs to be a match between the child's temperament and the caregiver's parenting style in order to improve functioning and to avoid behavioral and emotional problems.

TABLE 3.7 Chess and Thomas' Nine Behavioral Dimensions for Temperament

Activity Level

Rhythmicity

Approach or Withdrawal

Adaptability

Intensity of Reaction

Threshold of Responsiveness

Quality of Mood

Distractibility

Attention span and persistence

By the second month of life, the child becomes more interactive with parents and develops a social smile. This is followed by the ability to examine and reach for objects in the midline by three months, rolling over by four months, and being able to hold the head up and coo (produce long vowel

sounds in musical fashion) soon after. These activities provide positive reinforcement to parents who in turn respond with additional attention and affectionate behavior toward the child.

During this time, Erikson's **Basic Trust vs. Mistrust** stage (birth to 1 year) comes into play, as infants learn whether their needs are being met. The availability of a supportive and responsive parent allows the formation of a secure attachment and a sense of basic trust. Inconsistent parenting leads to mistrust and feelings of despair in the child. Bowlby's study of attachment behavior in infants demonstrated that the lack of a secure attachment with the caregiver (usually the mother) could negatively affect the child's emotional and intellectual development. Bowlby found that three stages exist during mother-infant separation. Initially, the child protests and cries for the caregiver. This is followed by despair when the child believes that the caregiver will not return. With continued separation, detachment occurs as the child loses emotional connection to the caregiver.

At 6 months, the child can sit unsupported, lift a cup, and transfer objects. At 9 months, the child develops a **pincer grasp** (e.g., uses his thumb to help grasp tiny objects), pulls himself to standing, says "mama" or "dada," and plays interpersonal games like "peek-a-boo." The ability to manipulate objects with better motor control allows the child to place objects in his or her mouth. As the child successfully maneuvers different objects, he or she achieves a sense of mastery, which creates an increased desire for autonomy (e.g., feeding self). The child's focusing of libidinal and aggressive energy toward oral pleasure zones is explained by Freud's **Oral Phase** (birth to 1 year). The child is receiving oral gratification from the act of nursing while attempting to control aggressive urges to bite, chew, or spit. During this phase the child develops trust in the caregiver. *A child who adequately resolves these conflicts develops the ability to give and receive from others, trust others, and experience self-reliance. A child with poor resolution of this stage may exhibit dependent features, low self-esteem, envy, and jealousy.*

Piaget's **Sensorimotor Stage** (birth to 2 years) refers to the development of sensory awareness which allows the child to gain better control over motor functions. Children use their new-found skills and motor abilities to explore and manipulate their environment in an effort to build new skills. As the child receives sensory input, his or her motor system responds in a stereotyped, reflexive way. As this happens again and again, the child gradually becomes aware of this stimulus-response loop. Piaget's theory refers to this stimulus-response awareness as a **schema**. Later, as the child's interaction with the environment increases, he or she develops specific schemas (mental categories of information) about different objects and experiences. Each of these schemas is built upon to construct more complex schemata. These schemata then serve as reference points for the actions of assimilation and accommodation to further progress development.

By 9 months, object permanence forms as the child becomes aware that objects continue to exist even when they can no longer be seen. This leads to stranger anxiety in which children find it hard to separate from parents and will protest if left with strangers. Mary Ainsworth developed the "Strange Situation" research project to assess the quality of infant-parent attachment in 1–2 year olds. In this attachment paradigm, infants were observed across episodes of increasing stress (a series of separations and reunions). Ainsworth identified three distinct types of attachment in these infants. **Securely attached** children were able to use their mother as a base for exploration of toys and the environment, were active in seeking contact with her, and were reassured after finding contact with her. Children with **anxious/resistant attachment** were unable to use the mother as a base for exploration, were not readily comforted by contact with her, and mixed contact seeking with anger. Infants with **anxious/avoidant attachments** withheld contact with the mother and ignored or avoided her following separation. Ainsworth believed that a caregiver's consistent responsiveness to the infant's needs leads to secure attachment. Insensitive care leads to the resistant pattern of attachment, and indifferent or rejecting care leads to the avoidant pattern of attachment. Ainsworth showed that the interaction between infant and caregiver during this early attachment period significantly influences both the child's current and future behavior.

By 12 months of age the child can walk independently, stack blocks, and speak 3–4 words. By 15 months, the child can creep upstairs, walk backwards, help in the house, and scribble by imitation. Play during infancy is primarily solitary (playing alone) or parallel (playing beside other children without interacting).

> A smart mother makes often a better diagnosis than a poor doctor.
>
> AUGUST BIER
> German professor of surgery

Toddler (18 months to 36 Months)

By the age of 18 months, the child has an improved sense of balance and a steadier gait. This improvement in motor skills leads to the ability to run and climb stairs. Cognitive development has also occurred allowing the child to solve problems in new ways. For example, instead of crying for a parent when a ball has rolled under the sofa out of reach, the child can now use a stick to get it.

CASE EXAMPLE

Jennifer is a 15-month-old Caucasian female who presented to her pediatrician with malnutrition and poor weight gain. Jennifer's visits to her pediatrician had been sporadic since birth, and on this visit her height and weight were noted to be below the 5th percentile.

Jennifer was admitted to the hospital for evaluation. A thorough medical workup failed to reveal an underlying physical cause for her malnutrition and poor weight gain. In the hospital, Jennifer responded rapidly to adequate feeding, and began gaining weight almost immediately.

Jennifer had no prior history of medical problems and no prior hospitalizations. She was the product of a normal full-term pregnancy, the youngest of four children, and lived with her mother. The Mother was 25 years old and had completed high school. She was unemployed, and reported that she had been dealing with a number of stressors including her boyfriend moving out of the home, limited financial resources, and the recent death of her parents in an automobile accident. She endorsed symptoms of severe depression and anxiety, and reported being unable to get out of bed on some days. Mother denied the use of alcohol or illicit drugs.

On examination, Jennifer was a cachectic appearing infant who was below the 5th percentile for height and weight, and in the 25th percentile for head circumference. She avoided eye contact, appeared to be disinterested in her surroundings, and resisted cuddling. She was able to sit alone, but was unable to walk. Mother described Jennifer as an irritable baby who cried frequently and awakened often during sleep. She reported that Jennifer had not yet spoken, and that she rarely smiled. Mother admitted feeling overwhelmed with Jennifer's care and often relegated it to Jennifer's 10-year-old sister.

The medical team requested a psychiatry consult to assess the mother's emotional functioning and a social work consult to assess Jennifer's social environment. The psychiatrist reported that Jennifer's mother met criteria for a severe depressive disorder as well as an anxiety disorder, and recommended treatment with medication and psychotherapy. The social worker reported that the mother had a history of domestic violence and was socially isolated, and that her level of poverty prevented her from providing her children with adequate nutrition.

The consensus of the medical team was that Jennifer met criteria for *failure to thrive*, a multifactorial syndrome characterized by weight gain deceleration, linear growth delay, and developmental delays. In Jennifer's case, weight gain and growth delays were thought to be the result of inadequate caloric intake, while her developmental delays were likely the result of emotional and socioeconomic deprivation. Because Jennifer's mother was so incapacitated by her depression and anxiety, the team decided to file a report with the state's Department of Social Services (DSS).

Together with DSS, the medical team developed a treatment plan that included referring the mother for treatment of her psychiatric disorders as well as for parenting classes, making a referral for early intervention services for Jennifer, and making arrangements for visiting nurses to go to the home to assist the mother in developing a feeding schedule for Jennifer. DSS was also able to make arrangements for daycare for the three other children, and assisted Jennifer's mother in setting up an appointment with a career counselor.

MEMORY TIP The "Bottom" Line

WET has three letters and most children should gain bladder control shortly AFTER age 3. MESS has four letters and most children should gain bowel control shortly BEFORE age 4.

This added functional ability gives rise to Erikson's stage of **Autonomy vs. Shame and Doubt** (1 to 3 years). In this stage, the child wants to explore the environment further as well as to develop greater anal sphincter control. In attempting these tasks, the child relies on basic trust to deal with the distress of being separated from parents and of having a bowel or bladder accident. Shame and doubt occur when a child is unable to achieve autonomy in these functions.

At 18 months, Mahler's **rapprochement** stage of separation-individuation occurs as the child's increasing awareness of helplessness and dependence leads to greater anxiety over separation from the caregiver. The child may test the waters by slowly moving away from the caregiver a short distance and then returning for additional support and reassurance. As the level of comfort increases and anxiety decreases, the distance from the caregiver also increases.

A **transitional object** assists the child in making the transition from complete dependence on the caregiver to independence. First described by Donald Winnicott, the transitional object may take the form of a blanket, pillow or stuffed toy. These objects remind the child of the caregiver and serve a soothing function while the child is falling asleep, or during times of stress or separation from the caregiver. *Attachment to a transitional object is a normal and healthy phase in the development of a toddler.*

Children at 18 months have a vocabulary of 15 words, which increases to 100 words by 24 months (speech is usually half-understandable by an unknown examiner at this stage). The newly emerging language development marked by this exponential increase in vocabulary signifies the end of Piaget's sensorimotor stage and the beginning of his **Pre-operational Stage** (2 years to 7 years). During this stage, children continue to function at a prelogical state, i.e., they are not yet able to use logical processes to arrive at conclusions. Piaget's experiment on **conservation of mass** illustrates this point. Children are asked to transfer water between two glasses that are shaped differently but hold the same amount of water. When asked which glass holds more water, children with prelogical thinking will pick the longer taller glass despite seeing the same amount of water being exchanged back and forth.

The emergence of symbolic play and magical thinking interweaves to affect the child's interactions in new situations. As opposed to play in the sensorimotor stage where little attention is paid to a toy's intended purpose, the child now understands the functional use of toys, and can even use them to represent other things. For example, a doll can be the mean mommy who gives time-outs for misbehaving.

Magical thinking can be troublesome as a blurred sense of reality testing in conjunction with prelogical thinking can make many things seem plausible. For example, children may fear sitting on a toilet for fear of getting swallowed down the drain.

At this time, greater sphincter control and erotic sensations in the anal area lead to Freud's **Anal Phase** (1 year to 3 years). This is a period marked by the need to separate and develop autonomy from the caregiver while obtaining greater bodily control and a capacity for speech and symbol formation. *The child's sense of autonomy is combined with ambivalent feelings about separating from the caregiver while acquiring new skills. This ambivalence may be expressed by holding in or letting out feces during a bowel movement, or by needy and clingy behaviors.*

At every step the child should be allowed to meet the real experiences of life; the thorns should never be plucked from his roses.

ELLEN KEY
The Century of the Child

CASE EXAMPLE

Sam was a 2- and- one-half-year-old boy who was referred for a developmental evaluation by his pediatrician because of concerns about language delay. Sam was the product of a normal pregnancy and delivery and lived with his parents and 5-year-old sister. The Parents reported that Sam had been a very fussy baby who was difficult to soothe and who often seemed to be "in a world of his own." Sam had never exhibited stranger anxiety, and had shown only mild interest in the social games of infancy such as peek-a-boo and pat-a-cake. He did not seem to take comfort in being held, and in fact would stiffen when his parents picked him up. Sam had no interest in pretend play or social interactions, and seemed happiest when sitting by himself lining his crayons from end to end. He had always exhibited very poor eye contact.

The parents described Sam as a "rigid" child, who was very sensitive to sounds and food textures and who insisted on the same routine every day. He would have severe behavioral outbursts if his routine was changed or when asked to try new foods. Sam's motor development had been normal, although he exhibited repetitive motor behaviors such as hand flapping when excited. Parents reported that his vocabulary consisted of only several words, however, he did appear to have an age-appropriate understanding of language.

Sam had no history of medical problems and took no medications. There was no family history of medical or psychiatric disorders. A comprehensive medical workup, which included a hearing test, EEG, CT scan, genetic screening, and chromosomal analysis, was negative.

On the basis of Sam's disturbances in social interaction, language, and communication, as well as his restricted, repetitive, and stereotyped patterns of behavior, the diagnosis of autism was made. Sam was enrolled in an intensive multidisciplinary treatment program that included speech and language therapy, occupational therapy, and behavioral therapy, and training in social skills.

The development of a sense of self is a critical developmental task.

Preschooler (3 Years to 5 Years)

The child's rate of growth slows during the preschool years. The average preschooler can be expected to gain 5–6 pounds annually until age 6, and grow 2–3 inches in height per year. The preschool child also experiences further improvement in gait and balance. During this time, children become more involved in self-care and activities of daily living, such as dressing themselves without help, preparing simple foods (e.g., cereal), and brushing teeth without help. The ability to throw, catch, and kick balls is seen in the common games of this age. *Bowel and bladder control develops by 30 months of age on average, with girls generally achieving control before boys.* Vocabulary continues to grow to nearly 2000 words by age five. By the start of kindergarten, children are speaking in sentences, using proper grammar, and are able to use speech to express emotions instead of acting them out.

There is also a shift from primarily parallel play at age 2 to cooperative play by age 4. During cooperative play, children must balance their egocentrism with the wishes of the group or playmate. To deal with this new form of interaction, rules are seen as absolute, with guilt assigned for bad outcomes regardless of the other child's intention. Behavioral limits are progressively internalized such that by age 5 the child can internally regulate what is considered appropriate behavior.

These skills are essential for success in the classroom. The ability to internalize limits and self-soothe helps the child to control behavior and emotions when away from his or her parents. Internalized images of trusted adults allow the child to experience comfort and security during times of separation and stress.

Children in this age group continue in Piaget's **Preoperational Stage** until 7 years of age, as described previously. Thinking is characterized by **egocentrism**, in which the child experiences every event in reference to him or herself. For example, the child may believe that night comes to make him sleep or that rain falls to keep him inside. Children of this age also believe they can alter reality by their thoughts or wishes (**magical thinking**). Children are better able to use their evolving language skills and creative endeavors, such as drawing and pictures, to share their experiences with others.

In Erikson's stage of **Initiative vs. Guilt** (3 years to 5 years), the child's basic task is to develop a sense of initiative and competence. He or she will develop a positive sense of self and ambition if allowed to initiate meaningful motor and intellectual activities and explore the environment. If children are made to feel inadequate about their interests they may emerge from this stage with a sense of guilt over self-initiated activity. *During this stage, the child also experiences sexual impulses toward the parent of the opposite sex,*

My dear Watson, you as a medical man are continually gaining light as to the tendencies of a child by the study of the parents. Don't you see that the converse is equally valid. I have frequently gained my first real insight into the character of parents by studying their children.

SHERLOCK HOLMES commenting to his physician colleague John Watson in *"The Adventure of the Copper Beeches"*

EMILY DROWNED

She asked me, aching-eyed.
I nodded. She sighed.
A twenty second silence followed,
Intense, explosive, hollowed
From the echo of the vaulted ceiling.
Charged with growing feeling
She screamed, "Oh! No. Oh! No,"
    and sank her nails
    into her husband's shoulder.
He, not much older,
Comforted her in vain
And stemmed his agony with a taut drawn rein.

A policeman came in haunting blue.
I left the parents to their loneliness
    and walked out through
The hall. In the grey street
My reluctant feet
    threw shattering steps upon the tar.
    We stopped.
The officer lifted the tailgate
Of his van and I heard him grate
His teeth. There, on a tartan rug, lay
Emily—three yesterday—

Pale and cold, she unmoving,
    I, so moved, I nearly cried.
    I had to touch her skin
    to certify her death.
I raised her eyelids. My misted breath
Dulled the already dull complexion of her eyes.
    She was dead.
I nodded to the officer and whispered, "She's
dead,"
And thought of my own small daughter
Asleep at home in bed.
    Emily had drowned in two feet of water
In the field behind
Her house. The weather signed
The sadness of the evening
With a bereaving
Winter shower.

I had to return to the parents
    who would sob for hour
On hour in each other's arms.
Gone were the infant charms
That dressed their home;
They cried together, but alone.

DUNCAN DARBISHIRE

which leads to fantasies of competing with the same-sex parent for a special relationship with the opposite sex parent. For example, a girl in this stage may become very jealous of her mother holding father's hand, or a boy may insist on taking a photo with mother alone to the exclusion of his father. By the end of this stage, the child's conscience has developed, which leads to the moral sense of right and wrong. The child has learned that aggressive impulses can be expressed in constructive ways, such as through play and sports.

Freud's **Phallic Phase** (3 years to 5 years) further explores this process. Children at this age are aware of the physical differences between boys and girls. Their focus is shifted toward the genitalia and play during this time is characterized by activities that reflect curiosity about the body's sexual functions. The child has strong libidinal and aggressive urges, which establish the **oedipal complex**. In the oedipal complex, the child seeks a relationship with the opposite sex parent and has aggressive urges to get rid of the same sex parent. In boys, this leads to **castration anxiety**, in which the fear of father cutting off his penis leads to repression of sexual interest in mother. Children can be-

come very possessive of the opposite sex parent with hostility toward the same sex parent during this time. This conflict is played out through fantasies and dreams, ultimately leading to resolution of the oedipal complex. This resolution permits the child to develop a healthy relationship with the same sex parent.

School-Age (5 years to 12 Years)

Increases in height and weight during the school-age years are gradual and steady compared with the earlier years and adolescence. Between the ages of 6 and 12, the average child will grow 2–2.5 inches and gain 3–6 pounds per year. The average 6-year-old child is approximately 3.5 feet tall and weighs about 40 pounds. By 12 years of age, the average child is almost 5 feet tall and weighs approximately 80 pounds. *Growth rates in boys and girls are equal until about age 9, when girls begin to grow more rapidly.*

By five or 6 years of age, children are less likely to employ magical thinking and are better able to separate fantasy

CASE EXAMPLE

Tommy was a 5-year-old boy who was referred by his pediatrician for psychiatric evaluation of "severe behavioral disturbance." Tommy had recently entered kindergarten, and was on the verge of being expelled for obstreperous behavior. His mother related that at a recent school conference, the teacher stated that Tommy "never sat still" and was constantly in motion throughout the day. In addition, she reported that Tommy talked incessantly and frequently blurted out answers to questions before hearing the entire question. He had difficulty waiting for his turn in classroom activities, and was disliked by the other children because of his inability to play cooperatively. The teacher also reported that Tommy was unable to sustain attention on anything for more than a few minutes, was easily distracted, and never listened to anything she said. Mother reported that the teacher called her almost every day because Tommy wouldn't follow simple routines and had difficulty playing with peers. He was sent to the "time-out corner" almost daily.

The mother described similar behaviors at home. She reported that Tommy had always been a very active and curious child who was constantly "on the go." Recently Tommy had started referring to himself as a "bad boy," and his mother worried that all of the negative interactions at school were affecting his self-esteem. He had no prior history of medical or psychiatric problems, and there was no family history of medical or psychiatric disorders. Tommy was on no medications. A complete medical workup to rule out a physical cause for his behavioral problems had recently been performed and was negative.

On evaluation, Tommy was a well-developed, well-nourished boy who appeared his stated age. He initially sat quietly in a chair next to his mother for several minutes, however he soon had difficulty sitting still and began to fidget. He walked to the toy chest and began to take out all of toys and place them on the floor without playing with any of them. He threw a ball across the room and nearly hit the window. For the remainder of the examination, Tommy displayed hyperactive and impulsive behavior.

On the basis of Tommy's history as well as medical and psychiatric evaluations, the diagnosis of Attention Deficit Hyperactivity Disorder, combined type, was made. A comprehensive treatment plan was developed which included behavioral therapy, social skills training, family therapy, school consultation, and parent training. The physician decided to avoid or at least postpone a trial of stimulant medication. Tommy responded well to this treatment regimen, with significant reduction in symptoms of hyperactivity and impulsivity, and improved relationships with parents, peers, and teacher.

A Boy is Beaten Because He Broke a Jar *Francisco José de Goya (circa 1800).* Courtesy of the National Library of Medicine. *Parents frequently use punishment to control the behavior of their children, but reinforcement is more effective in the long run.*

from reality. They are able to apply rules, to understand alternate points of view, and to sustain attention over 45 minutes for class. They can tolerate the increased demand from school as they begin the first grade. Children develop self-esteem and they can gauge their performance in class. They look for positive praise from adults outside of the home (e.g., school teachers and coaches) and focus on accomplishment. The irrational fears of the preschool child are replaced with more realistic concerns about everyday life, such as school failure and peer rejection. Children may cope with these fears by identifying with superheroes who are seen as invincible.

The beginning of school brings Erikson's stage of **Industry vs. Inferiority** (6 years to 12 years) to the forefront as the child seeks mastery at school. The level of success at school will affect self-esteem as the child looks for praise beyond that received from the child's parents. If the child feels competent in academic and social interactions, he or she will develop a sense of industry or confidence. If the child is unsuccessful in these areas he or she will develop a sense of inferiority.

Piaget's Preoperational Stage continues until roughly age 6 when the stage of **Concrete Operations** begins. The word operations refers to the logical principles (rules) we use to solve problems. During this time, the child's reasoning and conceptual skills develop, and thinking becomes more organized and logical. As abstract thought is lacking or very limited, school-age children are generally motivated to follow or to conform to rules. **Conservation** refers to the idea that a quantity remains the same despite changes in appearance. *With concrete operations in effect, the child is*

CASE EXAMPLE

Amy was a 10-year-old girl who was brought to her pediatrician's office for evaluation of persistent abdominal pain and vomiting of 4 weeks duration. The symptoms began during winter vacation, occurred on a daily basis, and were constant and severe. The abdominal pain and vomiting were worse in the mornings, and gradually subsided over the course of the day. Amy did not experience her symptoms over the weekends. She had been unable to attend school for the past month, and her mother was considering making arrangements for home tutoring. A complete medical workup performed recently showed no evidence of physical disease to account for the symptoms. Amy and parents denied history of recent or remote abuse or trauma. Amy was in the 5th grade and lived with her parents and younger brother. She had no history of medical or psychiatric disorders, was not sexually active, and took no medications. Her family history was significant for anxiety in Amy's mother and maternal grandmother.

Amy's pediatrician recommended a psychiatric evaluation to assess for an emotional contribution to her symptoms. The psychiatric evaluation revealed that Amy had functioned extremely well in school until this year, when her grades had dropped significantly. Amy reported that she had trouble concentrating on her schoolwork because "I just don't get it most of the time." She reported that her classmates made fun of her for being stupid and that her teacher was constantly reminding her to "stop daydreaming and get to work." Just prior to winter vacation, her group of girlfriends had "ditched" her, leaving her to eat lunch alone each day. Amy endorsed symptoms of mild depression including insomnia, decreased energy and low self-esteem.

The psychiatrist recommended that Amy undergo psycho-educational testing, which revealed a learning disorder. In addition, Amy met criteria for a depressive disorder and school phobia. The treatment plan included a return to school with implementation of remedial educational services, social skills training, and psychotherapy aimed at treating depression and improving self-esteem.

Father's Day card from Jeremy Wedding, age 9. *Parents typically cherish the cards and handmade gifts they receive from their children.*

The Golden Days *Balthus (1944–1946).* Hirshhorn Museum and Sculpture Garden, Smithsonian Institution, Washington D.C., Gift of the Joseph H. Hirshhorn Foundation, 1966. Photograph by Lee Stalsworth. Copyright © 2010, Artists Rights Society, Inc. (ARS), New York/ ADAGP, Paris. *This provocative painting captures the twin themes of emerging sexuality and preoccupation with self. Preoccupation with personal appearance is common in teens; in adults it can suggest the presence of a narcissistic personality disorder.*

able to conserve number, length and liquid volume. In addition, children tend to incorporate others views during this phase, becoming less egocentric than compared to the preoperational stage.

The child now enters Freud's **Latency Phase.** Freud postulated this to be a time of diminished sexual drive during which the child's attention turned toward societal endeavors. Although Freud described the disappearance of observable sexual behavior, children at this age do indeed engage in sexualized play, including masturbation.

The child begins to identify with the same sex parent and may imitate his or her behavior. There is an incorporation of more of the beliefs and values of the culture, and most children learn to distinguish between acceptable and unacceptable behaviors. During this phase, children tend to seek playmates of the same sex. They are interested in joint play, and make friendships on the basis of shared interests or experiences. *Play is often segregated by gender, with boys more likely to be engaged in aggressive competitive play, while girls participate in the more gentle competition of hopscotch, jump rope and "Simon Says."*

Children spend their days in school, where they must adjust to separation from parents, negotiate new relationships with teachers and peers, and begin the process of structured learning.

Adolescence (13 years to 18 Years)

Adolescence is the period of transition from childhood to adulthood. It is characterized by rapid growth, changes in physical appearance, and sexual development. *Puberty re-*

*fers to the period of adolescence that results in sexual maturation, while **adolescence** refers to the time from onset of puberty to the beginning of adulthood.* The adolescent **"growth spurt"** begins with the onset of adolescence and refers to changes in height, weight and body proportions. It typically begins earlier in girls than boys, and lasts about 4-and-one-half years. The adolescent growth spurt is accompanied by sexual maturation.

Sexual maturation in girls begins with breast bud development (**telearche**) between 8 and 13 years of age, followed by a spurt in height, pubic hair development (**pubarche**, average age = 11), and finally onset of menses (**menarche**) between ten and fifteen years of age. Recent studies in the United States have demonstrated earlier onset of sexual maturity in young women than previous decades. In boys, testicular enlargement occurs first (beginning at age 11), accompanied by changes in voice tone and the development of sexual interest. Testicular enlargement is followed by penile enlargement and later **adrenarche**. Male growth spurts tend to occur starting from 10.5–16 years of age and is generally completed by age 13.5–17.5. During this period, ejaculation occurs for first time during masturbation or sleep (**nocturnal emissions**).

Adolescents are acutely aware of the changes taking place in their bodies. The timing of maturation can play an important role in the adolescent's perception of him or herself. For example, early maturing boys tend to be respected by peers and treated more like adults. They may become involved in intimate relationships with girls sooner and have more confidence in boy-girl relations than late maturing boys. Overall, early maturing boys tend to be more poised and self-confident than late maturing boys. Early maturing girls, on the other hand, often feel different from

Adolescence *Gerald Leslie Brockhurst (1932). Etching on wove paper. Gift of Cloud Wampler, 1963.* Courtesy of the Syracuse University Art Collection, Syracuse, N.Y. *Sexual awakening is a critical part of the adolescent's development.*

and may be teased by their peers. Tobin-Richards and colleagues found that seventh grade girls who perceive their rate of development to be similar to their peers had higher self-esteem than late maturing girls.

During adolescence, individuals begin to view and perceive significant changes in society and the world around them, as detailed by Piaget's stage of **Formal Operations**. This stage marks the ability to use abstract concepts, consider real and hypothetical events, solve problems systematically, and use logic and deductive reasoning. This ability to consider divergent possibilities and what might occur often lead to idealism and grandiosity, coupled with interest in politics, religion, ethics, and philosophy.

Freud's **Genital Phase** (12–18 years) begins with the physiological changes associated with puberty. During this final phase of psychosexual development, there is a renewed interest and pleasure derived from excretory activity. In addition, masturbation takes place and is engaged in much more frequently at this time than during the latency stage. Initially, adolescents tend to spend most of their time with platonic friends, generally same sex peers. However as

adolescents become more sexually developed they may start dating and may engage in sexual experimentation with people of the same and/or the opposite gender, and spend less time with platonic friends. The primary objectives of this phase are the development of a sense of identity and self-reliance with less dependence on parents that will allow transition to adult roles and responsibilities. However, this search for autonomy can cause marked rebelliousness and struggling with limits (consistent or inconsistent) set by authority figures. Children in this stage question and analyze extensively and may have more strained relations with family. This process of fostering autonomy, termed **individuation**, can be a tumultuous period as adolescents seek to become unique individuals linked between both past experiences and future projections. The previously strong attachment toward parental figures can separate and reorient toward peer groups. These groups, or cliques, have a major role in adolescence as young men and women seek autonomy and their own identities.

During Erikson's stage of **Identity vs. Role Diffusion** (12 to 20 years), the primary task of the adolescent is to develop a sense of identity with respect to self and society in order to avoid role confusion (e.g., a lack of a clear identity). Identity is created by the alignment and control of id impulses through the ego and healthy superego along with external relationships with family and peers. In addition, identity is further shaped by completion of sexual maturation and establishment of an adult body image. Healthy identity develops with successful resolution of the previous three psychosocial stages, a firm understanding of personal history and future direction, and identification with healthy parents or other important adults. *Failure to successfully negotiate this stage leads to role diffusion (identity confusion) in which the adolescent questions his place in the world and does not have a firm sense of self.* This may lead to depression and behavioral problems such as running away, substance abuse, or to joining gangs or cults in order to develop a sense of identity.

SUMMARY

The development of children from birth through adolescence illustrates the marvelous interaction that exists between genes and the environment. Children are born with a biological trajectory, which is influenced by the nature of their experiences and their environment. A systemic method for studying development will aid in the thorough and thoughtful evaluation of children and adolescents. Early detection of developmental delays will allow for course correction before global functioning is affected. Most importantly, timely and developmentally appropriate interventions can lead to life long improvements in the life of that child.

CASE STUDY

Jay is a 16-year-old boy who presented to his pediatrician's office for a routine checkup. His mother told the pediatrician of her concerns, which included recent school suspension because of oppositional behavior and lack of respect for authority. She reported that Jay seemed to have a "very short fuse" lately, that he'd "sleep all day if he could," and that his irritability and sullen moods had made family life "impossible."

In the interview, Jay described himself as "always bored" and noted that he was unhappy with his life. He noted fatigue, lack of energy, irritability and hypersomnia while exhibiting a sad affect. Jay noted sometimes "thinking about" suicide; however, he denied any intent to harm himself. He reported a 6-month history of marijuana use with occasional binge drinking. The rest of his physical exam was benign.

Jay's mother reported a family history significant for depression in Jay's father and paternal aunt. There was a history of current psychosocial stressors including Jay's girlfriend's recent move across the country and parental conflicts related to his mother's recent acceptance into law school. He had been an honor roll student until this year, when his grades dropped to C's and D's. For the past six months he has seemed easily distracted in class and has been exhibiting increasing levels of oppositional behavior at school.

His pediatrician thought that Jay met the criteria for major depressive disorder and substance use disorder. Jay was referred for a psychiatric evaluation that confirmed these diagnoses. He was started on a multimodal treatment regimen, which included individual psychotherapy directed at helping Jay come to terms with his recent loss as well as addressing his marijuana and alcohol abuse. Family therapy was initiated and was aimed at addressing and resolving intrafamilial conflicts related to his mother's new career aspirations. Pharmacotherapy with an SSRI antidepressant was initiated based upon his symptom severity and his positive family history of depression. Psychoeducational testing was performed and revealed a learning disability for which remedial services were instituted. Within several months, Jay's symptoms of depression had significantly improved, as well as his relationships with the family and school performance.

SUGGESTED READINGS

Erikson, E. (1959). *Identity and the life cycle*. New York: International University Press.

This classic text can serve to provide further insight and knowledge into Erikson's theory of psychosocial development, including additional clinical information on each stage and repercussions from inadequate resolution during development.

Freud, S. (1953). Three essays on the theory of sexuality. In J. Strachey (Ed.), *The standard edition of the complete psychological works of Sigmund Freud* (Vol. 7). London: Hogarth Press.

Freud's three timeless essays serve as the groundwork for his views on sexuality and psychosexual development. This reference provides a complete review of Freud's theory and work.

Lewis, M. (2004). Overview of development from infancy through adolescence. In J.M. Weiner, & M.K. Dulcan (Eds.), *Textbook of child and adolescent psychiatry* (pp. 13–44). Arlington, VA: American Psychiatric Publishing, Inc.

This comprehensive text serves as a thorough guide for background, research, diagnosis and treatment in the field of child and adolescent psychiatry. Created and edited by leading clinicians and researchers, this text can be used to enhance and expand the information provided in this chapter.

Needleman, R.D. (2004). Growth and development. In R.E. Behrman, R.M. Kliegman & H.B. Jenson (Eds.), *Nelson textbook of pediatrics* (17th ed.). Philadelphia: Saunders.

For those interested in the study of pediatric medicine, this is an indispensable text covering the entire field. The chapter on development and growth explains the physiological changes seen during growth from birth through puberty and adolescence.

Piaget, J. (1962). The stages of the intellectual development of the child. *Bulletin of the Menninger Clinic, 26*(3), 120–145.

This sentinel article describes Piaget's views on childhood development, providing further insight into the different operational stages described in this chapter.

Sadock, B.J., & Sadock, V.A. (2003). Human development through the life cycle. In *Kaplan and Sadock's synopsis of psychiatry* (10th ed.). Philadelphia: Lippincott Williams and Wilkins.

An essential text for those interested in pursuing psychiatry, but created for those who are learning the craft for the first time. This textbook is focuses on the entire field of psychiatry and provides helpful citations and information on the field of human development.

Early Adulthood and the Middle Years

Joseph D. LaBarbera & Danny Wedding

> In youth you find out what you care to do and who you care to be ... In young adulthood you learn who you care to be with ... In adulthood you learn to know what and whom you can take care of.
>
> ERIC ERIKSON
> *Dimensions of a New Identity*

Only recently has a developmental perspective been applied to adults. A barrier in doing so is the great variability that characterizes the lives of adults, compared to those of younger people. For example, while the vast majority of 10 year-old children in the US may be spending much of their time in school or playing with peers, the life patterns of adults are more diverse: adults work at various jobs or not at all, some are married and some not, and some have children while others don't. That multiplicity of roles and activities complicates our ability to generalize about adult development.

Until the late nineteenth century, there was little appreciation of the factors that contribute to change in young people, much less adults; children were viewed at that time largely as unformed grown-ups. Freud's work, which emphasized the role of unconscious conflict in early psychological development, altered that, but psychoanalysis had little to say about the developmental stages and challenges associated with adulthood. Much later, after initial work on children, Erickson turned his attention to adult development. *Erikson suggested that the key developmental task of young adulthood is to achieve a capacity for* **intimacy**. A person who can sustain intimacy is capable of close friendships and of giving and receiving love in a sexual relationship. Such a person is also able to join in solidarity with his or her comrades when their values or interests are threatened by outside forces. On the other hand, the person who is incapable of intimacy is likely to become isolated and self-absorbed, with cold, stereotyped relationships, unable to join others in common cause. *Mid-adulthood for Erikson*

involves a resolution of the issue of **generativity**. This refers to an individual's ability to contribute in various contexts, as for example through reproduction and childrearing and through investment in work. Thus, embedded in Erikson's work is the idea that people change, often in predictable ways, throughout their entire life span, that adults are not the same at 65 years as at 25 years, and that understanding adulthood demands more than an appreciation for the events—career choices, marriage, parenting—that people typically experience.

Several authors have described a key task of adulthood as *emancipation from the family of origin*. As an infant, one had to separate and individuate from the mother as a step toward mastering the tasks ahead, such as attending school and establishing relationships outside the family. So too does the young adult need to branch out on his or her own, this time more completely, as parents are left behind. The task of leaving the adolescent world may require one to modify or terminate adolescent relationships, reappraise values and interests, and clarify aspirations. Entrance to college facilitates disengagement from the old and assumption of the new. For the person who seeks out separation too early, paradoxically there may be too little genuine internal separation; conversely, one whose emotional separation is delayed may ultimately reject the "old ways" more completely than he or she would otherwise have done.

On entering adulthood one is faced with conflicting demands. One must maintain hard-won independence and

> Wholly unprepared, we embark upon the second half of life ... we take the step into the afternoon of life; worse still we take this step with the false assumption that our truths and ideals will serve as before. But we cannot live the afternoon of life according to the program of life's morning—for what was great in the morning will be little at evening, and what in the morning was true will at evening have become a lie.
>
> CARL JUNG

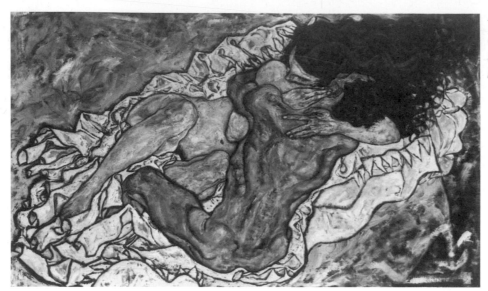

The Embrace *Egon Schiele (1917). Österreichische Galerie Belvedere, Vienna. Loving someone deeply and well is a fundamental parameter of mental health.*

keep options open, exploring the world and considering potential occupations, workmates, lovers, and friends. The same person must create a consistent life structure, avoiding chronic rootlessness. The expansiveness of adolescence gives way to adult commitment. In the end, most young adults will willingly give up part of their hard-won autonomy for the promise of satisfaction in work and love.

There are several fairly predictable crises or challenges of middle age. The heady dreams of young adulthood must often be abandoned in the face of the knowledge that time and energy are running out. In the best of cases these youthful dreams are replaced by an enjoyment of life as it is and by the anticipation of what it can realistically become. For some, the dreams of marriage and parenthood must be forsaken. Others find that their careers stall, with expected promotions going to younger coworkers. Still others succeed financially in mid-life but find they have little enthusiasm for their work or its rewards. Some sense the beginnings of physical and sexual decline or experience the death of romance through familiarity, and their marriages falter. Financial concerns and problems preoccupy many during the middle years, and plans for early retirement may have to be abandoned—this happened to many people during the financial crisis that occurred during the years 2007–2009. Although worrying about saving for their own retirement, the middle aged may also be concerned with financing children's college education and weddings and helping children launch their careers, and an increasing number of parents have had to continue to provide housing for adult children unable to find employment after graduation from college (e.g., 18% of men and 14% of women aged 25 to 29 still live at home with their parents). Late midlife is a time when parents, mentors, and friends die, and *people find themselves calculating their life in terms of the number of years they have left to live rather than the number of years that they have actually lived.*

The concept of "midlife crisis" was coined by Jacques (1965), and popularized in the 1960s and 1970s by Levinson's *Seasons of a Man's Life* and Sheehy's *Passages*. It referred to the frustration and impatience in the middle aged person who might therefore make some sudden and dramatic life adjustments, as for example quitting his job (it's almost always said to be a he), buying a sports car, and getting a divorce. While such patterns of behavior undoubtedly take place, the results of a large-scale study of the functioning of people in midlife (Brim, Ryff, & Kessler, 2002) have suggested that the midlife crisis is exaggerated in its frequency. Most middle-aged adults are guided by "psychological turning points," involving their recognition of their limitations, as for example the politician who realizes he will never attain a major office or the physician who realizes she will never be chief of staff. Such awareness prompts frequent but minor adjustments in attitude and behavior, obviating the pressure for an ultimate "crisis." Furthermore, the mid-life crisis, when it does occur, tends to be an affliction of the affluent; rosy illusions as to one's prospects are easier to sustain into middle age when one is shielded from unpleasant realities such as poverty.

MARRIAGE

Those who have reflected on the tasks of early adulthood have emphasized the importance of establishing intimate relationships. It is critical that, to affirm independence from the family of origin, the individual establish a mature relationship that recapitulates the closeness of a family. *Vaillant (1977) noted that those who have a stable marriage before age 30 and remain married until age 50 have the most favorable outcomes and are the best adjusted.* Successful marriage serves to facilitate autonomy from parents by replacing them as the primary sources of gratification. Hopefully, it is important that a new marriage not merely replicate the roles of parent and child. Levinson (1978) observed that the success of a marriage will be determined by several factors including conscious and unconscious needs relating to self-worth, intellectual stimulation, and the influence or pressures of family members and peers. Naturally, the degree to which spouses are able to react to each other, especially over time, contributes to success or failure. Because few people stay the same over decades, a strong commitment is required to deal with differences and misunderstandings, and failure to do so will weaken or even break the bond. Also critically important to the success of marriage is flexibility or ability to adjust over time to the changing needs, attitudes, and concerns of one's spouse. The husband or wife at ages 25 and 60 are very different persons.

Marriage, even during young adulthood, seems to traverse several distinct phases. Several authors have described an initial idealization, the earliest years bringing the highest level of satisfaction. What follows is typically a period of disenchantment. The experience of intense romantic love does not endure; once spent, it can leave the participants disillusioned. A renewed commitment may be required at that time, one based on factors that are more realistic than was the case initially. Those who are capable of doing so with a minimum of ambivalence will have the most successful marriages.

Levinson (1978) made the point that those who marry between adolescence and young adulthood have special problems with their relationships. A young man in that position is likely to view his wife, and a young woman her husband, as a powerful parenting figure. Such concerns are of less relevance for later marriages. Older people are capable of making choices less connected to parental pressures and "ghosts" and more in line with their true life goals and preferences. In other words, their spouses are more clearly partners rather than reminders of parents.

The early years of family life, filled with promise, enthusiasm, and the shared enjoyment of the challenge of parenting, do not end abruptly. However, many of the middle aged suddenly confront the financial burden of parenting, worry about relating to in-laws and relatives, and feel the impact of growing children on their sexual and marital relationships. The couple who either has opted not to have children or has been unable to have them faces somewhat different challenges. Their lives are filled with the need to balance careers, social responsibilities, and hobbies. Frequently, career demands may be so great that the partners fail to pay sufficient attention to each other's personal needs for attention and support, and they become entangled in tensions arising over changing needs for dependence or independence in the relationship.

Issues confronting the mid-life marriage include:

1. *Establishing boundaries:* Defining the extent to which family, such as in-laws, and friends impinge on family activities and decisions.
2. *Coping with careers and finances:* Dealing with the issues of dual career family, changes in work status (promotion, unemployment, and job satisfaction), financial competition between spouses, and the control of money.
3. *Parenting:* Deciding how many children to have and when to have them, allocating responsibility for child care, surviving the stresses of parenting, helping (or pushing) children into adulthood, and adapting to the empty nest.
4. *Sex and romance:* Finding time and energy for sex and intimacy, adjusting to the effects of aging on normal sexual functioning, overcoming sexual dysfunction, preventing or surviving infidelity.
5. *Facing chronic illness, disability, or both:* Shifting the nature and extent of the partners' responsibilities; seeking support from health-care professionals, friends, and community; adjusting to shifts in power and dependency needs; and dealing with depression and changes in self-image.

Women's employment, especially when career oriented, slightly decreases the likelihood of marriage. The rise in divorce rates has been linked with the increased participation of women in the work force, although it is unclear which is cause and which is effect; that is, whether women seek employment in response to a troubled marriage or whether the stress of the wife's employment contributes to marital failure. The risk of separation or divorce increases with the amount of the woman's income. In spite of the negative association between women's employment and marital stability, *general satisfaction with life, mental and physical health, and satisfaction with work are consistently found to be higher in women employed outside the home.*

Not to be overlooked is the impact of children on married adults both young and middle-aged. Marriage requires intimacy and sharing. Habits, cherished ways of doing things, and traditions are established by adults and shaped by their own personalities and expectations. However, the arrival of a child complicates matters, and sometimes results in disillusionment. Children *do* affect marital satisfaction, often for the better, but sometimes for the worse.

Rearing children inevitably consumes a large share of many married couple's financial, emotional and temporal resources. Parents must learn to balance limit setting and parental control with a willingness to give up authoritative control while the child accepts and demonstrates the ability to handle increasing responsibility for his or her own behavior. The development of self-discipline is the long-term goal. In many situations a fatigued parent will settle for immediate peace rather than confront a child in the interest of his or her long-term development. In other families, firmness slips into domination and results in forcing pa-

Drought Refugees from Oklahoma Camping by the Roadside *Photograph by Dorothea Lange (1936). Courtesy of the Library of Congress, Washington, D.C., Prints and Photographs Division, FSA/OWI Collection, LC-USF34-009666-E. One of the most demanding challenges of young adulthood may be meeting your family's health-care needs with a limited income.*

rental will on the child, leading to rebelliousness. *Successful parents temper their firmness with flexibility and have enough humility to acknowledge when they are wrong.* Highly successful adults often attribute their effectiveness to the influence of their parents. They report parental characteristics such as firmness (as opposed to permissiveness or rigidity), direction without dictation, rules that made sense, high expectations, and mutual trust and respect. Although as children and teenagers they occasionally rebelled against their parents' demands and values, the rebellion was generally verbal and rarely took the form of acting out or of destructive behavior.

The recent trend toward postponement of marriage and parenting has produced a new class of middle-aged parents with young children. Although little research is available concerning the "older" parent of young children, some trends are obvious. The parents are likely to have greater maturity and experience on which to draw, for example, although this is offset by a decline in the total energy available for parenting and the possible sense of loss and sacrifice that a couple may experience after having grown accustomed to the relative freedom, independence, and wealth they enjoyed as a childless couple. Most parents in their middle years, however, follow the traditional pattern and confront the issues of raising adolescents and coping with the "empty nest" during the middle years.

Eventually children leave home, and the nuclear family is reduced to the parents alone. The child-rearing phase is over, and the nest is emptied. The change, although often a hoped-for relief, is not always easy. Much of the success in negotiating this transition is determined by whether husband and wife have accomplished the tasks of parenthood, how they have grown, how well they have maintained their marital relationship, and how they take up their new roles as a childless couple. Traditionally women, especially those who have stayed at home to raise the children, are most at risk to develop the **empty nest syndrome**, a personal crisis marked by depression and a loss of the sense of identity. Working mothers and fathers may suffer profoundly as well, although men are less likely to articulate their feelings of loss or seek professional help in dealing with those feelings.

MARITAL PROBLEMS

Although the highest divorce rates occur during young adulthood, approximately half of the first marriages of those in their third decade of life also end in divorce. *Most who divorce eventually remarry, although women are less likely to do so.* Middle-aged adults are much quicker to marry their second spouses than are the younger divorced. *About half of these marriages will falter, resulting in a second divorce. However, remarried couples are no less satisfied with their marriages than are first-married couples.* The equal satisfaction and stability of first and second marriages might represent a simple unwillingness to repeat the highly traumatic experience of divorce, but it seems more likely that this statistic represents true gains. Given the myriad complexities and potential for conflict that are inherent in second marriages (with their constellations of former spouse, stepchildren, and additional financial burdens), a greater level of maturity and cooperation is certainly demanded.

The occurrence of divorce is frequently linked with the issue of fidelity. *It is estimated that 60% to 75% of husbands have been unfaithful to their wives and that 30% to 50% of wives have had affairs.* Considering the frequency with which couples divorce, it is perhaps easy to trivialize the event and to overlook the personal disruption associated with it. Divorce poses challenges on several levels. It involves psychological loss, as partners are compelled to give up completely their love objects and roles as wife and husband. That grieving process sometimes takes years. A couple must negotiate the legal system which, even in this era of no-fault divorce in many states, frequently provokes antagonism and distress. The two, especially the wife, frequently suffer severe financial loss and lowered standards of living. Divorced couples must re-configure their social networks. Those with children must perform the responsibilities of parenting without the presence of a partner.

Coping with the causes and effects of infidelity is an important task for many married individuals. The intense

> One can live magnificently in this world, if one knows how to work and how to love, to work for the person one loves, and to love one's work.
>
> LEO TOLSTOY

shock, anger, and depression that result from learning of a partner's betrayal require resolution, either through the rebuilding of the relationship or through its dissolution. Several life events or stressors that are likely to precipitate sexual infidelity have been identified. These risk factors exist when *either* partner is experiencing one of the following:

1. Selection or initiation of a new career
2. Expansion or success at work
3. Changing jobs
4. Traveling extensively alone
5. Depression linked with failure
6. Monotony associated with work or fatigue produced by dull overwork
7. Retirement

Additional risk factors exist when the *couple* is having experiences such as:

1. Pregnancy or the birth of a child
2. Young children at home demanding considerable attention
3. Bereavement from the death of a parent, sibling, child, or friend
4. Emotional crisis such as an accident or diagnosis of illness
5. Children leaving home
6. Stressful changes such as moving, buying a home, or undergoing a major change in lifestyle

Traditionally women were responsible for caring about and working on relationships. Although research has shown that men benefit considerably from marriage, even more than their wives, men are often less attuned to the priority of developing emotional connectedness. Not surprisingly then, it is often the women who overfunctions in the relationship, struggling for change, however, ineffectively. A **systems model of family functioning** (Lerner, 1989) proves useful in understanding the particular problems that often beset marriages during the middle years. The **overfunctioner** focuses much emotional energy, such as anger, strategizing, or worry, on the other or on the relationship, attempting to change or blame the other. Meanwhile, the other partner typically **underfunctions**, avoiding the experience of intensity by distancing, or withdrawing, from the partner or from a particular issue. This pattern seriously impedes the functioning of the relationship, resulting in

The Discovery of Sex

We try to be discreet standing in the dark
hallway by the front door. He gets his hands
up inside the front of my shirt and I put mine
down inside the back of his jeans. We are crazy
for skin, each other's skin, warm silky skin.
Our tongues are in each other's mouths,
where they belong, home at last. At first

we hope my mother won't see us, but later we
don't care,
we forget her. Suddenly she makes a noise
like a game show alarm and says Hey! Stop that!
and we put our hands out where she can see them.
Our mouths stay pressed together, though, and
when she isn't looking anymore our hands go
back inside each other's clothes. We could

go where no one can see us, but we are
good kids, from good families, trying to have
as much discreet sex as possible with my mother
and father
four feet away watching strangers kiss on TV,
my mother and father who once did as we are doing,
something we can't imagine because we know

that before we put our mouths together, before
the back seat of his parents' car where our skins
finally become one—before us, these things
were unknown! Our parents look on in disbelief
as we pioneer delights they thought only they knew
before those delights gave them us.

Years later, still we try to be discreet, standing
in the kitchen now where we think she can't see us. I
slip my hands down inside the back of his jeans
and he gets his up under the front of my shirt.
We open our mouths to kiss and suddenly Hey! Hey!
says our daughter, glaring from the kitchen doorway.
Get a room! she says, as we put our hands
out where she can see them.

DEBRA SPENCER

discontent and a diminished ability to cope with the inevitable crises and transitions that occur in the middle years. Successful marriages involve the coupling of two individuals "expressing strength and vulnerability, weakness and competence, in a balanced way" (Lerner, 1989).

The **triangulation of relationships** is another concept that is useful for understanding family interaction. It refers to an attempt to deflect emotional energy or anxiety about important issues between the partners onto a third party. The third party can be a child, in-law, or, very frequently, an extramarital affair. In essence, *triangles allow direct confrontation to be avoided and thereby stabilize, at least temporarily, the relationship.* Emotionally intense and conflictual relationships often represent disguised problems in the primary, or couple relationship. The child-focused triangle, for example, is common. The previously reliable teenager may rebel against family rules when the parent's level of stress as a result of a grandparent's death becomes unbearable, thus triggering the father's fury and the mother's overprotectiveness, allowing the parents to avoid having to experience their grief. According to Lerner (1989)

> Whenever adults are not actively working to identify and solve their own problems, children may volunteer to deflect, detour, and act out adult issues in most imaginative ways. Indeed, children tend to inherit *whatever* psychological problems we choose not to attend to.

BEING SINGLE

Marriage rates have dropped to a record low. Postponement of marriage, divorce, and cohabitation have resulted in what some call a "postmarital society," and these changes are perhaps most apparent in the statistics on marriage. In 1970 in the United States, only 21% of the 25-year-olds were unmarried; by 2005 the figure was 60%. A majority of couples, 65%, now cohabit before marriage, and behavior that was once viewed with considerable social opprobrium ("living in sin") is commonplace. Likewise, *sex before marriage is now considered acceptable by almost all young people and most of their parents*, and 90% of 20–24-year-olds have had sexual intercourse, most often in the context of a romantic relationship.

It should be noted that for many, being single is a matter of choice, a preferred state. Also, among those usually counted as single are members of homosexual couples whose long-term, committed relationships closely resemble marriages but who in most states are not allowed that legal sanction. The common perception of America as a country of couples forces single adults into a second-class status that is more likely to affect women than men. *As a result of disparate death rates favoring women and customary marriage of older men to younger women, the number of single men of the same age or older who are available for marriage is not sufficient and decreases with each decade of life.* The likelihood of marriage or remarriage drops drastically as a woman ages.

Clearly a number of issues and challenges face the single middle-aged adult, particularly the woman. Some women postpone marriage to complete their education and advance their careers and, when entering their thirties, hear the ticking of the biological clock only to discover that "all the good men are already taken." Dreams of eventual marriage and children may be shattered. Other obvious victims of recent social changes are the men and women in their forties and fifties who entered marriages years ago with a clear understanding of what was expected of them, only to find later that they must make serious adjustments. Most tragic, perhaps, is the displaced homemaker who cultivated only the skills of wife and mother and then was suddenly made vulnerable by divorce or widowhood and found herself unprepared to provide for her income. Blumstein and Schwartz (1983) summarized displaced homemakers:

> They actually have fewer resources and less confidence than they did twenty years before. Not only must they enter a new and inhospitable world of work, with few of the necessary qualifications, they must also face a romantic or sexual marketplace for which they are unprepared.

WORK

Work cannot be considered effectively in isolation; if so, we could refer simply to the various stages of career, namely, the preparatory stage involving education and training, the point at which the individual is committed to a particular line of work, and so forth. However, career development is intimately intertwined with the individual's development as a person. Work interacts with identity. Work determines how we live, compels us to select different traits for further development, determines and maintains status, and undergirds our values. Levinson (1978) has described the typical person in his or her twenties as poor in self-reflection but fairly skilled when it comes to performing tasks, careful at following rules, anxious for promotion, and willing to accept "the system." The typical 25-year-old is determined to "make the grade" and, by contrast, not particularly con-

> The great majority of us are required to live a life of constant, systematic duplicity. Your health is bound to be affected if, day after day, you say the opposite of what you feel, if you grovel before what you dislike and rejoice at what brings you nothing but misfortune ...
>
> BORIS PASTERNAK
> *Dr. Zhivago*

cerned with psychological conflicts about success. The individual must identify an occupational "dream" and set goals to achieve that dream. This process may be marked by conflict and uncertainty, which can be inhibited or suppressed; if so, such feelings may appear full-blown later on in life. Mentor relationships are also forged during this period. The mentor plays the role of a teacher who takes a special interest in enhancing the younger individual's skill.

The mentor plays other roles as well, sponsoring the young adult's career, inducting him or her into the social scene, and serving as an exemplar. Mentor relationships are intense and may be difficult to terminate at the end of early adulthood when guidance is no longer needed. Thus, abrupt or painful terminations of these relationships may occur.

Career choices during the early twenties are often characterized by ambivalence. The 25-year-old may feel uncomfortable with any choice, because choice brings a narrowing of the opportunity and freedom which, as an adolescent, were hard won. However, successful choices involve single-mindedness, and choose the person must. Although a commitment made too early may be regretted, one made too late places the individual at a distinct disadvantage. One cannot always delay a career choice until one is ready.

> O, how full of briers is this working-day world!
>
> WILLIAM SHAKESPEARE
> *As You Like It*

Career choices made during the twenties often amount to a merely preliminary definition of interests and values; reconsideration often takes place toward the end of the twenties or early thirties. Thus, the person in the early thirties enters a period of settling down, which amounts to establishing a second life structure. At this point there may be a redoubling of investment in career and a desire to realize youthful goals and ambitions. There are often two main tasks during the early thirties period. First, one must establish a niche in one's chosen area, a "project" of some sort that sets one apart from coworkers. A second task is to advance or make it in the system as reflected by an enhancement of social rank, income, and power. Toward the end of the thirties, the young adult can "become his or her own person," a senior member, capable of speaking with real authority within the organization. Such a sequence of events does not always lead to success, because there are always other, less fortunate, consequences of development. Aside from advancing consistently within the newly defined life structure, one might fail in pursuing one's dream. Other people break out of the mold and rewrite their life script. For some, success leads to a dramatic change in life structure. For example, a physician may be promoted to medical school dean, a position requiring vastly different social and occupational skills than was previously the case.

Note that the emphasis in the previous discussion is on the experience of men. Studies of early adulthood, like development in general, have been primarily male centered. The lives of women during early adulthood have been relatively ignored. Recent studies have begun to redress this imbalance. Gilligan's (1982) work emphasized fundamental differences between men and women from the standpoint of career development. Women, she claims, tend to value caring and sensitivity over autonomy. In addition, success on the job, including financial success, may be less critical to the psychological well-being of women. *Although Levinson and Vaillant believe that work is the central developmental concern of men, Gilligan underscored that for women nurturance and attachment may be just as critical, if not more so.* Gilligan also discusses the female sense of morality, which arises from an emphasis placed on genuine need and inclusion rather than the balancing of claims. Mercer and her colleagues (1989) have reflected on transitions in women's lives, including those of early adulthood. They made the point that, in general, women's transitions are more varied than those of men. Women may or may not elect to work outside the home, which almost all men do or at least attempt to do.

In any case, the early adult years involve emancipation from the family for women as well as men. A woman enters college, marriage, or the workplace during this period, and dependence on others turns into reliance on others, such as husband and coworkers. A few women may, in Levinson's terms, follow a life dream, but many do not. Some return to their dreams in middle age, seeking the professional training or artistic fulfillment that has been delayed by the responsibilities of the child care. The leveling phase during the end of the twenties is a time when many women change their earlier life pattern, confirming their commitment to family as opposed to work, or vice versa.

> I have now no relief but in action. I am becoming incapable of rest. I am quite confident I should rust, break, and die if I spared myself. Much better to die doing.
>
> CHARLES DICKENS (who died of heart disease thought to have been exacerbated by his work habits)

Issues related to work and career occupy much of the attention of the middle aged, as well as the young adult. What once was a stimulating test of the ability to succeed can become a tedious routine undertaken only to provide the necessary paycheck. The ambitious aggressiveness that characterized the early working years may give way to a "don't make waves" attitude and a preference for the tried and true methods of the past. Unsure that he or she can keep abreast of new advances, the middle-aged worker may begin to focus on issues of job security and pensions and hesitate to take risks. *Research suggests that the most satis-*

factory transition occurs when the role of ambitious "young turk" is exchanged for that of a mentor who "passes the torch" to the young, fostering their professional growth and guiding their careers. In contrast, women who return to school or work after their children are older often find themselves invigorated by the new challenges of the workplace. They may, however, find little support or encouragement from husbands who have already established successful records in the workplace and who are currently in the process of beginning to disengage from the world of work.

Losing a job can be a major stressor in mid-life. Many employees who are fired or laid off eventually find other positions, but a Labor Department study found that only 20% of those retrained under a federal program for dislocated workers got a job paying at least 80% of their former position's salary or wages. Other workers, faced with the possibility of termination, elect to take early retirement for which they are often emotionally and financially unprepared. In short, their expectations that hard work and years of loyal service would guarantee secure employment or that a college education or years of experience would secure managerial positions have proved naive.

ADAPTING TO CHANGES IN HEALTH

Whether it is greeted with mild apprehension or outright panic, the recognition of physical decline and eventual mortality faces each of us in the middle years. Some react to the first signs of aging with a hypochondriacal preoccupation with changes in body appearance, functions, and sensations. Others embark on self-improvement programs of diet and exercise, and still others valiantly attempt to modify self-destructive behaviors such as smoking or drinking. Concerns about health, physical attractiveness, fitness, and mortality surface frequently in both the healthy and the ill.

Contrary to the expectations of many, the middle years are not marked by illness. In a study by Verbrugge (1986) the number of days on which people noticed health problems (symptoms requiring rest, absence from work, self-medication, visits to a physician, or hospitalization) was not higher in the middle-aged group than in the younger. In fact, 78% of middle-aged women and 79% of middle-aged men reported their overall health as being good or excellent.

Although good health is the norm, chronic illnesses often make their initial appearance during the middle years. Development of a chronic illness can involve threats not only to life and physical well-being but to self-image, social and occupational functioning, and emotional equilibrium. For a satisfactory adjustment to chronic illness, the middle-aged adult must undertake several adaptive tasks:

1. Changing harmful behaviors and modifying his or her lifestyle

Heavy the Oar to Him Who is Tired, Heavy the Coat, Heavy the Sea *(1929) Ivan Le Lorraine Albright, American, 1897–1983.* Oil on canvas, 135.3 × 86.4 cm. Gift of Mr. and Mrs. Earle Ludgin, 1959.12. Photography © The Art Institute of Chicago. Reproduced by permission of the artist's estate. *Work can be viewed as a blessing or a curse. Read Ernest Hemingway's* The Old Man and the Sea *for an example of someone whose life is defined by his work.*

2. Tolerating and accepting loss of body parts, functions, or potential; compensating or replacing if possible
3. Maintaining self-image and a sense of worth
4. Maintaining satisfaction in relationships with family, friends, and health care providers; accepting a realistic degree of dependence
5. Maintaining emotional equilibrium and a positive outlook in the face of depression, fear, anxiety, and anger, which are normal responses to threat and loss

Coping with the psychological demands of a chronic illness is challenging at any stage of the life cycle. For the middle aged it intensifies the evaluation of life, personal worth, goals, and values. Successfully managed, the crisis of a chronic illness may even accelerate progress through the introspective developmental tasks of the middle years.

> "When you come to a patient's house, you should ask him what sort of pains he has, what caused them, how many days he has been ill, whether the bowels are working, and what sort of food he eats." So says Hippocrates in his work *Affections*. I may venture to add one more question: What occupation does he follow?
>
> BERNARDINO RAMAZZINI
> *Diseases of Workers* (circa 1700)

SUMMARY

Adult psychological development is a recent area of study as developmentalists have traditionally focused on earlier stages. Erik Erickson suggested that the primary developmental task for early adulthood involves achievement of the capacity for intimacy and for middle adulthood generativity or the ability to contribute to the welfare of others including younger people. Moving into the adult world, one separates from the family of origin, yet is pressed to make new commitments including those made to a spouse. The success and gratification derived from married life is determined by many factors, including the age of the couple at the time of marriage, the duration of the marital relationship, the presence or absence of children, and the response of the participants to children's eventually leaving home. Marriages falter when spouses are unable to adjust to demands that change over time or when conflictual issues are not effectively identified or addressed. Young adults are pressed not only to find mates, but also to decide on careers, even when not entirely prepared to do so. During early and middle adulthood good physical health is the norm, although chronic illness does often make its introduction during this time.

CASE STUDY

Sue Clifton, a 34-year-old patient in your family practice, brings her 14-year-old daughter to your office for diagnosis and treatment of a strep throat. You are shocked by how tired and thin Sue appears. You recall that she has generally been in good health, seeking help only for minor, episodic illnesses. You express your concern, and she responds, "I'm just stressed out right now, but everything's fine. I started back to school in September, and I plan to go into nursing. It's stressful, but I love it." You congratulate her but encourage her to come in for a physical examination because she hasn't had one in more than two years.

When you next see Mrs. Clifton, what possibilities will you want to explore?

On her return visit you note that Sue has lost 13 kg without dieting since her last visit 14 months ago. Your review of systems and physical does not reveal any problem, although you must wait on laboratory results to rule out anemia and thyroid disease. Sue admits she feels tired much of the time, but she attributes her fatigue to a "sleep shortage" since she studies late into the night after the family retires. She states that she is smoking a lot more now and drinking coffee almost continuously. She admits to frequently skipping meals.

Your feeling of unease, that you may be missing something important, persists. What other areas of inquiry should you pursue?

You remember that Sue's husband, John, is a machinist you had treated for a gastric ulcer. You recall being concerned that he was a moderately heavy drinker. You ask, "Is John being supportive of your going back to school?" She responds, "Who are you kidding . . . he's the main reason I'm doing this. The shop has cut him back to part time and he could be a big help around the house, but all he does is hang out with his buddies and drink beer." You wish her luck with her finals and tell her that you'll be in touch when you get her laboratory results.

What directions should you be considering regarding future discussions with the patient?

Stress management training, nutritional planning (with or without supplementation) and referral for marital/personal counseling or support groups should all spring to mind.

SUGGESTED READINGS

Brim, O.G., Ryff, C.D., & Kessler, R. (Eds.) (2004). *How healthy are we: A national study of wellbeing in midlife*. Chicago, IL: University of Chicago Press.
This reports results from a large scale study sponsored by the MacArthur Foundation on the functioning of people in midlife.

Gilligan C. (1982). *In a different voice: Psychological theory in women's development*. Cambridge, MA: Harvard University Press.
This book attempts to redress the imbalance in developmental theories which have been built on observations of men's as opposed to women's lives.

Lerner, H.G. (1989). *The dance of intimacy*. New York, NY: Harper & Row.
Based on the author's interpretation and application of Bowen's theory of family systems, this book focuses on intimate relationships. Case studies illustrate how we get in (and out) of trouble with the most important people in our lives.

Levinson, D.J. (1978). *The seasons of a man's life*. New York, NY: Ballantine Books.

This is a longitudinal study of men resulting in detailed description of adult developmental stages, with an emphasis on occupational success and failure.

Mercer R.T., Nichols E.G., & Doyle G.C. (1989). *Transitions in a woman's life: Major life events in developmental context*. New York, NY: Springer-Verlag.

This developmental study of the life trajectories of women underscores the importance of non-normative or unexpected life events such as illness, divorce, and death of loved ones.

Shifren, K. (Ed.). (2009). *How caregiving affects development: Psychological implications for child, adolescent, and adult caregivers*. Washington, DC: American Psychological Association.

Recent advances in medicine have resulted in people living longer, but often living at home with chronic illnesses. Most of these individuals will require care and support from other family members. This edited volume examines the role of caregiver at each stage along the developmental spectrum.

Vaillant, G.E. (1977). *Adaptation to life*. New York, NY: Little, Brown.

A landmark longitudinal study investigating ways in which some men cope effectively with variations in their lives while others cope badly or not at all.

5 Old Age

Randall Espinoza & James Randy Mervis

> Like a morning dream, life becomes more and more bright the longer we live, and the reason of everything appears more clear. What has puzzled us before seems less mysterious, and the crooked paths look straighter as we approach the end.
>
> JEAN PAUL RICHTER

WHO IS OLD?

The later stages of life can be positive and fulfilling, replete with rich experiences, fond memories and expressions of gratitude, happiness, and love. Relationships spanning decades alongside new connections add to the vibrancy and color of the lives of older persons. However, mystery, myths, and misconceptions about the aging process abound. In contrast to the common belief that a person's later years are uniformly fraught with disease and decline, in fact the vast majority of older persons continue to function proficiently and sufficiently. Indeed, *the heterogeneity of many aspects of individuals increases with aging, due not only to intrinsic genetic and biologic variation, but also as a result of the variety and multitude of experiences, exposures, and challenges encountered and lived.* Changes in culture and sociological mores have also evolved over time so that expectations of living into one's later years healthier, still capable and independent are more common.

Aging of the U. S. Population

America is graying. The 2000 U. S. census indicated that there were presently about 34.9 million Americans, or just about 13% of the total population, over the age of 65 years.

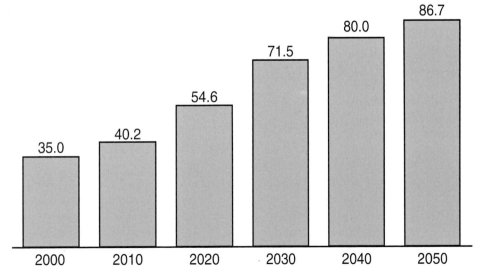

FIGURE 5.1 Growth of the 65+ population. Source: US Census Bureau, 65+ in the United States, 2005

2000	2010	2020	2030	2040	2050
35.0	40.2	54.6	71.5	80.0	86.7

Note: The reference population for these data is the resident population (in millions).

In 2010 the first of the baby boomers began to turn 65, adding over the next few decades an additional 76 million older individuals. By 2030, people over age 65 will comprise about 1/5 of the total population, or about 70 million citizens, nearly double the number of today.

However, the elderly are not a monolithic group, and there are significant changes in the size and growth rate among the **young-old** (persons aged between 65 and 74 years), the **middle-old** (persons aged between 75 and 84 years) and the **oldest-old** (persons aged 85 and above). Compared to the 1900 census, the young-old group in 2000 was 8 times larger, the middle-old group was 16 times larger, and the oldest-old group was 31 times larger. In fact, *the oldest-old group is growing the fastest* (see Figure 5.1). By 2050, there will be over 800,000 individuals in the United States older than 100 years of age (see Figure 5.2). These increases in life expectancy are due to gains both at birth

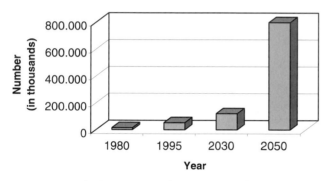

FIGURE 5.2 Growth of the oldest-old (U.S. Census Data).

and at age 65 years. Additionally, death rates are at a record low according to the most recent report from the Centers for Disease Control and Prevention. A child born in 2007 could expect to live 77.9 years, or about 30 years longer than a child born in 1900. The gains in life expectancy at age 65 are even more remarkable. Between 1900 and 1960, life expectancy at age 65 increased by 2.4 years, but since 1960, life expectancy increased by 3.4 years, or by 140% in less than 40 years.

While age 65 is usually considered the beginning of old age, it is important to keep in mind that the demarcation between middle age and older age at 65 years is arbitrary and reflects social legislation of the early part of last century. *Age by itself is often an inaccurate indicator of a person's underlying physical, cognitive and mental capability and sense of well-being.*

Gender Differences

Men and women in the U.S. do not share uniformly in these gains in life expectancy (see Fig 5.3). In general, women maintain a slight advantage in life expectancy earlier in

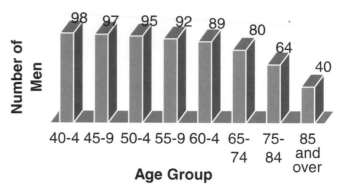

FIGURE 5.3 Number of men per 100 women by age group (1996).

life, but by age 50 the differences in life expectancy begin to more noticeably diverge and rapidly accelerate in the 8th and 9th decades of life so that *by age 85 or greater there are only 40 men for every 100 women*. Much of the difference is due to higher male mortality from heart disease, lung cancer, industrial and motor vehicle accidents, and violence.

Socioeconomic Status

Income and other economic factors bear upon the quality and extent of life of the older person. For example, *increased income results in higher life expectancy*. Having wealth and status positively affects means and access to healthcare. Wealthier individuals typically are able to maintain health and to treat illness. Being poor has the opposite effects. After children, the elderly have some of the highest poverty rates in America. People who were poor throughout early and adult life typically become even poorer in later life. However, many others, because of rising healthcare costs, retirement and loss of income, and dwindling investments face impoverishment only after becoming old. *While by numbers the vast majority of the poor are white, a greater proportion of ethnic and racial minority elderly are poor and their poverty is more severe.* Additionally, women of all racial and ethnic groups, and especially the oldest-old, are particularly susceptible to impoverishment.

NORMAL CHANGES WITH AGING

As related earlier, myths and misconceptions abound about aging. Distinctions in the past were often not made between **normalcy**, i.e., a biomedical notion of what is observed in the absence of disease, and **normality**, i.e., a statistical notion of what is usual or typical for a group. Thus, previous concepts of the effects of aging were confounded by the lack of control for the underlying effects of disease, contributing to the erroneous belief that aging and disease were synony-

> To resist the frigidity of old age, one must combine the body, the mind, and the heart—and to keep them in parallel vigor, one must exercise, study, and love.
>
> KARL VON BONSTETTEN

mous. Current modern notions view normal aging in broader nonpathological terms that cover life satisfaction and morale, survival and good health. Normal aging encompasses not just physical health and absence of disease but also behavioral competence, psychological well-being, perceived quality of life and a person's objective environment. The body retains a tremendous capacity for resilience, especially if given the appropriate time, care and support to recover and heal. Along these lines, there are several ways to conceptualize processes and groups of aging.

Concepts of Aging

One distinction describes groups according to **usual aging** and **successful aging**. Applying to the vast majority of people, **usual aging** describes the aging of individuals who have one or more medical conditions that become prevalent in later life. Here extrinsic factors heighten the effects of intrinsic aging processes. **Successful aging**, in contrast, applies to a smaller select group of individuals who do exceedingly well physically, mentally and cognitively into their latter years with many retaining active and full lives into their 90s and 100s and experiencing very little illness. Here extrinsic factors counteract intrinsic aging factors such that there is minimal or no functional loss.

Another distinction is between primary and secondary aging. **Primary aging** refers to those processes that appear to be most highly regulated or expressed by genetic influences. People may have better health outcomes and preserved health due to inheritance of "good" genes, or conversely, may be more susceptible to disease or effects of degeneration due to inheritance of "bad" genes. **Secondary aging** refers to processes that are not influenced directly by genetics, and includes results from accidents, injuries or traumas, the cumulative effects of life-long habits like smoking and heavy drinking (negative) or exercise and healthy diet (positive), the effects from environmental exposure, e.g., from toxins and smog, and finally, behaviors that are modulated by sociocultural beliefs, e.g., ageism.

In the end what matters to most people is the achievement of **optimal aging**, which means continuing to function at the highest possible level despite the inevitable limitations that growing older brings, or getting the best of what is possible for as long as possible across physical, cognitive, psychological and social domains.

NORMAL CHANGES IN AGING
Physical and Physiologic Changes

In general, a person experiences changes in all body parts and bodily functions over a lifetime with most of these changes beginning in early adulthood. Body parts vary naturally in the extent and pace of change with illness and disease influencing the type, degree and rate of change. However, changes in a body part may not relate to a similar change in body function. Visible physical changes of aging

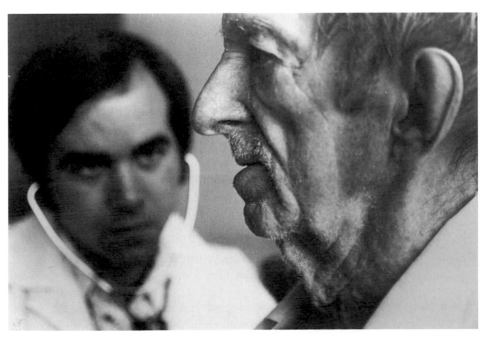

Young Doctor Courtesy of the National Institute on Aging. *Young physicians often feel uncomfortable counseling patients older than themselves.*

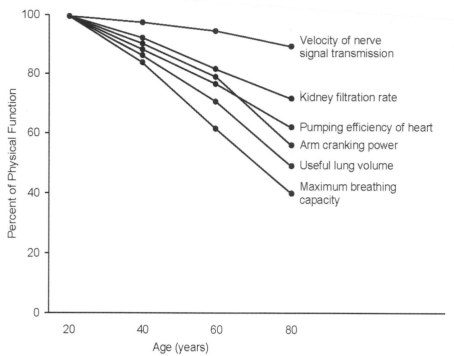

FIGURE 5.4 Average declines in bodily functions with increasing age for sedentary individuals. Source: Modified from Weg (1983) and Spirduso (1995).

include gray hair, loss of teeth and hair, wrinkled skin, elongation of ears and nose, postural changes and loss of height. Other changes are loss of muscle mass and subcutaneous fat and declining eyesight and hearing. Importantly, not everyone experiences all of these changes or experiences them at the same rate. The physiologic changes in bodily functions have been well described (see Figure 5.4.)

Brain and Intellectual Changes

As in the body, the brain also undergoes transformations in structure and function. Common alterations in brain structure found in aging include brain atrophy manifested by a decrease in brain volume and an increase in cerebrospinal fluid volume, ventricular enlargement, and decline in the density of gray and white matter. Deep white matter changes are of varying significance and various patterns and frequencies of change exist in an aging brain. Cerebral metabolic rates of glucose and oxygen utilization seem stable across age but cerebral blood flow diminishes, although the data are contradictory. However, one consistent finding is the loss of the usual pattern of frontal cerebral blood flow being greater than parietal cerebral blood flow that is seen in earlier life. Finally, there are age-related decrements in various neurotransmitter receptor-binding sites across several brain regions. *However, the brain changes described above do not necessarily result in loss of mental and cognitive capacity and function in the older person.*

Despite these morphologic, and functional brain alterations, cognitive and neuropsychological abilities appear to vary with age, and sometimes no loss of abilities is apparent. For example, the domains of *primary and tertiary memory appear better preserved in older adults than secondary memory, manifesting in difficulties in encoding and retrieval processing.* Additionally, older adults remain capable of learning and benefit from encoding strategies, from longer exposure to the stimulus that is to be remembered, and from techniques to enhance motivation. Cognitive abilities that remain stable include attention span, every day communication skills, lexical, phonological and syntactic knowledge, discourse comprehension and simple visual perception. Interestingly, studies suggest that some abilities such as judgment, accuracy and general knowledge may actually increase with age. However, abilities that appear to decline with age include selective attention, cognitive flexibility, ability to shift cognitive sets, naming of objects, verbal fluency, more complex visuoconstructive skills and logical analysis. **Crystallized intelligence**, which is the result of experience, tends to increase throughout life in healthy and active persons. In contrast, **fluid intelligence**, being more biologically determined, may be more susceptible to decline with age. Nonetheless, the mental and intellectual capabilities of older individuals, in the absence of medical or neurological disease, remain relatively intact with only minor deficits described that are usually not functionally or socially impairing. For example, while reaction time studies show a loss of speed of response in the central nervous system with age, if older persons have enough time on tests, they function as

A physician shown at two points in his life journey.

well and as accurately as younger persons. *Assessments of cognitive and mental capacity must take account of health status as poor health can adversely affect cognitive performance.* In general, with good physical health, adequate education, and intellectual stimulation, older persons do not appear to decline in intellectual abilities.

> For age is opportunity no less than youth itself, though in another dress, and as the evening twilight fades away, the sky is filled with stars, invisible by day.
>
> HENRY WADSWORTH LONGFELLOW

HEALTH PROMOTION AND PREVENTION

Activities and behaviors that promote healthy living and disease prevention are receiving increasing attention. *Maintenance of an active lifestyle throughout adult and later life with regular, and preferably vigorous, exercise results in lower risks for heart disease, some types of cancer, and dementia.* Also, maintaining a productive mental life by reading, by delving into novel subject areas, and by actively learning new skills is associated with better overall health outcomes for a variety of medical conditions and with a lower risk of development of a cognitive disorder. Likewise, maintaining social connections and having extensive social supports through networks of friends and family result in increased life satisfaction, lower prevalence of depression and improved overall health status and quality of life.

ADAPTATIONS TO AGING

Cultural Attitudes and Ageism

The elderly inevitably must face multiple changes and losses that impact self-image and their ideas of how they can function and live in the world. An individual's march through the later stages of life is an interplay between sociocultural biases and internal cumulative life experiences. Thus, the physiologic changes of aging described previously are accompanied by transitions in roles that the older person has in society, families, and work and by alterations in interpersonal relationships. Focused on youth, athleticism and a rapid pace, modern American society often diminishes the older person. Perceived as taxing or hindering the progress of modern times, the elderly may not be valued for their sagacity and wisdom.

Ageism is discrimination against a person based on age. For the older individual this means that negative attitudes and stereotypes of aging are likely. Ageism permeates contemporary culture from seemingly innocuous jokes about dentures and adult diapers to more insidious portrayals of the elderly in movies, commercials and novels as doddering, dim-witted, or incompetent individuals. Yet, with the entry of the baby boomers, a youth oriented generation born between 1946 and 1964 into the early stages of older age, these negative notions of growing older will be rightly challenged. This cohort appears deeply invested in maintaining good health, a positive physical image, and high levels of activity and of independence.

Life Transitions

Family Relationships Across the Life Cycle

For many elderly, the importance of family cannot be overstated. Greater longevity allows individuals to experience more marriages, divorces, and more complex and blended family structures. Increased longevity has led to an increase in "beanpole" families, characterized by more generations with fewer members in each generation. Their children may have their own families with extended familial relationships. This change in structure may provide opportunities for rich family interactions with closer relationships, or simply for more conflicts, disagreements and family discord. Having a greater number of relationships potentially subjects the older person to more important losses. The elderly experience the death of their parents, often of their own siblings, and of many other important relatives and friends who may have been central figures in their lives since youth. Conversely, if an older person has not yet lost her parents, she often faces the daunting task of taking care of them physically and financially. Some studies note that *a 60 year old has a 44% chance of having and caring for an elderly parent.* Centenarian parents are often cared for by their retired children who are themselves in their 70s and 80s. A spouse may be the most important relationship that a person ever has, as a spouse is a primary emotional and social support provider representing security, familiarity and comfort. Marital roles change over the years, however, and if not successfully transitioned, resentment and breakdown in communication, sometimes expressed in verbal or physical abuse, may ensue. *At the beginning of the 20th century marriages, on average, lasted 28 years, ending with the death of a spouse. One hundred years later marriages may last 45 years or more until the death of one of the partners.*

New diverse family structures present challenges in the interactions within and across generations. Children with alternative life styles may be a source of pride or shame for the elderly. Financial pressures may at times force older children in their 40s, 50s and even 60s to return to their parents' homes. Family members living together again may rekindle old dysfunctional patterns or present new problems as aging parents and their children confront reversed caretaking roles. This can result in older individuals being treated inappropriately, dismissively, or disrespectfully.

Retirement

Nearly two million people retire in the United States every year. Longevity has changed retirement patterns, and *today an individual can expect to live one quarter or more of life in retirement.* Planning and preparation for retirement can facilitate a successful transition to a new life stage, but a lack of such planning can create hardships across generations.

Beginning new hobbies and cultivating new interests should not be left until retirement. Some elderly continue to work as a source of enjoyment and of supplemental income, while many are forced to retire or are subtly eased out of their careers. Retirement can bring a focus on one's health and financial status. Social Security benefits were not intended to be the sole source of secure retirement income to retirees. Yet in 1998, according to the Social Security Administration, 16% of Social Security recipients received 100% of their income from this source and another 45% received between 50–90% of their income from Social Security alone. Thus, many elderly are living at poverty levels, and must continue to work or to seek additional employment to make ends meet. There are now proposals to change the present form of Social Security and to increase the age of eligibility for full benefits, which would reduce projected deficits in the Social Security Trust Fund, but which would have the greatest adverse impact on low income workers who are less able to save, have greater health care needs and are often not able to work into their later years. Sadly, a financially safe and comfortable retirement may not be an option for many. Mounting financial pressures have left many low-income elderly having to choose between medications, other essential medical treatments, food or shelter. Not surprisingly, a higher economic status at retirement is associated with more positive health outcomes and more satisfaction.

Successful retirements are not totally depended on health and financial matters, however. Making creative use of time influences quality of life to a great degree. There are many physiological and psychological benefits the retiree gains from leisure activities and volunteer work. Leisure activities such as gardening, dancing and traveling add a sense of fun and entertainment while enhancing the quality of retirement. Membership in volunteer associations and volunteer work allow the elderly to share their expertise and skills while continuing to contribute to society. While it has been estimated that 40% of the elderly do some form of volunteer work, elderly women are more likely to volunteer their time. Much of the volunteer activity done by the American Red Cross is by retirees who continue to share their skills and compassion while working with those in need. Other types of volunteer work include tutoring, helping religious organizations, raising money for charities or social and political causes, handiwork, office work, and hospital work. Helping others in need provides a way to achieve a sense of purpose and greater life satisfaction, which can significantly enhance retirement years.

Housing

Our homes provide a refuge of security and safety, and for the elderly, the form and structure of their living situations

Nursing Home Room Courtesy of the National Institute on Aging. *Many people desire a simpler and more stable life-style as they grow older.*

may change significantly. There are many types of housing arrangements for the elderly. More than 21 million people over the age of 65 live in their own homes. Nearly 80% of the elderly own their homes and about 50% have owned their homes for more than 25 years. Moving to a smaller residence after a spouse's death or as a result of financial need may be very difficult. On the other hand, voluntarily downsizing to a smaller residence can bring a sense of relief by lessening financial obligations and reducing worry about the physical burden of the upkeep in an aging house. Most elderly prefer independent living with options ranging from condominiums to cooperative apartments. Elder Cottage Housing Opportunity (ECHO), Accessory Units, and "Granny Flats" refer to housing arrangements where seniors share a single family home, a separate apartment, or a rental unit on a single family lot with another person or family. There are also age-segregated retirement communities, senior housing developments and retirement hotels, and mobile homes and recreation vehicles that are all available at various costs. For those needing assistance in their living arrangements, Continuing Care Retirement Communities (CCRCs) allow individuals and couples to enjoy independent living in apartments until they need further help or a change in the level or intensity of care. Short and long term nursing care is often available on site as needed. **Assisted living** is for those elderly who do not need nursing home care but who desire a facility where housing and meals are provided along with help with everyday living activities and transportation. Board and care homes are usually located in a private home setting where rooms, meals and supervision are provided for a monthly fee.

Institutionalization

According to the 2000 U.S. Census Bureau, only 5% of elderly above age 65 live in nursing homes. However, the rates of admission to nursing homes go up with age; for example, *almost 50% of those elderly older than age of 95 live in nursing homes.* Entering a nursing home has many ramifications. Families and spouses often feel as though they have failed their loved one, and family dynamic issues surrounding the decision for nursing home placement can be difficult and painful. However, *caregivers who attempt to provide total care for their family members have high rates of morbidity and mortality,* as they often neglect their own health and succumb to stress. The transition to a nursing home is difficult but the care received in this setting is usually more successful and less stressful for both patient and family. The nursing home can never be the same as home, nor can the care delivered be the same as that from a devoted family member. However, now an entire cadre of nursing home staff provides the care formerly delivered by one or two family members, which results in an enhanced quality of life for all. Concerns about abuse, neglect or exploitation by nursing home personnel are real, but sometimes overblown. State and federal regulations and guidelines help ensure the safety and quality of care.

There are high rates of psychiatric disorders in nursing homes. Although healthy community-dwelling elderly have lower rates of depression, *between 25% and 50% of elderly residing in nursing homes have or will develop clinical depression.* Nearly two thirds of elderly patients in nursing homes exhibit some element of dementia. One of the issues confronting society is where the demented patient who exhibits problematic neurobehavioral symptoms should be placed. These patients are not appropriate for acute adult psychiatric units, where they are at risk of being abused or injured, but remain a danger to themselves and/or to others in a conventional nursing home setting. Currently, there are not enough dedicated and locked dementia facilities capable of managing this growing population of often physically robust but cognitively impaired patients who are no longer capable of controlling their behavior or of navigating an environment safely and unsupervised.

Finally, for terminally ill patients, **hospices** and **palliative care settings** and programs are now increasingly available for use by patients and families to help them through the final days, weeks or months of life. These programs aim to maintain dignity and compassion in the experience of death and in the dying process. In the year 2000, about 2.4 million Americans died and nearly 600,000 received hospice care. Eighty percent of these hospice patients were over the age of 65. These settings promote and foster comprehensive and compassionate care in hopes of avoiding another acute but futile hospitalization, another abrupt change of surroundings, the introduction of new providers who are not familiar with the patient and family, or additional traumatic and stressful experiences.

Driving

Driving represents independence, freedom and personal power in our society. Curtailing or discontinuing unfettered access to an automobile can represent a significant social and psychological loss for an older person. Compounding the difficulty of this transition, *older persons with cognitive deficits and impaired realty testing often cannot make an accurate assessment of their driving competence.* The challenge of identifying and removing the impaired and incompetent older driver before a tragedy strikes confronts many states, and there is no national standard or law for evaluating or reporting an older individual who is no longer fit to operate an automobile. The role of the physician or healthcare provider is not to determine driving competency, which is the purview and obligation of the state licensing agency or department of motor vehicles, but is to identify those persons who may be unsafe to drive as the result of a physical, mental or cognitive disorder that might hinder safe operation of a vehicle. Tactics employed by states legislatures and state licensing departments to standardize evaluation of the older drivers include more frequent evaluations beyond a certain age and more comprehensive physical, visual and cognitive assessments.

Sexuality

Physiological and psychological changes may affect sexuality in the later stages of life. These changes occur in the context of a society that does not promote or accept sexuality in the elderly, and sexual expression at this stage is either ignored or, more often, ridiculed. This bias is reflected in the paucity of studies looking at sexuality in the el-

THE PLEASURES OF OLD AGE

When my grandmother Lisette turned ninety-nine,
all she could think of was men—
how they would enter her room during the night
from the vast mixer of the mind, wild
with desire, drunk with a desperate love
for only her. All day she sat, spectacle-less,
over romance magazines, until, at night,
she could dream them back into her arms,
those beautiful men, and, when morning came,
rise from her immaculate bed, pink
with the glow of the newly deflowered,
to enter the world again. All over our island
that was Manhattan, bachelors sprouted like
    dandelions
in the field of her hungers—Baruch Oestrich, stifled
by shyness at eighty-eight, for whom she would
    primp for hours;
Hugo Marx, a youthful seventy-seven, but too
    tired to notice;
Walter Hass, a sprightly eighty, who had sat shivah
for his wife for thirty years. Afternoons,
like a young girl dateless at prom time,
she would wait by the phone, sure that deliverance
would come in the voice of some stranger, resolved
that her double digits would grow centuried
in a whirl of romance. I don't know what she
    was thinking
that day, when she fell from the top of the stairs
to die at the bottom, but I like to imagine
it was of who would enter her room that night,
and of her great joy in beautiful men—
how she had trembled for them once,
how she would gladly tremble for them again,
even now.

MICHAEL BLUMENTHAL

derly. Physiological changes may make sex less spontaneous or carefree for the elderly, but clearly, *the yearning for closeness, sexual pleasure and sexual release are still part of the lives of older persons.* Issues of love and intimacy, homosexuality, and masturbation remain important parts of the daily lives of many elderly people. Increasingly, research in the area of human sexuality in the elderly supports the notion of "use it or lose it," meaning that *those who maintain active sex lives as they age can expect to remain so and to derive pleasure from sexual activity long into the latter stages of life.* An unusual but possible concern is sexual exploitation of the cognitively impaired individual in an institutional setting. These problems are often not addressed or discussed, although there is increasing evidence for their occurrence as more people become cognitively impaired while remaining physically and sexually robust.

COPING WITH LOSS

A series of changes and losses accompanies aging. Erik Erikson, a noted psychologist, wrote of eight stages of personality development from birth to death. Each life stage had a conflict that had to be resolved for successful completion. Postulated to occur in the last decades of life, the final stage of development involves the struggle between **ego integrity and despair** in the face of death. Integrity occurs when a person accepts life's accomplishments and accepts death as inevitable. Those persons who have the ability to accept life's joys and pains in perspective and with resolve have an easier time accepting death. Those living in despair view life as misspent and are full of regrets. They fear death as an unacceptable aspect of life.

Shame is a universal human emotion that occurs throughout the life cycle and that may become more pronounced in the aged. Shame is a painful emotion resulting from an awareness of inadequacy or guilt. The stigma of ageism and existential issues inherent in the aging process form the basis for shame in the elderly. Thus, shame in later life is the reaction felt to multiple losses and deviations in appearance, status, role, and ability from the idealized youthful, healthy, and powerful "self." Society also shames individuals about diseases and frailty, both of which happen more in older age. Shame in these circumstances becomes more intense when the elderly person feels invisible or is treated with rejection, impatience, disrespect, and derision. Patients may experience physical or psychological limitations as defects or inadequacies that threaten treasured ideals of the self such as youth, beauty, strength, stamina, dexterity, self-control, independence, and mental competence. Some conditions and treatments may further jeopardize self-image. For example, loss of hair and weight, mastectomies, and erectile dysfunction from cancer inter-

ventions can be degrading to patients. *Reactions to shame may take many forms and are often masked by anger, sadness, depression, or noncompliance.*

Physical Health

Many people over time will develop a chronic illness, which often begins in middle age. Most elderly patients learn to live with one or more chronic illnesses for the rest of their lives. Degenerative musculoskeletal diseases, loss or decline in primary sensory function (vision/hearing/taste), gastrointestinal conditions like ulcers or acid reflux, cardiovascular diseases, endocrinologic disorders like diabetes and hypothyroidism, genitourinary problems like incontinence, urgency, or prostate enlargement, and several types of cancer, commonly present in older age. These changes and decrements in function, while common, may precipitate a psychiatric disorder as the elderly person attempts to cope with these losses and signs of degeneration. In addition, chronic health neglect and poor hygiene begin to show detrimental cumulative effects as the person ages. Lifelong smoking, drinking, substance abuse, lack of exercise, poor dental hygiene and poor eating habits often take years to affect gross health, and with the onset of older age, these behaviors begin to harm the physical and mental condition of an older person. Unfortunately, making significant changes in poor lifelong habits is frequently difficult to achieve.

Cognitive Functioning

The public is now aware of Alzheimer's disease, and many elderly are understandably concerned and afraid of losing their cognitive abilities. Former President Ronald Reagan's announcement of his diagnosis and the subsequent media coverage of his illness over the years highlighted the ravages of this disease. The fear of developing dementia when an occasional memory lapse occurs, such as misplacing keys or being unable to remember a person's name, can lead to increased anxiety and depression. *A single or occasional lapse rarely signifies a dementia process, and without other evidence, the older individual should be reassured and counseled about some of the t normal cognitive changes with aging.* Conversely, anxiety and depressive disorders may affect an older person's abilities, and clearly, these need to be addressed. Perhaps surprisingly, many elderly are reluctant to participate in a cognitive assessment. Some may even become insulted when asked to answer questions about their cognitive state. Others may fear that their deficits will be exposed or that they will be ridiculed for appearing stupid

Aging Scholar Courtesy of the National Institute on Aging. *Although some individuals experience cognitive decline with aging, the more common experience is to remain intellectually active and alert.*

or dumb. Finally, some elderly are concerned that poor test results will have some adverse effect on their ability to remain independent. Therefore, evaluation of cognition should be performed with sensitivity to the potential issues uncovered and involved.

If diagnosed with a cognitive disorder, an individual may respond in a variety of ways. Common responses are denial that test results are correct or that memory problems are significant, and projection that others are mistaken or that others are having difficulties coping. Confrontation of denial is often met with further resistance due to impairment of insight, termed **anosognosia**, and lack of judgment, both of which may accompany cognitive loss. On the other hand, some elderly are keenly aware of their problems and cognitive struggles, and become anxious and depressed. *Approximately 25% of patients with early stage Alzheimer's disease present with symptoms of depression that should be treated.* A cognitive disorder in the elder head of household will impact all family members. The necessary changes in family structure and responsibilities for decisions will create new challenges as shifts in family dynamics and power differentials add caregiver burden and stress.

Competency

Independence and the ability to make decisions is an important and defining characteristic of being an adult. Losing the ability to make decisions about one's health care, finances and legal matters is a serious infringement of the basic rights of an adult individual. The task of assessing whether to deny a person of her rights cannot be taken lightly. Confusion surrounds the difference between the terms capacity and competency, which are often used interchangeably if imprecisely. **Capacity** refers to the ability or inability of an individual to make decisions, whether concerning medical, financial or legal matters of estate or of person, and is a conclusion reached usually after a medical or clinical evaluation. **Competency**, on the other hand, is a legal definition and reflects the decision of a court or judge, based on evidence concerning the proposed question, including the findings of a professional evaluator such as a physician, psychologist, religious arbiter or attorney. Thus, the terms are not entirely synonymous.

Competency assessments should focus on the specific decision or task that is being questioned, since incompetence or competence in one area may not predict or correlate with ability in another. Typical concerns arise when an older adult with a possible cognitive, medical or psychiatric illness that impacts decision-making is changing or writing a will, signing a contract, distributing property, or considering a potentially dangerous or experimental medical treatment or procedure. In truth, any time an older patient is making or considering a choice on any matter, competency is a factor.

Legal authorities and forensic experts use several processes for determining competency. Essentially, to be legally valid, any decision made by an individual must be voluntary, informed, and competent. Voluntary decisions are freely given and not the result of coercion, threat or undue influence. Additionally, the person must evidence a choice either explicitly in writing or by speech or implicitly by actions and behaviors. The decision must also be informed, which entails, for medical decisions, disclosure of the condition being treated and indication(s) for treatment, discussion and description of the recommended intervention or treatment, review of the risks, benefits and side effects of the recommended treatment, disclosure of alternative therapies including doing nothing at all, and the consequences of those choices. The clinician should assess for understanding of information presented and *ask the patient to repeat and describe the discussion in her own words.* In short, the clinician must determine if the older person has the ability to assimilate relevant facts, and if the person appreciates or rationally understands his or her own situation as it relates to medical circumstances. For older patients with cognitive impairment or serious medical or psychiatric illness, information may have to be presented multiple times or in multiple formats. Importantly, the state of competency can vary over time, e.g., during delirium or during a period of grave illness in which a patient was not able to make decisions or to participate in discussion. Conversely, with dementia, other cognitive disorders, and pervasive unremitting psychiatric conditions, cognitive abilities may be so impaired that competency will never be regained. In this situation may require guardianship or conservatorship, in which case a court formally appoints and charges another person with the responsibility and authority to make all medical, financial and/or legal decisions.

Standardized tools may help facilitate the evaluation of competency, but these need to be used in conjunction with a thorough clinical evaluation that might entail a complete medical history, review of medications, physical and psychiatric evaluations, and laboratory tests. A diagnosis, if established, may impact the determination of the decision-making ability and guide further work-up. Finally, evaluation of family structure and social network, and frequently, interviews of family members, caregivers and friends are necessary for a complete competency assessment.

Into the World There Came a Soul Called Ida (The Lord in His Heaven and I in My Room Below) *(1929/1930) Ivan Le Lorraine Albright, American, 1897–1983.* Oil on canvas, 142.9 × 119.2 cm. Gift of Ivan Albright, 1977.34. Photograph by Robert Hashimoto. © The Art Institute of Chicago. Reproduced by permission of the artist's estate. *Physicians have to be able to deal with patients who present with somatic concerns related to fading beauty, declining physical prowess, and loneliness.*

Separation and Death

Loss of loved ones, especially of a spouse or child, is devastating for most people. There are often changes in the survivor's social and financial situation. *The death of a spouse is associated with high rates of morbidity and mortality in previously healthy people.* Depression, anxiety and insomnia are common psychiatric features of bereavement. Studies suggest that the stress of bereavement produces changes in the body's immune system creating negative health outcomes. Women generally adjust better than men do to the loss of a spouse, and males are much more likely to die within a year after being widowed. Widowhood is difficult, but in many cases, after the period of grief passes, survivors adjust and find that they can regain a sense of normalcy, if not enjoy a new sense of independence. Some elderly find new experiences and new relationships in the aftermath of a death of a spouse or partner. *The losses of parents and adult children can be extremely painful for the elderly. Having a strong social net-*

work of close and valued relationships with friends and family provides the best means of coping with these losses. Early psychological treatment of complicated bereavement may prevent the development of clinical depression. Grief support groups available through pastoral counseling, hospice programs, or community organizations are helpful in providing or creating a sense of security and of sharing and are sources for new relationships. For many the role of spirituality and religion cannot be underestimated as a source of comfort, strength and solace.

MENTAL HEALTH AND ILLNESS

Psychiatric Assessment of the Older Adult

Psychiatric assessment of older individuals entails an evaluation and analysis of a person's thoughts, emotions, behaviors and cognition. The presenting psychiatric symp-

> You're only as young as the last time you changed your mind.
>
> TIMOTHY LEARY

toms must be analyzed comprehensively and placed in the appropriate medical and psychosocial contexts. Importantly, *psychiatric evaluation of the older individual must balance respect for personal autonomy, dignity and privacy with the need to gather information from a variety of collateral sources*, including spouses, partners, adult children, extended family and friends, and usually multiple medical care providers. The older person is considered competent until proven otherwise and, except in an emergency, his or her permission must be sought to discuss their care and treatment with others. However, there may be cultural differences and sensitivities to observe, and ideally, the clinician should be aware of these at the outset. Lastly, some elderly persons may shun psychiatric evaluation due to the stigma of mental illness or to a tendency to express psychological difficulties as somatic complaints as a means to avoid the perception of character flaws or weaknesses.

Medical or neurologic comorbidity may also complicate the psychiatric evaluation of an older individual. Psychiatric symptoms by themselves are relatively nonspecific and may develop in practically any medical disorder. That is, *medical conditions may present with psychiatric symptoms*, e.g., pancreatic cancer or hypothyroidism presenting with depressed mood, and conversely, *psychiatric disorders may present with medical symptoms*, e.g., clinical depression presenting with weight loss or panic disorder with chest pain. Medications, over-the-counter drugs, herbal remedies and supplements may cause an alteration in cognition, thinking, emotion or behavior as the result of drug side effects, drug-drug or drug-supplement interactions or toxicities. A careful systematic and comprehensive approach is necessary when evaluating an elderly patient, and includes query for past medical and neurologic history, review of medication lists, family medical and psychiatric history, social history, and review of systems. The physical examination focuses on acute processes and must include at least an elemental neurologic examination (cranial nerves, reflexes and motor exam). The **mental status exam**, which starts when the patient enters the room, continues throughout the interview, and incorporates observation of the interaction between patient and interviewer as well as between patient and environment, should specifically assess for suicidality, psychosis, and impaired thinking.

An older person may be experiencing an exacerbation of a pre-existing psychiatric disorder, present since earlier in life, or may be developing a psychiatric disorder for the first time only later in life. The former group is said to have an early-onset disorder and the latter to have a late-onset disorder. Patients with early-onset disorders have positive

psychiatric histories, although details may be sketchy or hard to corroborate, as well as higher genetic or biological load with positive family histories of mental disorders. Patients with early-onset disorders, in general, tend to have poorer physical health in later life compared to their peers without any prior psychiatric history. In contrast, patients with late-onset disorders typically have negative past and family psychiatric histories and carry a lower genetic or biological load. Late-onset psychiatric disorders appear to be associated with the development or worsening of an underlying medical or neurological condition. Many of the same conditions found earlier in life can develop later in life, although the likelihood, risk and prevalence of disorders are different.

Psychiatric Disorders in Late-Life

Anxiety Disorders

Anxiety disorders are among the most common yet poorly recognized and diagnosed mental conditions in later life. While de novo anxiety disorders are relatively rare in elderly persons, many patients live decades without accurate identification. These patients in particular are at high risk for self-medication with or abuse of alcohol, prescription drugs such as benzodiazepines or opiates, or over-the-counter sedatives and pain relievers. Often, these patients are only identified because of an alcohol-related or medication-induced medical problem or withdrawal syndrome. However, it is important to appreciate that anxiety may be a normal response to a stressful life event or serious medical problem. Only when anxiety symptoms become too overwhelming, interfere with daily functioning or impair health or safety, is psychiatric evaluation or intervention needed. Finally, anxiety may be a component of a variety of medical conditions or a manifestation of drug side effect or drug toxicity.

Mood Disorders

Mood disorders are common in the elderly population, albeit at a lower prevalence than generally thought. Mood disorders include unipolar and bipolar depression, dysthymia, subsyndromal depression, substance-induced depression, and mood disorder due to general medical conditions. In fact, *in community-dwelling healthy elderly the prevalence of clinical depression is only about 1/3 the rate of the general adult population. However, the prevalence rates of depression increase across more medically ill populations and in various medical settings* (see Figure 5.5).

Depression should be recognized because it is a diagnosable and treatable condition. Unfortunately, studies continue to show that *depression in the elderly remains under recognized, misdiagnosed, and both poorly and less intensely*

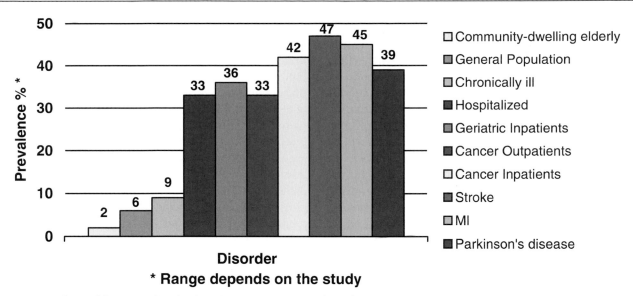

FIGURE 5.5 Prevalence of depressive disorders in various patient groups and populations.

treated. Many older persons, their families or healthcare providers may also show therapeutic nihilism and attempt to explain away the reasons for depression. However, an untreated mood disorder is associated with poorer medical and psychiatric outcomes. Depression in later life is associated with lower quality of life, prolonged suffering, more disability, increased healthcare utilization and costs, and increased morbidity and mortality. Psychiatric consequences of late life depression include mental health related disability, increased risk of substance abuse, and increased risk of suicide.

Diagnosis of depression or any mood disorder in the medically ill elderly patient may be particularly difficult due to the overlap of many physical complaints with the symptoms of depression. Evaluation for the psychological symptoms of depression such as depressed mood or sadness, **anhedonia** or loss of interests, feelings of guilt or worthlessness, suicidal ideation, or of behavioral equivalents such as crying, social regression or withdrawal, can increase the specificity of diagnosis. Neurovegetative symptoms like sleep disturbance, loss of appetite or weight, psychomotor retardation or fatigue are less specific for depression in medically ill elderly, but may be considered attributable to depression if these worsen or co-vary with mood. An older person with depression may develop severe cognitive impairment and appear demented. These patients may be either in the prodrome of a dementia syndrome or at higher risk of subsequently converting to a dementia syndrome, and in any case merit particular close attention. Screening instruments are available for use in the elderly population and include the **Geriatric Depression Scale**, which is available in several item and language versions and is validated across different settings, and the **Cornell Scale for Depression in Dementia**. However, *the gold standard for diagnosis of depression remains a thorough clinical interview.*

Psychotic Disorders

Primary psychotic disorders in the elderly include schizophrenia, schizoaffective disorder, and delusional disorder. However, symptoms of psychosis may manifest in other psychiatric conditions such as major depression, substance-induced intoxication and withdrawal states, and cognitive disorders such as dementia or delirium. Since DSM-IV, there is no longer an age specification for schizophrenia onset, although interestingly, it appears that older women may be at higher risk. Elderly patients with late-onset schizophrenia, whose illness typically begins after age 60, tend to have positive symptoms like paranoid delusions or hallucinations, while negative symptoms, like alogia and apathy, and disorganized states occur, in general, less frequently in older groups compared to younger adults and compared to those elderly with early-onset disorder. The original assumption that all patients with early-onset schizophrenia suffered unrelenting cognitive deterioration, i.e., **dementia praecox**, is likely wrong, and some patients remain remarkably stable over a lifetime. Late-onset schizophrenia, also termed **paraphrenia**, may be more common in women and in patients with primary sensory (vision and hearing) impairment, and is marked by predominance of paranoid symptoms and less bizarre ideation. *De novo psychotic symptoms in later life may be a manifestation of underlying central nervous system disease such as dementia, other neurodegenerative disorders like Parkinson's or Huntington's diseases, stroke, inflammatory processes, infection, primary or metastatic cancer, seizure disorder, or trauma.*

Substance Abuse and Dependence Disorders

Substance abuse and dependence disorders in the elderly remain poorly understood, appreciated and studied. The elderly may abuse alcohol, prescription drugs like opiates and benzodiazepines, or over-the-counter drugs and supplements. Like in younger populations, *substance abuse in the elderly significantly increases the risk for medical and psychiatric morbidity and mortality.* Prevalence estimates of the extent of substance abuse in older populations are difficult to ascertain for a variety of reasons. For example, identification of problem drinking in older patients is challenging because alcoholism may be a hidden condition, diagnostic criteria developed for younger populations may not apply to older groups, and physicians may be reluctant to make a diagnosis in an older adult. While most problem drinkers began in early life, about 1/3 to 1/2 of older people developed a problem with alcohol only later in life. Periods of high risk include time around the death of a spouse or companion, stresses around illness, loss of function or life transitions, and development of clinical depression. Additionally, many elderly may minimize or conceal their extent of alcohol or drug use. Elderly patients with multiple conditions may visit multiple providers and obtain multiple prescriptions.

The elderly are more prone to the toxic effects of alcohol and drugs. Due to physiologic changes of aging, older people have higher blood levels of alcohol and drugs and manifest toxic effects more readily, e.g., confusion, disorientation, memory loss, poor motor coordination, unsteady gait and more falls. Chronic alcohol use is associated with poor nutritional status and with vitamin and protein deficiencies, which may lead to peripheral and central nervous systems disorders like motor palsies, neuropathies, Wernicke's encephalopathy, or Korsakoff's psychosis. Finally, consequences of alcoholism and unsupervised or inappropriate drug use are serious, leading possibly to early deaths. In the elderly, drug-alcohol interactions and withdrawal syndromes from central nervous system depressants can be lethal.

Cognitive Disorders

With the increasing elderly population, dementias and other cognitive disorders are now major problems confronting the elderly population. *Current estimates of the number of Americans with dementia number around 4 million, and by 2020 the number may reach between 11 to 14 million.* **Dementia** refers to a variety of acquired conditions that involve impairments across multiple domains, usually including a primary deficit in memory function. These deficits develop for the first time in later adulthood and impair functioning in daily life, work or social relationships. **Amnesia**, in contrast, refers to dysfunction only in the domain of memory that can occur any time in life. While age by itself is not synonymous with dementia, *aging is the greatest risk factor for development of dementia* with incidence and prevalence rates increasing rapidly with age. Diagnostic schemas are predicated upon descriptions of presenting symptoms, clinical course of illness, and increasingly, an understanding of epidemiology, risk factors, and neurogenetics. Dementias are either primary or secondary. **Primary dementias** are further classified as cortical or subcortical. The prototypic primary neurodegenerative dementia is Alzheimer's Disease, which is also the most common form of dementia in later life. The second most common dementia syndrome is **vascular dementia**, which actually is comprised of several subtypes. Although the primary presenting symptoms of dementia involve memory loss and at least one or more neuropsychological impairments, many patients will also develop psychiatric symptoms such as depression, anxiety, psychosis, personality changes, or behavioral disturbances.

Delirium is another important cognitive disorder that occurs more frequently in the elderly population. Delirium if unrecognized may lead to death. Delirium, also-called altered mental status or acute confusional state, usually presents closely to an acute medical insult such as myocardial infarction, pneumonia, stroke, metabolic derangement, systemic infection, or drug toxicity or withdrawal syndrome, although *frequently the cause of delirium is multifactorial,* meaning that a single definitive etiology may not be found. Delirium presents with impaired consciousness and attention deficits and may include psychiatric symptoms and behavioral disturbances. *Risk factors for delirium include older age, serious medical illness, multiple active illnesses, use of multiple drugs, and pre-existing cognitive or psychiatric disorder.* In contrast to dementia, delirium develops quickly over hours to days, fluctuates throughout the course of the day, and if the underlying cause is identified and treated, will usually reverse. Elderly delirious patients are very difficult to manage and treat because of the many possible etiologies involved. Elderly delirious patients are also prone to neglect, dehydration, aspiration pneumonia, poor nutrition, deconditioning, pressure sores and strangulation from entanglement in intravenous lines and monitoring equipment. A sitter or family member is ideal to have at the patient's bedside to provide reassurance and calming and obviates the need for restraints and the excessive use of sedatives or tranquilizers.

Psychiatric Intervention

Psychotherapy

When Sigmund Freud, the father of psychoanalysis, was himself 68 years of age, he described those over the age of 50 as unsuitable for individual psychotherapy because he thought that older individuals, given a set character structure, no longer had the capacity or motivation for change and that the duration of treatment required to produce change portended an interminable therapy. It is interesting that Freud completed the majority of his work and prolific writings on psychoanalytic theory and treatment after the age of 50. However, his dismissal of insight-oriented therapy for older adults led to a long period of neglect and of limited study of this age group. *Over the past two decades renewed interest and research from several studies indicate that several forms of psychotherapy can be as effective as pharmacotherapy in treating several types of depression in the elderly patient, and more importantly, the combination of both modalities has better outcomes than when either is used alone.* There is, however, a striking disparity between the estimated need for mental health care of the elderly and the availability of privately and publicly funded services and providers. Older adults are much more likely to be treated in primary care settings rather than in mental health settings. Many fear dependency and mockery when seeking help for mental problems. They may also fear appearing weak and needy if they see a mental healthcare provider, as it is perceived to be more acceptable to seek medical or physical care. Talk therapy focuses on exposing and confronting disavowed feeling states, whereas medical care offers treatments aimed at curing physical suffering. Psychological issues represent a problem of self-image, whereas medical treatment displaces perceived injury of self onto an isolated body part. A shame response is possible in both milieus, but it is in the psychiatric setting where a patient may feel more vulnerable or exposed, and understandably, may avoid going to see a psychiatrist or therapist. Previously considered negative indicators for successful psychotherapy, may, in fact, be positive predictors of success. As people age and face a limited future, they have less time for, less use of and less patience for counterproductive attitudes and poor interpersonal strategies. In the hands of a savvy therapist, the urgency for change may speed the therapeutic process; in addition, *the elderly bring to therapy a lifetime of experience, which can be used productively to explore dynamics and achieve resolutions.*

Besides psychodynamic or insight-oriented psychotherapy, several other forms of therapy are effective and available for use in older populations. Cognitive-behavioral, interpersonal and brief psychodynamic therapy studies show efficacy in the elderly. Beyond individual modalities, couples, family and group therapy are variations to consider. The latter may be especially useful for caregivers. Groups provide the opportunity for sharing experiences, giving and receiving support, and social interaction. Groups for demented patients focus on improving memory and enhancing cognitive skills through music and art therapy, life reminiscing, and motor skills training and physical activity.

Somatic Treatment of the Older Patient

Compared to younger groups, elderly patients use more medications. Americans older than 65 years fill an average of 13 prescriptions per year, which is twice the national average and three times the average of individuals younger than 65 years. In general, the number of prescribed medications increases with age but so does the number of nonprescription over-the-counter (OTC) medications used. Nearly two-thirds of elderly patients report routine use of OTC medications. Somatic therapies in geriatric psychiatry consist of psychopharmacologic interventions and several types of brain stimulation therapies such as electroconvulsive therapy (ECT), vagus nerve stimulation (VNS) therapy, and repetitive transcranial magnetic stimulation (rTMS). When used appropriately and for the conditions indicated, both psychotropic medications and, of the brain stimulation therapies, ECT are safe and effective in older patients. Efficacy data for VNS therapy and rTMS in the older adult are still not definitive. All treatments work best when matched to the disorder for which efficacy is demonstrated.

Unfortunately, studies of psychotropic drug use in the elderly show inappropriate use of many classes of medications. For example, in the recent past *elderly patients residing in skilled nursing facilities were frequently overmedicated, primarily for behavioral reasons, despite the fact that psychotropics, mainly antipsychotics and benzodiazepines, show limited efficacy for these purposes and cause untoward and serious side effects.* Other studies show that many elderly patients are reluctant to take psychotropic drugs because of fear or misunderstanding of their purpose and because of the stigma associated with having a mental condition. Finally, other studies suggest that elderly patients are less intensely treated for their mental disorders in healthcare settings, causing unnecessarily prolonged suffering and increased disability. For ECT, the matter is similar. ECT, the most effective treatment for depression, especially psychotic depression, carries an immense stigma. In fact, *ECT has low morbidity and mortality rates, and recent studies suggest that older age may be a positive predictor of response.*

Managing and treating an older patient can be very challenging. Increasing numbers of medical problems, both acute and chronic, make older patients less responsive to treatment for a variety of reasons. Comorbid medical burden is a predictor of poorer response to acute psychotropic treatment, limits the choices of potential medications, may limit the extent of response and may leave the patient with greater residual symptoms and increased functional impairment. Additionally, medical conditions may be chronic or progressive, implying a high risk of intercurrent illnesses, interruptions in treatment, and need for frequent review and adjustments. More medical burden may make patients less tolerant to treatment due to less physiological reserve, less functional capacity, and a lower threshold for decompensation. Finally, *with increasing number of medications there is a higher risk for medication errors, inappropriate drug prescribing, drug-drug or drug-OTC interactions, and medication noncompliance due to complex drug schedules, drug interruptions, and cost.*

With an increased likelihood of more medical comorbidity and of being on several medications or supplements, an older patient may be at greater risk for an adverse outcome from a psychotropic drug. Alterations in pharmacokinetics and pharmacodynamics with aging increase the risk for an untoward or idiosyncratic drug reaction. **Pharmacokinetics** describes what the body does to the drug, i.e., absorption, distribution, metabolism and excretion. Changes in aging can affect each one of these areas. **Pharmacodynamics** involves what the drug does to the body, i.e., side effects, toxicity, and withdrawal reactions. Changes in body and brain receptor sensitivity and receptor availability with aging account for many of these effects and presentations. Common aging and pharmacodynamic effects are listed in Box 5.1 below.

BOX 5.1 Aging and pharmacodynamics

- Central nervous system: sedation, confusion, disorientation, memory impairment, delirium, agitation, mood and perceptual disturbances, headache
- Cardiovascular: hypotension, orthostasis, cardiac conduction abnormalities (arrhythmias, QTc prolongation)
- Gastrointestinal: nausea, vomiting, appetite changes, abdominal cramps, loose stool
- Peripheral anticholinergic effects: blurred vision, dry mouth, constipation, urinary retention
- Motor effects: tremor, impaired gait, increased body sway, falls, extrapyramidal system effects
- Other: sexual dysfunction; metabolic, endocrinologic, and electrolyte disturbances

---

General principles for use of psychotropic agents in an older person include matching the right drug to the right disorder, having clear target symptoms at the outset, and monitoring for improvement, lack of response, or deterioration. All are clearly important to successful management. Additionally, *the starting dose is lower, typically about 1/4 to 1/2 of the younger adult initial dose.* Adjustments continue gradually, made every 3 to 5 days as tolerated, being certain to reach the usual therapeutic range. Some side effects may not be evident in the beginning and only develop after the drug accumulates in the body. Medications continue until the patient reaches remission or maximal improvement. Whether to maintain a medication depends upon the disorder being treated and the patient's history of relapse and stability. Some patients may require chronic treatment.

Hospital and Day Programs

Adult day care is a newer option for elderly patients who prefer to remain in their homes, but who need or could benefit from a range of services, including medical, rehabilitation, occupational, and social activities. Senior centers and day programs coordinate many of these services and also help prevent social isolation. These programs provide respite for caregivers, allowing them a chance to recharge,

relieve stress, return to work or to take care of other daily needs and routine tasks like marketing, shopping, or banking. Many of these programs are run by charitable or religious organizations and may be free or relatively inexpensive and others may be covered by insurance. Families can also receive grants and other funds from social agencies or government programs to help defray costs.

Suicide

Considering the many losses that the elderly experience, it is not surprising that this group has very high suicide rates. *Although the elderly make up about 13% of the population they comprise 25% of the annual suicides in the United States. Men account for 80% of the elderly suicides and approximately 85% will use a firearm, a very lethal means of suicide.* Suicide rates are the highest for older white males and elderly African-American males have lower rates of suicide. Risk factors for suicide include a history of divorce or loss of a spouse, poor or failing health, a history of alcohol or substance abuse, a history of major depression, social isolation, and having access to firearms.

There are many reasons an elderly person may want to end his or her life. Some possible reasons include multiple losses of loved ones, chronic illness and poorly controlled pain. An older person may also fear becoming a burden on his or her family. Not uncommonly, an older person may want to end his life because of worry that an inheritance intended for family will be spent instead on mounting medical expenses. The fear of losing cognitive and physical abilities to make, execute and control decisions is another common precipitant of suicidal thinking. Indeed, suicide provides the ultimate act of control over how life ends, avoiding the unknown and uncertainty of death. Finally, suicide may be viewed as the only realistic means of ending uncontrollable and unremitting pain.

Physician-assisted suicide (PAS) is a social and political subject being debated in this country and around the world. Physician-assisted suicide was recently legalized in the Netherlands, and approximately 2% of deaths in the Netherlands result from PAS. The experience there shows that over 85% who request PAS change their wishes when provided adequate pain medications and when given counseling and pharmacologic treatments for depression. Thus, the majority of people who are interested in this option are suffering unnecessarily from untreated pain and depression.

As opposed to PAS, **passive euthanasia** entails the withholding or withdrawing of medical treatment in the terminally ill. The case of Terri Schiavo, a Florida woman in a chronic vegetative state for many years, is one example. Her husband wanted to honor her unwritten wish that she not to be sustained by medical means, specifically by a feeding tube. Many social, legal and emotional issues were debated and the eventual decision, after lengthy and dramatic court and political actions, was to withdraw her feeding tube. Questions of the "right to die" and the definition of brain death became front and center. Court litigation and treatment decision controversies are avoidable if individuals specify in writing what future treatment preferences are and note these in a **living will** or an **advanced life directive**. *Many patients and families find the topic hard to confront and broach, but the problem is made harder when clinicians unknowingly collude by avoiding discussion of these serious matters.* Importantly, the elderly should be encouraged to complete an advanced life directive or living will while they are still cognitively capable. Completion of these documents is a way to initiate a dialog about end of life issues. Fears about death and dying can then be openly addressed and relieved by proactive discussion of a frightening topic.

Elder Abuse

Physical frailty and cognitive impairment may make the elderly more dependent on families and others, which possibly exposes them to abuse. Elder abuse occurs in many forms including physical or sexual abuse, psychological abuse, financial exploitation, medical abuse and general neglect. The abuse can occur in any setting. These abuses may be the continuation of a lifelong pattern of abuse from a spouse or family member. Often, elder abuse stems from the breakdown of normal boundaries, as children or others assume caregiving roles, for which they are untrained, and experience caregiver stress, especially while attempting to maintain their previous lives and schedules.

Caregiver stress is a well-recognized risk factor for any type of abuse. As with other types of mistreatment and cruelty within the family or in professional settings, elder abuse may be subtle and difficult to detect. The victim frequently is fearful of reporting actions to authorities or others. The majority of states have laws protecting the elderly and have made reporting elder abuse mandatory if the suspicion arises. Exacerbation, relapse or recurrence of an older person's underlying psychiatric condition, or development of new problem behaviors may be warning signs of abuse. Other signs include repeated trips to emergency rooms with evidence of recent trauma, and illnesses and wounds that do not respond to treatment. Financial exploitation and undue influence over an elderly person who is no longer competent is, sadly, not uncommon. These patients lack the means and the insight to recognize that their persons or estates are being victimized. Physicians and healthcare providers have a duty to identify, protect and advocate for vulnerable older patients who are dependent, scared and defenseless. Legal authorities, social services and other governmental agencies such as Adult Protective Services should be contacted to provide further evaluation and protection.

> I like spring, but it is too young. I like summer, but it is too proud. So I like best of all autumn, because its tone is mellower, its colors are richer, and it is tinged with a little sorrow. Its golden richness speaks not of the innocence of spring, nor the power of summer, but of the mellowness and kindly wisdom of approaching age. It knows the limitations of life and its content.
>
> LIN YÜ-TANG

SUMMARY

The elderly are the most rapidly growing segment of the US population and there are multiple social and economic forces confronting this growing population. Gerontology is the study of the elderly and the aging process itself, and covers the social, psychological and biological aspects of aging. Geriatrics is the branch of medicine that studies the diseases, disorders and syndromes that occur in later life. Importantly, research funding for both the basic and clinical sciences of aging is increasing. Geriatric subspecialty training occurs formally in medicine, psychiatry, and family medicine, but many other specialties increasingly recognize the value and importance of this unique group of individuals. The clinical practice of geriatrics includes and integrates many disciplines across healthcare, involving professionals from medicine, nursing, social work, rehabilitation and occupational therapy, dietary and nutritional services, dentistry, pharmacy, psychologists, chaplains and others. Treatment and management of the elderly encompasses legal, ethical, moral, medical, psychological, and even political issues. As this age group grows, interest in caring for, understanding and treating the elderly also grows. Working with the elderly provides for an immensely rich and gratifying experience, and promises to be an area of immense healthcare need for the foreseeable future.

CASE STUDY

Part I. Over the past 6 months Mrs. Mary Jones, who is 74, has become more forgetful and irritable. She was an attorney and considered for a judgeship, but instead retired early about 15 years ago to care for an ailing husband. She gradually lost contact with many colleagues and professional friends. Her husband died last year after a long illness. She was the primary caregiver until 2 years ago when he went to a skilled nursing facility because she was unable to manage him at home after he suffered a fall and broke his hip.. She blames herself for his demise and subsequent death, believing she could have done more, and she is angry at herself for ever agreeing to his placement at her children's urging.

Shortly after her husband's death, Mrs. Jones experienced a mild heart attack and her recovery was complicated by pneumonia. After a brief stay in a rehabilitation facility she moved, at her children's behest, from New York City to Los Angeles where she lives in her own apartment close to her daughter and grandchildren. During an office visit her daughter reports that she is worried that her mother, previously a bright and energetic woman, now appears lost, confused and mentally dull.

Q1. What losses must she confront? Are there concerns about competency? What are useful courses of action to take?
Her life changed dramatically both in the short and long term. She gave up a professional practice and retired not because she was ready to, but instead, to care for an ailing spouse. She no longer had the stimulation of complex work in a field that provided prestige and intellectual challenge and she also lost contact with friends who supported her professional identity. Additionally, Mrs. Jones, after experiencing a prolonged period of caregiver stress, lost her spouse, is grieving, and must adjust to widowhood. She is at high risk for complicated bereavement or depression. She feels she failed as a caregiver having placed her husband in a nursing home where he died. She wonders if she were pressured into the choice of placement.

Concerns about problems with competency are difficult to discern. The patient recently had to make various types of decisions, e.g., the care and placement of her husband, type and extent of medical treatment she received after a heart attack and her own placement in a rehabilitation facility, and relocation to a different city to receive more help and support from an adult daughter. Apparently, she made most decisions voluntarily, and although she may have been influenced by her family, there is no evidence that her choices resulted in worse outcomes medically, legally or financially, caused anyone immediate danger or harm, or were made under threat or coercion. In the absence of any other evidence she must be presumed competent. Nonetheless, keep in mind that competency may vary over time and addresses specific questions or situations that must be assessed individually. If there is a specific concern, a clinical evaluation would strive to assess her **capacity** to make informed decisions which could then be used to make a determination of her **competency** to manage a specific medical, legal or financial affair.

However, she also has significant medical problems that may have been neglected as she focused more on her husband's ailments and nursing home placement. Caregivers often experience worse health outcomes, as they neglect their own health problems, or suffer physical setbacks because of the added burden of stress. She requires a thorough clinical medical evaluation including medical history, assessment of functional capability and of other psychiatric symptoms, review of prescribed medication and over-the-counter supplements, and reviews of psychiatric history,

family history, substance abuse history and of general systems. Furthermore, a physical exam assesses for acute medical processes and includes both an elemental neurologic exam and a mental status exam. Pertinent laboratory studies should be checked.

Part II. On clinical interview Mrs. Jones reports that she has hypothyroidism and hypertension. She relays that she forgot to fill her prescriptions and has not taken any medication for about 1 month. She complains of cold intolerance, constipation and fatigue. As you discuss the need to treat her medical problems, she appears to fall asleep. You tell her daughter that a careful physical exam, vital sign check, and basic labs are needed. She agrees to let her mother be examined and tested. The patient's blood pressure is low despite not taking any medications, but her temperature is mildly elevated. Her exam reveals no emergent medical process and is otherwise unremarkable. Her laboratory studies reveal several problems. Her urinalysis shows evidence of a serious urinary tract infection and a complete blood count shows a mild leukocytosis with a left shift. Her thyroid stimulating hormone level result is also mildly elevated.

When awakened and told of her problems, Mrs. Jones agrees to be admitted to hospital, where her infection is quickly treated with antibiotics and her low blood pressure stabilized after fluid hydration. She resumes her usual medications. On the day of discharge you notice the patient is quietly crying as she looks out the window. She says, "my life is falling apart," and complains that her thinking is "not right," as she has never before forgotten to take her medications. She worries that she has Alzheimer's, and she does not want to end up in a nursing home like her husband. Upon further questioning, Mrs. Jones reveals that she regrets moving to Los Angeles. She misses her church, her few close friends, and her home of 40 years. She resents not being able to drive since she sold her car. She complains of not sleeping well and feels bored, but she is worried that with all her recent health problems she is becoming a burden to her family. She says, "life would be easier if I weren't around to cause trouble."

Her daughter, while sympathetic, is also clearly frustrated. She has a young family at home and struggles to keep everything on schedule. Her brothers are not helping with their mother's care as they said they would. She discouraged her mother from driving in Los Angeles, as she is worried that she will have an accident. Since she has durable power of attorney, she instructs you to tell her mother that she can no longer drive. The apartment does not appear to be working out, but there is no room at her house. She wants her mother to move to senior retirement housing where she can meet other people.

Q2. What issues and problems should be explored now? What approaches, treatments or resources could be useful at this point? What is her prognosis?

Mrs. Jones does not seem to be handling the move from New York to Los Angeles well. She also appears to be struggling with the transition from independent living at home to an apartment and misses the independence of having an automobile. Her health setback raises worries about other potential losses and she raises the fear of dementia and of nursing home placement. Her daughter may have her hands full with a young family and she receives limited help from her brothers, so family tensions may be running high. Her daughter is experiencing her own level of caregiver burden and stress, and while thinking she is coming up with solutions and recommendations, she may be overstepping her bounds of authority and role by insisting that her mother not drive and that her mother move to another living arrangement.

While not a crisis per se, the situation presents several needs and areas of concern to prioritize. First and foremost is the issue of patient safety, which has medical, psychiatric and social components. One question is whether the patient is capable of being managed as an outpatient, which requires that she be able on her own or with additional supervision to attend to her basic needs. Her medical problems appear stable but do require consistent taking of medication and regular medical follow-up. Her understanding of this should be confirmed. If warranted, a visiting nurse can stop by and assess the home for safety and patient compliance. However, given the patient's despair and distress, the question of depression must be formally assessed prior to her discharge. A psychiatric consultation in hospital or soon after could be useful. If she is actively suicidal, outpatient management may not be possible without adequate supervision and follow-up. Options to review with the patient and family include inpatient psychiatric hospitalization, medication for depression, and psychotherapy to help her through unresolved bereavement and grief over the losses of her spouse, independence, home, and self-image. The family can also benefit from counseling to help adjust to their new roles and responsibilities. In particular, the family must appreciate that, absent a determination of incapability or finding of incompetence, their mother must be offered an opportunity to make choices and to participate in her own care. Finally, the patient and family may benefit from referral to social work to explore community, hospital day, and senior center programs.

Late-life depression is quite treatable as long as it is identified. While Mrs. Jones has many reasons to be depressed and several of her medical problems presented with symptoms similar to those of depression, she persists with complaints and sadness even after medical care. Her worries about cognitive dysfunction are very common, especially with the lapses demonstrated. She and the family should be reassured that there were other explanations for her confusion and memory complaints and that a thorough medical review, exam, and laboratory *screen revealed no evidence for another cause. Thus, dementia appears unlikely. With adequate treatment and monitoring, once her depression improves and she settles into a new and normal* routine, she can expect to live life happily, enjoying her grandchildren, learning new hobbies, volunteering, and making new friends.

SUGGESTED READINGS

Blazer, D.G., & Steffens, D.C. (2009). *The American Psychiatric Press textbook of geriatric psychiatry* (2nd ed.). Washington, DC: American Psychiatric Press.
Edited by leaders in geriatric psychiatry, this book provides a detailed guide to the current research, evaluations, and interventions in the field.

Butler, R.N., Lewis M.I., & Sunderland T. (1998). *Aging and mental health: Positive psychosocial and biomedical approaches* (5th ed.). Boston, MA: Allyn and Bacon.
This book provides a clear overview of evaluation and interventions for mental health issues presenting in aging patients.

Coffey C.E., & Cummings J.L. (2000). *The American Psychiatric Press textbook of geriatric neuropsychiatry* (2nd ed.). Washington, DC: American Psychiatric Press.
This textbook, edited by two prominent experts in neuropsychiatry of the elderly, provides a comprehensive overview of current knowledge in this area.

Hayslip, B., & Panek, P.E. (2002). *Adult development and aging* (3rd ed.). Malabar, FL: Krieger.
This book provides an excellent overview of aging form a developmental rather than pathological perspective.

6 Death, Dying, and Grief

John Edward Ruark

To-morrow, and to-morrow, and to-morrow,
Creeps in this petty pace from day to day,
To the last syllable of recorded time;
And all our yesterdays have lighted fools
The way to dusty death. Out, out, brief candle!
Life's but a walking shadow, a poor player,
That struts and frets his hour upon the stage,
And then is heard no more. It is a tale
Told by an idiot, full of sound and fury,
Signifying nothing.

WILLIAM SHAKESPEARE
Macbeth Act 5, Scene 5

Less than a century ago physicians had little to offer beyond simple supportive care for most life-threatening medical conditions, and the processes that caused human illness, suffering, and death were largely mysterious. Most of the physician's art consisted of comfort and palliation in the face of disease processes that would run their courses regardless of the efforts of those attempting to treat them. In all but the most recent history of medicine, physicians have regarded death less as an opponent to be ceaselessly fought than as a colleague to be welcomed—a humane and kindly collaborator who could place a final limit on human suffering. Nineteenth century medical texts even referred to pneumonia as "the old man's friend" that brought a relatively painless end to lives that had lost their quality.

Times have changed to an amazing degree. At present it is only at the literal end of life that medicine has no life-extending treatment to offer. From relatively simple interventions, such as antibiotics, diuretics, corticosteroids, and pressors, through transplant technologies involving every vital organ system outside the central nervous system, to mechanical devices replacing (at least temporarily) all of the nonnervous vital functions, it is almost always possible to buy some additional amount of life until the actual mo-

ment of total body failure. However, the quality of the life so purchased, and the cost paid in suffering, human effort, and money to achieve it, must be questioned. Our planetary resources are rapidly becoming insufficient to provide even the most basic needs for one third of the earth's inhabitants, and people are more aware of the trade-off between quality and quantity of life. We can no longer thoughtlessly do whatever is technically possible to address every pathophysiological problem for every patient. This chapter addresses some basic facts about death, dying, and grieving to assist physicians in dealing more thoughtfully and appropriately with issues surrounding death.

DEATH AT THE BEGINNING OF THE TWENTY-FIRST CENTURY

Life Expectancy

At the beginning of the twentieth century the life expectancy from birth for the average American was about 49 years. *Advances in public health and medical technology have since increased life expectancy to 78.0 years in 2006, when women lived 80.4 years, and men 75.5.* Such advances spawn the hope that eventually we may vanquish death totally. However, life expectancy from age 75 years increased only 3 years during the last century, and normal deteriorations in important body functions threaten life by the mid-eighties. In the absence of such fundamental breakthroughs as the resetting of a genetically programmed "aging clock," even with optimal medical care we can hope for a life span of only 85 years, with a standard deviation of about 5 years. Advances in preventive medicine and new treatments for conditions currently disabling the elderly are likely to result in a **compression of morbidity** into the last few years of most people's lives in the next century.

> Death has to be waiting at the end of the ride before you truly see the earth, and feel your heart, and love the world.
>
>   JEAN ANOUILH
>
> The right to happiness is fundamental.
> We live so little time and die alone.
>
>   BERTOLT BRECHT

Many patients think that life is virtually over once they are in their sixties. However, in 2006 *the average 65-year-old woman can expect to live another 20.0 years and the average 65-year-old man another 17.3 years.* Although early death causes a large reduction in the life expectancy from birth, adult patients can expect far more life than simple examination of total life expectancies might indicate. The physician's advice to elderly patients should reflect this reality, especially since the "use it or lose it" dictum has been so well demonstrated in medical practice. We should encourage the elderly to maintain active lives as long as possible and to plan for much longer lives than simple life expectancies from birth would indicate.

Location of Death

In 1900, more than 80% of people died in their homes, and a large fraction of those dying in institutions had tuberculosis, a disease for which isolation was the only known public health measure. *The opposite is now the case, with more than 80% of people dying in institutional settings.* Although the **hospice movement** and the extreme costs of institutional care are motivating some persons toward dying at home, most Americans can expect to die in an institution. This is one reason that the attitudes and efforts of health care personnel have such a critical effect on the dying process.

Any human service involving an institution requires a compromise between values dictated by the well-being of the individual served and values dictated by the requirements of the service institution. This inherent conflict of interest is most evident in institutions providing care to the critically and terminally ill. Federal and third-party funding seldom suffices to support optimal care, and many of these institutions, especially those providing chronic care, have significant limitations in number, training, and quality of staff. Thus it is not surprising that a majority of patients would prefer to die at home rather than in an institutional setting. If physicians work to promote their patients' interests above those of the institution, they can have a profound impact on the experience of dying patients and their families.

> In the depth of his heart he knew he was dying, but not only was he not accustomed to the thought, he simply did not and could not grasp it.
>
> The syllogism he had learnt from Kiezewetter's Logic: "Caius is a man, men are mortal, therefore Caius is mortal," had always seemed to him correct as applied to Caius, but certainly not as applied to himself. That Caius—man in the abstract—was mortal, was perfectly correct, but he was not Caius, not an abstract man, but a creature quite, quite separate from all others. He had been little Vanya, with a mamma and a papa, with Mitya and Volodyn, with the toys, a coachman and a nurse, afterwards with Katenka and with all the joys, griefs, and delights of childhood, boyhood, and youth. What did Caius know of the smell of that striped leather ball Vanya had been so fond of? Had Caius kissed his mother's hand like that, and did the silk of her dress rustle so for Caius? Had he rioted like that at school when the pastry was bad? Had Caius been in love like that? Could Caius preside at a session as he did? "Caius really was mortal, and it was right for him to die; but for me, little Vanya, Ivan Ilyich, with all my thoughts and emotions, it's altogether a different matter. It cannot be that I ought to die. That would be too terrible."
>
>   LEO TOLSTOY
>   *The Death of Ivan Ilyich and Other Stories*

Definition of Death

The definition of death is surprisingly unclear. Before the last few centuries, death was defined by the absence of the most obvious evidence of life: breathing. The fundamental nature of the **pulmonary definition** of death is apparent in such phrases as his or her "last gasp" or "the patient has expired." The pulmonary definition of death was more widely used than the **cardiac definition,** because the pulse is slightly harder to observe than respiration; however, with the evolution of the stethoscope, emphasis shifted to auscultation of the heart as the final arbiter of the presence or absence of life. The development of the electrocardiogram led the determination of death even further into the technological era. The ability to artificially maintain cardiopulmonary function has shifted the focus to a **neurological**

TABLE 6.1 Criteria for establishing death

1. Unreceptivity and unresponsiveness, even to intensely painful stimuli
2. No movement or spontaneous respiration for 3 minutes after being removed from a respirator
3. Complete absence of reflexes, both deep tendon and central
4. A flat electroencephalogram for at least 10 minutes of technically adequate recording, without response to noise or painful stimuli
5. All of the above tests repeated in 24 hours with no change
6. No history of hypothermia or use of central nervous system depressants before onset of coma

What is the worst of woes that wait on age?
What stamps the wrinkle deeper on the brow?
To view each loved one blotted from life's page,
And be alone on earth, as I am now.

BYRON
Childe Harold

I take it that no man is educated who has never dallied with the thought of suicide.

WILLIAM JAMES
US psychologist

definition, and the electroencephalogram became the ultimate criterion of death. The concept of "brain death" became particularly critical with the evolution of transplant technologies enabling the replacement of hearts and lungs. Currently a presidential commission has set uniform criteria for the definition of death that are listed in Table 6.1.

Although the neurological definition of death has been useful, it is far from perfect. It is not uncommon for disruptions of circulation or oxygenation of the brain to destroy large areas of the cerebral cortex while preserving function in the midbrain and brain stem. These types of patients do not meet the criteria in Table 6.1, but meaningful life clearly has ended. This situation illustrates the need for an expansion of the concept of brain death into a more realistic **neocortical definition,** because it is well established that most of the functions that give life meaning depend on the integrity of the neocortex. As demonstrated by the recent Terry Schiavo case, this issue remains fraught with controversy, though more for political and religious than medical reasons. Such cases have led medical ethicists to propose "nonreductionist" definitions of death that include biological, moral, and cultural considerations on a case-by-case basis rather than seeking a global "one-size-fits-all" definition.

Causes of Death

An examination of the principal causes of death in 1900 compared with 2006 reveals some interesting trends. In 1900 the three leading causes of death were influenza and pneumonia, tuberculosis, and gastroenteritis (accounting for 31.4% of all deaths), followed by cardiovascular disease (14.2%). In 2006 cardiovascular disease was the leading cause of death, responsible for 26% of all deaths, followed by cancer (23%) and stroke (5.6%). At the turn of the century *infectious* disease was the most likely killer. Currently, even in the era of AIDS, *degenerative* diseases end most lives. *Advances in public health, antisepsis, and antibiotics have resulted in a situation in which infectious diseases kill primarily persons with compromised immune systems, the elderly, or the chronically ill.* The resulting increased life span has brought us to the limits of the circulatory system, and its failures account for half of all current deaths. Modern

death is much more likely to result from chronic wear and tear or abuse of the body than from an acute attack by an external pathogen.

It is disturbing to note that suicide is included in the list of the top 11 causes of death. It is also ironic that the danger of dying by gunshot is far greater in modern America than it was in the Wild West. Particularly troublesome is the fact that suicide is the third leading cause of death among Americans 15 to 24 years old, accounting for 12% of deaths in that group. Health professionals should be especially careful in investigating depression in young patients, and *physicians must openly and diligently pursue suicidal thoughts or plans when evaluating a distraught young person.* Threats or gestures should be taken seriously, and errors should be made on the side of being overly conservative to ensure the safety of such individuals. There is a one or two month window of risk shortly after beginning antidepressant drugs (which in the long term will decrease likelihood of teen suicide) that there may be increased suicidal ideation. This problem should be dealt with by increased vigilance and robust contact with patients until their depression has remitted sufficiently that they are out of danger, rather than avoiding these medications when they are indicated.

DYING

Thoughts and Fears about Death

We think about death in three sharply divided ways: impersonal, interpersonal, and intrapersonal. The **impersonal** death is the death of the stranger, whose death does not touch us personally. We can read the reports of casualties from wars or natural disasters without paralyzing horror because our minds do not allow these deaths to become real. We refuse to consider seriously the possibility that events this horrible could happen to us. The terrorist attacks of September 11, 2001 have challenged this defense for many Americans.

When we lose someone who matters to us, we shift to the **interpersonal** manner of thinking about death. When myriad experiences with another individual are part of the fabric of our lives, the loss of that person constitutes a disruption of some part of ourselves. The degree to which each loss affects us parallels the importance of the deceased person's role in our lives.

That Which I Should Have Done I Did Not Do (The Door) *(1931–1941) Ivan Le Lorraine Albright, American, 1897–1983.* Oil on canvas, 246.4 × 91.4 cm, Mary and Leigh Block Charitable Fund, 1955.645. Photograph by Robert Hashimoto. © The Art Institute of Chicago. Reproduced by permission of the artist's estate. *Physicians can encourage family members to express love and deal with unresolved family issues while there is still time.*

Patients and families who have lost a loved one often feel alienated by the perceived impersonal attitude of professionals. This is unfortunate and ironic, because most people who enter the health care field do so because people *matter* to them. We do ourselves and our patients a service when we can clearly communicate this caring. *Contrary to the advice of some authors, I believe physicians, nurses, and other health care providers should strive to make each death with which they are closely involved an interpersonal rather than an impersonal one.*

The necessary delicate balance involves letting each death be personal enough so that we can be emotionally connected to patients and families but not so personal that our professional judgment is compromised. The ability to strike this balance consistently is one of the characteristics of truly gifted practitioners. Patients and families recognize and respond to our personal involvement, as recognized over a century ago by William Osler, who said "Patients don't care how much you know until they know how much you care." The issues of caregiver burnout and 'compassion fatigue' come up strongly in end-of-life settings. There are practical and effective strategies that emphasize physician self-awareness and self-care to mitigate these common but unfortunate sequelae of working with patients who are dying (see Kearny et al, suggested readings).

The concept of **intrapersonal death** is perhaps the most crucial concept for health professionals to grasp. The available evidence suggests that *death anxiety is significantly higher in those who choose a career in medicine than in others who choose similarly intellectually challenging fields.* Particularly for physicians, the thought of confronting our own mortality may be overwhelming, and the belief that "knowledge is power" may have unconsciously motivated many of us to seek careers in a field that fosters the illusion of power over death. Perhaps this accounts for the frequency with which physicians collude with or even press for inappropriate persistence in efforts to cure obviously terminal conditions. It also may lead to the tendency toward emotional aloofness around critical illness that patients find alienating.

Those of us who care for patients confronting death are ethically bound to face the issue of our own death and to achieve enough internal peace that we are confident that our own anxiety is not affecting patient care.

> The whole of his life had prepared Podduyev for living, not for dying.
>
> ALEXANDER SOLZHENITSYN
> *Cancer Ward*

The Dying Process

Since the publication of Kübler-Ross's book *On Death and Dying*, popular attention has been increasingly focused on issues surrounding death. This work, along with Waugh's *The Loved One* and Mitford's *The American Way of Death*, made death an acceptable topic of conversation and study in the 1960s. Kübler-Ross's work should be required reading for anyone entering a health profession, and it remains worthwhile reading for all educated adults.

One of the key concepts Kübler-Ross introduced was that of **stages of dying**. Although she presented them with appropriate disclaimers as to the unpredictability of their order or importance in any particular case, her stages have become more of a law than she intended. These stages are as follows:

1. Denial
2. Anger
3. Bargaining
4. Depression
5. Acceptance

Kübler-Ross's first stage of dying is denial. **Denial** is a primary primitive defense mechanism and is a predictable reaction to sudden overwhelming news of any sort. Patients or family members may manifest this response in ways ranging from shocked rejection of the physician's "verdict" to complete repression of any memory of the conversation in which they were confronted with the likelihood of death. Most patients seem to experience such responses fairly often during a terminal illness. *It is not useful to challenge the patient each time denial occurs; in fact, the response may be adaptive, and sometimes a few moments or hours of denial affords a vital respite from an overwhelmingly negative reality.* It is only when denial becomes *dysfunctional,* when it leads to poor decisions or family problems, that it requires confrontation. When such problems arise, careful exploration of the inner logic motivating denial will often be valuable to patients by enabling their emotional adaptation to impending death.

Anger, the second of Kübler-Ross's stages, is as ubiquitous as denial among terminal patients. It is an equally natural response to the threat against personal integrity posed by our own critical illness or that of a loved one. Unfortunately, it is also an emotion with which few of us are comfortable (either in ourselves or in others), and health professionals receive little training in managing anger. *The key to handling patients' or family members' anger successfully in terminal care settings is simple: let it be.* If anger is viewed as the individual's natural response to unmet needs for protection or nurturance, we can see that the critically ill have a right to be angry. We should assume that our patients' anger is valid, regardless of the inappropriateness with which it is expressed. Clinicians will be most effective if they remain nondefensive while conducting thoughtful inquiry into how they might more fully meet the needs of patients and families.

Bargaining, the third of Kübler-Ross's stages, consists of an effort to retain at least the illusion of control in a situation in which one is powerless. Manifestations range from vows to survive only until a personal landmark or anniversary, such as a graduation, to making deals with physicians to accept treatments only under certain circumstances. *The physician who can accept bargains that do not substantially compromise patient care can ameliorate the sense of powerlessness that inevitably accompanies life-threatening illnesses.*

The fourth of Kübler-Ross's stages is **depression**, which is as universal among terminal patients as denial and anger. Any psychologically healthy individual is bound to experience depression at times during the course of a terminal illness. However, *the clinician must distinguish between this normal mood variation and a more serious clinical depression that demands medical intervention*. The latter is characterized by neurovegetative symptoms, which are disturbances of the functions necessary to maintain life and requires pharmacological intervention as the standard of care. However, disturbances of sleep, appetite, and libido are difficult to assess in critically ill patients, especially in the hospital. It is somewhat easier to assess **anhedonia** (the inability to experience pleasure from usually pleasurable stimuli) and **psychomotor retardation** (especially increased speech latency). Special care must be taken when using any psychoactive chemical in patients with complicated medical conditions. In my clinical practice with dying patients, I am too often dismayed by the degree to which physicians and medical institutions seem to forget that the limited moments left are precious. Given how destructive untreated clinical depression can be to quality of life, it is particularly important to treat this condition in terminally ill patients.

Kübler-Ross's final stage is **acceptance** of death. She points out that most patients fail to achieve a truly clearheaded acceptance of their death. What appears to be a

---

One cannot help a man to come to accept his impending death if he remains in severe pain, one cannot give spiritual counsel to a woman who is vomiting, or help a wife and children say their goodbyes to a father who is so drugged that he cannot respond.

MARY BAINES
Palliative care physician

But when all usefulness is over, when one is assured of an unavoidable and imminent death, it is the simplest of human rights to choose a quick and easy death in place of a slow and horrible one.

CHARLOTTE PERKINS STETSON GILMAN
US writer on social and economic subjects

state of acceptance is often a combination of exhaustion and advancing organic brain dysfunction. A sense of resignation that death must be preferable to persisting in a painful and futile struggle is common as vital energy wanes and death approaches. This is not to say that certain rare patients cannot uplift everyone around them with the nobility and serenity with which they face their own deaths.

Weisman has addressed the issue of coping with dying by defining his own phases of dying. His phases roughly parallel those of Kübler-Ross and include:

1. **Existential plight** at the confrontation of an individual's own mortality
2. **Mitigation and accommodation** of an individual's illness and its treatments
3. **Decline and deterioration** of an individual's physical and mental abilities as the illness advances
4. **Preterminality and terminality** in which waning physical powers increasingly dictate quality of life

My experience involves many thousands of hours of contact with dying patients over the last 28 years. I have found that most individuals alternate between denial and acceptance of their conditions. The tenor of each person's reaction to the first revelation of a life-threatening condition tends to be repeated with subsequent recurrences or exacerbations of the illness. Furthermore, the historical reactions of a patient to losses or threats earlier in life provide valuable clues as to how that individual will cope with the challenge of a life-threatening illness.

Protecting Patient Rights During Terminal Illness

When patients become terminally ill, particularly if they are not medically sophisticated, issues of **informed consent** and the protection of individual rights become particularly critical. Since many professionals are unaware of the exact rights their patients have, it is important to summarize relevant portions of the **Patient's Bill of Rights**, as promulgated by the American Hospital Association and enacted into law in most states.

The most important patient right is the right to receive *considerate and respectful care*. If this right is thoughtfully maintained, all of the others follow directly from it. The second right is to receive *information about the illness,* its treatment, and its likely outcome, in a language patients can understand. The third right involves *informed consent;* patients are entitled to information about proposed treatments or procedures, their potential risks and benefits, and the risks and benefits of reasonable alternative treatments, including no treatment at all. The fourth right is the right

to *active participation in decisions* regarding medical care, including the right to refuse any or all treatments. The last right is the right to *transfer all of the previously mentioned rights* to a legal surrogate if an individual should become incompetent to make decisions for himself or herself. If these rights are thoughtfully preserved, it is hard to go too far wrong.

Health care professionals can provide invaluable support for patients and families as they deal with terminal illness. The primary way in which we can be helpful is by actively supporting patients or their legal surrogates in exercising authority over their medical care. *Physicians should regard themselves as consultants employed to advise patients of their options regarding medical problems; they can assume authority only after it is explicitly granted.* We are also wise to re-confirm major decisions periodically even when we have been given authority to decide.

Support is also possible through communication. Physicians are responsible not only for attempting to communicate but also for ensuring that the communication necessary to foster optimal decision making takes place. Important discussions should be held in a private, comfortable environment. We should anticipate that the stress of the situation may impair reasoning, and simple language is often adequate and usually more effective. Expression of questions and feelings should be actively encouraged, because many people are intimidated by physicians and hospitals. Given the multicultural complexity of many patient care settings, clinicians must learn to take culture and ethnicity effectively into account in order to achieve adequate communication. Patients or surrogates should be asked periodically to summarize what they have heard so the professional can check the accuracy of communication and correct any misconceptions. Finally, professionals should make specific efforts to sharpen their communication skills. These skills are crucial to medical practice, but they are not always systematically taught.

The final principle in the protection of the rights of patients in medical crises is the important concept of **proportionality**. Proportional treatment is that which, *in the view of the patient,* has a reasonable chance of providing benefits that outweigh its attendant burdens. *Although the issue of costs and benefits is present throughout medical practice, it is especially significant in the context of life-threatening illness.* The intensity of interventions required to treat many serious conditions is great enough that quality of life, if not life itself, can be significantly endangered by treatment. It is vital that patients, not professionals or family members, ultimately answer these difficult questions. Physicians tend to be invested in fighting and curing disease, and family members tend to be invested in anything that offers hope of holding on to their loved ones. These forces militate against the best interests of the patient in many critical care settings. Thus, the explicit early determination and ongoing review of each patient's views about proportionality are

> Euthanasia is a long, smooth-sounding word, and it conceals its danger as long, smooth words do, but the danger is there, nevertheless.
>
> PEARL S. BUCK
> *The Child Who Never Grew*

vital to optimal management of life-threatening conditions. Physicians must be candid in presenting realistic assessments of likely benefits and costs of proposed interventions. Previous decisions must be reassessed with major clinical changes, because each patient's willingness to fight can change with advancing debilitation or realization of the limited likelihood of an absolute cure. In short, physicians should seek to prolong useful living *as defined by the patient.* Medical intervention not guided by this principle may serve only to prolong the dying process, which is generally undignified and painful for all involved.

The recent Terry Schiavo case highlights a few important issues surrounding the end of life. First of all, the absence of any legally recognized documentation expressing her wishes, termed an "advanced directive" set up a potential for the unfortunate events that followed. Second, the lack of a professionally guided process between her loved ones toward achieving consensus about her wishes and who was empowered to represent her made the resulting conflict almost inevitable. Most critical care facilities have trained personnel who can be called in to facilitate a humane negotiation where, hopefully, consensus can be reached.

GRIEF AND MOURNING

Human life consists of a never-ending process of coming into and out of relationship with everything in our world. The possessions we hoard, the youth we covet, the food, water, and air we consume, and even the molecules that compose us are with us only transiently. This is most poignantly true of the people we love. Those who master efficient and effective ways to gracefully let go of that which they are losing are enabled to find renewed vitality in new attachments. Grief and mourning are the natural emotional healing mechanisms that restore our ability to enjoy life after any serious loss.

The loss of a loved one constitutes the greatest challenge to human coping that most of us face short of, perhaps, our own death. The psychological processes that lead to eventual resolution of bereavement are vital to mental and emotional health and the resumption of useful functioning. These processes begin with **grief**, which we define as a *clinical syndrome* characterizing the acute psychological and physiological reaction of human beings to significant losses. It is useful to regard grief as the initial phase of a more

The Wisdom of WILLIAM SHAKESPEARE, 1564–1616

Our remedies oft in ourselves do lie.
Which we ascribe to heaven.
All's Well That Ends Well

Last scene of all.
That ends this strange eventful history.
Is second childishness and mere oblivion.
Sans teeth, sans eye, sans taste, sans everything.
As You Like It

By medicine life may be prolonged, yet death will seize the doctor too.
Cymbeline

To sleep–perchance to dream: ay, there's the rub!
For in that sleep of death what dreams may come.
When we have shuffled off this mortal coil.
Must give us pause.
Hamlet

It is not strange that desire should so many years outlive performance?
Henry IV, Part II

It provokes the desire, but it takes away the performance. Therefore much drink may be said to be an equivocator with lechery.
Macbeth

Macduff was from his mother's womb
Untimely ripp'd.
Macbeth

global phenomenon of **mourning**, defined as a complex *intrapsychic process* in which a person withdraws attachment from a lost object and works through the emotional pain and injury of that loss.

Although grief and mourning are eloquently described in literature dating at least as far back as Homer, systematic attempts at understanding these processes began in 1917 with Sigmund Freud, who posited that grief required an investment of emotional energy (libido) in the lost object. Mental health and intrapsychic stability could not be restored until this attachment was withdrawn, an inherently painful process. Uncomplicated mourning proceeds when the reality of the loss is increasingly accepted and the bereaved person is gradually able to let go of memories and expectations attached to the deceased person. Pathological grief occurs when the bereaved person is unable to fully comprehend or work through the loss.

Bowlby explained grief and mourning in terms of a phenomenon he called **attachment behavior**, that is, any behavior that results in attaining or retaining closeness to a preferred individual. Many of the most intense human emotions arise as a result of the formation, maintenance, and disruption of these bonds ("falling in love," "being in love," and "mourning"). Thus, **separation anxiety** may be the basis of grief and leads to efforts to regain the lost object. Rage and frustration are likely to persist among mourners until emotional nurturance becomes available through new attachments to replace what was lost.

More psychologically mature defense mechanisms, such as **identification**, that provide a link to the lost loved one may bring comfort during the process of reattachment to a new object. We see identification in action when bereaved persons wear clothing or adopt mannerisms belonging to the deceased. More primitive defense mechanisms, such as **introjection** (the wholesale enactment of traits of a lost loved one), may cause problems because new sources of emotional attachment can be unconsciously regarded as threats to the life of the internalized lost person. An extreme cinematic example of introjection would be the character of Norman Bates in Alfred Hitchcock's *Psycho*. Persons who have experienced difficulties with attachments and losses can be anticipated to continue to have problems of this sort with each new mourning process, and they are likely to require professional assistance to cope with the period of mourning.

Grief

Lindemann conducted a systematic examination of acute grief in his study of the survivors of the Cocoanut Grove fire in Boston and his description of the acute grief syndrome remains a classic. Common symptoms of grief Lindemann observed included sensations of somatic distress that came in waves at least hourly, tightness in the throat, choking, shortness of breath, sighing, sensations of abdominal emptiness, muscular weakness, and intense emotional distress best characterized as **psychic pain**. The syndrome also included a sense of unreality, gastrointestinal complaints, preoccupation with the deceased, emotional distance from others, guilt, irritability, and anger. *Lindemann concluded that the five basic pathognomonic symptoms of grief were somatic distress, preoccupation with the deceased, guilt, hostility, and the loss of habitual patterns of conduct.* He observed that within 4 to 6 weeks, given op-

timal emotional support, the acute grief reaction could be settled for most people. However, this adjustment required the resolution of the conflict between the desire to remain attached to the lost person and reality testing that confirmed the loss.

Practicing health professionals need to appreciate that human beings are innately endowed with the resources necessary to negotiate all of the expectable traumas of life, including grief and mourning. Barring psychological developmental injuries, such as the sort of childhood physical or psychological abuse or deprivation that often accompanies personality disorders, most people are able to resolve acute grief if they have adequate emotional support. Such support involves validation of the strong primary emotions (anger, grief, terror) of the acutely bereaved and avoidance of psychochemical suppression of these feelings, even when they are disruptive to routine medical practice.

Health professionals are likely to be the targets of free-floating anger associated with normal grief. If we can nondefensively accept this rage, reflecting only how frustrating it must be for the bereaved to encounter how little power we actually have over death, we can continue to meet the needs of our patients and ourselves. The healthiest message we can send to the majority of patients encountering acute grief and mourning is that we are there to support them in the completion of a normal process that requires them to experience many uncomfortable feelings. Patients should be encouraged to rely on both professional and proven nonprofessional sources of emotional support to get them through this difficult period.

All men live enveloped in whale-lines. All are born with halters round their necks; but it is only when caught in the swift, sudden turn of death, that mortals realize the silent, subtle, ever present perils of life.

HERMAN MELVILLE
Moby Dick

I am not mad: this hair I tear is mine;
My name is Constance; I was Jeffrey's wife;
Young Arthur is my son, and he is lost:
I am not mad: I would to heaven I were!
For then, 'tis like I should forget myself:
O, if I could, what grief should I forget!
Preach some philosophy to make me mad,
And thou shalt be canonized, cardinal;
For being not mad but sensible of grief,
My reasonable part produces reason
How I may be deliver'd of these woes,
And teaches me to kill or hang myself:
If I were mad, I should forget my son,
Or madly think a babe of clouts were he:
I am not mad; too well, too well I feel
The different plague of each calamity.

WILLIAM SHAKESPEARE
King John
Act III, Scene IV

Mourning

John Bowlby divides the mourning process into three phases that occur after the resolution of the acute grief reaction. These phases parallel the reactions of the dying described by Kübler-Ross and Weisman; in many ways the dying person is simply mourning the loss of the whole world. Bowlby's first phase is **protest**, a period characterized by spontaneous reactions of disbelief focused on the deceased. Bereaved persons may cling tenaciously to thoughts of the deceased and may direct strong anger or despair toward the deceased and others. Particular anger may focus on those who encourage the bereaved to let go of the deceased and to resume normal life. This anger may disrupt important relationships at exactly the worst time, resulting in dangerous isolation for mourners.

Bowlby's initial phase of protest is followed by a period of **despair**. This period is usually precipitated by the intuitive realization that the deceased person is indeed lost. Free-floating anxiety and depression tend to overwhelm any compulsive activity that may have allowed the bereaved person to tolerate the previous reactions. Indeed, it may be that this disintegration, marking the abandonment of patterns centering on the deceased, is a necessary prelude to the development of new and more viable structures leading to eventual resolution of the loss.

The final phase of mourning that Bowlby characterizes is **detachment**. In this phase the personality of the bereaved is reorganized in such a way that the emotions that previously focused on the deceased are reoriented toward other people or activities. This process eventually leads to the resolution of serious interpersonal losses, and the bereaved individual is able to resume a more satisfying life.

Parkes studied the process of normal bereavement and reached a number of important conclusions. He observed that the usual period of protest lasts a few months and usually resolves, in the absence of grief pathology, within the course of the first year. He also observed that inhibited feel-

---

How do I help someone grieve?

Grieving is active. It is *work*. It requires remembering repetitively experiences shared with the dead person, over a long period of time; *talking about* and *expressing* the mixed emotional ties-particularly the anger, remorse, and sadness, perhaps, even relief-until the devastating potency of the loss is neutralized.

The most important balm a counselor can offer is presence and concern. *You are facilitating the grieving process by being there:* by listening, nonjudgmentally, and by reassuring the bereaved persons that they are not "going crazy." You can affirm that the acute pain they are experiencing is grief in process, and that it will not last forever.

1. Encourage the saying of goodbyes at the bedside, before death, whenever possible.
2. Encourage active participation in the care of the person dying, in being present at the moment of death, and even in preparing the body for burial. There is great solace in knowing "I was there and I did all that I could."
3. Encourage involvement with the mourning rituals of funeral, eulogy, celebration, and memorial services. Such rites provide outlets for the expression of sorrow and help delineate the grieving process. Viewing the dead body helps one accept the fact of death. Unveilings and anniversary rites also mark the progress of grief.
4. Listen, nonjudgmentally, realizing, as Samuel Coleridge's Ancient Mariner reminds us, that the albatross of grief falls off with retelling the story. Encourage reminiscences, the painful as well as the positive, and expression of the hostile, angry, and negative feelings that seem so incompatible with the genuine love for the dying or dead person. Again, offer reassurance that such ambivalence is normal.
5. Monitor your own feelings. You are not immune to sadness, anxiety, or the need to express personal concern. Your reactions are conditioned by your own experiences with earlier losses and by your ability to handle hostile reactions from those you are counseling: friend, patient, client, student, or family member.
6. Be informed about self-help support groups such as "Candlelighters," "Living with Cancer," "Sibs with Cancer," "People with AIDS," "Widow-to-Widow" and bereavement programs sponsored by churches, hospitals, hospices, and civic organizations in your community. Such groups assist in answering practical questions, in understanding feelings, in providing networks, and in enabling participants to reach out to others as they gain mastery in their own personal experiences.
7. Know when referral is necessary. You are in a good position to detect unresolved and complicated grief and pathological mourning and, when you suspect a severe problem, you should enlist additional psychotherapeutic help.

Grief is not a disease. It is love not wanting to let go. It can be likened to a "blow" or a cut in which the wound gradually heals. For a while, one is acutely vulnerable, physically and emotionally. Though grief can be temporarily disabling, working through it ultimately brings strength. Colin Murray Parkes sums it up nicely in his book, *Bereavement*, reminding us just as broken bones may knit together more strongly, so the experience of grieving can strengthen or mature those who have previously been shielded from misfortune: "The pain of grief is just as much a part of life as the joy of love; it is, perhaps, the price we pay for love, the cost of commitment. To ignore this fact ... is to put on emotional blinders which leave us unprepared for the losses that will inevitably occur in our own lives and unprepared to help others to cope with the losses in theirs."

Copyright © 1991. From *Facing death: Images, insights, and interventions. A handbook for educators, healthcare professionals, and counselors,* by Bertman, S. Reproduced by permission of Routledge/Taylor & Francis Group, LLC.

ings associated with grief and mourning tend to be more intense and difficult to manage when they finally surface. Loneliness, sadness, anger, despair, and reactive depression constitute natural and appropriate responses to any serious loss. Those who do not experience these emotions may be ignoring a vital biological imperative and may be exposed to far-reaching and potentially devastating consequences.

Physician consultations, physical illnesses, hospitalizations, and physiological abnormalities all increase significantly during bereavement. Furthermore, increased mortality has been demonstrated in many instances, sometimes exceeding the mortality rates of age- and health-matched non-bereaved cohorts by a factor of five or more. Parkes summed up these findings in his poignant description of the **broken heart phenomenon**, observing that *heart disease caused three fourths of bereavement-associated early mortality.*

In conclusion, it is clear from the literature that widowers and widows are more likely than their cohorts to seek medical help and that they are at greater risk for physical illness and death during the year after their loss. Not surprisingly, many studies reveal that the bereaved are also at greater risk for psychiatric illness.

Grief Pathology

Pathological variants of normal grief are quite common in medical practice. These variations include absence of grief, delayed grief, dysfunctional denial, the "manic escape," dysfunctional hostility, and clinical depression.

*The **absence of grief** phenomenon is particularly prevalent in death-denying cultures such as our own.* The grieving and mourning processes are inherently painful, and many people are reluctant to engage fully in them. This resistance is overcome in many cultures by institutionalized rituals surrounding death, and modern American culture is strikingly deficient in such supportive structures. Bereaved individuals should be supported in resisting social pressures that compel them to go on with life as if nothing had happened; however, many people in our culture continue to believe a person is "handling it well" if he or she is not making others uncomfortable by overt manifestations of distress.

Professionals should be alert to the absence of the signs of acute grief described previously, and gentle inquiries should be made within a few weeks if it appears that a bereaved person is not grieving. Many times the inquiry itself triggers a flood of emotion, but if not, counseling may be necessary. The main therapy for the absence of grief is the provision of a safe, supportive context in which bereaved persons are encouraged to express their sadness, despair, fear, and rage. Expert psychotherapy is required in the presence of more severe psychopathology, because supportive counseling alone is unlikely to be adequate.

> So death, the most terrifying of ills, is nothing to us, since so long as we exist, death is not with us; but when death comes, then we do not exist. It does not then concern either the living or the dead, since for the former it is not, and the latter are no more.
>
> EPICURUS
> Greek philosopher

The second most common form of grief pathology is **dysfunctional denial**. Although some denial is probably necessary for dealing with any catastrophic stress, dysfunctional denial interferes significantly with normal human functioning. Both intrapersonal and environmental forces may conspire to encourage bereaved persons to deny the seriousness, or even the existence, of a major loss. Manifestations of dysfunctional denial range from reluctance to participate in rituals surrounding a death, to refusal to devote time or energy to the grieving process, to frank delusions that the death has not occurred. Gentle exploration of the patient's thoughts and feelings about the deceased is the most effective therapeutic approach. As this painstaking exploration proceeds, most patients without severe psychopathology are able to restore reality testing and move on with their grief.

A third type of grief pathology is termed the **manic escape**, characterized by the classic "merry widow," and marked by frenetic activity, often accompanied by an inappropriately cheerful demeanor. It may represent an attempt to regain at least the illusion of power over an overwhelming situation. The brittle quality of this defense is unmistakable and leaves the observer feeling that the bereaved would crumble if the defense was challenged. Therapy involves gentle exploration of the loss and reflection of the feeling of powerlessness underlying the defense. Frequently exploration of the loss of control opens up more complex esteem and control issues relating to the deceased and the bereaved person's family of origin.

The next common grief pathology is **dysfunctional hostility**. Here again the term "dysfunctional" reflects the observation that significant hostility is normal in grief and mourning, and is pathological only when it interferes with essential functioning. In fact, *acknowledging and working through anger are two of the most important tasks in grief work.* However, when anger is poorly managed, it can drive away potential sources of support at exactly the wrong time. The anger in the grieving process is frustrating because its target is the deceased person, and yet most people have difficulty allowing their anger to consciously center on the deceased, so their rage is apt to be displaced toward less threatening targets. Given the negative associations most bereaved persons have with the failure of medical care to save their loved one, it is not surprising that physicians and nurses are particularly likely to come under fire in these situations. The key for therapy is validation of the rage, even when its manifestations are inappropriate and harmful. However, firm limits must be compassionately set against abusive expressions of rage, since they endanger patient care by alienating caregivers and increasing risk of professional burnout. Patients typically feel guilty about their irrational outbursts and seldom need chiding. The physician can give overt permission for anger directed at the caregivers or the deceased, and safe physical outlets can be encouraged for aggressive feelings.

> Doctor, doctor, shall I die?
> Yes, my child, and so shall I.
>
> Skipping rhyme, circa 1894

Clinical depression is the final manifestation of grief pathology to be discussed. *The importance of a therapeutic alliance in treating clinical depression cannot be overemphasized.* All the medications for depression are fraught with side effects that often manifest most strongly before therapeutic benefits appear, and some can be lethal in the hands of a suicidal patient. Frequently, the conviction that their physician is a competent, collaborative ally is sufficient to carry patients through the few weeks when the side effects of medication may offset the therapeutic benefits experienced from antidepressants.

Many of the grief pathologies described can be prevented if professionals encourage patients and families to support expression of the strong, often negative emotions of grief. Ongoing caring and contact initiated by the professional can often minimize pathological grief. However, it is usually the patient's support network that offers the greatest solace and comfort, and professionals should actively support this important safety net.

SUMMARY

In this chapter we have examined the inescapable medical reality of death from a variety of perspectives relevant to physicians in training. We began with a survey of the facts of death—when, where, and how it takes place for our patients (and for us!). Then we turned to the dying process, including how people think about it and fear it. Next we focused on the rights of patients during life-threatening illness and how physicians can and should act to safeguard these rights. Finally, we reviewed normal and pathological variants of the grief and mourning processes whereby people are enabled to recover from significant losses. If this material is incorporated and applied to interactions with patients facing death, the result will be a more humane and optimal experience for all concerned.

CASE STUDY

Mr. B was a 41-year-old married computer consultant with one preschool child who was referred for psychiatric evaluation by his hematologist during hospitalization for treatment of an acute myelogenous leukemia of ominous prognosis. The purpose of the referral was to assess for possible depression and to provide psychological support during a very arduous course of therapy. When I was called, Mr. B had been in the hospital for more than 4 weeks longer than expected because of complications that occurred when blood clots caused a series of intracardiac catheter failures. During the week before my consultation, the nurses and Mrs. B had observed Mr. B to become lethargic, less cooperative with vital self-care procedures, and alternatively withdrawn and uncharacteristically irritable.

After standard infection control procedures (scrubbing, gowning, gloving, and masking), I entered Mr. B's darkened room and introduced myself. I found a thin, tall, completely hairless man resting flat on his back in bed, who greeted me with reserve and apparent wariness. I asked him if he knew why I was there, and he said, "I guess they all think I'm crazy." I asked him what *he* thought, and he said, "I think I'm sick to death of this prison and everyone and everything connected with it." When I responded that based on what I had read in his chart I thought he would be more likely to be crazy if he *didn't* feel that way, he perceptibly relaxed and became more engaged in our conversation.

Can you determine which Kübler-Ross stage best describes this patient? How should a physician respond? What would happen if you confronted this patient and told him his anger was inappropriate?

In the next hour, Mr. B recounted with increasing energy his frustrations around this illness that had derailed what he termed his "perfect yuppie life." He focused a disproportionate wrath on minor technical errors by nurses, house officers, and surgical consultants, to which he inaccurately attributed the complications that had prolonged his hospitalization. I observed that it must be highly disturbing to have his life entrusted to people who demonstrated that they could make mistakes; he must feel even more out of control of a situation that makes most people feel extremely powerless. Once again an accurate **empathic reflection**, coupled with my failure to "rise to the bait" by defending the staff, caused a palpable increase in his energy and sense of engagement in our conversation. The foundation for a therapeutic alliance between us had been formed by my demonstration that I could find a sensible way to "be on his side" even when he was being critical of my friends and colleagues.

Mr. B and I explored the specific areas of his medical

evaluation and treatment over which he felt the least control. Most of these centered on confusing or inadequate information which did not enable him to understand what was going on and why. Because I was familiar with his unit and the treatments and procedures it employed and had read his chart carefully, I was able to explain most of his concerns to his satisfaction and to refer him to specific persons for answers to the questions that exceeded my expertise.

This patient is potentially depressed. What symptoms will you want to assess before making a diagnosis?

We then moved on to examine issues more specific to the evaluation of depression: his personal and family psychiatric and medical histories and the details of his symptomatic response to his leukemia and its treatments. It became clear that although his sleep and appetite had been typically compromised during his hospitalization, Mr. B's enjoyment of his toddler son had persisted. He visibly brightened as he showed me pictures of his son and described their daily telephone conversations (which were the limit of their contacts because of infection control procedures). Likewise, he admitted that his interest in sex had persisted, and on direct inquiry, he admitted concerns that nurses might accidentally interrupt him while he was masturbating or when he and his wife were "cuddling." Finally, the increase in his animation and the enthusiasm with which he spoke during our conversation was inconsistent with a clinical depression. Thus, I was comfortable reassuring Mr. B's physicians that he would probably not benefit from a trial of antidepressants at that time.

Is sexual intimacy appropriate in a hospital? Would it be therapeutic in this case? Would you feel differently if the visitor was the patient's girlfriend rather than his wife?

Toward the end of our initial consultation, Mr. B responded with enthusiasm to my suggestion that I visit him every few days to help him deal with his situation on an ongoing basis. In these visits, in addition to providing a safe environment in which he could ventilate his frustrations and fears, we focused on areas of his treatment that he *could* control. These included my visits, which we decided would be left up to him to request (and which I always took pains to conduct at prearranged appointment times to support the belief that his time was as valuable as mine). Because his mental status could fluctuate at times due to infections, medications, or metabolic abnormalities, we always wrote down any specific plans or questions he wanted to pursue so that he would be more likely to remember them.

I continued to meet with Mr. B and his wife periodically throughout the remainder of his initial hospitalization and his subsequent bone marrow transplant. We also met in my office during times when he was out of the hospital, and on one occasion I mediated a conflict between Mr. B's mother and Mrs. B regarding the manner in which they were sharing the responsibility of supporting him in the hospital. As this patient's condition worsened, our therapeutic alliance enabled me to be helpful through each of the harrowing complications and medical decisions he and his wife had to face before his death.

SUGGESTED READINGS

Bertman, S.L. (1991). *Facing death: Images, insights, and interventions.* New York, NY: Hemisphere.
This is a remarkable little book full of images, poems, and literary vignettes used by the author in her teaching and counseling as Director of the Program in Medical Humanities at the University of Massachusetts Medical Center.

Chochinov, H.M. (2006). Dying, dignity, and new horizons in palliative end-of-life care. *CA: A Cancer Journal for Clinicians, 56,* 84–103.
An excellent and thorough practical guide to managing the psychiatric and medical challenges of end-of-life care.

Fries, J., & Crapo. L. (1981). *Vitality and aging.* San Francisco, CA: Freeman.
Two distinguished geriatricians take a scholarly and practical look at the realities of life during advancing age.

Gonda, T. (1989). Death, dying, and bereavement. In H.I. Kaplan & B.J. Sadock (Eds.), *Comprehensive textbook of psychiatry,* (pp. 1339–1351). Baltimore, MD: Williams & Wilkins.
One of the giants of modern thanatology in his last publication before his own death provides a coherent and accessible summary of the field.

Gonda, T., & Ruark J. (1984). *Dying dignified: The health professional's guide to care.* Reading, MA: Addison-Wesley.
This is a readable award-winning summary that applies theoretical concepts to the clinical realities of terminal care.

Green, J.W. (2008). *Beyond the good death: the anthropology of modern dying.* Philadelphia: University of Pennsylvania Press.
An excellent wide-ranging anthropologic look at the current state of death in America.

Kearney, M.K., Weininger, R.B., Vachon, M.L.S., Harrison, R.L., & Mount, B.M. (2009). Self-care of physicians caring for patients at the end of life. *Journal of the American Medical Association, 30,* 1155–1165.
A poignant, practical guide to understanding and counteracting the risks caregivers encounter in caring for the dying.

Kubler-Ross, E. (1969). *On death and dying.* New York, NY: Macmillan.
This is a ground-breaking classic that first introduced America to the realities of death. The observations of this master clinician remain fresh, moving, and insightful.

Nuland, S. (1994). *How we die: Reflections on life's final chapter.* New York, NY: Knopf.
A remarkable analysis of death written by a physician.

Psychiatric Annals. (1990). *20.*
This entire issue contains valuable updates by such leaders in thanatology as Parkes, Zisook, Schucter, and Rynearson. A concise review of the field by its key contributors.

Puchalski, C. M. (2006). *A time for listening and caring: spirituality and the care of the chronically ill and dying.* New York: Oxford University Press.

A comprehensive survey of spiritual issues surrounding end-of-life, written by a physician and chaplain who is a leader in the field.

Ruark, J., & Raffin, T. (1988). Initiating and withdrawing life support: Principles and practices in adult medicine. *New England Journal of Medicine, 318,* 25–30.

This position paper of the Stanford University Medical Ethics Committee garnered national attention as the first widely publicized guideline to ethical issues involved in life support. It remains a useful summary for practicing clinicians.

Spiegel, D. (1993). *Living beyond limits.* New York, NY: Random House.

Based on voluminous research and clinical experience, this thorough and readable guide directed toward patients is also valuable for clinicians caring for those facing life-threatening illness.

7 Chronic Pain

Beverly J. Field, Robert A. Swarm, & Kenneth E. Freedland

> Pain is perfect misery, the worst
> Of evils, and excessive, overturns
> All patience.
>
> JOHN MILTON
> *Paradise Lost*

We have all experienced pain—the splitting headache, an aching tooth, a throbbing toe stubbed on a nightstand. It dominates our attention, makes it difficult to think and concentrate, and leaves us short-tempered and impatient with colleagues and family. Pain can interfere with our motivation to exercise, work, or even get out of bed. We anxiously await the time when the pain will finally stop. And when the pain is gone, without a backward glance, we continue on with our lives as usual. But what happens if the pain does not stop? What if we would come to know that it will be there every morning upon awakening, day after day, without any hope of relief?

WHAT IS PAIN?

Pain is a basic biological warning mechanism that signals physiological harm, increases awareness, and often calls for an action or response such as withdrawing a hand from a flame. Acute pain is of brief duration, generally has a known etiology, and in most cases is associated with tissue damage. When healing is complete, acute pain resolves, and the impact it has on an individual's life is usually minimal. Fear and anxiety are often the initial emotional responses to acute pain and serve to motivate careseeking and limitation of movement. Examples of acute pain include bone fractures, sprains, puncture wounds, childbirth, various acute disease states, and postsurgical pain. Chronic noncancer pain is defined as pain lasting 6 months or longer, or pain that persists

beyond the expected time of healing. Chronic pain is persistent, resistant to treatment, and in many cases lasts for the rest of one's lifetime. Because the underlying pathophysiological process is either unknown or not amenable to a cure, the goal of treatment is not to "fix" the pain, but rather to reduce pain severity and improve function. Chronic pain is associated with changes in the central nervous system (CNS) and often has a significant impact on physical and emotional well-being. Examples of chronic noncancer pain include chronic low back pain, postherpetic neuralgia after shingles, osteoarthritic pain, and fibromyalgia.

While acute pain generally signals tissue damage and physiological harm, chronic pain often does not. Bedrest, cessation of usual activities, careseeking, and the use of analgesics are appropriate adaptive responses to acute pain. In contrast, similar avoidance of exercise and daily activities over long periods often leads to deconditioning and exacerbation of chronic pain. Behaviors that are adaptive for acute pain become maladaptive when the pain becomes chronic. Acute pain behaviors such as avoidance of activities and careseeking are maintained by nociceptive factors. As pain transitions from acute to chronic, psychological, social, and environmental factors come to play a more prominent role in the maintenance of pain behaviors. Feelings of apathy, despair, and hopelessness emerge as prospects of a cure diminish. Increased familial attention to the patient's limitations can positively reinforce illness behaviors and avoidance of responsibilities. Eventually, the sick role comes to dominate the life—and often the self-image—of the person struggling with chronic pain.

The International Association for the Study of Pain Subcommittee on Taxonomy defined pain as follows:

> An unpleasant sensory and emotional experience associated with actual or potential tissue damage, or described in terms of such damage.

This definition recognizes several of the complexities of chronic pain, the first of which is its subjective nature. Be-

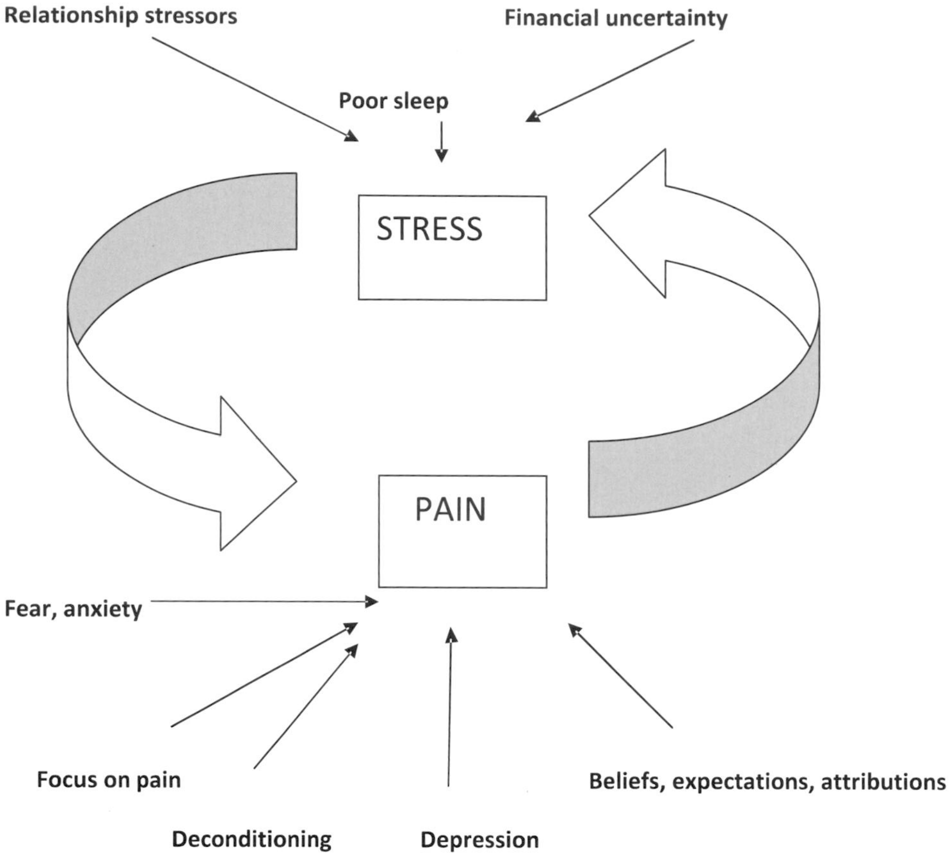

Relationship stressors   **Financial uncertainty**

FIGURE 7.1 The chronic pain-stress cycle

Poor sleep

STRESS

Fear, anxiety

PAIN

Focus on pain

Beliefs, expectations, attributions

Deconditioning   **Depression**

cause there are no reliable tests or biomarkers of chronic pain, it is necessary to rely on the patients' subjective narrative in order to understand their personal experience of pain. Second is the acknowledgment that pain has both sensory and emotional dimensions. Third is the recognition that disabling pain often occurs in the absence of objective physiological findings. The traditional distinction between "real" (somatogenic) and "it's all in your head" (psychogenic) pain is obsolete: A person's report of pain should be accepted as "real," regardless of the objective findings.

NEUROPHYSIOLOGY OF PAIN SIGNAL TRANSMISSION

Nociception is the process of detection and transmission of pain signals from the site of injury to the CNS. In the process of transduction, a noxious stimulus (thermal, mechanical, or chemical) is converted into nerve impulses by receptors called nociceptors. These nerve impulses, or pain signals, are then transmitted from the site of injury to the spinal cord and brain, leading to the perception of pain in the brain. Pain-signal transmission is continuous-

> It is by poultices, not by words, that pain is ended, although pain is, by words, both eased and diminished.
>
> PETRARCH, 1359

ly modulated by factors that either facilitate or inhibit transmission throughout the nervous system. The processes of pain-signal transduction, transmission, and perception are dynamic and may vary greatly within an individual over time as well as between individuals. Factors that may facilitate pain-signal transduction and transmission include nociceptor activity itself, tissue injury and inflammation, damage to nerves as in neuropathic pain, and chronic opioid use (opioid tolerance hyperalgesia). Hyperalgesia, an increased response to normally noxious (painful) stimuli, and allodynia, the perception as painful of normally nonnoxious stimuli, are common clinical findings that suggest the activation of mechanisms of pain-signal facilitation. In many cases in which pain might be described as out of proportion to that which is expected, the explanation lies not in undiagnosed psychopathology, but in mechanisms of neural facilitation of pain-signal transduction and transmission.

Nociceptive pain results from tissue damage, the source

of which may be mechanical, thermal, or chemical. It occurs when pain-specific neurons (nociceptors) are activated in response to noxious stimulation. Nociceptors are specifically sensitive to pain-enhancing substances associated with inflammation. Depending on its etiology, nociceptive pain may be described as dull and aching, sharp and burning, or cramping and pulling. Examples of nociceptive pain include burns, cuts and bruises, bone fractures, appendicitis, and pancreatitis.

Neuropathic pain results from damage to a peripheral nerve or to from a dysfunction in the CNS, and it often occurs in the absence of tissue damage. It can result from direct damage to nerves (cutting, stretching, or crushing injuries), from inflammation, from pressure, such as may result from tumor infiltration, or from compression or entrapment by damaged spinal disks, joint disorders, or scar tissue. Neuropathic pain is usually described as sharp, shooting, burning, or lancinating, and it is often associated with abnormal sensations such as "electrical shocks" or "pins and needles." The presence of chronic hyperalgesia and/or allodynia in the absence of tissue injury or inflammation should raise the suspicion that nerve injury or disease (i.e., neuropathy) is the cause of the pain.

> It is not true that suffering ennobles the character; happiness does that sometimes, but suffering, for the most part, makes men petty and vindictive.
>
> W. SOMERSET MAUGHAM
> *The Moon and Sixpence*

PREVALENCE OF CHRONIC PAIN

It is difficult to obtain accurate epidemiological data on the prevalence of chronic pain. The multiple dimensions of chronic pain conditions lead to highly diverse presentations of its biological, psychological, and social components. Without objective tests for pain, it is often difficult to obtain a consensus about whether or not a specific condition is present. For example, classification of low back pain could be based on objective findings, such as disk herniation on MRI, or on functional status and disability. The use of one or the other—or both—classifications would influence prevalence rates. Despite these limitations, prevalence estimates of chronic pain in the general population of Western countries range from 10% to 55%, with slightly higher rates among females. Approximately 70 million Americans report chronic pain, 10% thereof experiencing pain for more than 100 days per year.

MODELS OF PAIN
Gate Control Model

In 1965, Ronald Wall and Patrick Melzack questioned the model of pain transmission that had prevailed for the previous two centuries, by which pain had a direct one-to-one relationship with the degree of injury. They proposed that pain intensity is determined by both physiological *and* psychological variables. Their gate-control model suggested that the transmission of pain-related nerve impulses is modulated by a gating mechanism in the dorsal horn of the spinal cord. They proposed that both central and peripheral factors could open and close this gate, i.e., facilitate or inhibit the transmission of pain-related nerve impulses. Large diameter nerve fibers inhibit transmission and small diameter fibers facilitate transmission. Central factors such as attention, mood, attributions, and expectations were proposed as modulators of pain perception. For example, attention directed toward pain was thought to open the gate, whereas attention directed away from pain was believed to close it.

> The greatest challenge of pain continues to be the patient who has received every known treatment yet continues to suffer.
>
> RONALD MELZACK and PATRICK D. WALL

Biopsychosocial Model

The psychiatrist George L. Engel proposed the biopsychosocial model in the 1970s and further developed it in the 1990s. It emphasizes dynamic interactions between biological, psychological, and social variables in chronic pain which are continuous and reciprocal. Biological components include ascending and descending neural pathways and biochemical processes; psychological components include attention, thoughts, emotions, expectations, beliefs, and attributions. The social aspects range from sociocultural expectations to interpersonal interactions that shape learned responses to pain.

Operant Conditioning Model

In 1976, Wilbur Fordyce proposed a behavioral model of chronic pain based on theories of operant conditioning. Fordyce was a pioneer in the behavioral treatment of chronic pain and was instrumental in establishing one of the first pain-management centers in the country. In the operant conditioning model, acute pain behaviors, although initiated by a traumatic injury or disease, are reinforced by interpersonal and environmental factors. Over time, with continued reinforcement, patients develop pain (or illness) behaviors. Fordyce proposed a behavioral treatment paradigm based on extinguishing specific pain behaviors (e.g., excessive rest or requests for medication) and positively reinforcing adaptive behaviors (e.g., resumption of normal daily activities.)

Cognitive-Behavioral Model

The cognitive-behavioral model extended the operant model. It integrated principles of operant behavior modification (e.g., changing contingencies of reinforcement, building skills, and including families), with cognitive theory and therapy. A basic premise of cognitive theory is that perceptions of the world are filtered through personal history, beliefs, expectations, and attributions. Cognitions influence our perception, emotions, and behavioral responses, including those involved in the experience of pain. Cognitive therapy challenges distorted or dysfunctional cognitions and restructures them to improve patients' self-image and to create a more adaptive view of their problems and circumstances. Negative cognitions that contribute to feelings of depression, helplessness, and lack of control are identified, challenged, and restructured; misperceptions, maladaptive beliefs, unrealistic expectations, fears, and negative assumptions are addressed. Treatment includes developing techniques for redirecting attention away from pain, helping patients learn coping skills for managing pain, integrating coping skills into everyday life, and formulating plans for relapses.

COMORBIDITIES OF CHRONIC PAIN

Individuals with chronic pain often present with a number of additional physical and emotional problems. These conditions may or may not be secondary to the pain. Regardless, they can influence pain perception and adaptive coping. Depression, alcohol abuse, and substance abuse are common comorbidities found in the chronic pain population and should be treated when present.

Depression

Depression is a common comorbidity in patients with chronic pain—as with patients who have other chronic medical conditions. Patients with chronic pain suffer not only from pain, but also from physical limitations and multiple losses. They may be unable to maintain employment,

which can lead to adverse changes in the economic status of the family, loss of structured daily activities, and diminished self-image and self-worth. Physical limitations often result in the inability to participate in sports and recreational activities—or even less physically demanding activities such as gardening, walking the dog, shopping, or self-care. For a variety of reasons, including feeling "outside of things" and misunderstood by others, people with chronic pain may become socially isolated and withdraw from family and friends. Banks and Kerns (1996) present a diathesis-stress model of the association between pain and depression and suggest that individuals bring to the experience of chronic pain certain vulnerabilities, or diatheses. When multiple stressors of chronic pain are experienced, these diatheses are activated. A negative or helpless view of life, feelings of lack of control, or inadequate coping resources may produce a dysphoric mood or even trigger a full-blown major depressive episode.

Several factors make it difficult to determine the prevalence of comorbid depression in persons with chronic pain. Estimates vary depending on the definition of depression and on whether depressive disorders such as dysthymia or adjustment disorder with depressed mood are included or excluded. Prevalence estimates are also affected by the stringency of the criteria with which depression is diagnosed. Assessment methods may range from self-report questionnaires to structured interviews with strict diagnostic criteria. The second difficulty is that of overlapping symptoms between chronic pain and depression, which also exists with other medical populations. The DSM-IV-TR criteria for major depression include symptoms such as insomnia, fatigue, changes in appetite and/or weight, and changes in memory and concentration—all of which may be partially or entirely attributable to the pain itself or to the medications used to treat the pain. Modifications of the DSM-IV diagnostic criteria which would omit or substitute alternative symptoms have been recommended by some authorities. However, most attempts to modify the criteria have either not truly improved diagnostic accuracy or have resulted in a high rate of false negatives. Presently, the DSM-IV criteria remain the best choice for diagnosing depression in the chronic pain population.

The DSM-IV symptoms of major depression include sadness, loss of interest in usual activities (anhedonia), diminished ability to think or concentrate, excessive guilt, fatigue or loss of energy, poor sleep, appetite and weight disturbances, psychomotor agitation or retardation, and suicidal thoughts or behaviors. The symptoms must cause significant distress or impairment, and must not be attributable solely to the direct, physiological effects of a medication or a general medical condition. A meta-analysis by Banks and Kerns (1996) estimated the prevalence of depression in pain patients to be 30–54% based on selected studies using stringent criteria for major depression.

Evaluating and treating depression in patients with

chronic pain is important not only from a quality of life standpoint, but also because the rates of suicidal ideation and completed suicides are higher in persons with chronic pain than in the general population. Completed suicides occur at a rate of 2–3 times that of the general population. However, the actual rates may be underestimated as there is rarely any follow-up after patients have been discharged from pain clinics. Antidepressants, including tricyclics, SSRI's and SNRI's, and psychological therapies such as cognitive, cognitive-behavioral, interpersonal, and insight-oriented therapy can all be used effectively for the treatment of depression.

Substance Abuse

Individuals with a history of substance abuse often become patients in pain-management centers. They are at risk for developing chronic pain because of injuries and accidents associated with substance abuse, e.g., driving while intoxicated, and other high-risk behaviors. Active substance abuse can undermine attempts to treat pain. Furthermore, substance abuse is potentially life-threatening if alcohol and/or illicit drugs are taken in combination with pain medications. If substance abuse is present, the patient should be referred to a rehabilitation program and subsequently to a recovery program such as Alcoholics Anonymous (AA) or Narcotics Anonymous (NA). It is possible to manage chronic pain for a patient with a history of substance abuse if expectations regarding proper use of medications are clearly established, analgesic use is closely monitored, and random drug screens are taken in the context of a trusting doctor-patient relationship.

Addiction to opioids among patients prescribed opioid analgesics for pain is uncommon. The exact prevalence of addiction to opioids among chronic pain patients is not known, although a 1992 study by Fishbain, Rosomoff and Rosomoff suggested a prevalence range from 3% to 19%. Even defining what behaviors constitute addiction to opioids among patients prescribed opioids for pain is controversial. "Drug-seeking" behaviors such as taking pain medications faster than prescribed, requesting an increase in dosage, or obtaining pain medication from more than one doctor may reflect nothing more than poorly controlled pain. This drug-seeking behavior is known as "pseudoaddiction" and commonly resolves when pain is adequately managed.

Although patients being considered for pain treatment with opioid analgesics should be assessed for the risk of abuse or addiction to opioids, no strong predictors of misuse and addiction have been identified. One investigator found that patient and family histories of substance abuse and histories of legal problems predicted behaviors such as claims of lost or stolen pain medications and urine toxicology screens positive for illicit substances. Because abuse of, and addiction to, opioids is potentially life threatening, a careful assessment should be made of a patient's substance use history. Although there are no established predictors of who might abuse pain medications, the presence of multiple risk factors suggests the need for careful monitoring.

EVALUATION OF ALCOHOL AND DRUG USE HISTORY

- Past and current alcohol and illicit drug use history
- Age at which substance abuse began
- History of legal problems (incarceration, DWIs and DUIs) related to substance use
- History of attendance at rehabilitation programs
- Attendance at recovery programs such as AA or NA
- Family history of substance use
- History of opioid analgesic use
- How often patient has taken more pain medication than prescribed
- Number of times patient called for early refills
- Whether patient ever obtained pain medications from sources other than the prescribing physician such as from the Internet, friends, family or from the street
- Were pain medications ever lost or stolen? More than once?

TOLERANCE AND DEPENDENCE VERSUS ADDICTION

Patients, their families, and their physicians may have different concerns about the patient's use of opioid analgesics for chronic pain. Physicians may fear losing their license to practice for prescribing opioids for chronic pain, lawsuits for alleged over- or underprescription of opioids, and patient diversion of prescribed pain medication. Concerns about side effects and worsening pain from long-term use of opioids (opioid tolerance hyperalgesia) also influence whether, and to what extent, physicians prescribe opioid analgesics. Patients and their families often fear addiction to opioids prescribed for chronic pain.

Many patients who have been prescribed opioid analgesics for pain had been diagnosed with opioid addiction based on the DSM-IV-TR criteria for Substance Dependence. In order to fulfill the criteria for this diagnosis, patients must have three of seven criteria present. One of the criteria is tolerance, another is dependence, both of which occur with long-term administration of opioids. Tolerance refers to the need for ever higher doses of opioid to achieve the same level of pain relief, something that occurs with most patients over time. Withdrawal symptoms occur in patients who are physically dependent on opioids, if opioids are suddenly decreased or discontinued. Because tolerance and physical dependence are not uncommon with chronic use of opioids, patients prescribed opioids for pain readily meet two of three criteria for the diagnosis of Substance Dependence. The third criterion often met entails unsuccessful efforts to cut down on the use of opioids either because of withdrawal symptoms and/or increased pain.

In order to address the problem of unwarranted diagnoses of opioid addiction, the Liaison Committee on Pain and Addiction met in 2001 to develop definitions that would more accurately reflect tolerance, dependence, and addiction in patients prescribed opioids for pain. The committee included members of the American Academy of Pain Medicine, the American Pain Society, and the American Society of Addiction Medicine.

DEFINITIONS FROM THE LIAISON COMMITTEE ON PAIN AND ADDICTION

- **Tolerance** is a state of adaptation in which exposure to a drug induces changes that result in a diminution of one or more of the drug's effects over time.
- **Physical dependence** is a state of adaptation manifested by a drug-class-specific withdrawal syndrome that can be produced by abrupt cessation, rapid dose reduction, decreasing blood level of the drug, or administration of an antagonist.
- **Addiction** is a primary, chronic neurobiological disease with genetic, psychosocial, and environmental factors influencing its development and manifestations. It is characterized by behaviors that include one or more of the following: impaired control over drug use, compulsive use, continued use despite harm, and craving.

PAIN TREATMENT

Pain is one of the most frequent reasons why patients seek medical care. Over the past 20 years, there have been remarkable advances in our understanding of the pathophysiology of pain and tremendous growth in access to pain therapies. Despite these promising developments, pain is still undertreated, and pain treatments are often inadequate. Although many disease-related, individual, societal, and environmental factors influence pain and its management, a few realities broadly limit the provision of effective treatment for pain. These include the neurobiology of pain,

THE KNITTED GLOVE

You come into my office wearing a blue
knitted glove with a ribbon at the wrist.
You remove the glove slowly, painfully
and dump out the contents, a worthless hand.
What a specimen! It looks much like a regular hand,
warm, pliable, soft. You can move the fingers.

If it's not one thing, it's another.
Last month the fire in your hips had you down,
or up mincing across the room with a cane.
When I ask about the hips today, you pass them off
so I can't tell if only your pain
or the memory is gone. Your knitted hand
is the long and short of it. Pain doesn't exist
in the past any more than this morning does.

This thing, the name for your solitary days,
for the hips, the hand, for the walk of your eyes
away from mine, this thing is coyote, the trickster.
I want to call, come out, you son of a dog!
and wrestle that thing to the ground for you,
I want to take its neck between my hands.
But in this world I don't know how to find
the bastard, so we sit. We talk about the pain.

JACK COULEHAN

the individual psychosocial complexities of pain, and the high cost of pain therapy. Although clinical pain management is not a simple undertaking, the humanitarian mandate to provide relief of pain is obvious.

Because chronic pain is a complex, multifactorial experience, multidimensional and multidisciplinary therapies are often required. In general, chronic pain therapies strive to help the patient better manage pain and related symptoms, while maintaining or developing a meaningful and active lifestyle within optimized physical limitations. Multidisciplinary management of chronic pain involves a wide range of treatment approaches including analgesic medications, injections and interventional procedures, psychological interventions, and physical therapy. Psychological interventions address the consequences of living with pain, and teach techniques and strategies for managing pain and improving daily function. Physical therapy addresses musculo-skeletal contributions to pain and promotes general conditioning for strength and endurance. Medical management therapies include adjuvant analgesics, neurolytic techniques, spinal steroid injections, spinal facet joint injections, medial branch nerve blocks, spinal cord and peripheral nerve stimulators, and spinal analgesic infusion pumps.

PSYCHOLOGICAL INTERVENTIONS

The primary psychological interventions for chronic pain are behavioral (operant) therapy, cognitive-behavioral therapy, and self-regulatory therapies such as biofeedback, meditation, and self-hypnosis.

Operant Conditioning and Behavioral Therapy

Wilbur Fordyce, working at the University of Washington in Seattle in the 1970s, developed one of the first behavioral treatment programs for chronic pain. It was based on Skinnerian operant conditioning principles, which proposed that the frequency of a behavior could be increased or decreased by modifying environmental contingencies. Operant conditioning research showed that the frequency of a behavior can be increased by positive or negative reinforcement or decreased by punishment or extinction procedures. Positive reinforcement works by providing a reward when (and only when) a particular behavior occurs. Negative reinforcement works by contingently withdrawing an aversive stimulus when and only when the behavior occurs. Punishment works by contingently administering a negative stimulus when and only when a behavior occurs, and extinction decreases the frequency of a behavior by discontinuing whatever was reinforcing it. Fordyce extended Skinner's paradigm to pain behaviors, proposing that pain behaviors are often positively reinforced, and thus tend to increase them, by attention and assistance from family and friends, avoidance of aversive activities and responsibilities, financial incentives such as Workers Compensation or disability payments, and the administration of as-needed pain medication. Pain (or illness) behaviors that operant treatment programs seek to decrease or eliminate include verbal communications of pain such as complaints, moaning and groaning; pain behaviors such as limping or guarding; "downtime," or time spent lying or sitting down; and requests for assistance and/or pain medications.

In a behavioral treatment program, illness behaviors, such as pain complaints and groaning, are not attended to (that is, they are extinguished) by the program's staff. According to Skinner's model, these behaviors should decrease in frequency over time. Conversely, "well" behaviors, such as exercise and socializing, are positively reinforced with attention and encouragement from the staff. Pain medications are provided on a time-contingent schedule to reduce the positively reinforcing effect of pain medications being administered following complaints of pain. Exercise is performed toward "success" as opposed to "tolerance" as the endpoint. Performing toward success means that patients perform a specified number of repetitions, then rest as a positive reinforcement for success rather than resting in response to increased pain (a negative reinforcement for avoidance). The goals in a behavioral treatment program are functional in nature, that is, patients become more active and involved through positive reinforcement, shaping, and gradual approximation of well behaviors. Families are involved in these programs in order to learn how to help patients maintain gains and stop inadvertently reinforcing illness behaviors.

Self-Regulatory Techniques

These are techniques that patients learn for self-management of pain. They include diaphragmatic breathing, progressive and passive relaxation, imagery, meditation, autogenic phrases, hypnosis and self-hypnosis, and biofeedback. Although each technique has its distinctive elements, all aim to reduce stress, increase physical relaxation, and focus attention.

Relaxation therapies are methods for learning how to slow respiration and decrease muscle tension thereby counteracting the physiological response to stress. In addition, these techniques help patients become more aware of their physical responses, thereby learning to distinguish states of tension from states of relaxation. A third benefit of relaxation techniques, particularly hypnosis, relaxing imagery, and meditation, is the requisite mental focus that can help to reduce awareness of pain via distraction.

Biofeedback is a method of monitoring a patients physiological responses (muscle tension, peripheral skin temperature, heart rate, and/or electrodermal responses), and then feeding this information back to the patient via an auditory or visual modality. By having immediate feedback of, for example, muscle tension at a specific site, patients can learn how to reduce (or increase) tension in specific muscle groups. Electromyographic biofeedback is commonly used with chronic pain disorders in which muscle tension plays a significant role in the etiology or maintenance of the pain complaint. Examples include "tension" headaches and low back pain. Thermal biofeedback is the preferred modality for migraine headaches and reflex sympathetic dystrophy and can help patients learn how to modulate peripheral skin temperature.

Cognitive-Behavior Therapy

Cognitive-behavior therapy (CBT) grew out of behaviorally oriented programs. Rather than focusing solely on changing overt behaviors, these programs address how patients perceive and understand their pain and what expectations and hopes they hold for treatment, control of pain, and for the future. They also address the personal losses that so often co-occur with chronic pain, and patients' emotional responses to pain and loss. Whereas B. F. Skinner considered the mind to be a "black box," unamenable to study as it was not observable, CBT embraced thoughts as influential factors in emotional and behavioral responses.

CBT programs may differ in a variety of ways, but they all tend to have core elements in common. They may be disorder-specific (e.g., low back or fibromyalgia programs), they may include medical treatment and/or physical therapy in a multidisciplinary approach, and may or may not include therapies such as biofeedback. A CBT program may be offered as an inpatient or outpatient service, and in individual or group formats. An advantage of individualized CBT is that it enables the therapist to give undivided attention to the patient and to tailor the treatment to the patient's specific needs. Group sessions have the advantages of social interaction, peer support, sharing of ideas, modeling of adaptive behaviors, and opportunities for mutual validation of experiences.

Although the specific components of CBT programs can vary with the nature of the program and/or the needs of the individual patient, there are core components that are usually included in most CBT programs for chronic pain.

- **Education:** an introduction to pain transmission and modulation, with an emphasis on the affective, cognitive, and behavioral factors that influence pain perception.
- **Goal-setting:** individual long-term and short-term goals.
- **Self-regulatory techniques:** to manage stress, reduce muscle tension, aid in distraction from pain, and help with sleep.
- **Skill acquisition:** to improve communication skills, introduce activity pacing, and improve sleep hygiene.
- **Cognitive restructuring:** identify and modify pain-related cognitions, attributions, beliefs, fears, and expectations, and develop pain-coping statements
- **Maintenance:** identify or strengthen the patient's social

support network, anticipate problems and develop strategies for coping with setbacks and relapses.
- **Exercise:** general conditioning and proper body mechanics to address deconditioning, poor endurance, and fatigue. This part of the program is usually led by a physical therapist.

Physical Therapy

For many, if not most, individuals who suffer from chronic pain, activity and exercise worsen their pain. However, lack of exercise can also worsen pain over time due to protective responses such as guarded postures, muscle tension, and deconditioning. Physical inactivity can cause significant loss of muscle tone, and as the muscles become deconditioned, exercise (and even simple movement) becomes increasingly painful. Deconditioning also affects cardiovascular fitness, leading to fatigue and decreased endurance. Exercise and conditioning programs must be tailored to the individual and should be lead by a knowledgeable physical therapist. An exercise regimen should be implemented with the goals of improving strength, flexibility and endurance without exacerbating pain. This is not to imply that exercise will never be painful, but patients need to learn to distinguish "good pain," i.e., harmless pain associated with building muscle, from "bad pain" or exercise that seriously exacerbates the underlying painful condition. Exercise can help strengthen and stabilize muscles around the spine and painful joints. It can also improve sleep and energy, and help with weight loss, which in turn reduces stress and strain on painful joints.

Graduated exercise protocols can help patients to increase their exercise tolerance and fitness with minimal exacerbation of pain. A good physical therapy program includes several, or all, of the following approaches: learning to maintain postural alignment, relaxation to reduce muscle tension, flexibility exercises, resistance training for strength, and aerobic exercise training to improve endurance. Many physical therapists also have training in fitting, and instructing patients in the use of, transcutaneous electrical nerve stimulation (TENS) units, which use pulses of electricity to stimulate painful areas. They are small enough to be worn on a belt and are programmable. TENS is thought to relieve pain by stimulating myelinated nerve fibers, which in turn inhib-

> I commenced inhaling the ether before the operation was commenced and continued it until the operation was over. I did not feel the slightest pain from the operation and could not believe the tumor was removed until it was shown to me.
>
> JAMES VENABLE
> *Account by first ether patient who underwent public demonstration of ether at the Massachusetts General Hospital, 16 October 1846*

its the transmission of pain signals along unmyelinated C fibers.

Medical Treatments

Although analgesic medications are the most commonly used medical treatment for pain, currently available analgesics have significant limitations including incomplete pain relief, adverse effects, and tolerance. Fortunately, a wide range of medical therapies, which include but are not limited to analgesics, are available for chronic pain. A detailed description of the clinical use of medical therapies for pain is beyond the scope of this text; further information is available in standard pain texts.

Analgesic Medications

Among the analgesic medications with pain-relieving effects are nonopioid analgesics (acetaminophen, nonsteroidal anti-inflammatory drugs), opioid analgesics (morphine-like agents), and adjuvant analgesics (anticonvulsants, antidepressants). Opioid is the preferred term for all analgesics that have a mechanism of action similar to morphine. Opiate refers to the subset of opioids derived from opium and/or with a chemical structure similar to morphine.

In most clinical settings, analgesic agents are used empirically. In other words, even the best available research findings do not necessarily provide clinicians with sufficient guidance as to what will or will not work in any given case. Consequently, a trial-and-error approach is often needed to determine the optimal treatment for an individual patient. In addition, there are some areas of pain management in which there is little evidence to support commonly used therapies. The long-term use of opioid analgesics for the management of chronic, noncancer pain is a notable example. The use of any kind of medical therapy must be based on careful consideration of the potential benefits and risks. Because analgesics reduce pain intensity only temporarily—and generally do not contribute to the long-term resolution of pain—they must be used cautiously in order to minimize adverse effects.

Nonopioid analgesics include acetaminophen, aspirin and other salicylates, and nonsteroidal anti-inflammatory drugs (NSAIDs). These agents are widely used in the management of acute and chronic pain of mild to moderate severity although they have limited efficacy, even at maximal therapeutic doses, for moderate to severe pain. While reasonably safe for most individuals, all nonopioid analgesics have potential toxicities that limit their utility.

Acetaminophen is a modestly effective analgesic that appears to dampen pain-signal transmission in the CNS. In typical doses, it is generally safe and well-tolerated, although excessive doses of acetaminophen—or even standard doses in individuals with chronic alcohol use or liver disease—may result in potentially fatal hepatotoxicity. **Aspirin** (acetylsalicylic acid, ASA) has been in clinical use since 1899 and remains a widely used analgesic, the efficacy of which, for both chronic and acute pain, has been well documented in randomized controlled trials. Gastrointestinal toxicity (gastritis, bleeding, and peptic ulceration) are more common with aspirin than with other nonacetylated salicylates and NSAIDs. Because of the increased risk of gastrointestinal bleeding, chronic alcohol use is a relative contraindication to chronic use of aspirin. Because of risk of worsening renal function, aspirin should also be avoided in patients with renal insufficiency. Based on randomized controlled trials, **NSAIDs** appear to be more efficacious than acetaminophen in controlling pain from osteoarthritis and rheumatoid arthritis. As with aspirin, gastrointestinal toxicity is the most common adverse effect limiting clinical use of NSAIDs. Because of risk of worsening renal function, aspirin should be avoided and NSAIDs are contraindicated in individuals with renal insufficiency. NSAIDs may trigger or exacerbate hypertension and may increase the risk of cardiovascular thromboembolic events (e.g., myocardial infarction, stroke).

Opioid analgesics include all agents that have an analgesic effect similar to that of morphine, acting through specific opioid receptors in the peripheral and central nervous system. Opioid analgesics include naturally occurring agents derived from opium (morphine, codeine), chemically manufactured agents (e.g., hydromorphone, fentanyl, methadone), and the body's own endogenously produced endorphins. Although the analgesic effect of opium has been known for over 2000 years, opioids are still the most potent and most widely applicable analgesics for moderate to severe pain. Although extensively used in clinical practice for control of both acute and chronic pain, there is relatively little clinical research data regarding the long-term use of opioid analgesics in chronic pain. Most of the available evidence supporting the use of opioids for chronic pain comes from uncontrolled clinical case series, with follow-up periods of 1–2 years. A few RCTs of up to 6 to 8 weeks' duration have demonstrated the efficacy of opioids in chronic pain. Other than isolated case reports, however, there are no published data regarding the benefits or risks of using opioid analgesics for the control of chronic pain over the time course of several years.

There is no "correct dose" of any given opioid that is safe and effective for all patients; rather, the dosage must be titrated for each individual. The correct dose is one that reasonably controls pain with only minimal adverse effects. The required daily dose of an opioid can range over 2 to 3 orders of magnitude, depending on such factors as pain severity, the degree of opioid tolerance, and medical comorbidities.

The use of opioid analgesics for control of acute pain is often limited by adverse effects including respiratory depression, sedation, nausea, pruritus, urinary retention, and constipation. With the exception of constipation, patients tend to develop tolerance or resistance to these adverse effects with chronic use of opioid medications. Long-term use of opioids may be associated with additional adverse effects including:

- Impotence and loss of libido due to decreased levels of sex hormones
- Sweating and/or chills due to alteration of hormonal regulation of basal body temperature
- Depression (although the overall risk of depression may be lessened if pain is controlled)
- Physical dependence
- Opioid addiction
- Tolerance (decreased effectiveness of a given dose of opioid to control pain).

It has long been clear that analgesic tolerance (i.e., decreased pain relief from a given dose) limits the utility of chronic opioid therapy. Although there is individual variability in the rate and extent to which tolerance develops, most patients who use opioid analgesics on a daily basis for chronic pain over several weeks to months will require dosage escalation to achieve continued pain relief. The risk of developing opioid tolerance increases with the dose and duration of opioid therapy. Unfortunately, uncontrolled pain due to opioid tolerance may necessitate opioid dose escalation to regain pain control, which in turn can cause further opioid tolerance, etc. In order to keep the dosage as low as possible, and in order to limit the development of tolerance and preserve the utility of opioid for future pain control, it is often necessary to employ a wide range of multidisciplinary pain therapies.

One of the fundamental mechanisms of opioid tolerance appears to be that opioid analgesics not only inhibit, but paradoxically also facilitate or amplify, the neurotransmission of pain signals. With chronic administration of opioid, the transmission of pain signals is enhanced, gradually and increasingly undermining the inhibitory (analgesic) effects of opioid. Although convincingly demonstrated in experimental animals, the significance of opioid tolerance-induced hyperalgesia in humans is unclear. However, methadone maintenance patients as well as chronic pain patients requiring high doses of opioid clearly develop increased sensitivity to normally noxious stimuli (hyperalgesia). Minimizing, or even avoiding, the use of opioid analgesics appears to be the best way to avoid the development of opioid tolerance and opioid tolerance hyperalgesia.

Adjuvant analgesics, including several anticonvulsants, some antidepressants, and a few miscellaneous medications, have an analgesic efficacy, especially in neuropathic pain. These agents may be used alone or in combination with other opioid or nonopioid analgesics. In addition to pain relief, adjuvant analgesics may have other beneficial effects for chronic pain patients, including relief of insomnia, control of irritability, and, with antidepressants, management of comorbid depression and anxiety.

Gabapentin, an FDA approved drug for postherpetic neuralgia, is now widely used as a first-line analgesic for neuropathic pain, and its analgesic efficacy has been extensively studied for acute and chronic pain. It is generally well tolerated and relatively free of drug-drug interactions that can complicate the use of other anticonvulsants. Common adverse effects, including sedation, cognitive impairment, and weight gain, are usually modest and resolve once the drug is discontinued. **Pregabalin** (Lyrica) is a newer anticonvulsant thought to have a similar mechanism of action as gabapentin; it is FDA approved for postherpetic neuralgia, diabetic neuropathy, and fibromyalgia.

Other anticonvulsants, especially carbamazepine, have been used and extensively studied for pain control, but must be employed cautiously due to risks of adverse effects and drug-drug interactions. Anticonvulsants should be tapered over a period of 1–2 weeks, since abrupt discontinuation has been reported to be associated with new onset withdrawal seizures.

Antidepressants are widely used in the management of chronic pain, due in part to the high prevalence of depression among patients with chronic pain. In addition to managing comorbid depression, some antidepressants have analgesic efficacy, at least in management of neuropathic pain. The analgesic effect of tricyclics may be seen at doses lower than typically prescribed for the treatment of depression. Amitriptyline is the best studied antidepressant in terms of pain relief, but other tricyclic antidepressants (such as nortriptyline and desipramine) also have analgesic efficacy. Duloxetine, a relatively new antidepressant, is FDA approved for pain from diabetic peripheral neuropathy and fibromyalgia. There is less evidence supporting the use of selective serotonin reuptake inhibitors (SSRIs), but these agents are often reasonably well tolerated and should be considered if tricyclic antidepressants are poorly tolerated. The SSRIs may be especially useful in management of the dysphoric mood and irritability that often accompanies chronic pain.

Milnacipran (Savella) is a new serotonin norepinephrine reuptake inhibitor (SNRI) that is widely used in Europe and Asia for the management of depression. It was recently approved by the FDA for the management of fibromyalgia.

Interventional Therapies

Interventional therapies for chronic pain management include surgeries, injections, and other procedures. The goal of many interventional therapies, including most surgical procedures, is to correct or at least modify specific anatomic abnormalities causing the pain. Other interventions, such as localized injections, are not designed to cure the underlying disease, but rather to temporarily decrease the neural transmission of pain signals. Local anesthetics and steroid injection therapies such as **trigger point injections** for muscular/myofascial pain or **intraarticular joint injections** for osteoarthritis may offer temporary relief. They are used to control severe exacerbations of chronic pain and to provide periods of pain relief designed to enable the patient to participate in physical therapy and rehabilitation. Excessive use of steroid-based injection therapies can lead to steroid toxicity, hyperglycemia, fluid retention, pituitary-adrenal suppression, osteoporosis, or Cushing's syndrome.

In general, **neurolytic techniques** to destroy nerve pathways transmitting pain signals are not appropriate for the control of chronic, noncancer pain. Although permanent interruption of pain-signal transmission might seem to be desirable in some cases, the risks of inadequate relief, worsened pain, and other iatrogenic effects of this approach are often prohibitive. Specific examples in which intentional neural destruction may be of benefit include radiofrequency ablation of spinal medial branch nerves (for cervical or lumbar spine pain due to facet joint arthritis) and interventions for the management of analgesic-resistant trigeminal neuralgia.

Spinal steroid injections (epidural, selective nerve root, or transforaminal epidural) are commonly used for neck, back, and radiating arm or leg pain due to displaced intervertebral disks, spondylosis (degenerative arthritis of spine), spinal stenosis, or chronic pain that may occur following spine surgery. The long-term benefits of these procedures are modest, but they can provide short-term relief that can help to facilitate rehabilitation. The risk of needle trauma or spinal drug toxicity is very low, but similarly rare postinjection infections may have severe consequences including spinal cord damage and death. Spinal steroid injections and the other procedures listed below are minimally invasive and are usually performed on an outpatient basis.

Spinal facet joint injections and local anesthetic **medial branch nerve blocks** that innervate those joints are indicated for pain from facet arthropathy, i.e., osteoarthritis of the spinal facet joints. Local anesthetic or steroid injections may help to corroborate the clinical diagnosis of facet arthropathy as the cause of pain, or to provide temporary pain relief to facilitate physical therapy. **Radiofrequency (RF) ablation of the medial branch nerves** is an important exception to the proscription against neural destruction to control noncancer pain. It can provide long periods of relief (4–6 months or longer) from neck or back pain due to facet arthropathy. If pain returns due to neural regeneration, the RF treatment can be repeated.

Implanted **spinal cord stimulators** and **peripheral nerve stimulators** are occasionally used for control of moderate to moderately-severe neuropathic pain that has not responded to analgesics. With spinal cord stimulation, electrodes are positioned in the spinal canal, posterior to the spinal cord, so that electrical current through the device produces paresthesias in the areas affected by chronic pain. Peripheral nerve stimulators are similar implanted medical devices, with the stimulating electrodes implanted next to a peripheral nerve supplying the nerve input to the area of pain. Most patients perceive the stimulation paresthesias created by the stimulator as a tingling, warm, and soothing sensation that decreases pain intensity.

Spinal analgesic infusion pumps are typically used for advanced cancer pain. Pumps are, at times, used for palliative care of otherwise intractable noncancer pain. Compared to systemic administration, spinal administration of a solution containing an opioid, local anesthetic, or other appropriate medication can provide more effective analgesia. The cost, complexity, and risks of spinal analgesics generally limit use to cases of truly intractable, incapacitating pain.

SUMMARY

The treatment of patients with chronic pain can be a challenging yet rewarding process. Patients often come in tired, angry, deconditioned, demoralized, and apathetic, having lost much of what was of value in their lives. Across disciplines, there are a variety of treatment approaches that can help patients manage their pain. Yet even with comprehensive, multidisciplinary treatment, what we can at best offer is a reduction of symptoms and an improvement in functioning. It can be difficult for both patients and health-care professionals to accept a less than totally satisfying solution to a problem. Progress must be measured by whatever small successes can be achieved. Patients often approach pain management as the "end of the road," but with patience and understanding, management of pain can be, instead, the first step on a new road.

CASE STUDY

Mr. J. is a 52-year-old, married, white male who developed back pain following a fall at work, which ruptured a disk. He underwent lumbar spine surgery but continues to experience aching and grinding pain at his low back with burning pain radiating into his right leg. For the past 2 years (since the surgery), he has been unable to work at his job as a construction worker, has settled a claim with the company for which he worked, and is presently receiving Social Security disability. He has tried numerous medications for management of his pain and is currently prescribed propoxyphene/acetaminophen 100/650, 2 tablets per day, and gabapentin 300 mg 3 times a day. He believes these medications "help a little bit" when he is inactive and sitting in his recliner. Mr. J. stated that he has taken extra propoxyphene/acetaminophen when he is more active, for example, while on vacation with his family. He ran out of an opioid prescription early and said that his family physician will no longer prescribe his pain medications because of his excessive use of opioid analgesics. He has had no injection therapies but has attended physical therapy, consisting primarily of passive modalities, and he believes they provided only modest relief. Exercises increased his pain. He has no home exercise program or general conditioning regimen. He rates his pain as between a 6/10 and a 9/10, increasing when he is more active and decreasing with rest. A hot shower provides some modest relief.

Mr. J. spends his days watching TV and "puttering" in the garage where he used to enjoy working on cars as a hobby. His wife has returned to work because of the financial problems they have experienced since his unemployment, and to keep up with the tuition for their two children who attend college. Ms. J. attended the initial evaluation and expressed anger and resentment about having the responsibility for managing the household both financially and physically. She works, cares for the household and yard, and is feeling overwhelmed. She believes that her husband can do more than he presently does and has "gotten lazy" since he stopped working. He says that he tries to help, but doing housework or yardwork worsens his pain and he has essentially stopped trying.

During the evaluation, Mr. J. sat toward the edge of his chair, shifted his posture, and directed his gaze toward the floor. He presented as a modestly obese man whose grooming was somewhat negligent—he has several days' growth of beard and his torn shirttail was untucked and unbuttoned. His affect was sad. He described himself as "frustrated" and "worthless" because he can no longer do what he did in the past. His wife believes that he has been depressed since he was unable to return to work. Due to pain, he is no longer involved with activities he previously enjoyed such as working on cars and bowling, although he believes he would still enjoy doing these things if he were able. He no longer visits with family, sees his bowling buddies or goes with his wife to the movies saying he "would just rather stay home." He is "tired of explaining that [he's] not better" and believes that "people think [he's] faking because [he] looks OK." He described his sleep as poor, stating that he stays up and watches TV until he is tired, then sleeps in 2-hour stretches, getting up to smoke a cigarette or watch TV. He is "up and down" all night and believes that he averages 3–4 hours of sleep a night. He denied napping during the day, but his wife says he nods off while watching TV. He stated that is rarely hungry, although he snacks or eats quick foods throughout the day. He "picks at" his dinner, which his wife prepares. Despite decreased appetite, he reported a 40-pound weight gain, which he believes to be attributable to change in activity. He described his short-term memory as "terrible," saying that he forgets appointments and chores his wife asks him to do during the day. He reported that he is unable to concentrate like he did in the past but "doesn't have much to concentrate on anyway." He "doesn't know how long [he] can go on like this," although he denied frank suicidal thoughts, plan, or intent. He denied psychiatric history in himself or family of origin, and is not prescribed an antidepressant with the exception of amitriptyline 25 mg to help with sleep.

Mr. J is the third of six children. His parents are now both deceased and he has little contact with his siblings. He completed high school, began working with his father in construction and worked at this profession until his injury. He resides with his wife of 32 years. They have two children, both of whom are attending college. Mr. J. smokes 1–1 ½ packs of cigarettes per day, having smoked for over 30 years. He denied current use of alcohol although he reports a history of alcohol use (a 6-pack of beer nightly, with two DUI's) dating back 25 years. He denied use of illicit drugs.

Considerations for Treatment Planning

- Medical treatment has been minimal.
  - He has had no injection therapies, is prescribed limited opioids analgesics, and has had an inadequate trial of gabapentin.
  - He has some risk factors for developing addiction, such as past history of alcohol abuse and unsanctioned dose increases of his opioids analgesics. However, his alcohol abuse history is remote, and opioid dose increases appear to be limited to times when he tries to be more active. Pseudoaddiction, or inadequately treated pain, may be the principle reason for his increasing use of pain medications.
  - Mr. J. may be considered for interventional pain therapies such as injection techniques or spinal cord stimulation if conservative treatment fails to provide relief.

- Physical therapies have been inadequate, and Mr. J. is clearly deconditioned
  - His physical therapy to date has consisted primarily of passive modalities.
  - Previous exercise therapy resulted in increased pain, and he is not engaging in a home exercise program or conditioning exercise.

- The impact of pain on Mr. J's life has been significant. He is no longer employed, and this has affected his family's income, his self-image, his relationship with his wife, and his daily routine.
  - His recreational activities were physically demanding, and he no longer engages in activities he previously enjoyed. This also limits his social contact.
  - He presents with symptoms of depression including sad affect, social withdrawal, feelings of worthlessness, nonrestorative sleep, diminished appetite (although he has gained weight), and changes in memory and concentration. He acknowledges suicidal thoughts, without plan or intent, and he presents some future risk for suicide. He is prescribed amitriptyline 25 mg for sleep although it is clearly ineffective with sleep and too small a dose to be effective for depression.

Treatment Recommendations

- Refer to a pain management specialist for consideration of injection therapies and for medication recommendations.
- Refer for physical therapy with a therapist trained in the treatment of chronic pain. Mr. J. may benefit from instruction in individualized exercises but most certainly requires instruction in a slowly progressing conditioning program. He may benefit from a trial of transcutaneous electrical nerve stimulation (TENS).
- Consider the addition of an antidepressant, such as an SSRI to treat depression, and either increasing amitriptyline or changing to trazodone to help with sleep and decrease risk of further weight gain.

SUGGESTED READINGS

Fishman, S.M., Ballantyne, J.C., & Rathmell, J.P. (2009). *Bonica's management of pain* (4th ed.). Philadelphia, PA: Lippincott Williams.
This volume is a leading textbook and clinical reference in the pain-management field. It includes chapters on the physiological, psychological, cultural and environmental aspects of pain, specific pain syndromes, and evaluation considerations. This comprehensive text also covers treatment including pharmacological and psychological approaches, interventional therapies, physical therapies, and implantable devices. There are chapters on the legal, ethical, and political issues surrounding pain management.

Gatchel, R.J., & Turk, D.D. (Eds.) (1996). *Psychological approaches to pain management: A practitioners hand book.* New York, NY: Guilford.

Gatchel, R.J. (2005). *Clinical essentials of pain management.* Washington, DC: American Psychological Association.
These two books cover a broad range of topics including the evolution of pain theories, and psychosocial factors that influence pain perception and coping. Topics include the impact of depression and anxiety, family issues, expectations, and beliefs. Also covered are psychological techniques and strategies for the management of pain.

Part 2

Patient Behavior

8 Stress and Illness

William R. Lovallo & Margaret L. Stuber

I think that we must admit that, although physicians have not infrequent occasions to observe instances of functional disturbance due to emotional excitement, there is an inclination to minimize or to slight that influence, or even to deny that it is part of a physician's service to his patient to concern himself with such troubles. The doctor is properly concerned with the workings of the body and their disturbances, and he should have, therefore, a natural interest in the effects of emotional stress and the modes of relieving it.

WALTER B. CANNON

The objective of this chapter is for the reader to understand the concept of stress as it applies to brain mechanisms and peripheral physiology, and to appreciate how these stress mechanisms influence the diagnosis and treatment of illness. The focus is on how thoughts and feelings become physiological events that interact with peripheral physiology and with brain function.

DEFINITION

Stress refers to the presence of significant physiological or psychological threat resulting in acute or persistent strain on the body's compensatory systems. All deviations from normal function call for some compensation to restore normalcy. When compensatory responses begin to deviate from a poorly defined "normal range," we classify these as stress responses. There is no predetermined level at which a normal response becomes a stress response; however, some stress researchers use the presence of an acute cortisol response to a discrete event as evidence of a true stress response. Such cortisol responses are usually associated with negative emotions such as fear, anxiety, or anger, as well as physical or mental distress.

In everyday speech, the word stress often is used to refer to psychologically induced strains rather than physical threats. Indeed, psychological stress responses are perhaps more common in daily life than purely physical stressors.

These comments illustrate two points. First, the concept of stress emerged naturally from the study of normal physiology. *It is impossible to understand how the body works as an organized self-sustaining system without also considering how it deals with external stimuli and threats to its integrity.* As such, stress is a central topic in physiology and medicine. Second, psychologically induced stress responses can act through the body's regulatory systems to alter physiological functions.

HISTORY OF THE STRESS CONCEPT

The concept of stress is embedded in the history of physiology. Stress reactions are extensions of the normal physiological regulation that sustains life. Stress responses protect living things against severe threats (**stressors**). By the 1850s, Claude Bernard, the French physiologist and physician, argued that variations in both the external environment and the internal environment, meaning the chemical makeup of blood and other bodily fluids, could damage cells and organs. He saw physiology as the study of the regulatory mechanisms that respond to these internal and external imbalances, and how these are corrected to maintain a relatively constant internal environment to support cells, organs, and bodily systems.

We are simply not accustomed to the conceptual handling of complex entities where many factors, all vital, maintain a balance. The human body is one such entity, and disease...can be viewed as any persistent harmful disturbance of its equilibrium.

ALASTAIR CUNNINGHAM

In the 1930s, Hans Selye brought the word stress into widespread popular usage. In medical school Selye had discovered that rats exposed to severe systemic threats such as heat, cold, toxic agents, and the like always had elevated levels of corticosterone. Selye argued that activation of the **hypothalamic-pituitary-adrenocortical response** was at the center of the response to stress. In particular, although corticosterone signaled that a stress response was occurring, Selye argued that high levels corticosterone helped to keep the stress response under control. The regulatory role of corticosterone in the stress response is substantiated by the fact that animals deprived of corticosterone by adrenalectomy are susceptible to death from exposure to even minor stressors because the stress response runs unchecked. Following Selye's lead, *activation of the cortisol response is now considered a definitive, generalized sign of stress that is not specific to a given type of stressor.*

> Bernard was right; the pathogen is nothing; the terrain is everything.
>
> Louis Pasteur's deathbed words

Following Claude Bernard's idea that physiological regulation serves to correct deviations from a normal internal state, the American physician and physiologist, Walter Cannon, coined the term **homeostasis** to refer to the collective processes that maintain an internal equilibrium. Cannon also recognized that autonomic and endocrine responses alone could not always maintain homeostasis. Some threats could only be removed by behavioral activity. Cannon further noted that severe threats are accompanied by negative emotions that can motivate corrective behaviors, and that positive feelings of satisfaction might accompany a return to normal. These two insights fostered the understanding that *behavior and emotions act in concert with autonomic and endocrine regulation to maintain homeostasis.* A simple example of this continuity of responses from physiological regulation to emotions and behavior is the sensation of hunger that starts out as a mild drop in blood glucose, which, without our conscious awareness, can be counteracted by cortisol and insulin secretion. Eventually at a greater degree of internal need, the person may feel discomfort and recognize the need to find food to eat. The discomfort motivates the behavior and the feeling of satisfaction rewards it.

PSYCHOLOGICAL AND EMOTIONAL CONTRIBUTIONS TO STRESS RESPONSES

Cannon also recognized that severe physiological changes occurred following psychological shocks and long-term emotional strains, and that these changes could lead to ill-

ness. In one case, Cannon noted, a diabetic man who was hospitalized, kept on a controlled diet, and given regular insulin suddenly began excreting sugar in his urine although there was no change in his diet or insulin dose. Inquiry revealed that the patient had just discovered that his company was about to make him retire; the emotional strain apparently complicated his diabetic control. In another case, a young woman's husband committed suicide in her presence in order to punish her for extramarital affairs. She soon developed an elevated basal metabolism along with hyperthyroidism and a large goiter. She later became diabetic and hypertensive. The striking thing about these cases is that the precipitating events were not physiological injuries but rather life events that evoked their fears and insecurities. Nonetheless, the physiological consequences were very real.

Psychologists Stanley Schachter and Jerome Singer substantiated the role of thoughts and perceptions in shaping emotional reactions. They found that they could manipulate the emotional and physiological reactions of their research subjects by exposing them to other persons displaying either neutral behavior or strong emotions such as euphoria, anger, or irritation. This **emotional biasing** provided strong evidence that social processes and our thoughts and perceptions color our interpretation of physiological states and shape our emotions. This work forms the basis of our modern concept of **psychological stress.**

BOX 8.1 Concepts of physical versus psychological stress

Physical stressors include cold, heat, infection, and extended exercise. These challenges to homeostasis provoke significant physiological reactions using what we might call "bottom-up" mechanisms. That is, signals from the body reach the brainstem and hypothalamus to evoke reflex responses to maintain homeostasis. Psychological stress responses originate as thoughts or learned reactions to events at higher levels in the nervous system, but they act on the body through the same hypothalamic and brainstem mechanisms as physical stressors. We refer to psychological stress reactions as "top-down" because they originate in these higher cognitive centers in the brain. Both top-down and bottom-up stressors may affect health if they are severe or prolonged.

The psychologist Richard Lazarus examined how thoughts might contribute to stress responses. His primary insight was that a life event might become a stressor if the person appraises the event as harmful, an obstacle to achieving goals, or violating expectations about the world. This "primary appraisal" of potential threat is aggravated if the person believes he or she has a limited ability to cope with (i.e., reduce or eliminate) the potential threat. *These dual appraisals of threat and limited coping resources form the beginning of a psychological stress response.* A common example is the familiar emotional reaction and physiological state that accompanies a poor test grade. The grade cannot cause harm by itself, but it may result in a failure to achieve a major goal, such as graduation or a desired residency, and the student may not be able to alter that negative consequence. The low grade thus becomes a stressor with physiological consequences due to these negative appraisals. *The most severe psychological stressors accompany fear of potential physical harm and concomitant feelings of helplessness.*

A key factor in understanding the impact of psychological stress is that the bodily responses may be similar to those accompanying physical threats. Appraisals of threat and of limited personal coping resources lead to negative emotions that are grounded in brain functions. These brain mechanisms have outputs through the same regulatory systems that maintain homeostasis in response to physical threats. For this reason, both physiological and psychological stress responses have ample avenues for engaging mechanisms of illness.

> Mental tensions, frustrations, insecurity, [and] aimlessness are among the most damaging stressors, and psychosomatic studies have shown how often they cause migraine headache, peptic ulcers, heart attacks, hypertension, mental disease, suicide, or just hopeless unhappiness.
>
> HANS SELYE

PHYSIOLOGICAL AND PSYCHOLOGICAL STRESS

In introducing the brain mechanisms associated with psychological stress, it is instructive to begin with physiological stress responses. Stress physiology can be considered most readily by considering a bottom-up view of **physiological regulation**, starting with local tissues, progressing to the spinal cord and the brainstem, followed by the hypothalamus, and ultimately by the limbic system and prefrontal cortex. Each higher level in the system lends a greater level of complexity to the organization of the response to threat, with the top levels supplying behavioral and emotional characteristics to the response repertoire. In discussing the effector systems and formulation of the endocrine and autonomic responses during stress, we will focus here on constructing a general model. Neuroscience texts can provide more detailed information about afferent information, reflex loops, and efferent regulation of tissues via the autonomic nervous system and endocrine outflow for different effector systems.

The cardiovascular system is useful for illustrating the layered, bottom-up structure of the regulatory apparatus of the human body and how it makes adjustments during

periods of physiological stress. The blood vessels provide oxygenated blood to all tissues along with energy-supplying nutrients, and they remove waste products in order to maintain homeostasis. Much of the regulation of blood flow and redistribution of body heat in soft tissue results from local autoregulation by the small blood vessels. This acts to balance vessel constriction due to sympathetic outflow and forms an elegant system ideally suited to distributing blood flow as needed and with little or no intervention by the spinal cord or any higher center.

A different picture emerges when local, spinal, and medullary mechanisms cooperate during situations that threaten short-term regulation of blood pressure. In a common example, rising from a seated to a standing position (orthostasis) threatens to cause a loss of consciousness if blood pools in the legs and fails to reach the brain. The baroreceptors detect the incipient pressure drop and act through medullary centers to greatly increase sympathetic outflow and suppress parasympathetic activity. The net effect is increased heart rate and improved left ventricular performance, vasoconstriction leading to reduced pooling of blood in the lower extremities, increased blood flow to the heart, and sustained perfusion of the brain. In this example, the added contribution of brainstem mechanisms through the baroreflex provides a higher level of integration in the regulation of the heart and blood vessels than would occur if each were to rely only on its intrinsic mechanisms. This interplay between local and brainstem reflexes allows a far wider range of adjustments in the service of homeostasis.

However, these higher reflex mechanisms are not adequate for all purposes. *Adaptive reactions may require integration of autonomic, endocrine, and behavioral response systems.* The hypothalamus is well adapted to this complex role. It is capable of regulating autonomic outputs at the level of the brainstem, it controls endocrine function, and it also has motor response centers. Because the hypothalamus has such a wide range of adaptive response capability, it can regulate homeostasis during periods of considerably increased demand, such as during extended aerobic exercise, when longer-term cardiovascular adjustments are called for along with increased availability of both glucose and fatty acids for energy.

Less well appreciated is the ability of the hypothalamus to generate behavioral outputs via the skeletal muscles. Philip Bard and Walter Cannon cut the central nervous system of a cat immediately above its hypothalamus and studied the cat's behavior. Observation showed that the cat was viable as long as food and water were provided near at hand. The animal had relatively normal sleep-wake cycles and good physiological regulation. Most interesting, the cat could produce an elaborate emotional display if stroked vigorously to provoke it. The response was a threatening defensive display, including an arched back, erect hair, and hissing. Bard referred to this reaction as a "sham rage." This observation by Bard and Cannon suggested that the *hypo-*

thalamus responds to threats that call for elaborate physiological and behavioral responses that supersede basic reflexes. These inborn physiological and behavioral responses provide a ready-made response prototype designed to support extreme vigorous escape or defense behaviors in life-threatening situations.

Although this study outlined the large range of controls that emanate from the hypothalamus, it provided perhaps more striking information about the role of structures above the hypothalamus. Considering Bard and Cannon's decerebrate cat, we should note that, lacking a cortex, the cat was deprived of sight, smell, and hearing, and so could not perceive anything beyond the surface of its own body. Lacking such perception—although it had programmed motor patterns at the level of the hypothalamus—it could not produce a meaningful behavioral response directed toward an external threat. These facts tell us that the hypothalamus and brainstem are capable of sustaining life in a relatively constant environment. However, brain structures higher up than the hypothalamus are necessary for dealing effectively with the external world. *Regulating behavior to external events relies on elaborate visual, auditory, and olfactory systems as well as an equally elaborate motor system, which together allow for perception and effective behavioral response generation to external threat.* Accompanying these perceptual and motor systems are those that classify stimuli as safe or desirable or as dangerous and aversive. This includes the limbic system and the prefrontal cortex along with several critical brainstem nuclei.

BRAIN MECHANISMS OF EMOTIONS AND STRESS RESPONSES

Figure 8.1 illustrates the flow of information through these systems that classify stimuli and make response choices, beginning with sensory inputs and ending with bodily expressions. The systems between inputs and outputs are responsible for developing emotional responses and stress reactions to those inputs. Following the pathways, external events are processed in cortical projection areas and then the increasingly high-level association cortex. Information from all external sensory modalities as well as the viscera is directed to the parahippocampal gyrus. Here, this information becomes accessible to the hippocampus and the amygdala. The hippocampus allows this input to form new declarative memories and also to aid in the retrieval of declarative memories. The amygdala is usually described as an emotion-related structure: Its emotional significance depends on the role in forming classically conditioned associations.

During an environmental encounter with a known threat—or with a novel event of uncertain outcome—the

---

BOX 8.2 Role of the Amygdala in Forming Conditioned Associations

The amygdala is the brain's focal structure in producing innate and acquired emotional responses. The acquired emotional responses result from experience; for their development, they depend on classical conditioning, also referred to as Pavlovian conditioning. Classical conditioning is a learning process by which sights, sounds, and smells signaling external events become associated with internal bodily states and responses. In the common example of Pavlov's dog, the sound of a bell was paired repeatedly with the delivery of food directly into the dog's mouth. Soon, the dog began making behavioral and visceral responses to the sound of the bell; for example, the dog would look around and begin to salivate. This illustrates that Pavlovian conditioning serves to motivate behavior by giving meaning to external events. Events that signal positive outcomes acquire different behavioral responses than ones that signal aversive outcomes. Bilateral destruction of the amygdalae results in the inability of the animal to form both positive and negative Pavlovian conditioned associations. In addition to amygdalar responses that are acquired through experience, the amygdala possesses innate, hardwired responses. A classic example is the innate fear of snakes exhibited by young primates. This fear is also eliminated by bilateral destruction of the amygdalae. The actions of the amygdala and its role in classically conditioned responses lead to the recognition that experience with life events can produce emotional memories.

---

amygdala becomes activated through its innate and classically conditioned responses to threat. The amygdala then signals the bed nuclei of the stria terminalis, the nucleus accumbens, the anterior cingulate gyrus, and the paraventricular nucleus of the hypothalamus. In addition, the amygdala's inputs to the prefrontal cortex provide essential signals that reach the level of consciousness and play a crucial role in the development of appraisals that underlie psychological stress responses. In a reciprocal fashion, the orbital prefrontal cortex provides feedback to the amygdala and bed nuclei (not shown) and to the hypothalamus. These descending inputs to the amygdala can help regulate the response to psychological stressors. During periods of stress, the net effect of this reciprocal interaction determines autonomic outputs at the level of the pons and medulla, stress endocrine outputs (especially epinephrine and cortisol), and motor patterns.

In addition to these relatively direct outputs to the body, stress-related activation of the amygdala also results in the activation of brainstem aminergic nuclei that alter the state of the entire central nervous system. These nuclei found in the pons include the locus ceruleus, with widespread noradrenergic outputs, the dopaminergic ventral tegmental nuclei, and the serotonin-containing raphe nuclei. These systems function to produce states of generalized arousal (norepinephrine outputs), motivate approach behaviors

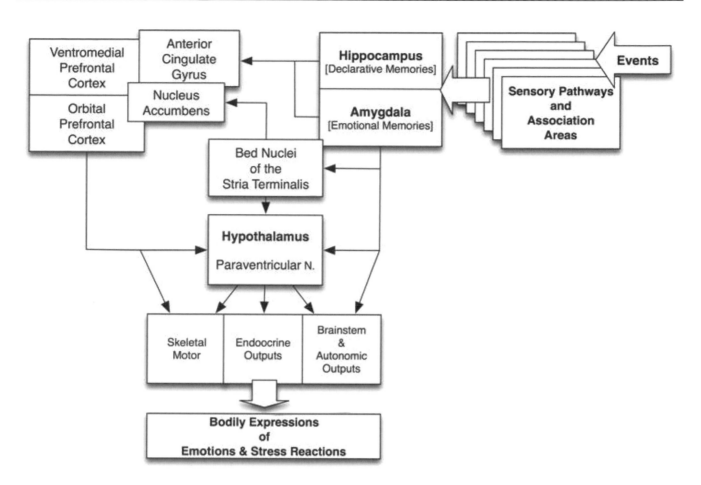

FIGURE 8.1 Psychological stress responses. This diagram shows major pathways from sensory inputs to emotion formation, stress responses, and bodily outputs. External events are processed through sensory pathways in the brain, beginning with primary input areas and increasingly elaborate areas of association cortex. All sensory pathways feed into the temporal lobe, which contains the hippocampus and amygdala. These two structures form memories of past events and help to define responses to events based on that experience. In doing so, both structures interact with subcortical structures (including the bed nuclei of the stria terminalis [BNST], closely associated with the activities of the amygdala, and the nucleus accumbens). The BNST and nucleus accumbens interact extensively with several areas of the prefrontal cortex. The outcome of these subcortical-prefrontal interactions form the basis for outputs to the hypothalamus and brainstem. These are sometimes in conjunction with conscious processes and sometimes are out of consciousness. The resulting skeletal motor patterns, autonomic responses, and endocrine responses determine the impact of emotions and stress reactions on the body.

> These changes—the more rapid pulse, the deeper breathing, the increase of sugar in the blood, the secretion from the adrenal glands—were very diverse and seemed unrelated. Then, one wakeful night, after a considerable collection of these changes had been disclosed, the idea flashed through my mind that they could be nicely integrated if conceived as bodily preparations for supreme effort in flight or in fighting.
>
> WALTER B. CANNON

and orient attention to meaningful stimuli (dopamine), and regulate long-term moods (serotonin). In particular, the noradrenergic fibers interact with a widespread system of neurons that use corticotropin releasing factor (CRF) as a peptide neurotransmitter, and these are considered responsible for the well-coordinated fight-or-flight response.

Of central importance in the stress response is the release of high levels of **glucocorticoid** *hormones during negative emotional states that accompany events that cause fear, anxiety, and anger.* CRF neurosecretory cells of the paraventricular nucleus are responsive to amygdalar outputs and are responsible for activating the hypothalamic-pituitary-adrenocortical core of the stress response. Cortisol is capable of acting on all bodily tissues, and it is a crucial regulator of the stress response at the level of the brain. Cortisol acts on glucocorticoid receptors found in high numbers in the paraventricular nucleus, parahippocampal gyrus, amygdala, and medial and orbital prefrontal cortex. These areas are all associated with evaluating inputs and generating emotional and stress responses. Feedback by cortisol to these areas is accordingly crucial in shaping responses to stress. Cortisol feedback generally reduces activity in areas supplied by glucocorticoid receptors. A notable exception is the amygdala, where stress levels of cortisol act to increase levels of reactivity, acutely and chronically. High levels of cortisol at the central nucleus of the amygdala also cause activation of CRF neurons located in widespread areas of the prefrontal cortex, limbic system, and brainstem. These **positive feedback effects** of cortisol on the amygdala and then on the CRF system are considered to be long lasting and illustrate an important consequence of stress exposure.

The model of psychological stress pioneered by Lazarus places primary importance on cognitive processes, but similar effects may occur without conscious awareness. Given the role of the amygdala in classical conditioning and the amygdala's connections to subcortical structures, some effects of amygdalar activation may occur out of consciousness and may be difficult to regulate intentionally. These activities may therefore underlie symptoms such as anxiety and fear that seem to have few obvious antecedents and are difficult for the patient to control. As noted, a key consideration in thinking about the effects of stress on the brain is that *it is irrelevant whether autonomic activation or a high level of cortisol secretion occurs in response to a physical stressor or a psychological stressor. The effects are the same.*

STRESS RESPONSES, BIASING OF PHYSIOLOGICAL OUTPUT SYSTEMS, AND ILLNESS

Stress responses engage brain mechanisms that are associated with learning via the amygdala and hippocampus. These learning processes mean that stress responses can alter brain function throughout life. Two brief examples illustrate this process.

The first concerns brain mechanisms controlling stress responses that are modified by early experience in rat pups and in humans. Work by Michael Meany and others shows that some rat mothers are naturally highly nurturing to their young and will frequently lick and groom them. Highly nurtured pups grow into adults that display a nonanxious behavioral temperament and are rapidly able to dampen stress responses. Meany's work shows that licking and grooming causes the pups to have high levels of serotonin released in their central nervous systems. When this stimulation occurs early in life, the serotonin causes promoter regions of the glucocorticoid receptor gene to be demethylated, allowing those genes to be easily turned on. This **epigenetic** alteration to the DNA facilitates the production of glucocorticoid receptors throughout the rat's life. In contrast, animals reared by naturally

neglectful mothers produce lower numbers of central glucocorticoid receptors during their lives. The two sets of animals differ in response to future anxiety-provoking challenges, with the nurtured animals rapidly regulating response to stress and the neglected ones remaining more readily activated by stress provoking stimuli. The effect of experience and maternal nurturing on the developing pups is not genetically inherited. Instead it results from the tactile stimulation provided by the mother.

Another example of early life experience influencing long-term outcome is seen in work with humans exposed to common early life stressors, such as separation from a parent or physical abuse. A cohort of adults born in New Zealand has been under continuous study since the 1970s, when these individuals were 3 years old, and early life events are now being examined in relation to genetic characteristics and life outcomes. One aspect of this study found that persons with a particular variant allele of the serotonin transporter gene are vulnerable to negative consequences of early life stress and were more likely to have significant clinical depression as young adults. In another study from this same cohort, persons with a particular allele of the gene for monoamine oxidase were shown to be prone to antisocial behavior and violence as young adults, but only if maltreated as children.

These examples from animals and humans illustrate the long-term consequences of early stress exposure, and *they highlight the potential importance of genetically conferred vulnerabilities to the effects of stress.* It should be noted that at least some of the stressors in question were psychological in nature, such as early loss of a parent.

Chronic or numerous stressors over time that repeatedly challenge the body appear to be associated with physiological changes. **Allostatic load** is the term used to refer to the physiological wear and tear on the body that results from ongoing adaptive efforts to maintain stability (homeostasis) in response to both physical and psychological stressors. This adaptive cost is measured using quantitative assessments of endocrine, immune, autonomic, and brain systems such as hippocampal volume, salivary cortisol, vagal tone, and the number and activity of specific white blood cells.

The long-term effects of stress and the lingering effects of stressful experiences on future stress reactivity provide a background for examining a selection of medical conditions the severity of which may be affected by stress. The material below is a partial list of medical and psychiatric conditions that are known to interact with stress.

CARDIOVASCULAR DISORDERS

Episodes of acute stress can precipitate sudden death in vulnerable individuals, and chronic stress can enhance progression of atherosclerosis and hypertension. Regardless of environmental causes, studies show persons with large cardiovascular reactions to standardized stressors in the laboratory are at *an increased risk of future atherosclerosis, myocardial hypertrophy, and hypertension*. However, there is little evidence from animal or human research to suggest that stress alone can cause cardiovascular disorders.

In the case of sudden death, underlying rhythm disturbances or advanced atherosclerosis can leave affected persons vulnerable to the physiological effects of severe stress, including autonomic responses and high levels of circulating epinephrine. A well-documented example is seen in several reports of increased sudden death following catastrophic events such as earthquakes. *In the 1994 Los Angeles earthquake, most deaths on that day were not due to physical trauma, but rather to sudden cardiac death*, with mortality rates reaching five times the normal rate. In England, hospital admissions for myocardial infarction were significantly above normal for three days following a national team loss in World Cup soccer. Other surveys of stressful events preceding sudden death indicate significant episodes of extreme anger and emotional agitation involving family conflicts, confrontation with an intruder, or returning home to find one's home burglarized and in disarray. In all such cases, preclinical or clinically recognized disease is strongly suspected.

In other instances, chronic exposure to a crowded and potentially stressful environment may contribute to elevated death rates for the population, as seen in high rates of death in New York City relative to other areas. Similarly, persons identified as having a hostile temperament and followed for health outcomes in epidemiological studies have been repeatedly shown to have high death rates due to cardiovascular causes and to all-cause mortality.

Emotional distress may be a cause of changed clinical status in patients with previously well-managed hypertension. Hypertension incidence and progression is known to be greater in persons with apparent genetic vulnerability to hypertension, as seen in follow-up studies in persons with moderately elevated resting pressures (e.g., 125–135/78–85 mmHg), or in those who have large rises in blood pressure in response to moderate stress in the laboratory. Again, the stress response does not appear to be causal, but in these instances *the large responses associated with physiological factors or a hostile disposition appear to highlight underlying vulnerability*.

WOUND HEALING AND SURGICAL RECOVERY

Psychological stress can slow wound healing and recovery from surgery. In 1995, a landmark paper demonstrated a relationship between psychological stress and slowed wound healing. Older women in a study of life-stress exposure were given a simple punch biopsy of their forearm skin and were then followed to assess the speed at which their wound healed. Healing was defined as a lack of foaming after hydrogen peroxide was applied to the wound site. Women undergoing the stress of caring for a husband with Alzheimer's disease required 25% longer to fully heal their skin lesions relative to unstressed controls. Related work shows substantial stress-related increases in time for soft palate healing to occur following oral surgery. Other work shows that psychological responses to surgery, such as anxiety, can influence all facets of surgical recovery, including the need for pain medication, length of hospitalization, speed of recovery, and patient satisfaction.

GASTROINTESTINAL DISORDERS

High levels of stress and associated anxiety may cause or aggravate several categories of gastrointestinal disorders. Stress may be implicated in cases of otherwise unexplained diarrhea, or aggravation of symptoms of irritable bowel syndrome, and increases in pain due to peptic ulcer. *Studies of women with irritable bowel syndrome (IBS) find that approximately 70% have a history of prior sexual or physical abuse*. Work using animal models shows that helplessness during exposure to traumatic stress exposure is related to subsequently increased sensitivity to visceral pain stimuli. This increased pain sensitivity appears to be caused by high levels of activation in the limbic system and in the amygdala in particular. Autonomic output accompanying pain may alter bowel function and lead to increased stomach acid secretion. Acute physical or psychological stress may exacerbate the symptoms of IBS, but is neither necessary nor sufficient to cause IBS.

Early adverse life events, such as childhood traumatic events or abuse, are associated with poorer outcomes and higher levels of distress in adult patients with IBS. The mechanism is believed to be persistent changes in the central stress response systems, including the hypothalamic-pituitary-adrenal (HPA) axis. Hyperreactivity of the HPA axis to a visceral sensation has been demonstrated in adults with a history of childhood trauma.

PAIN

Pain can influence emotions and cognition; cognitive processes, in turn, can increase or reduce sensations of pain. These reciprocal relationships among pain, emotion, and cognition are mediated by the same brain structures responsible for psychological stress responses. Acute and chronic pain can increase stress reactivity in patients. Recent animal studies show that ascending nociceptive signals engage the amygdala and the orbital prefrontal cortex, resulting in the activation of CRF fibers in these regions. This activation of the brain's central stress system increases the reactivity of the amygdala and interferes with activity of the medial prefrontal cortex. For example, humans with chronic arthritis pain have higher levels of activation in the amygdala and reduced function in the medial prefrontal cortex as seen in neuroimaging. Therefore, chronic pain increases the sensitivity of the amygdala to sensory stimulation and reduces the ability of patients to exercise cognitive control over their pain.

Stress can also exacerbate pain. The occurrence of negative emotional responses along with ascending pain sensations can cause long-term enhancement of amygdala reactivity. In turn, activation of CRF fibers causes enhanced responses to stressor exposure in general. This pain-enhanced activation of the stress system and its effects in the prefrontal cortex has cognitive consequences. Patients suffering chronic neuromuscular pain show 5–10% reductions in gray matter volume in the temporal lobe and prefrontal cortex on structural MRI examination. In such patients, decision-making tasks show a shift toward a preference for immediate, small rewards over delayed, larger ones—a pattern similar to that seen in substance abuse. *Pain changes emotional reactions to the environment, alters cognition, and changes the reward value of environmental events*, rendering the patient vulnerable to future stress exposure and increasing the risk of anxiety and depression.

> Stress is not necessarily bad for you: it is also the spice of life, for any emotion, any activity, causes stress.
>
> HANS SELYE
> *The Spice of Life*

IMMUNE SYSTEM DYSFUNCTION

The full topic of stress and its effects on the immune system is beyond the scope of this chapter. However, several research findings of reduced immune system function in persons under stress are relevant and deserve brief mention. Stress is known to reduce the ability of the immune system to respond adequately to the administration of influenza and hepatitis vaccines. A mechanism underlying this appears to be high levels of sympathetic nervous system activation and elevated levels of cortisol. In laboratory tests, persons with large sympathetic and cortisol responses to acute stress exposure also had the poorest responses to hepatitis B vaccine. *Life stress is shown to increase the reactivation of latent viruses*. In several studies, medical students were studied during examination periods to note the effect of stress on immune system function. In these studies, immune system impairments are seen in two ways: In one research model, circulating antibodies to latent viruses, such as herpes or Epstein-Barr, indicate that these normally latent viruses had been activated recently. Students reporting the highest levels of perceived life stress were indeed found to have the highest antibody titers. In both herpes and Epstein-Barr, latency of the viruses is maintained by immune system surveillance, and apparent reductions in surveillance associated with high levels of cortisol appears to result in reactivation of virus and recruitment of an antibody response. In a related experimental model, immune system suppression during stress is documented by a failure of the person to develop a normal immunity following vaccination against hepatitis B. Again, persons undergoing the greatest levels of stress usually produce less immunity to the virus. Therefore, although stress can interact with immune system function in various ways, there is good evidence that naturally occurring stressors can impair the body's ability to keep latent viruses at bay and mount a successful immunity to vaccination.

ASTHMA

Asthma has long been viewed as a "psychosomatic" illness, one that was clearly exacerbated by stress. Today we know more about the mechanism by which this happens. The airway inflammation and hyperresponsiveness of asthma can be worsened by cholinergic activation, which can be initiated by sadness. Airway inflammation has been found to correlate with measures of psychological distress in people with asthma. A family history of affective disorders has been associated with increased morbidity and mortality in children with asthma. Major depressive disorder appears to be a risk factor for some diseases like asthma which involve chronic inflammation and pain as well as autonomic reactivity. Substance P has been proposed as the mediator between chronic inflammation and mood states.

POSTTRAUMATIC STRESS DISORDER

Posttraumatic stress disorder (PTSD) is a persistent set of symptoms that stem from exposure to events that posed a threat to life or body integrity, resulting in emotional responses of extreme fear, horror, or helplessness. Events such as exposure to combat, rape, sexual abuse, and physical abuse will result in PTSD in some people but not in others. Symptoms of PTSD include persistent, intrusive recall of the original event, often accompanied by the experience of vividly reliving the event during wakefulness.

These "flashbacks" may be triggered by cues (sights, sounds, smells) associated with the event and may lead people with PTSD to avoid such reminders. Sufferers may experience frequent periods of hyperarousal (jitteriness, increased startle reflex) associated with high levels of sympathetic nervous outflow. Persons with PTSD may have difficulty evaluating danger in situations, resulting in social isolation and avoidance—or in risk-taking and impulsive behaviors. These individuals are at high risk of substance use disorders, depression, and panic attacks. As might be expected from what has been discussed about stress responses, people with PTSD often have trouble concentrating and are at greater risk for gastrointestinal pain disorders. A decrease in hippocampal volume has also been seen in both adults and children with PTSD and elevated cortisol.

GENERALIZED ANXIETY DISORDER AND PANIC DISORDER

Generalized anxiety disorder (GAD) is a persistent feeling of anxiety and worry associated with a range of normal, impending life events or activities in the person's life, such as financial challenges or job responsibilities, and is not associated with prior traumatic exposure as occurs in PTSD. *GAD is not a reaction to stress, but is an exaggerated response to the threats of usual life events, and a perception of normally innocuous events as highly stressful.* GAD is a risk factor for depression, substance use disorders, and poorly defined physical disorders such as muscular pain, headache, and irritable bowel syndrome.

DRUG AND ALCOHOL ABUSE, PATHOLOGICAL GAMBLING, AND EATING DISORDERS

The experience of stress leads to a tendency to engage in a number of behaviors that may impair health. These include increased consumption of alcohol, nicotine, caffeine, and fatty, salty, or sweet foods, as well as choosing to engage in risky activities. *A growing body of evidence in animals and humans suggests that the release of dopamine in the nucleus accumbens, sometimes referred to as the brain's "pleasure center," is a common denominator of all these activities.* This may be the mechanism by which enhanced feelings of well-being (euphoria) counteract the dysphoria accompanying exposure to stress. The reduced dysphoria and increased euphoria accompanying all of these behaviors then activates the brain's reward circuitry, increasing the likelihood of such behaviors in the future. The individual becomes "addicted" (although not necessarily physiologically dependent) on repetitions of these behaviors, resulting in a variety of health consequences.

HIPPOCAMPAL FUNCTION AND MEMORY

The effect of stress on the hippocampus and memory function has received much attention. As noted above, the hippocampus is essential for laying down new declarative memories and for activating stored memories during the process of recall. Systemic cortisol feeds back to the dentate gyrus of the hippocampus, where it exerts negative feedback on subsequent cortisol secretion by acting through hippocampal outputs to the hypothalamic PVN. To function normally, the hippocampus continually produces new precursor cells in the dentate gyrus, which in turn migrate to portions of the hippocampus where they mature into cells that generate the long-term potentiation of new synaptic connections needed for establishing memories. Stress levels of cortisol have two undesirable consequences on hippocampal function.

Work in rats shows that *exposure of the dentate gyrus to high levels of corticosterone reduces production of the precursor cells and renders their mature counterparts vulnerable to cell death (apoptosis).* In addition, loss of dentate gyrus cells impairs negative feedback leading to progressively higher levels of cortisol. In aging humans, high levels of circulating cortisol are associated with poorer declarative memory retrieval and with reduced hippocampal volumes.

INTERVENTIONS

On the basis of the relationships between stress and illness described above, stress reduction interventions are being developed and tested. Relaxation response training over a period of 8 weeks has been found to be four times as successful as lifestyle modification training in reducing diastolic blood pressure enough to eliminate the need for medication in some adults with hypertension. Experimental evidence suggests that even a brief psychological intervention to increase coping and a sense of control can reduce the cortisol response to a pharmacological HPA axis activator. Biofeedback has also been found to be effective in giving children and adults an added sense of control and decreased stress response, resulting in fewer headaches, less GI distress, and lower blood pressure. Mindfulness meditation is another successful intervention for reduction of the physiological stress response and the associated health problems.

SUMMARY

The field of stress and health is complex and a rapidly growing one. As medicine becomes more sophisticated in the identification of genetic vulnerabilities, it is increasingly important to intervene so as to prevent disabling or life-threatening illnesses related to stress.

CASE STUDY

Situation: Steve, a 42-year-old businessman, has always been a runner. He has been competing in marathons since he was in college. About 6 months ago he had an episode of extreme back pain while running, which left him writhing on the ground. Many tests later he was told that he had a herniated disc, but that it would be better to try to avoid surgery. He was advised to stop running. He now states that he is constantly afraid that the pain will start again. His back hurts whenever he gets anxious, such as when he is up against a deadline, or has a conflict with a coworker. Recent financial problems at his business have worried him, with ensuing exacerbation of his back pain. Although there is no evidence of any new damage, his pain has at times been bad enough that he could not get out of bed. His wife is losing patience with him, and he is now afraid he may lose his job. He misses the alone time and opportunity to think that running offered him. He is aware that his body feels more stiff and tense than when he was running regularly.

Discussion: Steve has an underlying structural medical problem and has experienced the major physiological and psychological stressor of acute and severe pain. He also has a number of other psychological stressors, at home and at work. Meanwhile, he has lost his major coping strategy for dealing with physical and psychological stressors. He needs to learn some new coping strategies to reduce the physiological stress response that is leading to his disabling pain.

Follow-up: Over a period of months, Steve tries out several stress-reduction techniques. He finds writing and meditation are the most comfortable and effective for him. His wife is more supportive as she understands how his anxiety translates into arousal of his autonomic and endocrine systems, and then into the muscle tension and inflammation that result in pain.

SUGGESTED READINGS

Lovallo, W.R. (2005). *Stress and health: Biological and psychological interactions* (2nd ed.). Thousand Oaks, CA: Sage.
  This book provides an overview of the biology and research in the burgeoning area of stress and health, providing more detail on each of the areas addressed in this chapter.

Uhart, M., & Wand, G.S. (2009). Stress, alcohol, and drug interaction: An update of human research. *Addiction Biology, 14*, 43–64.
  This recent review examines the research on the complex interactions between traumatic exposure, chronic stress, and use or abuse of alcohol and drugs.

Weaver, I.C., Cervoni, N., Champagne, F.A., D'Alessio, A.C., Sharma, S., Seckl, J.R., et al. (2004). Epigenetic programming by material behavior. *Nature Neuroscience, 7*, 847–854.
  A concise review of work showing the influence of early experience on brain regulation of stress reactivity.

9 Addictive Disorders

Timothy W. Fong

"Why can't they just stop?" That is the fundamental question asked by physicians, families, patients and anyone else whose life has been touched by someone with an addiction. *Each year, abuse of drugs, alcohol, tobacco and behavioral addictions claim over 540,000 lives and cost American society nearly $500 billion in combined medical, economic, criminal and social costs.*

People from all age groups and classes of society suffer from addictive disorders. Infants and children exposed to drugs of abuse are at risk for cognitive and psychological developmental problems. Teenagers who are addicted to drugs and alcohol do poorly in school, commit crimes and act impulsively, resulting in unwanted pregnancies and behavioral problems. Adults impaired by addictive disorders struggle with employment and social functioning, and often develop medical problems such as HIV/AIDS, hepatitis and other preventable medical problems. One of the emerging populations where addiction is occurring is in the elderly, who are susceptible to memory impairment, falls, accidents and health problems related to years of abuse. Even though addiction touches an enormous number of individuals and families, one of the prevailing explanations over the past 50 years has been that addicts are morally weak, greedy, or lazy. *Research over the last 20 years has challenged this belief by characterizing the biological basis for addictive disorders and using the medical model to explain such seemingly irrational behaviors.*

Despite this, training on how to screen, diagnosis and manage addictive disorders is often neglected during medical training. This is due in part to the limited number of specialists and researchers in addiction but also results from long-standing beliefs that addiction can only be treated by 12-step self help groups or when the patient has hit "rock bottom." Addiction psychiatry and addiction medicine are new subspecialties of medicine, and as these fields mature, there will be a substantial increase in the number of qualified and trained professionals. Since 2000, there has been a significant increase in the number of FDA-approved medications for substance abuse disorders, along with a rapidly growing database of evidenced-based psychosocial treatments. The end result is that *there are now effective treatments for all addictive disorders.* These treatments are available and will work if patients commit to follow treatment recommendations. When used properly, outcomes from these treatments of addictive disorders will equal or surpass treatment outcomes for other medical disorders.

DEFINITIONS AND TERMS

The origins of the term "addiction" suggest it means "surrendering one's legal rights to another." However, since the mid 1950s, the term has been used to refer to people who fail to control their drug or alcohol use. As currently conceptualized, there is no universal, scientific definition for addiction. Addiction is a broad concept that has many different components, including tolerance, withdrawal, compulsive use, urges and loss of control. *A working definition of addiction that has been posited by researchers and clinicians in the field is a "chronic, relapsing brain disease characterized by compulsive behavior in spite of harmful consequences."*

This definition highlights much of the work that has been done in research and clinical fields to increase the understanding of addictive behavior. "Chronic and relapsing" suggests that this condition comes and goes, waxes and wanes, much like other chronic medical illnesses such as diabetes, hypertension and asthma. Furthermore, it suggests that addiction is not curable but, rather, controllable. In one of the most influential articles in this field, Thomas McClellan recommends that clinicians and researchers view addiction as a chronic medical illness that has similar outcomes to other medical illnesses. By viewing addictions in this way, the false expectation that addicts can just stop once they are sufficiently motivated or in the right circumstance starts to fade. The negative energy generated by a relapse can now be replaced with an emphasis on keeping relapses to a minimum and on restoring functioning as soon as possible. *It is no more reasonable or effective to shame someone with an addiction for relapsing than it is to scold a diabetic for not taking insulin or to chastise a patient with high blood pressure for not making lifestyle changes.*

The second part of the definition is the concept of addiction as a "brain disease." This idea became popular during the mid 1990s and was promoted by the National Institute for Drug Abuse (NIDA); it resulted from research that highlighted genetic predispositions for addiction and the neuroanatomical regions involved in drug abuse. Loss of functioning in specific areas of the brain (in this case the limbic system and frontal lobes) appeared to create symptoms which were consistent and could be replicated. Much has been written about how drugs of abuse can damage, sometimes permanently, a wide range of brain tissues and neural networks. It makes sense that *as drug use progresses, the increased brain damage or scarring makes it more difficult for addicts to stop using.* A clinical example of this is can be seen in methamphetamine patients who present with obvious impairment in attention, memory and language skills. These cognitive problems make it more difficult for them to attend and sit still in group sessions, making treatment less effective.

The idea of addiction as a brain disease represents a significant cultural shift, medicalizing a behavior and an entire patient population previously not addressed by the medical community. As recently as the early 1990s, addictive behaviors were thought to be an issue of morality, willpower and conscious choice. Psychiatric perspectives of addiction explained it as unresolved psychological conflicts centered on avoidance of life's responsibilities or as a by-product of antisocial traits. The shift to viewing addiction as a brain disease was a direct result of work done in the research lab, using animal models and neuroimaging. *Researchers now believe that a combination of genetic vulnerabilities and direct toxicities of compulsive drug use fundamentally change brain structure and functioning.* Much as heart disease develops as a result of years of poor nutrition, lack of exercise and physical and emotional stress, the brain disease of addiction develops from ongoing and continued exposure to drugs and alcohol. The end result is interruption and disruption of normal bodily functioning – in this case, those regions of the brain responsible for balancing pleasure-seeking, rewarding behaviors and self-control are affected. Once those areas are destroyed or damaged, the disease of addiction will show itself, consistently and predictably.

This concept of addiction as a brain disease leads naturally into the third element of the definition of addiction, which focuses on "compulsive behavior despite harmful consequences." *This loss of control over rewarding behaviors is one of the true hallmarks of addiction – persistent and repetitive participation in an activity that brings continued harm to one's life.* Even though surrounding signs and problems in one's life scream "stop," those with addictive disorders persist in their maladaptive behavior. Recent re-

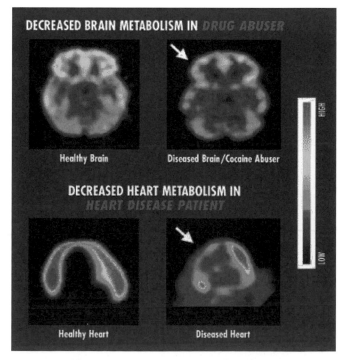

FIGURE 9.1 Addiction as a Brain Disease. From the Laboratory of Dr. Nora Volkow and H. Schelbert (www.nida.nih.gov). Addiction is similar to other diseases, such as heart disease. Both disrupt the normal, healthy functioning of the underlying organ, have serious harmful consequences, are preventable, treatable, and if left untreated, can last a lifetime.

Drunkenness is temporary suicide: the happiness that it brings is merely negative, a momentary cessation of unhappiness.

BERTRAND RUSSELL

search in neuroscience suggests that the biological centers in the brain responsible for this control are the frontal lobes, especially the orbitofrontal cortices. When damaged, these metaphorical "brakes" in the brain are worn down, leading to ongoing engagement in primal and appetitive urges for pleasure (see Figure 9.1).

ADDICTION IN THE DSM

In the first (1952) and second (1968) versions of the American Psychiatric Association's *Diagnostic and Statistical Manual* (DSM), alcoholism was classified as a personality

---

TABLE 9.1 DSM-IV Criteria for Substance Abuse

A. A maladaptive pattern of substance use leading to clinically significant impairment or distress, as manifested by one (or more) of the following, occurring within a 12-month period:

(1) Recurrent substance use resulting in a failure to fulfill major role obligations at work, school, or home (e.g., repeated absences or poor work performance related to substance use; substance-related absences, suspensions, or expulsions from school; neglect of children or household);

(2) Recurrent substance use in situations in which it is physically hazardous (e.g., driving an automobile or operating a machine when impaired by substance use);

(3) Recurrent substance-related legal problems (e.g., arrests for substance-related disorderly conduct);

(4) Continued substance use despite having persistent or recurrent social or interpersonal problems caused or exacerbated by the effects of the substance (e.g., arguments with spouse about consequences of intoxication, physical fights).

B. The symptoms have never met the criteria for Substance Dependence for this class of substance.

---

disorder. The third DSM introduced scientific criteria for substance abuse and dependence, which were expanded in the fourth version, the currently used DSM-IV. However, the DSM-IV does not list any formal criteria for the term addiction. Instead, substance-related disorders exist as the larger parent condition, divided up into substance-induced disorders (comprised of substance intoxication, substance withdrawal, substance induced mood disorders, etc) and substance use disorders (comprised of substance abuse and substance dependence). The DSM describes substance-specific features for eleven classes of drugs including alcohol, amphetamines, caffeine, cannabis, cocaine, hallucinogens, inhalants, nicotine, phencyclidine (PCP), sedative-hypnotics/anxiolytics and other/unknown.

In the DSM-IV, substance abuse and substance dependence are two distinct and separate diagnoses (see Tables 9.1 and 9.2). *Substance abuse is characterized by recurrent, maladaptive patterns of drug or alcohol-taking behavior that results in harmful external consequences*, such as hazardous situations or failing to fulfill role obligations. In contrast, *substance dependence lists seven separate criteria that result as a byproduct of continued, ongoing drug or alcohol use, including pharmacological adaptations such as tolerance and withdrawal*.

DISTINGUISHING BETWEEN SUBSTANCE ABUSE AND DEPENDENCE

Substance abuse can be thought of as a precursor to substance dependence, but it is important to recognize that the two conditions are not the same. For instance, all of the medications currently approved are indicated for treatment of substance dependence, not abuse. Secondly, a diagnosis of substance abuse does not require the pharmacological/physiological adaptations that most people think of as a part of addiction. The term addiction, as used by most clinicians and researchers, is generally synonymous with substance dependence.

TABLE 9.2 DSM-IV Criteria for Substance Dependence

A maladaptive pattern of substance use, leading to clinically significant impairment or distress, as manifested by three (or more) of the following, occurring at any time in the same 12-month period:

(1) Tolerance, as defined by either of the following:

    (a) a need for markedly increased amounts of the substance to achieve intoxication or desired effect; or

    (b) markedly diminished effect with continued use of the same amount of the substance.

(2) Withdrawal, as manifested by either of the following:

    (a) the characteristic withdrawal syndrome for the substance (refer to Criteria A and B of the criteria sets for Withdrawal from the specific substances); or

    (b) the same (or a closely related) substance is taken to relieve or avoid withdrawal symptoms.

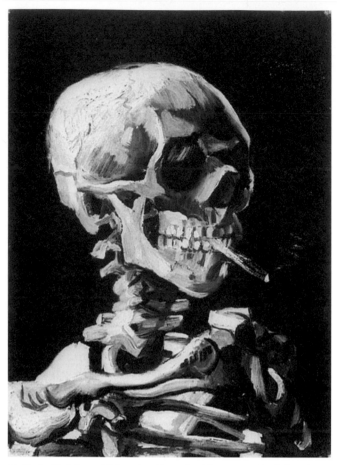

Skull of a Skeleton with Burning Cigarette *Vincent van Gogh (1886).* van Gogh Foundation Museum, Amsterdam. *The medical profession has played an important role in alerting the public to the addictive potential of nicotine and the lethality of tobacco.*

The DSM-V is currently being developed, and there is on-going debate as to what changes are likely in the classification of substance abuse related disorders. The term addiction may come to prominence with specific scientific criteria based on biomarkers. Additionally, some have argued for a dimensional rather than dichotomous approach to diagnosis. As it stands, if a patient meets only two out of the seven criteria for substance dependence, they are not considered to have the disorder. There are no defined subclinical or subsyndromal conditions. However, in clinical practice, it is often unclear if patients have or do not have this disease. The symptomatic person not meeting full criteria will still require ongoing treatment and monitoring.

Behavioral addictions such as gambling, compulsive sexual behaviors, video game addiction, compulsive shopping and Internet addiction are not listed in the DSM-IV section on substance-related disorders. Pathological gambling is listed under the section on impulse control disorders. The other behavioral addictions do not have any formal criteria listed in the DSM. This does not mean that they do not exist or that they are not real problems. Research is

beginning to uncover the behavioral and physiological processes that are similar or different between behavioral addictions and substance use disorders.

CLINICAL CHARACTERISTICS AND NATURAL COURSE OF ADDICTION

Addiction is a disease of the young. *The majority of those who develop an addictive disorder start using or engaging in the addictive behavior before the age of 21* (see Figure 9.2). The first step to developing an addiction is introduction and access. The earlier someone is exposed to drugs and alcohol, the more likely addictive substances will have a negative impact on brain development and the greater the likelihood of addiction. The time it takes to develop full criteria of substance dependence depends on a host of factors including frequency of use, number of life responsibilities, social context and financial support. Pharmacologically, tolerance and withdrawal from specific substances can occur within a few weeks of use. Lifelong consequences such as legal, financial or relationship harm can occur as a result of a single day of substance abuse.

As a general rule, *men appear to be more vulnerable to addictive disorders than women.* This is thought to be due to a combination of differences in help-seeking behaviors, genetics and gender roles played in society. The face of who becomes addicted is ever changing and diverse. Addictive disorders impact every ethnicity and culture, but in different ways. Some, such as Asian and Pacific Islander cultures, tend to bury the consequences within the family, creating further shame and stigma. Although lower socio-economic groups feel the harm of addictions more acutely, addictive disorders remain highly prevalent across all classes of society.

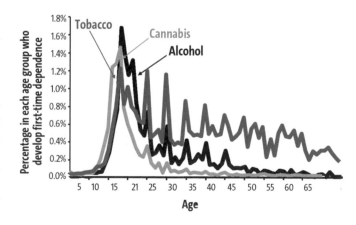

FIGURE 9.2 Addiction is a developmental disease that starts in adolescence and childhood: Age at tobacco, alcohol, and cannabis dependence per DSM-IV (source: *National Epidemiologic Survey on Alcohol and Related Conditions*, 2003.)

From an epidemiological perspective, addiction is a common disorder. Close to 13% of the adult population meet criteria for substance abuse or dependence in the last 12 months. One of the largest challenges in the field of addiction treatment is that most people never seek treatment, and it is estimated that only 10% of individuals who are addicted to substances ever seek treatment on their own. Little is known about the ability of those who are addicted to recover without treatment, but smoking cessation rates for unaided attempts at quitting are around 7% per year. There are many reasons for not seeking treatment including denial, lack of available treatment providers, lack of insurance, not believing treatment will work and not wanting to stop using. Some individuals are not even aware that their use or behavior is problematic, believing instead that continuing to use drugs is the solution, not the problem.

The consequences of this are enormous. *Patients with addiction have much shorter life spans compared to the general population.* The cause of death is not usually acute overdose but rather long-term health consequences such as heart disease, cirrhosis, dementia or infectious diseases.

ETIOLOGICAL FACTORS

Both genetic and environmental factors play a role in the development and expression of addictive disorders. Exactly how these factors intertwine with one another is just beginning to be worked out, but there has been some remarkable progress in this area. For instance, research has shown that individuals with a specific genotype for a serotonin transporter gene who are born into high stress environments (i.e., suffer more adverse life events) are more vulnerable to developing psychopathology than those individuals born with a different allele who were raised in the same environment.

Genetics

Although scientists still debate the presence of an "addiction" gene, *twin studies have clearly documented a genetic predisposition to the development of addictions.* What is more likely are that there are a number of genes that predispose to addictive behaviors. For instance, alcohol researchers have shown that those who are born with a predisposition to be low responders to alcohol (i.e., those who require more drinks to feel an effect) are at higher risk to develop alcohol dependence. Genetic changes in dopamine, catecholamine synthesis, and serotonin have been shown to be altered in patients with addictive disorders, all indicating a neurochemical link. However, the biology of addiction is more complex than simply having too much or too little of any given neurotransmitter. Drugs of abuse

will also alter bioavailability and levels of these chemicals transiently and may leave a lasting effect. Another newer hypothesis involves the genetics of connexin, leading to alterations in frontal lobe formation that can impair executive functioning and impulse control.

Neuroanatomy

Evidence is accumulating to show that addictions affect similar brain regions. The fibers and centers associated with the ventral tegmental region of the brain stem and ending in the nucleus accumbens of the striatum and prefrontal cortex are known as the **mesolimbic and mesocortical pathways**. *Lesions in these pathways have been shown to block the rewarding behavioral effects of addictive drugs.* The primary neurotransmitter associated with these pathways is dopamine. This area, sometimes called the *"pleasure center" of the brain*, has been shown to influence attention, pleasure, euphoria, reinforcement salience, and motivation.

In addition to the areas that control reward and natural motivation for reinforcing behaviors, recent addiction research has highlighted dysfunction in the frontal lobes, primarily the **orbitofrontal cortex**. *This region is largely responsible for self-control, for weighing immediate versus future options and for, essentially, "putting on the brakes" of the brain.*

Individuals with impairments or dysfunction in these two regions of the brain are prone to developing addictions due to higher threshold for experiencing reward coupled with loss of self-control. Ongoing drug use and stress are likely to continue to weaken and perhaps scar these neural systems, further damaging already vulnerable areas in the brain. Neuroimaging data suggest methamphetamine damages these brain regions, perhaps permanently. Without these structures and fibers operating, the end result will be continued use and an inability to adapt and learn from past behaviors and mistakes.

Psychosocial Risk Factors

Alan Leshner, former director of the National Institute on Drug Abuse (NIDA), was fond of saying that *people use drugs for one of two reasons, to feel high or to feel normal.* The latter reason implies the presence of a psychiatric condition such as major depression, anxiety disorder or attention-deficit disorder. In fact, the *presence of a psychiatric disorder is one of the strongest risk factors for a co-occurring addictive disorder.* There are many different possibilities to explain this link, ranging from shared genetic risks to overlapping symptoms. Whatever the exact reason, it has been conclusively shown that psychiatric conditions are associated with an increased risk for developing addictive disor-

The Drinkers *(1890) Vincent van Gogh, Dutch, 1853–1890. Oil on canvas, 59.4 × 73.4 cm.* The Joseph Winterbotham Collection, 1953.178. Post-treatment. Photograph by Robert Hashimoto. © The Art Institute of Chicago. *Both genetics and modeling influence a child's future drinking habits.*

ders, and vice versa. For instance, those with severe mental illnesses, such as schizophrenia, have nearly three times the rate of nicotine dependence compared to the general population. People with bipolar disorder have nearly three times the rate of alcohol dependence as the general population. This increased risk is also true for people with personality disorders, an often overlooked group of psychiatric conditions seen in patients in the primary care sector. Antisocial personality disorder, characterized by a persisting pattern of the disregard for the rights to others, has been shown to be associated with much higher rates of all substance-related and behavioral addictions.

Family studies have shown that family members of those with addictive disorders are at eight-fold risk for having addictions themselves. This results from the influence of the environment as well as genetics. Other social factors that have been identified as directly influencing the risk of addictive disorders include peers that use, lower socioeconomic status, lack of structured activities and lower educational attainment.

RECENT TRENDS IN ADDICTIVE DISORDERS

Alcohol

Alcohol consumption remains a very common activity in America, and approximately 60% of the population have

had at least one drink in the last year. The average age of first consumption of alcohol in America is around 16 years of age, despite the national age limit of 21 for legal alcohol consumption. Alcohol's mechanism of action is complex and includes modulation of gamma-aminobutyric acid (GABA) receptors that produces sedative and anxiolytic effects. Other neurotransmitter systems, such as inhibition NMDA receptors and serotonergic and dopaminergic systems, are also directly affected, which explains why alcohol can be stimulating and sedating at the same time.

Epidemiological studies have put the percentage of the general population meeting criteria for alcohol use disorder at 9% (alcohol abuse 4%, alcohol dependence 5%). This means that *alcohol use disorders are as common as major depressive disorders.* This impact of alcohol related disorders on society is enormous; its influence is reflected in statistics on accidents, traumatic brain injuries, unintentional overdose, domestic violence and criminal behaviors.

Because of this enormous impact, screening for alcohol use is necessary during every patient visit. There are several common screening instruments that can be used by clinicians such as the Alcohol Use Disorders Identification Test (AUDIT) and the Michigan Alcohol Screening Test (MAST). On clinical interview, simply asking "do you drink?" is inadequate as it fails to illicit more information about drinking. *Open-ended questions such as "tell me about your drinking habits" or "how has drinking affected your life recently?" are more likely to begin a discussion about drinking.* The National Institute on Alcohol Abuse and Alcoholism (NIAAA) have established guidelines with upper limits of recommended drinks – no more than 7 standard drinks per week for women and no more than 14 standard drinks per week for men. Another way of phrasing this is a limit of no more than one standard drink per day for a woman and no more than two standard drinks per day for a man. Women metabolize alcohol less efficiently, and therefore they are more affected by a given amount of alcohol. It is important to remember the definition of a standard drink: a 12 oz beer, 8–9 oz of malt liquor, a 5 oz glass of wine or 1 ½ oz of hard liquor. Another helpful screening question is "during the last year, has there ever been an occasion where you had more than 5 drinks in a single day?" Answering "yes" indicates a risk of harmful drinking and a more detailed alcohol use history should be conducted. Exceeding the daily recommended amounts of alcohol does not make one an alcoholic, but it does indicate a pattern of risky drinking. Patients who drink excessively may minimize the amount consumed (or may not be able to accurately recall), signaling the importance of further in-depth examination of the impact of alcohol across life's domains.

Nicotine

In the 1960s, the general population rate of smoking in the United States was approximately 50%. Through years of public education, health regulations and other public health measures designed to curb tobacco use, *the national prevalence rate of smoking has fallen to approximately 20%.* In California, where there are much stricter clean air laws and population measures (e.g., no smoking in bars and restaurants, and separate taxes for cigarettes), the smoking rate is around 13%. *Tobacco and smoking-related illnesses cause the greatest harm of all the addictive substances and disorders.* Nearly 500,000 people die each year in the United States because of tobacco-related illnesses such as cancer, emphysema, and cardiovascular diseases. This harm comes not from the nicotine, but from the numerous chemicals and pyrogens released in the smoking process. Chewing tobacco does not allow the user to avoid health consequences, as this practice has been associated with increased risk for oral and throat cancers.

Nicotine, in and of itself, is a powerful reinforcing substance; animal studies have shown that intravenous nicotine is as powerful as intravenous cocaine, amphetamine or opiates. Nicotine binds to receptors located in many brain regions, including to the $\alpha4\beta2$ subunit in the nucleus accumbens, which can release dopamine. Because of its short half-life, nicotine withdrawal can be particularly vexing, inducing further use to diminish irritability and anxiety.

Screening for smoking should occur at every visit, as *studies have shown that even three minutes of counseling can double the quit rates of smokers.* Screening for smoking includes questions about the total number of cigarettes smoked per day and the number of years your patient has smoked. This will yield the quantities of packs per day and total pack years. One of the shortcomings with this screening tool is that it does not measure severity of the addiction to smoking. A simpler, more powerful screening question to assess for the presence of nicotine dependence is "from the time you wake up, how long does it take before you smoke your first cigarette?" If someone answers 10 minutes or less, this indicates severe nicotine dependence (because the person is waking up in nicotine withdrawal), and this signals the need for nicotine replacement therapy.

> There is in all men a demand for the superlative, so much so that the poor devil who has no other way of reaching it attains it by getting drunk.
>
> OLIVER WENDELL HOLMES, JR.

Opiates

Opioids are any substances that can bind to the body's opioid receptors in the brain, namely the mu, kappa and delta receptors. Opioid receptors are located in the brain and body and are responsible for pain, reward, mood and also automatic functions like respiration. Opiates are substances that are derived from naturally occurring opium; examples include morphine, heroin and codeine. *All opiates are opioids but not all opioids are opiates.*

The two primary forms of abusable opiates in America are heroin and prescription opiate pills. Heroin is derived from opium and the majority of the world's supply is grown, processed and distributed from Southeast Asia. Heroin can be injected, smoked, sniffed or popped into the skin. Once in the body, heroin binds quickly and tightly to the opioid receptors in the brain and body and begins to exert its effects.

After injecting heroin, users report feeling a euphoric rush accompanied by emotional numbness, heaviness of the arms and legs and a warm feeling in the stomach. Depending on the purity of heroin, the effects can last anywhere from one hour to six hours. As tolerance develops, users need heroin more frequently in order to stave off the effects of cravings and opiate withdrawal. Heroin users are at an extremely high risk for addiction – it is estimated that about 23 percent of individuals who use heroin become dependent on it. Heroin abuse is associated with serious health and psychiatric problems, most notable fatal overdose, HIV/AIDS and hepatitis. Chronic users often develop repeated skin infections, endocarditis, malnutrition and liver or kidney disease.

According to the National Survey on Drug Use and Health, the number of people over the age of 12 who used heroin for the first time in the United States in 2008 was 114,000. This was not a significant decrease from the number in 2007, of 117,000. The average age at first use was 23.4 years. The number of people in the United States who had used heroin in the past twelve months was 453,000 in 2008, from 2007 (366,000) but lower than the 560,000 in 2006, which was a 10 year high.

Marijuana (Cannabis Sativa)

The use of marijuana continues to be a common practice, especially with adolescents. According to national surveys, marijuana is now the second most popular drug of abuse (prescription pill abuse is number one), according to national estimates. Nearly 30% of high school seniors over the last year have used marijuana. Many communities and towns across America report that marijuana is very easy to obtain and may be more accessible than alcohol. Marijuana's psychoactive effects come from binding of Δ^9-tetrahydrocannabinol (commonly abbreviated as THC) to brain cannabanoid receptors.

The highest density of cannabinoid receptors are located throughout the brain in a wide number of regions that influence pleasure, memory, thoughts, concentration, sensation, time perception, and coordinated movement. In addition to THC, there are at least 65 other psychoactive compounds derived from marijuana, which explains in part why there are so many different varieties of marijuana.

Historically, there has been a debate about the existence of a marijuana withdrawal syndrome. Recent research has now shown that this syndrome does occur and that it is similar to nicotine withdrawal. It is characterized by anxiety, irritability, craving, flu-like symptoms and insomnia. Proponents of legalizing marijuana point to its anxiolytic, analgesic and calming effects. However, research has found that marijuana's adverse effect on learning and memory abilities can last for days or even weeks. Additional research on the long-term effects of marijuana abuse documents changes in the brain similar to those seen after long-term abuse of other major drugs. Long-term use of marijuana has been shown to affect cognitive performance and functioning as well as influence mood disorders and psychoses.

One recent development in the availability and rise in popularity of marijuana has been in the form of medical marijuana. In California, medical marijuana was made legally available by a voter proposition in 1996. The intent of this initiative was to exempt patients and defined caregivers who possess or cultivate marijuana for medical treatment from legal sanctions. Physicians who prescribe medical marijuana, with a good faith examination, will not be prosecuted nor will they lose their medical licenses. Since its inception, tensions between state and federal agencies flared over the operations of these clinics and cooperatives. However, California has continued to operate medical marijuana clinics, thereby increasing the accessibility of marijuana throughout the state.

The THC content of most marijuana grown today is 9–10%, approximately twice the THC content of marijuana in the 1960s (4–5%). The end result of this increase in potency translates to an increased risk for adverse effects such as psychosis, mood symptoms, dependence, and impaired neurocognitive skills.

Marijuana has been considered by many to be a gateway drug, meaning that initiation of marijuana use will lead directly to use of other, more serious illicit drugs. However, research has failed to demonstrate this conclusively. More than likely, *marijuana use is a symbol of a constellation of conditions that promote ongoing drug taking behavior*. Risk factors such as peers using drugs, antisocial traits and family history of drug addiction tend to be much more important contributors to likelihood of drug use.

Prescription Pills (Sedative-Hypnotics, Stimulants, Opiates)

Prescription drugs that are misused, abused or used for nonmedical reasons can lead to dependence and harm. Commonly abused classes of prescription drugs include opioids, and central nervous system depressants such as benzodiazepines and stimulants. Approximately 52 million people (ages 12 and older) in the United States had used psychoactive prescription drugs for nonmedical reasons in their lifetimes according to the 2008 National Survey on Drug Use and Health. This represents almost 21 percent of the U. S. population.

Inappropriate use of prescription pills can be categorized as misuse, abuse or dependence. The term *misuse is defined as purposely ingesting prescribed medications without a prescription*. The terms abuse and dependence apply to prescription drugs with the same criteria as other drugs of abuse. Patients obtain prescription drugs from a variety of sources, principally their physicians. Training in the recognition of pain as the fifth vital sign and the emergence of a variety of narcotic formulations have given physicians a wide number of options to prescribe opiates. Furthermore, many of these medications are inexpensive, come in generic forms, and are covered by insurance plans without the need for further authorization. Patients can also order medications through the Internet, an activity that is not regulated and prone to unscrupulous business practices.

Because of widespread availability and ease of access, it is not uncommon to have addicted patients state that their primary source of prescription pills are one or two physicians. This can occur due to lax prescribing practices such as authorizing multiple refills at one time or authorizing refills without a face-to-face evaluation. Physicians should not only educate patients about the addictive risks of medications, but should remind patients to be mindful of where these medications are being stored. Providers should note any rapid increases in the amount of a medication needed or frequent requests for refills before the quantity prescribed should have been finished, as these may be indicators of abuse.

Stimulants

The primary forms of abused illicit stimulants in the United States today remain cocaine and methamphetamine. An estimated 1.9 million Americans were current (past month) users of cocaine in 2008 (0.7% of the population) while another 314,000 Americans were current (past month) users of methamphetamine (0.1 percent of the population). Approximately 0.4% of people between the ages of 12 and 17 were current (last month) cocaine users in 2008. and 0.1 were current users of methamphetamine.

Psychoactive signs and symptoms are similar for all stimulants, including increased wakefulness, increased physical activity, decreased appetite, increased respiration, rapid heart rate, irregular heartbeat, increased blood pressure, and hyperthermia. In spite of this, cocaine and methamphetamine do not have identical effects.

Cocaine is derived from the coca plant and is ingested by smoking (crack), injection or snorting (powder cocaine). Cocaine acts to increase dopamine by blocking dopamine reuptake transporters, thereby keeping more dopamine available. The half-life of cocaine is very quick, less than 20–30 minutes and the psychoactive effects may be much shorter than that. Physical signs of intoxication include dilated pupils, elevated heart rate and blood pressure, emotional intensity, hyperactivity and euphoria.

In contrast, methamphetamine is a synthetic drug manufactured from a variety of precursor elements, including nasal decongestants and over-the-counter products. Like cocaine, methamphetamine can be smoked, snorted or injected. *The psychoactive effects of methamphetamine tend to last much longer, as the half-life of this drug can be as long as 24–30 hours.* Methamphetamine also increases the availability of dopamine in the synaptic cleft via blockage of dopamine reuptake mechanisms and by releasing more dopamine from intrasynaptic vesicles. Over the last 15 years, due in part to its potent effect, cheap price and its availability, the use of methamphetamine has escalated In America, centered primarily in the western United States. Long-term methamphetamine abuse has many negative health consequences, including extreme weight loss, severe dental problems ("meth mouth"), anxiety, confusion, insomnia, mood disturbance, and violent behavior. Chronic methamphetamine abusers can also display a number of psychotic features, including paranoia, visual and auditory hallucinations, and delusions (for example, the sensation of insects crawling under the skin).

Behavioral Addictions

In addition to drugs of abuse, there are certain behaviors that have the potential to grow from a hobby or habit into an addictive disorder. Sometimes called behavioral addictions, they are also known as process addictions, and include gambling, compulsive sexual behaviors, video game addiction and compulsive shopping. Of these behaviors, gambling has been studied the most while we have relatively little data on the others.

Even during challenging economic times, gambling is common. Surveys indicate *approximately 60% of the general population has gambled within the last 12 months* The majority of those who gamble do so socially and do not incur lasting adverse consequences or harm. However, approximately 1–2% of the population currently meets the DSM criteria for pathological gambling. Pathological gambling, otherwise known as compulsive gambling, gambling addiction or disordered gambling, can be easily hidden. As a result, clinicians may not recognize the signs and symptoms of pathological gambling. The course of pathological gambling can vary from a chronic relapsing condition to one with a short time course. Vulnerable groups include males, those with co-occurring psychiatric disorders, especially substance abuse, ADHD and antisocial personality disorder, the elderly, adolescents, the disabled, and those from low socioeconomic classes.

The consequences of pathological gambling will vary with each case and can range from financial loss, divorce, substance abuse, and lost time or productivity, to domestic violence and illegal activity. Suicidal ideation is common in pathological gamblers, affecting nearly 25% of this population. Medical consequences of pathological gambling include insomnia, sleep deprivation, lack of exercise, stress-related illnesses and decreased attention to self care.

TREATMENT

The primary goal in treatment for addictive disorders is to engage and retain the patient in treatment. *The strongest predictor of who will be able to achieve abstinence and reduce harm in their lives is active involvement in formal treatment.* Treatment for addictive disorders requires a comprehensive approach that utilizes multiple professional disciplines to address the consequences of addiction. Treatment involves much more than saying "no" and attending 12-step meetings. Treatment can occur in a variety of settings, including inpatient, outpatient, partial hospitalization or res-

TWO SUFFERING MEN

I sat across, behind my desk,
and told him I thought
he might be alcoholic.
"I never been drunk," he said.
I made a note on the medical chart.

I could see him getting irked.
His liver sick;
his wife gone with the kids!
I made a note on the chart.

I saw him gaining rage.
He clenched his fists,
leaned forward,
his arms on the desk.
He held his breath
until he turned red,
then, sighing, fell back
in his chair and cried.

Breaking a long pause,
he asked, "You're telling me
I'm alcoholic? How in hell
would you know, in your
'pretty' white picturebook
middleclass hospital coat?"
His face suddenly tensed.
He pursed his lips
and lifted himself from the chair.
He stood tall, straight up,
bulging with pride
for all the ground-in years
of his laboring trade,
shouting,
"Stay out of my head.
Stay OUT of my head!"
and slammed the door behind him.

I longed to lower my eyes and cry.
But, from the bottom drawer
of my desk, just one small glass
of vodka and a chlorophyl candy
taste so damn good in the morning.

EUGENE HIRSCH

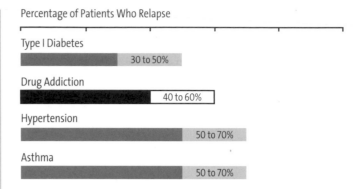

Percentage of Patients Who Relapse

Type I Diabetes	30 to 50%
Drug Addiction	40 to 60%
Hypertension	50 to 70%
Asthma	50 to 70%

FIGURE 9.3 Comparison of relapse rates between drug addiction and other chronic illnesses. Adapted from: *Principles of Drug Addiction Treatment: A Research Based Guide.* National Institute on Drug Abuse

idential treatment. Because addiction is a chronic, relapsing disorder, a short-term, one-time treatment is not likely to have a lasting impact. For most patients and families, treatment is a long-term activity that requires multiple interventions, ongoing monitoring, and starts and stops to treatment. The fact that one treatment session fails does not mean the patient is hopeless or will not get better. Comprehensive treatment for addiction will 1) address the biological underpinnings of addiction through medications, 2) deal with psychological conflicts such as denial, ambivalence and lack of motivation, and 3) increase social support to develop healthy peer networks and coping skills. *The end result is that those who complete treatment for substance abuse will get substantially better.* In fact, the majority of patients with addictive disorders improve. This is quite different from the stereotype that suggests addicts are constantly utilizing healthcare resources without remorse or change (for a comparison of relapse rates in different types of chronic illness, see Figure 9.3).

MEDICATIONS

Over the last 10 years, there have been several new medications that have been approved by the FDA for the treatment of addictive disorders, signaling a new era in treatment. These medications are designed to be used by addiction specialists and by primary care providers, and will increase the number of patients with addictive disorders who seek and receive treatment.

ALCOHOL

Disulfiram (Antabuse)

This was the first medication to be approved for alcohol dependence by the FDA and has been available since 1951.

Disulfiram's mechanism of action is to block the second step in alcohol metabolism, which will result in the accumulation of acetaldehyde if a person consumes alcohol. Acetaldehyde triggers a physically adverse reaction, manifested by flushing, tachycardia, nausea, vomiting, anxiety and dizziness. *Disulfiram is prescribed to create an aversive response to the desire to drink by creating awareness in patients that if they drink, they are going to get sick.* The antabuse reaction is not typically life-threatening but does carry some cardiac risk.

The efficacy of disulfiram has been established primarily for highly motivated patients and for patients who are receiving the medication in the context of directly-observed therapy. Clinical experience has shown that antabuse is effective in establishing early abstinence, but that as soon as ambivalence or urges to drink return, patients stop taking it. The main side effects of disulfiram include elevated liver enzymes, dizziness, nausea, paresthesias, and in rare instances, psychosis. Disulfiram has received recent attention as a possible treatment for patients with cocaine dependence because of its indirect effects on increasing dopamine.

Acamprosate (Campral)

FDA-approved in 2003, acamprosate is a taurine-derived compound that targets NMDA receptors and glutamate in alcohol dependent individuals. Extensive data were collected in Europe prior to US approval, and this medication has a long history of safety and efficacy. Clinical trials conducted in the United States have shown that *acamprosate is effective in increasing the number of drinking-free days, increasing time to relapse and decreasing the number of heavy drinking days (defined as consuming more than 5 drinks per day).*

Acamprosate should only be started once alcohol detoxification has been completed and then the target dose is 666 mg three times a day (1988 mg per day). It is not a medication to use during alcohol detoxification. In its current formulation as a tablet, the medication has to be taken 6 times a day, which raises issues of compliance with many patients. Acamprosate is well-tolerated with the major side effects being diarrhea and nausea. Patients should be told that if they drink while on acamprosate, they should continue take the medication.

Naltrexone Oral (Revia)

Naltrexone is an opioid antagonist that appears to target the positive reinforcement properties of alcohol. Clinical trials have shown that it is helpful in increasing the time to first drink, decreasing urges and craving to drink and decreasing the priming effect of alcohol (i.e., one drink that triggers ongoing drinking). Side effects from Naltrexone include hepatitis, dysphoria (separate from an underlying depressive disorder), fatigue and nausea. Naltrexone is also quite expensive, and although many insurance plans cover it, the *monthly costs of Naltrexone can still range in the hundreds of dollars.*

Naltrexone Injectable (Vivitrol)

Although oral naltrexone has been shown to be effective if taken properly, compliance rates with the medication have been low. This led to the development of a long-term, injectable version of naltrexone, which came to market as Naltrexone (§Vivitrol), FDA-approved in 2006. This formulation works identically in the brain as the oral version, although steady states are much more consistent because of the once-a-month dosing.

Injectable naltrexone is administered once a month at a dose of 380 mg, as an intramuscular gluteal injection. It is started once alcohol detoxification is completed. The obvious advantage to this medication is compliance and assurance that patients are receiving the proper dose of medications. The side effect profile of the injectable version is similar to oral naltrexone. Some physicians hesitate to prescribe because of concerns that if side effects emerge, one cannot simply stop the medication. Physicians do not need special certification and training to prescribe or inject naltrexone and can do so in their office.

OPIATES

Methadone

Methadone is a long-acting opioid agonist and is FDA-approved for the treatment of opioid dependence. It has long been the gold-standard for treatment and remains an effective and viable option for patients. Methadone minimizes the effects of detoxification and helps patients avoid drug use because of the medication's long-acting agonist effects. In order to start someone on methadone a patient must be enrolled in a federally-licensed and regulated methadone program. If patients are admitted to a hospital, for medical or psychiatric reasons, methadone can be continued by the admitting team only after confirmation has been made that the patient is an active patient, registered with a methadone clinic.

Methadone remains highly effective for opioid dependence and is safe when dispensed properly. The concerns about methadone remain overdose potential, long-term effects on mood or cognitive functioning, dependency and stigma. Drug interactions also remain a concern, especially with benzodiazepines that can increase sedation.

Buprenorphine (Subutex and Suboxone)

As effective as methadone is, the tight regulation of its dispensing along with the limited availability of clinics have left a significant number of patients with opioid dependence without access to treatment. It is estimated that only 10% of patients with opioid dependence ever seek care. To address this, the availability of buprenorphine as an office-based treatment for opioid dependence emerged in 2004. *Buprenorphine is a partial mu-agonist that binds tightly to the opioid receptor.* By definition, partial agonists have a ceiling effect and additional medication does not increase the effect once this ceiling is reached. This limits the number of overdoses and the fatalities that would result if a full opioid agonist was used.

Buprenorphine is FDA-approved for opioid dependence, including the treatment of withdrawal. In order to prescribe, physicians must obtain a waiver from the Drug Enforcement Agency. In order to qualify for this waiver, physicians must have completed either an 8-hour in-person training or an online course offered by certified experts in the addiction field. When a physician first becomes certified to prescribe buprenorphine, there is a 30-patient maximum prescribing limit, but that number can increase to 100 with ongoing experience.

During opiate withdrawal, buprenorphine is administered to reduce and attenuate all signs of withdrawal. It does this through the partial agonist effect. Once the withdrawal process is complete, buprenorphine can serve as a maintenance agent by reducing urges, cravings and preoccupation for opiates. Also, because buprenorphine is a powerful binding agent, if exogenous opiates are introduced in the presence of buprenorphine, they will not have an effect because they will not bind to the opioid receptor. Clinically, patients describe this as a blocking effect in which they are not able to experience any subjective effects of opiates while they have buprenorphine in their system.

Smoking Cessation

Natural quit rates from smoking for those attempting to quit without any formal behavioral or pharmacological treatment is approximately 7% after one year. *With three to five minutes of counseling from a physician, these natural quit rates can double.* Adding pharmacological and psychological treatment to smoking cessation practices can increase the quit rates to as high as 30–40%, which is significantly higher than most people would think. Smoking cessation

is particular challenging because of the high availability of cigarettes, peers who are still smoking, ingrained habits and the short half-life of nicotine which contributes to repetitive and frequent use.

Nicotine Replacement Therapies

During the mid-1990s, nicotine replacement therapies gained FDA approval, initially requiring a prescription, but then phased into an over-the-counter drug. There are several different formulations of nicotine replacement therapy, including gums, lozenges, inhalers, patches, and nasal sprays. The mechanism behind each product is the same, which is to *introduce a steady state of nicotine replacement and then gradually taper off nicotine in a matter of a few weeks.* The tapering is supposed to occur according to a fixed schedule, and the patient should not show signs of nicotine withdrawal. There are no differences in efficacy between the different types of nicotine replacements. Each piece of nicotine gum contains approximately 1 to 3 mg of nicotine, which is similar to the amounts of nicotine contained in one cigarette. The starting dosages of the transdermal patches range from 7 to 21 mg of nicotine.

Patients have to be taught not to chew nicotine gum like regular chewing gum. Instead, they must chew the gum only until a peppery tingle starts. They are then to "park" the gum between the cheeks and gum to absorb the nicotine. If patients chew the gum like regular chewing gum, they will not absorb nicotine, or more likely, they will absorb it in the upper GI tract which can lead to side effects like nausea or diarrhea.

Nicotine replacement therapies can be mixed. For example, passive use of nicotine patches can be combined with active use of nicotine gum for breakthrough urges or cravings. When used properly, nicotine replacement therapies carry a 15 to 20% success quit rate one year after beginning of treatment.

Bupropion (Zyban)

Marketed under the trade name Zyban, bupropion is also available for smoking cessation. Bupropion's mechanism of action remains largely unknown but it is thought to restore dopaminergic tone as well as regulating nicotinic receptors. Under a different trade name, Wellbutrin, bupropion is approved for the treatment of major depressive disorder. *Studies have shown that bupropion, when used correctly, can lead to an approximately 20% quit rate for smokers.* This effect is independent of any impact on mood. The most important side effect of bupropion is an increased risk of seizures. Like many antidepressant medications, it also carries a firm warning to physicians to monitor for any signs of suicidal ideation, agitation or hostility.

Varenicline (Chantix)

The most recently approved medication for smoking cessation is varenicline. This is a partial nicotinic agonist that binds to the alpha-4, beta-2 nicotine receptor located within the nucleus accumbens. *During clinical trials Varenicline established a 40% continuous abstinence rate after 12 weeks,* which is significantly higher than other treatment modalities for smoking cessation. Varenicline works by attenuating nicotine withdrawal and by reducing smoking urges and cravings. It is not a controlled substance and can be used in conjunction with other psychotropic medications. Varenicline's main side effects are nausea, insomnia and headache. In 2009, a black box warning was added for both bupropion and varenicline related to the possibility of suicidal ideation and behavioral agitation. As a result, clinicians need to inform patients and monitor their behavior carefully in the first few weeks after starting the medications.

STIMULANTS

There are no FDA-approved medications for cocaine or methamphetamine dependence. Over the last 15 years, numerous medications, from many different classes, have been tried in clinical trials without clear and convincing treatment effects. A cocaine vaccine is likely to become available by 2011, which would offer significant promise. Until then, clinicians should emphasize behavioral treatments for stimulant dependence and aggressive treatment of co-occurring disorders.

MARIJUANA

There are no FDA-approved medications for marijuana dependence. Some candidate medications have been researched and proposed, but there are no medications that clearly stand above the others. Psychosocial interventions remain the most effective treatment for marijuana dependence.

BEHAVIORAL ADDICTIONS

Pathological gambling, compulsive sexual behaviors and compulsive shopping have all had medication trials con-

> **The Wisdom of THOMAS JEFFERSON, 1743–1826**
> **US president and philosopher**
>
> Not less than two hours a day should be devoted to bodily exercise.
>
> I wish to see this beverage (beer) become common instead of the whiskey which kills one-third of our citizens and ruins their families.
>
> Bodily decay is gloomy in prospect, but of all human contemplations the most abhorrent is body without mind.
>
> We never repent to having eaten too little.

ducted, but to date, no FDA-approved medication has been approved for these problem behaviors. There have been research trials using antidepressants, opiate antagonists and mood stabilizers that have shown efficacy and promise. At this time, clinicians are encouraged to use medications for co-occurring disorders with the hope that will reduce behavioral addictive disorders.

PSYCHOSOCIAL TREATMENT

In addition to medications, psychosocial treatments are indicated for patients with all forms of addictive disorders. *Psychosocial treatments can come in a variety of different styles from self-help materials, individual counseling, group therapies and residential treatments.* Evidenced-based treatments that have shown effectiveness for addictive disorders include cognitive behavioral therapy, motivational therapy and relapse prevention techniques. Contingency management, which is a form of providing incentives (usually in the form of money) for remaining sober, has been shown to be a highly effective form of treatment for substance-related disorders. Manualized treatment by therapists who have been trained in this area and receive ongoing supervision is the optimal treatment delivery format.

Individual therapy or counseling not only focuses on reducing or stopping addictive behaviors, but also addresses employment status, legal support, restoring family/social relationships and increasing healthy lifestyle choices. Through its emphasis on short-term behavioral goals, individual counseling helps patients develop coping strategies and tools to abstain from drug use and maintain abstinence. Many treatment programs also offer group therapy as a way to increase peer interaction and to help promote drug-free lifestyles. Research has shown that when group therapy is offered in conjunction with individual drug counseling, positive outcomes are more frequently achieved. Twelve-step groups such as Alcoholics Anonymous, Narcotics Anonymous and Gambler's Anonymous are social support groups that provide peer support, advice and reflection. They are not usually facilitated by a healthcare provider. Evidence shows that 12-step programs are an important component of recovery, and patients should be encouraged not just to go to meetings, but also to find a sponsor and make a commitment to full participation in the meetings (such as setting up chairs or passing out books). In general, the recommended frequency of meetings is at least 2 to 3 times per week at the beginning of treatment, and then as often as required by the individual to reduce craving and urges to use.

Primary care clinicians can also provide psychosocial therapy through brief interventions in their office. The Substance Abuse and Mental Health Services Administration (SAMHSA) has created an initiative called Screening, Brief-Intervention and Referral to Treatment (SBIRT) to make screening for substance abuse a routine part of medical care. This requires a paradigm shift in which primary care providers and healthcare providers from all fields learn to follow a series of prescribed SBIRT steps with patients with addictive disorders. The goal of SBIRT is to make screening for substance abuse a routine part of medical care.

The first step is screening to quickly identify patients who need further assessment or treatment for substance use disorders, especially if their presenting complaint does not appear to be related to substance abuse. Screening is not a way to establish a diagnosis or treatment plan.

Screening involves using patient reports (through questionnaires) and laboratory studies. A number of substance abuse screening instruments have been developed and are easily available for use. Examples of commonly used screening instruments are the Alcohol Use Disorders Identification Test (AUDIT), the Drug Abuse Screening Test (DAST) and the World Health Organization's Alcohol, Smoking and Substance Involvement Screening Test (AS-SIST). Laboratory studies that are used for screening for addictive disorders include urine drug screens, liver function tests, and physical examination findings (e.g., unexplained skin lesions).

The second phase of SBIRT is *Brief Intervention, which refers to a single session or multiple sessions that are designed to increase insight and understanding of addictive behaviors and to directly increase motivation toward making a change.* Brief interventions can be flexible and come in a wide variety of forms, including help lines, self-help workbooks or time-limited group therapy. One does not have to be a mental health practitioner nor an expert in addictions to implement brief interventions. The essential components of brief interventions involve engaging the patient in openly discussing their addictive behaviors and providing accurate information about what needs to be done to reduce harm.

Finally, SBIRT ends with referral to, and treatment by, addiction specialists. This may include arranging an appointment, providing a list of qualified and accessible providers in the area, and/or following up with the patient to ensure that he or she actually followed up on the referral and visited the addiction specialist.

FUTURE DIRECTIONS

The field of addiction treatment is rapidly developing in the areas of medication and psychosocial interventions. Improved screening, early intervention and referrals will be critical to reducing the harm and stigma of these diseases. In time, genetic profiling and screening to match patients to the appropriate treatment modality offer the promise of truly individualized treatments.

CASE STUDY

William Barrington is a 19 year old white male who presents to the student health service at his college campus because of concerns about insomnia and anxiety. He reports to his primary care team that he has had some trouble adjusting to college and is finding it hard to make friends, do well in school and balance his time. He joined a fraternity during his freshman year, lives there and finds himself very much involved in their activities. He states his mood is "fine" and that he is motivated to do "stuff," but finds himself not actually doing things. A physical examination is unremarkable and his initial blood work is also normal, including thyroid tests and a comprehensive metabolic panel.

What is in the differential diagnosis at this time?
The initial impression is that this is some form of depressive disorder and perhaps an anxiety disorder. The plan is to start an antidepressant and refer him to student psychological services for therapy. William follows-up with student psychological services; during his intake, he reports that he does not like alcohol or use drugs like marijuana, cocaine or amphetamines. However, he does describe taking prescription pills regularly, including "a few vics (Vicodin), some oxys (Oxycontin) . . . Whatever is around." He goes on to say that his mother has a severe medical problem, and that he takes her medications from time to time. When asked how many per day, he reports that he doesn't keep track, but thinks it's approximately 4 – 5 times per day.

What are the next steps in assessment?
A urine toxicology screen is ordered and it is positive for benzodiazepines and opiates. William does not think that taking these prescription pills constitutes an "addiction"

because he says it's legal and everyone around him seems to be doing it.

This part of the interview is critical to determine how much impact and harm these drugs may be causing William. After applying the DSM-IV criteria for opioid dependence, it becomes clear that William meets the criteria for tolerance, withdrawal, and spending large amounts of time trying to obtain the drug. Because this is a student psychological service, there are few groups on addiction and although there are several physicians on staff, none of them are certified addictions experts. The team decides to refer William to a different physician who is an addictions specialist.

What happens at the office of the addictions specialist?
William follows-up with an addiction specialist for an intake about a week later. There, he is given a whole battery of tests that examine his drug-taking behavior as well as other addictive behaviors. On further questioning, William reveals that he has been gambling over the Internet with his parents' credit cards since he started college. He played poker during high school with friends and thought that he was getting pretty good because he usually won. Once he got to college, he started playing more in the fraternity and continued to win. Because he was not 21, he could not go to the local casinos to play and an upperclassman showed him how to open an account online. He states that he has been losing over the last 3 months but that it's not that much and it "doesn't take much time." After applying some problem gambling screening instruments, it becomes apparent that William is losing about $2,000 per month and spending up to 20 hours per week gambling. He reports that some of his opiate use is related to his gambling as a way of dealing with the anxiety that results from his gambling losses.

The treatment plan, as determined by the addictions specialist, includes detoxification off of opiates and treatment as an outpatient with buprenorphine. At the same time, William is encouraged to enroll in a partial hospital program to address both his gambling and opiate abuse. At first he maintains that he cannot participate in the program because of school, but after some encouragement, he begins to understand that he can dedicate 9 hours per week toward recovery.

Medications to address his mood symptoms are deferred until his detoxification is complete. William is also encouraged to discuss what happened with his parents, which will begin the process of dealing with the guilt related to lying. From a social perspective, William is encouraged to continue to stay active in school and with extracurricular activities. Structure, feeling needed, and being responsible to others is important for William and will be reinforced the more active and participatory he becomes.

What would happen if an addictions specialist were not available?

Cases like William's are more common than most healthcare specialists realize, especially given the hidden nature of addictive disorders. Although William presented for vague physical and emotional complaints, there were two addictive disorders that were present underneath the initial presentation that were clearly the causes of his presenting symptoms. The first step to helping patients like this is to help them recognize and identify the source of their symptoms, which explains why screening is so critical. If specialty-level care for addictions is not available, primary care physicians are left to manage a case like William's by themselves. In that instance, it is important for primary care providers to link up with local mental healthcare and addictions treatment programs.

What happens during treatment and what is william's prognosis?
The strongest predictors of who will do well in treatment and have a positive outcome are length of time in treatment and commitment to the recovery process. A well-thought out and comprehensive treatment plan asks the patient to invest a large amount of time, energy and resources to treatment. Most patients with addictive disorders do not stay to complete the treatment cycle for a variety of reasons, including ambivalence, denial, lack of time, lack of insurance coverage or other treatment barriers. During ongoing treatment for addictions, William will receive medical, psychiatric and social treatment to address the consequences of his addiction and to develop healthier ways of dealing with life stressors and better problem solving skills.

SUGGESTED READINGS

Ries, R.K., Miller, S.C., Fiellin, D.A., & Saitz, R. (2009). *Principles of addiction medicine* (4th ed.). Philadelphia, PA: Lippincott Williams & Wilkins.
A comprehensive guide to current treatment of addictive disorders.

National Institute on Drug Abuse: www.nida.nih.gov
NIDA's mission is to lead the nation in bringing the power of science to bear on drug abuse and addiction.

National Institute on Alcohol Abuse and Alcoholism: www.niaaa.nih.gov
NIAAA provides leadership in the national effort to reduce alcohol-related problems by conducting and supporting research and translating research findings to health care providers, researchers, policymakers, and the public

Substance Abuse and Mental Health Service Administration: www.samhsa.gov
The Substance Abuse and Mental Health Services Administration (SAMHSA) has established a clear vision for its work – a life in the community for everyone. To realize this vision, the Agency has sharply focused its mission on building resilience and facilitating recovery for people with or at risk for mental or substance use disorders. SAMHSA is gearing all of its resources – programs, policies and grants – toward that outcome.

American Academy of Addiction Psychiatry: www.aaap.org
   AAAP is an international professional membership organization founded in 1985 with approximately 1,000 members. Membership consists of psychiatrists working with addiction, faculty at various academic institutions, medical students, residents and fellows, and related health care professionals.

American Society of Addiction Medicine: www.asam.org
   ASAM is a professional medical organization that seeks to increase access and improve the quality of medical treatment for addictive disorders.

http://pubs.niaaa.nih.gov/publications/Practitioner/PocketGuide/pocket_guide2.html
   This publication on the National Institute on Alcohol Abuse and Alcoholism website describes what is a standard drink and provides examples.

10 Psychodynamic Approaches to Human Behavior

Peter B. Zeldow

> Every man has some reminiscences which he would not tell to everyone, but only to his friends. He has others which he would not reveal even to his friends, but only to himself, and that in secret. But finally there are others which a man is even afraid to tell himself, and every decent man has a considerable number of such things stored away.
>
> FYODOR DOSTOYEVSKY
> *Notes from the Underground*

> All the art of analysis consists in saying a truth only when the other person is ready for it, has been prepared for it by an organic process of gradation and evolution.
>
> ANAÏS NIN
> *The Diary of Anaïs Nin*

> Every life is, more or less, a ruin among whose debris we have to discover what the person ought to have been.
>
> ORTEGA Y GASSETORTEGA Y GASSET

For many people, psychoanalysis conveys the image of a patient lying on a couch, speaking endlessly (that is, session after session, and for many years) about dreams and sexual fantasies to a bearded and elderly psychoanalyst who remains relatively silent, except for an occasional oracular comment known as an interpretation. For those who have been superficially exposed to Freud in undergraduate psychology courses, psychoanalysis is both a largely discredited theory of personality and form of treatment for which there is little empirical justification.

Yet psychoanalytic theorizing and psychoanalytically influenced psychotherapy remain viable and continue, over a century after Freud's first publications, to have an influence not only in psychiatry and clinical psychology but in the arts and humanities in intellectual communities throughout the world. Contemporary psychoanalytic theory and practice have both changed dramatically since Freud's death in 1939 and can no longer be considered the work of a single man. They have evolved in many different directions, some of which represent radical departures from orthodox Freudian formulations. A very small sample of psychoanalytic theorists and concepts is provided in Box 10-1.

Another view of psychoanalytic theory, popular in some academic circles, considers it worthless because it is based on a biased sample (neurotic, middle class, nineteenth-century residents of Vienna) and because its concepts cannot be subjected to empirical testing. These criticisms are simplistic, and a rebuttal is beyond the scope of this chapter. Suffice to make the following comments. First the history of science suggests that those theories richest in explanatory power have often proved most difficult to study empirically. Newton's Second Law, for example, could not be demonstrated in a reliable, quantitative way for 100 years. Psychoanalytic theory is derived primarily from the experience of psychotherapy, and, in the eyes of those who have experienced it, provides a vocabulary and conceptual map for a set of experiences that are intense, highly personal, and otherwise hard to explain.

Furthermore, it is not true that all the theories of Freud and his followers are untestable. **Psychoanalytic hypotheses may be difficult to subject to scientific scrutiny, but** the same can be said about any psychological hypotheses involving complex phenomena and worthy of being tested. Psychoanalytic ideas have possibly inspired as much empirical research as any theory in the behavioral sciences, and they have not always fared badly. Interested readers can consult Fisher and Greenberg (1996) or Kowalski and Westen's (2008) introductory psychology text for balanced discussions of the empirical status of contemporary psychoanalytic ideas.

BOX 10.1 Selected psychodynamic theorists

Sigmund Freud (1856–1939); Vienna; psychoanalysis

Creator of psychoanalysis as a theory, research method, and psychological treatment

Psychosexual theory of development, emphasizing vicissitudes of biological drives through *oral, anal, phallic,* and, ultimately, *genital* stages

Carl Gustav Jung (1875–1961); Zurich; analytical psychology

Early disciple of Freud who disputed sexual nature of psychic energy, or *libido*

Developed psychological types: *introverts* and *extroverts*

Interested in spiritual crises of midlife

Formulated theory of *archetype,* a universal, emotionally charged mythological image in the *collective unconscious*

Alfred Adler (1870–1937); Vienna; individual psychology

Early disciple of Freud who deemphasized sexual strivings in favor of *social interest:* "man is inclined towards the good"

Emphasized conscious capabilities of humans

Interested in effects of *birth order* and *earliest memory*

Formulated theory of compensation for *organ inferiority*

Harry Stack Sullivan (1892–1949); New York and Washington, D.C.; interpersonal psychiatry

Eminent and influential American psychiatrist

Defined the psychiatrist as an expert in interpersonal relations

Formulated theories:
    Anxiety results from threats to one's security
    Self-system develops as guardian of security but limits personal growth
    Good-Me remains conscious; Bad-Me is *dissociated*

Erik H. Erikson (1902–1994); Germany, Vienna, and United States; psychosocial theory of development

Emphasized *psychosocial* implications of Freud's psychosexual stages

Extended developmental theory throughout adulthood (**Eight Ages of Man**)

Wrote psychohistorical studies of Luther and Gandhi

Developed concepts of *identity* and *identity crisis*

Donald Winnicott (1896–1971); Great Britain; object relations theory

Transitional objects such as blankets and teddy-bears, which soothe and comfort the child in its early efforts to separate from mother

Capacity to be alone as a psychological achievement reflecting a cohesive self and successfully *internalized objects*

Margaret Mahler (1896–1985); United States; object relations theory

Central dimension of development from complete dependence (*symbiosis*) to differentiation of self (*separation-individuation*)

Heinz Kohut (1913–1981); Chicago; psychoanalytic self psychology

Emphasized *narcissistic* line of development from immature grandiosity and exhibitionism to more mature modes of self-enhancement

Developed taxonomy of transferences classified according to type of experience patient is trying to recreate (*mirroring, idealizing, twinship*)

Formulated theory of *self-object,* defined as any object (person, thing, ideal) that lends sense of cohesion, strength, and harmony to self

My intention in what follows is to provide a clinically useful introduction to what I prefer to call the *psychodynamic* perspective on human behavior. As future physicians and health-care professionals, most readers of this book will inevitably find themselves in clinical situations that will require them to empathize with patients, to understand patients' motivations and adaptations under stress, and to understand their own intensely personal reactions to their patients. I believe that psychodynamic formulations of human behavior often provide the most experientially useful roadmaps for clinical work.

PSYCHODYNAMIC ASSUMPTIONS

Unconscious Motivation

Any psychodynamic formulation of human behavior must include the notion that human lives are governed by internal forces of which they are unaware and that these forces, which may be images, thoughts, or feelings, are the primary determinants of who they are and what they do. Psychodynamic theorists emphasize the limits of self-report and self-awareness; they are more impressed with the all-too-human capacity to cut ourselves off from certain emotions, wishes, and fears which, if acknowledged, would disrupt our psychological equilibrium. This is demonstrated in the following vignette.

A patient on a coronary care unit witnessed the fatal cardiac arrest of his roommate. Although the nursing staff expected that this would be traumatic for the patient, he denied any fright and eagerly accepted the staff's reassurance that he was not at similar risk. Only one seemingly minor event suggested that there was anything more to this situation: When patients were surveyed as to whether they would prefer single rooms or roommates should another hospitalization be required, all patients chose to have roommates, except for this patient and others who had witnessed cardiac arrests.

In this situation it is easy to see how the patient's denial of fear served to reassure him and maintain his psychological equilibrium. However, it is also difficult to believe that he was not terribly upset *at some level,* although the only evidence for this (his preference for a single room) is admittedly tenuous. Perhaps if the staff were to insist that he share a room, his protestations would increase and his anxiety would come closer to the surface.

Experimental psychologists once objected to the notion of unconscious cognitive processes. In recent years, however, such processes have become the subject of numerous experiments under the rubric of implicit memory. It is now widely accepted that we learn and remember without awareness. Still, it is fair to say that the dynamic unconscious of psychoanalysis and the cognitive unconscious of experimental psychology are different from each other. Nowhere is this more apparent than in the controversy surrounding the recovery of repressed memories of childhood sexual abuse. Most victims of repeated or severe abuse of this type do have some memory – however vague – of the abuse prior to entering psychotherapy. Experimental psychologists have demonstrated quite persuasively that false memories can be created in the laboratory and presumably in the therapist's consulting room as well. Nonetheless, responsible clinicians continue to observe patients who recall, in the course of psychotherapy, long forgotten events from their early lives. Such remembrances can be vivid, highly emotional, and cathartic. Although it is important to retain a heathy skepticism about the veracity of such remembrances, it is equally important to respect the opinion of the experienced clinicians, to re-frain from overgeneralization from the laboratory to the real world, and to remain humble and curious in the face of phenomena that we cannot yet explain.

Conflict

Psychodynamic formulations of human behavior begin with the inevitability of conflict, both intrapsychic and interpersonal. To speak of conflict in this way is simply to note that humans are complex organisms, capable of having incompatible goals and engaging in paradoxical actions.

Conflict can take many forms. There can be conflict between two impulses (love and hate); conflict between an impulse and a prohibition ("I want to kill" vs. "Thou shalt not kill"); conflict over a vocational choice (medicine vs. creative writing); or conflict over one's sexual identity ("Am I gay or am I straight?"). This is far from an exhaustive list. Furthermore, conflict can be experienced fully, partially, dimly, or not at all. In the psychodynamic perspective, conflict is considered to be the basis of most forms of functional (i.e., nonorganic) psychopathology.

It is easier to speak of psychological conflict if a hypothetical psychological structure is created, the parts of which may operate more or less smoothly (more or less conflictually). Such is the purpose served by Freud's heuristic division of the human personality into three components. **Id** is the repository of all biological urges and instincts, including hunger, thirst, and sexuality. Under most conditions, humans are unaware of its contents and functions. It is governed by the **pleasure principle**. This means that it attempts to avoid pain and obtain pleasure and cannot tolerate delay of gratification. The id is said to operate according to **primary process**, a primitive form of wishful and magical thinking. For example, if the organism is hungry, primary process provides a mental image of food, a wish fulfillment. Dreams and the hallucinations of psychotic patients are other examples of primary process thinking. Although they satisfy the id, such experiences do not enable the organism to deal with objective reality.

Ego develops to permit more effective transactions with the environment. In contrast to the id, the ego is governed by the **reality principle**, which aims to postpone gratification until an appropriate object is found. In other words, the ego will not accept a mental image of food or any wish-fulfilling fantasy. It operates according to **secondary process** thinking, which is basically synonymous with realistic thinking and problem solving. Ego functions include cognition (perceiving, remembering, speech and language, reality testing, attention, concentration, and judgment), interpersonal relations, voluntary movement, and defense mechanisms (discussed in this chapter). However, because the ego develops from the id, it is always beholden to it, and its various functions may be disrupted if the demands of the id are insufficiently addressed.

For humans to function effectively, they must learn not only to negotiate a balance between their bodily needs and the limitations of physical reality but also how to deal with the norms of society. The **superego** is the internal representation of the values, norms, and prohibitions of an individual's parents and society. It has two components: **conscience**, which both punishes the person for engaging in forbidden actions and thoughts and rewards morally acceptable conduct, and **ego-ideal**, which represents the moral perfection that humans strive for and never attain.

Intrapsychic conflict occurs when the demands of these three mental agencies are at odds. When id impulses threaten to become overwhelming, anxiety is generated. Anxiety, in this perspective, is a signal of impending danger. It may be experienced directly or may serve as a stimulus to new efforts by the ego to keep the id impulses unconscious. Some of these efforts of the ego to respond to signal anxiety are discussed in the section on defense mechanisms.

Developmental Perspective: The Past in the Present

A third assumption common to psychodynamic formulations is that the *events of the past, particularly the events of childhood, have a profound influence on our behavior as adults.* This influence appears in two distinct ways. First, humans are viewed as "repeating machines," playing out (as adults) crucial early experiences in an effort to master them and obtain the gratification that was unavailable in childhood. Second, modes of thinking characteristic of childhood remain with individuals as adults, unconscious and ready to be activated under appropriate conditions. Both of these influences are evident in the case study at the end of this chapter.

Respect for the Body

A fourth assumption inherent in most psychodynamic formulations is that *an individual's body plays a crucial role in personality development.* However controversial Freud's view that "anatomy is destiny" may be as an explanation of psychological differences between the sexes, two related points are clear. First, the anatomical differences between men and women are objects of no small interest to children, who notice the differences and wonder and fantasize about them. The possibility that these differences may have different consequences for boys and girls does not seem unreasonable. Certainly events such as menstruation, lactation, pregnancy, childbirth, and menopause are unique to the female life cycle and have profound effects on self-esteem and

the ways in which needs and emotions are expressed. Anyone who has spent any time in a men's locker room knows that men, too, have some curious rituals (such as teasing each other about the size of their penises), which seem comprehensible only when some sort of genital anxiety is assumed. Second, all humans have to come to terms with their sexuality and their capacity to be hurtful and destructive. The notion that psychoanalytic theorizing reduces everything to sex and aggression is caricature. It is equally ludicrous to pretend that characteristic ways of satisfying and inhibiting various bodily needs have nothing to do with the development of personality and psychopathology.

PSYCHODYNAMIC THEORIES OF DEVELOPMENT

When unconscious motivation is being considered, questions such as what precisely are the "contents" of the unconscious that motivate human beings and are the sources

Sigmund Freud *(1856–1939).* Courtesy of the National Library of Medicine. Freud's throat cancer was associated with a lifetime history of smoking cigars, a habit he was unable to discontinue, despite repeated attempts to stop smoking. Freud's physician collaborated in his death by giving him, at Freud's request, a lethal dose of morphine. How would you have responded to this request?

> The little girl likes to regard herself as what her father loves above all else; but the time comes when she has to endure a harsh punishment from him and she is cast out of her fool's paradise. The boy regards his mother as his own property; but he finds one day that she has transferred her love and solicitude to a new arrival.
>
> SIGMUND FREUD

of conflict and inner divisiveness should be asked. In a consideration of the role of the past in the present, the aspects of human development that exert the most formidable influence and provide the greatest challenge should be determined. Unfortunately, psychoanalysts disagree considerably on these issues.

Freud's theory of psychosexual development represents an attempt to describe the path of the instincts through various erogenous zones and phases of childhood. Sexuality for Freud refers to a "primary, distinctively poignant pleasure experience" derived from the stimulation of an area of the body. Infantile sexuality has nothing but this sensual pleasure in common with the variety of experiences that we think of under the rubric of adult sexuality (or *genital sexuality,* to use Freud's terminology). During the **oral stage**, sucking, biting, and other oral activities are primary sources of pleasure. During the **anal stage**, at roughly age 2 to 3 years, pleasure is obtained through the expulsion and retention of excretion. During the next 2 or 3 years, in the **phallic stage**, the predominant erogenous zone is the genitalia. During the **latency period**, from 6 years to adolescence, drive activity presumably subsides. Only at the end of adolescence do we find psychosexual development culminating in sexuality as adults know it, with a capacity for orgasm and unambivalent, mutually gratifying relations with others. This so-called **genital stage** is not attained by all persons but represents the highest possible level of human development for Freud.

What is not apparent in so sketchy and abstract an account are the implications of this theory for personality development. Suffice to say that particular personality traits are associated with excessive gratification or deprivation at each stage. Problems at the oral stage, such as insufficient opportunity for oral gratification, can leave a legacy of pessimism, dependency, and excessive need for approval, as well as an inclination to eat, drink, and smoke excessively. Problems at the anal stage, such as toilet training that is too early or too severe, can result in compulsive neatness, stubbornness and defiance, ambivalence and indecisiveness, and stinginess. During the phallic phase, boys and girls must come to terms with their possessive love of the parent of the opposite sex and their murderous fantasies toward the same-sex parent. One purported outcome of difficulty in containing such feelings can be a lifelong pursuit of failure. In such a view, success is unconsciously equated with the gratification of the Oedipal fantasy and must be studiously avoided.

Several years ago a medical student came to see me after having failed an examination in one of his basic science courses. He had had no earlier academic difficulties during medical school and expressed the belief that he had unconsciously sabotaged his own performance. He explained that he was ambivalent about becoming a physician and that there were many unresolved tensions in his relationship with his father, an eminent physician-educator. He also reported that earlier in his life, he had failed to perform as well as expected in numerous important sports events. In retrospect, he thought that his history of underachievement was related to his relationship with his father, and he used the occasion of his academic difficulties to take a leave of absence from school to work out these problems in psychotherapy.

Erik Erikson has reformulated (some would say "sanitized") the psychosexual theory in psychosocial terms. For him the oral stage is the time at which a child ideally develops a basic sense of **trust vs. mistrust**, an outlook on life as essentially good, nourishing, and predictable, based on his or her early experiences with the mother. Similarly, the demand for bowel control that society imposes in the anal stage can leave a child with either a healthy sense of **autonomy**, rooted in mastery of his or her body, or a lifelong and pervasive sense of **shame and doubt**. Erikson spoke of the phallic stage in terms of **initiative vs. guilt** and defined the latency stage in terms of a child's sense of **industry** (i.e., learning the basic skills of society) **vs. inferiority**. He described adolescence as the time in which an individual establishes a firm sense of **identity** or becomes confused about his or her role in society. Erikson also made a major contribution by extending the notion of growth beyond adolescence. In contrast to Freud, he described adulthood not only as a stage for the playing out of infantile conflicts but as a series of new opportunities and dangers. The following are Erikson's developmental tasks of adulthood:

1. To develop a trusting and enduring relationship (**intimacy vs. isolation**)
2. To develop in midlife a concern with guiding the next generation (**generativity vs. stagnation**)
3. To develop in old age an acceptance of an individual's own life as a necessary and valued experience, lived with dignity (**ego integrity vs. despair**)

With such formulations, a clinician has a framework for evaluating the developmental progress of a patient at any stage of life.

Freud believed all behavior was ultimately in the service of, or an expression of, basic sexual and aggressive instincts. In contrast, a number of psychodynamic theorists have argued that the most significant lines of human growth and development concern self and **object relations** (objects are significant others or their intrapsychic representations). To these theorists, who have serious divergences of opinion among themselves, the understanding and treatment of psychopathology take very different forms from the traditional Freudian model. Mahler and Winnicott, two proponents of object relations theory, stress movement from the absolute dependence of the newborn to the independence and autonomy of the adult as the primary and lifelong developmental task. Development proceeds from a symbiotic fusion with the mother through various stages of partial differentiation of self and others toward a state of increased individuality and independence. The internalized images of others (or objects) in the infant (and the psychotic adult) are primitive, engulfing, devouring, and otherwise menacing. Only in maturity, when separation from the mother has been successfully achieved, is seen a capacity for empathy and for seeing others as they actually are and not as projections of an individual's primitive fantasies.

Even in maturity, there remains, more or less consciously, the eternal longing to lose separateness and be blissfully reunited with the "all-good, symbiotic mother." Ideally this is manifested in the capacity for loving and true intimacy. However, in persons who have failed to establish a firm sense of self and in those who, when under duress, find themselves losing this sense of separateness, love may become an attempt to recapture some of the primitive gratification characteristic of the earliest feelings of fusion with the maternal object. In such instances a desperate style of love relations may ensue wherein the lover is idealized, separations are intolerable, and rejection may be life threatening. The lover is not perceived in an accurate way as a separate person with strengths and imperfections but as the sole source of nurturance and need satisfaction. There is really no room for personal growth in such a relationship, and bitter disappointment is an inevitable consequence.

Kohut has been more concerned with the narcissistic line of development and the concomitant changes in the self as the individual moves from the grandiose and exhibitionistic fantasies of immature narcissism to the more realistic modes of action associated with healthy narcissism. He stresses that certain experiences (which he calls self-objects) are as vital to the developing self as are food and water to physical well-being. These experiences include the need to be confirmed and prized for who we are (the need for mirroring), and the need to look up to, admire, and feel a part of a source of calm infallibility and strength (the need for idealizing). In a child, these needs are expressed in unsocialized ways. As long as the child's caretakers provide a milieu in which such expressions are welcomed, the child will develop a healthy, self-assertive ambition and a viable set of values and ideals by which to live. If the child's needs are misconstrued, ignored, or disparaged, the child (and later the adult) will lack the internal sense of self that is so essential for psychological well-being. Lacking these emotional nutrients, such a person resorts to a variety of strained, desperate, and developmentally primitive measures to bolster a defective self. For example, if a

parent continually responds to a child's *age-appropriate* expressions of aggression and sexuality with anger and contempt, it is difficult to imagine the child becoming an adult capable of expressing affection and assertiveness in a conflict-free way. Similarly, a drug addiction, which Freud might consider a direct attempt to satisfy oral cravings, would be seen by Kohut as an attempt to compensate for a defective self, the consequence of parental failure to provide the mirroring and calming functions so necessary for the child to learn to regulate his or her own feelings.

CLINICAL CONCEPTS AND APPLICATIONS
Defense Mechanisms

The concept of the defense mechanism was borrowed from immunology to describe the ways and means by which the ego wards off anxiety and controls unacceptable instinctual urges and unpleasant affects or emotions. The first systematic treatment of defense mechanisms was written in 1936 by Freud's daughter Anna Freud, an eminent child analyst. More recently, George Vaillant has introduced a classification of defenses based on the degree to which these mechanisms distort the perception of reality.

The defense mechanism of **denial** *is commonly seen in general medical practice.* It is a primitive defense wherein the facts or logical implications of external reality are refused recognition (denied) in favor of internally generated, wish-fulfilling fantasies. Denial involves a major distortion of reality and is common in healthy children until around age 5 years.

An example of denial is seen in the 50-year-old physician who ignores the classic signs and symptoms of an acute myocardial infarction and continues to clear his driveway of snow. Another is found in the woman who examines her breasts daily for lumps until she discovers one, ceases her self-examinations, and fails to report her findings to her physician. Denial in these examples is life threatening and clearly maladaptive. However, it can be adaptive at times: For example, a cardiac patient may refuse to accept that he or she has had a heart attack and appear incredibly cheerful and serene after admission to an intensive care unit.

Projection is another defense associated with considerable reality distortion. *In projection, an individual's own repressed (or unacceptable) impulses and desires are disowned and attributed to another person.* Most typical are projection of sexual and aggressive impulses, such as when, all evidence to the contrary, a patient is convinced that his or her physician is making sexual advances or that the physician is plotting with the nursing staff to have the patient killed. *Projection is the dominant defense mechanism employed by people with paranoid personality disorders.* It also plays a part in many prejudicial attitudes. When bigots assert that members of some minority group are all lazy, cheap, dirty, untrustworthy, immoral, etc., they are very likely projecting attributes that they need to disavow in themselves.

Regression is a partial return to an earlier stage of development and to more childish and childlike forms of behavior. Its purpose is to escape anxiety by returning to an earlier level of adjustment in which gratification was ensured. Like denial, regression is an extremely common response to severe and chronic illness and to hospitalization. Whenever confronted in clinical practice with a patient whose symptoms and incapacities are disproportionate to the physical disorder that underlies them, the clinician is probably dealing with a regressed patient. These are the patients who make insatiable demands on physicians and nurses, complain insistently, demand medication (and meetings with their lawyers), request special privileges, and accuse all those around them of indifference to their plight.

Regression is not necessarily a sign of psychiatric disturbance and short-lived reactions of the kind described here occur frequently. But when extended in time, such signs of emotional distress make it difficult for health providers to maintain their professional attitudes of equanimity and detached concern.

Regression can be precipitated by fatigue, drugs, chronic pain, stress, or any circumstance that deprives a patient of his or her autonomy. It is not uncommon to witness mildly regressive behavior in a group of students who have stayed up late to study the night before an examination. Psychoanalytic theories of creativity consider **regression in the service of the ego** to be one of the hallmarks of creativity. But when regression is prolonged and severe, it is associated with psychotic levels of functioning in which the ability to separate reality from fantasy is blurred.

Viederman (1974) uses the concept of regression to explain the behavior of patients on a renal transplant unit. He likens hemodialysis treatment to the mother-child relationship in two ways. First, the patient lives in a type of symbiotic fusion with the machine, and is attached to it by a plastic tube ... not too dissimilar to an umbilical connection. Patients readily enter into a love-hate relationship with this machine, which becomes both the preserver of their life and the tyrant that symbolizes the limitations of their freedom.

Second, because dietary and fluid limitations are severe, oral deprivation is a constant element in treatment. Viederman uses case material to demonstrate that successful adaptation to dialysis depends on the patient's ability to effect a partial regression to the stage of oral dependency, which in turn depends on a reasonably successful mother-child relationship during the patient's earliest years. The patient who, as a helpless child, was able to develop a hopeful and trusting relationship with his or her mother is more comfortable with the enforced dependency on the dialysis machine than the patient whose earliest years were characterized by less than adequate maternal care.

Fixation refers to a persistent inability to give up infantile or childish patterns of behavior for more mature ones and may occur because of either excessive deprivation or excessive gratification at the stage where development has ceased. When we say that a 40-year-old person has the mind of a 15-year-old person, we are implicitly saying that in some important ways (perhaps in capacity for intimate interpersonal relations), this person does not act as expected for someone of his or her chronological age. Various psychoanalytic theories emphasize different lines of human development (psychosexual, psychosocial, narcissistic), and an individual's progress can be stunted along any of these lines. For example, every human has a need for recognition, attention, and affirmation of worth. However, there are different ways of obtaining such so-called narcissistic gratifications at different points in time. A 4-year-old child who engages in blatantly exhibitionistic activity may be seeking such affirmation in an age-appropriate way. It may be the only way he or she knows. Adults should not feel that they have to outgrow such needs, but are expected to seek gratification in more mature ways. Recently a celebrity was quoted as saying that he loved his girlfriend because "she never makes demands on him." From a psychodynamic perspective, this is a rather selfish form of love. Mature people are not afraid of making demands on others, nor are they afraid of having demands made on them. Although it would not serve any purpose to say as much to the celebrity in question, his comment reflects a fixation at an immature level of psychosocial development.

It is somewhat inaccurate to speak of all the behaviors described herein as defense mechanisms. It is more accurate to describe them as having, among other things, *defensive aspects.* The "defense" of **identification** provides a good example. Identification is the psychological mechanism by which some traits or attributes of another individual are taken on as an individual's own (more or less permanently). This process is a major factor in the development of the superego, the moral dimension of personality. According to Freud, during the Oedipal phase, children relinquish their troubling attraction to the opposite-sex parent for fear of its consequences. By identifying with the parent of the same sex, the child is able to resolve this conflict. "Instead of replacing Daddy (or Mommy), I will become like him (her)." Such a resolution has its defensive side, to be sure, but it is also adaptive and plays a major role in personality development.

Identification is seen in its predominantly defensive aspects in pathological grief reactions–reactions to loss of a loved one in which the normal work of mourning, grieving, and truly accepting the loss is blocked. *For many people the death of a parent is a profoundly ambivalent experience.* At the same time an individual experiences acute pain and sadness, he or she may be more dimly aware of less admirable and more disturbing feelings: anger from being abandoned, relief if a long siege of suffering has ended or unconsciously wishing for the parent's death, and possibly guilt over such hostile wishes. Under such circumstances, normal grieving may be inhibited and identification can contribute to this process. For example, if the parent suffered a heart attack, the child may have chest pain. If the parent walked with a limp or spoke with a stutter, the child (even the adult child) may unintentionally adopt the same characteristic. In so doing, the child keeps the parent alive in a magical kind of way through identification. The new symptom also helps to distract the mourner from the pain of the loss.

A common variant is **identification with the aggressor** in which an individual masters the anxiety generated by being victimized through involuntary imitation. Anna Freud (1966) describes the case of a 6-year-old boy whom she interviewed shortly after he underwent a painful dental procedure:

> He was cross and unfriendly and vented his feelings on the things in my room. His first victim was a piece of India rubber ... Next he coveted a large ball of string ... When I refused to give him the whole ball, he took the knife again and secured a large piece ... Finally, he ... turned his attention to some pencils, and went on indefatigably sharpening them, breaking off the points, and sharpening them again.

As Anna Freud points out, this was not a literal impersonation of a dentist; rather, it was an identification with the dentist's aggression.

Concentration camp victims and terrorist hostages sometimes identify with their captors, taking on their characteristics and converting to their political points of view. Some medical educators have even described the occasional harsh treatment of medical students by residents as the result of a similar process. In these cases a resident who has been mistreated by an attending physician may be similarly abusive to a medical student clerk. Such an identification with the attending physician may temporarily reduce the hurt of his or her own mistreatment, but at the expense of the victim.

Repression refers to motivated forgetting, the process by which memories, feelings, and drives associated with painful and unacceptable impulses are excluded from consciousness. Repression is the basic defense mechanism, according to Freud. Only if repression fails or is incomplete do the other mechanisms come into play. Denial and repression are sometimes confused. Denial, however, is a reaction to external danger; repression always represents a struggle with internal (instinctual) stimuli. Repression must also be distinguished from suppression. Suppression reflects a voluntary or intentional effort at forgetting. It is as if the person knows the forgotten material is there but ignores it.

Suppression is considered to be one of the more mature defenses and has been shown empirically to correlate with various measures of adult mental health. I have always admired my wife's ability to use suppression appropriately. Once we were driving home from work on a Fri-

day afternoon, and she was reviewing some stressful events that she fully anticipated would continue to preoccupy her during the next workweek. Because the weekend was on us, however, she declared that she would put it all out of her mind for now. It has always seemed to me that the emphasis on the volitional nature of suppression is not entirely accurate. My wife did successfully suppress the unpleasant thoughts about her work. But how many of us, having made the same declaration of intent, would be able to carry it out?

Reaction formation is the defense mechanism by which repressed motives are translated into their opposites. For instance, have you ever found yourself disliking someone who is overly kind and good? Much to your embarrassment you question the purity of their motives. Perhaps there is something to your intuitions. Unless this person qualifies for sainthood, a psychodynamic formulation of such behavior might involve a reaction formation against hostility: Repressive defenses were insufficient to keep hostile impulses from consciousness, so the defense of reaction formation is enlisted to aid in this effort by camouflaging the original aggressive intent of the behavior. In a reaction formation against dependency, a person who is unconsciously very needy often lives a life of exaggerated independence, refusing all help from others. In a reaction formation against sexual impulses, all sexual desires are repudiated. The individual takes up the cause of celibacy and lives a life of asceticism.

In all of the preceding examples it is fair to ask how an individual knows that these formulations are true or valid. *The psychodynamic clinician would point to the dreams and slips of the tongue (**parapraxes**) of the patient for evidence of the underlying impulse.* The patient's words (or associations) are another rich source of evidence. Excessive reliance on first-person pronouns and frequent allusions to power and status may reflect a narcissistic orientation. Themes of supply and demand and frequent use of food imagery may reflect an oral orientation. I was recently struck by a male patient's discussion of dating and its attendant risks. He constantly spoke of his fear of "sticking his neck out" and referred to singles bars as "butcher shops." Such imagery suggests castration anxiety to the psychodynamic clinician. Observations of how the individual in question handles unexpected life changes are another source of evidence. If an independent man were to sustain a minor injury and react with disproportionate emotion and distress, taking to his bed for the next 6 months, this would enhance our suspicion that dependent impulses lay beneath his pseudoindependence. With some regularity, the media treat the American public to scandalous revelations about the unconventional sexual preferences of some well-known sports figure, televangelist, politician, or entertainer. The psychodynamic clinician who is not surprised by such revelations is not a cynic and does not simply believe that base impulses alone underlie our noblest ideals. But such a clinician does know that human behavior has multiple determinants and that our bodies (including our sexual and aggressive impulses) cannot be ignored. Rare indeed is the individual who negotiates his or her childhood so smoothly that "no troops are left behind" to handle some problem on one or another path of development.

Isolation and **intellectualization** are two related defenses whose common purpose is to seal off feelings, or **affects**, to use a technical psychiatric term. *In isolation of affect, only the emotional component of an idea is repressed, whereas the cognitive component (or the idea itself) remains conscious.* People are often better off not experiencing the full extent of their emotional involvement in a situation. The capacity for logical thinking itself depends on isolation of affect. For physicians and other health professionals, isolation provides the distance and objectivity toward the suffering of patients that is needed to allow treatment to proceed. But if isolation is used too rigidly and pervasively, an individual is in danger of becoming unduly dispassionate and distant.

The distinctive feature of intellectualization is its "shift of emphasis from immediate inner and interpersonal conflict to abstract ideas and esoteric topics" (Schafer, 1954). When medical students enter the anatomy laboratory for the first time and begin to dissect cadavers, they must find ways to cope with the feelings of revulsion and disgust that are common reactions in the presence of the dead. By focusing intently and narrowly on the assigned anatomy lesson for the day, they are able to deflect many of these feelings in the service of learning. This is a perfectly acceptable use of intellectualization.

The following example illustrates a less adaptive use of intellectualization. An oncology resident had just informed a young man of approximately the same age as himself that he (the patient) had liver cancer. In response to questions from the patient concerning his prognosis and the alternative courses of treatment, the resident launched into a lengthy and technical discussion of "age-corrected mortality rates" and "double-blind clinical trials of chemotherapy." It is not difficult to appreciate the physician's anxiety. Nobody likes to be the bearer of bad news, and undoubtedly the similarity in age enhanced a troubling sense of identification with the patient that only compounded the problem. Unfortunately, the net result of such an abstract and intellectualized response was to increase the patient's anxiety level and to confuse him more about his prognosis and treatment. Were he to meet again with this resident, he might hesitate to express his deepest concerns or to ask the necessary questions. *Patients are often sensitive to the emotional states of their physicians and will go to great lengths to avoid burdening physicians (e.g., with difficult questions), even at the risk of jeopardizing their own care.*

Displacement involves redirecting an emotion from its original object to a more acceptable substitute. The emotion most commonly involved is anger. The classic example of displacement is the story of the milquetoast who comes home from the office where his boss has berated him mercilessly and displaces his pent-up aggression by yelling at his wife and kicking his dog.

Turning against the self is a special form of displacement in which impulses and fantasies directed at someone else are self-directed. It is a common feature in some depressed patients who have been provoked or wronged by another person but who do not display any overt anger. Instead, they grow increasingly depressed. Patients with postoperative complications and those who undergo painful procedures frequently become depressed through the use of this mechanism. These patients are angry and resentful toward their caretakers but do not express such feelings publicly for fear of jeopardizing these important relationships. Instead, they turn their rage on themselves. An individual can alleviate depressive symptoms that are generated in this way by giving the patient permission to turn the anger outward with assurance that such feelings will not alienate the hospital staff.

Undoing refers to a defense mechanism designed to negate or annul (undo) some unacceptable thought, wish, or actual transgression of the past. The neglectful parent who showers presents on his or her children and the underworld godfather who makes generous charitable donations may both be said to be engaged in undoing, that is, atoning for or attempting to counteract past misconduct. Undoing can become the predominant defense mechanism and virtually paralyze its victim, as illustrated in Carson's (1979) example:

Before going to school each day, a 13-year-old male went through an elaborate series of rituals that served no practical purpose. He checked his closet and checked under his bed exactly three times before leaving his room. On his way out of the house, he always straightened a picture on the living room wall until it looked just right. On his way to and from school, it was important to him to walk in definite pathways in relation to several telephone poles he passed. If he deviated from this routine, he became quite anxious. He was sexually inhibited, and experiencing guilt about masturbatory fantasies. His ritualistic behavior served the purpose of decreasing guilt and anxiety by magically undoing his unacceptable sexual fantasies and urges.

Sublimation may be understood as a relatively mature defense in which various instincts are displaced or converted into socially acceptable outlets. Normal sexual curiosity, for example, can become voyeurism under adverse circumstances. Under more favorable circumstances, the same impulse may be sublimated into an interest in photography. Similarly, a sadistic impulse to inflict pain can be sublimated into the socially acceptable and necessary practice of surgery. The surgeon can cut and hurt the patient in the service of a higher goal. Note that in both of these examples of sublimation, the infantile and sexual origins of these behaviors are nearly completely disguised.

Humor, altruism, suppression, and anticipation complete most lists of mature defenses.

Transference

Transference may be defined as "the attitudes, feelings, and fantasies which patient's experience with regard to their doctors, many of them arising, seemingly irrationally, from their own unconscious needs and psychological conflicts rather than from the actual circumstances of the relationship" (Nemiah, 1973). *The analysis of transference is the focal point of psychoanalytic treatment,* but our interest in it concerns its expression in a broader variety of health-care settings.

The physician-patient relationship is not entirely (or even primarily) rational. Patients attach all sorts of wishes, expectations, and sentiments to their physicians, the majority of which remain unknown to the physician. For example, when a patient is angry for having had to sit in the waiting room for 2 hours, this is not an inappropriate reaction and need not fall under the rubric of transference. But if this same patient were raised in a household with numerous siblings competing for the parents' attention and had to endure more than his or her share of delayed gratification, sitting in the waiting room might stir up all sorts of painful memories and associated feelings that, whether conscious or not, would serve to intensify and color an otherwise legitimate resentment. Every interpersonal encounter has both realistic and transference components.

Transference is a double-edged sword. It can provide the physician (or any other health-care provider) with leverage in influencing a patient to comply with an unpleasant or inconvenient treatment regimen. It can also lead a patient to trust a physician long before he or she has an objective basis for such confidence.

A positive transference can help carry a patient through the anxieties that accompany most illnesses. I was once asked to see an elderly woman who was terrified of radiation treatment. She was upsetting her family and disrupting the nursing staff with her histrionic refusals. After a brief interview during which I simply allowed her to express her anxieties, she announced that I reminded her of her favorite grandson and promptly consented to the treatment.

Transference, whether positive or negative, can create great difficulties when it is not recognized and successfully managed. *The same transference that permits patients to imbue the physician with magical therapeutic powers also leads them to make impossible demands,* to rage when the physician disappoints them, to resent his or her authority, and to fear and rebel against the physician.

Transference is basically a regressive phenomenon based on psychological factors and not on reality. For that reason, it is important not to take *personally* one patient's confession of undying love–just as it is important not to be offended by another patient's equally unjustified expressions of hatred and contempt. Such expressions must be acknowledged and understood, and the physician must help the patient separate reality and fantasy. To act on initial impulses in either of the preceding situations would disrupt the relationship with the patient and render the physician ineffective.

*When such understandable but unprofessional feelings interfere with a physician's work, it is known as **countertransference**.* Despite its exclusive reliance on male pronouns, I can find no better statement concerning the role of feelings in a clinician's professional life than the following by Nemiah:

> It would be unwise if not impossible for a doctor to avoid having any feelings for his patients. One cannot help at times being annoyed at a particularly hostile patient, pleased at praise that may not be entirely warranted, anxious and uneasy with some, warm and comfortable with others, charmed by the seductive behavior of an attractive

Melencolia I (Melancholy) (1514) *Albrecht Dürer, 1471–1528.* Engraving, 24 × 19 cm. Courtesy of the National Library of Medicine. Depression has been called the "common cold of mental illness," and every primary care physician will encounter and need to treat depressed patients.

woman, overcome by a feeling of helplessness in the face of hopeless situations. It is, however, of particular importance that the doctor have enough self-awareness to recognize how he is feeling. He must be able to judge whether his attitudes are really appropriate to the situation in which they arise, or whether they are a result of his countertransference. It is even more important that he be able to refrain from acting according to the dictates of his impulses and feelings, if such actions would conflict with the rationally determined goals of treatment. It is part of the physician's job to recognize the irrational in both himself and his patients; he must be able to provide the objectivity they lack, without losing his human warmth, understanding, and empathy.

SUMMARY

This chapter can only hint at the complexity and range of psychoanalytic ideas. My hope is that readers will find some of the ideas herein to be both thought-provoking and useful in understanding some of the less rational aspects of human behavior that one observes in patients and physicians as they cope with illness. The psychodynamic perspective may not provide the most scientifically rigorous approach to human behavior, but it offers a comprehensive conception of human concerns with room for all psychological phenomena. No other perspective is so successful at weaving together such disparate domains of experience: past and present, waking thought and dreaming, conscious and unconscious, will and compulsion, love and hate.

CASE STUDY

A third-year medical student began his clerkship year with a rotation in internal medicine. It soon became apparent to his supervisors that he overly identified with his patients, spending inordinate amounts of time engaging them in conversation, giving them false reassurances, and complaining to all who would listen that the nursing staff had been negligent in its duties. He was tactfully and justifiably confronted with his behavior by the chief resident, but his immediate reaction was a combination of resentment and denial. The next day he was temporarily overcome by feelings of depression and worthlessness, and he considered dropping out of medical school.

How can a psychodynamic perspective help you understand the student's behavior?
A psychiatric consultation revealed that this young man was the only son of a chronically depressed mother of

four who rarely had sufficient energy or mental health to attend to her children's' needs. Over the course of his childhood, he and she established an unspoken arrangement, the essence of which required that he subordinate his own needs to hers in return for her approval. In other words, as long as he was a good little boy, uncomplaining and attentive, willing to listen to her lengthy complaints and to provide unrealistically optimistic feedback, he could avoid alienating her. His sisters coped with their mother's psychopathology in an entirely different way, by distancing themselves both physically and emotionally as best they could.

Repeated interviews with this student helped to delineate further the picture of an individual whose choice of vocation and whose characteristic ways of relating to patients could both be understood, in part, as efforts to win maternal approval by assuming the roles of healer, listener, and cheerleader. As an adult, he was still trying to master an impossibly complicated relationship with his mother. His perception of the nurses, too, was colored by his perception of his sisters as derelict in their responsibilities to their mother. To the degree that his concern for his patients was free of conflict, he was capable of being an unusually empathic physician. But to the degree that his self-esteem was at the mercy of his patients' well-being, he was at risk of impairment himself.

Childlike modes of thinking are most apparent in the student's denial and in his subsequent depressive reaction. He was unable to absorb criticism and keep it in perspective. Instead he exaggerated and overgeneralized, concluding on a flimsy evidential basis that he was no longer worthy of becoming a physician. This is an example of what is sometimes called *pars pro toto* thinking in which the part (in this case, one episode of problematic behavior) is mistaken for the whole (his worth as a person). Fortunately, a brief course of psychotherapy was sufficient to improve the student's morale and restore a mature perspective on the situation. He completed the clerkship (and the rest of medical school) uneventfully.

SUGGESTED READINGS

Fisher, S., & Greenberg, R.P. (1996). *Freud scientifically reappraised: Testing the theories and therapy.* New York: Wiley.
This book reviews the social science research conducted to prove or disprove some of Freud's most influential ideas, including the nature of dreams, the Oedipal complex, the origins of depression and paranoia, and the outcome of psychoanalytic treatment.

Gabbard, G.O. (1985). The role of compulsiveness in the normal physician. *Journal of the American Medical Association, 254,* 2926–2929.
An application of psychoanalytic thinking to the psychology of medical students and physicians, this article shows how personal traits

can be adaptive or maladaptive in a physician depending on the uses to which they are put.

Kowalski, R.M., & Westen, D. (2008). *Psychology* (5th ed.). New York: Wiley.

An excellent introductory psychology text with unusually good coverage of psychoanalytc perspectives.

Leichsenring, F., & Rabung, S. (2008). Effectiveness of long-term psychodynamic psychotherapy: A meta-analysis. *Journal of the American Medical Association, 300,* 1551–1565.

Mitchell, S.A. (2002). *Can love last? The fate of romance over time.* New York: Norton.

A thoughtful and optimistic book by a brilliant psychologist who demonstrates the relevance of contemporary psychoanalytic thinking to a subject of interest to us all.

11 Facilitating Health Behavior Change

Adam Aréchiga

> Habit is habit, not to be flung out of the window but rather coaxed downstairs, one step at a time.
>
> MARK TWAIN
>
> The unfortunate thing about the world is that good habits are much easier to give up than bad ones.
>
> W. SOMERSET MAUGHAM
>
> My doctor told me to stop having intimate dinners for four. Unless there are three other people.
>
> ORSON WELLES

With improvements in medical care, and the resultant aging of the population, chronic care models have become an increasingly important component of medical care. Long term problems affecting multiple organ systems, such as diabetes, hypertension, and obesity, are widespread and account for much of the utilization of healthcare resources. Successful treatment and management of these problems require lifestyle modification on the part of the patient.

TABLE 11.1 Common lifestyle changes that healthcare professionals advocate

Eat a healthier diet (e.g., decrease sodium intake, increase consumption of fruits/vegetables)

Increase physical activity

Quit smoking

Drink alcohol only in moderation

Change medication or medication regimen

Monitor blood glucose or blood closer

Adapted from Rollnick, Mason, & Butler (1999)

Physicians are responsible for the diagnosis and treatment of such chronic illnesses. They can also play a crucial role in facilitating behavior change on the part of the patient. Unfortunately, physicians often fail to take advantage of opportunities for effective interventions when they arise. This chapter provides a basic understanding of effective ways to help patients begin the process of lifestyle change.

TRANSTHEORETICAL MODEL

In the past few years the **transtheoretical model** (TTM) of Prochaska & DiClamente has increasingly been used to understand and teach health behavior change, especially in the field of addictions. The TTM or **"stages of change"** theory is based on the idea that change occurs in well-defined, predictable stages or time periods, each of which is associated with specific tasks. These stages are defined as precontemplation, contemplation, preparation, action, maintenance, and termination.

Individuals in the **precontemplation** stage tend to resist change. They may use denial and place responsibility for their problems on factors such as genetic makeup, addiction, family, or society. They may lack information about their problem. They really have no intention to change their behavior any time soon.

Individuals in the **contemplation** stage acknowledge that they have a problem and have begun to consider some kind of behavior change. While many contemplators may consider taking action in the next 6 months, they may be far from doing so. Individuals can remain stuck in this stage for months or years.

Individuals in the **preparation** stage plan to take action in the next month and are making the final adjustments before they begin to change their behavior. While they may appear committed and ready to change their behavior, they may not have resolved their ambivalence toward change.

TABLE 11.2 Recommended interventions for each stage of change	
Stage of Change	Intervention Strategies
Precontemplation	Inquire about past attempts at behavior change Use patient-centered, empathic approach Discuss health problem Explore the "cons" to change
Contemplation	Discuss the history of the problem behavior Discuss health consequences of the behavior Discuss benefits of change Build self-confidence of change (self-efficacy)
Preparation	Match patient to appropriate behavior change model Refer to appropriate treatment provider Facilitate development of realistic goals
Action	Use standardized self-help materials Give support for health behavior change Problem solve for barriers to change Give relapse prevention training
Maintenance	Provide on-going support for lifestyle changes Give health feedback, emphasizing improvements Address "pros" of behavior change Discuss other related behavior change issues (e.g., possible negative consequences of change)

Adapted from Clark & Vickers (2003).

God and the Doctor we alike adore
But only when in danger, not before;
The danger o'er, both are alike requited,
God is forgotten, and the Doctor slighted.

ROBERT OWEN

at maintaining their healthier behavior(s) for the rest of their lives.

While the progression through the stages of change appears linear in nature, in reality change more closely follows a spiral path. Individuals who have progressed to the action stage may suffer a setback and return to the contemplation or precontemplation stage. *Patients rarely work through each stage of change without some kind of setback or relapse.* The majority of people who are trying to change their behavior struggle for years to find an effective solution to their problems.

The **action** stage is where real behavior change begins. This stage requires the greatest commitment in terms of time and energy. Changes made during this stage are the most visible to others and thus receive the most recognition. The danger of this stage is that *many health professionals equate action with change, ignoring the important preparation for action and the efforts to maintain the changes that follow action.*

In the **maintenance** stage any gains achieved in the preceding stages need to be consolidated. *It is important to understand that change does not end in the action stage.* This stage requires a strong commitment to maintenance of the behavior change if relapse is to be avoided, and it can last from 6 months to a lifetime. Any program that promises an easy change or a "quick fix" does not acknowledge that maintenance is a long, ongoing, and sometimes difficult task.

The **termination** stage is the final goal for anyone who is trying to change their behavior. Individuals who eventually reach this stage have complete confidence in their new or healthier behavior and do not fear relapse. They are able to maintain their new behaviors with minimal effort. *Many individuals might not reach this stage and will have to work*

King Death's distribution of prizes. Bacchus takes the first premium (1870) *Wood engraving after Thomas Nast.* Courtesy of the National Library of Medicine. *Most of us will die sooner than necessary because of bad decisions we make about food, alcohol, and exercise.*

TABLE 11.3 Counseling for behavior change

How *Not* To Do It	A Better Method
Practitioner: Have you though about losing some weight?	Practitioner: Have you thought about losing some weight?
Patient: Yes, many times, but I can't seem to manage. It's my one comfort, my eggs in the morning, my fried chicken at lunch. I'm stuck in the house so much these days.	Patient: Yes, many times, but I can't seem to manage. It's my one comfort, my eggs in the morning, my fried chicken at lunch. I'm stuck in the house so much these days.
Practitioner: It would certainly help your blood pressure	Practitioner: It's not easy.
Patient: I know, but what do I do when I really want my two eggs for breakfast? It's a family tradition. [sighs] I always get told to lose weight when I come here.	Patient: You can say that again!
Practitioner: Have you thought about a gradual approach, like leaving out just one of the eggs for a while, and seeing what a difference it makes?	Practitioner: Some people prefer to change their eating, others to get more exercise. Both can help with losing weight. How do you really feel at the moment?
Patient: Yes, but what sort of difference will that make?	Patient: I'm not sure. I always get told to lose weight when I come here.
Practitioner: Over time, as you succeed with one thing, you can try another, and gradually your weight will come down.	Practitioner: It's like we always know what's good for you, as if it's just a matter of going out there, and one, two, three, and you lose weight!
Patient: Not in my house. The temptations are *everywhere*; you should just see what's on the table to munch any time you want.	Patient: Exactly. I'm not sure I can change my eating right now. I used to get a lot more exercise, but life's changed and I've gotten lazy.
Practitioner: Have you talked to your partner about leaving these off the table, just to make it easier for you?	Practitioner: Well, I'm certainly not here to harass you. In fact, all I want to do is understand how you really feel, and whether there is some way you can keep your blood pressure down. Perhaps there isn't at the moment?
Patient: Yes, but . . .	Patient: Well, I could think about . . .

Adapted from Rollnick, Mason, & Butler (1999)

MOTIVATIONAL INTERVIEWING

Motivation Interviewing, developed by Miller and Rollnick, is a therapeutic method or approach for enhancing behavior change in individuals. It is a directive, client-centered counseling style that is intended to help a client or patient become "unstuck" and to begin the process of changing a behavior. The "spirit" of motivational interviewing can be described as collaborative, evocative, and respectful of patient autonomy. *It is not so much a set of techniques as a way of being with people.* Motivational interviewing has four main principles that guide clinical interactions: (1) **roll with resistance** while resisting the "righting reflex," (2) understand the patient's own motivations to **develop discrepancy**, (3) **express empathy**, (4) **enhance self-efficacy** to empower the patient.

Roll with Resistance, Resistance is to be expected and should not be directly opposed; instead, the physician or other healthcare provider should "flow" with the resistance. In motivational interviewing, reluctance and ambivalence toward change are noted and acknowledged as natural and

Better to hunt in fields, for health unbought,
Than fee the doctor for a nauseous draught,
The wise, for cure, on exercise depend;
God never made his work for man to mend.

JOHN DRYDEN

understandable. Humans naturally resist persuasion. The health provider's role is not to impose new views or goals, but to invite their patient to consider new information and new perspectives. To this end it is vital that clinicians resist the natural desire to inform patients that they are doing something wrong (the "righting reflex"). Patients are invited to do what works best for them. This may involve turning a patient's question or problem back toward them ("Yes, but . . ."). *When a health provider rolls with resistance they are actively involving the patient in the problem solving process.*

Develop Discrepancy. Motivational interviewing is intentionally directive. It aims to resolve ambivalence toward positive health behavior change, and gets patients unstuck

TABLE 11.4 Six kinds of change talk

Desire	Statements about preference for change ("I want to . . .")
Ability	Statements about capacity for change ("I can . . .")
Reasons	Specific arguments for change ("I would be healthier if . . .")
Need	Statements about feeling obliged to change ("I have to . . .")
Commitment	Statements about the likelihood of change ("I plan to . . .")
Action	Statements about specific actions taken ("I walked . . .")

Adapted from Rollnick, Miller, & Butler (2008).

TABLE 11.5 Sample questions to elicit change talk

Disadvantages of the *status quo*

- What worries you about your current situation?
- What makes you think that you need to do something about your blood pressure [or weight]?
- What difficulties or hassles have you had in relation to your drug use?
- What do you think will happen if you don't change anything?

Advantages of change

- How would you like for things to be different?
- What would be the good things about losing weight?
- What would you like your life to be like five years from now?
- If you could make this change immediately, by magic, how might things be better for you?
- The fact that you're here indicates that at least part of you thinks it's time to do something. What are the main reasons you see for making a change?
- What would be the advantages of making this change?

Optimism about change

- What makes you think that if you did decide to make a change, you could do it?
- What encourages you that you can change if you want to?
- What do you think would work for you, if you decided to change?
- Have you ever made a significant change in your life before? How did you do it?
- How confident are you that you can make this change?
- What personal strengths do you have that will help you succeed?
- Who could offer you helpful support in making this change?

Intention to change

- What are you thinking about your weight [or other behavior] at this point?
- I can see that you're feeling stuck at this moment. What's going to have to change?
- What do you think you might do?
- How important is this to you? How much do you want to do this?
- What would you be willing to try?
- Of the options I've mentioned, which one sounds like it fits you best?
- Never mind the "how" for right now, what do you want to have happen?
- So what do you intend to do?

Adapted from Miller & Rollnick, (2002).

and moving toward positive change. One way to do this is to *create and amplify any discrepancy between the patient's current behavior and their broader goals and values.* For example, a physician might note the discrepancy between a patient's current state of health and his or her desired state of health. The reality is that *many patients may already perceive such a discrepancy, but are ambivalent about changing their behavior.* The goal of the health provider is to make good use of the discrepancy, increasing and amplifying it until the patient becomes unstuck and is able to move toward change. This process is often facilitated by identifying and clarifying the patient's own goals and values that conflict with his or her current behavior. It is the patient's own reasons for change that are most likely to trigger behavior change. *It is imperative for the patient to present his or her own reasons for change and not feel coerced by the health professional.*

Express Empathy. The foundation of motivational interviewing is a client-centered, empathic counseling style based on "acceptance." The counselor attempts to understand the client or patient's perspectives and feelings without judging, blaming or criticizing. It should be noted that you can understand or accept a patient's perspective without endorsing or agreeing with it. Likewise, acceptance does not stop the counselor from expressing an opinion different from the patient's. The interesting thing is that *when you accept patients for who they are, it frees them to change.* Conversely, if you adopt a nonaccepting attitude, it will typically halt the change process. The client or patient is not viewed as incapable of change, but rather as having become "stuck" through understandable psychological processes.

Enhance Self-Efficacy. One of the keys of behavior change is **self-efficacy**, which is a person's belief in his or her ability to change and/or meet goals. One goal of motivational interviewing is to enhance or increase the patient's confi-

> A person should not eat until his stomach is replete but should diminish his intake by approximately one fourth of satiation.
>
> MOSES BEN MAIMON (MAIMONIDES)
> *Mishneh Torah*
>
> The rich ate and drank freely, accepting gout and apoplexy as things that ran mysteriously in respectable families . . .
>
> GEORGE ELIOT
> *Silas Marner*

dence in his ability to achieve successful change. This can be accomplished by letting patients know that you *can* help them change versus telling them that you as the health provider *will* change them. Self-efficacy may also be enhanced by looking at the success of others or building upon the patient's own past success. *It is vital that health providers support the patient's hope that change is possible and that it can make a difference in their health.*

Throughout the interaction with the patient, it is important to listen for and elicit change talk. By listening to what the patient says, you gain insight into the likelihood of change. As a rule when you hear positive change talk you are doing it right. If on the other hand you find yourself arguing for change and patient defending the status quo, you need to get back on course.

CLINICAL APPLICATIONS

Example of Motivational Interviewing Techniques Applied to Smoking Cessation

Introduce Topic and Assess Readiness for Change

- **Introduce topic**—Use open-ended, nonjudgmental question or comment to invite the patient to discuss smoking:
  "I'm interested in hearing you talk a little bit about your smoking."
  "I want to understand what it is like for you to be a smoker, please tell me about it."
  "How do you really feel about your smoking these days?"

- **Rate motivation**—Ask the patient to rate their motivation to quit smoking:
  "I'd like to have you rate for me, on a scale from 1 to 10, your current motivation to quit smoking. If 1 is not at all motivated to quit smoking and 10 is completely ready to quit smoking, what number are you right now?"

- **Rate confidence**—Ask the patient to rate confidence to quit smoking:
  "Again on a scale from 1 to 10, how confident are you that you could be successful at quitting smoking if you decided you wanted to quit right now? If 1 is not at all confident that you could quit and stay quit, and 10 is absolutely confident that you could be successful, what number are you right now?"

Address Motivation and Confidence

- **Discuss motivation**—Elicit patients' self-statements about change by having them explain their motivation rating:
  "Why are you a . . . . . . and not a 1 on the scale?"
  Note: asking the question in the other direction (why are you a . . . . . . and not a 10?) will encourage the patient to argue against change and thus should not be used.
  "What would it take for you to move from a . . . . . . to a [higher number]?"

- **Weigh the pros and cons**—Explore with the patient both the benefits of change and the barriers to change:
  "What do you like about smoking?"
  "What concerns you about smoking?"
  "What are the roadblocks to quitting?"
  "What would you like about being a nonsmoker?"

Summarize both the pros and cons provided by the patient and then ask: "So where does that leave you now?"

- **Provide personal risk information**—Share nonjudgmental information about risk and/or objective data from medical evaluation, then ask the patient's opinion of this information (Avoid giving advice or attempting to shock or frighten the patient into change):
  "What do you think about these results?"
  "Would it be helpful for you if I gave you some information about the risks of smoking?"
  "What do you need to hear from me about this?"

- **Discuss Confidence**—Get the patient to make self-statements about his or her confidence to quit smoking by discussing their confidence rating:
  "Why are you a . . . . . . and not a 1?"
  "What would help you move from a . . . . . . to a [higher number]?"
  "What can I do to support you in moving up to a [higher number]?"

Offer Support and Make a Patient-Centered Plan

- Work with the patient to create a patient-centered plan that matches the patient's readiness to quit.

TABLE 11.6 Recommendations for behavior change counseling

Frame plan to match patient's perceptions.

- It is important to assess the beliefs and concerns of the patient and to provide information based on this foundation. Remember that behavior change interventions need to be tailored to each patient's specific needs.

Fully inform patients of the purposes and expected effects of interventions and when to expect these effects.

- This will help limit discouragement when the patient cannot see immediate effects. If side effects are common, tell the patient what to expect specifically, and under which circumstances the intervention should be stopped.

Suggest small changes rather than large ones.

- Individuals experience success just by achieving a small goal; this will initiate a positive change.

Be specific.

- Explain the regime and rationale of the behavior change; it is often useful to write the regime down for the patient to take home.

It may be easier to add a new behavior rather than eliminate an established one.

- For example, it may be more effective to suggest that patients increase their physical activity rather than change their current dietary patterns.

Link new behaviors to old behaviors.

- For example, suggest using an exercise bike while watching television.

Use the power of your profession.

- Patients see physicians as health experts, so be sympathetic and supportive while giving a firm, definite message.

Get explicit commitments from the patient.

- Asking the patient how he plans to follow the recommendations encourages him to think about how to integrate a specific behavior into his daily schedule

Refer.

- Sometimes it is not possible to counsel patients properly. In those cases, refer patients to behavioral specialists, clinical health educators, or support groups to review the appropriate intervention.

Adapted from the *Guide to Clinical Preventive Services*, 2nd Ed. 1996.

- Encourage the patient to consider what could work, rather than focus on what could not.
- Provide options (referral, nicotine replacement, patient education materials, etc.), but not direct advice.
- Ask patient to select the next step.
- Reinforce any movement toward making a change.
- Follow-up on subsequent visits.

Example of Motivational Interviewing Techniques Applied to Adolescent Dietary Adherence

- **Establish Rapport**
  "How's it going?"

- **Opening Statement**
  "We have . . . minutes to meet. So here is what I thought we might do:
  Hear how your new diet is going.

Give you some information from your last diet recall and cholesterol values.
Talk about what, if anything, you might change in your eating.
How does that sound? Is there anything else you want to do?"

- **Assess Diet Adherence and Progress**
  "On a scale of 1—10, if 1 is not following the recommended diet at all, and 10 is following the recommended diet all the time, what number are you at right now?"
  "Tell me more about the number you chose."
  "Why did you choose a . . ., and not a 1?"
  "What times do you follow your diet, and when don't you?"
  "How are you feeling about the recommended diet?"
  "The last time we met, you were working on . . . How has that been going?"

- **Give Feedback**
  Show patient test data.
  Compare participant results with normative data or other interpretive information.
  "This is where you stand compared to other teenagers."

TABLE 11.7 Examples of tailored intervention responses

Not Ready	Unsure	Ready
Goal: raise awareness	Goal: to build motivation and confidence.	Goal: to negotiate plan.
Major task: inform and encourage	Major task: to explore ambivalence.	Major task: facilitate decision making.
Ask open-ended questions. "What would need to be different for you to consider making additional changes in your eating?" "You said you were a ___ on the scale. What would have to happen for you to more from a ___ to a ___ ?"	Explore ambivalence. "What are some of the things that you like (and dislike) about your current eating habits?" "What are some of the good (and not so good) things about changing your diet?"	Identify change options "What do you think needs to change?" "What are your ideas for making a change?" "Which option makes the most sense to you?"
Respectfully acknowledge the patient's decisions. "I respect your decision to not make any new or additional changes in your eating."	Look into the future. "I think I can understand why you're unsure about making new or additional changes to your diet. Let's just take a moment and imagine that you decided to change. Why would you want to do this?"	Help patient set a realistic and achievable short-term goal. Develop a plan to eat healthier diet. Summarize the plan.
Offer professional advice. "It should come as no surprise that my recommendation is for you to _____. But, this is your decision. If you should decide to make some changes to your diet, I'm here to help you. Regardless, I would like to keep in touch."	Refer to other teens. "What do your friends like to eat?" "What would your friends think if you ate this way?"	
	Ask about the next step. "Where does this leave you now?" (Let patient raise the topic of change)	

Elicit patient's response information.
"What do you think of all this information?"
Offer information about the meaning or significance of the results (note: only do this if the patient shows interest or asks questions about the information).
"Most teenagers who have cholesterol values around . . . are more likely to . . . ."

- **Assess Readiness to Change**
 "On a scale of 1–10, if 1 is not ready to make any new changes in your diet, and 10 is completely ready to make changes such as eating foods lower in saturated fat and cholesterol, what number are you at right now?"
 "Tell me more about the number that you chose."
 "What made you choose a . . . instead of a 1?"

- **Tailored Intervention Approach**

- **Close the Encounter**
 Summarize the session.
 "Did I get it all?"
 Support self-efficacy.
 "I can tell that you are really trying and I know that you

> Those who think they have not time for bodily exercise will sooner or later have to find time for illness.
>
> EDWARD STANLEY, EARL OF DERBY
> *The Conduct of Life—Address at Liverpool College*

can do it. If this plan doesn't work so well, we can adapt it or change it so that you are more successful."
- Arrange next appointment.

SUMMARY

Lifestyle change is a necessary step for patients with chronic illnesses. Unfortunately behavior change can be difficult. Health care providers have an important role in facilitating this change in their patients. Two of the most relevant models for counseling for behavior change are the **Transtheoretical Model** and **Motivational Interviewing**. The TTM posits that health behavior change occurs in distinct stages (precontemplation, contemplation, preparation, action, maintenance, and termination) each of which has its own tasks that need to be accomplished before an individual can effectively progress. Motivational Interviewing is a directive client-centered counseling approach that is used to get patient "unstuck" and begin the process of behavior change. The four main principles of this approach are expressing empathy, developing discrepancy, rolling with resistance, and supporting self-efficacy. When used successfully, these models can help facilitate and foster behavior change in patients.

CASE STUDY

Mr. Brown is a 51-year-old accountant who has a number of health issues. He experiences fatigue, depression, and insomnia. He is concerned about his heart because of a family history of heart disease (his father died of a myocardial infarction at age 59). He is obese (BMI 34 kg/m^2), has hypertension, elevated cholesterol and is sedentary. When given this feedback, Mr. Brown sighs and says that he has tried to lose weight in the past but that nothing has worked. When you ask about his eating and exercise habits, he responds, "I work 80+ hours each week, eat when I can (usually out of the vending machines at work), and have no time to exercise."

What would be the best approach with this patient?
Mr. Brown is unsure about any health behavior change. If you confront this patient, it will most likely lead to denial and resistance. The best approach would be to start by establishing rapport and expressing empathy toward the difficulty of lifestyle change. Open-ended questions, such as "Tell me more about your concerns of heart disease" "What are your thoughts about your weight?" and "What weight loss methods have you tried in the past?" can help highlight past successes and failures in terms of lifestyle change. Questions such as these may also reveal the patient's readiness to change, and identify the pros and cons of such a change. The main goal for this initial appointment might be to have Mr. Brown examine his problem behaviors more closely and to begin thinking about what would be necessary for him to change. At a following appointment it may be possible to present Mr. Brown with different lifestyle options that would positively affect his risk factors, and help him develop a plan of action once he had identified the behavior that he felt most comfortable attempting to change.

SUGGESTED READINGS

Berg-Smith, S.M., Stevens, V.J., Brown, K.M., Van Horn, L., Gernhofer, N., Peters, E. et al. (1999). A brief motivational intervention to improve dietary adherence in adolescents. *Health Education Research, 14*(3), 399–410.
This article describes specific alterations in the motivational interviewing approach that are helpful when working with adolescents.

Clark, M.M., & Vickers, K.S. (2004). Counseling for health behavior change. In R.S. Lang, & D.D. Hensrud (Eds.). *Clinical preventive medicine* (2nd ed., pp. 59–67). New York, NY: AMA Press.
This chapter provides a basic outline of motivational interviewing as applied in a medical setting.

Miller, W.R., & Rollnick, S. (2002). *Motivational interviewing* (2nd ed.). New York, NY: Guilford.
The authors and creators of motivational interviewing have written a book that explains their method of counseling for health behavior change. In addition to providing a detailed description of the foundation for motivational interviewing, they provide easy to follow examples of the clinical application of their counseling method.

Prochaska, J.O., Norcross, J.C., & DiClemente, C.C. (2002). *Changing for good.* New York, NY: Quill.
This book explains the transtheoretical model of behavior change in a way that can be used with the lay public.

Report of the U.S. Preventive Services Task Force/U.S. Department of Health and Human Services, Office of Public Health and Science, Office of Disease Prevention and Health Promotion (1996). *Guide to clinical preventive services* (2nd ed.).
This report was written by a task force from the U.S. Department of Health and Human Services, Office of Public Health and Science, Office of Disease Prevention and Health Promotion. The report is a reference source on the effectiveness of clinical preventive services including counseling for risk reduction.

Rollnick, S., Miller, W., & Butler, C. (2008). *Motivational interviewing in health care.* New York, NY: Guilford.
This book provides a practical and stepwise approach to using Motivational Interviewing in health care.

12 Human Sexuality

Jeannine Rahimian, Jonathan Bergman, George R. Brown, & Salvador Ceniceros

> I believe in the flesh and the appetites,
> Seeing, hearing, feeling are miracles
> And each part of me is a miracle.
>
> WALT WHITMAN
> *Song of Myself*

Sexual functioning is an important aspect of human life and interaction. However, sexual health is also highly susceptible to the effects of many illnesses and medications. For example, impotence is among the many problems faced by diabetics secondary to neuropathy and microvascular disease. The newer antidepressants may have few adverse effects, but a decrease in sexual desire causes many patients to stop taking these medications. The public's interest in enhancing sexual function is evident in the glut of advertising (including computer spam) for medications to help men with erectile dysfunction. One measure of the importance of sexual functioning in the United States is that most insurance plans will cover the cost of drugs for erectile dysfunction, despite their high cost. *Evaluation of sexual function is a critical part a physician's evaluation of patients, particularly when patients have illnesses or medications that are associated with sexual dysfunction.*

Despite its importance, it is estimated that only 35% of primary care physicians often or always take a sexual history as part of routine patient evaluations. The reasons given for this lack of attention to sexual health include time constraints, embarrassment, the belief that a sexual history is not relevant to the chief complaint, or the physician feeling ill-prepared. Medical schools are now more systematically addressing these issues, and medical students actively practice taking sexual histories to help them feel more prepared and less embarrassed. Questions that are tailored to the specific needs of the patient are highly relevant and not unduly time consuming.

This chapter will outline the types of questions that are best used for screening, describe how to determine when to ask more questions, and illustrate how to get specific information when it is needed. In addition, the chapter will address some simple interventions that a clinician can use to help patients who have problems with sexual function. Most such problems are relatively easily addressed, reducing yet another obstacle to asking questions about sexual function—a physician's sense of helplessness about doing anything helpful.

> Sex is not an antidote for loneliness, feelings of inadequacy, fear of aging, hostility, or an inability to form warm friendships.
>
> ISABEL P. ROBINAULT
> *Sex, Society and the Disabled*

THE SEXUAL HISTORY

The sexual history should be a part of a general assessment and would rarely be the first set of questions asked. *A physician should always establish rapport with a patient prior to asking personal questions about sexual health.* Once ready to ask the sexual questions, a transition statement can be helpful. For example, one might say:

> Now I am going to ask some questions which may be a bit more personal. I ask these questions as a part of a total medical history. Your answers are confidential, and you don't need to answer any questions if you are uncomfortable.

Generally the patient will not be embarrassed as long as the doctor is matter-of-fact, sensitive, and nonjudgmental. *Sexual orientation or behavior should never be assumed, and the way questions are worded should provide permission to give honest responses.* For example, questions such as "how many partners have you had in the past year?" are more likely to elicit accurate information than questions about whether a patient has a girlfriend or boyfriend. Normalization of specific activities or problems may help patients feel more comfortable giving information that they may otherwise find embarrassing. For example, one might ask if the number of lifetime partners was "about 5, 10, 20, or more?" This gives permission for the patient to acknowledge it if he or she has had more than a few partners. Similarly, telling a diabetic patient that "many people with diabetes experience changes in sexual function" may ameliorate some of the patient's potential embarrassment.

Screening *questions for a sexual history should be included in the patient's initial evaluation*, as an important component of a comprehensive history and examination. Some relevant questions might include the following:

- Are you currently sexually active, or have you been in the past?
- Do you have sex with men, women, or both?
- Do you use contraception? If so, what type?
- Do you desire a pregnancy in the near future?
- How many partners have you had in the past month? In your lifetime?
- What type of sex activities do you participate in (oral, vaginal, anal, other)?
- Are you satisfied with your sexual functioning?
- Is there an area in which you would seek improvement?
- Do you have difficulty achieving orgasm or ejaculation?
- Do you ever have pain with intercourse?
- Do you use any toys or devices during sex?
- Have you ever been tested for a sexually transmitted infection (STI)? Have you ever had an STI?
- Have you ever been tested for HIV? Would you like to be tested today?
- What is your understanding of STI transmission, including HIV?
- Are you ever pressured into having sex when you do not want to?

In situations in which sexual dysfunction is suspected, open-ended questions such as "How can I help you?" or "What is the problem?" can be quite helpful. These can be followed with more specific questions after the patient has had an opportunity to explain the problem(s) as he or she perceives them. *Silence can be a powerful tool in taking a sexual history, and repetition of what the patient has said shows empathy and attentiveness to the patient's needs.*

INTERVENTIONS

Once a problem has been identified, it is important to let the patient know that it is good that he or she shared this

> Venus found herself a goddess
> In a world controlled by gods,
> So she opened up her bodice
> And evened up the odds.
>
> HARVEY GRAHAM
> *A Doctor's London*

information. Following this, the physician can address the patient's concerns. Often the intervention is very simple, although in some cases consultation with an expert in sexual function is indicated. Jack Annon's **PLISSIT** model offers a graduated series of responses to sexual concerns raised by patients.

1. *Permission:* Most sexual concerns can be addressed with simple permission, such as assuring the patient that there is no "correct" position for intercourse, or explaining that problems with decreased libido can often be addressed by simply switching to a different antidepressant.
2. *Limited Information:* Sexual concerns that require more than permission are often handled with simple and limited information. For example, a woman with orgasmic problems may be "cured" with information about the role of clitoral stimulation in female orgasm, or a man with erectile dysfunction may need to be told that alcohol decreases sexual performance.
3. *Specific Suggestions:* The physician can provide suggestions specifically tailored to each patient's problems and desires. This may include prescriptions for medications for erectile dysfunction, or vaginal cream for painful intercourse. In some cases, this is the point at which a primary care physician would seek consultation from a specialist, such as a urologist or gynecologist.
4. *Intensive Treatment:* If the less intensive interventions are not sufficient, individualized therapy by a trained sex therapist or couples therapist is sometimes needed. The physician's recommendation that the patient get help can add significantly to the likelihood that the patient will follow through with treatment.

The remainder of the chapter will provide more details on what is known about "normal" and problematic sexual response. However, it is important to note that *the concept of "normal" or healthy sexual functioning is profoundly influenced by the time and culture in which the patient and physician are functioning.* For example, some sexual behaviors labeled as psychiatric disorders by the American Psychiatric Association 30 years ago are now considered to be within the range of "normal" behavior. Laws regarding sexual behavior differ by state within the United States. The powerful and intimate nature of sexuality leads it to be the focus

TABLE 12.1 Major physical changes occurring in the sexual response cycle

Male	Female
Excitement (mechanism: vasocongestion) *Appearance of sex flush over neck, chest, face, torso, and genitals; increase in heart rate and blood pressure; increase in muscular tension*	
Erection of penis	Clitoris increases in size
Swelling and elevation of testes	Vaginal lubrication
	Inner two thirds of vagina lengthens and expands
Plateau (mechanism: vasocongestion) *Continuation of increases that began in excitement phase*	
Continued enlargement and elevation of testes	Clitoris retracts under hood
Rotation of testes	Outer one third of vagina swells, forming the orgasmic platform
Secretion of a few drops of fluid from Cowper's gland	
Orgasm (mechanism: neuromuscular) *Muscular contractions throughout the body; respiratory rate and pulse may double, and blood pressure may increase as much as 30%; vocalizations may occur*	
Contractions extending from testes to penis itself	Muscular contractions (2-4/sec) beginning in outer one third
Three or four strong ejaculatory contractions occurring at 0.8-sec intervals, followed by two to four slower contractions of the anal sphincter	of vagina followed by 3 to 15 contractions occurring at 0.8-sec intervals
	Uterine contractions
Resolution *Rapid reduction in vasocongestion occurs; respiration, pulse, and blood pressure return to normal; muscles relax*	
Gradual return of penis to its unstimulated state	Clitoris, vagina, and external genitalia return to normal
Testes descend and return to normal size	

of intense moral and spiritual debate throughout the world.

THE SPECTRUM OF SEXUAL RESPONSE

Prior to the work of **Masters and Johnson** in the 1960s, men and women were thought to be very different in their physiological sexual responses. However, the pioneering work of Masters and Johnson established that most of the physiologic changes during sexual response were similar for both sexes (Table 12.1). Masters and Johnson did report two dramatic differences between men and women: (1) male sexual functioning is characterized by a lengthy **resolution phase**, whereas many women are capable of experiencing multiple orgasms in a single sexual episode; and (2) male orgasms are punctuated by ejaculation, whereas female orgasms are not. More recent research has suggested that even these differences may not be universal, with some men capable of multiple orgasms and some women reporting ejaculation during orgasm.

Masters and Johnson proposed that the intensity of sexual response in men did not vary widely, but they did report a wide variety in the relative length of various sexual response phases (Figure 12.1). At one end of the spectrum is premature ejaculation, with a very rapid progression through the excitement and plateau phases, culminating in an abrupt orgasm much earlier than either the man or his partner wishes. At the other end of the spectrum, men and women can exhibit a pattern of greatly delayed or absent orgasm, often in the context of otherwise typical arousal and excitation.

Sexual Dysfunction in Men

Premature ejaculation is defined as ejaculation that occurs before it is desired, without reasonable control over the timing of ejaculation. There are many factors associated with this problem, which may occur more often in less experienced men. The prevalence of premature ejaculation is estimated at 30%. In practice, the term premature ejaculation is only used if there is associated distress or relationship difficulty (e.g., if this is a regular and unwanted aspect of the man's sexual response cycle). The key to ejaculatory control is the recognition of signals occurring just before ejaculation be-

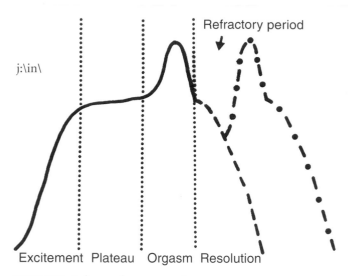

j:\in\

Refractory period

Excitement Plateau Orgasm Resolution

FIGURE 12.1 Male sexual response cycle

gins (the point of **ejaculatory inevitability**). Men who ejaculate prematurely may suffer from constitutionally hypersensitive sympathetic nervous systems, a concept described as constitutional vulnerability or somatic vulnerability. Treatment is usually behavioral, with techniques such as the "**start-stop**" technique and **squeeze technique**, or with medications such as antidepressants, which have the specific side effect of delaying ejaculation.

Behavioral techniques are very effective when used alone or with medication. The "**start-stop**" (or "stop-go") technique can be done alone or with a partner. The man is instructed to stimulate his penis to erection and then masturbate until he senses he is about to ejaculate. He is then to stop and wait for several minutes to let the intense sensation subside. He should repeat the procedure until he has approached orgasm four separate times. He learns to control his timing by learning his point of ejaculatory inevitability and internalizing his body's response to stimulation.

The **squeeze technique** involves being brought just to the point of ejaculatory inevitability and then delaying additional pleasurable stimulation. At this point, the man or his partner applies a firm squeeze to the penis with the thumb and first two fingers, on either side of the coronal ridge between the glans and shaft of the penis. The squeeze should be firm enough to cause partial or complete loss of erection and should last 15 to 20 seconds. After 1 minute, the stimulation is repeated and the entire procedure is repeated four separate times. The man should abstain from intercourse during the initial treatment phase. When intercourse is recommended, the woman should be on top to reduce the stimulation to the male and to reduce his control over body movements during intercourse. Initially, the man should permit intravaginal containment of his penis without thrusting, and the woman should control the pace and rhythm.

Antidepressant medication has also been shown to help delay ejaculation. Specifically, several studies have documented the efficacy of **clomipramine**, a tricyclic antidepressant, in treating premature ejaculation. **Selective serotonin reuptake inhibitors** (SSRIs) have also shown considerable efficacy, as premature ejaculation may be related to diminished serotonergic neurotransmission and 5-HT_{2C} or 5-HT_{1A} receptor disturbances. Meta-analyses have shown that paroxetine is clearly superior to clomipramine, sertraline, and fluoxetine for treatment of premature ejaculation. Pharmacological treatment of premature ejaculation is recommended when the etiology is indicative of biological origin, the patient wishes to pursue pharmacotherapy, traditional sex therapy has failed, relationships have failed with premature ejaculation as an important factor, or when religious or cultural considerations preclude sex therapy.

Inhibited ejaculation may result from psychiatric conditions, medical conditions (e.g., multiple sclerosis, diabetes, and vascular disease), or the use of medications. This disorder affects approximately 2–8% of the general population, with varied etiology including spinal cord injury, multiple sclerosis, pelvic surgery, severe diabetes, and medications that inhibit adrenergic innervation of the ejaculatory system such as phenothiazines, alcohol, some antidepressants, antihypertensives, anxiolytics, zolpidem, and antihistamines. Alternatively, inhibited male orgasm may reflect relationship distress when it is associated with the inability to achieve orgasm with a specific partner, while retaining the ability to reach orgasm with other partners or with self-stimulation. Attention to relationship issues in the form of counseling by a trusted healthcare professional or referral to a specialist can often help resolve this problem. **Orgasm triggers** that are sometimes helpful in facilitating orgasm include breathing rapidly and then stopping (breath holding); tilting the head back (glottal displacement); pointing the toes and contracting the pelvic muscles; stimulating the scrotal, testicular, and perianal areas; and anal stimulation with massage of the prostate by the partner.

Male sexual dysfunction may be caused by psychological concerns, physical problems, or a combination of these etiologies. Previous teachings held that the majority of cases of sexual dysfunction were psychologically based. However, newer diagnostic techniques have prompted urologists and sleep researchers to report that a majority of all cases have predominant somatic etiologies. *The most likely etiology with any particular patient is a combination of both somatic and psychological elements, with possible primary and secondary etiologies.*

Evaluation of the patient with **male erectile dysfunction** should include hormone levels of a pooled sample of serum (especially prolactin and testosterone), vascular examination, and a nocturnal penile tumescence test, although the latter is expensive and not always accurate. Medical

UNREQUITED LOVE

Salivating like Pavlos' dogs, I respond to signals
of distress, not food, put on my clinical hat,
offer you anti-depressants for a wound too deep
for chemistry to touch, and try in vain to find you.

I have to accept that you will always be just
out of reach, that to lie between paper sheets
is the nearest we shall ever get to love. Turn
a computer cross just slightly, and it makes a
kiss.

In the end, as they say, words seem to fail me,
and putting on my poet's hat I could wish it was
the plastic bag which now is the ultra-modern way
out of all the stanzas of free-fall delusion.

I never thought my bitch's drooling mouth
would be so eager for the meal that never came,
that you would be my white-coated master,
calling me to heel, wearing your laboratory hat.

These animals, they copulate so rapidly.
Perhaps we should have done the same,
a forceful thrust against the railings
of the hospital, but, no, that's not the way.

You never liked my colloquial way with words.
I mock the only gods I ever had this way,
knowing that they are all I really cared for,
and all the rest is just a tale of unrequited love.

ELIZABETH BARTLETT

form, he is less able to do so. A vicious cycle soon develops in which failure begets failure, and the man becomes more and more sexually inhibited.

The treatment of male erectile dysfunction has been revolutionized by the discovery of the role of **nitric oxide** as a neurotransmitter in the physiology of erection. This finding led to the development of **sildenafil citrate** (*Viagra*), the *first widely effective oral treatment for erectile dysfunction*. Sildenafil citrate works by inhibiting phosphodiesterase, preventing the breakdown of cGMP and prolonging smooth muscle relaxation. Tadalafil (**Cialis**) and vardenafil (**Levitra**) work by the same mechanism, although the half-lives of tadalafil (36 hours) and vardenafil (72 hours) are longer than that of sildenafil citrate (6 hours). Patients are instructed to take these medications on an empty stomach, ideally 1 hour prior to sexual activity. Other agents that may be effective include androgens, yohimbine, intracavernosal injections of papaverine, prostaglandins, and sensate focus exercises. Vacuum constriction devices (pumps) and surgical management such as arterial revascularization, venous ligation, or penile implants can also be considered.

Sexual Dysfunction in Women

Women demonstrate considerable variety in the length and intensity of their sexual response phases. Mood, effectiveness of sexual stimulation, distractions, and previous experiences all affect overall sexual responsiveness. Masters and Johnson described numerous patterns of female sexual response and discovered that a woman may have a pattern that is typical for her, whereas others may respond with different patterns on different occasions (Figure 12.2).

Women may experience a pattern that resembles the sexual response of men, i.e., multiple orgasms sufficiently far apart that they are experienced as separate events (pattern

conditions that should be considered include nicotine addiction, diabetes, coronary artery disease, heart failure, and alcoholism. Moreover, patients undergoing dialysis or taking medications (e.g., antihypertensives, antipsychotics, corticosteroids, or opioids) can also experience erectile disorders.

Anxiety, guilt, or anger toward the sexual partner are the most common psychological contributors to erectile dysfunction. Furthermore, feelings of inadequacy and shame can lead to an intellectualization of the sexual act and "**spectatoring**"; that is, treating sexual intercourse as a performance at which the man is a spectator and not an emotionally involved participant. As the man tries harder to per-

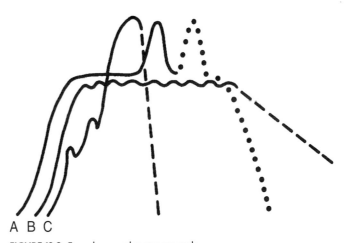

A B C

FIGURE 12.2 Female sexual response cycle

A). Women with less sexual experience may have a gradual and somewhat tenuous increase in arousal and a slow resolution phase (pattern B). Some women have an "escalating effect" with continued stimulation after orgasm, resulting in several orgasms each building on the intensity of the previous one (pattern C).

This variability in female response undoubtedly contributed to the notion that psychologically mature women obtain orgasm with men through vaginal stimulation by the penis rather than from clitoral stimulation. Masters and Johnson maintained that clitoral stimulation, direct or indirect, is the primary source of orgasmic stimulation and that the types of orgasmic response are physiologically indistinguishable. However, in contrast, at least three types of female orgasm have been identified by a small body of research:

1. **Vulvar orgasm** is characterized by contractions of the outer one third of the vagina as a result of coital or noncoital stimulation. No refractory period occurs with this type of orgasm.
2. **Uterine orgasm** is characterized by altered breathing distinguished by gasps and climaxing with an episode of involuntary holding of the breath that is exhaled at orgasm. This response is then followed by a refractory period characterized by deep relaxation and a feeling of satiation. This type of orgasm occurs during repeated deep stimulation involving deep thrusting.
3. **Blended orgasm** contains features of both vulvar and uterine orgasms, resulting from simultaneous stimulation of the clitoris and the vaginal wall.

There is little research on the sexual response disorders of women. Available data suggest that drugs and illnesses exert similar effects on sexual function in the same phase of the response cycle in men and women. For example, *about half of men taking serotonergic antidepressants experience delayed ejaculation and orgasm and a similar percentage of women experience treatment-emergent orgasmic difficulties.* Most disorders occur in both men and women, although certain disorders may be more prevalent or troublesome in one gender or the other. Men are more likely to seek professional advice than women with regards to sexual dysfunction. Women whose sexual arousal disorder involves a failure to lubricate may resort to self-help measures such as over-the-counter remedies with some success, thereby avoiding the need for professional help.

*Recurrent or persistent genital pain experienced during or after sexual intercourse is called **dyspareunia**.* Pain may be felt at the entrance to the vagina (the **introitus**) or deep in the vagina or pelvis, and can result from either physical or psychological problems. Women will often become concerned if they are evaluated by a physician and informed that there is nothing physically abnormal. However, although no anatomic abnormality may be present, physicians can often identify a physiological basis for sexual

problems if they conduct a careful examination. For example, scars from previous episiotomies or from adhesions due to previous pelvic inflammatory disease may result in pain during intercourse. A vaginal infection or insufficient lubrication also may cause irritation and inflammation of the vaginal walls. Similarly, a dry, thinning vagina in a postmenopausal woman will often lead to dyspareunia.

Psychologically, sexually inexperienced women who were taught that men are insensitive and uncaring or that sex is to be tolerated but not enjoyed may expect pain, with their fear and anxiety leading to subsequent dyspareunia. The influence of sexual abuse or trauma on many women's sexuality cannot be overstated, especially given the high prevalence of these problems.

*The involuntary contraction of the pubococcygeus muscles that surround the outer third of the vagina is termed **vaginismus**.* Spasm of these muscles can interfere with coitus and can prevent penetration of the penis. *More than half of women with vaginismus also have a history of dyspareunia.* The majority of women with this disorder will contract their pubococcygeus muscles in response to anything inserted into the vagina (e.g., a finger, speculum, or tampon). These contractions of the pubococcygeus muscles are not under voluntary control. Attempts to penetrate the vagina can produce pain and associated anxiety. Some women avoid the possibility of such pain by avoiding all sexual encounters. Obtaining a thorough medical and psychological history is essential for these women, to discover whether rape or sexual abuse as a child has occurred. A history of either suggests psychotherapy may be required in addition to sex therapy.

Treatment of vaginismus is highly effective, with success rates reported at up to 100%, with no relapse at 5-year follow-up. Treatment should combine education, counseling, and behavioral exercises. Treatment begins with self-discovery, masturbation, and relaxation learned via exercises and audio tapes. The next step involves insertion of successively larger dilators into the vagina while controlling the pace of treatment. The exercises and insertion of dilators are then explained to the partner, who takes over the insertion, with the woman guiding her partner's hand. Sexual intercourse should not proceed until she feels ready. *The majority of unconsummated marriages result from vaginismus,* and many couples remain together for years without having sexual intercourse.

Societal attitudes toward female orgasm have changed markedly with time. In Victorian times, orgasm was considered abnormal and harmful, which is not the case today. This shift in cultural norms has produced increased emphasis on orgasm, and diagnostic precision, including development of appropriate differential diagnosis, must be applied before labeling a woman as anorgasmic. However, some women are simply unable to reach orgasm, despite adequate sexual stimulation. They may look forward to sex and experience a high level of sexual excitement, with vaginal swelling and lubrication, but still be unable to experience the release of orgasm.

Inhibited female orgasm is divided into two major subtypes: global and situational. **Global** or generalized orgasmic disorder refers to the inability to experience orgasm in all situations and with all partners. **Situational** orgasmic disorder refers to the ability to experience orgasm only in specific circumstances, e.g., during masturbation but not with intercourse, or with one partner but not another. The treatment for inhibited female orgasm consists of helping the patient progress through nine basic steps:

1. Self-examination.
2. Genital touching.
3. Identification of pleasurable areas.
4. Learning of masturbation (with or without assistance of a training film).
5. Experience of arousal from erotic pictures, stories, or fantasies.
6. Use of a vibrator.
7. Observation by a partner.
8. Participation by a partner.
9. Intercourse.

Hypoactive sexual desire disorders affect both sexes and may result from a wide variety of conditions, such as obsessive-compulsive personality traits or disorder, and **anhedonia** (a symptom of depression). Gender identity problems or specific sexual phobias may also contribute to lack of sexual desire. In addition, numerous physical conditions can result in low sexual desire. For example, diabetic women may have repeated yeast infections, leading to difficulty in lubrication and decreased sexual response. Psychiatric illness can also be an integral part of this form of sexual dysfunction. *Anxiety disorders, mood disorders, and substance abuse must be treated before or concomitant with treatment for hypoactive sexual desire.*

Deficiency in sexual desire is also strongly tied to the complexity of relationships. Some people are no longer attracted to their partners, or their partners may have poor sexual or communications skills. Power struggles between sexual partners may diminish sexual desire. Treatment is therefore difficult, given the multifactorial etiology of the problem. In these cases, the psychosocial aspects of the sexual problem have to be addressed, including development of verbal and nonverbal communication between the sexual partners, developing new ways of thinking about the relationship, and potentially increasing the frequency of sexual play.

Sexual aversion is a sexual desire disorder where the patient experiences an aversion to and avoidance of specific sexual activities, organs, or sexual content. These patients initially have a normal level of interest in sexual activities. However, if left untreated, their specific aversion may reduce libido, resulting in a difficult to treat desire

disorder. In fact, the majority of patients who present for treatment already have reduced sexual desire. Aversion frequently occurs in conjunction with panic disorder and with sexual phobias. This extreme level of anxiety triggered by sexual activity can be connected to cases of sexual victimization, such as rape or abuse in childhood. Because many of the treatment techniques used in sex therapy may escalate these anxieties, these patients often seem unable to benefit from therapy. If the problem is recognized, the integration of anxiolytic medication and brief psychotherapy into overall treatment can increase the likelihood of success.

Nocturnal Arousal and Morning Sex

The sexual excitement and response that occur while a person sleeps are referred to as **nocturnal arousal**. *Many men and women experience multiple episodes of sexual excitement (erection with and without ejaculation in men and vaginal lubrication and clitoral enlargement in women) during rapid eye movement sleep.* The potential contribution of this response to reproductive success is unclear, although nocturnal arousal may provide adequate sexual outlet if waking sexual experience is diminished or absent.

One effect of nocturnal arousals is that males frequently have erections upon waking. For men who encounter difficulty having erections when awake, morning erections are vital to the clinical history and may also present an opportunity to engage in sexual activity. The interpretation of some women of morning erections as being caused by a reflex rather than a response to the sexual partner must be addressed if treatment is to be successful.

Effects of Aging on Sexual Function

Age affects the sexual function of both men and women. Men generally experience a gradual but steady decline in sexual functioning after the early twenties, with some potential decrease in drive as well. Women reach their sexual peak in their thirties or forties, with a gradual decline in their fifties. After age fifty, sexual performance in men and women declines in each successive decade. For women, the sentinel event in sexual decline is menopause. Reduced estrogen levels may lead to vaginal dryness and thinning, resulting in dyspareunia. The use of **water soluble lubrication** during intercourse is highly recommended, and hormone replacement therapy can be considered, although the benefits of the latter must be weighed against the medical risks associated with this treatment. The psychological effect of menopause varies across different women, but potential feelings of de-

Nearly 4 centuries ago, Shakespeare described the enduring quality of a commitment of love, despite the ravages of changing circumstance, fading beauty, or time.

Let me not to the marriage of true minds
Admit impediments. Love is not love
Which alters when it alteration finds,
Or bends with the remover to remove:
Oh, no! it is an ever-fixed mark,
That looks on tempests and is never shaken,
It is the star to every wandering bark,
Whose worth's unknown, although his height be taken.
Love's not Time's fool, though rosy lips and cheeks
Within his bending sickle's compass come;
Love alters not with his brief hours and weeks,
But bears it out even to the edge of doom.
If this be error and upon me proved,
I never writ, nor no man ever loved.

WILLIAM SHAKESPEARE
Sonnet 116

creased femininity must be addressed to maximize sexual function and pleasure.

In men, the **refractory period** *begins to lengthen at around 30 years of age, increasing yearly.* Typical refractory periods are 20–30 minutes in teenagers, and 3 hours to 3 days in 70-year-old men. Additional stimulation is typically required to achieve erections in older men. Men's partners should be made aware that this is a normal physiological response and does not represent decreased attraction toward the partner.

Women's higher life expectancy compared to men results in a disproportional number of elderly women without sexual partners. Widows and widowers who resume sexual activity after long periods of abstinence often experience considerable difficulty with sexual function and desire. Generally, however, *although sexual function declines with time, sexual interest typically remains constant later in life.* Large national surveys have shown that 75% of men and 58% of women in their seventies have a moderate to strong interest in sex. Eighty-one percent of married couples in their seventies are still sexually active, while 75% of unmarried men and 50% of unmarried women in their seventies remain sexually active. *It is, therefore, important to address sexual function in the elderly, as sexual desire is often substantial later in life.*

Sexual Pleasure: Masturbation

Masturbation is defined as self-stimulation for the purpose of sexual excitation and/or orgasm. Children may

masturbate because they enjoy the sensation. Adults may masturbate when they are lonely, tired, bored, or sexually aroused. Masturbation may help relieve sexual tension, stress, or anger, or may aid in initiation of sleep. Masturbation is typically accompanied by sexual fantasies, many of which will never be acted upon, providing a safe outlet for sexual desires. *Masturbation is a normal, healthy activity that enhances the quality of life of most individuals;* in some cases, however, it may dull the desire for interpersonal sexual interaction. Excessive masturbation is associated with several psychiatric disorders, although the majority of people who masturbate more frequently than twice per day do not have a psychiatric disorder.

Patterns of masturbatory activity can provide insight into sexual problems. For example, women who are anorgasmic rarely masturbate. Orgasm during masturbation but not during intercourse suggests a psychosocial etiology or a deficiency in the sexual interaction between a woman and her partner. Women with vaginal spasm often masturbate to orgasm without difficulty. Men with premature ejaculation may masturbate to release tension, not merely for pleasure. Men with delayed ejaculation may masturbate compulsively and become overly engaged in autostimulatory activity. Ideally, masturbation is an affirmation that an individual is worthy of pleasure. Sharing sexual experiences with other people is a matter of choice. Masturbation is a satisfactory sexual outlet for many individuals; however, for others it may not provide the emotional satisfaction of an interpersonal sexual relationship.

Sexual Fantasies

Sexual fantasies usually begin during early adolescence and decrease in middle age. Men report more frequent sexual fantasies than women, and these fantasies occur during both masturbation and intercourse. Fantasies can relieve monotony, increase arousal, and permit one to imagine behavior that would be unacceptable or undesirable in reality. People sometimes find fantasies intolerable, humiliating, or frightening. Men with sexual dysfunction may visualize another person making love to their partner; this second person is often who the dreamer wishes to be. Some individuals have violent fantasies, which may or may not be undesired, while others may have fantasies that involve humiliation or degradation. Most self-described heterosexuals have occasional same-sex fantasies.

Specific fantasies may precede a new romance or sexual encounter. Individuals who are contemplating an out-of-relationship affair may fantasize about the affair before it happens, and this may be a stressor for both partners. When the fantasy becomes ineffective, the likelihood of acting on the fantasy increases.

Hylas and the Nymphs (1896) *John W. Waterhouse, British (1849–1917). © Manchester City Galleries, Manchester, UK. Fantasy is a natural and important part of our sexual being, and physicians frequently need to reassure patients that fantasies are harmless.*

Sexual Pleasure with a Partner

When combined with communication and guidance, exploration of each other's bodies can provide information on techniques that increase a partner's pleasure. Mutual masturbation provides an often satisfying alternative to intercourse, and mutual caressing of the breasts and genitals can be an enjoyable prelude to intercourse. Oral sex may also serve as a precursor or alternative to intercourse. **Fellatio** involves oral stimulation of the male genitals; **cunnilingus** refers to oral stimulation of the female genitals; **analingus** is oral stimulation of the anus; and **soixante-neuf** (French for **sixty-nine**) involves simultaneous fellatio and/or cunnilingus. The desirability of oral sex differs from person to person, although recent surveys of sexual behavior in U.S. teens suggests that this practice is becoming increasingly common and accepted among young people.

For many people, the anus, which is supplied by the same nerves and spatially related to the pelvic organs and muscles involved in sexual response, may be a source of sexual pleasure and eroticism. For other individuals, anal sex is not enjoyable because of association with defecation, rape, or prior painful attempts with rectal penetration. Some heterosexuals may be uncomfortable with the association of anal sex with male homosexuality. However, *anal sex forms part of the sexual repertoire of at least one fourth of the heterosexual population and at least three fourths of the male homosexual population.*

The risk of infection with the **human immunodeficiency virus (HIV)** and other **sexually transmitted infections (STIs)** is particularly high with anal sex because of the presence of delicate blood vessels in the anal-rectal region. For this reason, the use of a lubricated condom is recommended in all nonmonogamous relationships. In all cases, lubrication is recommended because of the lack of natural lubrication; in addition, the penis should be carefully washed after anal penetration before insertion into another body cavity.

While some primates use the rear entry position almost exclusively, humans use a wide variety of positions during intercourse. Different sexual positions allow exploration of a variety of methods of stimulation and also introduces novelty into the sexual experience. Face-to-face positions allow kissing and observation of the partner's facial expressions. Rear entry with the partners lying on their sides is the least physically demanding position, and it is recommended for those with medical problems that limit vigorous sexual activity. Masters and Johnson reported that a woman's excitement develops more rapidly and intensely when the woman is on top, which allows the man's hands to provide additional stimulation.

Sexual Orientation

Sexual orientation is defined as an erotic affinity and engagement in sexual activity with those of the opposite sex (heterosexuality), the same sex (homosexuality), or either sex (bisexuality). Homosexuals tend to have stronger spontaneous erotic feelings for members of the same sex, while heterosexuals tend to have stronger spontaneous erotic feelings for members of the opposite sex. Many individuals have the ability to become aroused by members of both sexes, although for most people arousal from one sex or the other predominates. *A sizable portion of people who self-describe as exclusively homosexual or heterosexual report the capacity to be sexually aroused by or to have engaged in sexual activity with members of both sexes.* A self-identified heterosexual has not necessarily had sex exclusively with members of the opposite sex, nor has a self-identified homosexual had sex exclusively with members of the same sex. People who engage in **situational homosexuality**, such as in a prison setting, do not typically persist in this behavior once they leave the restricted setting. They do not necessarily consider themselves homosexual, nor do they define their situational homosexual behaviors as gay sex. Fantasies may allow them to dissociate their actual partner from the envisioned partner.

The **Kinsey Report** estimated that approximately 5–10% of American men and 3–5% of women were homosexual. Kinsey and his colleagues reported that 37% of men and 14% of women had had homosexual experience to the point of orgasm before the age of 45, with 4% of men and 0.03% of women remaining exclusively homosexual. However, problems of definition, classification, and reporting hamper efforts to provide precise estimates. For example, is anyone who has engaged in same-sex activity homosexual? In 1994 The National Health and Social Life Survey found that 2.8% of men and 1.4% of women identify themselves as exclusively gay. Reports of voluntary same-gender sexual contact within the past year, however, range from 2%–15%, with a trend toward increased reporting of same-gender sexual activity over time when the same methodology is employed.

The prevalence of **bisexuality** is also difficult to estimate with accuracy. Bisexuality involves a tendency toward some combination of same-sex and opposite-sex sexual expression. Many individuals who consider themselves to be either heterosexual or homosexual are capable of being sexually aroused by members of both genders. One study in 1978 found that 52% of exclusively homosexual men and 77% of exclusively homosexual women had engaged in intercourse with a member of the opposite sex on at least one occasion. Although not precise, *estimates project that a small number (roughly 6%) of marriages involve one heterosexual and one homosexual spouse.* Comparable data do not exist for bisexual individuals. Additionally, it is estimated that 1% of marriages involve a homosexual man and homosexual woman in a marriage of convenience.

A considerable body of research has failed to provide definitive evidence of any specific biological or psychological basis for any sexual orientation. *An individual's sexual orientation appears to be deeply ingrained at an early age and is generally immutable.* Nevertheless, negative attitudes toward homosexuality and bisexuality still prevail across different societies and ethnicities. "Sexual preference" is a misnomer because it implies that individuals actively choose their sexual attraction, while the vast majority of research suggests that sexual attraction is not a choice. *In 1973, the American Psychiatric Association removed homosexuality from its list of recognized mental disorders,* largely based on the absence of evidence of any direct correlation between sexual orientation and mental disorder. However, when sexual orientation of any type

leads to psychological distress or impairment, the psychiatric diagnosis of "Sexual Disorder Not Otherwise Specified" can be made.

Potential psychological differences between homosexuals and heterosexuals have not yet been completely elucidated. *Homosexual teenagers have a significantly higher rate of depression and suicide that their heterosexual peers,* although the cause of this disparity is clearly multifactorial. Early awareness of same-sex arousal may be accompanied by a sense of isolation from peers, possibly accompanied by either self-imposed social isolation or being ostracized by heterosexual peers. Differences in the parietal cortex of homosexuals and heterosexuals have recently been reported, as have varying responses to pheromones between the two groups. Many researchers believe that sexual orientation will eventually be explained exclusively on a genetic or hormonal basis. Previous teachings that homosexuality and bisexuality result from an early conflicted parent-child relationship are unfounded and speculative. The factors that contribute to the development of an individual's sexual orientation remain unknown.

Homosexuals and bisexuals tend to have different psychosocial support networks than their heterosexual peers. For both gays and lesbians, the presence of social support is positively related to good psychological adjustment. However, the rates of depression and substance abuse are still higher in the homosexual and bisexual population than it is in the heterosexual population.

PARAPHILIAS

Paraphilias, or deviant attractions, are consuming sexual fantasies or activities characterized by erotic exclusion of an adult partner and significant distress or dysfunction as a direct result of these fantasies or activities. It is inherently problematic to define any sexual behavior or fantasy as deviant or abnormal, given the wide array of normal human sexual interests. However, when sexual activities harm others, involve nonhuman objects in a way that erotically and emotionally excludes an adult partner, require the participation of animals or nonconsenting adults, or cause an individual significant distress or impairment, such activities are generally considered evidence of a psychiatric disorder rather than part of a healthy, varied sexual appetite. The fourth edition of the Diagnostic and Statistical Manual of Mental Disorders of the American Psychiatric Association explicitly requires a clinical significance criteria be met before a sexual activity can be labeled a disorder.

Individuals with one or more paraphilias (see Table 12.2) often spend considerable time, energy, and money satisfying their all-consuming urges. For example, a voyeur may prowl the streets in search of unsuspecting persons disrobing or engaging in sexual activities that can be viewed

TABLE 12.2 Paraphilias described in DSM-IV

Paraphilia	Description
Exhibitionism	The exposure of one's genitals to strangers
Fetishism	Sexual use of nonliving objects, such as underwear, shoes
Frotteurism	Touching and rubbing against a nonconsenting person
Pedophilia	Sexual activity with a prepubescent child by a person who is at least 16 years old and at least 5 years older than the child; including activities with children in an individual's own family (incest)
Sexual masochism	The act (real, not simulated) of being humiliated, beaten, bound, or otherwise made to suffer
Sexual sadism	The act (real, not simulated) in which the psychological of physical suffering (including humiliation) of the partner is sexually exciting
Transvestic fetishism	Dressing in the clothes of the opposite sex is required for sexual excitement
Voyeurism	Observing people who are disrobing, engaging in sexual activity, or naked, without their consent
Others	Paraphilias not already specified, such as telephone scatologia (obscene phone calls), necrophilia (sexual activity with corpses), zoophilia (with animals), partialism (exclusive focus on a specific body part), and klismaphilia, coprophilia, and urophilia (respectively, arousal from enemas, feces, and urine)

through open curtains or telescopes. This may be time-consuming to the point of interfering with other life activities. **Pedophilia** involves sexual interaction of an adult with a child for sexual gratification. *These children are nonconsenting minors; even if they agree to the interaction, a power dynamic exists in which the child is not capable of knowledgeably consenting to the interaction.* Of note, pedophilia, much like rape, is now believed to be a crime of aggression, violence, and power, rather than a crime of sexual lust. That is, an adult male may molest a young boy not because the adult is a homosexual who is sexually attracted to the young boy, but as an expression of aggression. Many pedophiles desperately seek treatment. There have been several reports of suicide as an alternative to relapse, as the pedophile wants to avoid the future crime but does not trust him or her self to abstain.

The vast majority of paraphiles are men and since most never come to clinical attention, information about paraphilias has come from the minority of individuals who do seek treatment. These individuals typically have multiple paraphilias. *Contrary to public belief, effective treatment reg-*

imens do exist for a majority of paraphiles, including pedophiles. The most successful treatments consist of multimodal approaches incorporating social skills training, group or individual psychotherapy, and antiandrogen medication (e.g., leuprolide acetate, medroxyprogesterone acetate, or cyproterone acetate).

HIV AND SEXUALITY

When the HIV epidemic began in the early 1980s, it was labeled a "gay disease." As evidence of transmission accumulated, it became clear that HIV could be transmitted through vaginal intercourse, anal intercourse, blood to blood contact (including intravenous drug use), and even oral intercourse. Today, *the worldwide rate of heterosexual transmission exceeds all other routes of infection.* In 1996, with the development of protease inhibitors and delineation of the **highly active antiretroviral therapy (HAART)** protocol, significant suppression of HIV replication, partial restoration of immunity, reduction of morbidity, and extension of lifespan was achieved. Projected life expectancy for individuals on HAART is believed to be greater than 10 years, although only preliminary data are available. However, because HIV is currently a noncurable and ultimately mortal disease, it has changed the way many individuals consider sexuality as related to sexually transmitted infections (STIs).

Several studies have found that approximately 70% of HIV-positive patients report one or more sexual problems. Erectile dysfunction has been reported in 25–55% of these individuals, hypoactive sexual disorder in 25–60%, and delayed ejaculation in approximately 25%. Women with HIV are more likely than men to have unresolved hypoactive sexual desire disorder, although the multifactorial psychological and medical causes of this dysfunction have yet to be entirely elucidated.

HIV is not incompatible with sexual health. Honest communication with sexual partners is of paramount importance, especially when the partner is HIV-negative. Several authors have shown that *HIV-negative individuals often risk unprotected sex with their HIV-positive partners in order to show empathy toward the HIV-positive individual.* However, many safe sex practice options are available, including mutual masturbation, interfemoral intercourse (insertion of the penis between tightly clenched thighs), use of adult sex toys, and total body massage. Vaginal sex, anal sex, and oral sex can all involve use of a condom, and each of these practices are safer than sex without a condom; however, these practices are not totally without risk, even when a condom is used.

SUMMARY

Knowledge of sexual behavior has increased significantly in the past century, but the spectrum of human sexuality has only been partially illuminated. The etiology of the vast individual differences in sexual desire, sexual orientation, and sexual activity remains unknown. What is clear is that sexuality is a central part of an individual's sense of self and remains, for many people, one of the most satisfying and gratifying aspects of the human experience.

CASE STUDY

Patient J.Y. is a 54-year-old female who presents complaining of a lack of desire for sexual activity with her husband. They have been having less frequent intercourse over the past 3 to 4 years and now only have intercourse about twice a year. She reports that she is still very much in love with her husband and they have not had any marital difficulty but she feels that their lack of intercourse has reduced their level of intimacy.

She denies any history of medical problems and is not taking any medications other than occasional Tylenol for headaches. She has not had a menstrual cycle in three years. She had hot flashes and night sweats for about two years before and one year after her last menses. She reports that she has had increasing vaginal dryness and irritation over the past three to four years, which is bothersome during intercourse. She feels that this discomfort has decreased her desire to be intimate.

She is given the name of an over the counter water-based lubricant to use with intercourse. She returns one month later and reports that the lubricant helped with intercourse but she still feels some discomfort with intercourse and some vaginal dryness throughout the day. After a discussion on the risks and benefits of vaginal estrogen cream and oral hormone replacement therapy, she opts to try a topical vaginal estrogen cream. She is given a prescription for a vaginal estrogen cream to be applied every other night.

She returns to the office one month later and reports great improvement in her symptoms since initiation of the vaginal estrogen cream. She has been using it only twice a week, but now has no discomfort throughout the day or with intercourse. She has already noticed great improvement in her relationship with her husband and they have been having more frequent intercourse.

SUGGESTED WEB SITES

http://www.nlm.nih.gov/medlineplus/sexualhealthissues.html
This website is provided as a service of the U.S. National Library of Medicine and the National Institutes of Health. It provides current information on sexual health for people of all ages, including a glossary, specific conditions, statistics, and information about relevant organizations.

http://www.cdc.gov/node.do/id/0900f3ec80059b1a
This website is maintained by the Centers for Disease Control and Prevention and has information on women's and men's health, as well as information on reproduction and sexually transmitted diseases.

http://www.ejhs.org/
The *Electronic Journal of Human Sexuality* is a publication of the Institute for Advanced Study of Human Sexuality, and posts peer-reviewed research papers and book reviews on a broad range of sexual topics.

Part 3

The Physician's Role

DOCTOR'S ROW

Snow falls on the cars in Doctors' Row and hoods the headlights;
snow piles on the brownstone steps, the basement deadlights;
fills up the letters and names and brass degrees
on the bright brass plates, and the bright brass holes for keys.

Snow hides, as if on purpose, the rows of bells
which open the doors to separate cells and hells:
to the waiting-rooms, where the famous prepare for headlines,
and humbler citizens for their humbler deadlines.

And in and out, and out and in, they go,
the lamentable devotees of Doctors' Row;
silent and circumspect—indeed, liturgical;
their cries and prayers prescribed, their penance surgical.

No one complains—no one presumes to shriek—
the walls are very thick, and the voices weak.
Or the cries are whisked away in noiseless cabs,
while nurse, in the alley, empties a pail of swabs.

Miserable street!—through which your sweetheart hurries,
lowers her chin, as the snow-cloud stings and flurries;
thinks of the flower-stall, by the church, where you

wait like a clock, for two, for half-past two;
thinks of the roses banked on the steps in snow,
of god in heaven, and the world above, below;
widens her vision beyond the storm, her sight
the infinite rings of an immense delight;

all to be lived and loved—O glorious All!
Eastward or westward, Plato's turning wall;
the sky's blue streets swept clean of silent birds
for an audience of gods, and superwords.

CONRAD AIKEN

13 Medical Student and Physician Well-Being

Margaret L. Stuber

> Let us emancipate the student, and give him time and opportunity for the cultivation of his mind, so that in his pupilage he shall not be a puppet in the hands of others, but rather a self-relying and reflecting being.
>
> SIR WILLIAM OSLER

> If you listen carefully to what patients say, they will often tell you not only what is wrong with them but also what is wrong with you.
>
> WALKER PERCY

Entrance into medical school is for many students the fulfillment of a long-held dream. The path to medical school always involves a great deal of effort. Often it also requires competition, and a drive to be the best. Once in medical school, however, students are expected to work and learn in teams and small groups. Personal best, rather than competition with peers, is encouraged—at least officially. The amount of information that must be mastered is overwhelming, as is the responsibility of making life or death decisions. It is often difficult for medical students, driven to care and to know, to cope with the significant pressures they encounter during medical school. Unfortunately, the result, too often, is depression or even suicide. *The chances of dying by suicide are higher for physicians than nonphysicians, particularly in women.* Male physicians have a rate of suicide 1.41 times that of male nonphysicians. Female physicians have a suicide rate 2.27 times that of female nonphysicians.

These increases in suicide are partly a result of the fact that doctors are more likely to actually die when making a suicide attempt; ironically, this results in part from their enhanced understanding of physiology and drugs. Few of the physicians who died by suicide were receiving psychiatric treatment just before their death. *These numbers also reflect a greater prevalence of depression in physicians.* A re-

cent study of over 2,000 medical students and residents found that 12% reported symptoms of major depression, and 6% reported suicidal ideation. Both depression and suicidal thoughts were more common in medical students than in residents. Medical students and residents report "burnout", defined as emotional exhaustion, diminished sende of personal accomplishment, lack of empathy, and a feeling of depersonalization.

This chapter will examine what is needed to make the transition from college graduate to physician. It will also examine the factors that predict well-being as a physician, and the obstacles to achieving these goals. Unlike the other chapters in this book, which emphasize the context of clinical care or physician-patient interactions, this chapter will focus on you, and your own behavior.

> Nothing will sustain you more potently than the power to recognize in your humdrum routine...the true poetry of life—the poetry of the commonplace, of the ordinary man, of the toil worn woman, with their joys, their sorrows, and their griefs.
>
> SIR WILLIAM OSLER'S advice to medical students (circa 1905)

A NEW LANGUAGE AND A NEW ROLE

Even for students who have had in-depth training in some aspect of science, medical school requires learning a new and technical language. In the first 2 years this new learning involves learning numerous multisyllabic Latin terms for anatomy and various new uses of common words for pathology (e.g., "cheesy necrosis"). Clinical work brings an onslaught of abbreviations, many of which are used in different ways by different specialists (e.g., MS can refer to either multiple sclerosis or morphine sulfate).

Students are often amused or offended about having

Medical Students at Work on a Cadaver, 1890 From the collection of the Minnesota Historical Society, Minneapolis. *Human dissection is a unique learning experience that links every freshman medical student with previous generations of physicians.*

formal courses in which they are taught how to "interview" patients. Surely you know how to talk to people, be friendly, communicate information, and ask questions? Quickly however, it becomes apparent that *you are now expected to ask total strangers about intimate and often unpleasant topics in a way that would be considered totally inappropriate in any other context.* Conversations between doctor and patient commonly focus on topics such as diarrhea, vomit, blood, itching, bloating, and "discharge" from a variety of orifices. In many clinical situations, the physician must engage in a matter-of-fact conversation about whether someone has sexual interactions with men, women, or both, and about the details of those interactions. Obvious advice—often unwanted and unappreciated—has to be offered about the need to stop smoking, lose weight, or improve personal hygiene. These are precisely the things you have been taught *not* to talk about in polite society since early childhood, and so these interactions are naturally uncomfortable and often awkward.

Similarly, you are asked to notice and report details about people that genteel people would overlook. You need to consider not only the smell of alcohol on someone's breath, but also the earthy odor of upper GI bleeding or Candida, and the sweet smell of ketosis. A person's gait, posture, and facial expression are all potentially important data, to be noted, evaluated, and used. Slips of the tongue, restlessness, or confusion cannot be politely ignored, as one might socially. For many of you, this is a new, uncomfortable, and intrusive way of relating to others.

YOU CAN'T KNOW EVERYTHING

Medical school has been compared to drinking from a fire hose—the volume is high, the pressure intense, it is impossible to completely consume the product, and the experience is often less than completely satisfying. Although most medical schools have changed the ways they present material, genuinely trying to reduce the vast amount of minutia to memorize and the number of dense readings to plow through, *it is simply not possible to know, understand, and remember everything that is presented to you in medical school.*

The intense pressures of medical school are, to some extent, purposeful. You will never have the security of knowing all there is to know about your field. There will always be the need to look up some detail, or to seek new information, or seek out consultation. You will have to be able to say "I don't know, but I will find out" thousands of times throughout your career. *An important task in medical school and in your continuing medical education is to learn what you really do have to know, and figure out how to look up everything else.*

THE CULTURE OF MEDICINE

Professional schools, such as law and medicine, are action oriented. This is a very different orientation than other graduate schools in which contemplation and deliberation

Sir William Osler Lecturing to Medical Students at Johns Hopkins Courtesy of the National Library of Medicine. *Master teachers have always been appreciated by medical students. Note that almost all of the students appear to be male.*

are highly valued. Obviously, the actions that are necessary are radically different for different specialties. Physicians such as those in the Emergency Department or Anesthesia must make instant decisions in acute situations, and rarely spend more than a few hours with a patient. In contrast, Family Medicine physicians engage in long-term planning aimed at health maintenance and illness prevention. Nonetheless, physicians are evaluated primarily on what they do or do not do for their patients. Since time is almost always at a premium, this creates a situation in which efficiency is highly valued.

Most inpatient medical teams in academic medical centers operate in a very hierarchical system. Each member of the team has a specific job or area of expertise and contributes to patient care, but one person ultimately is responsible for final decision-making. Decisions by consensus are rarely used; the process simply takes too long to be useful in this setting. Some teams, however, operate with a blend of these two systems, having differentiated responsibility for team members, and regular means of communication for coordination.

In medical school, interns and residents report to attending physicians, and medical students report to the interns and residents. This means that as a medical student you are at or near the bottom of this hierarchy. This stands in stark contrast to the rest of your life, when you have very likely been one of the smartest of the members of every group, and a leader in many settings and situations. Indeed, you are in medical school training so that some day you can actually lead a medical team. This situation—the hierarchy, the time pressure, and your personal

> There is within medicine, somewhere beneath the pessimism and discouragement resulting from the disarray of the health-care system and its stupendous cost, an undercurrent of almost outrageous optimism about what may lie ahead for the treatment of human disease if we can only keep learning.
>
> LEWIS THOMAS (1979)

history—creates a perfect set up for misunderstandings, frustration, and power abuse.

Other chapters in this book make the point that *you must understand the cultural and experiential world of a patient in order to effectively communicate and negotiate treatment.* This is also true in the culture of medicine. However, this does not mean that medical students should expect or accept that they will be abused by the attending physicians, residents, and nurses with whom they work. It is inevitable that your coworkers and teachers will occasionally be irritable, they may sometimes be rude, and some may make racial or sexual jokes that you believe to be in very bad taste. However, *you do not have to tolerate other physicians systematically degrading or insulting you, throwing things at you, or repeatedly making unwanted sexual advances.* All medical schools have systems in place to deal with such problems. So why do they still happen? It is a two-fold problem. First, medical students are very reluctant to say anything, to the perpetrators or to anyone else, knowing that students are vulnerable. The residents and attending physicians write student

BOX 13.1 Attitudes that influence the happiness of medical students and physicians*

Path 1 These coping attitudes will not be very useful to you in medicine, in the long run.	Path 2 These coping attitudes will lead to more long-term satisfactions and enjoyment in medicine.
The strong silent approach. Don't tell others what you are thinking.	Learn to listen to the feelings of others, and to share your own.
Success means good grades and, later, wealth and material goods.	That's okay, but it doesn't compare to enjoying your work and people.
Your needs must take a second place to more important things in life.	You must fill your own needs at the same time you are accomplishing your other goals.
Your worth depends on what you accomplish. When you don't accomplish as much as others or as much as you can, you are basically inadequate.	There is a source of self-worth that cannot be measured by your accomplishments, that is non-negotiable and fundamental.
Mistakes are the result of ignorance, apathy, carelessness, and general basic worthlessness.	Mistakes aren't exactly okay, but they are a fact of life, even in medicine. Mistakes are your chief source of wisdom. Learn from them and don't make them twice. Perfectionism leads to burnout.
Criticism is a demonstration to the world of your inadequacy. Defend, justify, explain, and attack!	Criticism isn't exactly pleasant, but get used to the idea that it doesn't imply inadequacy. Learn to use it.
You are helpless in a world that controls your behavior.	You are in charge of what you do; it's no use blaming anyone else. What you do is up to you.
When you are feeling overwhelmed, lonely, anxious, depressed, and can't study, it is up to you to "snap out of it." Be strong, work hard, and keep a stiff upper lip. It's just a matter of willpower.	There is nothing wrong with you; everyone has trouble coping and could use some help. It may be embarrassing to find that you don't know everything yet. A sense of self-worth that keeps you from getting help may lead to real trouble.
Results are more important than people. (Type A behavior is goal oriented.)	People are more important than results. (Type B behavior is "process" oriented.)
Thinking is the highest function.	There is more to you than thinking. Don't let your feelings and intuition atrophy; don't become an intellectual nerd.

* From *Coping in Medical School* by Bernard Virshup. Copyright © 1985, 1981 by Bernard B. Virshup. Used by permission of W.W. Norton & Company, Inc.

evaluations, and can make life very difficult. However, the administration can only act if there is evidence of repeated or outrageous offenses. Second, in some settings, particularly those that are very high-stress or time-sensitive, it is considered acceptable to abuse medical students, interns, and residents. In some areas, such as Pediatrics, verbal abuse of students appears to be rare, whereas in others, such as Surgery, it appears to be far more frequent. Medical school deans, department chairs, and administrators are working hard to change this aspect of these cultures. However, as with all cultural change, this will take time.

So what do you do in the meantime if you feel you are being abused? A few basic guidelines follow:

1. First, take a deep breath, and make sure you are not taking something out of context or personally when it was not meant that way.
2. Calmly let the person know that this was uncomfortable for you, and why.
3. Wait for a response. If there is an acknowledgment or apology, great! If not, but the behavior is not repeated, no further action is needed unless the abusive behavior is then directed at someone else.
4. If the response is only further abuse, or the abuse is repeated despite acknowledgment or apology, seek help. Help is available from the medical school ombudsman's office, the Student Affairs Office, or the Chair of the course or clerkship.

ASKING FOR ACADEMIC HELP

Everyone who is accepted to medical school has the academic ability to complete medical school. Those who have such serious academic difficulty in medical school that they do not graduate generally do so because they were not willing or able to ask for help when they needed it.

"My family/friends need me." Medical students are smart and hard-working people, and their family and friends admire and count on them—sometimes too much. However, medical school is a full-time job. It may have been possible to run the family business while in college, or you may have always been the one that all of your family depended on to make important decisions or to host all family events. Medical school is much less flexible about absences than undergraduate school. You may be expected to be in the hospital by 5 a. m. each morning to round on your patients. Being pulled in too many directions can cause serious problems for a medical student.

> This is all very fine, but it won't do—Anatomy—Botany—Nonsense! Sir, I know an old woman in Covent Garden who understands botany better, and as for anatomy, my butcher can dissect a joint full and well; no young man, all that is stuff; you must go to the bedside, it is there alone you can learn disease.
>
> THOMAS SYDENHAM

"I have always been able to do it, and I will be able to do this too." Some medical students have overcome significant obstacles on their way to medical school. They may come from families with few financial resources, or limited educational background. They may have had medical or psychological problems to cope with, or learning disabilities to overcome. They may have dealt with tragedy or violence. The fact that these students made it to medical school is a testimony to their hard work, determination, and intelligence. They deserve to be proud of their accomplishments. It is, therefore, a terrible loss when such students do not avail themselves of any supports they need once in medical school. All too often a student will refuse to meet with anyone after they fail an exam or course, thinking that all that is needed is to work harder. It is not until a pattern has emerged, and the student is forced to agree to an evaluation, that he or she is found to need a quieter test setting, different study approaches, or help in coping with anxiety. Medical schools are required to supply accommodation to any otherwise capable student for any documented learning disability or sensory impairment—but only if the student requests such accommodation. It is up to you as a student to request the evaluation and accommodations.

"I can't let anyone know that I can't do it." Although most students have worked hard to get to medical school and are there because they want to be, some are not. Some students are in medical school because that is what their parents expected or demanded, and many of these students are not sure they want to be there. Other students are convinced they are not capable of succeeding academically. These students experience embarrassment and shame when they encounter academic difficulty, and it may feel like they have let their friends and family down. These students often find it difficult to admit that they need help.

ASKING FOR NONACADEMIC HELP

Academic difficulty is not the only reason students do not graduate from medical school. For some students, the work load and the sense of never knowing enough can precipitate or uncover depression or anxiety. Trouble sleeping, difficulty concentrating, or not having enough energy to get to class or the hospital can exacerbate a situation that already felt overwhelming. Although help is available, it is often resisted. This is understandable: if you are having trouble functioning on your surgery rotation, the last thing you may want to do is to ask for time off to see a counselor. A less short-term assessment, however, shows that *it is far better to deal with such responses earlier rather than later.* The time lost when a student fails a course or clerkship is much more consequential and costly than any time invested in solving a problem before it gets out of hand.

> The physician himself, if sick, actually calls in another physician, knowing that he cannot reason correctly if required to judge his own condition while suffering.
>
> ARISTOTLE
> *De Republica*

Substance abuse, suicidal ideation, depression, and anxiety are much more wide-spread among medical students and physicians than is commonly believed, especially given how bright and accomplished medical students are. It is important for you to understand that *these problems are generally quite treatable*—if the individual seeks help. However, studies of medical students have found that less than 25% of those who were clinically depressed used mental health services. Barriers students most frequently cited included lack of time, lack of confidentiality, stigma, cost, fear of documentation on academic records, and fear of unwanted intervention.

All medical schools are required to have confidential counseling services. These services include access to medications, addiction counseling, and psychotherapy. However, *once out of medical school up to 35% of physicians do not have adequate mental health care.* Given that physicians do not adequately diagnose or treat depression in 40 to 60% of patients with depression, it is perhaps not surprising that they have difficulty overcoming psychological barriers to treatment and seeking help for themselves.

There are also some real risks to seeking treatment. Medical students often are very concerned that any diagnosis or treatment they receive will be recorded in their files. These concerns are partially justified; for example, in one study, residency directors stated that they would be less likely to invite a hypothetical applicant to interview if he or she had a history of psychological counseling. Medical licensing boards in most states ask about significant medical conditions, and expect disclosure of any diagnosis or treatment that might impair ability to practice. Although it is unlikely that a state board would prevent someone from getting a license because of a history of treatment for depression, some states may require a letter from the applicant's treating physician documenting that the applicant is coping with his or her disorder.

Occasionally a medical student will have a serious underlying psychiatric or medical illness that may be exacerbated by the stresses of medical school. Examples include bipolar affective disorder and ulcerative colitis. In these cases, although the illness is quite treatable, the treatment as well as the symptoms of the illness can interfere with concentration and the student's ability to work as a part of a team. It is wisest for students to seek out help and guidance early, to determine if a leave of absence is preferable to the possibility of poor evaluations or failed exams, which eventually can cost more time than would be lost by taking a semester or a year off from medical school.

Students often can be the best advocates for one another, and in many cases you will know before the faculty if another student is struggling with anxiety or depression or is drinking too much. Often simply letting your classmates know that you consider it to be acceptable and honorable to seek help, and reminding them that help is available, can be enough to make a difference in someone's academic success, career—and life.

Character and Medicine

Most medical schools are now also evaluating students on their professionalism or **"physicianship."** Pioneered by the University of California, San Francisco, this type of evaluation is an addendum to the usual evaluations of knowledge and skills done in each course or clerkship. This type of evaluation was born out of concern about some of the abusive behaviors that appeared to be tolerated within the "culture of medicine" described above. A systemic approach to student abuse was necessary to communicate (to both students and faculty) the schools' condemnation of

---

TABLE 13.1 Physicianship expectations from the David Geffen School of Medicine at UCLA Reporting Form

Professionalism

1. **Reliability and Responsibility:** Fulfills responsibilities to peers, instructors, patients, other health professionals, and oneself; Provides accurate, nonmisleading information to the best of one's abilities.

2. **Self-Improvement and Adaptability:** Accepts constructive feedback, and incorporates this feedback when making changes in his/her behavior; Accepts responsibility for one's failures.

3. **Relationships with Patients and Families:** Establishes rapport and demonstrates sensitivity in patient care interactions; Maintains professional boundaries with patients or members of their families.

4. **Relationships with Peers, Faculty, and Other Members of the Health-Care Team:** Relates well to fellow students, faculty or staff; Demonstrates sensitivity to other members of the health care team.

5. **Professional Behavior:** Respects diversity in patients and colleagues; Resolves conflicts professionally; Dresses and acts in a professional manner.

---

abusive or insensitive behavior. Culture change takes a long time, and this is one of the more effective ways to do it.

At UCLA, for example, using the expectations outlined in Table 13.1, students are counseled by the attending physician or faculty teacher if there is an egregious violation, or repeated examples of more minor infringements, of these expectations. If the student is able to accept the counseling and modify his or her behavior, a written report is given to the course chair, but no further action is taken. If, however, there is repetition of the behavior or another violation of the expectation, the course chair also counsels the student, and the report form is sent to the Student Affairs Office and put in the student's file. Two such forms in the student file will result in a notation in the Medical Student Performance Evaluation, and more than two can be grounds for dismissal.

Examples of violations of the expectations would include:

1. The student cannot be depended on to complete tasks in a timely manner.
2. The student is resistant or overly defensive in accepting criticism.
3. The student does not protect patient confidentiality or privacy.
4. The student does not establish and maintain appropriate boundaries in work and learning situations.
5. The student misrepresents or falsifies information and/or actions.

The response of students to these types of guidelines has generally been supportive, but students have been understandably quick to ask for similar guidelines for the faculty. Such expectations also exist for faculty, but the process of enforcement is not always as obvious or rapid. However, recently there has been far more focus on these types of expectations in medical settings. For example, mandatory training about sexual harassment is now provided for faculty and staff at most medical centers. The gender and ethnic diversity of current medical students and physicians has created a situation in which some long-standing problems are no longer tolerated by the majority of physicians. It is unfortunate that lawsuits have been necessary to make some of these changes become widespread. However, the result will be a better environment for the practice of medicine.

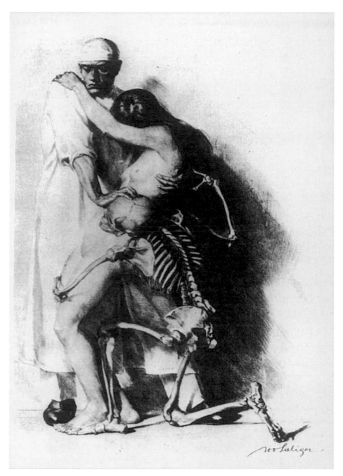

The Physician Ivo Saliger (1920). Courtesy of the National Library of Medicine. *Although the image is appealing, physicians who adopt grandiose self-images are at high risk to burn out and become frustrated and embittered.*

TAKING CARE OF YOURSELF

As medical students and physicians, you will frequently give excellent advice to your patients about lifestyle issues. However, a number of research studies have documented that *you are extremely likely to ignore this good advice when it comes to your own life.* After all, you are young. You are busy. You are stressed. Unfortunately, although you will not stay young, you are very likely to continue to be busy and stressed unless you choose to do something about it. *Medical school is the best time to set up habits that can help you to be a better doctor and a happier, healthier person for the rest of your life.*

Here are a few recommendations for maintaining your well-being that are best started now, not after you finish training.

1. Prioritize your Time

Without this, nothing else will work. Realizing that there really is not time to do everything, figure out what you need to do. This means saying no to some things, often things that would be enjoyable or tasks that someone else thinks only you can do. It also means having some idea as to how long it will really take to do a given task. This is a life-long goal, as you will see if you observe any of your teachers or mentors. However, you are in a field where you should be able to enjoy your work. This will be much less true if you try to do too much.

2. Friends

Having people in your life is an essential part of being human. Depending on your personality, this may be a lot of people or just a few very close friends. You may have a huge extended family with whom you communicate daily, or your family may communicate primarily by email or through intermittent visits. Your social network may be within your neighborhood, your place of worship, your children's school, or at work. What matters is that you are able to relax and be yourself with someone who knows and likes you. *Isolation makes it much harder to get the support that is essential to the very emotionally demanding job you have chosen.*

3. Exercise

Taking care of your body is always a wise investment of time and energy. Exercise can be a wonderful way to deal with the tension of a day, or provide a moment of peace or thoughtfulness in a day filled with demanding patients or petulant coworkers. It is also a great way to be with people, whether you enjoy team sports or more individual activities such as swimming, hiking, or biking. Trips with organizations such as the Sierra Club can provide both exercise and a sense of belonging and community.

4. Relaxation

Exercise is one way to relax, but it should not be the only way. Relaxation is partly about changing the pace of your activities, but it also about changing the ways in which you are thinking. Reading or travel can take you into a different world, figuratively or literally, and help you develop new perspectives and experiment with different "ways of being." *You will be a better and more interesting person, but also a better and more sensitive physician, if your time is not spent solely with your patients and your journals.*

Different people find different ways to relax. Some physicians are uncomfortable when they have unscheduled time, and if this applies to you, you may need to have your weekends and vacations very structured. Some people are happy spending all of their free time with other people, while others have a genuine need to spend some time alone. Getting to know what works for you is an important step in taking care of yourself.

5. Sleep

The amount and timing of sleep needed is different for different people, and these needs change as a person ages. What is true for all is that some amount of restful sleep is essential for well-being, and most of us do not get as much sleep as our bodies need. This means it is important to understand and respect your own personal needs, and watch how these needs change over time. *Teenagers and people in their twenties often have an internal diurnal pattern that makes it easiest for them to concentrate and work at night,* and difficult to function effectively in the early morning. This pattern changes over the years, until by the age of 60 or 70 the early morning is the most active time for the majority of people. Most people need approximately 8 hours of sleep a night. However, some adults do very well on 6 or even 4 hours, while others really need 9 or 10 hours.

> Today's trainees have different values and demand a more balanced lifestyle than those who believed the only thing wrong with every other night-call was that you missed half the good cases.
>
> H. SANFEY
> Contemporary US surgeon, University of Virginia
> *British Journal of Surgery*

Probably more important than the amount of sleep is what interferes with sleep. Coffee and other caffeine-containing drinks are an integral part of the culture in the United States, and they have become an expected part of medical culture. However, these beverages can have a significant effect on sleep, particularly when they are used to artificially induce alertness when the body is exhausted. Alcohol is especially likely to affect sleep patterns. *Often used as a relaxant, alcohol is actually disruptive to sleep.* Although a drink may help induce sleep, it also interferes with deep sleep, leads to wakening during the night, and interferes with restful sleep. Similarly, because of their ready access to sedatives, physicians often use drugs to induce sleep. The dangers of this are obvious, and yet the temptation is strong.

SUMMARY

In choosing to become a physician, you are starting on your way to a life which promises to be challenging and rewarding, intellectually and emotionally. Learning to handle the new language, culture, and stresses of the world of medicine can be as difficult as learning anatomy and the physical examination. A realistic approach to medical school, which allows one to ask for help and includes some relaxation, will provide an excellent preparation for a long and satisfying career.

CASE STUDY

A first-year medical student failed an important Anatomy examination in the first semester of medical school. She told the course director that she had an anxiety attack, but she reported that she was now fine, did not need treatment, and only requested an opportunity to retake the exam. She passed the makeup exam. However, the next semester she fails a midterm. When she is asked to see the course chair, she acknowledges that she has been extremely anxious, and she has had difficulty concentrating when she tries to study. She reluctantly agrees to go to Student Health. A counselor at the Student Health Center learns that she is the first one in her family to ever go to college, much less graduate school. Her family is very proud of her, but cannot be very emotionally supportive, as they do not understand the pressures and demands of medical school. She also feels conflicted because her family is experiencing financial distress, and she feels she should be working and supporting her family. She is trained in relaxation skills, and she is given medication for an underlying depression that has never been treated. However, it is the counseling about her professional goals and her obligation to the family that are ultimately the most helpful.

SUGGESTED READINGS

Epstein, R.M., & Hundert, E.M. (2002). Defining and assessing professional competence. *Journal of the American Medical Association, 287*, 226–235.
   This article reviews the expectations now made of medical students, including those having to do with professionalism, and how these are assessed.

Hampton, T. (2005). Experts address risk of physician suicide. *Journal of the American Medical Association, 294*, 1189–1191.
   This is an overview of a recent report from a group of experts in medicine, health insurance, and physician licensing convened to identify those factors that discourage physicians from seeking treatment for depression.

Krasner, M.S., Epstein, R.M., Beckman, H., Suchman, A.L., Chapman, B., Mooney, C.J., & Quill, T.E. (2009). Association of an educational program in mindful communication with burnout, empathy, and attitudes among primary care physicians. *Journal of the American Medical Association, 302,* 1284–1293.

This article reports on a study of the benefit to primary care physicians who were taught mindfulness meditation, self-awareness exercises, and wrote narratives about meaningful clinical experiences. Participants demonstrated short-term and sustained improvements in well-being and attitudes associated with patient-centered care.

Rosenthal, J.M., & Okie, S. (2005). White coat, mood indigo—depression in medical school. *New England Journal of Medicine, 353,* 1085–1088.

This article outlines the incidence and probable causes of depression in medical school, as well as the obstacles to treatment, and what some schools are doing to address this.

14 Medical Ethics

Sarah J. Breier

> Surgeons must be very careful
> When they take a knife!
> Underneath their fine incisions
> Stirs the Culprit – Life!
>
> EMILY DICKINSON

The learning, understanding, and practice of medical ethics in the clinical setting require many of the same constructs as the learning, understanding, and practice of clinical medicine itself. Like medicine, the hands-on application of medical ethics must be preceded by considerable study of ethical principles, theories, and approaches. The study of ethics and ethical behavior in medicine has been substantially developed over the past two decades, and there is now an abundance of primary and secondary texts as well as numerous journals devoted to this topic; ethical issues such as genetic engineering, confidentiality, and allocation of funds have been treated in great breadth and depth in the medical literature. These topics are discussed most often from the viewpoint of either utilitarian or deontological ethics, yet these core theoretical foundations are often missing in medical training curricula. This chapter provides a general overview of the fundamental ethical principles that shape ethical behavior in physicians, a discussion of ethical qualities of exemplary physicians, medicine's social contract, and the development of much needed ethics training in medical education.

REVISITING THE PRINCIPLES

Complete reviews of the principles of medical ethics and how they influence the behavior of physicians are well beyond the scope of this chapter. However, ethical issues frequently arise in the care of patients in any clinical settings, and a basic familiarity with these principles is essential for all medical students. Although physicians can rely on scientific research, accepted standards of clinical care, laws, and legal guidelines in making decisions, each ethical dilemma is unique to the patient and his or her own physical, emotional, and cultural circumstances.

Most physicians practice within the limits of a professional code of ethics that provides guidelines for working with patients and families. However, technological advances in medicine and increasingly complex systems of health care delivery have generated situations in which the application of different professional, legal, and ethical principles often lead to different conclusions. However, the fundamental ethical framework for ethical medical practice can be founded on the following all-encompassing principles.

Autonomy refers to the principle of self-determination—a principle that is prominent in Western cultures. Self-determination means that it is essential to know the patient's wishes with respect to his or her illnesses. In addition to respect for individual autonomy, it is critical to appreciate that individuals are interrelated and interconnected members of a human community. This far-reaching principle (emphasized particularly in public health) recognizes that many of the decisions we make as individuals affect others directly or indirectly.

Every effort should be made to respect a patient's autonomy. Nevertheless, autonomy may be compromised if the patient has diminished decision-making capacity or is deemed incompetent by a judge, such as patients with certain psychiatric or neurological illnesses. To act with utmost autonomy, a patient is also entitled to give **informed consent**. This mandates that a patient must receive a thorough and understandable explanation of his or her illness and be fully informed about possible benefits and burdens of the various proposed treatments, including the option to refuse treatment. *The ability to give informed consent for a medical intervention rests on the patient's capacity to understand his or her illness, to comprehend the* *prognosis, proposed treatment, and other options, and the ability to balance the benefits and burdens of receiving the treatment.*

Autonomy also extends to the patient's right to **privacy and confidentiality**. Physicians are occasionally obligated to "break" confidentiality in the event of emergencies such as suicidal or homicidal intent, or in cases involving minors. Likewise, despite their respect for autonomy, physicians must sometimes override an informed and consenting patient's decision because they consider this decision not to be in their patient's best interests (e.g., a depressed patient's wish to die). This is often referred to as **paternalism**. Paternalism per se has a long and hallowed tradition in medicine, evolving from the *fiduciary duty of the physician to act within the best interests of the patient*. "Old-time physicians" are traditionally portrayed as making wise and prudent decisions for their patients, with patients following those decisions unquestionably and respectfully. However, with the advent of self-determination and enhanced societal respect for the role and respect for patient autonomy, the connotation of physician paternalism has become negative. In fact, contemporary descriptions of physician paternalism often produce images of the physician arrogantly and egotistically proceeding with a course of treatment without respect for the patient's wishes.

Beneficence is the principle that requires the physician to help patients and to weigh the burdens of treatment vis-à-vis the benefits. The basic interpretation of this principle is *the duty of the physician to be of benefit to the patient as well as to take positive steps to prevent and remove harm from the patient*. These ethical obligations are deemed self-evident and are widely accepted as the right and proper objectives of medicine. These objectives are applied to both individual patients and to the benefit of society as a whole. However, the optimal health of individual patients is the proper goal of medicine. The prevention of disease through research and the employment of vaccines, for example, is simply this same goal expanded to society at large.

Health care is deemed to have a positive value if it promotes health and welfare, such as the prevention of illness, deterrence of injury, or avoidance of premature death. Balancing the benefits and burdens in patient care, decision making, human subject research, or policy development must be considered as part of the thoughtful and careful action mandated by the principle of beneficence. Burdens must be measured and weighed up against potential benefits to the patient from the perspective of the patient or persons affected—not from the perspective of the physician. Consequently, the principle of autonomy significantly influences and may override the principle of beneficence.

Nonmaleficence is based on the time-honored Hippocratic principle *primum non nocere—first, do no harm*. This involves the physician and patient balancing the benefits and burdens of a given procedure. Physicians must be certain that they are extending care that is unlikely to result in

---

BOX 14.1 Setting appropriate boundaries and limits presents vexing dilemmas for physicians. Consider the following situations and discuss how you would respond:

- Several of your patients ask to follow you on Twitter and to be listed as your friend on Facebook.
- A longtime patient dies, and her sister asks you to say a few words at your patient's funeral.
- Your patient, a travel agent, offers you a free upgrade to first class when you are only paying for an economy-class seat.
- A patient you have seen for many years commits suicide, and the patient's sister – a trial attorney who has been paying her sister's bills for many years – asks to have a private session to "get closure on Susan's death."
- A patient reveals that she is in fact "Maria," a woman you have been flirting with on an Internet dating site for the past 2 months without knowing her true identity.
- A state trooper – who also happens to be one of your patients – stops you for speeding, but tells you he is only going to give you a warning ticket because you've been such a good doctor over the years.

---

illness or death. When risk of injury or death is inevitable, physicians must make certain that the benefits of treatment truly outweigh potential harm. The principle of nonmaleficence sometimes can be a negative duty that results in the physician deciding *not* to treat a patient's illness or injury. Nonmaleficence necessitates that the physician not intentionally imposing unnecessary harm or injury to the patient, either through acts of commission or omission.

Society at large considers it negligent if one imposes a careless or unreasonable risk of harm or injury upon another person. Providing an appropriate standard of care that avoids or minimizes the burdens of harm is supported by our commonly held moral convictions and by law.

In a professional model of health care delivery, the physician may be ethically and legally guilty if he or she does not meet "community standards of care," which are increasingly being defined by practice guidelines. In addition, nonmaleficence underscores the necessity for medical competence. It is understood and accepted that medical errors will sometimes occur. However this principle articulates a deep-seated commitment on the part of all physicians to do everything possible to protect their patients from harm.

TABLE 14.1 The legal criteria for determining professional negligence in medicine

1. The physician must have a duty to the affected party
2. The physician must breach that duty
3. The patient must experience a harm
4. The harm must be caused by the breach of duty

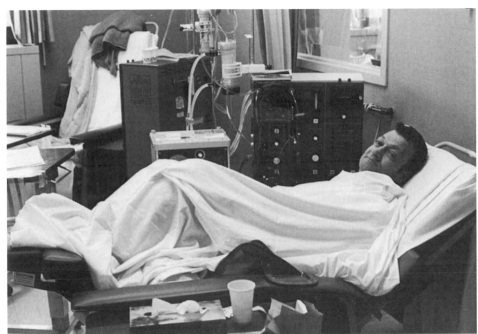

Used with permission from the National Kidney Foundation, Inc., New York. *Renal dialysis has provided tremendous health benefits but at considerable cost. Deciding if expensive benefits such as dialysis should be available to everyone who needs them is one of the major challenges of health policy.*

Justice in health care is a complicated ethical issue that demands *consideration of the fairness of a proposed treatment or intervention*. While the principles of autonomy, beneficence, and nonmaleficence have obvious applications at the level of the physician-patient interaction, the ethical principle of justice is more routinely employed at a community or public health level. The range of concerns under the principle of justice are far-reaching and would include such issues as establishing the number and category of nursing home beds that will be authorized and provided in a specific geographical region, deciding who is the most appropriate candidate for a kidney transplant, or determining the number of influenza vaccines to be distributed and deciding who would be the first to receive them. There are countless ways of considering justice in our pluralistic society, and we do not currently have a social consensus as to what constitutes justice, although it is recognized that most people have a "sense" of justice as an ethical principle.

QUALITIES OF AN ETHICAL PHYSICIAN AND THE SECONDARY PRINCIPLES

Most of us have our own basic assumptions of the qualities that make up the ideal physician. There are a limited number of qualities that, if possessed or practiced, would ensure that patients held their trust and confidence in their physician. These include *veracity, maintenance of confidentiality, fidelity, trustworthiness, integrity, compassion, and discerning judgment*. While these qualities are implied by the aforementioned ethical principles of autonomy, beneficence, nonmaleficence, and justice, they are worthy of separate consideration.

Veracity and truth-telling are synonymous. The departure from physician paternalism toward patient autonomy should clarify that patients expect physicians to tell them the truth. It would be unusual for an ethical physician to intentionally lie to his or her patients. However, some physicians find it difficult to distinguish between obfuscation and compassionate provision of information. This is compounded in many parts of the United States and similar settings, where physicians are dealing with patients (and their families) from virtually all world cultures. It is possible to practice veracity while still believing that "beneficent deception" is justified at times to reduce patient anxiety, that neither patients nor physicians can ever know the whole truth, and that indeed not all patients want the whole truth. The existence of these arguments emphasizes that *effective medical practice requires compassion, patience, discernment, and excellent communication skills*.

A commitment to truthfulness, veracity, and frankness raises other difficulties for physicians, including how to explain to patients that something has "gone wrong" during a procedure, and whether one should notify the Medical Board regarding a colleague whose ability to practice may be impaired. This latter issue in particular opens up an important discussion on the ethics of "whistle-blowing," and every medical student should be thinking about the circumstances under which he or she would be willing to report concerns about an impaired colleague.

Privacy and confidentiality were first based on the ethical principle of nonmaleficence, arising from the fact that a release of information could harm the patient. Today, it is the ethical principle of autonomy that most clearly shapes decisions about privacy and confidentiality. Even if an ethical principle were not involved, the practical need for trust as a basis for a satisfactory physician-patient relationship makes confidentiality of paramount concern. However, there are legal and ethical conflicts that influence decisions about confidentiality, particularly when a physician possesses confidential information that, if released, might prevent harm or injury to others. Yet in daily practice confidentiality is frequently breached either knowingly (with implied consent) or thoughtlessly, systematically, and deliberately (without implied consent). Conversations in the elevators are a classic example of thoughtless breaching of confidentiality. *Systematic failure to protect the confidentiality of computerized medical records has allowed violations of confidentiality to happen on an unprecedented scale.*

Fidelity, trustworthiness, and integrity are essential to the primary ethical principles of autonomy, beneficence, nonmaleficence, and justice. These are the qualities or behaviors that can make the practice of medicine so burdensome. These qualities underlie why physicians must not abandon their patients without making other suitable arrangements; why physicians must never use the physician-patient relationship to achieve sexual or other self-serving goals; why they must leave their families and loved ones when on call; and why the profession has long claimed that the patient's interests must always come first.

> Sexual relationships with patients are problematic, not only because they may be unethical and may compromise patient care, but because they may lead to civil actions for damages, criminal actions, and disciplinary proceedings by state medical boards ... While concern focused originally on relationships between patients and psychiatrists, it is now generally recognized that the problem extends to nonpsychiatric physicians as well.
>
> MAXWELL J. MEHLMAN

The intimate nature of the physician-patient relationship may give rise to sexual attraction. However, a fundamental rule of traditional medical ethics is that such attraction must be resisted. The Oath of Hippocrates includes the following promise: "Whatever houses I may visit, I will come for the benefit of the sick, remaining free of all intentional injustice, of all mischief and in particular of sexual relations with both female and male persons ..." In recent years many medical associations have reiterated this prohibition of sexual relations between physicians and their patients. The reasons for this are as compelling and defensible today as they were in Hippocrates' time, 2500 years ago: Patients are vulnerable and place their trust in physicians to help them get well. They may fear retribution if they resist sexual advances of the physician. Additionally, the clinical judgment of a physician can be negatively affected

by emotional involvement with a patient. This latter reason also applies to physicians treating their own family members, which is a practice strongly discouraged and prohibited by many medical codes of ethics.

Compassion and discerning judgment are all-embracing virtues that assist physicians in developing and maintaining effective relationships with their patients. Physicians with compassion and discerning judgment are able to act in ways that are acceptable to all parties, and to avoid potential breaches of ethical duties. *Compassion in medical practice encompasses perceptivity and sensitivity to the needs of the patient.* Kindness and a caring acceptance of both human frailty and finitude are pivotal to the principle of compassion. The absence of compassion is evident in thoughtlessness, rudeness, disrespect, abruptness, and insensitivity. *Discerning judgment implies that the physician is able to discern the real needs of the patient based on the physician's intuition, communication skills, and experience.* It is a quality that is more willingly developed by some physicians than others, and a skill that will never be developed without a deliberate decision to do so. Nevertheless, discerning judgment can never be perfected: Even the most experienced and compassionate physicians will sometimes get it wrong. Misunderstandings, misconceptions, and being "lost in translation" in the midst of clashing cultures are inevitable outcomes in the practice of medicine.

> Don't think of organ donations as giving up part of yourself to keep a total stranger alive. It's really a total stranger giving up almost all of themselves to keep part of you alive.
>
> Anonymous

CROSSING CULTURES

Immigration and globalization have connected world populations geographically, economically, digitally, and socially, creating multicultural communities at both local and global levels. Consequently, physicians must be appropriately prepared to attend to patients who differ from them in ethnicity, language, religion, education, socioeconomic status, and cultural beliefs and norms. Sensitivity to cultural differences promotes effective communication with patients from diverse backgrounds, and hence provides improved and enhanced care for them.

Cultural competence curricula recently have proliferated throughout medical schools. Appreciation of the moral foundation of this development sheds light on the purpose of such curricula for educators and trainees, and provides a way to evaluate the relationship between the ethics of cultural competence and normative Western medical ethics. The fundamental tenets of cultural competence are the acknowledgment of the importance of culture in people's lives, respect for cultural differences, and minimization of any negative consequences of cultural differences. There are myriad cultures found in the medical setting—the cultures of patients, their families, and caregivers; the cultures of our diverse health care provider population; and the culture of Western medicine. Culturally competent physicians learn about culture, embrace pluralism, and adapt to cultural differences, knowing that culturally competent care will promote patient autonomy, beneficence, nonmaleficence, and justice.

MEDICINE, ETHICS AND SOCIETY

The social contract, a concept originating from political science, has recently been used to describe the relationship between the medical profession and the society that it serves. This social contract of medicine with society has far-reaching implications for physician ethics and professionalism. Historically, medicine's social contract has been more implicit than explicit, and functioned most effectively when the values of both medicine and society were virtually homogeneous. The obligations of physicians necessary to maintain this social contract were passed on by respected role models. *Society expected that those responsible for the care of the infirm will be competent, altruistic, and moral, and that they will address the health care needs of individual patients and society. In exchange, society granted physicians status, respect, autonomy, the privilege of self-regulation, and high incomes.* This understanding continues to be the quintessence of the social contract today, despite the fact that the role of the physician in modern society has undergone an extraordinary modification in the past few decades.

Until the mid-20th century, the structure of health care delivery evolved gradually. Trust in medicine remained high, and the term "social contract" did not feature in medical discourse. Believing that members of the profession would be altruistic, the public looked favorably upon the professions, and medicine's influence on public policy was significant. However, in the 1960s and 1970s, all forms of authority were called into question. Social scientists argued that medicine had abused its monopoly to further its own interests, had not self-regulated appropriately, and that its organizations were more interested in serving their members than society. In the 1980s Paul Starr coined the term "social contract" to describe medicine's relationship to society, stating that this contract was being renegotiated to cope with the complexities of both modern medicine and contemporary society. Since then, societal expectations of medicine and physician behavior have continued to develop and augment the need for increased ethical deliberation regarding professional practice, education, and life-long learning.

Society's foremost expectation is that individuals will re-

PEAU D'ORANGE

We barter the difference
between black and gray.
"Surgery, radiation or
death," you say and leave
the decision to me,

while I insist you are the gods
I believed in as a child.
I prayed you to pull magic
out of your black leather bags
to wave away the rattling
in my bones.

I accept your calling
my breast an orange peel,
let you lay hands on this fruit
my mother said no man
must touch. In this disease
there is no sin.

If you lift the chill
that unravels my spine,
I will send you stars
from the Milky Way,
send them spinning down,
dancing a thousand-fold. Please
let me grow old.

MARCIA LYNCH

ceive assistance from healers. Society wants—and deserves—professional and compassionate health care, with patients' confidentiality being respected and their dignity preserved. Furthermore, individuals want to maintain control of the direction of their own treatment. Medicine has an obligation to meet these expectations.

Society also expects that the medical profession will guarantee the competence of each physician by establishing and enforcing standards for education, training, and practice, and by disciplining incompetent, unethical, or unprofessional conduct. The obligation of the individual physician is to maintain his/her own competence and to engage in the process of self-regulation.

Physicians are empowered to ask intrusive questions and carry out invasive procedures. However, along with this power come clear expectations: Patients must believe that their physicians will put their patients' needs ahead of their own. This does not have to be an open-ended commitment incompatible with a healthy physician's lifestyle; rather, it is important for medical students and physicians to realize that *altruism is central to the social contract between doctors and patients.*

Other societal expectations of physicians include that of morality and integrity in their practice and day-to-day lives. Physicians who do not act morally and with integrity will, without question, lose trust, causing the public to lose confidence in the medical profession. Promotion of the public good is another expectation of physicians. To the extent that physicians are granted control over the practice of medicine, it is expected that they will address the problems faced by individual patients and issues of substance to society, rather than just the concerns of medicine itself. What is expected of the physician as healer and moral agent is largely determined by what it means to be a professional in contemporary society. Physicians must understand professionalism and the obligations that are necessary to sustain the professional and ethical behavior essential to the social contract. Yet this is not as easy as it sounds. The social contract is jeopardized by many ethically questionable concerns (and behaviors) including, but not limited to, the corrupting influence of financial incentives, fierce market competition, and the gradual diminution of patient trust. Unfortunately, many physicians are ill-equipped to deal with these concerns. Other ethical struggles often encountered by physicians include challenging clinical situations, where their preferred action may conflict with the expectations of patients, demanding families, or third-party payors. When ethical, competent, and compassionate physicians succumb to such demands and to questionable expectations, being complicit in actions they perceive to be ethically inappropriate, their integrity is compromised. Education in medical ethics is essential to "ethically empower" physicians to behave appropriately, beneficently, and justly.

CAN WE TEACH ETHICAL BEHAVIOR IN MEDICINE?

Until the late 1970s, ethics, professionalism, and humanism were not part of the formal medical school curriculum. However, formal training in medical ethics has become increasingly common, and medical ethics has been a highly successful addition to educational curricula in most medical schools around the world. This resulted from the realization that all physicians must be equipped with skills to enable them to recognize ethical distress, identify ethical dilemmas, conduct a problem-based ethical analysis, and work through the complex ethical issues

> **BOX 14.2** Education in medical ethics should include the following subject matter:
>
> - Informed consent, both for medical treatment and participation in research
> - Confidentiality and when it can justifiably be breached
> - Assessment of decision-making capacity or lack thereof
> - Disclosure and justification for withholding information (therapeutic privilege)
> - Medical futility/do not resuscitate (DNR) orders/limitation of treatment
> - Advance care planning
> - Terminating the therapeutic relationship between physician and patient
> - The noncompliant patient and refusal of recommended treatment, including life-sustaining treatment
> - Quality-of-life issues
> - Management and stewardship of costly and scare medical resources
> - End-of-life care and the distinction between:
>   - withholding and withdrawing life-sustaining treatment, including nutrition and hydration
>   - ordinary and extraordinary care
>   - hastening the death process versus allowing death to occur naturally
>   - assisted suicide and euthanasia
>   - brain death and persistent vegetative states
> - Genetic testing and genetic manipulation issues
> - Impaired physician issues
> - Ethical, moral, cultural, and religious differences regarding such issues as reproductive technology, abortion, contraception, and birth control

they will confront in practice. Some medical schools have very little ethics teaching, while others have highly developed programs. Various approaches have been taken over the past several decades to introduce medical ethics into undergraduate, graduate, and postgraduate training. Formal training in clinical ethics has become a central part of residency curricula in the United States in order to prepare future physicians to manage the many and varied ethical dimensions of patient care and health care delivery.

The goals and objectives of medical ethics education include gaining the skills in ethical analysis that are essential to meet the demands associated with moral medical choices, increased responsibility for ethical issues in everyday clinical practice, and enhanced critical reflection of one's personal values and obligations as a physician. Such training will assist physicians and physicians-in-training to develop a thorough theoretical and practical working knowledge of ethics and ethical behavior. However, the onus for ethical behavior will always rest with the individual physician.

CASE STUDY

A 32-year-old woman, in her 12th week of a pregnancy with twins, tells her obstetrician that she is extremely fatigued. The obstetrician counsels her that fatigue is quite common in the first trimester, but orders a complete blood count with differential, thinking she may be anemic. That evening her obstetrician calls her at home, obviously upset. "You have leukemia. It is in an acute phase and needs to be treated right away." The young woman says that this is a much-wanted pregnancy, and she also thinks it would be immoral for her to do anything that might damage her unborn children. She announces that she will refuse to have any treatment for the leukemia until after the babies are delivered. She does not want to involve her husband in the decision. She and the obstetrician agree to meet the next day.

What are the medical ethical principles to consider in this case?

- *Autonomy:* Respect for the autonomy of the young woman would suggest that she should be able to make her own decision s about her health care, even if her doctor disagreed. However, the usual rules of informed consent apply. That is, the doctor must ascertain that she understands her diagnosis, the options she has, and the potential consequence of each option. In this case she has to understand that if she refuses treatment both she and the twins might die.
- *Beneficence:* In any case which involves more than one person, there are competing "good" or beneficent approaches. In this case, treatment of a life-threatening illness in the young woman would be the usual beneficent approach. However, in this case that conflicts with the immediate good for the fetuses, and potentially with beneficence to the father, who is at least an interested party. However, one may argue that beneficence to the woman is of more importance here than to the twins, who are not independently viable beings. Given that the young woman is refusing treatment, beneficence is also in conflict with respect for autonomy.
- *Nonmaleficence:* It does seem clear in this case that to treat this young woman with the systemic toxins which are the usual treatments of leukemia would be doing harm to the twin fetuses, and thus violate nonmaleficence. The mother is also asking that everything be done to preserve the life of the twins, so it could be argued that to damage or kill the fetuses, even with the purpose of saving her life, would be doing harm to the young woman.
- *Justice:* In general, women are allowed to make their own decisions about healthcare during pregnancy, and people with serious illnesses are allowed to refuse treatment, provided they understand the consequences. It could

thus be argued that it would not be fair or just to make this young woman either take or forgo treatment.

This type of case would often be presented to a formal ethics committee, given the complexity and the possible ramifications of any decision. However, less serious variations on this situation are commonly encountered in clinical care.

SUMMARY

Throughout almost all of recorded history and in virtually every part of the world, being a physician has meant something honorable, principled, and good. People come to physicians for service, benefit, and simple help with their most pressing needs—alleviation from pain and suffering and restoration of health and wellness. People allow physicians to see, touch, and manipulate every part of their bodies, even the most intimate. People entrust in physicians the care of their normal—and not so normal—bodily functions. They do this because they trust their physicians to act in their best interest, and to respect and honor their autonomous decisions without fear of retribution, discrimination, or less than optimal care. The ethical behavior of the physician must encompass the ancient Hippocratic traditions all the way through to our most contemporary understandings of personal and professional integrity and humility. This appreciation of ethical behavior in medicine is too important to be confined to a "hidden curriculum" of medical training, whereby the ethical comportment of the physician is developed by way of an experiential rite of passage. Although there is much to be gained by experience, ethics must also be valued as a solid theoretical and applied clinical construct.

SUGGESTED READINGS

Bryan, C.S., & Babelay, A.M. (2009). Building character: a model for reflective practice. *Academic Medicine, 84*, 1283–1288.
  The authors examine the use of reflective practice in medical schools as a way to teach the skills needed for resolving ethical dilemmas and promoting virtue and professionalism among physicians. This is meant to be a partial answer to the question as to whether ethical character can, indeed, be taught.

Goold, S.D., & Stern, D.T. (2006). Ethics and professionalism: What does a resident need to learn? *American Journal of Bioethics, 6*, 9–17.
  Qualitative methods were used to assess what residents, faculty, training directors, and ethics committees should learn about medical ethics. As suggested in this chapter, the study found that consent, interprofessional relationships, family interactions, communication skills, and end-of-life care were essential components of training.

Wilkinson, T.J., Wade, W.B., & Knock, L.D. (2009). A blueprint to assess professionalism: Results of a systematic review. *Academic Medicine, 84*, 551–558.

This paper examines the work that has been done in assessment of professionalism for physicians. The authors identify a set of attri-butes and behaviors associated with professionalism, and describe the ways in which they currently are being assessed. They also iden-tify elements of professionalism for which there are not yet good assessment measures.

Part 4

Physician-Patient Interactions

15 The Physician-Patient Relationship

Howard Brody

CASE STUDY 1: TWO VERSIONS OF THE ELECTRONIC MEDICAL RECORD

Dr. Green, a primary care physician, is seeing Mrs. Jones on a return visit to evaluate a new medication and exercise regimen she has recommended for her osteoarthritis of the knee. Mrs. Jones is very pleased and mentions that she is now able to work in her garden again.

Dr. Green uses a version of the electronic medical record (EMR) that facilitates narrative notes as well as offering check-off options. She adds the comment, "Able to work in garden again," to her progress note for the visit.

On the next visit, Dr. Green reviews her previous note and then asks Mrs. Jones at the beginning of the session, "And how is your garden coming along?" Mrs. Jones is pleased that the doctor remembered her favorite hobby.

Dr. Gold, another primary care physician, has an identical encounter with his own osteoarthritis patient, Mrs. Smith. The form of EMR he uses makes it very complicated to add narrative notes and favors check-off boxes. He clicks on the box, "Joint function: improved."

On the next follow-up visit, Dr. Gold cannot remember whether it was Mrs. Smith or one of his other patients who likes to garden. He decides to play safe and not bring up the subject.

CASE STUDY 2: THE PHYSICIAN'S WORDS AND THE PATIENT'S BRAIN

In 2002, Fabrizio Benedetti, a neuroscientist at the medical school of the University of Turin, wrote a review called "How the Doctor's Words Affect the Patient's Brain" (Benedetti, 2002). The theme he addressed has an ancient lineage, which the Spanish medical historian, Pedro Lain-Entralgo, addressed in a book called *The Therapy of the Word in Clas-*

> There, I think, is the oldest and most effective act of doctors, the touching. Some people don't like being handled by others, but not, or almost never, sick people. They need being touched, and part of the dismay in being very sick is the lack of close human contact.
>
> LEWIS THOMAS

sical Antiquity (Lain-Entralgo, 1970). Yet there was nothing antiquated about Benedetti's review–he summarized recent investigations of his neuroscience group at Turin and referred to other studies using neuroimaging techniques to explore brain chemistry.

One research finding from Turin was particularly intriguing. Benedetti and his colleagues studied a group of patients who had recent major surgery and were receiving heavy-duty pain medications, such as morphine, intravenously. The medication, however, was administered under two different conditions. In one, the patient witnessed a health worker injecting the medication into the intravenous line, and was told that this was a potent analgesic and would soon take effect. In the other condition, the patient was hooked to an intravenous pump which was programmed to give the same dose of the medication at specified times, but with no way for the patient to know when the medication was being infused. All patients had their pain levels continuously monitored.

The analgesic medication administered with the patient's knowledge and awareness had just about twice the pain-killing effect as the same chemical compound administered blindly (Amanzio et al., 2001).

It is worth taking a minute to think about this. The vast majority of studies of drugs look only at the first type of situation—the patient takes a medicine, and knows that she is taking the medicine, and what it is supposed to be for. Virtually no such study has a control group in which other patients have the medication slipped into their morning cups of coffee without their knowledge. (There is good reason why we do not do such studies; they would, as a rule, be unethical.) But suppose such studies were routinely done. And suppose the findings mirrored those of the Turin investigators that *fully half of the effects of most drugs rely on the patient's awareness of taking the medication, and the expectation that it will do them good; and only half of the efficacy of the drug depends solely on its chemical properties.* This is only an intriguing hypothesis at present. But imagine how this finding would change the way we think about medical practice—and the importance of the physician-patient relationship.

Benedetti pointed out in his review that it is not merely the case, today, that we can observe these effects. It is now also true that we have a much better idea of how to account for such results. A key finding from the Turin research group's work was that when patients experience pain relief because they expect to, the effect appears to be mediated by **endorphins**, opiate-like neurochemicals manufactured by the brain that bind to the same receptor sites as do morphine and other exogenous opiates. As part of a larger study that included the work with post-operative pain relief, the group conducted laboratory studies on experimentally-induced pain. They used a different drug, ketorolac (a nonsteroidal anti-inflammatory drug chemically unrelated to opiates) as a pain-reliever, and again compared the effect size of open vs. hidden administration. But, in an especially elegant twist, they added an injection of naloxone to the open injection of ketorolac. Naloxone is an opiate antagonist. It blocks the effects of both exogenous opiates such as morphine, and the brain's naturally occurring endorphins. Since ketorolac is not an opiate, naloxone will not reverse the pain-relief effect of that drug. But when given along with the open injection of ketorolac, the naloxone reduced the effectiveness of the injection to the same level as the hidden injection of ketorolac.

The Turin group interpreted these results as sorting out two separate healing effects. The first is the purely chemical analgesic effect of ketorolac. This is not reversed by naloxone, and is the same whether the patient knows he is getting the medication or not. The second is the extra boost, as it were, that the patient gets from *knowing* that the drug is being given and *expecting* that it will help. This extra boost, Benedetti and colleagues concluded, is mediated by endorphins in the brain; therefore it is subject to reversal by naloxone. And, again, this "extra boost" was responsible for about half of the total analgesic response.

Before we consider any more examples, let's contrast Case Studies 1 and 2. The latter has all the elements that we typically associate with scientific research, including careful measurement of administered chemicals and the resulting outcomes. By contrast, Case Study 1 seems to have nothing to do with the *science* of medicine at all. Whether Dr. Green manages to remember that Mrs. Jones likes to garden is the sort of thing that is commonly referred to as "the art of medicine" or, more disparagingly, as "bedside manner." So long as EMR software allows the physician to

record important objective measurements (such as improvement in joint function), who cares whether it facilitates noting down the patient's favorite hobby?

Let's keep these questions in mind as we consider yet another example of research.

CASE STUDY 3: LISTENING TO THE PATIENT AND LATER HEALTH OUTCOMES

The ketorolac-naloxone study, by its nature, could be done only in an artificial laboratory setting, and so one should use caution in extrapolating those results to clinical work with real patients. That caution need not be applied to an older study done by family physicians at the University of Western Ontario. They asked a disarmingly simple question. Suppose that you have a group of patients, all coming to the family physician's office with a wide variety of common complaints. What happens during the visit with the physician that *best* predicts that one month later, the patients will report that they *feel better*?

The research group looked at a number of such visits and carefully analyzed what went on. Most of the variables they studied had no correlation with the patient's later outcome. The thoroughness of the history and physical; what laboratory and x-ray tests were done; what treatment was prescribed; how complete a note was written in the chart—none of these variables correlated well with later improvement. It seemed that virtually everything we try to teach in medical school and residency made little difference.

One factor, however, was highly associated with later improvement. This was the patient's perception that *the physician had listened carefully enough so that both physician and patient agreed on the nature of the problem* (Bass, Buck et al., 1986). This result was actually not surprising, since a study done a few years earlier at Johns Hopkins University had similarly shown that the patient's sense of being carefully listened to was the crucial variable in later improvement (Starfield et al., 1981).

The Western Ontario physicians, however, were not fully satisfied. They took one group of patients—those coming in for the first time complaining of headache—and followed them for a full year. What would predict that the headache was improved one year later? Once again the answer was clear: the patients' perception that at the first visit, they had the chance to discuss the headache problem fully with the physician.

If we compare Case Studies 1 and 3, we can start to see a greater advantage to a version of the EMR that allows us to make a note to ourselves that Mrs. Jones likes to garden. How much better Mrs. Jones feels in the future may be directly tied to how well she feels listened to during her physician visits—and remembering her gardening hobby helps to reassure her that she is truly being listened to and treated as a unique individual.

Still, skeptics may object that we are still stuck in an unimportant domain—the "art of medicine" or "bedside manner"—when we should be talking about something important, like the physiology of the body in disease. This skeptical objection, however, is at odds with what we know today about mind, brain, and behavior (see Chapter 1). As we dig deeper, we'll see that the "physiology of the body in disease" is exactly what we *are* talking about.

> What we see ultimately is that the placebo isn't really necessary and that the mind can carry out its difficult and wondrous missions unprompted by little pills. The placebo is only a tangible object made essential in an age that feels uncomfortable with intangibles, an age that prefers to think that every inner effect must have an outer cause. Since it has size and shape and can be hand-held, the placebo satisfies the contemporary craving for visible mechanisms and visible answers. The placebo, then, is an emissary between the will to live and the body.
>
> NORMAN COUSINS

THE PLACEBO EFFECT IN EVERYDAY PRACTICE

Bass and colleagues at Western Ontario did not have a special name for what they were studying in 1986. Later they summarized their research findings into what they came to call the "patient-centered clinical method" (Stewart et al., 1995). Benedetti and his group at Turin, on the other hand, believed that their studies of open vs. hidden injections were part of their larger inquiry into the *placebo effect*.

The idea that the quality of the physician-patient relationship—or what words the physician utters to the patient—can have an important effect on health and disease goes back to the time of Hippocrates. At least as long ago as the Renaissance, physicians had become used to using dummy or imitation medicines in some circumstances, observing that the unknowing patient often responded just as if he had received the actual drug. Eventually such dummies came to be called **placebos** and the resulting impact on the patient, the **placebo effect**.

Modern research into the placebo effect demonstrates that the power of words, and of the patient's expectations, to alter the course of a symptom or illness is not confined to situations in which a fake medicine is administered. (Recall that in Case Study #2, all the patients received "real" morphine.) So it is reasonable to believe *the placebo effect is ubiquitous and exists whenever a physician encounters a conscious patient*. The physician does not necessarily have to be present—it is very likely that if patients who strongly believe in the power of alternative medicine order products from an Internet site, they will have an equally powerful placebo effect when they take it. In other words, the placebo effect is a much more widespread and important phenomenon than the administration of placebos—which, again for ethical reasons, is hardly ever justified in clinical practice. Box 15.1 summarizes what is now known about the placebo effect.

BOX 15.1 Summary of research into the placebo effect

1. On average, about one-third of research subjects given a placebo will demonstrate improvement. This rate varies considerably among studies and the reasons for the variation are unclear.
2. Placebos can be powerful agents in relieving pain or anxiety, but their effectiveness is not restricted to those conditions. Virtually every potentially reversible symptom has been shown at one time or another to respond to placebos.
3. Placebos can affect both "organic" and "psychogenic" symptoms, and response to placebo does not provide any help in distinguishing which is which. Indeed, as we come to find out more about the neurophysiology and neurochemistry of symptoms like pain, *it is increasingly questionable whether the so-called organic/psychogenic distinction makes any sense*.
4. Placebos can alter physiologically measurable variables such as blood sugar, and not merely the individual's subjective state.
5. The application of neuroimaging techniques to the study of the placebo effect is still in is infancy. What has been learned so far suggests that when a placebo effect occurs, it involves the same neural structures and pathways as would pharmacologic treatment of the same disease. There is also strong scientific support for the hypothesis that expectancy-related placebo pain relief is endorphin-mediated.
6. Placebo effects can be as striking, and occasionally as long-lasting, as any effect produced by drugs. Some studies have documented a powerful placebo effect from a sham surgical procedure.
7. Placebos can also mimic many of the side effects seen with pharmacologic therapy.
8. As a general rule, research aimed at identifying a "placebo personality type" has been futile. *Most people seem to be potential placebo responders given the right set of circumstances.*
9. Older research often overestimated the size and frequency of the placebo effect because other effects were confused with it—most notably, the natural tendency of the human body to heal itself (natural history of illness). Even when these other effects are controlled for, a placebo effect often can still be demonstrated.
10. Placebo effects can be triggered by two different sorts of psychological processes. In one, people can experience a placebo effect because they expect a positive outcome to occur (expectancy). In the other, people can experience a placebo effect because they are placed in similar circumstances where healing has occurred in the past (conditioning).

BOX 15.2 Possible biochemical pathways for placebo effects (the "inner pharmacy")

Endorphins Endorphins were among the first neuropeptides studied in relation to the placebo effect; early research showed that the placebo effect could be reversed by naloxone, an endorphin antagonist. Subsequent research, particularly studies by Benedetti and colleagues (see text), has demonstrated consistently that endorphins play an important role in placebo pain relief (so long as expectancy is an important psychological mechanism) and probably in a number of other symptoms. Neuroimaging studies confirm that the brain nuclei involved in placebo effects for pain include centers known to be responsible for endorphin secretion.

Catecholamines and serotonin Catecholamines were the first hormones shown to be highly responsive to stress and emotional state. Besides their effects on heart rate, blood pressure, and other manifestations of the "fight or flight" response, adrenocortical hormones have also been shown to be linked to altered immune responses. This suggests that ultimately, catecholamine and psychoneuroimmune pathways (see below) may come to be viewed as a single complex pathway.

Psychoneuroimmune responses Immune function can be altered experimentally through changes in stress or relaxation. Neuropeptide receptor sites have been identified on immune cells, illustrating how catecholamines and endorphins may all "talk" to each other and to the immune system. While psychoneuroimmunology remains a promising route for future placebo research, to date there have been few studies directly linking placebo effects with immune system function and with measurable health outcomes in human disease.

BOX 15.3 The Meaning Model

A positive placebo effect is most likely to occur when the patient's meaning of the experience of illness is altered in a positive direction.
A positive change in meaning is most likely to result when the following elements are present:
- Patients feel listened to
- Patients are provided with a satisfactory explanation for their symptoms
- Patients sense care and concern in those around them
- Patients are helped to achieve a sense of mastery or control over the illness

---

What happens when my body breaks down happens not just to that body but also to my life, which is lived in that body. When the body breaks down, so does the life.

ARTHUR FRANK

Thanks to the work of groups such as Benedetti and colleagues in Turin, we also know a good deal more today about the biochemical pathways (including the endorphin system) that appear to be responsible for the placebo effect (see Box 15.2). It is not too far-fetched to say that the human body is supplied with its own inner pharmacy, capable of dispensing its own healing medications when people find themselves in the right sort of environment and are presented with the right stimuli (Bulger, 1990). We are now in a position to place inquiry into "the art of medicine" on a more scientific footing. We can ask in what ways the physician needs to behave—and what sort of relationship with the patient needs to be created—in order for the physician to best turn on this inner pharmacy.

The available research suggests that *the inner pharmacy, or placebo effect, is likely to be turned on optimally when the patient's meaning of the experience of illness is altered in a positive direction.* What counts as a positive alteration in the "meaning of the experience of illness"? Thanks to the research at Western Ontario and elsewhere, we can say with some confidence that *the patient's sense of being fully listened to is one such "turn-on."* Adding the results of other studies, we can expand this list into what we call the

Meaning Model (see Box 15.3). The Meaning Model describes those behaviors and social conditions that are most likely to turn on the physiologic mechanisms listed in Box 15.2.

Our ability to investigate the placebo effect in a scientific manner was further developed by a research group at Harvard led by Ted J. Kaptchuk. They were using a somewhat unusual placebo condition—acupuncture administered with special needles that withdrew back into their stems, so that the patient thought the needle was piercing the skin when it actually was not—and measuring the outcomes of symptom relief for a common medical condition, irritable bowel syndrome. As part of their study, they randomly assigned subjects to one of two conditions—the sham acupuncture was given by a cold, impersonal technician or administered by a warm, supportive, and attentive individual. For all symptom measures, the warm interpersonal relationship added to the sham acupuncture alone. Indeed, much as in Case Study #2, *the "extra boost" of symptom relief attributable to the warm relationship roughly doubled the symptom relief produced solely by the sham acupuncture* (Kaptchuk et al., 2008).

It would be nice if we could say that everywhere medicine is practiced, the "positive meaning" elements listed in Box 15.3 are fully present. Sadly, we know that in our complex and often impersonal medical care system, this is not true. All too often patients have the opposite experience. Their problems remain mysteries to them, and their physicians often fail to explain what their illness *means* in understandable language. No one listens. The patient might perceive healthcare providers as cold and distant rather than caring and concerned. The end result may be a patient

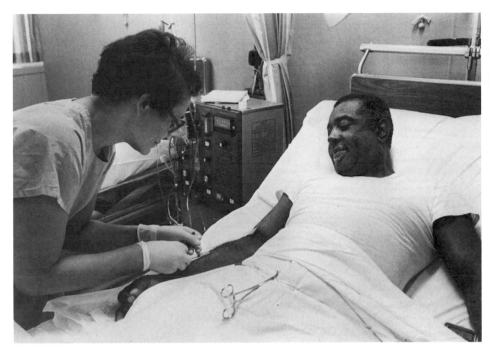

Expectations help determine outcome in any clinical setting. Copyright © National Kidney Foundation, Inc. *Learning how to shape patient expectations will help you become "a healing sort of person."*

who feels helpless and victimized. When these negative-meaning elements are present, it is reasonable to expect that the patient would suffer worse outcomes. Some investigators refer to this unfortunate result as the **nocebo effect**, the harmful opposite of a positive placebo effect.

AN EXAMPLE OF POSITIVE MEANING: "WOMEN'S COMPLAINTS"

Here's a practical example in which a physician saw a serious nocebo effect occurring, and worked to change it to a positive placebo effect.

At about the same time that the Western Ontario family physicians were puzzling over what made patients better, Kirsti Malterud was starting out as a general practitioner in Bergen, Norway. She soon found she had a number of patients suffering from "women's complaints," who had symptoms relating to the genital tract or pelvic area. The symptoms in some cases were crippling in their impact on the women's lives. The gynecologists and internists in Bergen had performed numerous investigations on these women, but had been unable to make any firm diagnosis. Eventually they told many of them that their pains were "all in their head" or in one way or another suggested that they should not come back.

These desperate women hoped that a woman physician would be better able to care for them. At first, however, Malterud had no idea of what to do. She had, after all, been trained in the same tradition, and she believed that if you did not have a diagnosis, you could not offer treatment. Besides, when the women were given medications in a

"shotgun fashion," they hardly ever got better and kept coming back with the same symptoms.

Eventually Malterud scored a breakthrough in her thinking when she came to view what her colleagues had been doing as creating a nocebo effect. The sort of care these other physicians had given, with all the best of intentions, had the net result of making these women feel powerless. They suffered from their symptoms but had been told, in effect, that they could only get better by letting physicians "work on them." The physicians undressed them, poked and prodded their genitals, and subjected them to a variety of uncomfortable procedures. After all was done, the women were told that they were even more defective than had first been thought. They had severe symptoms, but they did not have the good sense to have a diagnosable disease. Obviously, if they were so uncooperative, the problem was theirs, not the physicians'. They left the office empty-handed, with the clear message that nothing could be done for them and that nothing would ever get any better.

Armed with this insight, Malterud asked how she could alter these women's experience of their illness. She eventually found that she obtained the best results if she made sure that at each visit, she asked these women four questions (Malterud, 1994):

- What would you most of all want me to do for you today?
- What do you yourself think is causing your problem?
- What do you think that I should do about your problem?
- What have you found so far to be the best way of managing your problem?

This list of questions lines up with the recommendations

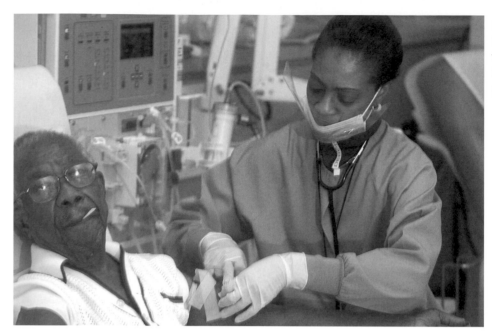

Health-care providers sometimes forget how alien and strange it feels for a patient to be in the hospital © National Kidney Foundation, photo by Erica Berger. Reprinted with permission.

from a classic paper on how to apply knowledge from the social sciences to everyday medical practice (Kleinman, Eisenberg & Good, 1978).

Malterud's way of approaching her patients gradually started to turn the nocebo effect into a positive placebo effect. Suddenly these patients found themselves looked to as experts instead of as defective bodies. Somebody actually wanted to know what they thought, and somebody actually was turning to them for guidance as to what should be done about their problems. Somebody, it seemed, was finally willing to listen to them. And, if something they themselves had done might hold the clue to how to better manage their problems, maybe they were not powerless after all. Maybe, if they put their minds to it, they could come up with even better ways of taking care of themselves in the future. Malterud found that treating her patients as thoughtful and creative problem-solvers, rather than as bundles of defective tissue, produced the best outcomes.

MEANING AND THE IMPORTANCE OF STORY

We've seen that ideally, a positive placebo effect could be a part of every physician-patient encounter, even if placebos are never administered. This has led some commentators to argue that the term "placebo effect" is too misleading to be useful any more. One systematic review of the literature suggested the term "context effects," since the entire healing context, and not merely the chemical content of the pill, is responsible (Di Blasi et al., 2001). Other authors, using a model very similar to ours, propose calling these responses "meaning effects" (Moerman and Jonas, 2002).

> The ultimate indignity is to be given a bedpan by a stranger who calls you by your first name.
>
> MAGGIE KUHN
> *Observer*

We might next ask how patients attach meaning to the experience of illness in the first place. The most basic human way we can assign meaning to any set of events in the world is to tell a story about it (Brody, 2003). A story organizes events into both a chronologic and a cause-effect sequence. A story situates events within the context of the life of the individual and of the larger community or society. When patients tell the story of an illness, they take a stab at explaining what caused the illness; what future results will arise from it; and what impact all of this has on their past, present, and future lives and activities. *Experts in medical interviewing have suggested that we ought to think of the process of "taking a medical history" as being better characterized as eliciting the patient's story* (Smith and Hoppe, 1991).

Patients go to physicians for many reasons. Obviously, they want something they can take or do that will resolve their ailments. Some want something as simple as a piece of paper saying it is okay for them to go back to work. But many patients seek a physician's care while laboring under some degree of distress or anguish. A way of characterizing this distress is as follows: "Something is happening to me. I have constructed a story to try to make some sense of it. But my own story either doesn't make much sense; or else it has really scary implications for my future. Can you help me tell a better story, that will make sense and also provide me with some comfort and reassurance?" We could summarize this succinctly as, "My story is broken; can you help me fix it?"

The notion of "fixing stories" brings us back to the "patient-centered clinical method," the proposal that emerged from the research begun by the family physicians at the University of Western Ontario. This "method" assumes that two stories of the illness will eventually be told. The patient will describe the illness in terms of the symptoms he has felt and the impact these have had on his life. The physician, after the appropriate investigations, will tell a medical story of the illness. Often this medical story will be told using terms of diseases and tissue damage, such as, "you have strep throat," or, "it sounds as if you may be having gastroesophageal reflux; I may have to suggest some further tests to be sure." Both the patients' and the physicians' stories are valuable and are essential to a good outcome. What makes the method "patient-centered" is that *the physician's job is not done until she has worked with the patient to reconcile the two stories*. The patient, in the end, is the "expert" in whether or not the reconciliation has occurred. If the physician's story of the illness or disease is not acceptable or meaningful to the patient, more work remains to be done, no matter how elegant a diagnosis the physician may have made, or no matter how scientifically sound the treatment plan.

Let's look at the patient-centered clinical method from the vantage point of "fixing a broken story" and making optimal use of the Meaning Model. How should the reconciliation occur? What would count as the ideal cooperation between physician and patient in *constructing a better story*?

CONSTRUCTING BETTER STORIES— A CASE ILLUSTRATION

Here's a case that could be almost a daily occurrence in the office of a primary care physician during the winter season (see Case Example on next page). How would we analyze this physician-patient encounter, given our goals of utilizing the Meaning Model and constructing a better story?

First, let's recall that *our overall objective is an effective and healing physician-patient relationship, not merely a satisfactory encounter*. This suggests that the physician has two agendas. First, the disease, if one is present, should be satisfactorily identified and treated, and the patient should feel listened to, cared for, and more in control of events. Second, all of those things should happen in a way that lays a positive groundwork for future collaboration and cooperation. The physician should be looking ahead down the road to the sorts of problems this patient might encounter in the future. This visit, ideally, should set the stage for the physician and patient to work together as a team to address those problems.

PATIENTS

Not the official ones, who have been
Diagnosed and made tidy. They are
The better sort of patient.

They know the answers to the difficult
Questions on the admission sheet
About religion, next of kin, sex.

They know the rules. The printed ones
In the Guide for Patients, about why we prefer
No smoking, the correct postal address;

Also the real ones, like the precise quota
Of servility each doctor expects,
When to have fits, and where to die.

These are not true patients. They know
Their way around, they present the right
Symptoms. But what can be done for us,

The undiagnosed? What drugs
Will help our Matron, whose cats are
Her old black husband and her young black son?

Who will prescribe for our nurses, fatally
Addicted to idleness and tea? What therapy
Will relieve our Psychiatrist of his lust

For young slim girls, who prudently
Pretend to his excitement, though age
Has freckled his hands and his breath smells
old?

How to comfort our Director through his
Terminal distress, as he babbles of
Football and virility, trembling in sunlight?

There is no cure for us. O, if only
We could cherish our bizarre behaviour
With accurate clinical pity. But there are no

Notes to chart our journey, no one
Has even stamped CONFIDENTIAL or Not to be
Taken out of the hospital on our lives.

U.A. FANTHORPE

CASE EXAMPLE

The patient complains of a cough that has persisted for several days. The physician's careful interview elicits, along with the usual description of symptoms, the absence of fever and the presence of nasal congestion. When the physician asks the patient what he is most worried about, the patient says that his aunt recently nearly died of pneumonia and he is worried that he might have the same disease. Examination reveals no fever, nasal congestion, some irritation of the posterior pharynx, and clear lung fields. The physician reassures the patient that he has no signs of pneumonia, and that the cough is probably related to postnasal drainage. She recommends a vaporizer and other simple home measures to try to relieve the nasal congestion. She also lists danger signs of possible pneumonia for the patient to watch for "just in case."

Now let's return to addressing what happened in the visit itself. For the physician's reassurance to be satisfying to the patient, and for the patient to feel adequately listened to, *the new story* ("post-nasal drip" instead of "pneumonia") *must emerge from a true therapeutic collaboration.* The physician must indicate to the patient, both verbally and nonverbally, that she is fully attentive to the history and physical and that she carefully considered alternative possibilities before coming up with her final explanation. (Even if this is the tenth case of post-nasal-drip-cough the physician has seen today, the patient wishes to believe that he has received the same attention as if he had walked in with a rare complaint previously unknown to medical science.) The physician must be alert during this entire process to the patient's verbal and nonverbal feedback. If the patient looks relieved and nods his head, the physician can proceed to conclude the visit. If the patient raises an eyebrow or looks more worried, the physician must stop and more carefully explore what the patient is thinking.

If the patient feels that he has been a full collaborator in constructing the new story, he will perceive the story as meaningful from his point of view. That is, he must be able to imagine what was said actually going on in his own body. The explanation offered by the physician must square with the patient's previous life experience. If, for instance, he has had allergies in the past, and had a tickle in his throat that made him cough, he may readily accept the idea that the cough is due to a nasal process. If, by contrast, the patient feels wheezy and tight in his chest, he may resist any explanation of his cough that attributes the symptom to upper respiratory problems. In any case, the time and care that the physician took in eliciting the history and offering the explanation will help determine whether the patient ends up feeling that the new story is about *his* cough, or is a stock explanation that the physician is handing out to all patients that day.

Patients come to physicians for *medical* care, not mere emotional reassurance. To be worthy of the trust the pa-

tient places in the physician, the latter must help to create a story that is *biomedically sound*. It must be scientifically correct that post-nasal drainage can cause a cough. If the physician actually fears that this patient is developing lung cancer, she must not offer the post-nasal drip explanation merely to make the patient feel better. In our case, the patient might be immensely relieved if the physician were to prescribe an antibiotic. But if no antibiotic is truly indicated, the physician ought not send the patient out of the office with an inappropriate story such as "I must have needed an antibiotic." If the biomedically sound story is "post-nasal drip not requiring an antibiotic," the physician must negotiate that correct story with the patient, even if it takes some extra time. Later, in an ongoing relationship, that extra time will pay dividends. By contrast, prescribing an unnecessary antibiotic just to save time will come back to haunt the relationship in the future.

Another feature of the best sort of healing story is that it will *promote the right sorts of healthy behaviors*. If the physician has recommended a vaporizer and perhaps a saline nasal spray, with an over-the-counter decongestant if those do not work, then the patient must imagine himself actually doing these things, and must imagine that doing them will produce the desired outcome. In other words, the story mutually constructed by physician and patient must end (in the patient's version) with, "And I went home and did what the doctor recommended, and in just a few days my symptoms were gone." This part of constructing a new healing story is relatively easy when the measures required are simple and the disease is self-limited. As patients increasingly face multiple chronic illnesses demanding major lifestyle changes, this aspect of constructing a new story becomes much more challenging.

The final requirement of the ideal healing story is also made more challenging by serious or chronic illness. This requirement is that *the new story must help the patient get on with his life*, either after the illness has resolved (for acute illnesses) or with the illness as a constant presence (chronic illness). Eric Cassell, in his classic study of the dangers of highly technological and impersonal medical practice, describes what happens when physicians adequately diagnose and treat the patient's disease, but fail to relieve the patient's suffering (Cassell, 1991). Suffering, as Cassell relates, is often due to a basic sense of being split apart where one was formerly whole. When healthy, the patient viewed herself as one with her own body, and as a functioning member of her community within her network of assigned roles and relationships. When chronically ill, this patient may see herself as alienated from her body, which will no longer do what she wants it to, and which now places new demands on her for its care. The patient may also see herself as alienated from her family and community, as the illness makes it impossible for her to perform some of her role responsibilities, and as she feels that others around her simply cannot understand what is happening to her.

In the face of this sort of suffering, the physician's care and compassion, and willingness to listen, may help the patient feel that a lifeline has been tossed to her, drawing her back into a whole relationship with the human community. But the ultimate relief of the suffering will probably require that the patient constructs a new story of the rest of her life. She will have to give up the old "healthy" life story in which she could simply do what she wanted without thinking. She will have to construct a new story in which she lives a life that is still satisfying in terms of her core values and relationships, and that permits her to carry on with her most cherished life projects. But in this new story, her illness will be a constant companion as she lives her new life. She will have to follow a new diet, exercise, take the correct medications, and see her physician more often. The physician who works carefully and consistently with the patient over a number of visits to help in the construction of this new healing story is doing some of the most important work that can be done in medicine.

AN EVIDENCE-BASED PHYSICIAN-PATIENT RELATIONSHIP

So far, we have seen that a number of general principles can effectively guide us in creating the sort of physician-patient relationship that is most likely to assure positive healing outcomes:

- **The Meaning Model:** Ways to promote a positive placebo effect as part of each patient encounter
- **Collaborative construction of stories:** Working with patients to tell better stories about their illnesses, realizing that story is the major way we have of assigning meaning to our lives
- **Patient-centered care:** Incorporates both the Meaning Model and collaborative story construction, reminding us that *we should approach medical diagnosis and treatment through our relationship with patients, rather than seeing diagnosis and treatment as somehow separable from those relationships*

Today medicine is under increasing pressure to become more evidence-based. Some fear that this trend will undermine humanism in medicine and believe "the measurable will drive out the important." They imagine that since we can more easily measure whether (for example) a drug lowers blood pressure or whether a spiral CT scan can effectively detect appendicitis, physicians will focus solely on technique and ignore medicine's human relationships.

It is admittedly hard to study the physician-patient relationship in the same rigorous way we evaluate new pharmaceuticals. Imagine trying to do a study in which you ran-

---

The Wisdom of HIPPOCRATES, 460–375 BCE
Greek physician

Sleep and watchfulness, both of them, when immoderate, constitute disease.
(Aphorisms II)

Persons who are naturally very fat are apt to die earlier than those who are slender.
(Aphorisms II)

He who desires to practice surgery must go to war.
(Corpus Hippocraticum)

I will not use the knife, not even on the sufferers from stone, but will withdraw in favour of such men as are engaged in this work.
(Corpus Hippocraticum)

The art has three factors, the disease, the patient, and the physician. The physician is the servant of the art. The patient must co-operate with the physician in combating the disease.
(Epidemics I)

I will neither give a deadly drug to anybody if asked for it, nor will I make a suggestion to this effect.
(The Oath)

So do not concentrate your attention on fixing what your fee is to be. A worry of this nature is likely to harm the patient, particularly if the disease can be an acute one. Hold fast to reputation rather than profit.
(Precepts I)

Sometimes give your services for nothing. And if there be an opportunity of serving one who is a stranger in financial straits, give full assistance to all such. For where there is love of man, there is also love of the art.
(The Art VI)

The physician must have a worthy appearance; he should look healthy and be well-nourished, appropriate to his physique: for most people are of the opinion that those physicians who are not tidy in their own persons cannot look after others well.
(Attributed)

---

domly assigned thousands of patients to either good or poor relationships with their physicians, and then came back in ten years to see what outcomes had occurred. Or imagine that you tried to do a randomized controlled trial in which you kept all other elements of the physician-patient relationship constant, only in half the cases the patient received a meaningful explanation for their illnesses, while in the other half they received a confusing explanation. In some ways, our understanding of the physician-patient relationship is destined to fall short of good evidence.

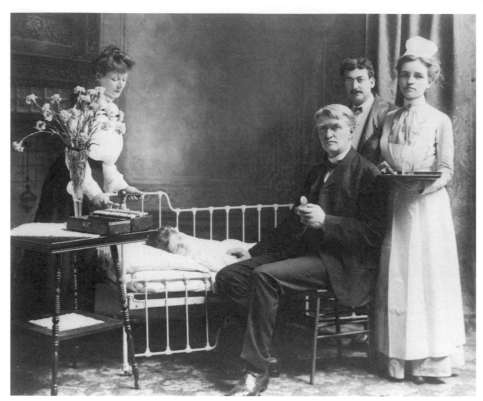

Courtesy of the Library of Congress, Washington, D.C. *Professional and gender roles were once firmly established in the healing professions, and physicians tended to be white, male, and clearly in charge.*

Yet this need not mean that we cannot pursue two important goals. First, we can continue as best as we can to document what happens to our patients' health when they experience different sorts of encounters and relationships—as Ted Kaptchuk's research elegantly demonstrates. Second, we can try further to refine our understanding of what works and what doesn't, so that ultimately our teaching of ourselves and of future physicians will be better grounded scientifically.

We have already seen how the family physicians at the University of Western Ontario based their "patient-centered clinical method" on measurable patient outcomes. Later, a massive study in the United States called the Medical Outcomes Study documented repeatedly how certain ways of interacting with patients produced better health outcomes in a variety of chronic conditions. Patients who were encouraged to become active participants in their own care, using a patient-centered approach, had better results, while their medical care generally cost less (Kaplan et al., 1996). Surveying this literature, a group of primary care experts concluded that "sustained partnerships" with patients had been proven to produce better health outcomes in a wide variety of diseases and conditions (Leopold, Cooper & Clancy, 1996). In 2001 when the Institute of Medicine of the National Academy of Sciences issued its influential report called *Crossing the Quality Chasm*, it included *patient-centered* as one of six essential criteria for assessment of the quality of medical care. Similarly, a task force describing the "Future of Family Medicine" singled out patient-centered care as the key element for the future devel-

opment of that primary care specialty (Future of Family Medicine, 2004).

THE FUTURE: TOWARD THE PATIENT-CENTERED MEDICAL HOME

In summary, we have solid evidence today on which to argue that the sort of physician-patient relationship we have described in this chapter is:

- Humane and compassionate
- Ethically respectful of patients' rights
- Well-grounded in a scientific understanding of the human brain
- Effective in producing superior health outcomes
- Efficient in holding down the costs of medical care

How can this sort of superior care best be packaged? Leaders of primary care medicine and health policy analysts are increasingly discussing the concept of the **primary care medical home**. The central features proposed for this medical home are listed in Box 15.4.

As valuable as the medical home concept is, and as reassuring as is the initial research on its benefits, we can still go awry if we follow the pattern of too much of American medicine and focus only on technology or financing and not on human relationships. If the medical home deteriorates into the place where we have electronic medical re-

---

BOX 15.4 Features of the ideal patient-centered medical home

- Patient-centered care such as same-day scheduling and ease of access by telephone, e-mail, and internet
- EMR and aggressive quality monitoring
- Interdisciplinary team care, ideally led by a primary care physician
- Coordination of care, whether delivered on-site or referred outside
- Focus on prevention and health education, including group visits
- Focus on management of chronic illness

Future of Family Medicine Project Leadership Committee (2004)

---

cords only to save money, it will fail to live up to its promise. Recall Case Study 1 –the critical question is *which* version of the EMR will the future medical home use?

If it's the good version of the EMR, and one that makes it easy for Dr. Gold to write down a note about Mrs. Jones and her garden, then we have reason to think that Mrs. Jones will *feel welcome* when she comes to her "medical home" to seek help from Dr. Gold and other members of the team of caregivers. And so long as everyone keeps firmly in mind that *home* means a place where you *feel welcome*, whatever else is true of any particular "home," then we can be hopeful that the relationships encouraged by the medical home of the future will be the truly meaningful, healing relationships that the best scientific evidence today endorses.

REFERENCES AND SUGGESTED READINGS

Amanzio, M., & Benedetti, F. (1999). Neuropharmacological dissection of placebo analgesia: expectation-activated opioid systems versus conditioning-activated specific subsystems. *Journal of Neuroscience, 19*, 484–494.

Amanzio, M., Pollo, A., Maggi, G., & Benedetti, A. (2001). Response variability to analgesics: A role for nonspecific activation of endogenous opioids. *Pain, 90*, 205–215.

Bass, M. J., Buck, C., Turner, L. et al. (1986). The physician's actions and the outcome of illness in family practice. *Journal of Family Practice, 23*, 43–47.
An excellent, pioneering study showing that the patient's and physician's agreement on the nature of the problem (which in turn requires that the physician listen carefully to the patient) predicts later resolution of common symptoms.

Benedetti, F. (2002). How the doctor's words affect the patient's brain. *Evaluation and the Health Professions, 25*, 369–386.
A review of much recent research on the placebo effect, and on how the medical setting and context (including the physician-patient relationship) affects neural systems.

Benedetti, F. (2009). *Placebo effects: understanding the mechanisms in health and disease.* New York, NY: Oxford University Press.

Brody, H. (2000). The placebo response: Recent research and implications for family medicine. *Journal of Family Practice, 49*, 649–654.
Elaborates the Meaning Model and evidence supporting it, and recommends actions to implement the model in primary care practice.

Brody, H. (2003). *Stories of sickness* (2nd ed). New York, NY: Oxford University Press.
Explores the importance of story and narrative in medicine and in medical ethics.

Bulger, R.J. (1990). The demise of the placebo effect in the practice of scientific medicine—a natural progression or an undesirable aberration? *Transactions of the American Clinical and Climatological Association, 102*, 285–293.

Cassell, E.J. (1991). *The nature of suffering and the goals of medicine.* New York, NY: Oxford University Press.
An important book on the nature of suffering as it involves the whole person and the person's social relationships, and how medicine can both ameliorate and exacerbate suffering.

Di Blasi, Z., Harkness, E., Ernst, E. et al. (2001). Influence of context effects on health outcomes: A systematic review. *Lancet, 357*, 757–762.

Future of Family Medicine Project Leadership Committee (2004). The future of family medicine. *Annals of Family Medicine, 2*, S1–S32.
A report on the future of family medicine that stresses the importance of patient-centered care.

Hahn, R.A. (1997). The nocebo phenomenon: scope and foundations. In A. Harrington (Ed.) *The placebo effect: An interdisciplinary exploration* (pp. 56–76). Cambridge, MA: Harvard University Press.

Institute of Medicine. Committee on Quality of Health Care in America. (2001). *Crossing the quality chasm: A new health system for the 21st century.* Washington, DC: National Academy Press.
A major report on quality care, arguing that "patient-centered" is one of six essential elements of good quality.

Kaplan, S.H., Greenfield, S., Gandek, B. et al. (1996) Characteristics of physicians with participatory decision-making styles. *Annals of Internal Medicine, 124*, 497–504.
One of a series of publications from the Medical Outcomes Study, describing a style of physician-patient communication associated with health improvements.

Kaptchuk, T.J., Kelley, J.M., Conboy, L.A. et al. (2008). Components of placebo effect: randomized controlled trial in patients with irritable bowel syndrome. *British Medical Journal, 336*, 999–1003.
Well-designed study showing that different elements contributing to a placebo effect in ill patients can be distinguished and their relative contributions measured.

Kleinman, A.F., Eisenberg, L., & Good, B. (1978). Culture, illness and care: Clinical lessons from anthropological and cross-cultural research. *Annals of Internal Medicine, 88*, 251–258.
A classic study of the application of social-science insights to everyday physician-patient encounters.

Lain-Entralgo, P. (1970). *The therapy of the word in classical antiquity* (trans. L.J. Rather & J.M. Sharp). New Haven, CT: Yale University Press.

Leopold, N., Cooper, J., & Clancy, C. (1996). Sustained partnership in primary care. *Journal of Family Practice, 42*, 129–137.

Describes the model of "sustained partnership" and assesses evidence that it produces superior health outcomes.

Malterud, K. (1994). Key questions—a strategy for modifying clinical communication: transforming tacit skills into a clinical method. *Scandinavian Journal of Primary Health Care, 12,* 121–127.
Malterud describes her method of asking key questions that empower female patients as part of the routine office visit.

Moerman, D.E., & Jonas, W.B. (2002). Deconstructing the placebo effect and finding the meaning response. *Annals of Internal Medicine, 136,* 471–476.

Smith, R.C., & Hoppe, R.B. (1991). The patient's story: integrating the patient- and physician-centered approaches to interviewing. *Annals of Internal Medicine, 115,* 470–477.

Starfield, B., Wray, C., Hess, K. et al. (1981). The influence of patient-practitioner agreement on outcome of care. *American Journal of Public Health, 71,* 127–132.

Stewart, M., Brown, J.B., Weston, W.W. et al. (1995). *Patient-centered medicine: Transforming the clinical method.* Thousand Oaks, CA: Sage.

Communicating with Patients

Gregory Makoul & Peter B. Zeldow

Medicine was once the most respected of all the professions. To-day, when it possesses an array of technologies for treating (or curing) diseases which were simply beyond comprehension a few years ago, medicine is under attack for all sorts of reasons. Doctors, the critics say, are applied scientists, concerned only with the disease at hand but never with the patient as an individual, whole person. They do not really listen. They are unwilling or incapable of explaining things to sick people or their families.

LEWIS THOMAS
House Calls

Longstanding notions of communication as bedside manner or history taking have given way to viewing communication as a fundamental clinical skill that is vital to both patient well-being and to diagnostic and therapeutic success. This is the case throughout the continuum of medical school, residency, and clinical practice. In fact, the Accreditation Council for Graduate Medical Education, which oversees U.S. residency programs, and the American Board of Medical Specialties, the umbrella organization for specialty boards that certify physicians, have designated that *interpersonal and communication skills that result in effective information exchange and teaming with patients, their families, and other health professionals are a core area of competency for all physicians.*

Effective communication has been linked to increases in physician and patient satisfaction, adherence to treatment plans, more appropriate medical decisions, better health outcomes, and decreased incidence of malpractice suits. Moreover, attention to interviewing skills can enrich the practice of medicine over the course of a lifetime, ensuring that the patient is treated as a living, breathing, feeling human, and not just a collection of malfunctioning organ systems. This point deserves close consideration because it is often overlooked in everyday clinical practice. When people become patients, they enter a world in which their sense of control is threatened. Not only can perceived control be diminished by the illnesses that cause patients to seek help, but opportunities to regain control can be limited by the consultation itself. This is especially true if physicians view patients as cases to be treated, not people to be helped. Cases require no information, no explanation, no choice. However, people do, because information, explanation, and choice enhance the sense of perceived control. In other words, with regard to the consultation, patients can maintain control by obtaining information about their situation and participating in decisions about treatment.

Obviously the nature of an interview depends on the setting and on the relationship between the physician and patient. A delirious patient in an emergency room cannot engage in the kind of dialogue possible during an office visit with a patient who has chronic heart disease. Interviews with children and adolescents also require modifications in technique. Of course, an initial diagnostic interview has different objectives than a follow-up appointment designed to provide emotional support, manage medication, or discuss lifestyle. Reading about interviewing is only a first step toward becoming a competent interviewer; supervised practice is also important. *Simply conducting many interviews does not improve technique, but only consolidates preexisting habits.* Observation, feedback, and self-reflection are keys to more effective interviewing skills. Videotaped interviews with real or simulated patients provide incontestable evidence of verbal and nonverbal strengths and weaknesses as an interviewer. Reviewing such tapes, particularly with supervisors, can have a profound effect on developing skills.

THE PATIENT

The first thing to remember about the patient is that he or she is anxious. This may or may not be apparent. It is

An eighty-four-year-old woman living in Maine has never had a complete medical exam. Her kids insist that she go to the doctor, and although she's never been sick, she goes. She's not a very sophisticated woman, and the young doctor is amazed she's in such good shape.

After the exam he tells her, "Everything seems to be in good order, but there are additional tests I'd like to run. Come back next week and bring a specimen."

The old woman doesn't know what he is talking about.

He says, "What I need is a urinary sample. Would you bring that in and we'll run some additional tests." She still doesn't understand. The doctor says, "Before you come in, void in a jar." The woman responds quizzically, "What?"

The doctor finally gets exasperated and says, "Look, lady, go piss in a pot." She gets red in the face, smacks him over the head with her pocketbook, replies, "And you go shit in your hat," and promptly walks out.

RICHARD S. WURMAN
Information Anxiety

important to recognize that the patient is ill or subjectively distressed and may have already developed their own theories about what is wrong. The possibility of having disease evokes fear of death and disability, fear of bodily harm, fear of separation from loved ones (e.g., through hospitalization) and, consequently, concerns about the ability to fulfill day-to-day responsibilities. In addition, physicians often intimidate patients. No matter how kind and eager to help the physician may be, the patient's reaction to the physician's *presence* cannot be controlled. Patients expect great things from their physician and feel a strong sense of dependence on the physician to meet their physical and emotional needs. It is critical for physicians to realize that these realities complicate the interview. The physician cannot simply ask questions and assume that the desired answers will be returned in a straightforward manner. Moreover, it is not enough for a physician to provide information in what he or she perceives to be an understandable manner. They must check with patients to ensure that the information was heard and understood as intended. *Patient anxiety and the emotion-laden nature of the physician-patient relationship require putting the patient at ease, establishing a trusting relationship, actively listening to what patients say and ask.*

A related point is that patients and physicians may have different agendas during the interview. Typically patients are seeking relief from subjective complaints (symptoms) and speak the **language of illness**. Physicians are seeking to elicit the objective signs that aid in diagnosis and speak the **language of disease**. Although the physician might prefer that the patient present his or her complaint and history in precisely the sequence required for write-up,

this rarely happens and need not be encouraged. With increased experience, the interviewer gradually becomes more comfortable taking the occasionally vague and disorganized words of the patient and transforming them into a comprehensive, meaningful, and orderly medical history. While this medical history will be useful for the health-care team, team members need to subsequently translate clinical information and options back to the patient.

THE PHYSICIAN

The role of the physician entitles him or her to inquire into private and intimate details of the patient's life and to conduct a physical examination on a relative stranger. It also obliges the physician to be professionally competent, to put the patient's interests ahead of personal interests, and to provide help and comfort whenever possible.

Although the primary purpose of the interview from the physician's perspective may be diagnostic, *an interview can and should also be therapeutic for the patient.* Depending on the physician's conduct, the patient can potentially come away from every physician encounter feeling better understood, better informed, and reassured of the physician's interest and availability. Alternatively, he or she can come away feeling misunderstood, confused, and alienated.

The following vignette exemplifies an exchange with little therapeutic content:

The interviewer failed to knock at the patient's door. He introduced himself in a hasty mumble so that the patient never had his name clearly in mind. He mispronounced the patient's name once and never used it again. The physician conducted the interview while seated in a chair about 7 feet from the patient. There was no physical contact during the interview. On several occasions the patient expressed her emotional distress. On each occasion the interviewer ignored the emotional content of her statements. For instance:

- *Doctor:* Exactly where is this pain?
- *Patient:* It's so hard for me to explain. I'm trying to do as well as I can. (Turning to husband:) Aren't I doing as well as I can?
- *Doctor:* Well, is the pain up high in your belly, or down low? (Platt & McMath, 1979)

Several aspects of this vignette are worthy of comment. The failure to knock and to learn the patient's name and the hasty introduction indicate a neglect of the most basic amenities. *The physical distance between physician and patient may also have been excessive, paralleling the emotional distance created*

The Wisdom of OLIVER WENDELL HOLMES, 1809–1894
US humorist and physician
Medical Essays

The truth is, that medicine, professedly found on observation, is as sensitive to outside influences, political, religious, philosophical, imaginative, as is the barometer to the changes of atmospheric density.

A man of very moderate ability may be a good physician if he devotes himself faithfully to his work.

The most essential part of a student's instruction is obtained, as I believe, not in the lecture room, but at the bedside.

I would never use a long word where a short one would answer the purpose. I know there are professors in this country who "ligate" arteries. Other surgeons only tie them, and it stops the bleeding just as well.

The bedside is always the true center of medical teaching.

Specialized knowledge will do a man no harm if he also has common sense, but if he lacks this, it can only make him more dangerous to his patients.

BUT HER EYES SPOKE ANOTHER LANGUAGE

The door opened.
She walked towards the waiting seat.
She sat.
Her hands wrestled in her lap.
She crooked her fingers to conceal the nicotine stains and bitten nails.
She chewed the inner side of her lower lip.
She plucked at the clasp of her handbag.
"I have a cold," she said
but her eyes spoke another language.

"No, no trouble at home."
She flinched before the subtle onslaught.
She danced and weaved through the questions.
She fell.
Tears welled and filled her eyes.
The comforting arm went unnoticed.
The hell she lived erupted from her lips.
She discharged herself and her shoulders crumpled.
She sobbed to a halt and dried her eyes upon a paper handkerchief.
"Thank you," she whispered and left by the back door.

DUNCAN DARBISHIRE

---

by the physician's failure to pursue the emotional content of the patient's statement. Most of all, notice the physician's insistence on eliciting the site of the pain. This is certainly a necessary aspect of the interview, but at this moment the patient is incapable of answering. *If the physician had been more willing to explore the patient's difficulty in explaining, he might have learned something of critical importance about the symptom and about the patient.* The patient would be more likely to experience the physician as a person who has patience and pays attention, which could only enhance the patient's confidence in the ability to describe her symptoms. Instead, the physician has learned very little, and the patient is no better off than before this exchange. These are the consequences when a physician is narrowly devoted to eliciting disease-related information at the expense of learning about the patient who hosts the disease.

Physician anxiety can also be an obstacle to effective interviewing (and may have played a role in this vignette). Although anxiety on the part of the patient should always be assumed, somehow a clinical encounter is supposed to be a routine and entirely rational interaction for the physician. This is simply not true. Insecurity with the role of a physician, discomfort with sudden access to the bodies of patients, concerns about age and sex differences, and anxiety about exploring certain topics may be perfectly natural at early stages of professional development. The danger arises when such anxieties lead the physician to avoid asking necessary questions or pursuing important leads.

THE SETTING

The setting for an interview can either facilitate or inhibit the spontaneous and open transmission of information. *Privacy, comfort, and sufficient time are three desirable aspects of setting that may be difficult to achieve.* In a hospital setting, privacy may be threatened by the presence of roommates and by the intrusions of visitors and other health-care professionals. In a busy outpatient clinic, an interview conducted in a cubicle may be hampered by limited privacy, physical discomfort (including extraneous noise), and time limitations. These factors are not completely under the physician's control. However, being aware of their potential to affect the interview, the physician should exercise control when possible. For example, if the interview is being conducted in an austere office with uncomfortable chairs, the physician can briefly acknowledge the problem and at least offer the more comfortable of the two chairs to the patient. If the problem is a noxious level of noise, it may

> The sad truth is that our trillion-dollar medical care system seems to feel that time spent with patients is a luxury it simply can't afford.
>
> FRANK DAVIDOFF
> *Annals of Internal Medicine*

> Touching with the naked ear was one of the great advances in the history of medicine. Once it was learned that the heart and lungs made sounds of their own, and that the sounds were sometimes useful for diagnosis, physicians placed an ear over the heart, and over areas on the front and back of the chest, and listened. It is hard to imagine a friendlier human gesture, a more intimate signal of personal concern and affection, than these close bowed heads affixed to the skin.
>
> LEWIS THOMAS
> *House Calls*

have to be endured, but perhaps the effort to give the patient undivided attention can be doubled and freedom from other intrusions can be provided. Privacy and comfort are important, but the physician can compensate for their absence with a combination of consideration and attentive listening.

A physician's time is valuable. In some practices, financial success is predicated on a policy of limiting office visits to 12 minutes. It is difficult to believe that the needs of patients can be handled adequately when physicians are encouraged to focus on the clock. *However rushed the physician may feel and whatever the reason, he or she must be aware that the sense of time urgency is antithetical to professional obligations.* Patients know when they are being hurried along and can recognize when the practitioner's mind is not entirely on them. Some react with resentment and others react by trying to extricate the physician from the situation. This may take the form of omitting critical symptoms from their statement of the problem, failing to ask questions that could clarify an instruction, or canceling a future appointment out of a genuine, albeit somewhat masochistic, desire not to overburden the physician. None of these reactions is acceptable, and all can be avoided if the Type A impatience and irritability that medical environments often impose is controlled. While the physician is with the patient, full attention and unhurried participation in the interview must be practiced. Having command of the interviewing techniques to be discussed helps make efficient use of the time spent with patients.

The best interview is a collaborative process between two people of equal status, no matter how different their roles. It is better not to sit behind a desk during an interview because the desk imposes a barrier between the participants that is both real and symbolic. Similarly, it is better to sit at the same level as the patient rather than to stand, which makes the patient feel dominated. Finally, interviewing a patient who is unclothed, partially dressed, or dressed in a hospital gown contributes to the patient's sense of unequal status. It is usually best to keep the interview portion of an examination separate from the physical examination as another means of emphasizing equal status. It may sound paradoxical, but *the more a patient perceives himself or herself to be an equal partner in this health-care relationship, the more likely he or she will be to accept the physician's influence.* Along these lines, it is useful to recognize that you may be the relative expert in terms of medicine, but patients are the experts on their lives.

THE SEGUE FRAMEWORK: INTEGRATING COMMUNICATION AND CLINICAL TASKS

At this point, it is important to provide a very tangible sense of how effective communication can be integrated into clinical work. The SEGUE Framework, a research-based checklist developed by one of us (GM), has become one of the most widely used models for teaching and assessing communication skills in the world. In addition to serving as a reminder of the general areas on which to focus (i.e., Set the Stage, Elicit Information, Give Information, Understand the Patient's Perspective, End the Encounter), the SEGUE acronym connotes the transition or flow of the medical encounter: from beginning to end, and from problems to solutions. The SEGUE Framework provides a common vocabulary for teaching, learning, assessing, and studying communication in medical encounters.

The checklist highlights a set of essential communication tasks (i.e., things that are important to do during a medical encounter). Since the tasks themselves can be accomplished in a variety of ways, it is important to develop a repertoire of communication skills and strategies that will work for you and your patients. This built-in flexibility with respect to the skills and strategies required to accomplish relevant tasks reflects the reality and individuality of human communication. In other words, *SEGUE offers a flexible framework, not a script.* While things might not progress in the order presented, the brief explanations and examples offered below are intended to provide a better understanding of each SEGUE task.

Set the Stage (S)

1. Greet the patient appropriately.

The key is to decide upfront what "appropriately" means, and then stick to that definition. Here are examples of the criteria for this task:

If you and the patient have not met

You should confirm (i.e., ask or say) the patient's name and introduce yourself using your first and last name. For instance, if Dr. Robert Franklin is meeting Ms. Jane Smith, it is often better to walk into the room and say: "Jane Smith? Hi, I'm Dr. Bob Franklin," rather than assuming that she prefers to be called Jane. A medical student or resident should provide both his/her name and role (e.g., "I'm Ellie Brown, a first-year medical student working with Dr. Franklin.").

If you and the patient have met previously

You should acknowledge this in greeting ("Hi Ms. Smith; good to see you again" or "I don't know if you remember me from last time; I'm Dr. Janet Jones, a resident working with Dr. Franklin.").

2. Establish the reason for the visit.

You can accomplish this task in a number of ways by asking such questions as: "What brings you in today?," "What can I do for you today?," or "So this is your 6-month recheck?"

3. Outline an agenda for the visit (e.g., issues, sequence).

Oftentimes, the patient has different priorities than you do. *The key to this task is to ask the patient if there is anything he or she would like to discuss beyond the stated reason for the visit* ("Anything else?"). This negotiation should occur before you begin exploring specific issues in detail. Providing an outline of how the encounter will flow is also helpful. Outlining an agenda lets both parties know that their issues will be addressed.

4. Make a personal connection during the visit (e.g., go beyond medical issues at hand).

This task focuses on treating/acknowledging the patient as a person. While it is probably best if this happens early in the visit, it can occur at anytime during the visit, as long as it is sincere. This is something patients notice, and appreciate. Example:

> Patient: "I'm in college"
> Doctor: "Oh, what are you studying?"

→ *5. Maintain the patient's privacy (e.g., knock, close door).*

Self-explanatory: If there is no door, you can maintain the patient's privacy by standing or sitting nearby. This is also a consideration in physical exam situations (e.g., draping).

Elicit Information (E)

6. Elicit the patient's view of health problems and/or progress.

Since patients have their own ideas about health and their own hypotheses about what might be causing and/or exacerbating a health problem, it is important to elicit their perspectives.

You can accomplish this task by asking the patient an open-ended question such as "Can you tell me how you're doing?," "How have things been going?," or "How are you doing now that you've started the treatment?" The patient's ideas, worries, and concerns can often be elicited if you remain silent after asking the "What brought you in today?" question.

7. Explore physical/physiological factors.

You can accomplish this task by asking about signs or symptoms regarding the health problem (e.g., duration, location, intensity, etc.).

8. Explore psychosocial/emotional factors (e.g., living situation, family relations, stress, work).

The key here is learning about relevant factors in the patient's life that might influence his or her health problem and health status.

9. Discuss antecedent treatments (e.g., self-care, last visit, other medical care).

The point of this task is to find out what the patient has done for the health problem before coming to see you for this visit.

10. Discuss how the health problem affects the patient's life (e.g., quality of life).

Quality of life is subjective and is best assessed by discussion. Here, instead of exploring how the patient's life affects the health problem, you are trying to learn how the health problem affects the patient's life. This task can be accomplished by asking general questions like "How has the problem affected your life?," "How has this affected your daily life?," "Tell me about a typical day," "Is this preventing you from doing things you like to do?," or more specific questions (e.g., about activities of daily living).

11. Discuss lifestyle issues/prevention strategies (e.g., health risks).

The idea here is that you identify health risks, as well as the extent to which the patient is managing them. Diet, exercise, alcohol or drug use, smoking, and safe sex are examples of the topics that could be discussed. This task is often facilitated when you provide the patient with a preface such as "I'm going to ask some questions to get a better picture of your overall health."

→ *12. Avoid directive/leading questions.*

"You're not having chest pain, are you?" is an example of a directive, or leading, question. This kind of question sometimes sounds like a statement ("No problems with your chest?"). *The problem with these questions is that they put words in the patient's mouth, and it is often very difficult for patients to correct their provider.* Similarly, if a physician asks a directive question about an uncomfortable topic (e.g., "So, no drugs?"), patients might take the opportunity to let the topic slide. Directive/leading questions are distinct from closed-ended questions like "When did it start?," "Is the pain sharp, dull, burning, squeezing, or does it feel like something else?" that are very helpful when asked at appropriate junctures.

→ *13. Give the patient the opportunity/time to talk (e.g., don't interrupt).*

We are all familiar with explicit interruptions and their effect on conversations. It is also important that you avoid "jumping" on the patient's last word, which sometimes cuts patients off before they are really finished talking. If patients go off on a tangent, try to let them know that you are interested, but need to focus on their main concerns.

→ *14. Listen. Give the patient your undivided attention (e.g., face patient, give feedback).*

As Sir William Osler said about 100 years ago: "Listen to the patient, for he [or she] is telling you the diagnosis." Facing the patient, giving verbal acknowledgment, and providing nonverbal feedback (e.g., nodding, "uh huh") are examples of ways you can show you are paying attention.

Patients notice, and tend to become less forthcoming, when a clinician is not facing them, rarely looks up from taking notes, is reading the chart while the patient is talking, or is otherwise distracted from what the patient is saying.

→ *15. Check/clarify information (e.g., recap, ask "How much is not much?").*

At issue here is the accuracy of information. Checking means that you recap what the patient has said to ensure that you interpreted it correctly ("OK, so swelling tends to be worse in the morning, is that right?"). Clarifying means

that you ask the patient to be more specific about vague information. Example:

Doctor: "How much do you smoke?"
Patient: "Not much."
Doctor: "How much is not much?"

Give Information (G)

16. Explain the rationale for diagnostic procedures (e.g., exam, tests).

You should let the patient know why you are conducting procedures. Examples include: "I'm going to listen to your lungs" before using a stethoscope, "Let's check the range of motion in your leg" before moving a patient's leg, and "I think we should check for strep" before swabbing the patient's throat.

17. Teach the patient about his or her own body and situation (e.g., provide feedback and explanations).

The medical encounter provides an excellent opportunity for giving information that can help the patient learn about his or her body or situation. You can accomplish this task by telling the patient what you found in a physical exam ("You seem a bit weaker on this side") or laboratory test ("Your strep test came back negative—that means you don't have strep throat"). You can also accomplish this task by explaining relevant anatomy ("The rotator cuff is really a set of muscles ..."), the diagnosis ("It looks like you're having tension headaches—they're often related to stress and it sounds as if your new job is pretty stressful ..."), or treatment ("This kind of antibiotic works on a wide variety of bacteria, but has a few side-effects ...").

18. Encourage the patient to ask questions/Check his or her understanding.

It is useful to actively solicit questions from the patient ("Do you have any questions?," "Is that clear?," or "Does that make sense?"). This is a very effective way to check the patient's understanding. NOTE: Asking "Is there anything else?" is *not* the same as encouraging the patient to ask questions.

→ *19. Adapt to the patient's level of understanding (e.g., avoid or explain jargon).*

Self-explanatory: There is no need to say "ambulate" when you mean "walk."

Understand the Patient's Perspective (U)

20. Acknowledge the patient's accomplishments/progress/challenges.

At issue here is whether or not you respond to a patient's overt statement about something perceived as very positive or very difficult, or to an expression of emotion. Your response (or lack thereof) very clearly suggests to the patient the degree to which you are listening and the extent to which you care.

21. Acknowledge waiting time.

If the patient has been waiting (or will have to wait) for a long period of time, you can accomplish this task by letting the patient know that you are aware of the wait.

→ *22. Express caring, concern, empathy.*

The focus here is on attention to the patient's subjective experience. You can accomplish this task by letting the patient know that you understand—or at least appreciate—the patient's perspective. This can be accomplished either verbally or nonverbally; the key is to respond. Patients tend to become less forthcoming when you appear detached, aloof, or overly businesslike.

→ *23. Maintain a respectful tone.*

Whether or not you agree with or like the patient, it is most inappropriate and unprofessional to be condescending, patronizing, or rude.

End the Encounter (E)

24. Ask if there is anything else the patient would like to discuss.

Sometimes patients feel they need permission to bring up issues beyond the "chief concern" or the main reason they've been hospitalized. Even if you do this as part of outlining the agenda toward the beginning of the encounter, you should explicitly ask the patient about this at the end of the encounter as well. In order for the patient to feel that it is actually permissible to raise another issue, you should ask this question before getting up to leave. If time is a factor—and it often is—you can always suggest discussing new issues that come up in a subsequent visit.

25. Review next steps with the patient.

You can accomplish this task by saying either what you will do for the patient *or* what the patient should do once the visit is over. Examples include:

"I will check on the test results for you."

"Please make an appointment to come back in 6 months."
"You can get dressed now."
"The nurse will be in to show you how to do that."
"Don't forget to pick up your prescription at the pharmacy."

If You Suggested a New or Modified Treatment/Prevention Plan

26. Discuss the patient's interest/expectation/goal for the plan.

Does the patient see and/or agree with the need for this plan?

27. Involve the patient in deciding upon a plan (e.g., options, rationale, values, preferences, concerns).

Not all patients want to be involved in decision making, but all should be involved to the extent they are comfortable. In addition to providing options and discussing rationale, it is especially important to explore the patient's values, preferences, and concerns.

28. Explain likely benefits of the option(s) discussed.

Do the specific benefits relate to the goal for this plan?

29. Explain likely side-effects and risks of the option(s) discussed.

In addition to providing the information, let the patient know what to do if he or she experiences a problem.

30. Provide complete instructions for the plan.

Make sure that the patient understands your instructions.

31. Discuss the patient's ability to follow the plan (e.g., attitude, time, resources).

This is an essential, and often neglected, component of the process. A patient is unlikely to follow—or even start—a treatment plan unless he or she thinks it is do-able. At the same time, many patients are unlikely to spontaneously offer their views on this subject.

32. Discuss the importance of the patient's role in treatment/prevention.

It certainly helps if patients understand that they are partners in the process. Talk about what they can do to facilitate improvement (e.g., monitoring details of their situation and letting you know how things progress).

The SEGUE Framework

Patient: _____   Physician or Student: _____

Set the Stage		Yes	No
1.	Greet patient appropriately		
2.	Establish reason for visit		
3.	Outline agenda for visit (e.g., "anything else?," issues, sequence)		
4.	Make a personal connection during visit (e.g., go beyond medical issues at hand)		
→ 5.	Maintain patient's privacy (e.g., close door)		

Elicit Information		n/a	Yes	No
6.	Elicit patient's view of health problem and/or progress			
7.	Explore physical/physiological factors			
8.	Explore psychosocial/emotional factors (e.g., living situation, family relations, stress)			
9.	Discuss antecedent treatments (e.g., self-care, last visit, other medical care)			
10.	Discuss how health problem affects patient's life (e.g., quality-of-life)			
11.	Discuss lifestyle issues/prevention strategies (e.g., health risks)			
→ 12.	Avoid directive/leading questions			
→ 13.	Give patient opportunity/time to talk (e.g., don't interrupt)			
→ 14.	Listen. Give patient undivided attention (e.g., face patient, verbal acknowledgement, nonverbal feedback)			
→ 15.	Check/clarify information (e.g., recap, ask "how much")			

Give Information		n/a	Yes	No
16.	Explain rationale for diagnostic procedures (e.g., exam, tests)			
17.	Teach patient about his/her own body & situation (e.g., provide feedback from exam/tests, explain rationale, anatomy/diagnosis)			
18.	Encourage patient to ask questions/Check understanding			
→ 19.	Adapt to patient's level of understanding (e.g., avoid/explain jargon)			

The SEGUE Framework continued

Understand the Patient's Perspective	n/a	Yes	No
20. Acknowledge patient's accomplishments/progress/challenges			
21. Acknowledge waiting time			
→ 22. Express caring, concern, empathy			
→ 23. Maintain a respectful tone			

End the Encounter	Yes	No
24. Ask if there is anything else patient would like to discuss		
25. Review next steps with patient		

If suggested a new or modified treatment/prevention plan:	n/a	Yes	No
26. Discuss patient's expectation/goal for treatment/prevention			
27. Involve patient in deciding upon a plan (e.g., options, rationale, values, preferences, concerns)			
28. Explain likely benefits of the option(s) discussed			
29. Explain likely side-effects and risks of the option(s) discussed			
30. Provide complete instructions for plan			
31. Discuss patient's ability to follow plan			
32. Discuss importance of patient's role in treatment/prevention			

Comments:

Items without an arrow focus on *content*; mark "Yes" if done *at least one time* during the encounter.

Items with an arrow (→) focus on *process* and should be maintained throughout the encounter; mark "No" if at least one relevant instance when not done (e.g., just one use of jargon).

SHARING INFORMATION

A primary purpose of the clinical interview is to share information, an activity that takes two forms: (1) eliciting information from patients to diagnose their condition and understand them, and (2) providing patients with information such as diagnoses, prognoses, prescriptions, and treatment recommendations. The interview also helps establish a positive relationship with the patient that can be the foundation of the eventual therapeutic relationship.

Information about patient symptoms is necessary before a diagnosis is made, but it is not sufficient for effective treatment. *A broader aim of the interview is to understand the patient more fully and to develop hypotheses about personality, life experiences, assets and liabilities, and reactions to illness.* If a physician cannot anticipate that a patient will have difficulty adhering to a treatment regimen or will be at risk to develop psychiatric complications, an accurate diagnosis by itself hardly guarantees successful treatment.

A physician seeking diagnostic and psychosocial information from a patient should make every effort to elicit information that is as *full-bodied* and *spontaneous* as pos-

> Doctors don't get paid for talking to patients. In a medical economy dominated by third-party paymasters—insurance companies, the government, health plans, etc.—the harsh reality is that doctors get paid mostly for tests and procedures. It is not surprising, therefore, that patients should be subjected to a multitude of encounters with expensive medical technology, not all of which is essential or without risk ... Even more serious, of course, is the reduced time for the careful questioning by the physician that has held such a high place in medical tradition.
>
> NORMAN COUSINS
> *Head First: The Biology of Hope*

sible. Patient descriptions that are full-bodied have a live and organic quality to them that is unmistakable. The physician can sense the effort that has gone into making the description accurate and elaborate. Patient descriptions that lack this quality tend to be brief, flat, unidimensional, and stereotyped, and they make it more difficult to diagnose the condition or understand the patient. Similarly, spontaneity in patient verbalizations indicates that the patient is speaking freely, without hesitancy and without editing his or her remarks. This is the ideal to which an interviewer should aspire because it means that the broadest range of information is being elicited. Patients who edit their responses to inquiries are withholding information and depriving the physician of the opportunity to do what he or she is trained to do—to separate essential from irrelevant details. The creation of such full-bodied and spontaneously offered information is a joint product of the physician and the patient. It may be impossible to change a patient's innate descriptive abilities, but it should also be evident that *how questions are posed and how the physician listens profoundly influence the quality of the information the patient provides.* Information giving is the second way in which information is shared during a clinical interview; it will be considered in more detail later in this chapter.

INTERVIEWING TECHNIQUES: FOCUS ON ELICITING INFORMATION

The interviewing techniques discussed in this section form a continuum of interviewer control. At one end of the spectrum is the use of silence, which imposes minimal interviewer control over the patient and affords the patient a wide range of response alternatives. At the other end of the spectrum is the kind of direct question that affords the patient the opportunity to answer only yes or no. *Both of these techniques have their place in the clinical interview* (although not at the beginning), along with facilitation, confrontation, and a variety of other clinical

Sorrow *Vincent van Gogh (1882).* Drawing, 38.5 × 29 cm. van Gogh Museum Foundation, Amsterdam.

tools. Because the physician is seeking a full-bodied and spontaneous account of the patient's difficulties, the best use of these techniques often involves moving through a cycle of information seeking that begins with modest control and proceeds to progressively greater use of authority. Whichever technique you choose, the key to successful interviewing lies in remembering to *listen* to the information elicited.

Open-Ended Questions

Starting the interview with questions such as "What brings you in today?," "How are you?," "How can I help you?" and "What kind of problems have you been having?" communicate to the patient that he or she can begin anywhere, without restriction. They also put the momentary burden of responsibility on the patient (which is perfectly appropriate), and they minimize bias. To begin an interview with more specific or direct questions ("Tell me about your headaches.") restricts the field of discourse prematurely and may suggest to the patient that other topics are inappropriate or not medically relevant.

Starting an interview with an open-ended question facilitates the diagnostic process because the answer that the patient chooses to give in response to the open-ended question has a special significance. However, two observational studies indicate that few physicians give patients the opportunity to make a complete opening statement of their concern. In only about 25% of office visits studied did physicians allow patients to complete their opening statement. *Most of the time, physicians interrupted and redirected patients to discuss the first concern expressed.* As the authors of one of these studies noted, physicians "frequently and perhaps unwittingly inhibit or interrupt their patients' initial expression of concerns."

Medical students sometimes justify their avoidance of open-ended questions by claiming they take up too much time. (Presumably the students are referring not to the questions themselves but to the time patients take to answer them.) This is a rationalization based on a misunderstanding of interviewing technique and purpose. An interview that employs open-ended questions is using those questions to elicit a free flow of information in the service of making a diagnosis and understanding the patient. It is the interviewer's responsibility to guide the patient's discourse if needed. While open-ended questions can indeed be efficient, they are only effective if used appropriately.

Students and physicians sometimes come away from an interview in which they used open-ended questions unimpressed with their yield. However, *an open-ended question does not guarantee an elaborate answer; it merely increases its likelihood.* Children, adolescents, and even some

adults may not be able to respond to such questions with elaborate accounts. For example, some very literal-minded patients (as well as those with organic mental disorders) respond to a question such as "What brought you to the clinic today?" with an answer such as "I drove my Toyota." Physicians should not be discouraged by their early efforts to use a new skill and should not be seduced into asking only direct questions when some open-ended questions fail.

Silence

If a patient responds to an open-ended inquiry with a minimal response, consider using silence to signal that you want to hear more. Silence imposes minimal control on the patient. It communicates to the tight-lipped patient that the physician wants to hear more and is willing to wait. Sometimes patients are guarded in responding to open-ended questions simply because they imagine that a brief response is required or because that has been their experience with physicians in the past. An expectant and attentive silence on the part of the interviewer is often all that is needed to get the patient to elaborate on his or her problems.

When a patient is talking in a full-bodied and spontaneous way, silence is the most appropriate response. When the patient becomes silent, a brief silence on the interviewer's part is again appropriate, because the patient may have stopped speaking to collect his or her thoughts or to find the right word to describe a concern. Interruptions or interjections would likely be premature. The patient whose pause signals the end of a train of thought often turns his or her gaze on the physician, indicating a willingness to give him or her a chance to speak. Whether the physician decides to do so or remain silent depends on his or her assessment of the situation. Early in the interview, the physician may deem it essential to pursue what the patient said. Or the physician may decide that he or she wishes to give the patient more time to talk. Silences are less likely later in the interview after a full account of the patient's difficulties has been gathered. At such times, the physician may more confidently proceed with direct questions with very specific aims.

When a patient is overwhelmed with emotion, often the best thing to do is to remain silent. To say something at such a juncture is to run the risk of inhibiting the expression of the emotion that is almost always therapeutic or cathartic. To say nothing, to simply *be* with the patient while he or she weeps, for example, gives the patient control over how much or how little emotion to display.

In certain situations the use of silence is not advised. Patients with neurological disorders, for example, often need a fair amount of structure to permit them to respond adequately and may become confused and disoriented if silence is used where guidance is needed. Adolescents may be intolerant of ambiguity for other reasons and find an interviewer's silence discomforting. Occasionally a patient is overly talkative, although paradoxically such patients never seem to be very informative. Here is a clear case in which silent indulgence of the patient does little good, and the physician may have to interrupt the patient to gain control of the interview and guide it in more meaningful directions.

Facilitation

"Encouraging communication by manner, gesture, or words that do not specify the kind of information sought is called facilitation" (Enelow & Swisher, 1986). Facilitation involves slightly more control than silence and subsumes a wide variety of interventions that require little expenditure of energy on the part of the interviewer. *Despite their seeming simplicity, facilitating techniques play a powerful role in both eliciting information and guiding the interview to desired topics.* An attentive facial expression, a raised eyebrow, a shrug of the shoulders, and a nod all are mannerisms or gestures that can encourage a patient to continue with his or her associations. The physician does not speak a word, yet the patient knows that the interviewer is interested in what is being said and is curious to hear more. Words such as "yes," "okay," "go on," and "I see" serve essentially the same function, as does the utterance "mmm-hhh." Such vocalizations serve as reinforcers and increase the probability that the patient will talk more freely about the subject that has been reinforced in this way. However, interviewers must guard against employing such easy-to-use and potent techniques mechanically or in stereotyped ways that may have the unintended effect of distracting and inhibiting the patient. Listening to interviews on audiotape or watching them on videotape provide safeguards against abuse of these techniques.

Another set of facilitating techniques that involves a bit more control on the interviewer's part is any intervention, verbal or nonverbal, that conveys to the patient that "I don't understand" or "I am puzzled by what you are telling me." This communication can be made directly or indirectly (e.g., a quizzical look).

A very *powerful facilitating technique, if used appropriately and in moderation, involves the judicious repetition of key words spoken by the patient.* Words condense and summarize patient experiences. They can sometimes be taken at face value; in other situations they need to be explored in greater depth for what they connote. An economical and effective way of inviting patients to elaborate on the meaning of their words is simply to repeat words that are of interest, with a slight interrogative vocal inflection.

The following are the responses of three physicians with a patient whose initial complaint is expressed by the words, "My head is killing me." Physician A asks, "Have you had headaches before?" This is a reasonable question, but it is likely that the answer will emerge naturally if the patient is given the opportunity to give an account of his or her difficulties without physician interference. By asking this question at this time, the physician is interrupting the patient's flow of ideas and narrowing the range of response alternatives.

Physician B responds by saying, "Tell me more about how your head is killing you." This is a legitimate request, but it is 10 words long and may be too formal and professional sounding to facilitate good rapport.

Physician C responds by noticing the violent imagery in the patient's brief description of her headache. She decides that such an emotion-filled word deserves to be articulated at greater length ("**unpacked**"), and she replies, "Killing you?" This imposes only modest control over the patient's next response and follows the patient's lead as closely as possible. It increases the probability that the patient's responses will provide a fuller account of this symptom, one that spontaneously includes the information about site, onset, duration, and history that any physician desires. It may also elicit significant material concerning the patient's fears and fantasies regarding what is wrong, fears legitimately assumed to exist if the patient's description is taken at face value.

Two additional facilitating remarks are "How do you mean?" and "How so?" They serve the same function as the repetition of key words and phrases, can be used in the same situations, and put a little more variety into the interviewing repertoire. Variety is important because as soon as a patient becomes conscious that the physician is employing these techniques, the interview suffers.

> If your news must be bad, tell it soberly and promptly.
>
> SIR HENRY HOWARTH BASHFORD
> *The Corner of Harley Street*

Confrontation

Confrontation involves pointing out to patients aspects of their behavior of which they were unaware. It represents a moderately high degree of control on the part of the interviewer. *It is a technique to be used sparingly.*

Confrontation can be appropriate in several circumstances. If a patient continues to offer only brief, unelaborated responses to open-ended questions, silences, and facilitations, and if this seems related to some distress that the patient is experiencing, a comment along the lines of "You seem uncomfortable talking about this" makes the patient aware that the discomfort has been noted and that somewhat lengthier responses are expected. The comment is made in the form of an observation by the interviewer. This allows the patient more latitude in responding. By using the tentative phrase "you seem," rather than the more presumptuous "you are," the interviewer avoids coming across as all knowing and can retreat from the observation more gracefully if it proves to be wrong.

Once the confrontation has been made, the patient can either admit or deny it. If the confrontation is acknowledged, the patient can proceed to elaborate on the nature of the difficulty. A patient might say, for example, "Yes, I am uncomfortable; I really don't know how much detail to go into." Or, "Yes, I am uncomfortable; I haven't told you something that I think you need to know." Whatever the reason for the patient's reticence, confrontations of this sort help to clear the air and set the stage for the resumption of more open discussion. Should the patient be genuinely confused by the confrontation, he or she can simply ask for clarification. If this happens, the interviewer should describe the patient behaviors that led to the inference of patient discomfort; this helps to clarify the situation and promote greater understanding, and the patient can easily deny the observation if he or she desires. The observation may be correct, but the patient does not trust the interviewer sufficiently to admit such private concerns. Even in this case, the fact that the interviewer made the appropriate inquiry, used the appropriate technique, and did not insist on a certain answer signals to the patient that this is an observant physician interested in removing obstacles to a better physician-patient relationship and not afraid to tread (gently) into potentially delicate areas. This augurs well for the future of the relationship.

Other circumstances in which confrontation is useful occur when a disparity is observed in different aspects of the patient's behavior. For example, the disparity may be a contradiction between two of the patient's remarks, and the confrontation could take the following form: "You say your foot doesn't bother you, but just a moment ago you said you can't put any weight on it." Notice how gentle such a confrontation can be. It is not accusatory; the physician is simply juxtaposing two of the patient's statements. *Implicit in this statement is the same exhortation that underlies all the other interventions just discussed: "Tell me more."* The only difference is that in the case of confrontation, the interviewer is exerting more control over the nature of the material to be elicited.

Often the disparity to be confronted is between what the patient says and does. For instance, a patient may blandly discuss suicidal thoughts or discuss the most seemingly insignificant matters with great trepidation. These discrepancies between verbal and nonverbal aspects of behavior must be investigated. The physician might confront the suicidal patient by saying, "You seem so nonchalant." To the nervous patient, the physician might say, "You're shaking"

or "I hear such fear in your voice." Many other situations exist in which the patient's nonverbal behavior communicates something that is not being addressed. Confrontation gives the patient both permission and the opportunity to express emotions verbally.

Direct Questions

The highest level of control among all the interviewing techniques is found in closed, or direct, questions. An entreaty phrased as "Tell me how you're doing" is broader in focus and less controlling than "Tell me what is wrong," which, in turn, is broader in focus than "Tell me when the nausea began." For some patients and in some situations, interviewers may have to rely more heavily on direct questions. A question such as "How would you describe the pain?" may yield only an equivocal response. In this case it would be appropriate to give the patient a question with a multiple-choice format: "Is it a burning, aching, or pricking type of pain?" Direct questions are very helpful when used appropriately: they serve to fill in missing details, tie up loose ends, and sharpen the focus of the interview. They are also associated with a number of potential pitfalls.

One problem is the possibility that *a direct question can bias the patient's answer through the inadvertent use of an emotion-laden word or through poor phrasing.* For example, asking patients if they have a history of mental illness has a more pejorative quality than asking if they have ever seen a mental health professional (and following an affirmative response with a request for more detailed information). Asking married patients whether they have had any affairs is judgmental and may evoke a less honest answer than a question about other sexual partners. Similarly, asking about "illicit drugs" or "illegal drugs" is unlikely to yield an honest response; it is more appropriate to ask about "any drugs like marijuana or cocaine, that sort of thing." Similarly, it is often difficult for patients to provide honest answers to a common form of direct questions—leading questions—such as "So, no drugs?" or "You're not having chest pain, are you?" either because patients are reluctant to correct the physician or might prefer not to discuss the topic at all.

The other major problem with direct questions is the chilling effect they can have on the patient's narrative. The following exchange demonstrates how the excessive use of direct questions deprives the patient of the chance to develop a more full-bodied account of her problem:

Doctor: What sorts of troubles have you been having?
Patient: I've been going downhill for 2 years. Nothing seems to be working right.
Doctor: What is the worst part?

Patient: My legs. I have constant pain in my legs. It's gotten so bad I can't sleep.

Doctor: What about your breathing?

Patient: Oh, that's all right. I can breathe fine. I just hurt so bad in my legs.

Doctor: Are you still smoking?

Patient: Yes, with this pain I've gone back to cigarettes for relief. But I'm down to half a pack or so a day.

Doctor: Are you having pains in your chest?

Patient: No.

Doctor: How about cough?

Patient: No, I hardly ever cough.

Doctor: How much are you actually able to do?

Patient: Well, I was able to do everything until about 2 years ago, but now I can hardly walk half a block.

Doctor: Why is that?

Patient: My legs. They hurt.

Doctor: Do they swell up?

Patient: Well, they've been a bit swollen the last 2 or 3 weeks but the pain is there whether they swell or not.

Doctor: All right, I want to ask you some things about your medical history now. (Platt & McMath, 1979)

The physician's first question is fairly open ended. By following up with "What is the worst part?" he allows the patient an opportunity to describe the chief complaint. But his next four comments are all symptom-oriented questions imposed on the patient. They do not follow the patient's lead. She clearly wants to discuss her legs, and he clearly has an agenda of his own. By the end of this exchange he still knows little about her leg pain and is forced to endure a second round of description of the leg pain that is no more detailed than the first round. (Compare "I have constant pain in my legs" with "My legs. They hurt," six responses later.) The physician is working hard, but this interview has not gone anywhere. This encounter is an example of an interview style known as **high physician control-low patient control.** *According to empirical research this style is highly prevalent in clinical settings.* During such interviews the physician tends to talk more and the patient less as time goes on. This is in direct contradiction to good interviewing technique. After the preceding interview, the physician described the patient as "not wanting to talk." In fact, the interviewer's use of direct questions to control and limit the interview had forced her to this point.

Direct questions are an absolutely essential component of a clinical interview: Physicians and other health-care professionals cannot do without them. The problem is that they are easily misused and frequently used to the exclusion of other techniques that do a better job of eliciting unbiased information and developing a sense of productive collaboration.

> The doctor may also learn more about the illness from the way the patient tells the story than from the story itself.
>
> JAMES B. HERRICK, M.D.
> *Memoirs of Eighty Years*

STRATEGIES FOR GIVING INFORMATION: FOCUS ON CHECKING UNDERSTANDING

Physicians approach the interview with a primary interest in gathering information. Patients have a slightly different interest: they want to know what the physician thinks about their complaint and what course of treatment will be recommended. They want an explanation of their illness and a statement about the benefits and risks of treatment. *More often than not, patients leave the interview disappointed with the information received.* In the best study available on this topic, physicians spent little more than 1 minute (on average) of a 20-minute interview giving information. Yet they perceived themselves to spend more than 9 minutes informing their patients. This is a gross distortion of what actually takes place, and *this misperception is a major factor in both patient dissatisfaction with physicians and poor patient adherence to treatment regimens.* The problem was particularly acute when the patient was poorly educated or from a lower-class background, when the physician had a busy practice (defined as more than 20 outpatients per day), and when the physician was from a lower-middle-class or lower-class background. Male patients tended to receive less attention and fewer explanations than female patients, perhaps because female patients ask more questions and are more verbally active during an interview.

Even if the amount of time spent in explanations and other forms of information giving were increased, problems with the quality of information sharing would remain. *Instructions should be as simple, brief, and jargon-free as possible, but the patient must be more than a passive recipient.* Telling a patient to take medication on an as-needed basis is not a good idea without a discussion of what "as needed" means. Telling a patient to take medication four times a day is subject to misunderstanding, and requires a discussion with the patient to determine when (e.g., breakfast, lunch, dinner, at bedtime). The bottom line: "Telling" a patient to follow your plan is unlikely to yield good result; try working with patients to tailor a plan, and remember to check their understanding.

It can be difficult to anticipate all the potential misunderstandings that can occur when an already anxious patient is trying to assimilate your instructions. One colleague interviewed a longshoreman who had sought treatment at a clinic for patients with chronic pain. As he told his story about his earlier experiences with physicians, he suddenly began to cry. It seems that he had been told, 3 months earlier, that he had degenerative arthritis, and he had been depressed ever since. For this man, degenerative arthritis meant that his spinal cord was degenerating, or crumbling, and that he would soon be totally disabled, unable to walk, work, or support his family. His anguish could have been avoided if his physician had taken the time to explain the meaning of this diagnosis in terms that the patient could readily understand, and checked to make sure he understood.

Hospitalized patients are often particularly deprived of information concerning their condition and future treatment. This only imposes additional uncertainty in a situation that is already stressful and anxiety provoking. Several years ago, one of us (PBZ) was at the bedside of a cancer patient who was complaining about how his physicians were keeping him in the dark about their plans for him. As we spoke, the surgical resident entered, introduced himself, and announced that the patient would have surgery in the morning. He then turned and left the room. Such conduct is not only unprofessional, it is countertherapeutic.

Studies that compare the medical outcomes of patients with and without adequate information about their treatment frequently show that *provision of information is advantageous for both the physician and the patient.* In one such study, anesthesiologists visited patients in the experimental group preoperatively to describe what the patients would experience when they awoke after surgery. The physicians indicated that the patients would experience pain, told them where it would hurt and how it would feel, emphasized that this was normal and would be self-limiting, and urged the patients to ask for analgesics if the pain became too great. When compared with a control group, these patients were judged ready for discharge 2.7 days earlier and made 50% *fewer* requests for pain medication.

Patients almost invariably have a different frame-of-reference than that of their physicians. Moreover, there is a limit to the amount and complexity of information that humans can absorb in a short time span. Accordingly, checking patient understanding of explanations and recommendations is absolutely essential. We recommend the following technique to ensure that each patient has heard what was intended. *After an explanation or recommendation, ask the patient to repeat what has just been said in his or her own words, not verbatim.* Physicians will be surprised at what they hear and at the frequency with which explanations and instructions are distorted and misconstrued. More importantly, this exercise gives the opportunity to correct any misunderstandings and to clarify any earlier ambiguities. In addition, physicians can be more secure in the knowledge that patients understand the medical advice on their own terms.

HANDLING PATIENT EMOTIONS

Illness is frequently accompanied by negative psychological states. When patients are anxious, angry, or depressed, it can be difficult to elicit a full and spontaneous account of their difficulties. On many occasions, the patient's psychological state *is* the primary problem. The ability to handle such situations smoothly and therapeutically takes time and practice, but a number of general guidelines can be considered.

Anxiety

If a patient is fidgety, restless, or easily startled, seems nervous, or has a tremor in his or her voice, the patient may be anxious. Proceeding with the interview may be difficult until the anxiety is discussed. The technique of confrontation is most useful in these circumstances, with the physician simply saying to the patient, "You seem upset," or nervous, or whatever descriptor is most appropriate. Usually the patient seizes on this opportunity to speak about his or her anxiety. This sharing helps diminish anxiety and restore the alliance between physician and patient.

Some patients may be chronically anxious, but many others may be anxious as a function of the situation in which they find themselves. For some, the prospect of submitting to a physical examination with a relative stranger is anxiety arousing. For others, the passivity and loss of independence associated with being ill (and hospitalized) can be threatening. For still others, anxiety may be associated with earlier, unpleasant experiences with a physician or a procedure. In any of these instances, and in any other instance of patient anxiety, the prescription is the same: the physician's responsibility is to elicit the source of the patient's concern, understand it, and take appropriate measures to diminish it.

We spoke of diminishing rather than eliminating the patient's anxiety. Anxiety cannot be completely eliminated, and its elimination is not necessary for a successful interview. Once anxiety has diminished to a point at which the interview can proceed, the interviewer can conclude that he or she has handled the problem satisfactorily. With a patient who is anxious about being exposed during a physical examination, it might be best, once the nature of the anxiety has been established, simply to defer the physical examination until better rapport has been achieved with the patient. With a highly active patient, threatened by the enforced passivity and dependency of illness, the physician might acknowledge the discomfort that the situation entails, review why it is necessary, and promise to take the necessary steps to increase the patient's activity and sense of personal control. With a patient who anticipates an unpleasant procedure, accurate information is often enough to reduce anxiety. If the procedure is a painful one, and if anxiety is so high as to threaten patient participation, hypnosis, modeling, or medication might be helpful. In refractory cases, referral to a psychologist or psychiatrist may be necessary.

Anxiety often presents itself in subtle ways. For example, patient questions may actually be veiled expressions of anxiety. *When a middle-aged patient asks a resident how old he or she is, it is fairly certain that the patient doubts that someone so young, and presumably inexperienced, can be helpful.* When a mother of five beset by her children's behavioral problems asks a student on a pediatric rotation if he or she has children of his or her own, we can assume again that the question is not being asked out of idle curiosity. In ordinary social conversation it is considered rude not to answer a direct question. However, in a clinical context, to take such a question at face value and to answer it immediately and directly is to fail to address the underlying concern of the patient.

Such expressions of anxiety and concern masquerading as direct questions take many different forms. "Should I marry my girlfriend?" "Is a 20-pound weight loss anything to be concerned about?" "Should I accept chemotherapy?" "Can jogging cause a heart attack?" These may be perfectly legitimate questions, and they may even be within the expertise of a physician. But it is never appropriate simply to give an affirmative or negative answer and leave it at that. Instead, the clinician's responsibility is to clarify the precise nature of the question and, if appropriate, to provide the information needed by the patient to make an informed decision. For direct questions such as these, a response that puts the responsibility for clarification back on the patient (e.g., "You seem unsure" or "You seem concerned") is the most appropriate first step. Only when it is understood why the patient asks and how the patient intends to use the answer is it proper to respond. Even at this juncture *a distinction should be made between advice and information.* If a 40-year-old woman asks whether she should attempt to have a baby, it is one thing to provide her with information about the risks and something else entirely to advise or direct her in one direction or another.

Another response to patient anxiety that ought to be avoided is the falsely reassuring response that says to the patient that everything will be all right. **Reassurance** that is based on the facts of the case and does not raise unreasonable expectations is a useful way to allay patient anxiety. *Too often, however, reassurance is used to protect the feelings of the physician and does nothing to reassure the patient.* If the patient senses that the clinician's efforts at reassurance are not genuine, the clinician becomes still another person from whom the patient must conceal intimate feelings.

The following vignette demonstrates that responses to a patient that acknowledge his or her concerns and reflect true understanding are the most reassuring responses of all. Imagine how differently this encounter would have been if the physician responded with reassuring platitudes of the "Of course you're not going to die" or "I'm sure you don't have cancer" variety.

Patient:	I'm worried about these headaches. I know what headaches can mean.
Doctor:	What they mean?
Patient:	Brain tumors. Cancer. Deep down I think I'm already convinced I have an inoperable tumor.
Doctor:	It must be a frightening thought to live with.
Patient:	Well, I've probably lived with it most of my life. My father died of a brain tumor when I was 5.
Doctor:	(after a brief silence) And now you're worried that it's your turn.
Patient:	Mmm-mmm. Yes and no. I realize I'm jumping the gun. What my father died from was not a hereditary disease. And my symptoms could be the result of a million things. It's just hard not to think like this with my family history. If I were going to bet on what's wrong, I wouldn't really bet on cancer. I'd bet this whole thing is stress related.
Doctor:	How so?

Depression

Depressed mood is another common response to physical illness, one expressed in terms of hopelessness, guilt, low self-esteem, and fatigue. Interviews with depressed patients can be laboriously slow and unproductive. Here, too, confrontation can be a useful technique. Commenting on the slow process of the interview ("You seem to be having trouble keeping pace with me") or on the patient's mood itself ("You seem tired" or "You seem kind of blue") gives the patient a chance to discuss his or her difficulty with the interviewer if he or she so wishes. *Acknowledging that the patient appears to be on the verge of crying ("You look like you're about to cry") effectively grants the patient permission to cry or not to cry and can open the door to important emotional material.*

If the physician is concerned about the magnitude of depressive affect, the patient's **suicide potential** should be assessed. Usually it is best to begin indirectly, asking if the patient feels hopeless, derives any meaning from life, or has ever wished he or she were dead. Broaching the subject in a progressive or gradual fashion is not the same as being evasive. *If the patient senses that the physician is timid when asking about suicidal intent, he or she is more likely to give an evasive answer.* Eventually, if the answers convince the physician that the patient is contemplating suicide, direct inquiry must be made: "Have you thought about taking your life?," "Have you thought about how you would do it?," or "Have you thought about how other people would feel?" *Clear expressions of suicidal intent must always be taken seriously. The more lethal the method contemplated, the easier the patient's access to the method, and the more vivid his or her fantasies about how others would be affected, the greater the* *risk.* At this point the clinician must be frank with the patient, declaring the intention to plan for the patient's protection and recovery by involving family members and a mental health professional. Patients may object strongly, but as a rule they are grateful that the practitioner has assumed responsibility for the burden of the immediate future.

Anger

If a patient is covertly angry, the appropriate response of the physician is to use the technique of confrontation, just as a physician would respond in the case of the patient's unacknowledged anxiety or depression. One of the authors once interviewed a patient who was giving brief and unelaborate responses to his questions. All the while his face was reddening, his fists were clenched, and his voice was becoming more hostile. It was not difficult to sense his anger, and the interviewer braced himself for his response. It developed that he thought that his interviewer was in his hospital room to give him a spinal tap, and he believed the extensive questions and leisurely pace were part of an effort to delay the inevitable. The patient wanted to get on with the procedure. Had the interviewer not been willing to confront the patient, an altercation would have been likely. This encounter demonstrates the need for an interviewer to clarify the purpose of the interview at the outset as part of his or her introductory remarks.

Perhaps more common in clinical practice is the overtly angry patient for whom the use of confrontation may be redundant. Patients get angry for numerous reasons, but these reasons can be conveniently grouped into two categories. First, a patient may be angry because of something said or not said, or done or not done. The possibilities are legion and include the physician failing to introduce himself or herself, making the patient wait a long time, failing to remember some critical fact about the patient, hurting the patient, making accusatory or moralistic-sounding remarks, withholding information, or failing to allow the patient to think he or she has given a full account of the illness. If the physician is the source of the anger, whether or not by design, no alternative exists other than owning up to this responsibility, taking appropriate remedial measures, and, if appropriate, apologizing.

The second possibility is that the patient is the source of the anger and would be angry whether or not the physician did something provocative. *Anger is often a comparatively safe way for a patient to express fear.* Patients are often frightened by their illnesses or by the proposed treatments and may use anger as a means of both discharging and denying such anxiety. In addition, some patients are frightened by the loss of control that the sick role entails and respond with anger as a means of reasserting their authority. The sensitive clinician learns to listen for the feelings of powerlessness that underlie such overt anger and does not respond reflexively or in a way that merely engenders the same feelings of powerlessness that made the patient angry at the outset. In addition, the physician must appreciate that *anger is often displaced from another person who has frustrated the patient.* If the receptionist offended the patient or if the patient has been disappointed by physicians in the past, the clinician may well be the innocent recipient of unwarranted hostility.

In each of these cases the natural tendency is to become defensive and want to retaliate. Such responses might be momentarily cathartic but are generally ill advised because they are not in the patient's best interest. The ideal way to handle an angry patient is to make a concerted effort to understand the nature of the anger. If the anger is justified, the acknowledgment of responsibility is often enough to restore the physician-patient alliance to a productive level of functioning. If the anger is not justified by the physician's behavior, accepting the patient's anger and permitting its full expression are cathartic for the patient and give him or her greater insight into its actual source.

REFERRAL TO A PSYCHOTHERAPIST

Making referrals is a neglected but important aspect of patient care, and perhaps the most difficult referral is one to a psychiatrist or another mental health professional. *It is relatively certain that if the physician does nothing but say to the patient that consultation with a psychiatrist is recommended, that recommendation will not be followed.* Most patients find this threatening, and 20% to 40% of patients reject psychotherapy when it is offered. Such referrals are most successful when they are discussed over several sessions, when the physician is able to provide a straightforward and nonthreatening rationale, and when the patient is encouraged to express reservations.

Three common misconceptions about psychotherapy should be routinely addressed whenever the issue of a referral arises. *The first misconception is the notion that only crazy people need to see psychotherapists.* Whether or not the patients voice this concern, it is generally useful for the interviewer to say that he or she does not think they are crazy, does not believe their problems are all in their head, and *does* believe their complaints are real. Then, a nontechnical explanation of the recommendation should be offered: for example, that most illnesses have an emotional component and that even greater concern would be raised if the patient were displaying no psychological effects. Or the physician might say that almost anybody undergoing the same physical difficulties or stresses would be likely to experience psychological symptoms. At any rate, an expression of concern coupled with a statement to the effect that a mental health professional is better equipped to help with the problem ought to make the idea of a referral more palatable.

A second common misconception is the notion that psychotherapy is equal to psychoanalysis. The patient must be assured that referral does not mean a daily treatment of long duration in which he or she is asked to lie on a couch and free associate to a silent individual sitting out of view. Only a fraction of patients in need of psychotherapy are interested in and suited for this form of treatment.

A third misconception is the idea that the psychiatric referral is being used to get rid of the patient. This misconception is common among chronically ill patients who are especially dependent on their physicians and among patients whose relationships with their physicians have been characterized by disagreement and strain. *Such patients must know that the physician is not giving up on them and that this is not the end of the relationship.* It simply means that certain aspects of their lives are beyond the physician's competence and could be better handled by someone else.

Once the physician has given the explanation for the referral and discussed these common misconceptions, the patient needs an opportunity to ask questions and express additional concerns. Patients who characteristically deny emotional difficulties and patients who lack insight into the inappropriateness of their behavior are particularly resistant to referral for psychological evaluation or treatment. Therefore the physician must not feel compelled to complete discussion of a referral in a single session. Some physicians routinely mention the possibility of future referrals in their first contact with a patient if they have any reason to suspect that a referral may be necessary. If a referral to a psychiatrist or psychologist is mentioned in passing at this point, in conjunction with the possibility of referral to a neurologist, cardiologist, or other specialist, it becomes easier to reintroduce the idea.

SUMMARY

Attention to interpersonal and communication skills can facilitate effective and efficient clinical encounters. This chapter provides useful approaches, but *practice, reflection and feedback are the keys to developing and improving your interactions with patients.* The notion that patients and providers have different—but equally valuable—perspectives and roles in clinical encounters was captured in the title of a book by Tuckett et al. published 20 years ago: *Meetings between Experts.* Keeping this deceptively simple idea in mind as you progress in your training will help you and the patients you serve.

CASE STUDY

This is an excerpt from the second clinic visit of a 38-year-old plant foreman with intermittent chest pain. Extensive testing has not revealed any abnormality. All results were within normal limits.

Dr. Jones: How are you today, Mr. Smith?

Mr. Smith: Things are pretty bad at work. This is our busy time and everyone's stressed out. I'm doing okay, though.

Dr. Jones: Well, I've reviewed your tests with our cardiologist, and we agree that there really isn't anything wrong. Chances are it's just a combination of things, maybe stress or indigestion.

Mr. Smith: Okay, but I don't see it getting any better. Sooner or later, I'll have a blowout.

Dr. Jones: I don't think that's likely. You're young and in good health; you don't smoke or have a family history of heart disease. Some people get chest pain when they're under stress.

Mr. Smith: You say it's not likely, but I don't know. I've got a lot of problems, and all I hear from everyone is that it's in my head.

Dr. Jones: It's not in your head. The pain is real, but you're not having a heart attack. We can order more tests, but they're not going to show anything.

Mr. Smith: I don't know how you can be so sure. I've been having trouble catching my breath lately too. And my brother-in-law ran 10 miles a day and never smoked or drank, and he dropped dead of a heart attack just 1 month before I came to see you.

This is *not* an example of a good interview. Dr. Jones has a nice manner and was trying very hard in this instance, but the physician and patient were largely talking at cross-purposes. *Review this interview line by line, and see if you can improve on Dr. Jones' interviewing technique. Can you find examples of open-ended questions or facilitation? How might the interview have been different if Dr. Jones had used these techniques and tried to follow the patient's lead rather than convince Mr. Smith that he does not have heart disease? How might the patient feel when the physician is willing to order more tests despite his skepticism?*

SUGGESTED READINGS

Billings, J.A., & Stoeckle, J.D. (1999). *The clinical encounter: A guide to the medical interview and case presentation* (2nd ed.). Chicago, IL: Year Book Medical Publishers.

An introduction to the medical interview and to oral and written case presentation. The second half of the book considers more advanced topics such as the mental status examination, functional assessment, and various difficult relationships.

Platt, F.W. & Gordon, G.H. (2004). *Field guide to the difficult patient interview* (2nd ed.). New York, NY: Lippincott, Williams, & Wilkins.

Short chapters that cover topics that are relevant for medical trainees and practitioners at all levels. Each chapter offers principles and tangible procedures for dealing with difficult topics and situations.

Diagnostic Reasoning

Carl D. Stevens

> ...there is no one best way through a problem. The more one studies the clinical expert, the more one marvels at the complex and multidimensional components of knowledge and skill that she or he brings to bear on the problem and the amazing adaptability she must possess to achieve the goal of the effective care.
>
> GEOFFREY NORMAN
> 2005
>
>
> Symptoms are the cries of the suffering organs.
>
> GIOVANNI MORGAGNI
> 1761

As medicine enters its fourth millennium, diagnosis retains its primacy as the foundation of clinical care. Diagnosis lies at the heart of what patients seek from physicians, and what physicians have to offer in return. Now, as always, patients approach healers with their most urgent concerns, most private suffering and darkest fears. Long before effective treatments existed, physicians provided comfort through diagnosis- the simple act of giving a name to the patient's ills, and along with the name, some explanation of what caused the illness and what it portends. Now, as always, a correct diagnosis, well-reasoned and well-explained, opens the door to a successful clinical encounter. And now more than ever, with our vast armamentarium of medical technology, a mistaken diagnosis can send patients and their doctors on a costly and fruitless odyssey of testing and treatment. To summarize, *in clinical medicine, diagnosis always comes first: in time, in importance and in its potential to benefit or harm the patient.*

This chapter introduces diagnostic reasoning to early stage learners of medicine. It begins with a general explanation of the science of disease-naming, discussing the origin and development of the classification systems or "taxonomies" used in the various branches of medicine. Next, it turns attention to the logic of diagnosis, considering both qualitative and quantitative approaches and introducing the basic vocabulary necessary to understand current medical literature on diagnosis. The chapter closes with consideration of some pitfalls of the diagnostic process and how to avoid them, and some reflections on the future of diagnosis at the dawn of a new era of molecular medicine.

NOSOLOGY: THE SCIENCE OF DISEASE-NAMING

A basic understanding of "nosology," or disease classification systems, will help clarify the reasoning process clinicians use to arrive at diagnoses. Though patients present with an infinite variety of symptoms, physical signs and laboratory findings, the clinician must ultimately choose one or more diagnoses from a finite list, and the universe of possible diagnoses is bounded by the particular list the physician uses. To facilitate communication, data collection and health policy, public health agencies have formalized the process of disease classification by developing and regularly updating standardized taxonomies. In the West,

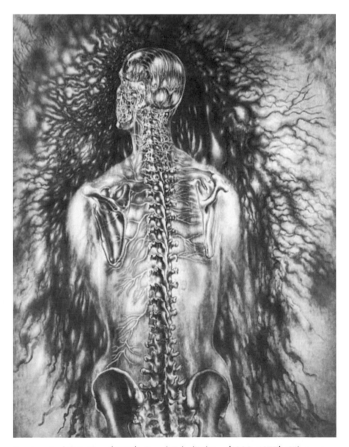

Anatomical Painting (1946) *Pavel Tchelitchew (1898–1957). Oil on canvas, Overall: 56 × 46 in. (142.2 × 116.8 cm). Whitney Museum of American Art, New York; gift of Lincoln Kirstein 62.26. This painting captures both the beauty and the complexity of the central nervous system and suggests the diagnostic challenges facing the physician.*

the World Health Organization's *International Classification of Disease*, 10th Revision (ICD-10) serves as the standard, encoding thousands of detailed diagnoses using a five-digit system. In the United States, a clinical modification of WHO's previous version, ICD-9-CM is most widely used to register clinical encounters. While the ICD does include diagnosis codes for behavioral disorders, in the United States and some other countries clinicians generally use the American Psychiatric Association's *Diagnostic and Statistical Manual Fourth Revision* (DSM-IV) as the preferred classification of diagnoses for behavioral health.

Disease classification systems are dynamic, changing over time as new entities are discovered and older terms are retired. As is the case in other sciences, nosology evolves through a series of minor adjustments and updates occasionally interrupted by major paradigm shifts that overturn an entire system for understanding and classifying human illness. In Europe, the humoral theory of illness that originated during the classical period with the writings of Hippocrates and Galen dominated clinical thinking and practice from the 2nd to the 16th century, before being overturned by the discoveries of Harvey, Morgagni and the other inventors of modern scientific medicine. While the diagnoses based on the humoral model -imbalances of the blood, phlegm and yellow and black bile—seem laughably antiquated to us today, they accurately reflected the dominant understanding of illness of their time, just as our own disease classifications reflect our present beliefs. Accordingly, we must expect that future generations looking back will find today's diagnoses equally amusing and quaint. Modest changes to disease taxonomies occur routinely as the classifications undergo scheduled updates. For example, Asperger's Syndrome, a subtype of autism, appears in the DSM-IV as a separate entity, but will not appear in DSM-V where it is subsumed within autism spectrum disorders.

> Time after time I have gone out into my office in the evening feeling as if I couldn't keep my eyes open a moment longer. I would start out on my morning calls after only a few hours sleep, sit in front of some house waiting to get the courage to climb the steps and push the front-door bell. But once I saw the patient all that would disappear. In a flash the details of the case would begin to formulate themselves into a recognizable outline, the diagnosis would unravel itself, or would refuse to make itself plain, and the hunt was on.
>
> WILLIAM CARLOS WILLIAMS
> *The Doctor Stories*

The Asperger's example illustrates another important truth about diagnosis: *Disease names represent social constructs, gaining their existence through expert consensus in addition to scientific developments.* For this reason, disease-naming systems are culture-specific, closely reflecting a society's understanding and beliefs about the nature of health and illness. Each of the "alternative" medicine systems practiced in the United States and elsewhere has its own diagnosis classification system based on its unique understanding of physiologic and pathologic mechanisms. For example, chiropractic medicine places an emphasis on the alignment of the spine and other joints as the underlying source of symptoms and therefore diagnoses may refer to specific skeletal derangements. Each of the major Asian medical traditions (Chinese herbal medicine, acupuncture, Aryuvedic) has its own disease names reflecting the understanding of illness and treatment characteristic of each of these disciplines. Cultural competency requires awareness on the part of the physician that the patient may understand illness in the concepts and language of an alternative medical tradition, and that Western allopathic diagnoses may require translation or explanation if they are to provide information of value to the patient and family.

> Symptoms are the body's mother tongue; signs are in a foreign language.
>
> JOHN BROWN
> *Horae Subsecivae*

Disease names or diagnoses in current use in Western medicine vary dramatically with respect to their sources and levels of precision. For example, when a patient develops pain in the lower back that radiates down one leg, the clinician may use a descriptiveness diagnosis based on the symptom pattern ("sciatica"), a mechanistic diagnosis based on the physical exam findings ("L5 radiculopathy"), or a structurally-based diagnosis ("herniated nucleus pulposus"). Other diagnoses may be based on biochemistry ("dyslipidemia"), or specific genetic disorders (trisomy 13). This broad range of specificity and derivation of diagnostic entities provides the clinician with the ability to achieve high precision in making a diagnosis. However along with the flexibility comes the challenge of accuracy. As a general rule of thumb, *clinicians should assign the most specific diagnosis that the clinical data support at the time the diagnosis is made.* Further evaluation may allow a more precise diagnosis to be made.

Finally, scientific advances continuously expand single diagnoses into multiple clinically distinct subtypes. The leukemias are rapidly being subclassified by cytogenetic markers with important implications for treatment. Since disease names track to the current state of basic and clinical science, physicians can expect rapid expansion of the ICD as the molecular underpinnings of common diseases come to light. However, despite this trend toward ever-greater complexity, the essential reasoning processes allow clinicians to make diagnoses have not changed. We turn our attention next to a consideration of clinical reasoning processes and methods.

> More is missed by not looking than by not knowing.
>
> THOMAS MCCRAE
> *Aphorism*

THE LOGIC OF DIAGNOSIS

Qualitative Diagnostic Reasoning

The process by which expert clinicians arrive at accurate diagnoses has received extensive study by psychologists and educational researchers, sufficient to prove only that no single reasoning strategy or heuristic captures the process completely. The research indicates that experts do employ various combinations of hypothetico-deductive reasoning, pattern recognition, illness scripts, schema, and other abstract problem representations. However, a substantial component of clinical reasoning by experts appears to take place outside of conscious awareness, and is best characterized as a form of clinical intuition that develops only with extensive practice possibly requiring as much as 10,000 hours of work in clinical settings. Unfortunately for students, no reliable shortcuts to attaining this level of diagnostic intuition have revealed themselves. Therefore, developing true expertise in diagnosis seems to require an investment of many hours of hands-on work in clinical settings where physicians perform the initial evaluation of a large and varied group of undiagnosed patients. In the current health care delivery system, emergency departments and urgent care or walk-in clinics offer medical students and residents the greatest opportunities for gaining this type and intensity of hands-on experience.

Beyond the importance of direct patient care experience, a few general concepts may help the early stage learner build clinical reasoning skills. The diagnostic process is highly iterative, beginning with an initial list of possibilities and then proceeding through multiple rounds of updating the hypothesis list as additional information becomes available. This iterative process presents two substantial challenges: First, the clinician must remain "on track"—that is, the new data sought at each round must effectively raise the likelihood of the correct diagnosis, while lowering or eliminating alternative diagnoses. Second, and equally challenging, the clinician must recognize when sufficient information gathering cycles have been completed to reach a "decision threshold": The point at which the clinician feels enough confidence in the diag-

> In the practice of medicine more mistakes are made from lack of accurate observation and deduction than from lack of knowledge.
>
> GEORGE HOWARD BELL
> *Experimental Physiology*

nosis to initiate treatment. Excessive iterations in search of diagnostic certainty can delay and complicate the process, while too few rounds can result in "premature closure," selection of a wrong diagnosis because of failure to sufficiently consider and evaluate alternatives.

In practice, the iterative diagnostic process begins as soon as the first pieces of data arrive, typically through the patient's chief complaint and initial history. However, in the information-rich 21st century practice environment, the clinical encounter can begin in a wide variety of ways, some of which don't require presence of the patient—online data review, referral information, a "panic" lab value or concerning imaging finding.

We close this section with a description of a prototypical clinical encounter, along with the disclaimer that a minority of patient care in the current practice environment follows this pattern. However, it remains a useful model for presenting an approach to diagnosis in patients with a new, unexplained complaint. The prototypic clinical encounter begins with the patient's own account of the onset and development of symptoms. During this initial history, the clinician tries to match the features of the unfolding story to illness patterns or "scripts" learned through study, clinical experience and practice. Following the patient's initial account—and quite often before it has finished-the clinician begins to guide the conversation with questions designed to elicit "pertinent positives and negatives." This next section of the interview has as its goal reducing the number of most likely diagnoses from five or six down to two or three, depending on how well the current patient's symptoms match descriptions of the diseases under consideration. As the clinician generates and refines hypotheses, two classes of conditions are considered: those most likely, given the patient's complaints, but also some less common but more serious disorders where if the diagnosis is missed, the patient would risk a (preventable) poor outcome. Next, the interviewer conducts a "review of systems" to elicit any details that the patient may have forgotten to mention or not previously noticed that might help complete the picture of the patient's illness based on symptom patterns. Next, depending on the type and scope of the encounter, the history is followed by a physical examination of greater or lesser detail, to test or confirm the hypotheses generated during the history. Expert clinicians generally hold that a correct diagnosis is identified through a skillfully elicited history in about 90% of undifferentiated patients. However, this has not received objective confirmation. Regardless, following the history and physical examination, the clinician will make one of two decisions: Either sufficient diagnostic certainty exists to allow treatment without further testing, or the clinician desires additional diagnostic tests to confirm the suspected diagnosis or to distinguish between multiple remaining possibilities. The need for additional testing, as well as the number and complexity of tests requested differs dramatically between expert and novice.

Inexperienced clinicians place greater reliance on diagnostic testing technologies to confirm their hypotheses. A consideration of diagnostic tests, when to use them and how to interpret their results leads us into a consideration of quantitative methods to support diagnostic reasoning.

> I rolled a quire of paper into a kind of cylinder and applied one end of it to the region of the heart and the other to my ear, and was not a little surprised and pleased to find that I could thereby perceive the action of the heart in a manner much more clear and distinct than I had ever been able to do by the immediate application of the ear. I saw at once that this means might become a useful method for studying, not only the beating of the heart, but likewise all movements capable of producing sound in the thoracic cavity.
>
> RENE LAENNEC
> *Auscultation Medicine*

Quantitative Diagnostic Reasoning

The concepts underlying diagnostic reasoning are so deeply rooted in probability that even a brief introduction to the topic must include a few simple mathematical principles. Fortunately for students of medicine, the calculations required for a basic understanding of diagnosis consist of simple arithmetic and require no higher mathematics. The payoff for mastering these simple calculations and definitions of terms is a much deeper understanding of the reasoning process underlying diagnosis, and an ability to accurately interpret and apply the results of diagnostic tests.

Consider the iterative reasoning process discussed in the previous section, in which the clinician forms a list of possible diagnoses very early in the clinical encounter, and then "updates" the list each time a new piece of information becomes available. The mathematics of diagnosis treats each of these bits of information as a "test result," regardless of whether they come from the history, physical or mental status exam, laboratory or imaging studies. As each "test" result comes in, some diagnostic hypotheses seem more likely, while others seem less probable. Sufficient iterations point to a single diagnosis and treatment proceeds.

The "test" data available to the clinician comes in several types, of which the simplest is categorical data, such as a point-of-care urine pregnancy test that has two possible results: positive and negative. For brevity, we will limit our discussion to this type of data. If this test is applied to a population of women of child-bearing age, each patient is either pregnant or nonpregnant, and each has a test result that is either positive or negative, creating four categories of patients: pregnant with a positive test (cell a, "true positives"), nonpregnant with a positive test (cell b, "false positives"), pregnant with a negative test (cell c, "false negatives") and nonpregnant with a negative test (cell d, "true negatives") (Table 17.1). By convention, we display this result in a 2 × 2 ("two by two") table, the standard method of analyzing diagnostic test results:

TABLE 17.1 2 × 2 contingency table for diagnostic test					
	Pregnant			Not Pregnant	
Test positive	True positive	a	b	False positive	a + b
Test negative	False negative	c	d	True negative	c + d
	a + c		b + d	a + b + c + d	

From this simple example, we can generate all of the vocabulary we need for a basic understanding of quantitative diagnostic reasoning. First, for the table to make sense, we must have access to an independent reference or "gold" standard to check the accuracy of the point-of-care urine test. In this example, a serum pregnancy test would serve this purpose, and we would know how well the point-of-care test performs relative to this gold standard from studies conducted in large populations. Applying this concept of a reference standard, we can now define the two most commonly cited measures of test performance, the sensitivity and specificity.

A test's **sensitivity** makes a statement about how well it performs in patients who have the target condition (according to the gold standard). Stated in prose, the concept could not be simpler: *A test's sensitivity is the proportion of all patients with the condition who are correctly identified* (positive test result), in our table, a/a + c. **Specificity** makes an analogous statement about how well the test performs in patients without the target condition: *the proportion of all patients without the disease who are correctly identified* (negative test result) in our table d/b + d. Of note, sensitivity and specificity are measures of the test's performance, and have values that range from zero to 1.0. Generally the higher these values are, (or in other words, the lower the proportion of false results to true results) the more useful the test is in clinical applications.

> The most valuable diagnostic instrument is the passage of time.
>
> HENRY GEORGE MILLER

However, while sensitivity and specificity provide a general sense of how a test may perform, they do not directly answer the pressing question that clinicians confront as they go through the iterative process of arriving at a diagnosis. Sensitivity tells us the probability that a patient with a disease will have a positive test, but clinicians need to know the opposite information: what is the probability that a patient with a positive test has the condition? For this, we need to calculate different measures, the test's

positive and negative predictive values. A complicating factor here is that, while a test's sensitivity and specificity are properties intrinsic to the test itself, the predictive values are highly dependent on the population in which the test is used. The proportion of patients in the population who have the target condition (also-called **disease prevalence**) has a dramatic impact on the information the test provides the clinician. For example, even when a test has fairly high sensitivity and specificity, when it is applied in a population with a very low prevalence, most of the positive test results will be false positives.

Fortunately, some shortcuts exist to help clinicians judge the likelihood of a disease using a test result and the sensitivity and specificity. The method most commonly used relies on using simple arithmetic to combine sensitivity and specificity into likelihood ratios, defined as follows: **Positive likelihood ratio** = sensitivity/(1-specificity) = [a/(a + c)] / [b/(b + d)] for the example table.

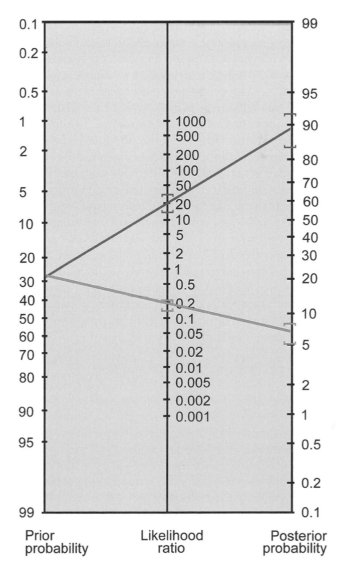

FIGURE 17.1 Fagan nomogram

TABLE 17.2 2 × 2 contingency table a single question screening test for unhealthy alcohol use

Result of single question screen	Unhealthy alcohol use confirmed by gold standard questionnaires	Unhealthy alcohol use excluded by gold standard questionnaire	
Positive (≥ 5 drinks on ≥ 1 day)	72	a	b
Negative (≥ 5 drinks on 0 days)	16	c	d
	88	a + c	b + d

Negative likelihood ratio = (1-sensitivity)/specificity = [c/(a + c)] / [d/(b + d) for the example table. Knowing the likelihood ratio, the clinician can use test results to carry out the central task of diagnostic reasoning: resetting or "updating" her initial estimate of the probability that her patient has a particular disorder—the "pretest probability"—to a new "posttest probability." Figure 17.1 (Fagan Nomogram) shows how the likelihood ratios help translate pretest to posttest probability of disease. An example will help illustrate how this would work in a real-world clinical encounter.

Imagine that you have volunteered to work in an urban clinic providing care to an underserved population. It is important to recognize patients with substance abuse disorders, as this may complicate their other medical problems, but the visits are brief and you need an efficient way to screen patients for alcohol dependency. You find and read a recent study that tested the usefulness of a single screening question for the detection of unhealthy alcohol use in an urban adult population. In this study, conducted in a primary care clinic in an inner-city neighborhood, 286 adult patients were asked a single screening question: "How many times in the past year have you had 5 or more drinks in a day (4 for women)?" The test was considered positive if the patient reported one or more days of consuming 5 or more drinks. After recording the answer to this question, all patients completed an independent "gold standard" evaluation for unhealthy alcohol use based on answers to validated questionnaires. The results are presented below in a 2 × 2 table (see Table 17.2).

Sensitivity = a/a + c = 72/88 = 0.82, or 82%

Specificity = d/b + d = 156/198 = 0.79, 79%

Positive likelihood ratio = sensitivity/(1-specificity) = [a/(a + c)] / [b/(b + d)] = 0.82/0.21 = 3.9

Negative likelihood ratio = (1-sensitivity)/specificity = [c/(a + c)] / [d/(b + d)] = 0.18/0.79 = 0.23

Now using the calculated values for the likelihood ratios, imagine that you estimate your patient's pretest probability of unhealthy alcohol use at around 30%, based simply on estimates of the prevalence of alcohol abuse in the population the clinic serves. Using the nomogram and a straight-edge, you can see that a positive test on the single question would give you a posttest probability of approximately 62%, more than double your pretest estimate. You might refer this patient for further evaluation and counseling for alcohol abuse. Conversely, a negative response on the single question would allow you to "update" your suspicion of unhealthy drinking to below 10%: You probably would not send this patient for counseling. To summarize, a "test" as simple as a single question posed to the patient can provide the clinician with valuable diagnostic information to guide patient care, as long as the test's likelihood ratios are known, and the pretest probability can be estimated. Finally, consider applying this same test to a very different population, with a much lower prevalence of alcohol use disorders of perhaps 5% (approximately the rate in a typical medical school class). Going back to the nomogram, a positive response to the single question gives a posttest probability of only about 20% for habitual unhealthy drinking. This provides a nice illustration of how dramatically disease prevalence affects diagnostic test performance. This principle holds for all diagnostic tests, including elements of the history, physical exam findings, laboratory tests and imaging. Each test has a likelihood ratio, and results always reflect both test characteristics and disease prevalence in the tested population.

> When additional information cannot possibly alter the decision, but only gives rise to a greater sense of comfort on the part of the physician, such additional information is of no benefit to the patient. Its only benefit is in reducing the discomfort of the physician.
>
> HAROLD M. SCHOOLMAN

SUMMARY

As this book goes to press, medicine finds itself on the cusp of the next great paradigm shift that will transform our understanding of human illness and our ability to treat it. Molecular biology has just now begun to deliver on the promise created during the middle years of the previous century, as the biochemical bases of inheritance, gene expression, the cell cycle and signaling were unveiled.

Our current disease names and classifications will one by one give way to precise categories linked to molecular mechanisms, as what we now consider single diseases separate out into several distinct entities with dramatically different prognoses and treatments. As they unravel the molecular basis of disease, laboratory researchers will give clinicians increasingly precise targets, along with ever more tailored therapies.

The advent of molecular medicine will transform the clinical encounter: Clinicians will gain the tools to make a "molecular diagnosis," and prescribe precise, targeted molecular treatments. The relative importance of making a precise diagnosis will rise, and the task of selecting treatment will become easier. Diseases we currently still quaintly refer to as "schizophrenia" and "mania" will eventually give up their molecular secrets and offer precise treatment targets. As this happens, the skilled diagnostician will rise again to the position of leader of the health care team. Naming the disease—the first activity to link patients and healers at the dawn of medical history—will carry medicine into its next epoch. In the future as in the past, gifted diagnosticians will continue to anchor the clinical enterprise and provide inestimable value to their patients.

CASE STUDY

An 83-year-old woman is brought to the clinic by her daughter for worsening confusion and the recent onset of urinary incontinence. By the daughter's history, the patient has a gradually progressing problem with short-term memory loss, but is generally alert and conversant, and able to carry out most activities of daily living independently. About one week prior to the visit, the daughter noticed urine stains on the couch where her mother has spent much of each day watching television since the death of her husband 2 years previously. Three days ago, the daughter reports that her mother stopped speaking spontaneously, and seemed to be talking and singing quietly to herself. She had trouble answering simple questions, and ignored the dog when he waited to go out for his afternoon walk. She also stopped bathing and dressing herself.

This case presents one of the most common and challenging diagnostic dilemmas that confront clinicians who care for elders: a fairly abrupt change in behavior, suggesting loss of cognitive capacity. To the unpracticed eye, the story represents little more than an elderly widow succumbing to the inevitable cognitive decline of senility. In contrast, an astute clinician sees a broad range of more concerning possibilities: worsening Alzheimer-type dementia, major depression with psychotic features, or an acute delirium resulting from metabolic disturbance, intoxication, adverse drug reaction or systemic or central nervous system infection, or stroke. Misdiagnosis in this setting has

dramatic and permanent consequences: when delirium is labeled dementia, the cause and solution often go undetected, with preventable bad outcome.

The past medical history is notable for hypertension, fluid retention in the ankles and a thyroid problem. The daughter has brought all of the medication bottles from her mother's bathroom: digoxin, 0.125 mg once per day, furosemide 20 mg once per day, clonidine 0.1 mg twice per day, levothyroxin 75 µg once per day, empty bottle, last filled 6 months previously. The patient denies dysuria or flank pain.

The medication list expands the possible causes of delirium: digoxin toxicity, central nervous system effects of a centrally-acting alpha blocker, electrolyte disturbances from loop diuretics, untreated hypothyroidism. Because delirium is dangerous and reversible and dementia generally is not, the clinician makes a presumptive diagnosis of a toxic, metabolic delirium and proceeds to try to elucidate the cause.

Physical exam: The patient is disheveled, with mismatched socks, but in no apparent distress. She acknowledges the physician, and answers questions briefly. She is oriented only to person and place ("the hospital") but not to time. She begins picking at her clothing, stating "where did all of this cat hair come from?"

Temperature: 36.2, pulse 48, respirations 12, blood pressure 110/66

Skin: dry and rough; hands cool to touch; diffuse alopecia; puffy face, hands, and feet; HEENT unremarkable; neck supple; thyroid midline, not enlarged, no nodules; voice slightly hoarse; chest: clear to auscultation; dullness right base on percussion; heart distant without murmurs, rubs or gallops; abdomen non-tender, without organomegaly, rectal hemocult negative, extremities moderate pretibial edema, DTR's 1 + and delayed, gait slow, shuffling, with negative Romberg, without ataxia, mental status testing: unable to perform serial 3's or spell world backwards, neurologic exam otherwise notable only for diffuse weakness.

We began with a broad and concerning differential. The physical exam has lowered the post-test probability of acute infection – the patient is afebrile, without signs of bacteremia or systemic toxicity. Evaluating a possible metabolic encephalopathy must await results of laboratory examinations, though the clinical picture is typical of untreated hypothyroidism. Like every patient with an undiagnosed delirium, this patient requires hospitalization until a life-threatening cause can be excluded. A metabolic screen reveals electrolytes in the normal limits, but the TSH is markedly elevated, consistent with hypothyroidism as the principal, or strongly contributive diagnosis.

A trial of thyroxine replacement therapy is initiated, despite the need for additional laboratory testing. Based on the clinical picture, the patient is restarted on her last known dose of thyroid supplement, 100 µg per day, and is observed in the hospital until additional blood tests and brain imaging studies exclude a life-threatening condition.

Nor bring to see me cease to live.
Some doctor full of phrase and fame.
To shake his sapient head, and give
The ill he cannot cure a name.

MATTHEW ARNOLD
A Wish

SUGGESTED READINGS

Gladwell, M. (2008). *Outliers*. New York: Little, Brown and Company.
    In a highly readable book, Gladwell examines how we think about real life statistics, variability, and deviance, and their impact on the world.

Simel, D.L., & Rennie, D. (2009). *The rational clinical examination*. New York: McGraw-Hill.
    This book offers a current look at how to use the clinical examination for systematic diagnostic hypothesis generation and testing.

Vergehese, A. (2008). *Culture shock–patient as icon, icon as patient. New England Journal of Medicine, 359*(26), 2748–2751.
    Dr. Vergehese is an internist and professor at Stanford, who has written and speaks on the importance of the interaction of the patient and the physician. In this paper he discusses the emergence of the "ipatient" the patient who appears in images and lab values on the computer, with the human body serving primarily as an icon.

18 Patient Assessment

John C. Linton & Steve Cody

Scientific medicine has hitherto paid much attention to disease and almost none to health, to causative agents rather than to the person or host, that is, to the seed rather than to the soil; and to the sick rather than to the people who become sick.

J. AUDY

Evaluating a patient's personality, behavioral characteristics, and capabilities is an important part of effective care. Sometimes these findings will apply directly to the determination of a diagnosis and treatment, as in cases of psychiatric disorder and mental retardation. At other times, factors such as intelligence and personality may place some patients at increased risk for certain medical conditions, or complicate effective treatment. Much can be learned about a patient through careful interviewing, but there are also formal techniques that are more focused and objective. These techniques range from the semistructured mental status examination, to highly structured and standardized tests of intelligence and neurocognitive functioning. Some techniques such as the mental status exam will be a routine part of an interview, while others such as personality inventories or intelligence tests will have to be administered and interpreted by a psychologist.

All of these techniques involve *sampling behaviors* in a more or less systematic fashion. Patients are presented with questions, tasks, or stimuli, selected to reflect a broader aspect of functioning, such as intelligence. Such procedures are useful because they allow one to predict how a patient will function outside the context of the assessment.

An attentive and observant physician will be aware of things patients are communicating that are not limited to the *content* of what they say. There is often much to be learned from the *process* aspects of communication; in other words, *how* patients express the things they share.

Patients reveal a great deal of themselves in the demeanor they adopt toward the physician, the kind of information they provide and when they provide it, and the tone of their responses to advice and information. Subtleties of attitude, emotion, and nonverbal behavior can be critical to psychiatric diagnosis, but are also important in understanding the unique patient with whom the physician is trying to establish and cultivate trust and cooperation. Attending to all this can seem overwhelming to the new physician, who may be struggling to remember all the important questions to ask, but these skills can be developed with practice.

Of course, the astute physician will also know the importance of being thoughtful about what the patient actually says. Some conditions directly affect the ability of the patient to comprehend what is happening and communicate effectively with an interviewer. In some situations, patients will be ambivalent about the information they share. More generally, one can be misled by assumptions that prevent the physician from understanding the specific situation of that person. For example, *it may be a mistake to assume that the patient means the same thing the physician meant by the word "depressed."* It is often better to ask for data than for conclusions (e.g., "How much do you drink?" rather than "Do you have a drinking problem?")

MENTAL STATUS EXAMINATION

For patients in psychiatric and some nonpsychiatric medical settings, it is necessary to conduct a psychiatric interview, which includes a comprehensive psychiatric history. The psychiatric history is an account of events from the past as recalled by the patient. As such, the history is highly subjective; the recounted *events* were not witnessed by the interviewer. Therefore, the clinician must also conduct a mental status examination, which is an objective report on the patient's current mental functioning as witnessed by the interviewer. In a sense the mental status examination is to the mental health clinician what the physical examination is to the internist. Just as the findings from the physical examination allow an objective appraisal of current physical status, *the mental status examination is an objective assessment of the quantitative and qualitative range of the patient's mental functioning at a specific point in time.*

Technically the mental status examination is conducted and reported on as a separate part of the clinical psychiatric interview. In fact, however, this separation is artificial because information gathered throughout the entire interview may be applicable to the psychiatric examination; conversely, specific mental status findings may prompt the clinician to reevaluate the medical or psychiatric history already obtained or to return to previous portions of the interview to re-examine specific details. The clinician often switches back and forth a number of times from one aspect of an interview to another while gathering information about a patient.

Importance of the Mental Status Examination

The mental status examination provides a system for organizing information, allowing diagnosis of different psychiatric disorders. Individuals with psychiatric problems who come to a psychiatric setting are the most clearly in need of such an assessment; however, patients with ostensibly nonpsychiatric medical problems sometimes have subtle psychiatric disorders that emerge only during such a structured examination.

In addition, *patients frequently change with time, and the mental status examination establishes a baseline against which to measure this change.* An individual may be treated by different clinicians in different places at different times, and the findings from his or her mental status examination offer a standard and widely accepted form of communication between professionals regarding the mental functioning of that patient. Thus, the mental status examination assists in understanding, diagnosing, and measuring the progress or deterioration of patients, and it facilitates communication among professionals.

Conducting and Interpreting The Mental Status Examination

Conducting a mental status examination requires the clinician to listen empathically to a person's description of his

or her subjective experiences while remaining aware of speech patterns and observing often subtle behavior. In emergency department settings and on medical floors the clinician is often required to gather complex information quickly and organize it into a cogent, accurate mental status evaluation. At the same time the clinician must develop a rapport with the individual, assist the individual to feel secure and understood, and maintain the confidentiality of the relationship. The clinician must cover a variety of specific examination areas through observation and questioning yet must not appear to be checking off items on a prepared list.

Weighty decisions often are made on the basis of mental status examination results, such as whether patients are capable of self-care, are competent to manage their financial affairs, are currently psychotic or at risk for psychosis, or are prone to commit suicide or some other violent act. It is important to gather information that is as accurate as possible and to consider variables that might reduce this accuracy. For instance, patients are sometimes emotionally upset and difficult to follow; they may be unable to attend to or concentrate on questions or tasks; or they may have perceptual difficulties, such as impaired hearing or eyesight, or expressive or receptive language disorders. Sometimes patients may not comply with the examination and may resist revealing information about themselves. Such noncompliance may result from a patient's particular personality or it may result from the nature of the evaluation, particularly if it involves legal issues or financial compensation.

Many mental status examinations are performed informally. A patient who is seeking only medical attention or outpatient counseling for adjustment problems may be evaluated quickly and show no need for further assessment. If a person shows symptoms of substantial disturbance or mood, perception, memory, or thinking, however, a formal mental status examination is required. An overview of the major parts of the mental status examination follows.

Presentation

General Appearance. The examiner's report should create a picture of the subject, so that anyone reading the report will be able to visualize the patient's unique appearance. The overall physical impression is recorded, including gait, posture, body shape, scars or tattoos, facial features and expression, grooming, and cleanliness. It is helpful to estimate how old the patient looks relative to his or her chronological age. Clothes, cosmetics, and jewelry often indicate how the subject wants to be perceived by others. The clothing's condition and appropriateness to the occasion and the weather should be noted.

And Man Created God in His Own Image, (1930–1931) *Ivan Le Lorraine Albright, 1897–1983.* Oil on canvas 121.9 × 66 cm. Gift of Ivan Albright, 1977.36. Photography © The Art Institute of Chicago. Reproduced by permission of the artist's estate. *Simply looking closely at your patients is the beginning of an effective mental status examination. What hypotheses would you have about this man?*

Level of Consciousness. It is important to describe how alert the patient was when he or she was interviewed. This is especially important when mental status examinations are conducted on hospitalized medical and psychiatric patients and on emergency department referrals. Clearly the presentation of the patient's mental functioning will be influenced by level of consciousness.

The examiner should be as descriptive as possible, stating in detail how the patient responded to questions, requests, prompts, and so forth. Level of consciousness is usually described on a continuum from comatose to alert. In a **coma**, neither verbal nor motor responses occur in response to noxious stimuli. Patients in a stuporous state require repeated energetic stimulation to be aroused. **Lethargic** patients are sleepy, inactive, and indifferent, responding to input from others in a fashion that is incomplete and delayed. The **drowsy** individual is sleepy but can be aroused by aversive stimuli. **Alert** wakefulness is the state in which the individual responds promptly and appropriately to all perceptual input.

Attitude Toward Interviewer. How the patient relates to the examiner and the interview situation affects the quality and quantity of information obtained. The examiner should give a descriptive summary of how the patient interacted during the session, commenting on both general attitude and changes in the patient's style of responding.

Sometimes in the course of an interview the examiner may discuss certain topics that affect the patient's attitude; the patient may show sudden resistance to further discussion or, conversely, show evidence of greater involvement in the process at that point. It is wise for the examiner to note what content areas caused which reactions because this can provide clues to the patient's mental status for further investigation. The examiner should also note his or her reaction to the patient. Awareness of personal reactions may help the examiner predict how others will respond to the patient.

Motor Behavior. The motor behavior section of the mental status report describes the specifics of patient behavior during the interview. The patient's gait, gestures, and firmness of handshake are noted, along with involuntary or abnormal movements such as tremors, tics, hand wringing, **akathisia**, or stereotyped mannerisms. The examiner should note if the patient mimics his or her movements (**echopraxia**) or if the patient's limbs remain in positions that are unnatural or uncomfortable once placed there (**waxy flexibility**). The clinician should also report on the pace of movements. Psychomotor restlessness or **agitation** is seen in the patient who has difficulty sitting still and who must constantly move about, scratching, biting his or her nails, or rising from the chair or bed and wandering around the room. At the other extreme, **psychomotor retardation** is indicated by a significant slowing of movement and speech. The patient sits quietly and seldom moves, and facial expression is flat. It is important to record specific behavior rather than merely summarizing global impressions. The behavior of most patients can be described as "normal;" however, evidence of any of the previously mentioned suggests significant emotional disturbance.

Speech. The speech section is devoted to describing *manner;* not content. The examiner listens for the rate of speech and notes characteristics such as rapid, slowed, pressured, slurred, or loud or soft speech. Speech problems such as stammering or stuttering are indicated, as are any symptoms of aphasia.

Emotional State: Mood and Affect

The description of emotion is typically divided between **mood**, *a subjectively experienced feeling that is fairly persistent, and* **affect**, *the emotional tone of the interview or the overt manifestation of mood as directly observed by the interviewer.* In other words, patients feel and complain of problems with mood, and their mood influences how they view the world. Patients do not complain about their affect. Clinicians see and evaluate affect, and it can change frequently during the course of an examination.

In addition to patient reports regarding emotion, the interviewer pays special attention to many cues, including facial expression, speech, and nonverbal cues such as gestures and body language. Here again, specific descriptions of the patient's emotional expressions are likely to be more valuable than summary impressions.

Range of Emotional Expression. The examiner should describe the predominant emotion as reported by the patient, such as sadness, depression, anger, guilt, or fear. It is wise to question patients further to determine what personal meanings are attached to these descriptors rather than assume their meaning.

Moods can vary in intensity. Normally happy individuals are known as **euthymic**; however, this positive mood can become exaggerated along a continuum in which the individual's mood first becomes elevated, then euphoric, then expansive. At the other end of the spectrum, unpleasant moods are dysphoric and can include **dysthymia**, anxiety, and irritability. Dysphoric patients commonly come to the interview with complaints about mood. Those who are euphoric or expansive seldom complain about their moods, but others do!

The range of the person's affect is important to indicate. A "normal" individual has a *broad* range of affect; he or she appears sad when discussing unhappy topics and laughs when things are funny. If affect is **blunted**, the patient has a significantly diminished and narrowed range of emotional responsiveness. With a **flat affect** the patient relates little or no feeling, seems devoid of emotion, and shows little or no change in facial expression, regardless of what is discussed. *This is a symptom classically associated with schizophrenia.* **Constricted affect** is commonly seen in depression. Emotions are present, but the patient is too depressed to act on them. **Labile affect** refers to emotion that shifts rapidly from one expression to another with the slightest provocation. Such individuals can be happy one minute, angry the next, and depressed the next. Labile affect is found in certain personality disorders and is prominent in

organic brain disease. Finally, clinicians are increasingly recognizing patients who are **alexithymic**, or seemingly incapable of discussing their emotions. Discussion of emotions and connections between their physical symptoms and feelings seem to elude them completely. Such patients are most often found in general medical settings, and they can be very frustrating for those caring for them.

> It is useful to remember that *affect* is to *mood* as *weather* is to *climate.*

Appropriateness of Emotions. The examiner should determine and note whether the affect and presentation are appropriate to the subject matter being discussed. At times there may be a wide discrepancy between the subject being discussed and the patient's facial expressions and projected emotional tone. A person who discusses problems for which the appropriate response would be sadness, anxiety, or anger, yet acts cheerful or silly, and smiles, shows inappropriate affect. Some patients feign this behavior, but if the finding of inappropriate affect is sustained, it usually reflects significant psychopathology.

Biological Indicators of Affect. The examiner should inquire about psychophysiological changes that may accompany the patient's emotional state. This is perhaps most salient with depression. It is important to determine whether the patient has **diurnal variation** in mood, that is, whether the person's spirits are worse in the morning and improved during the day or vice versa. *The examiner should note characteristics of the patient's sleep, paying special attention to problems with getting to sleep, waking too early and not being able to get back to sleep, or sleeping more or less than is usual* (however, the examiner should be careful not to use his or her personal standards for adequate sleep for comparison).

Changes in the patient's appetite, such as a reduction in frequency and amount from what is customary, should be noted. Significant recent weight changes should also be recorded. The examiner should determine whether the patient's **libido**, or sex drive, has changed and, whether there has been an increase or decrease in sexual activity. Changes in the patient's interest in everyday activities such as work, family, and hobbies should be noted, as should the patient's ability and motivation to carry out daily living activities.

Some clinicians also address **suicide** and **homicide** at this time. *No mental status examination is adequate without a statement about the patient's thinking with regard to suicide or homicide.* The clinician must always determine whether the patient is likely to harm or kill himself or herself or others. This is best assessed by asking *directly* about the history of such thoughts, or plans. The final report should state clearly that these issues have been explored and the nature of the findings. If they are positive, the examiner should offer some evaluation of the situation's urgency. A patient who "might tell my wife to ask a pharmacist for some pills that are poison" is probably less at risk than one who seems hopeless, lives alone, and has "a loaded pistol in the bedside drawer." However, *all suicidal ideation should be treated with clinical respect and appropriately evaluated.*

> The thought of suicide is a great consolation: with the help of it one got through many a bad night.
>
> FRIEDRICH NIETZSCHE

Perceptual Disturbances

Abnormal sensory functioning is described in the perceptual disturbances section of the report. At one time or another, most people have brief experiences with "dream states," a sense of depersonalization or **déja vu**, or the experience of falsely hearing someone call their name. This happens infrequently in "normal" individuals, most often during times of stress. However, this category also includes more significant perceptual disorders.

Hallucinations and Illusions. A **hallucination** is a sensory impression that exists in the absence of a real external stimulus. Patients may report hearing voices that no one else can hear, seeing objects that are not there, feeling sensations without tactile stimulation, and tasting or smelling things that are not present. Hallucinations involving the **vestibular sense**, in which the patient feels as if he or she is flying, occur occasionally. Some patients admit having hallucinations but many do not, and the examiner must infer their existence when patients seem preoccupied, as if listening to voices or sounds, or stare at something that seems real to them, sometimes moving their eyes around to follow it. When observing such behavior, the examiner should tactfully inquire about the experience.

Auditory hallucinations can include sounds, complete words and sentences, or commands to act. The voices can be strange or familiar. *A useful rule is that auditory hallucinations are most often found in functional disorders, typically schizophrenia, but also in affective (manic or depressive) psychoses.* Such hallucinations tend to be more consistent in schizophrenics and more transient in patients with affective disorders. They can also be found in organic mental disorders, such as **alcoholic hallucinosis**.

Hallucinations can be mood incongruent or mood congruent. The former hallucinations do not match the patient's mood; the latter hallucinations do. *Schizophrenic patients tend to have mood-incongruent hallucinations, whereas patients with affective disorders have more mood-congruent hallucinations.* Depressed patients may hear voices telling them that they deserve punishment, whereas withdrawn, frightened schizophrenics may hear that they are destined to rule the world with Jesus. *The clinician should determine whether the voices are telling the patient to harm himself or herself or others and whether this command can be resisted.*

Visual hallucinations are most common in organic mental disorders such as delirium but can also be found in a variety of other conditions such as brief reactive psychoses or severe grief reactions. Visual hallucinations can also result from the effects of drugs or sensory deprivation. They occur infrequently in schizophrenia and are often described as frightening. Patients with some forms of personality disorder describe experiences that sound like hallucinations, when in fact their imaginations are active and they relish the attention that comes with such discussions.

Illusions are misperceptions of real stimuli, such as thinking that a stranger is a familiar acquaintance until he or she gets closer. Such experiences are most common in states of anxiety or extreme fatigue. Persons without demonstrable mental disorder may have them; they can also accompany functional psychoses because such patients may be emotionally upset and exhausted as part of their clinical syndrome. Patients sometimes think that illusions are hallucinations, and the examiner should attempt to differentiate between the two.

Depersonalization and Derealization. Depersonalization refers to a strange feeling of change or loss of reality of the self and the accompanying feeling that there is something different about the self or the emotions that cannot be explained. *With **depersonalization** the individual feels that he or she is different; with **derealization** the person feels that the environment has changed somehow and that external reality is no longer familiar.* These conditions are best assessed by asking patients whether they feel natural, if they or their bodies feel different or unusual, or if their environment seems strange. Both of these conditions can occur in "normal" individuals under certain circumstances, but they most often accompany panic disorder, agoraphobia, or depression.

Thought Processes

The examiner cannot directly assess a patient's thoughts and so must depend on behavior and speech to evaluate how well a person's mental associations are organized and expressed and what they are about.

Stream of Thought. When assessing stream of thought, the examiner is interested in the quantity and rate of thought, again as measured by speech. At one extreme the patient produces little or no speech, perhaps saying only a few words. Unless there is reason to suspect that he or she is being purposefully resistive, such poverty of speech suggests a retardation or slowing of thoughts. At the other extreme the patient's speech is overabundant and accelerated or racing so that it is difficult to follow. This is usually referred to as **pressured speech** and is often seen in persons with acute anxiety or agitated depression who feel pressed to talk; it sometimes suggests the presence of flight of ideas, which is a diagnostic sign of mania.

Continuity of Thought. *Continuity of thought is assessed by determining to what extent the patient's thoughts are goal directed, as well as the nature of the associations between the patient's ideas.* Some abnormalities of thought continuity are extremely pathological, whereas others, although usually pathological, may also result from limited intelligence, cultural differences, or a severe reaction to overwhelming dysphoria. The abnormalities of thought that are always pathological include **clang associations**, in which thoughts are connected illogically by rhyming or puns; **echolalia**, a condition in which the patient repeats exactly what the clinician says; use of **neologisms**, which are invented or condensed words that have meaning only to the patient; **perseveration**, which is the apparently involuntary responding to all questions in the same way; and the presence of **word salad**, a nonsensical mix of words and phrases. Usually pathological, and certainly noteworthy, are **looseness of associations**, a condition in which the person jumps from one topic to another and the connection between thoughts is lost; **blocking**, which is the sudden cessation of thought in the middle of a sentence and the inability to continue or recover what was being said; **circumstantiality**, which is characterized by the absence of direction toward a goal in language and thought and the inclusion of details that are unnecessary and eventually tedious and which is common in obsessional individuals who do not want to leave anything out, no matter how trivial; and **tangentiality**, which is a severe form of circumstantiality, in which the patient strays completely from the topic and includes thoughts that seem to be totally unrelated and irrelevant. Tangentiality is most often seen in schizophrenia.

Because patients are often upset, they may present their thoughts poorly, and at first the thought process might seem to be disordered. Rather than assuming that this is the case, the examiner should ask the patient, "What does that mean to you?" or "Could you explain to me what you just said?" A patient's thoughts should be clear to an unbiased observer; if they are not, the examiner should be comfortable enough to ask about them.

Content of Thought. The content of thought section of the mental status examination assesses the integrity of the patient's thoughts. Most of this material will have already been developed during the general psychiatric interview or elsewhere in the mental status examination. However, a number of specific abnormalities of thought content must be investigated before certain diagnoses can be ruled out.

A **delusion** is a belief that is false and unique to the individual. It cannot be adequately explained by reference to the patient's cultural or subcultural background and in fact would be rejected by others with the same cultural background. Delusions can appear in many different guises. For example, a person with **delusions of reference** has a feeling of being watched, discussed, or ridiculed by others; **delusions of persecution** most commonly involve the belief that the person has been singled out to be plotted against or harmed in some way; **delusions of grandiosity** refer to the belief that the individual has assumed the identity of a famous person, living or dead, or has special talents or unique powers; **delusions of jealousy** result from false beliefs that a spouse or lover has been unfaithful; **delusions of guilt** refer to the feeling of having committed an unforgivable deed; and **erotomania** refers to the delusion that a stranger or a celebrity loves the person but cannot make it public. The examiner should ask patients objectively about delusional thoughts without attempting to dissuade them from or agreeing with their notions. The examiner should also determine the level of organization of the delusional system and assess whether it is a passing idea or a systematized way of viewing the world. *It is critical that the examiner ascertain whether the patient intends to act on a delusional belief.* For example, the examiner should determine whether the patient intends to retaliate in some form against others for their perceived persecution.

> If a patient is poor he is committed to a public hospital as "psychotic"; if he can afford the luxury of a private sanitarium, he is put there with the diagnosis of "neuroasthenia"; if he is wealthy enough to be isolated in his own home under constant watch of nurses and physicians he is simply an indisposed "eccentric."
>
> PIERRE MARIE JANET
> *Strength and Psychological Debility*

Obsessions are repetitive irrational thoughts. Patients dislike these thoughts and realize that they are not normal; they wish to be rid of the thoughts but are unable to stop the intrusion into their thinking. Obsessions are usually accompanied by a sense of anxiety or morbid dread, which patients find painful but irresistible. **Compulsions** are related to obsessions except that they involve behaviors instead of thoughts. Compulsions are stereotyped and repetitive rituals the individual is driven to perform even though the person knows the actions are senseless. Performing the ritualistic deeds is not enjoyable *per se*, but it reduces anxiety, thereby reinforcing the action; if compulsions are resisted, the patient becomes exceedingly anxious.

The clinician should try to determine the degree to which both obsessions and compulsions interfere with the patient's life. Is it a minor irritation, or is the patient in danger of losing a job because checking and rechecking the locks in the house dozens of times before leaving makes the patient chronically late for work? Finally, preoccupations involve the degree to which a patient is absorbed in his or her thoughts to the exclusion of reality. Brilliant but eccentric individuals are noted for absentmindedness when focusing on certain ideas. At the other end of the continuum is the person who can think about nothing but homicide or suicide or who has autistic fantasies. When present, preoccupations and their intensity should always be noted.

A **phobia** is a morbid fear of an object, animal, or situation that would not frighten the average person. The phobic individual goes to great lengths to avoid contact with the feared stimulus. If it is easily avoided (e.g., snakes in a large city), the patient's phobia should cause little disruption of daily activity, but if the phobic stimulus is regularly encountered (e.g., elevators in a large city), it is more problematic. Patients are seldom seen primarily for phobias, which often coexist with other syndromes. The examiner may have to question the patient about specific phobic anxiety because this information is seldom offered spontaneously.

Cognitive State

Some examiners choose to assess cognitive abilities early in the examination before determining emotional state and thought processes to ensure that what is observed *as* thought or mood disorder is not really an impaired cognitive state. However, this area is more commonly focused on at the end of the examination, when the information can be used in interpreting what was observed earlier.

Orientation. Orientation refers to the patient's ability to understand the nature of his or her current environment relative to time, place, person, and situation. For most patients this part of the examination is unnecessary, particularly if earlier in the interview the quality of the material communicated to the examiner indicates that the individual is well oriented. Disorientation can exist in functional psychoses such as schizophrenia and major affective disorders but is most common in organic disorders.

Orientation to time is assessed by asking the patient about the year, season, month, day of the week, and date. Occasionally someone who appears to be functioning well surprises an examiner with a time response that is incorrect by decades. Some believe that this is the most sensitive indicator of disorientation because time changes constantly, whereas the other spheres change less often or not at all. **Orientation to place** is determined by asking the patient to name his or her location by country, state,

county, city, type of building, and location in the building. Clinicians should use common sense and caution here, asking about easier locations such as country only after the patient cannot respond to the type of building or the city. One should also take into account the person's intelligence. **Orientation to person** involves the patient's awareness of his or her own name and the names and roles of those in the immediate environment. In some cases this is the last area to show deficit, and it is the first to reappear in reversible organic states. The patient who is oriented to situation is aware that he or she is a patient and that a clinical examination is taking place, rather than a social visit or job interview. If no deficits are noted in any of the previously mentioned areas, the individual is said to exhibit a clear **sensorium**.

Attention and Concentration. Attention refers to the patient's capacity to focus on one activity or task at a time. The clinician usually gets a sense of the patient's ability to attend during the other phases of the interview. Lack of attention is sometimes volitional. Patients may be purposely noncompliant and oppositional and may ignore the clinician or engage in some other behavior designed to compete with the interview process. However, patients may also be distracted by anxiety or psychotic preoccupations. In such cases the patient cannot distinguish between relevant and irrelevant stimuli and may attend to sounds outside the room or internal voices rather than to the examiner.

*Although the interview can never actually take place with a person who has serious attentional deficits, a patient with deficits in **concentration** is able to attend for short periods* and the examination may get off to a good start. However, he or she soon becomes distracted and must be guided back on track with repeated questions and restructuring of the interview task.

When a patient has a significant problem with attention or concentration, more formal testing is required. The most common test, known as **"serial sevens,"** asks the patient to subtract 7 from 100, then 7 from that answer, and so on as far as possible. However, some clinicians believe that this requires too much mathematical ability and instead suggest the use of "serial ones," a task that requires the patient to count backward by ones from any number (e.g., 62), and stop at another number (e.g., 19). This task provides a relatively pure measure of concentration.

Memory. Memory can be clinically assessed in five basic dimensions: *Immediate memory refers to the ability to recall what a person has just been told; **short-term memory** involves retrieving information received about 5 minutes earlier; **recent memory** involves recognizing material from the past several days to several months; **long-term memory** involves recalling data from the past few years; and **remote memory** involves recalling events from the distant past.* When an individual's memory fails, immediate memory typically fails first, remote memory last. Recent, long-term, and remote memory can usually be assessed by evaluating how well the patient remembers personal history and current happenings. However, some patients with organic mental disturbances **confabulate,** or invent plausible but false stories that mask their memory problem. Therefore, a patient's recollections should be independently verified by other sources, such as family members, if there is any doubt as to the veracity of the patient's statements.

Immediate and short-term memory can be assessed by formal testing. The most common method is to ask the patient to remember five neutral objects, such as a car, shoe, umbrella, teacup, and flashlight. The patient is asked to repeat them and, if correct, is then told that he or she will be asked about them again in 5 minutes. The examination continues for another 5 minutes, and then the patient is asked to repeat the items. Most patients remember four or five items. A score of three is borderline performance, and recall of less than three items suggests a need for further evaluation of organicity.

Finally, the examiner must not forget to record the items he or she asked the patient to recall or should use a standard list. More than one busy examiner has forgotten what the patient was asked to remember!

Intelligence. The only true measure of **intelligence** is derived from intelligence testing, which is seldom available at the time of the mental status examination. However, an examiner can at least estimate a patient's level of intellectual functioning by his or her comments during the interview. *The person's use of vocabulary is probably the best estimate of overall intelligence,* particularly if one considers level of education as well. A good vocabulary in a patient with limited schooling suggests that he or she is an academic underachiever, whereas a weak vocabulary in a college graduate suggests that the person's intellectual functioning may be declining.

The patient's **fund of information** encompasses general knowledge that can be assessed by asking questions about a wide range of subjects such as geography, history, and current events. It is important to remember that educational and cultural limitations can play a significant role in the patient's educational and knowledge base.

Testing **abstraction** is an additional measure of the patient's intelligence and is accomplished by asking the individual to find commonalties among apparently dissimilar objects, such as asking how a drum, guitar, and violin are alike. The patient who responds that they are all musical instruments shows good skill in abstraction; the patient who says simply that they all make noise is responding concretely. It is also useful to ask the patient to interpret proverbs, again controlling the test for the person's age and cultural background by avoiding dated or colloquial stimuli. Finally, if the examiner suspects significant intellectual impairment, a formal intelligence assessment should be requested.

Reliability. The examiner should give some estimate of the reliability of the patient as an informant or historian. Several factors must be considered, such as the individual's intelligence, contact with reality, and personality style and the purpose of the evaluation. For example, if the patient is being evaluated because of pressure from family or the court system, he or she is likely to tell a different story from someone who is seeking symptom relief. Patients with poor memories may wish to cooperate but be unable to recall vital information and confabulate stories that are quite believable. The clinician's notion as to the reliability of the data should temper and qualify all of the information gathered from the interview.

Insight and Judgment. *Insight is the capacity to understand that one has a problem, to conceptualize how it came about, and to think about how it might be solved.* The degree of a patient's insight is a general predictor of how well the individual will cooperate with treatment, especially if treatment is at all insight oriented.

The clinician can determine the patient's **judgment** by assessing the history gleaned from the interview and by directly assessing interview behavior. Judgment refers to the individual's ability to deal with social situations and to understand and adhere to reasonable social conventions. Obviously, the psychotic patient who goes without eating for days shows poor judgment. However, even individuals with normal intelligence and no major psychopathology can have notoriously bad judgment, repeatedly making disastrous romantic, vocational, and economic decisions. This finding should be noted and reported, because it has clear implications for treatment.

Summary

Conducting a comprehensive mental status examination is a mixture of art, social persuasion, and science. Knowing how, when, and at what level to conduct this examination is an invaluable clinical skill and is critical to superior patient care. Although the examination may appear complex and difficult, in reality it is relatively brief and easily learned by most physicians.

Unfortunately the mental status examination can also become perfunctory, cursory, and truncated to the point that it yields little information of value. However, *master clinicians routinely include a full mental status examination in their assessments of patients,* using a structured format such as the one outlined in this chapter. The few extra minutes it adds to the patient interview is a small price to pay for information that is structured, systematic, and easily communicated to other professionals.

PSYCHOLOGIC AND NEUROPSYCHOLOGIC TESTING

Testing offers the most structured and systematic approach to sampling behavior for learning about a patient's personality, abilities, and functioning. In some cases, formal testing is essential to a diagnosis, as is the case with intellectual assessment in the course of diagnosing mental retardation or learning disorders. In other cases, testing can be useful in differential diagnosis, illuminating the personality factors that contribute to a patient's situation, determining whether patients' capacities fit a given demand (e.g., driving), or establishing how an illness or injury has affected the patient. For purposes of discussion, it can be useful to consider three broad areas of psychological assessment: (1) measures of personality and psychopathology, (2) measures of intellect and academic functioning, and (3) neuropsychological assessment.

Criteria for Evaluating Testing Techniques

Just as medical tests are expected to meet scientific standards to be accepted for clinical decision making, so too must psychological tests meet basic standards. In order to be useful, tests must be **standardized**, **reliable**, and **valid**.

Standardization refers to the idea that the stimuli and materials, instructions and procedures, the way in which responses are scored, and interpretation of the results are consistent from one administration of a test to another. Holding all these things constant from one person to another allows the test results to reflect only the differences among people. Standardization permits the establishment of norms, much as normal ranges are defined for various medical tests. The clinician is able to identify behaviors and characteristics that deviate from the norm, and quantify the extent of deviation.

Reliability refers to the stability of test findings over time and repeated administration. Just as blood pressure readings should be essentially the same if taken twice or if taken by different clinicians, tests should yield stable findings in a stable characteristic, and yield essentially the same findings when given by different examiners. Establishing that a measure is reliable allows the clinician to conclude that a change in scores reflects some change in the person, rather than irrelevant variability.

Although reliability ensures a consistent valuation of what the test is claimed to measure, it does not ensure that the test, in fact, measures what is claimed. **Validity** is established by demonstrating that the test accurately relates to other measures of the construct, accurately predicts a person's status now or in the future, and differentiates among

people accurately. In practice, a test is only considered valid for certain uses and for certain populations, and understanding these limitations is critical to using a test correctly. The ultimate criterion for evaluating a psychological test is utility, but a test that is not valid, reliable, and appropriately standardized is unlikely to be useful.

Assessment of Personality and Psychopathology

A broad range of measures exists for evaluating personality characteristics, emotional state, and symptoms of psychiatric disorder. These measures vary widely in focus, extensiveness, and method. They may evaluate many different aspects of personality functioning, or focus on symptoms in a specific area of interest; some are aimed at evaluating "normal" aspects of personality functioning, while many others are used for clinical purposes.

Title Page of Anatomy Text This woodcut from Andreas Vesalius' *De humani corporis fabrica* (1543) shows the celebrated professor of medicine performing a dissection in a crowded anatomical theatre. Courtesy of the National Library of Medicine. *Most physicians perform in the superior to very superior range of intellectual ability.*

Most currently used instruments are considered *objective* in that they ask for specific answers to specific questions that have a given meaning and significance. For example, respondents read a statement (e.g., *I am often depressed*) and decide if it is true or false as applied to them. In **projective testing**, the stimuli are much more ambiguous and the range of responses is more diverse. Perhaps the best known example of a projective personality test is the **Rorschach Ink Blot Test**, where the designs are not intended to look like anything in particular and persons can theoretically see all manner of things in the patterns made by the blot. Because the stimuli have no obvious meaning and the possible responses are so diverse, it is thought that responses are a *projection* of a person's inner feelings and ways of thinking. Other projective tests ask the subject to generate stories in response to pictures of persons in ambiguous situations, to complete the stems of sentences such as "I am most afraid of ..." with a personally relevant answer.

The best known and most widely used of the objective tests of personality and psychopathology is the **Minnesota Multiphasic Personality Inventory** (MMPI), currently in its second edition. The 567 statements, identified as true or false by the subject, load onto 10 primary clinical scales, many more supplemental and content scales, and several *validity* scales. The purpose of the validity scales is to provide information about the person's approach to taking the test, and they can help determine if the person is exaggerating, minimizing, or responding inconsistently. The scores a person obtains on various scales quantify the extent to which the person deviates from expected norms.

Intellectual and Academic Skills

Formal assessment of intellect began just about 100 years ago with a test introduced in France in 1905 by Alfred Binet. Currently, the most widely used tests of intelligence are the measures originally devised by David Wechsler. These include the **Wechsler Adult Intelligence Scale** (WAIS-III, for subjects 16-years old and older), the **Wechsler Intelligence Scale for Children** (WISC-IV, for subjects 6-16), and the **Wechsler Preschool and Primary Scale of Intelligence** (WPPSI, for ages 4–6).

Intelligence tests yield a score called an *IQ* (intelligence quotient). The idea of an intelligence quotient originated with early formulations of IQ as a ratio of chronological age and a "mental age" exhibited in test performance. Students may have seen a description of this *ratio IQ* as Mental Age/Chronological Age × 100. For a variety of reasons, the ratio IQ has been superseded by the *deviation IQ*, in which scores can be directly interpreted in terms of departure from an average level. IQ scores, which are a type of *standard score*, have a mean of 100, and a standard deviation of 15. The scores compare a person with others in his or her age group; a score of 115, for example, places a person one standard deviation above the mean, at the eighty-fourth percentile for persons of a similar age. The use of age-group norms corrects for normal age-related change in different areas of functioning.

A global score called a Full Scale IQ provides a statement about overall functioning, but sometimes conceals significant underlying variability. The Wechsler tests traditionally included two broad groups of specific measurements. Verbal tests, yielding a **Verbal IQ**, included such things as vocabulary, general information, and social reasoning. Another group of tests emphasizing visual abilities and speed generated a **Performance IQ**. Current editions provide four index scores representing more specific domains of ability. These deal with verbal abilities, visual and visuospatial abilities, speed of processing, and working memory.

One situation in which formal intellectual assessment will figure prominently is in diagnosis of mental retardation and learning disorders. One essential criterion for diagnosis of mental retardation is a finding of subnormal intellectual functioning, typically defined as an IQ score of 70 or below (which falls at least two standard deviations below the norm, or in the bottom 2% of the age group). An essential criterion for diagnosing learning disorders is a finding of approximately normal intelligence, combined with failure to achieve at an expected level in one or more areas of academic ability.

A variety of standardized tests exist for evaluating academic skills. Some are best used for screening, some focus on a narrow area, and others offer an entire battery of tests examining a wide range of abilities. Scores are commonly expressed as standard scores with mean of 100 and a standard deviation of 15, and will have norms for age and education.

Neuropsychological Assessment

Clinical neuropsychology is an established specialty area in clinical psychology. The neuropsychologist assesses intellectual, cognitive, social, and emotional functioning and makes inferences about the integrity of cerebral functioning, and about the ability of the patient to perform in a variety of social, interpersonal, and vocational roles. The value of assessment rests in identifying the functional significance of brain impairment (how a lesion affects a person's behavior and capabilities), and in the assessment of disorders in which behavioral manifestations precede structural change in the brain (e.g., dementia) or involve no structural evidence of impairment (e.g., mild head trauma).

Evaluation will typically include interviews with the patient and perhaps with family members or other significant others, review of records, and formal testing of various dimensions of neurocognitive functioning. Testing may involve the use of standardized batteries of tests; the ones most likely to be encountered in practice are the **Halstead-Reitan**

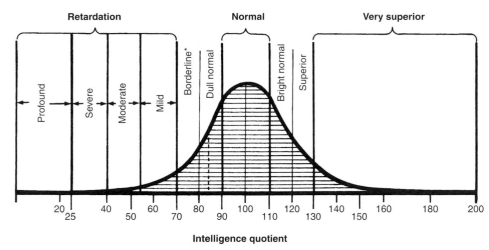

FIGURE 18.1 The distribution of IQ scores in the general population. Both the American Association on Mental Deficiency and the American Psychiatric Association use the range 71 to 84 to define borderline intellectual functioning.

Neuropsychological Battery and the **Luria-Nebraska Neuropsychological Battery**. The former is more widely used and better known; the latter is somewhat briefer and the required equipment is more portable and less expensive. In addition to measures that address issues of mental health and psychiatric diagnosis, a variety of instruments are available for evaluating attitudes and functioning in areas more relevant to health care in general. One widely used instrument is the Short Form Health Survey. Consisting of 36 items that can be completed in 10 minutes, it yields scores on eight scales related to functioning and well-being. These include general health, pain, vitality, physical and social functioning, and fulfillment of social and emotional roles as well as mental health.

Another such instrument is the Health Related Quality of Life. It provides measures of health perception, energy, participation in social and leisure activities, freedom from pain, social and sexual functioning, family life, and friendships. Tests such as the SF-36 and HRQOL provide valuable information about the impact of medical illness on the patient's life. Such knowledge can help the physician understand how the patient perceives his or her health status, and focus efforts on the concerns of particular importance to the patient.

Questionnaires and checklists can provide systematic collection of information that might be difficult to cover in time-limited patient visits. The ability to deal with the broad range of basic and instrumental activities of daily living (ADLs) is one example. Various rating scales are available that can be completed by patients (and/or family members) in the waiting room. Once again the benefit is in enabling the physician to focus on areas of particular concern. Examples include the Lawton Instrumental Activities of Daily Living Scale and the Bristol Activities of Daily Living Scale. While most of these instruments are relatively easy to use, the physician will commonly find it helpful to consult with a psychologist in selecting measures that will fulfill the desired purpose and meet appropriate psychometric standards.

SUMMARY

Understanding patients thoroughly underlies all efforts to diagnose and plan treatment. The techniques described in this chapter can be of invaluable assistance as clinicians work to comprehend the nature of the patients in their charge.

CASE STUDY

William H. is a 59-year-old man who comes in at the urging of his wife with problems including recurrent gastrointestinal distress, diarrhea, and headaches. Workup does not reveal any evident medical condition, but it comes out in conversation that his symptoms have stymied three attempts at taking the admission test for law school. He is eligible for retirement, and his wife is encouraging him to pursue a long-expressed dream of becoming a lawyer. He presents himself as exceptionally intelligent, but his grades were unspectacular in college. He has an engineering degree, and has worked in the same technical capacity for a state agency for over 30 years but he has never been promoted or received merit pay. He has had periods of depression for many years but never sought treatment. He lived with his mother for most of his adult life, marrying after her death 4 years earlier.

The physician makes a referral for evaluation, recognizing the possibility that anxiety, depression, and personality issues may contribute to this man's presenting problems. What factors lead the physician to think this?

The patient's academic and work history do not suggest a person of exceptional intellect. An objective appraisal of intellectual functioning may help the physician respond to the situation. Assessment of the patient's emotional status and personality can help clarify the extent to which his symptoms might represent anxiety over the prospect of actually following through on his dream, manifestations of underlying depression, or conflicts about dependency.

Intellectual assessment indicates that Mr. H. is a person of superior ability, with a Full Scale IQ of 128, which places him at the 97th percentile for persons in his age group. He has exceptional verbal abilities and excellent working memory, which involves mental manipulation of information in immediate memory. His visual and visuospatial abilities are above average. Simple speed of processing is average.

Mr. H.'s MMPI validity indices suggested that he might underestimate his problems, looking to appear more healthy than he is, but not to an extent that would invalidate the profile. The dominant features suggest depression and somatization. Persons with similar profiles are more likely than others to react to stress with physical symptoms and tend to present physical symptoms that medical findings will not adequately explain. They tend to be passive and dependent in relationships and have trouble expressing aggressive feelings overtly. They are often emotionally immature and rely excessively on denial and repression as defenses. The psychologist also administered the Millon Clinical Multiaxial Inventory (MCMI-III), which indicated dependent personality features.

The physician now knows that Mr. H. has the intellectual capacity to be successful in law school, but there are significant indications that he may be conflicted and stressed by the prospect of actually pursuing a law degree. He might be counseled about the natural stress that would be associated with such a drastic change in his life and the idea that some people react to this kind of stress with physical symptoms. These symptoms are no less genuine for being a reaction to stress. Referral to a therapist can help this patient address his conflicts and clarify what he wants, and can help him deal with the stressors if he wants to proceed with enrolling in law school.

SUGGESTED READINGS

Linton, J.C. (2004). Psychological assessment in primary care. In L. Haas (Ed.), *Handbook of Primary Care Psychology*. New York: Oxford University Press.

This is a chapter devoted to the special challenges of assessing patients in a fast-paced primary-care environment.

Rozensky, R.H., Sweet, J.J., & Tovian, S.M. (1997). *Psychological assessment in medical settings*. New York: Plenum.

This book discusses how a well-organized psychological assessment service should operate in a medical setting. Special emphasis is given to referral questions, efficiency, and quality control.

Stead, L.G., Stead, S.M., & Kaufman, M.S. (2005). *First aid for the psychiatry clerkship*. New York: McGraw-Hill.

This is a neat and tidy book for medical students who wish to learn the basics of patient assessment in an easy to read format.

Trzepacz, P.T., & Baker, R.W. (1993). *The psychiatric mental status examination*. New York: Oxford University Press.

While the date suggests this book is older, it remains a classic for students seeking the basics of conducting a thorough mental status exam.

Zimmerman, M. (1993). A 5-minute psychiatric screening interview. *Journal of Family Practice, 37*, 479–482.

This is a remarkably clever paper, which presents a very brief screening tool to be used by busy primary care physicians to identify patients who require further evaluation. This interview is concise and quickly covers the gamut of functioning using down-to-earth questions that are unlikely to offend the patient.

19 Recognizing and Treating Psychopathology in Primary Care

Debra Bendell Estroff, Denise Stephens, & Pilar Bernal

> In my father's time, talking with the patient was the biggest part of medicine, for it was almost all there was to do. The doctor-patient relationship was, for better or worse, a long conversation in which the patient was at the epicenter of concern and knew it.
>
> LEWIS THOMAS

In the context of today's rapidly changing health care, appropriate allocation of medical resources to improve quality of care and increase efficiency of services has become a priority. Traditionally, medical education has focused on organ systems. Medical specialties have evolved from the expertise clinicians developed treating specific organs or illnesses. However, the presence of co-morbidity (e.g., depression exacerbating diabetes or anxiety contributing to mitral valve prolapse) has made diagnosis and treatment more complex. In addition, the influence of a patient's level of functioning and social support systems often altered the outcomes for patients with the same diagnosis and given the same treatment. *It has become increasingly clear that good doctors treat whole patients and not simply diseased organs.*

THE PRESENTATION OF MENTAL ILLNESS IN PRIMARY CARE SETTINGS

The focus of treatment in medicine has shifted from treatment for acute conditions to treatment of chronic illness, and the prevention of psychological sequelae or iatrogenic complications of illness. The central problems that concerned early physicians included infection, nutrition, high infant mortality, and limited life expectancy. These problems have not disappeared, but significant advances have been made in each of these areas. Physicians increasingly confront the serious morbidity associated with psychosocial problems, and their practice often centers on the treatment of chronic illness and mental health problems.

More than 30 years ago it was shown that psychiatric illness was one of the most common reasons for consulting a medical practitioner, and of psychiatric disorders 95% were treated without specialist involvement. This trend has persisted through the years. Psychiatric illnesses are still among the most common disorders presenting in primary care medical settings. *The term "de facto mental health services system" refers to the fact that 50% of the nation's mentally ill receive treatment solely from primary care practitioners and not from psychiatrists or other mental health providers.* Recent epidemiological surveys confirm this trend, showing that psychiatric disorders, particularly depressive disorders, substance use disorders, and anxiety disorders are routinely treated in primary medical care settings.

Psychiatric illnesses such as depression, anxiety, posttraumatic stress disorder (PTSD), and substance abuse have been shown to be associated with significant psychosocial morbidity, excess mortality, and increased cost to society, yet these disorders frequently go undetected and untreated. Only a minority of patients with psychiatric disorders will ever receive treatment, whether from a generalist or specialist regarding these illnesses.

Posttraumatic Stress Disorder

It is important for every primary care physician to be able to recognize and treat PTSD. PTSD is an anxiety disorder that can develop after exposure to a terrifying event or ordeal. Recent studies indicate that as many as 60% of men and 51% of women in the general population report at least one traumatic event at some time in their lives, and 17% of men and 13% of women experience more than three such events. The most common traumatic events include witnessing someone injured or killed; being involved in a fire, flood, or natural disaster; being involved in a life-threatening accident; robbery; or the sudden tragic death or injury of a close relative or friend. Less common, but some times more traumatic, events included molestation, physical attack, rape, combat, and physical abuse. Despite these high rates of trauma, only 10.4% of women and 5% of men actually report experiencing PTSD.

PTSD is a chronic and highly comorbid condition. People who recover spontaneously from PTSD generally do so 3 months after the trauma. About one third of people with PSTD are recovered within a year. After 10 years, over a third of patients with PTSD still experience symptoms several times a week. *Individuals with any PTSD symptoms are at a higher risk for health problems and more likely to experience chronic illnesses.* Studies of combat veterans, rape victims, refugees, hostages, disaster victims, and women with a history of physical and sexual abuse have found that the physical complaints of trauma victims are numerous and serious, resulting in a disproportionate use of health care system and outpatient expenses up to two times as great as those of other health-care users. In many cases, the patient feels that the trauma has no bearing on the present physical complaint. One recent study found that veterans with a history of PTSD had a higher postoperative mortality than those who did not. Individuals with PTSD symptoms are no more likely to seek treatment through the mental health system than nonvictims and, in fact, appear to be even more reluctant than others with emotional problems to seek professional help.

People with PTSD have a high degree of comorbidity. Sixteen percent of patients with PTSD have one other psychiatric diagnosis, 17% have two other psychiatric diagnoses, and nearly 50% have three or more additional psychiatric diagnoses. Even the most conservative studies show that those with PTSD are two to four times more likely to have other psychiatric diagnosis including depressive disorders, anxiety disorders, phobias, substance abuse, or somatization disorders. Somatization was found to be 90 times more likely in those with PTSD than those without it, suggesting an important, but often overlooked connection between PTSD and physical complaints.

TABLE 19.1 Symptoms of PTSD

- Re-experiencing traumatic intrusive images, thoughts, dreams, or flashbacks
- Avoidance of thoughts, feelings, conversations, places, or people associated with trauma and inability to recall important aspects of trauma
- Heightened arousal, including difficulty falling or staying asleep, difficulty concentrating, hypervigilance, exaggerated startle response, and irritability or outbursts of anger
- Withdrawal, including diminished interest or participation in significant activities, sense of foreshortened future, restricted range of affect and feeling of detachment or estrangement from others

---

Depression and Anxiety

Depressive disorders, substance abuse disorders, and anxiety disorders are common in primary medical care settings and constitute a major source of disability. *Depression is without question the most common psychiatric problem that*

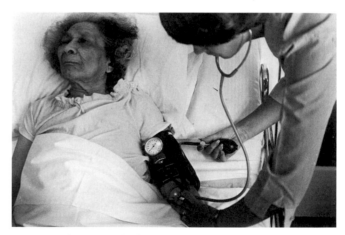

Woman with Depressed Affect Courtesy of the National Institute on Aging. *Learning to recognize depressed affect is a critical clinical skill.*

TABLE 19.2 Symptoms of depression and anxiety

Depression	Anxiety
- feelings of hopelessness	- excessive anxiety and worry, more days than not for at least 6 months
- poor appetite or overeating	- difficulty controlling the worry
- insomnia or hypersomnia	- sleep disturbance
- low energy or fatigue	- easily fatigued; restlessness or feeling keyed up or on edge
- poor concentration or difficulty making decisions	- difficulty concentrating or mind going blank
- low self-esteem	- anxiety causes significant distress or impairment in daily functioning
- suicidal ideation or attempts	- muscle tension
- in children/adolescents can manifest as irritability or angry outbursts	- irritability

Refer to *DSM-IV* for further symptomatology

primary care clinicians encounter. Major depressive disorders develop in 15% of the population (with a higher incidence for women) during their lifetime. An estimated 70% to 80% of these patients will seek treatment from their primary care physician. In addition, almost a third of all patients seeing their primary care physician have a diagnosable anxiety disorder.

TABLE 19.3 Likelihood of birth defects	
Down syndrome:	1/800 births
Cleft lip ± palate:	1/800 births
Spina bifida:	1/1000 births
Fetal alcohol syndrome:	1–2/1000 births

Substance Abuse

Abuse of both legal and illegal substances is common and debilitating in both adults and adolescents. Between 17 to 27% of Americans are affected by substance abuse and dependence over their lifetime. Even higher rates are found in hospitalized patients and in emergency departments. As with other psychiatric problems, substance abuse remains largely undetected and underdiagnosed and is accompanied by stigma and shame.

Substance abuse is linked with multiple health complications, as well as psychosocial problems. For example, smoking has been linked with cancer, cardiovascular disease, and pulmonary disease of various types. In addition, smoking causes complications in conditions such as peptic ulcers and pregnancy, and increased mortality.

Alcoholism, another common substance abuse problem, is the third leading cause of death in this nation. Alcohol is an important contributing factor in half of the motor vehicle accidents, half of homicides, a quarter of suicides, and in a substantial majority of deaths from drowning, fires, poisonings, and falls. Alcohol is also responsible for widespread toxicity of multiple organ systems, including the brain, heart, liver, endocrine system, gastrointestinal system, skeletal muscle, and skin systems. Neurotoxicity is another consequence of alcoholism. Seven organic mental disorders are associated with alcohol, including intoxication, uncomplicated withdrawal, withdrawal delirium, idiosyncratic intoxication, alcohol hallucinosis, alcohol amnestic disorder, and dementia associated with alcoholism. In addition alcohol, often in association with other drugs, is a major contributing factor in cases of domestic violence, child abuse and neglect, homelessness, and a broad range of criminal acts.

Fetal Alcohol Spectrum Disorder (FASD) refers to a range of mental and physical defects that develop in an unborn fetus when the mother drinks alcohol during pregnancy. This alcohol in the bloodstream crosses the placenta and interferes with normal development of the fetus. Some babies born with FASD have distinctive facial characteristics including short palpebral fissures, an indistinct philtrum, and a thin upper lip. With or without these facial characteristics, *children with FASD are often seriously handicapped with symptoms that include growth deficiencies, skeletal deformities, facial abnormalities, organ deformities, and central nervous system handicaps.* Primary care physicians are often the first health-care providers to identify the symptoms of FASD. They can play an important role in educating women of child-bearing age at risk for becoming pregnant about the importance of avoiding all alcohol exposure during pregnancy.

PRIMARY CARE DETECTION

Even though most patients with mental disorders are seen only in primary care settings, these disorders frequently go unrecognized by primary care practitioners. Mental health specialists provide services to only a very small percentage of those with mental health difficulties such as depression, anxiety, PTSD, and substance abuse. Between 15% and 40% of adult primary care patients have diagnosable mental disorders, yet fewer than 20% of these are treated by mental health specialists. Since primary care physicians are those most likely to see patients with psychiatric disorders, it is imperative that they ask patients about traumatic exposure and changes in their home, work, or social life. All competent primary care providers have to be familiar with the symptoms of psychiatric disorders, and they must continually decide whether to refer those patients to mental health professionals.

Adolescents

Adolescents are generally healthy. Few adolescents are hospitalized, and outpatient care typically focuses on relatively minor problems such as colds, sore throats, ear infections, skin and vision problems, and allergies. While adolescents have the lowest utilization of health care services of any age group and are the group least likely to seek care in traditional office-based settings, they are also more likely to be uninsured than any other age group. This is especially true for ethnic minorities and the economically impoverished. Ironically, uninsured adolescents tend to have the most significant health problems, as poverty is associated with increased risk of disease and chronic illness.

About 6% of adolescents between the ages of 10 and 18 years have a chronic condition that limits their daily activities. The major physical disabilities for this group include

> In my experience of anorexia nervosa it is exclusively a disease of private patients.
>
> SIR ADOLF ABRAMS
> British physician

chronic respiratory conditions such as asthma and diseases of the muscle and skeletal system.

The single leading cause of disability among adolescents is not physical disabilities, but mental disorders, which make up 32% of all disabilities for this age group. Approximately 20% of youth under age 18 suffer from developmental, behavioral, or emotional problems. The former U. S. Office of Technology Assessment (OTA) estimates that at least 7.5 million youth under the age of 18 are in need of mental health services, but less than one third of these children receive services.

The suicide rate has increased more rapidly among adolescents than in the rest of the population. Most adolescents who commit suicide have suffered from a psychiatric disorder, including affective disorders (especially depression), conduct disorders, substance abuse, anxiety disorders, eating disorders, and schizophrenia. In the past 60 years, the leading cause of death for adolescents has changed from natural causes to injury and violence. Overall mortality rates for young people rise by 239% when they reach ages 15 to 19, with violence responsible for this dramatic increase. Approximately 80% of the deaths in this age group are from accidents, homicide, or suicide. *With such a high mortality rate among adolescents, it is imperative for primary care providers to be acutely aware of symptoms that may indicate a need for mental health treatment.*

Children

The American Academy of Pediatrics has called for physicians to be more involved with the identification and treatment of chronic psychosocial morbidity in children. As with adults, the rate of identification of mental health problems in children is shockingly low. Primary care physicians vary widely in their ability to correctly identify children as behaviorally or psychiatrically disordered, identifying 0.6% to 16% in different medical settings. Although psychosocial problems are both common and disabling, fewer than 2% of children and adolescents receive care from mental health specialists in any given year. This lack of mental health services for children creates a burden on other service sectors, including schools, child welfare services, correctional facilities, and nonpsychiatric health care providers, particularly primary care physicians.

Many children experience difficulties with emotional regu-

TABLE 19.4 Common behavioral and emotional symptoms of children and adolescents

Internalizing Items

Tires easily, little energy

Is afraid of new situations

Feels sad, unhappy

Feels hopeless

Is down on him or herself

Worries a lot

Seems to have less fun

Externalizing Items

Is irritable, angry

Fights with other children

Takes unnecessary risks

Teases others

Does not listen to rules

Refuses to share

Does not understand other's feelings

Gets upset easily

Teases others Hits others

Blames others for troubles

Hard to control

Items from Child Behavior Checklist (Achenbach, 2009).

---

lation. Emotional regulation is the ability to direct and modify intense feelings. The central focus of emotional regulation is impulse control. One result of lack of control is what are called "externalizing problems," in which emotions are displayed in impulsive anger and attacks on other people or things. Examples of externalizing behaviors include: fighting with others, taking unnecessary risks, and not understanding other's feelings. Others children or adolescents will express their uncontrolled feeling in "internalizing problems," with inhibition or fear being the primary response. Examples of internalizing behaviors include worrying a lot, feeling hopeless, and feeling sad and unhappy.

The relationship between childhood mental disorders and parental mental disorders is strong, and appears to be of both genetic and environmental origin. Between 25 and 50% of the children of mentally ill parents also have psychiatric disorders that require evaluation and follow-up. Several studies have suggested that psychological disturbance in children is more closely related to the degree of parental functional impairment than to the presence of a parental psychiatric diagnosis. High levels of stress and low levels of cohesion and social support have been associated with psychiatric illness in both children and their parents.

As with the adult population, relatively few children are seen by mental health specialists. It is estimated that 5 to 15% of all children under the age of 18 have significant mental health problems, yet only 2% of children with mental health difficulties are seen by mental health specialists. Primary care physicians see about 75% of children with psychiatric disabilities. Pediatricians often play a central role in the detection and management of mental disorders in children.

IDENTIFICATION AND DIAGNOSIS

Some of the obstacles to the diagnosis and treatment of mental disorders in primary care medical settings include physician discomfort with discussions of patients' emotional problem, inadequate training, and economic and time pressures. Physicians who have been taught that psychiatry is somehow separate from the rest of medicine may feel this is not a part of their job. This mind-body split is built into the language of medicine, and dates back to the time of Descartes. Patient resistance to a diagnosis of a psychiatric disorder and mental health treatment is also common in primary care. Primary care patients often do not expect or desire psychosocial assistance for unrecognized mental health problems.

Even if they do feel it is appropriate for them to address mental health concerns, primary care physicians often feel they have not been adequately trained to recognize and manage psychiatric problems. Identifying mental illness is more difficult in primary care settings than in psychiatric settings. Patients in primary care clinics often present with ill-defined or somatic complaints that are not acknowledged or recognized as mental health problems. In psychiatric settings, the mental health problem is the sole focus of care, whereas in primary care, clinicians often manage multiple problems simultaneously and almost never address mental health difficulties separately from other health problems.

Time is also a serious problem. Demands made on physicians have increased steadily over the years. The fundamental demands of practice regarding health monitoring and supervision and management of acute medical problems have remained constant or become more complex. Preventive services including a wide range of screenings, health counseling, and immunization services are routinely expected of primary care physicians. Physicians are concerned about how they can now be also expected to recognize and manage developmental and behavioral problems (e.g., depression or learning and attention-deficit disorders), environmental threats (e.g., family violence, child abuse and neglect), and parenting and family relationship problems

> One evil in old age is, that as your time is come, you think every little illness is the beginning of the end. When a man expects to be arrested, every knock at the door is an alarm.
>
> SYDNEY SMITH
> British essayist
> *Letter to Sir Wilmot-Horton*

One response to the time demands has been an emphasis on screening within primary care settings. *Screening for mental health problems has been popular since 1985 when 46% of physicians reported using questionnaires in their practice.* Screening may be especially important because primary care physicians range so widely in their ability to recognize children with behavioral or psychiatric problems. Since the majority of children with behavioral problems are seen by primary care providers, researchers across the country have focused on screening in pediatric practices as a way to assist in proper identification of this population. For the adult population, screening for depression, anxiety, and substance abuse is critical in primary care settings.

Unfortunately, studies have consistently found that primary care physicians underrecognize mental health problems. For example, in one study of screening of 2 to 18-year-olds, pediatricians had low sensitivity and high specificity in their identification of psychiatric disorders; in other words, they failed to detect many positive cases but seldom misidentified negative cases. This is important because lack of recognition can be expensive in terms of money as well as human suffering. In a study of utilization and cost of health and psychiatric care the average cost of health care per child was $393 for one year of medical services within an HMO. The average health care cost for children with symptoms of anxiety and depression was more than twice as high. When psychosocial dysfunction was present, regression models showed that health care spending was highest for young children.

The social stigma associated with depression and the lack of integration of mental health services into primary care pose additional barriers to effective treatment. Part of the reason most patients with major depression are treated exclusively by primary care physicians is the poor response to referrals. When depressed patients are referred to mental health specialists, as many as half do not follow through and keep their appointment. In one study, only 19% of those children identified positively as having clinically sig-

> Everyone who is born holds dual citizenship in the kingdom of the well and in the kingdom of the sick.
>
> SUSAN SONTAG
> *Illness as Metaphor*

Home Health and Institutional Placement

Family members confronting the difficult decision of whether to place a relative in an institution often turn to their family physician for advice. Explicit criteria for the physician to use in counseling a family include regular incontinence of bladder and bowel, inability of the relative to cooperate in their care, inability of the relative to realize that a home with familiar caregivers is stable and secure, risk to the health or mental stability of others in the home, and primary caregiver burnout. Options available to families include assisted living facilities, general nursing homes, and nursing homes with locked units and mental health expertise. A midlevel alternative might be mental and physical health services in the home setting provided by a mental health nurse who has a sophisticated understanding of assessment tools and treatment protocols such as clinical pathways.

Rehabilitation Strategies

Chronic psychiatric disorders limit an individual's ability to function in multiple spheres, including practical aspects of daily living and coping strategies. For the more impaired psychotic and depressed patients, socialization, activities of daily living, time management, and organization are important areas of treatment. When integrated into a comprehensive treatment plan that includes psychotropic medication, psychotherapy, and other treatment modalities, psychosocial rehabilitation offers the patient and their families important assistance with these practical matters.

SUMMARY

It is essential to train physicians to recognize mental illness. Psychosocial and psychiatric conditions affect a large number of patients, and their pain goes unrecognized and untreated.

Medical science illuminates the delicate balance between mind and body. Learning to recognize and treat the whole human being is an essential skill for tomorrow's primary care physicians.

CASE STUDY

A 17-year-old female college student is brought to the emergency department of your hospital in a coma. She was diagnosed 2 years ago with diabetes mellitus. Several candy bar wrappers were found in her backpack at the time of her hospitalization as well as some writings in her notebook expressing suicidal thoughts. When she wakes up she refuses to speak to anyone. Her roommates report that lately she has been keeping to herself and hiding out in her room. She sleeps a lot, but still has trouble getting up for class. She is irritable and becomes angry easily, and her grades are slipping. She doesn't go out as much with friends anymore and seems to have gained weight in the last few months.

How would you manage this patient? Would behavior modification programs such as self-monitoring be appropriate? Should the patient be referred to psychiatry for evaluation of her depression and her potential risk for suicide? Are the patient's problems primarily psychiatric or medical? Do you need this young woman's permission to discuss her case with her parents?

Depression is very common and primary care physicians need to be aware of the symptoms in adolescents and young adults. Suicide is one of the leading causes of death for young adults, further underscoring the importance of vigilance on the part of physicians for the development of depression. In general, studies have shown that between 1 and 2 years after the initial diagnosis of a chronic illness, patients go through a second adjustment, realizing "this is for life." In cases of chronic illness, anticipatory guidance for families to understand that this period of adjustment may occur in the second year after diagnosis is helpful. Noncompliance with treatment is a very common issue during adolescence and may extend into young adulthood. Interventions that enable children and adolescents to deal realistically with the "this is for life" response are important, as is education on the short- and long-term consequences of noncompliance with treatment. Young adults and their families should be referred to psychiatry to deal with depression and for help adjusting to the realities of life with a chronic illness. At 17 the patient is still a minor even though she is attending college, so her parents will need to be consulted.

Your patient is discharged after a brief psychiatric consultation suggests she is not acutely suicidal. However, you schedule an appointment with her for the following week and discover she has continued to lose weight. Her vital signs and EKG are within normal limits.

Would a patient like this benefit from antidepressant medication? Is bed rest and a restricted diet advisable? Will you want this young woman and her parents and siblings to be in family therapy? Should she be hospitalized?

Your patient was able to recover from her acute symptoms and does not require a more intensive level of psychiatric care at this time. However, her progress should be monitored from both a physical and psychological perspective.

After 6 months you note that your patient has been only

partially compliant with treatment and she continues to lose weight. She returns for her weekly medical appointment and discloses to the RN who is weighing her that she knows how to access her father's gun and has been thinking about killing herself. She begs the nurse not to tell you about her suicidal thoughts, but the nurse feels you must be informed that your patient has a plan for killing herself and she has selected a method that is clearly lethal.

Is a suicide threat a medical problem or a legal issue? Should you call 911 or the police? Will you want this patient on antidepressant medication at this point? How long will you have to wait for the medication to take effect? Should she be hospitalized or simply seen the following day? Is this a case that a primary care doctor should handle or would it be advisable to ask for a psychiatrist, clinical psychologist, or social worker to consult on this case? What is your responsibility if you are convinced the patient should be in the hospital but her insurance company disagrees and refuses to accept your recommendation?

Suicidality is a common psychiatric emergency among patients with eating disorders. As such, it should be assessed and evaluated by a mental health professional. It is probably most prudent to consult with a psychiatrist in this case because of the likelihood that antidepressant medication will need to be prescribed. The psychiatrist in turn may elect to work with a social work or psychology colleague. It is your obligation to make the best medical decisions possible, and your patient will have to negotiate with her insurance company to ensure she receives appropriate coverage for her medical expenses. You can work as her advocate in these negotiations; however, your psychiatry colleague may be in a better position to argue that inpatient psychiatric care is essential for this young woman.

SUGGESTED READINGS

Gillespie, C.F., Bradley, B. Mercer, K., Smith, A.K., Conneely, K., Gapen, M., Weiss, T., Schwartz, A.C., Cubells, J.F., & Ressler, K.J. (2009). Trauma exposure and stress-related disorders in inner city primary care patients. *General Hospital Psychiatry, 31,* 505–514.
A current view on the prevalence of PTSD and stress in a primary care setting.

Kashikar-Zuck, S., Goldschneider, K., Powers, S., Vaught, M., & Hershey, A. (2004). Depression and functional disability in chronic pediatric pain. *The Clinical Journal of Pain, 34,* 341–349.
This article defines succinctly for physicians the quality of life issues associated with depression for children.

Nimalasuriya, K., Compton, M.T., & Guillory, V.J. (2009). Screening adults for depression in primary care: A position statement of the American College of Preventive Medicine. *Journal of Family Practice, 58,* 535–538.
These are the most recent recommendations on depression screening for adults in family medicine.

Managing Difficult Patients

Brenda Bursch

> It is not a case we are treating; it is a living, palpitating, alas, too often suffering fellow creature.
>
> JOHN BROWN
> Edinburgh physician and author

Most health-care providers have a desire and feel a responsibility to be helpful to their patients. It is typically assumed that the patients have a similar desire; they want to be cured, and they can and will act in their own best interests. It takes very little time and experience for most physicians to recognize that the practice of medicine is far more complex than this idealistic formula. *No matter how caring and tolerant you are as a physician, it is likely that you will have patients that you find yourself dreading*, patients with whom you feel frustrated or confused or angry. You might feel guilty about such feelings, or you might feel that it is not within your power to help these patients. The purpose of this chapter is to describe management strategies you can use to help challenging patients more effectively obtain the care they need from you.

WHO ARE THE "DIFFICULT" PATIENTS?

Approximately 15% of patient encounters are perceived as "difficult" by physicians. Physicians report they are most frustrated by patients who require much of their time and do not follow medical recommendations. Contrary to what might be expected, it is not the medically complex patients who are considered difficult, but patients who are seen as demanding, aggressive, rude, seeking secondary gain, or having multiple nonspecific psychosomatic complaints. Patients seen as "difficult" frequently have a depressive or anxiety disorders, alcohol abuse or dependence, a personality disorder, unexplained somatic symptoms, or more se-

vere symptoms. They also have poorer functional status, more unmet expectations related to their medical encounters, less satisfaction with their medical care, and higher use of health services.

Perhaps equally important, clinicians with poorer psychosocial attitudes rate more patients as difficult. Additionally, physicians who report high frustration with patients have been found to be less experienced and more stressed; they are more likely to be under 40 years old, to work over 55 hours per week, to practice in a subspecialty, and to have more patients with psychosocial or substance abuse problems.

In 1978 Grove proposed four categories to describe patients who are seen by physicians as difficult: dependent clingers, entitled demanders, manipulative help-rejecters, and self-destructive deniers. Although these category terms may be unnecessarily pejorative, the accompanying descriptions are useful. **Dependent clingers** exhaust their doctors and caregivers with requests and needs—for explanation, affection, analgesics, sedatives and attention. It is not uncommon for clinicians to feel aversion in response to a patient they view as highly needy. It is helpful to remember that individuals who have an insatiable need for attention are not happy and have no intention of provoking feelings of aversion in their clinicians. Regardless of the medical problems present in highly needy patients, *the most effective and helpful intervention can be to arrange predictable, limited, and appropriate types of attention for them.*

Entitled demanders often use guilt, intimidation, or threats to manipulate clinicians. Not surprisingly, such patients' threats are ultimately self-defeating since clinicians become fearful of them and often respond with anger, sometimes striking back at the patient. Surprisingly, *patients who appear angry or threatening are often quite frightened.* They may be extremely fearful of abandonment by the medical team, loss of control, receiving suboptimal care, or numerous other possible consequences of their situation. It is especially important that clinicians remain nondefensive and agree with angry and demanding patients that they have a right to a high quality of care. It can be very helpful to remember that these patients are fundamentally fearful and potentially in need of guidance regarding how to more effectively communicate with the treatment team.

Manipulative help-rejecters, sometimes called "crocks" by frustrated clinicians, have symptoms that seemingly can never be relieved or that continually change over time. Some even appear to derive satisfaction from the failures of the clinicians, perhaps pleased that they can maintain their relationship with the clinician as long as they have symptoms. *Common emotional reactions experienced by physicians to this type of patient include worry about overlooking a treatable illness, irritation with the patient, helplessness, and self-doubt.* Not surprisingly, patients often have the same feelings. They are worried about a potentially lethal disease being missed, they worry that they will not be believed, they worry that they really are crazy, they become frustrated with clinicians who cannot explain or fix their symptoms, and they feel helpless. It is essential that the clinician communicate with these patients using language which conveys a biopsychosocial model, and *avoid the temptation to dichotomize problems as either physical or mental.* If rapport is established, a focus on functioning with a rehabilitation approach can be effective.

Self-destructive deniers deny the need for self-care to the point of being self-destructive; they could be considered chronically suicidal, though they would be more likely to admit to hopelessness than acknowledge suicidal ideation. Some may appear to find meaning in observing their own demise. Clinicians may feel a desire to save these patients or they may sometimes covertly wish the patient would die. Because it is hard for these patients to see that they are potentially contributing to their own deterioration, it is important to gently confront their denial by being supportively explicit about the choices they have, by acknowledging any healthy decisions or actions they take, and by pointing out any unhealthy decisions they are making.

THE PHYSICIAN'S FRAME OF REFERENCE

It can be extremely rewarding to successfully treat, or minimize **iatrogenic harm** in, a patient that other clinicians have deemed difficult or untreatable. As might be clear from the previous section, *it is possible to use your reactions to patients as a diagnostic tool to help you discern what your patient is feeling and what he or she needs.* Not surprisingly, you may have some patients with elements of several of the emotions and actions previously described.

The first essential frame of reference to adopt is that *anyone can be difficult.* This includes you, especially when you are stressed. It is far more useful to think of an appointment as difficult, while refraining from labeling a person as difficult. After all, few people feel good about being angry, needy, or self-destructive. Some patients become difficult over time as they realize it is the only way to get their needs met within our healthcare system; essentially, we (doctors and health care organizations) have trained and rewarded them to be difficult during medical encounters.

It is possible to learn how to manage difficult patient encounters in a manner that will help both you and your patient. Once you adopt this frame of reference and develop good management skills, you might even find yourself fascinated, energized, or satisfied by initially difficult patient encounters.

The next step is to recognize that *you will see patients under unusual times of stress.* You have chosen a career that will require you to be in contact with highly distressed individuals. People are more vulnerable to illness and injury when extremely stressed. Additionally, *injury and illness is stressful to most people under the best of circumstances.* Most clinicians are not born with the intuitive knowledge about how to best handle these situations. Consequently, it is essential that you obtain training in managing difficult situations with a focus on behavioral responses when under stress.

It can be important to separate what is being said from how it is being said. It is normal to respond to both *what* your patient is telling you as well as *how* your patient is communicating with you. It is also normal to have a harder time hearing what is being said if you are disturbed by how it is being communicated to you. While much can be learned by how your patient is communicating, it is important to remember that important information can be easily be lost if communicated poorly. Making a conscious decision to consider the content of a message and the patient's communication style separately can be very helpful during difficult patient encounters. This simple technique can help you better understand your patient as well as the experiences of other involved clinicians. You can then decide, and discuss with your team members, which aspects of the communication are most relevant and require your response, and which aspects are best ignored.

You can respond in ways that improve the situation or make it worse. There will be days that challenge your patience and endurance. There will be patients that you feel are unaffected by your recommendations or concerns. There will be situations over which you have no control. Nevertheless, the choices you make in difficult patient encounters can significantly alter the course of the exchange, your day in general, and your relationship with your patient. Even with the most challenging patient encounter, you have choices in your responses that can potentially create a positive experience.

MANAGING PATIENT EXPECTATIONS

Unmet patient expectations can lead to difficult patient encounters, as well as decreased patient satisfaction and increased health care utilization. *Dissatisfied patients are less likely to adhere to medical recommendations, follow-up with appointments, or enjoy symptom improvement, and they are far more likely to change health-care providers.* Primary care patients frequently expect to obtain information during a medical appointment, and do not necessarily expect med-

---

CASE EXAMPLE

Mr. Eastman is the father of a 4-year-old girl undergoing a bone marrow transplant. The Director of the hospital calls you to let you know that Mr. Eastman complained that you did not sufficiently wash your hands before examining his daughter. When you get to the hospital room, Mr. Eastman starts to loudly complain about a stain on the floor. You are angry that he complained about you and feel he is being extremely unreasonable. You can respond in several ways; here are two options:

You can ask Mr. Eastman to refrain from complaining and inform him that he is being unreasonable in his expectations.	You can sincerely acknowledge Mr. Eastman's fear for his daughter's life and discuss the rationale behind and reasonable goals for contagion precautions.

While either approach might stop Mr. Eastman from complaining so loudly for the moment, the second approach is more likely to facilitate a beneficial (and perhaps enjoyable) discussion that will strengthen the trust in your relationship and help your patient's father cope with the stress and tension he is experiencing in this frightening situation.

CASE EXAMPLE

Mrs. Robinson, who is somewhat shy, comes in with flu-like symptoms. An appointment can take two directions from the start depending on your assessment of patient expectations.

APPROACH 1

"Good morning Mrs. Robinson, I see from the nurse's note that you aren't feeling well. What symptoms are you having today?" *Note: This question assumes she wants a diagnosis and treatment plan.*	You learn she is having flu-like symptoms. You are annoyed that so many people with the flu come in for antibiotics. You explain to her that she probably has the flu but does not need antibiotics.

APPROACH 2

"Good morning Mrs. Robinson, I see from the nurse's note that you aren't feeling well. What can I do for you today?" *Note: This question lets her set the agenda.*	You learn she is worried that she might have HIV and wants to learn more about how it is transmitted. You then do some patient education, take a risk history, and decide if an HIV test is indicated.

The second approach is far more likely to meet Mrs. Robinson's real needs, and she will be much more satisfied with both the physician and the encounter.

ical tests or referrals. However, physicians often fail to accurately perceive patients' expectations, and *an estimated 15% to 25% of primary care patients do not have their expectations met during a medical appointment.* Consequently, assessing patient expectations is an important first step to improving patient satisfaction and possibly other health outcomes. Patient expectations can include being examined, having medical tests ordered, being referred to another clinician, being given a prescription, receiving education about a problem (including the normal trajectory and available treatments for an illness), receiving education about a treatment (including administration instructions, expected effects/side effects, expected improvements, and related timelines), and/or ways to self-manage a problem. *Although simple, the best way to ensure you are meeting your patients' expectations is by asking them what they are hoping to get out of their appointment rather than simply assuming that they want what you have offered.*

It is also important to help your patient develop appropriate expectations about his or her health, illness, treatment, and/or need for self-care. Having expectations that are too high or too low can lead to less than optimal health and functioning. Written patient educational materials can be of great assistance in helping patients set realistic and appropriate expectations. Consider the following patient's expectations after hip replacement surgery:

CASE EXAMPLE

Expectations Too Low	Expectations Too High
Mr. Hart had heard that most people die within 1 year of hip replacement surgery. Therefore, he decided there was no need to put himself through physical therapy and it was pointless to try to walk again. He requested a wheelchair and started to get his affairs in order.	Mrs. McKinney had heard that hip replacement surgery was wonderful. However, she became very upset when her physical therapist asked her to engage in therapeutic exercises that caused pain. In addition, she was surprised that her recovery took so long. She knew some people took longer to improve, but had expected she would complete her recovery in no more than 2 weeks.

MANAGING DIFFICULT PATIENT ENCOUNTERS

The Angry Patient

Anger is almost always a secondary emotion, and a protective response to another emotion. It can be effective at

---

CASE EXAMPLE

Mr. Martellino is a 53-year-old man who has been in the waiting room for over 2 hours. This is partly because he was 45 minutes early, but it is also true that your last patient required considerable time and had to be hospitalized. Mr. Martellino is furious and yells loudly at you for wasting his time. He threatens to change health plans and wants to file a complaint. You have been on call all night and feel like walking out of the room.

Issues to consider:

- Safety. Is Mr. Martellino simply blowing off steam or is he being physically threatening too?
- Most people do not yell in this type of situation, and there likely is more to the story of Mr. Martellino's anger. For example, there might be something else he is angry or scared about; the delay may have seriously upset his schedule for the day; and/or Mr. Martellino's neurological functioning may be impaired.
- Most people would be angry and frustrated in a similar situation.

Communication tips:

- Avoid responding in an angry manner. This rarely improves a situation.
- Apologize and explain that an urgent patient issue delayed you.
- If the patient continues to yell, allow him to complete the outburst. Again, apologize and acknowledge the frustration. Respectfully ask the patient if he wishes to continue with his appointment or if he feels too upset or behind schedule to proceed.
- Help the patient switch topics by talking about the reason he came in today.
- Carefully document the exchange. While the outburst may have been situational, it is also helpful to track the episodes as part of your assessment. Additionally, it is helpful to have documented the event if a complaint is filed.

---

blocking the physical or emotional pain associated with fear, criticism, or perceived injustice. *Anger can also be a symptom of numerous emotional and neurological disorders.* Regardless of the etiology of the anger, it is helpful to remember that your angry patient might be feeling very vulnerable. Because an angry patient can create much distress for all clinicians involved, it is especially important to remember to check your frame of reference. Consider the anger as potentially part of the clinical presentation, and do not allow it to trigger an angry response from you.

The exchange will go best if you can remain calm, consider the message content and the communication style of your patient separately, and treat your patient respectfully. Regardless of the reason for the anger, it is important to first consider your safety. Do you need to have someone else in the room with you, have an escape route, or call security? If it appears there is no physical danger present, attempt to de-escalate the anger as quickly as possible. Potentially helpful interventions include remaining nondefensive; determining what the patient is angry about, apologizing for any errors or inconveniences, even if they were not your fault (apologies can prevent lawsuits); agreeing that all patients have a right to a high quality of care; smiling and maintaining a soft voice; asking what the patient would like at this time; and attempting to refocus the patient in a productive direction.

The Pain Patient

Clinicians often dread seeing patients with chronic pain or other symptoms that do not conform to an identifiable disease or do not respond as expected to treatment. Such patients often trigger worry in clinicians about having missed a diagnosis on the one hand or contributing to an addiction on the other hand. *You should assume that the symptoms are genuine and explainable, even when there is an absence of obvious tissue pathology or inflammation to explain the symptoms.* Persistent physical symptoms that are not fully explained by medical illness or tissue pathology are common and are often referred to as functional symptoms and disorders. These symptoms are caused by altered physiological function (the way the body works) rather than by structural abnormality.

Functional disorders are not diagnosed with x-rays or laboratory tests, but with symptom-based criteria. Examples of functional disorders include headaches, irritable bowel syndrome (IBS), and nonepileptic seizures. There is a growing research interest in identifying the biological mechanisms contributing to persistent somatic symptoms (for example, hypersensitivity in the gastrointestinal tract associated with IBS). The key to working effectively with patients with functional disorders is to *avoid the temptation to dichotomize problems as either physical or mental*, and to become highly adept at understanding all illness within a **biopsychosocial context**. The biopsychosocial model posits that illness is the product of biological, psychological, and social subsystems interacting at multiple levels. For example, biological factors contributing to functional abdominal pain include changes in intestinal wall sensory receptors, modulation of sensory transmissions in the nervous system, cortical perceptions, and physiological responses to pain memories. Psychological factors that might contribute include temperament, increased focus on pain-related stimuli, emotional responses to pain, pain memories, and efforts to cope with and manage pain. Relevant social factors can include family history of pain, family member responses to pain, and stressful life events. Other correlates of functional somatic symptoms include substance use, comorbid anxiety disorders, prior medical illness, physical injury, hospitalization, and a history of trauma.

A multimodal rehabilitation approach is recommended rather than a sequential single treatment approach. Interventions should address possible underlying symptom

---

CASE EXAMPLE

Mrs. Rockwood is a 35-year-old woman who experienced a severed Achilles tendon while playing tennis. She had an unremarkable surgery and appears to be healing well, but now complains of severe pain. There is no indication of an infection or other explanation for her pain. She requests a higher dose of pain medication than is normally prescribed at this point in time for such surgeries. You are worried about providing the higher dose of the medication.

Issues to consider:
- Did she over-use her limb, sustain another injury, or develop a complication?
- Does she have risk factors for development of a chronic pain disorder or for opioid intolerance (for example, past injuries, comorbid anxiety, or past opioid use)?
- Does she or another family member have a substance use problem?
- Does she recognize that physical therapy is normally painful?

Communication tips:
- Accept that the patient is experiencing more pain than is typical.
- Determine specific concerns and situations that elicit greater pain.
- Evaluate for complications, comorbid problems, and exacerbating factors.
- Evaluate past injury, surgery, and opioid use behavior. Patients who previously developed tolerance for opioids often require higher doses, even years later.
- Describe a rehabilitation approach to recovery. If indicated, *encourage a focus on functioning rather than pain*. Set expectations: Physical therapy may not improve pain while functioning is still improving.
- Provide recommendations that include medications and non-medication approaches to pain management.

---

mechanisms, specific symptoms, and disability. In general, treatment goals should focus on increasing independent functioning (activities of daily living, vocational, social, and physical); remediation of specific symptoms, deficits, or problems revealed in the assessment; enhancing communication, especially of distress, with peers and family members; and facilitating more adaptive problem-solving skills. Treatment techniques designed to address possible underlying specific symptoms and mechanisms include cognitive-behavioral strategies (e.g., cognitive behavioral psychotherapy, self-hypnosis, or biofeedback), behavioral techniques, family interventions, physical interventions (e.g., massage, acupuncture, transcutaneous electrical nerve stimulation (TENS), physical therapy, occupational therapy), and pharmacological interventions.

In general, *interventions that promote active coping are preferred over those that require passive dependence.* Evidence based treatments should be recommended whenever possible.

The Seductive Patient

Seductive patients solicit your interest and caretaking of them by exhibiting excessive admiration, affection, and flattery. These behaviors can initially seem comforting and benign to a clinician. The desire for a safe, supportive relationship is probably the most common motivation for patients to act seductively toward their physicians. However, clinicians can easily become over involved with patients who make them feel skilled, smart, attractive, or powerful, especially when the clinician is personally stressed. Clinicians need to be especially aware of their own vulnerability during times of acute or extreme stress, such as by a death or divorce, an ill family member, or excessive work. *It is important to remember that seductive patients may have a history of emotional problems and often have been victims of abuse, including incest, rape, and physical abuse.*

CASE EXAMPLE

Ms. Cooke is a 26-year-old unmarried woman who is new in town and comes in for her annual physical exam. She is highly attractive and very friendly. She brings you cookies and asks if you need any help in your office. She recently went through a difficult break-up and would like to take her mind off of it by doing some volunteer work for you. She found your name on the Internet and is impressed by your work. You are very flattered and feel tempted to take her up on the offer to organize your office.

Issues to consider:

• Safety. Is Ms. Cooke simply friendly and helpful, or could she be stalking you?
• Most people do not offer to volunteer to work for their physician, especially a new one; there is likely more to Ms. Cooke's offer. For example, she might be experiencing a personal crisis, have a history of becoming overly close to professionals, have a family member with the disease you are studying, and/or come from a very small town where this is normal behavior.
• What are some potential complications from working with your patient?

Communication tips:

• Avoid responding in an overtly rejecting manner. This rarely improves a situation.
• Thank the patient for her kind offer and state your policy on the topic (for example, not using patient volunteers, not using volunteers of any type, or not needing someone at the moment).
• Encourage volunteering through established community or hospital volunteer programs.
• Avoid sending conflicting messages to the patient. Maintain friendly, but professional communication and contact at all times.
• Carefully document the exchange. While the offer may have been perfectly innocent, it is also helpful to track the behavior as part of your assessment. Additionally, it is helpful to have the documentation if it ever becomes necessary to terminate treatment or in the event a complaint is filed.

The ethics codes of the American Medical Association (1995–2009) and the American Osteopathic Association (2003–2009) outline the physician's duty to act in the best interests of patients, including refraining from exploiting the doctor-patient relationship. *This duty includes "key third parties," such as those who may accompany your patients to medical visits or hospitalizations.*

This stance is based on two basic premises: (1) the patient-doctor relationship is nonreciprocal, and the physician has more power than the patient, and (2) professional medical objectivity is often lost when a physician enters into a personal intimate relationship with a patient. Research clearly documents that when physicians become intimate with patients, the patients often suffer lasting emotional harm. Warning signs that you may be becoming overly involved include telling your favorite patient about your personal problems, spending more time with the patient than is allotted for a minor problem, scheduling him or her for the end of the day, offering free or substantially discounted care, exchanging gifts, making plans to see the patient outside the office, and/or spending considerable time on the telephone with your patient.

CASE EXAMPLE

Mr. Finley, a 42-year-old man, who is new to your clinic, presents for a routine annual checkup. You perform the examination with your female medical assistant present. Two weeks later the patient returns and says, "I just had to see you again." During the office visit, he talks about a current difficult relationship and indicates that he is looking for someone new to care for him. He asks if you are interested in going out to dinner. You inform him that you are flattered, but not interested, and that you do not date patients. You document the behavior in the medical record. The next day, flowers and a card are delivered to you from the patient, again asking for a date and teasing that he won't take "no" for an answer since he feels you are meant to be together.

Issues to consider:

• Safety. Is Mr. Finley simply being friendly, or could he be stalking you?
• Do you need to obtain consultation from risk management, a colleague, or a mental health professional?

Communication tips:

• Do not meet alone with the patient.
• Avoid responding in an overtly rejecting manner; however, your message must be clear and definite. Restate your policy on the topic (not dating any patients *or former patients*).
• Remind your patient that it can sometimes be helpful to see a therapist when having painful and difficult relationship problems. Provide referrals.
• Inform the patient in writing that you wish to terminate care and that you recommend he see a physician of the other gender; provide referrals and offer to have records transferred.
• Carefully document the exchange in the medical record.
• Do not respond to future cards, flowers, or other gifts.

Beware of the young doctor and the old barber.

BENJAMIN FRANKLIN

It is important to understand what it is that the seductive patient is attempting to gain by his or her behaviors, to communicate clearly with the patient about your role as a physician, to avoid sending mixed messages, to discourage the seductive behavior, to document in the medical record any seductive behavior exhibited by your patient, to encourage your patient to obtain support from a mental health professional if indicated, to obtain consultation from a colleague if you unsure if a patient is being seductive, and to refer to another clinician if needed. Never ignore seductive behavior, even if you think it is likely to be harmless.

Likewise, *failing to document your patient's unusual behavior is like failing to document a fever. Not only is it clinically pertinent, but it will also be important to have the information in the medical record if the situation escalates into a legal problem.*

While some patients might be obviously inappropriate, it might be less clear in other situations.

In situations with clearly inappropriate attempts to seduce you, a more aggressive response can sometimes be necessary.

The Noncompliant Patient

Clinicians are often frustrated when they discover that a patient has not adhered to medical recommendations, perhaps not recognizing that roughly 75% of patients do not follow all medical recommendations all of the time. On average, adherence has been found to be best among patients with HIV, arthritis, gastrointestinal disorders, and cancer, and worst among patients with pulmonary disease, diabetes, and sleep disorders. Better adherence is associated with less complex recommendations (taking medication vs. changing health behaviors). Reasons for not adhering to medical recommendations vary and the patient is not always aware of the fact that he or she did not follow their physician's recommendations.

Possibilities to consider are that the patient

- does not understand the seriousness of the condition and/or the instructions provided. This can occur because of language problems, comprehension difficulties,

a physician's desire to maintain a positive attitude or protect a patient from bad news, inadequate patient education, and/or a patient feeling overwhelmed and, thus, being unable to absorb the information;
- forgets the recommendation or instruction;
- is angry, depressed, guilty, worn out, frightened, traumatized, or embarrassed by the condition or needed treatment;
- is uncomfortable with the physician;
- disagrees with the physician;
- meets emotional needs by visits to the doctor, and nonadherence increases contact;
- has treatment goals that differ from those of the physician.

It may also be that the medical recommendations

- cause unacceptable side effects;
- are too complex or time consuming;
- are too frightening or anxiety provoking;
- are too expensive, and/or transportation to obtain the treatment is too expensive;
- are not consistent with patient beliefs.

As with many of the problem encounters discussed in this chapter, careful planning pays off and prevention is always the best cure. To enhance adherence, during the initial evaluation and treatment planning and during subsequent points of treatment planning:

- Determine your patient's understanding of the problem or disease.
- Ask about religious or cultural factors that might influence thoughts about the problem and treatment.
- Assess the interest and ability of your patient, or the caregiver, to participate in decisions and self-care.
- Educate your patient and family (when indicated) about the medical condition.
- Develop treatment goals jointly with your patient.
- Include the patient and family (when indicated) in planning the treatment.
- Ask the patient if they think the plan will work for them.
- Provide your patient with specific, clear, and printed instructions.
- Review how you will communicate with your patient (appointments, calls, email).
- Document all instructions given to the patient and all discussions about the treatment regimen.

Once you have detected nonadherence, the following approaches may be useful:

CASE EXAMPLE

Mr. Golden is a 68-year-old man recovering from hip replacement surgery. He indicates that he no longer has the strength to ambulate and is requesting a wheelchair. The physical therapist reports to you that Mr. Golden is simply not interested in rehabilitation. Mr. Golden states that he is old enough to have wheelchair and it is wrong to push him into physical therapy. Mr. Golden is otherwise quite healthy; he is married, has several grandchildren living nearby, and he previously played golf 3 days per week. You are extremely frustrated by his reluctance to engage in physical therapy and understand that he is risking his Medicare coverage if he does not make progress.

Issues to consider:
- Does Mr. Golden have a comorbid medical condition interfering with adherence?
- Is he depressed, scared, angry, frustrated, in pain, embarrassed, or guilty?
- Have there been changes in his psychosocial situation?
- What does he believe about his prognosis? Does he believe that he will not live much longer?

Communication tips:
- Avoid responding in an angry manner. This rarely improves a situation.
- Attempt to engage him in conversation about his emotional response to his situation.
- Normalize his feelings (for example, it is normal to be fearful of falling again, angry at his physical therapist, or sad about his decline in health).
- Correct any information that is likely to be incorrect (for example, he might believe that all people die shortly after hip replacements, that physical therapy is not normally as frightening as he is experiencing it to be, or that he will die at age 70, just like his father did).
- Provide education regarding the normal course of recovery, the self-care requirements for optimal recovery, and the risks of not making progress.
- Point out the healthy decisions made by the patient (for example, making the decision to proceed with the surgery, completing all the postsurgical medications).
- Gently point out the unhealthy decisions made by the patient (for example, skipping physical therapy sessions and avoiding particular exercises).
- Assess his life goals and treatment priorities.
- Have a problem-solving discussion about what would help him engage in physical therapy.

Age and eyesight may be two factors affecting adherence Courtesy of the National Institute on Aging.

- Be willing to compromise.
- Prioritize the treatment goals.
- Simplify the treatment.
- Engage your patient in problem-solving to increase investment in adherence.
- Treat co-morbid symptoms or disorders interfering with adherence.
- Document observations and discussions.
- Consider terminating your relationship with the patient if you feel they would be better served elsewhere.

The Needy/Demanding Patient

Needy patients generally want frequent contact with you. They may have endless questions or concerns; they may have frequent requests for further assessments or specific treatments; they may expect that rules and schedules will be altered to accommodate them. In some cases, multiple family members may want contact with you. For clinicians who attempt to avoid disappointing patients and families at all costs, these patients can be enormously draining. The best way to ensure quality care and reasonable burden is to develop and adhere to practice guidelines. These guidelines

- Consider the nonadherence a symptom and develop a differential diagnosis to determine the underlying explanation.
- Ask the patient why they are engaging in a specific behavior. "Why are you skipping your evening medication?"
- Do not criticize your patient.

CASE EXAMPLE

Miss Gracie is a 44-year-old woman with recurrent urinary tract infections. She is highly concerned about this problem and spends much of her time researching her disorder. She makes frequent telephone calls to you to discuss her hypotheses about her medical problem (for example, a primary immune deficiency) and alternate treatment approaches (for example, herbs and acupuncture). You find yourself dreading these calls and even start to wonder if she really has recurrent UTIs. You want her to feel less anxious, but it seems nothing helps her anxiety. You really wish she would find another doctor.

Issues to consider:
- Why are you dreading her calls?
- Does Miss Gracie have good ideas?
- Do you need to do your own literature search or consult a colleague?
- Does she take your advice?
- Have there been changes in her psychosocial situation?
- Does she have any comorbid medical or psychiatric problems?

Communication tips:
- Be sure to take her questions seriously; it will not help the situation to train her that physicians are unhelpful.
- Do your research; a seemingly unconventional idea might have an evidence base to support trying it.
- Attempt to understand what you dread about this patient so that you can directly address the problem.
- Avoid responding in an angry or rejecting manner. This rarely improves a situation.
- Attempt to engage her in conversation about her emotional response to his situation. How is she coping with this recurrent problem?
- Make an agreement with her regarding when and how she can contact you. For example, you might ask her to make weekly appointments with you, but to restrain from calling with questions between appointments.

should be shared with every patient at the initial visit and should be repeated for those who ignore them. If multiple family members are involved, either have one designated family spokesperson or meet with the family as a group.

TERMINATING A PATIENT RELATIONSHIP

Once you have accepted a patient into your care, you have an ethical and legal obligation to provide services as long as the patient requires them. However, there are times when is it acceptable to terminate a patient relationship, as long as you do so in a conscientious manner. You may consider terminating a patient relationship when the patient is unmanageably noncompliant, unreasonably demanding, or

threatening, or when it is simply not possible to develop a good rapport. There are also times you may have to end the relationship because you are moving, retiring, or changing jobs. Patient abandonment is a legal term referring to the termination of a physician-patient relationship at a critical stage of treatment, without good reason, and without giving the patient adequate time to find another comparably qualified physician. The AMA's Council on Ethical and Judicial Affairs considers patient abandonment, as described above, to be unethical and explicitly states that the patient's failure to pay a bill is itself not sufficient justification for terminating a therapeutic relationship. To avoid the legal and ethical problems associated with patient abandonment, in 1998 the American Medical Association, Office of the General Counsel, summarized appropriate steps that should be taken to terminate a patient-physician relationship. They include:

1. Giving the patient written notification by certified mail, return receipt requested;
2. Providing the patient with a reason for the termination (e.g., inability to achieve/maintain rapport, noncompliance, or failure to keep appointments);
3. Agreeing to provide ongoing care for a reasonable period of time (typically 30 days; your letter should include an anticipated date of termination) to allow a patient to find another physician;
4. Providing general referrals (such as local medical societies, hospital medical staffs, or community resources) to help a patient locate another comparable physician; and
5. Offering to transfer records to the new physician (if provided signed consent to do so).

Particularly risky times to attempt a patient termination include when the patient is in an acute phase of treatment, such as immediately postoperatively or during the diagnostic workup, or when you are the only specialist available or the only source of medical care in the area. Additionally, if the patient is part of a capitated insurance plan, you might need to speak with the third party payor to request a transfer of the patient to another physician.

SUMMARY

No matter how caring and tolerant you are as a physician, it is likely that you will have patients that you find yourself dreading, patients with whom you feel frustrated or confused or angry. However, this is not necessary bad; in fact, *your reactions to patients can be used as a diagnostic tool to help you discern what your patient thinks, feels and needs.*

It is important to learn how to manage difficult patient encounters in a manner that will help both you and your patient. Once you accept this as part of your role as a physician and develop effective patient management skills, you might find yourself fascinated by the challenges and drawn to the rewards associated with difficult patient encounters.

CASE STUDY

Ms. Jetter, a 29-year-old woman with a 10-year history of intractable chronic pain of her lower extremities, was referred for evaluation and treatment after failing numerous previous rehabilitation programs aimed at helping her learn how to walk again. She was described as highly uncooperative and difficult. On one occasion, her behavior had escalated to the point of a physical altercation with a physical therapist.

On initial exam, Ms. Jetter appeared alert, oriented, cooperative, intelligent and verbal. She made good eye contact and was well groomed. She endorsed being irritable and a worrier. She indicated that she worries about her health, the health of her parents, and "everything else." When describing her previous physical rehabilitation programs, she reported that she was extremely traumatized because she had no sense of control and she didn't trust her clinicians. Because her fear and anxiety led to greatly increased arousal in the central nervous system, her pain was exacerbated and became more centralized.

It was unclear why Ms. Jetter seemed to be in more pain and have a more difficult time than other patients. The increase in pain caused by her extreme arousal impeded her recovery and caused others to view her as difficult. Naturally, this situation was quite confusing to both the treatment team and to Ms. Jetter (and her family).

After much investigation, cognitive testing conducted as part of a psychological evaluation of Ms. Jetter identified a specific deficit that made it difficult for her to anticipate the intentions of others. While this is a common deficit among autistic individuals, Ms. Jetter was not autistic and this deficit had not previously been identified. Once this deficit was defined for her, she gained an important insight and was quickly and easily able to recount numerous episodes in which her deficit contributed to her difficulty in relating to others.

When she thought back to the altercation with the physical therapist, Ms. Jetter realized that she experienced the normal behaviors of the physical therapist as assaultive because she could not understand that he was trying to help

her and trust that he would demonstrate restraint and not exacerbate her pain. The repeated exposures to this inaccurately perceived assaultive behavior led to the development of clinical Post Traumatic Stress Disorder (PTSD).

Effective interventions included treating Ms. Jetter's PTSD, educating the physical therapist about her cognitive deficit, clearly communicating intentions to Ms. Jetter before touching her, and allowing Ms. Jetter to set the pace of her rehabilitation. While she had been thought of as a "difficult patient" for years, Ms. Jetter's story demonstrates how curious clinicians can solve a long-standing and perplexing mystery. The treatment team was able to enjoy the satisfaction associated with helping a patient previously labeled as "difficult," and Ms. Jetter was finally able to work with a rehabilitation team to once again learn to walk.

SUGGESTED READINGS AND WEBSITES

http://virtualmentor.ama-assn.org/2009/03/hlaw1–0903.html; retrieved on July 17, 2009.
This article on the American Medical Association website reviews the risk of medical malpractice litigation within the context of a difficult patient-physician relationship:

http://www.aafp.org/afp/20051115/2063.html; retrieved on August 7, 2009.
This article on the American Academy of Family Physicians website reviews practice recommendations related to difficult patients using the SORT evidence rating system.

Haas, L.J., Leiser, J.P., Magill, M.K., & Sanyer, O.N. (2005). Management of the difficult patient. *American Family Physician, 72,* 2063–2068.

These websites contain the Ethics Codes for doctors:

American Medical Association, Medical Ethics Code (1995–2009). Retrieved on July 17, 2009, from http://www.ama-assn.org/

American Osteopathic Association, Medical Ethics Code (2003–2009). Retrieved on July 17, 2009 from http://www.osteopathic.org/

DiMatteo, M. R. (2004). Variations in patients' adherence to medical recommendations: A quantitative review of 50 years of research. *Medical Care, 42,* 200–209.
This review offers insights into the literature on patient adherence and provides direction for future research.

21 The Humanities and the Practice of Medicine

Steven C. Schlozman

> The humanities, which center on well-wrought narratives, can remind medicine what a depth of plight illness is, but also that this plight allows for joy . . . Medical workers—physicians, nurses, technicians, and administrators—need to be reminded that they are playing parts in the drama of the ill person's plight, and that how they play their parts shapes this drama just as consequentially as the disease—the cellular pathology—shapes it. The humanities can remind ill people that their private trouble is also a public plight, thus giving suffering a sense of consequence and scope. The universal message of well-wrought narratives of illness is that to be sick is not to be sequestered from life; instead, illness is privileged in the fullness of its participation in life–although most people have to be sick to realize that.
>
> ARTHUR W. FRANK

Since very ancient times, the practice of medicine has been equated with the study of the human condition. Classical mythology quite deliberately equated the exploration of artistic expression with the art of healing. Apollo himself was the god of music, poetry, *and* medicine. In this sense, medical practice has often been associated with the study of the humanities in general, and for many years physicians were as educated in classical studies as they were in diagnosis, prognosis, and therapeutics.

However, while many medical educators persist in pointing out the robust connections between an appreciation of the humanities and one's prowess as a healer, increasingly critical appraisals are emerging that suggest that medical curricula and, thus, current medical students ignore the humanities, much to their detriment as well as to that of their patients. Often, the growing body of knowledge that one must master to become a modern physician, coupled with the need for increasing one's technological expertise, can lead to a de-emphasis of the appreciation for everything that careful attention to art and literature might contribute to the overall perfor-mance of contemporary doctors. As one astute medical student has written, "students learn to treat patients as they might treat an experimental mouse. Idealistic notions of altruism, honesty, and integrity that attracted many to the calling of medicine are mentioned in the white coat ceremony, talked about by deans, and actively discouraged through the acculturation process." One might argue that we are currently at the crossroads of medical reductionism as it competes with the more broadly shaped goals of the study of the humanities as a means for educating better physicians.

Such claims, however, demand careful definitions. If one is prepared to argue that the study of humanities both informs and contributes to the effectiveness of physicians, one must first be clear about what the term humanities encompasses. Consulting current medical literature does not offer clear solutions to this initial inquiry. Humanities can be loosely defined as the study of literary, philosophical, and artistic expressions of the so-called "human condition." In this sense, literature, art, music, and even popular culture fall into this broad category. **"Medical Humanities,"** on the other hand, is a relatively recent term, reportedly first coined in 1976 by an Australian surgeon who hoped to enhance his students' appreciation for their surgical experiences by assigning relevant literary works as part of the surgical curriculum. Alternatively, the term humanities in some medical schools has been narrowly conceptualized to encompass only those aspects of the curriculum involving the study of ethics and professionalism. Clearly, any attempt at improving the integration of humanities into medical teaching and practice demands that one carefully wade through these various definitions and arrive at some consensus about what is most useful to our patients and to ourselves.

Men's Bath *Albrecht Dürer (1496). The German National Museum, Nuremberg. This work is an example of Dürer's preoccupation with the four temperaments. The man at the pump typifies the melancholic humor (and may be a portrait of Dürer himself). The man with the flower represents the sanguine temperament, whereas the choleric type is seen in the man with the scraper. Finally, the phlegmatic personality is represented by the man with the stein of beer.*

WHAT ARE THE HUMANITIES? WHAT IS THEIR RELATIONSHIP TO THE PRACTICE OF MEDICINE?

Turning again to antiquity, one should note that the formal study of humanities is essentially a renaissance phenomenon, referred to as the *studia humanitatis*. The roots of this academic pursuit were classical in nature, encompassing fields as diverse as literature, drama, poetry, law, theology, philosophy, and ethics. This is similar to current definitions, and this chapter will more or less adhere to this definition. In short, the study of the humanities here refers to the study of how individuals and cultures express themselves as human beings.

The pursuit of the humanities is a uniquely human endeavor. We are the only species that represents its experiences through metaphor and simile. This distinction is remark-

ably similar to Osler's famous distinction of humans from the rest of the animal kingdom as the only species for which medicines are desired and pursued. In other words, *the human desire for poetry is akin to the human desire for understanding sickness and health.* Both are elements that are unique to the fundamental experience of being human.

Where, then, does this leave the modern physician with regard to the role of the humanities in medical education and practice? Virtually no practicing or aspiring physician would doubt the utility of an appreciation and understanding of the expression of human experience in order to be a good doctor. However, how students and physicians pursue this goal, how much time is devoted to these principles, and to what extent these principles can effect change in the growing perception that doctors and patients float further and further apart remains to be seen. Fortunately, there is enormous interest in asking exactly these questions in current medical debate. This chapter will, therefore, focus on how the study of the humanities can positively influence modern medicine, and on some of the more promising resources and curricula that are addressing these complicated issues. Finally, a list of resources that can aid the physician in the integration of the principles of the liberal arts with the practice of medicine will be outlined and explored.

> Know then thyself, presume not God to scan.
> The proper study of mankind is man.
>
> ALEXANDER POPE
> *An Essay on Man*

THE CONTRIBUTIONS OF THE HUMANITIES TO THE ART OF MEDICINE

A great deal of enthusiasm and energy is currently being devoted to the rediscovery of the humanities as part of medical training. It is beyond the scope of this chapter to discuss these efforts in detail, but one should note that a genuine renaissance of interest in the humanities is currently successfully fighting for space in diverse medical curricula. The reasons for these changes are many, but in general there is a sense that a better grasp of the principles of critical inquiry into the arts and literature will lead to an overall improvement in fundamental issues such as the doctor-patient relationship, the appreciation and mastery of empathic skills, and the universality that the study of humanities contributes to one's own capacity to withstand powerful and sometimes uncomfortable feelings.

Doctors deal on a daily basis with the existential and experiential issues that are represented in the fine arts. To this end, many have suggested that doctors themselves will be better able to withstand the emotional assaults that can accompany routine exposures to human suffering if they have a better grasp of the ways powerful experiences in general have been represented throughout artistic expressions. To the extent that such explorations can lead to better self-awareness, many have postulated that the capacity to heal will be similarly improved through the honing of empathic skills in the displaced space that study of the humanities engenders. Consider, for example, the following passage from William Shakespeare's Richard II:

> Let's talk of graves, of worms, and epitaphs;
> Make dust our paper and with rainy eyes
> Write sorrow on the bosom of the earth,
> Let's choose executors and talk of wills:
> And yet not so, for what can we bequeath
> Save our deposed bodies to the ground?
> Our lands, our lives and all are Bolingbroke's,
> And nothing can we call our own but death
> And that small model of the barren earth
> Which serves as paste and cover to our bones.
> For God's sake, let us sit upon the ground
> And tell sad stories of the death of kings;
> How some have been deposed; some slain in war,
> Some haunted by the ghosts they have deposed;
> Some poison'd by their wives: some sleeping kill'd;
> All murder'd: for within the hollow crown
> That rounds the mortal temples of a king
> Keeps Death his court and there the antic sits,
> Scoffing his state and grinning at his pomp,
> Allowing him a breath, a little scene,
> To monarchize, be fear'd and kill with looks,
> Infusing him with self and vain conceit,
> As if this flesh which walls about our life,
> Were brass impregnable, and humour'd thus
> Comes at the last and with a little pin
> Bores through his castle wall, and farewell king!
> Cover your heads and mock not flesh and blood
> With solemn reverence: throw away respect,
> Tradition, form and ceremonious duty,
> For you have but mistook me all this while:
> I live with bread like you, feel want,
> Taste grief, need friends: subjected thus,
> How can you say to me, I am a king?
>
> *Act III, Scene II*

Within this extremely evocative passage, one senses the very questions that are central to the nuances of medicine. Without question, Richard is suffering greatly. At the same time, the passage can also be read as ripe with self-pity and narcissism, making it difficult to empathize with Richard's plight. Indeed, a major theme of the play involves the tragic difficulties Richard encounters as he at-

tempts to align his own court with his suffering in the setting of his persistent hubris and self-aggrandizing. And yet, does his suffering constitute signs and symptoms of a medical problem? What might be an appropriate intervention to alleviate Richard's clear thoughts of death, isolation, and fatalism? If medical students are taught to adhere strictly to medical nosology, they will note that his suffering exhibits narcissistic features and potential suicidality, but they will be hard pressed to identify clear symptoms of a mood disorder that would more accurately direct treatment However, the passage cries out for analysis and empathy, and it is the rare individual who is not gripped with a desire to help in some way with the desperation that Richard experiences. Similarly, one hopes that the visceral nature of Richard's suffering is experienced at least somewhat by whoever reads the passage. In this way, the analysis of the work itself engenders both a sense of self-awareness (what some clinicians have called **autognosis**) and a desire to act to alleviate suffering.

Thus, whether a reader determines that Richard is suffering pathologically or normally becomes less important. What takes precedence is a need to alleviate the suffering as much and as effectively as possible. To undertake this task, one must first examine one's own reactions to Richard's anguish, decide the extent to which these personal reactions are valid guides to how best to proceed and provide care, and then implement this care.

Many medical students have noted that the very act of reading such works is in and of itself therapeutic. This is not to say that physicians ought to prescribe literature for their patients in the same manner that they prescribe other therapeutics. However, the realization of the universality of feeling that art and literature engender can greatly help medical students recognize that *simply being with a patient can prove enormously therapeutic*. Indeed, it is this kind of empathic presence that many critics of modern medicine feel is most grievously lacking in current medical practice. If medical educators can help aspiring physicians understand that the act of carefully and viscerally reading a passage from literature or examining a painting can generate genuine emotion and cathartic healing, one moves much closer to helping those same aspiring healers appreciate the powers of empathy and connection in the doctor-patient relationship.

> I realize I have two professions, not one. Medicine is my lawful wife and literature my mistress. When I grow weary of one, I pass the night with the other. Neither of them suffers because of my infidelity.
>
> ANTON CHEKHOV
> Letter

> *Stupidity* ... seeps like a corrosive poison through every level of society, and lays it blighting hand on every aspect of social, professional, political and cultural life ... What can you—what, as humanist physicians, must you do—to fight stupidity? First, you must assure your own complete inoculation against this plague by massive daily applications of art, music, and literature. Then you must do the most difficult thing of all: you must be wholly honest with your patients.
>
> ROBERTSON DAVIES
> *Can a Doctor Be a Humanist?*

THE REBIRTH OF THE HUMANITIES IN THE MEDICAL CANON

In fact, many physicians recently have eloquently discussed the importance of incorporating the humanities into medical training and practice. For example, an innovative program directed by Abraham Verghese and Therese Jones at the University of Texas in San Antonio provides longitudinal and mandatory exposure to the humanities for all medical students. The directors of this program note that their goals are nothing less than to "create the kind of doctor one would be proud to have for one's self and one's family," by using the humanities as integral to a "new curriculum" that protects, nurtures and respects the "innate humanity, dynamic imagination, and precious individuality of students." In other words, students individually and dynamically pursue topics usually reserved for the liberal arts, and in so doing generalize what they learn to their overall capacity as complete healers.

> My "medicine" was the thing that gained me entrance to these secret gardens of the self. It lay there, another world, in the self. I was permitted by my medical badge to follow the poor, defeated body into these gulfs and grottos.
>
> WILLIAM CARLOS WILLIAMS
> *Autobiography*

Similar sentiments can be found in a wonderful essay written by Brian Hurwitz, a distinguished professor of medicine at Kings College in London and published by the Royal College of Physicians. Dr. Hurwitz notes that "productive clinical encounters depend on diverse sorts of communications: spontaneous and staged, verbal and nonverbal, intimate and detached interchanges, observations and interpretations." While much of these encounters demands the guidance of scientific and evidence-based principles, Dr. Hurwitz argues as well that attention to "arts and humanities" makes equal contributions to medical practice to the extent that such attention helps

ROCK OF AGES

This miner comes in
with hardly a story for anything
serious. A little pain
back where he busted his back,
sick to the stomach
since Easter, not enough
not to eat. Man's got to eat,
right? When he takes a smoke
his stomach rolls like a room
in Noah's ark. He's plain
apologetic. It's nothing,
it's the wife, she's always
looking for the worst.

Blue-black roots around his arms,
he stumbles, coughing,
from the elevator cage
covered with coal from head to foot,
clanging his lunch bucket.
He pulls off his black boots.
His feet are porcelain.
Crystals glisten
at the base of his neck.

I put my hands on his chest.
The skin, granite-like at first,
cracks and crumbles.
Shale! I listen
to his stony breathing,
and hear a man
scrambling the lip of an open mine
and kicking showers of shale
at the ominous figure
that follows him. The man
is running for his life. He's not
fast enough. It's nothing,
it's the dampness. . . . His skin
is translucent, revealing
cold, hard lumps of coal
that endure—I tell him, Yes,
you need some tests—

when the rest is gone.

JACK COULEHAN

doctors to emphasize "meaning and interpretation." He goes on to argue that "educationally, the arts and humanities develop a range of skills and capacities: from observation, argument, and analysis, to self-awareness; capabilities that are insufficiently nurtured by school science courses and conventional medical curricula. Caring for sick people frequently confronts nurses and doctors with intense questions about the meaning of life and exposes them to human tragedies and comic absurdities, sometimes simultaneously. The arts can tackle such issues with an immediacy and range of response often lacking in medicine." In this sense, the passage from Shakespeare offered above contributes greatly where a more analytic and scientific approach often falls short.

Finally, one must be wary of limiting attention to the humanities in medical training and practice to discussion and analysis of only so-called "fine arts and literature." Popular culture, from music to film to television to video games, are all expressions of the human condition. There is growing interest among medical educators to pursue a better understanding of both the risks to and benefits for our patients of increasingly pervasive media that bombard our daily lives. Patients and physicians express themselves through their feelings engendered not only by established poets, but also by pop music, the satisfaction of winning a virtual reality game, or the feelings inspired by very real identification with fictional television characters. Many patients cried when Buffy called off her relationship with Angel in *Buffy the Vampire Slayer*. Just as the *The Bell Jar* can prove both therapeutic or detrimental to a patient's health, so too can identification with the real or fictional stories that pervade popular culture. Ignoring these phenomena deprives physicians of a means by which they might better connect with and understand their patients as well as themselves.

> If I had to live my life again, I would have made a rule to read some poetry and listen to some music at least once a week; for perhaps the parts of my brain now atrophied would thus have been kept alive through use.
>
> CHARLES DARWIN

THE FUTURE OF THE HUMANITIES AND MEDICINE

The arguments for including the humanities in medical school curricula are growing in scope and volume. Nevertheless, what exactly one does with these ideas on a more systemic scale remains unclear. Rafael Campo, a poet and internist based at Harvard Medical School, has noted that those who advocate for a greater humanities pres-

ence in medical education and practice often seem somewhat conflicted about the role that humanities should play in medicine. Should humanities be taught alongside all medical courses, with relevant readings and experiences similar to the San Antonio model, or should emphasis on humanities inform more traditional questions in medicine such as ethical considerations around advanced directives and neonatal care? Are these agendas necessarily exclusive? Perhaps, as some have suggested, all medical schools should have separate departments of "medical humanities" with faculty from the liberal arts as well as physicians and allied professionals. These are issues that are evolving in a piecemeal way with little centralization of goals and agendas. However, both the public and those who are applying to medical school seem universally to favor increased integration of humanities within medical institutional practices. What remains to be seen is the extent to which these strongly held beliefs will manifest a cultural change within the practice of medicine itself.

ARE FORMAL STUDIES OF THE HUMANITIES APPROPRIATELY PLACED IN THE MEDICAL CANNON?

Despite a growing body of literature suggesting physicians benefit when they study humanities, some physicians have argued that the nature of modern medicine is simply not compatible with the inclusion of the humanities in the modern medical school curriculum. Ironically, some of these arguments come from clinicians and scholars who, in the past, have argued just as strongly for the inclusion of this material.

Jane McNaughton at the Center for Medical Humanities at Durham University suggests that the role of the doctor involves increasingly objectifying the patient so that the patient's illness can be understood dispassionately and scientifically; however, virtually all arguments for the inclusion of medical humanities in medical education aim to minimize this objectification. The disconnection students experience between the attempt to promote greater empathic skills through scrutiny of the humanities and their scientific and technological training is confusing for students.

The ongoing competition for curriculum time in medical education makes any attempt to introduce and study the humanities difficult. Students quickly figure out what is important and what can be glossed over, and they discover that what is presented in the context of medical humanities often seem to be merely platitudes. Students read poetry, see films, explore literature, and contemplate paintings that professors choose as relevant proxies for the existential crises that confront patients, but because so little time can be devoted to these endeavors in practice, students only take relatively simplistic reductions from these exercises: "Be nice to your patient," or "Try to know what your patients are feeling." As any serious contribution of the humanities to medicine is intended to convey a much greater level of profundity and contemplation, some scholars argue that current curricular limitations do not allow for anything other than a shallow, superficial, and therefore ultimately damaging introduction to the humanities.

Another problem involves the lack of expertise of those teaching the humanities in medical school. It is hard to challenge the appropriateness of a nephrologist who studies the kidney teaching about renal pathophysiology. However, medical humanities are, except in rare circumstances, taught by physicians with little or no formal training in either studying or teaching literature or the arts. Students note these inconsistencies, and, given the expectation of instruction from noted experts that characterizes the rest of medical education, students feel short changed by their introduction to the humanities during their medical education.

These are structural criticisms that beg important questions. Do we want modern medicine to de-emphasize the subjective nature of the doctor-patient relationship? Can students learn the technological issues that are increasingly stressed in medical cannons on their own – through online formats and self-study – and leave the careful examination of the humanities to potentially shallow tutorials? Is the modern physician simply too busy for the empathic connectedness that a serious study of the humanities promotes? Current surveys of patient satisfaction suggest that a substantial percentage of patients feel the sting of the increasing objectification that some clinicians feel is a sound and necessary aspect of modern diagnosis and treatment. Perhaps these are growing pains of a new kind of medicine, and these pains are in fact symptoms of a medical environment in which the humanities will have little or no role. The current pathos expressed on both sides of these issues in medical literature suggests that medicine is itself in the midst of an important and widening identity crisis.

POTENTIAL COLLABORATIONS OF MODERN SCIENTIFIC MEDICINE WITH THE HUMANITIES

A number of scientific studies have addressed the nature of empathy. Topics such as the "theory of mind" and a better understanding of mirror neuron theory allow doctors to lecture with genuine expertise when discussing the humanities. If clinicians and teachers suggest to students that an appreciation of the humanities in fact involves sophisticated and only recently understood complex neurological processes, perhaps students will take such discussions more seriously. In fact, theoretically, *the same neurological processes that are involved in connecting with patients are involved when we are deeply moved by art.* The humanities may offer a safe setting in which students can explore the potentially invasive and intimate neurological experiences that have traditionally made them uncomfortable when confronted with real patient suffering. Making it clear to students that an appreciation of the humanities involves neurologically complex and sophisticated processes can enhance students' willingness to accept the importance of the humanities to the practice of medicine.

> Our townsfolk were not more to blame than others; they forgot to be modest, that was all, and thought that everything was still possible for them; which presupposed that pestilences were impossible. They went on doing business, arranged for journeys, and formed views. How should they have given a thought to anything like plague, which rules out any future, cancels journeys, silences the exchange of views. They fancied themselves free, and no one will ever be free so long as there are pestilences.
>
> ALBERT CAMUS
> *The Plague*

SUGGESTIONS FOR APPLICATIONS OF THE HUMANITIES TO THE PRACTICE OF MEDICINE

There are many avenues through which medicine as a discipline can embrace an appreciation of the humanities as a means of improving the delivery of care. A few of these methods are suggested above, but it is useful to outline the central ways in which humanities can be utilized.

Encourage medical students to have greater exposure to the study of humanities as a condition for acceptance to medical school.

This notion is potentially controversial. The growing breadth of medical information often necessitates increased attention to scientific study even before medical school starts. As these needs grow, there will be inevitable and understandable tension between the desire that students master more and more science before starting their studies vs. the desire that they also demonstrate more proficiency in the study of liberal arts. The few studies that have examined those students applying for medical school with primarily humanities majors have found slightly worse performance among these candidates on standardized assessments, but improved performance on interpersonal assessments and a greater willingness to discuss abstract and complicated issues. Students in this group, perhaps not surprisingly, were also found to have a slightly increased likelihood of choosing psychiatry over other medical disciplines.

> The greatest enterprise of the mind always has been and always will be the attempt to link the sciences and the humanities.
>
> EDWARD O. WILSON

Humanities Training Throughout Pre- and Postgraduate Medical Curricula

Many of the references mentioned above and listed at the end of this chapter make passionate pleas for active implementation of humanities training for medical students. Scholars have argued that training in humanities can be helpful in areas as wide ranging as pattern recognition to the therapeutic nature of improved empathic connections. While students on the whole have received these additions to the medical canon favorably, there are few studies examining whether or not these changes effect real professional change. The new live-patient interview that is now part of the United States Medical Licensing Examination (US-MLE) offers an opportunity to study whether or not medical programs that actively combine the study of the humanities with medical training create more empathic, connected, and effective physicians. Similarly, the growing practice of the 360-degree evaluation of medical professionals might help to clarify whether postgraduate humanities curricula accomplish the goals of better, empathic doctor-patient relations. However, the qualities that are being sought by pursuing appreciation of arts and literature within medical practice are difficult to measure. Improvements in doctor-patient relations are to some extent qualitative changes, not always suited to the outcomes measures that characterize the standards for medical evidence.

These issues are not new, and much can be learned from experience.

The challenge of making objective observations concerning the subjective nature of the experience of illness has always been a central paradox in the practice of medicine. Patients have historically felt misunderstood, and it would be foolish to suggest that the current divide between doctors and their patients, which is often lamented, is purely a product of modernity. While technology and deemphasizing more abstract analyses certainly play some role, there are fascinating examples of misunderstood patients dating back hundreds of years. For example, the French physician and philosopher, Jean Marc Gaspard Itard, apparently realized this divide when he suggested that the misunderstanding of the plight of contemporary women was the primary genesis for an epidemic of hysteria in nineteenth century Paris. Similarly, examination of letters to the celebrated eighteenth century Swiss physician Samuel Tissot demonstrate remarkable similarities to the complaints of the modern patient. One patient wrote that the consulting physician "found me very well

indeed; for me, I was still feeling sick." Frustrated sentiments such as these are present throughout medical history, and it would, therefore, be disingenuous to bemoan a completely lost era of patient-doctor understanding. Instead, these examples provide potent arguments for the use of the humanities as a means of reshaping a very ingrained culture. The subjective nature of illness is by definition reconceptualized as objective when one discusses characteristics such as natural history, prognosis, and treatment. However, the melding of universal and deeply personal responses to inquiries into arts and literature holds real promise as a means of helping physicians to reconcile these competing forces. Humans experience art both internally and as it relates to their prevailing culture. To this end, the experience of art can help physicians to understand the unique perspectives of the individual with regard to the global conclusions that the study of illness and experience entails. As always, history is the most efficient teacher.

> Make it a point not to let your intellectual life atrophy through non-use. Be familiar with the classics of English literature in prose and verse; read the lives of the great men (sic) of the past, and keep pace with modern thought in books of travel, history, fiction, science. A varied intellectual life will give zest to your medical studies ... Let music and art shed their radiance upon your too often weary life and find in the sweet cadences of sound or the rich emotions of form and color a refinement which adds polish to the scientific man (sic).
>
> WILLIAM WILLIAMS KEEN
> The ideal physician. *JAMA* (1900), 34:1592–1594.

SUMMARY

Many physicians relish the opportunity to contemplate art, literature, and other aspects of human expression. Columns such as the very popular "A Piece of My Mind," published in the *Journal of the American Medical Association*, and now anthologized by the AMA press, clearly demonstrate the need that doctors feel to both express themselves artistically and to look to cultural expression as a means of understanding their own sense of purpose. In fact a huge number of these essays discuss poems, painting, plays, and books. Journals as esteemed as the *Lancet* review art exhibits, and the *American Journal of Psychiatry* has long reviewed books only loosely connected to the practice of medicine. Nevertheless, medical training and practice is increasingly crowded and burdened. Rather than considering a turn to the humanities as yet another hurdle for already beleaguered students and practitioners to endure, it makes sense to reconceptualize this endeavor as a rejuvenating and affirming experience. In this sense, attention to the humanities is synergistic and not at all burdensome. The study of the humanities can instead remind physicians of the essential humanity of their patients that is central to the doctor's calling.

SUGGESTED READINGS

Jones T., & Verghese, A. (2003). On becoming a humanities curriculum: the Center for Medical Humanities and Ethics at the University of Texas Health Science Center at San Antonio. *Academic Medicine, 78,* 1010–1014.
A wonderful summary of a very successful medical humanities curriculum integrated throughout all 4 years of a traditional medical education.

Campo, R. (2005). A piece of my mind. "The medical humanities," for lack of a better term. *Journal of the American Medical Association, 294,* 1009–1011.
A thoughtful and provocative essay on the many variations of medical humanities that are possible throughout medical training.

DasGupta, S., & Charon, R. (2004). Personal illness narratives: Using reflective writing to teach empathy. *Academic Medicine, 79*(4), 351–356.
This paper describes a program at Columbia University College of Physicians and Surgeons that uses illness narratives to enhance empathy. Second-year medical students wrote about a patient's illness from the standpoint of the patient.

Dolev, J.C., Friedlaender, L.K., & Braverman, I.M. (2001). Use of fine art to enhance visual diagnostic skills. *Journal of the American Medical Association, 286,* 1020–1021.
An innovative approach to the use of fine art and paintings in teaching pattern recognition to medical students for disciplines such as dermatology and radiology.

Schlozman, S.C. (2000). Vampires and those who slay them: Using the television program *Buffy the Vampire Slayer* in adolescent therapy and psychodynamic education. *Academic Psychiatry, 24,* 49–54.
An example of the ways in which popular culture can be utilized to better understand important medical and psychiatric concepts.

Shapiro, J., Coulehan, J., Wear, D., & Montello, M. (2009). Medical humanities and their discontents: Definitions, critiques, and implications. *Academic Medicine, 84,* 192–198.
This paper offers specific theoretical and practical ideas on how to integrate the humanities throughout the medical school curriculum as well as to enhance reflective thinking and the examination of values.

Part 5

Social and Cultural Issues in Health Care

THE HANDS

The Emergency Department is usually quiet early Saturday mornings. Things that hurt too badly have caused the owners of such pain to come in earlier—and the accidents haven't as yet had time to happen. But the early morning is a favorite time for the elephant-on-the-chest discomfort of a heart attack: it may come on during the rapid eye movement portion of sleep, that part of sleep associated with dreaming. With a thumping dream, good or bad, the eyes roll under the lids like marbles in oil. It can be as though you're running while lying down, your body tense, heart pumping wildly to no purpose, blood pressure up. Perhaps that's when it happened to him.

What we know is that he sat up on the side of the bed, still, as when he went to sleep, 39 years old. And complained of pain. An ambulance was called and got to him quickly: no question what he had or what must be done. Lying there, hurtling there under the siren, he stopped breathing. Resuscitation was begun: pump, breathe, pump, breathe. Two minutes from the hospital. Radio the Emergency Department: *Roger. Man with chest pain. Just arrested. ETA 1 minute. Get the doors open.*

Galvanized is the word for what happens then in the Emergency Department: a flurry of white coats, hands, legs, linen. Drugs, EKG ready. The whip of the siren. *They're on the ramp.*

39, I keep thinking. *Damn!*

As the EKG machine is hooked up, the tube for breathing pure oxygen is put down. *He's pinker. Keep pumping on the chest.* Nothing on the EKG. Not a thing, just the mechanical jumps of the needle as the Resident pumps a perfect 60 times a minute. Nothing to shock. Flat line. Drugs—that's what we need: *epinephrine, bicarb. Hurry. Keep pumping!*

The Resident is sweating heavily and is relieved when someone offers to take over for him. Nothing works. No drug is helping. Try another. *Try calcium.*

I swear his hand moved—no, his *arm* moved. *Both* arms are moving! His heart still dead, but he's moving his arms! *God. Never Saw That Happen Before.*

The hands come up on his chest to the hands of the pumping Resident and *push* them away. He's making a sound around the tube in his mouth.

Check the EKG. Stop pumping. Check it.

Nothing.

The hands fall down lifeless again. Pump.

Pump! Try some more epinephrine. Nothing. Straight line. Nothing on his own.

Get me a pacemaker.

The hands come up again, pushing away the doctor's hands.

Stop pumping so I can see the EKG. Nothing. The man's hands fall down again as the pumping is interrupted momentarily. We're keeping him alive but he won't let us.

Here's the pacemaker. Keep pumping. Check the blood gases.

The pacemaker doesn't help. He has no pump left. His heart muscle is gone. We keep trying, pumping. The hands come up and fall back down. Death is fighting off life and the living.

We work for hours. The hands are weaker; they do not rise as often; they do not rise at all; they do not move. We have lost in spite of everything. The something that waits inside us all for the first falter and stumble of the heart has won.

I hope his wife is a strong spirit. I'd like to tell her about the hands. About how he struggled. How we hurt with him in that purgatory until we were all rendered innocent of everything we might have been guilty of, then and tomorrow.

JOHN STONE

22 Culturally Competent Health Care

David M. Snyder & Peter Kunstadter

[R]educing racially or culturally based inequity in medical care is a moral imperative. As is the case for most tasks of this nature, the first steps, at both the individual and societal levels, are honest self-examination and the acknowledgment of need. That process, which is now well underway, will enrich physicians and patients alike.

H. JACK GEIGER

Human behavior in health and illness is shaped by physical, social, and cultural influences. It is often necessary to consider each of these "levels of analysis" in order to achieve a complete understanding of a patient's illness and his or her responses to medical advice and treatment regimens. Failure to do so can contribute to incorrect diagnoses, ineffective or harmful treatments and patient nonadherence with medical advice. This chapter focuses on the contributions of culture to patients' health status, their concepts of health and illness, and their behavioral expectations for themselves as patients and for their health professionals.

Culture and Health Care

"Culture" refers to the beliefs, values, social structures, situational behavioral expectations, language, and technology shared by a group of people. These attributes endure over time, but are not homogeneously held by all members of the group. Each group has formal and informal ways of passing its culture on to new members. Culture also changes over time and across generations as a result of technological and environmental change and contact with other cultures. When members of differing cultures encounter each other, they must negotiate their differences in order to achieve a mutually satisfying interaction. This is true whether the interaction is in the economic, political, or health-care domain.

The impact of an individual's life experience is filtered through his or her values, beliefs, and knowledge. These provide meaning for those experiences and become causal models that explain the rules governing how one should respond to changing circumstances. For example, the first contact some Hmong (refugees from Southeast Asia who now live in the United States) had with modern care was in refugee camps in Thailand. Health care in one of the camps was run by a fundamentalist religious organization. This organization discouraged traditional diagnostic and treatment methods, and carried out forced child immunization programs without adequate health education or consent of the parents. Some refugees came to believe that modern medical care represents an attack on their culture and when they saw that some children became febrile after they received immunizations they thought that immunizations were administered in order to make their children sick.

Attitudes toward health care are also shaped by the experiences of others with whom we identify. For example, if we hear that another person we perceive as being like us has had a bad experience at a particular hospital, we are less likely to seek care at that hospital.

Culture is usually thought of as an attribute of ethnic, religious, or national groups, but other social groups, including professional groups such as physicians, also have distinct cultures. For example, physicians must negotiate a mutual understanding—a common set of behavioral expectations —with patients. This can be a challenge, even when patients come from similar cultural backgrounds. It is an even greater challenge when the doctor and patient come from significantly different backgrounds. **Culturally competent health care** is health care that successfully accommodates such cultural differences, allowing effective communication between doctor and patient, a shared understanding of each other's behavioral expectations and, above all, mutual trust and respect.

Aside from the interests of physicians in providing the best possible care for their patients, increasingly *federal and state laws mandate culturally appropriate or competent care.* For example, "cultural and linguistic competence" is a requirement of California's Medicaid Managed Care program. The legal basis for this requirement is Civil Rights legislation and the **Americans with Disabilities Act**. Other laws mandate equal access and participation in federally funded programs through the provision of bilingual services. How these requirements should be operationalized, implemented, and evaluated is currently being actively debated by representatives of departments of health services, health-care providers, third party payers, ethnic minority organizations, and academics throughout the country.

> Doctors are men who prescribe medicines of which they know little, to cure diseases of which they know less in human beings of whom they know nothing.
>
> VOLTAIRE

THE CULTURE OF THE MEDICAL PROFESSION IN AMERICA

Values

The ethical foundations of modern medical practice have roots as old as Western civilization itself. The earliest written statements of the moral obligations of the physician such as the **Hippocratic Oath** (500 BC) reveal values which persist in Western medicine in the twenty-first century—e.g., the requirement that physicians do no harm to their patients, an emphasis on the confidentiality of clinical information and a ban on sexual relationships between doctor and patient. The core values we consider in making medical decisions today reflect changes in our society over the centuries, but they also demonstrate the conservatism inherent in value systems. This is clearly demonstrated in the current debates over abortion and euthanasia.

Some of the core values of modern medical practice are:

- *Autonomy:* The right of the patient to decide whether or not to accept recommended medical procedures or treatments. This value is embodied in our informed consent procedures. It assumes that a competent individual is best able to determine whether accepting a medical recommendation is in his or her best interest.
- *The value of human life:* The obligation to preserve life and to avoid actions that shorten life.
- *Honesty:* The obligation to be truthful with patients regarding diagnosis, prognosis, and the advantages and disadvantages of alternative treatments.

- *Confidentiality:* The obligation not to reveal information about patients to others not participating in their medical care.

Ethical dilemmas arise when a medical decision brings one or more of those values into conflict. For instance, our obligation to preserve life may conflict with the value we place on patient autonomy when a patient refuses a treatment we regard as essential to prevent his or her death. The value we place on honesty may conflict with the obligation to avoid actions that harm the patient, as occurs when the patient's culture interprets a fatal prognosis as a curse that will *cause* the patient to die.

The process of resolving ethical dilemmas entails three steps:

1. Establishing the facts regarding
   - The patient's clinical condition
   - The alternative clinical actions, the likely consequences of each, and the recommendations of the clinicians involved in the patient's care
   - The wishes of the patient and/or others who must consent to any recommended clinical actions
2. Identifying the ethical issues and associated values
   - The patient's values
   - The values of the health-care providers
3. Reconciling the facts and the values and identification of a preferred action

This process works well when the facts are clear, those who must consent to the recommended action are identified and participate in the decision-making process, and all participants know and share values and prioritize those values similarly. The strong Western value placed on the individual (as contrasted with other cultures that value the group over the individual) is pervasive in Western medicine and in the ethics (such as autonomy) which are stressed in Western medical practice. Cultural differences in values complicate ethical decision making, and they may also obscure assessment of the patient's clinical condition. In addition, *specific symptoms may be valued differently in different cultures.* For example, in many cultures, pain may be denied or minimized because of the value placed on "toughness," particularly in men. In Islamic patients, pain may be valued as a way of expiating sin. For many, fear of addiction to analgesics may be greater than fear of pain. Culture also influences how specific pathologic processes present symptomatically. For example, *depression may be experienced and expressed as feelings of sadness (in Northern Europeans), chest pain (in the Hmong), or denied in other cultures because of the shame associated with mental illness. Another example would be what is considered a "fate worse than death," such as a young unmarried Hmong woman who was diagnosed with uterine cancer. The oncologist informed her and her family that the condi-*

tion was life-threatening and that surgical removal of her uterus plus radiation could save her life. The young woman refused surgery and fled the hospital with the explanation that she would rather be dead than be unmarriageable because she would no longer be able to bear children and thus any husband of hers could not continue his family line.

Patients' health-care decisions reflect the values and behavioral expectations governing relationships and social roles. For example, a patient or his or her family may weigh the economic impact of various treatment alternatives and the effect of these costs on the family before making a decision about a particular treatment. Because a sick person is expected to decrease normal activities, lose some autonomy, and increase their dependency, some patients may delay admitting they are sick because of professional or family obligations that the patient believes take precedence over accepting the role of a sick person.

Beliefs

The culture of Western medicine shares many values with the culture of science. For example, most physicians believe that symptoms have causes that are amenable to discovery through the gathering and analysis of objective data and they often distrust that which they cannot measure. They strive to explain illnesses in terms of what they know about normal and disordered anatomy and physiology. They make distinctions between "objective" and "subjective" data and tend to devalue the latter. They follow a **dualism** first articulated by Descartes, the seventeenth century French philosopher, that distinguishes between body and mind. They believe in "progress" and often contend that medical science is continuously advancing. The latest (drugs, scanners, operative techniques) is often assumed to be the best. As individuals, physicians may have strong religious and spiritual beliefs, but they clearly separate the spiritual aspects of their patients' well-being from their physical health and tend to concern themselves exclusively with the physical.

Most non-Western and preliterate societies have very different beliefs regarding the causes of illness and their treatment. They may define symptoms that are not recognized by Western medicine as indications of disease and may not recognize symptoms as abnormal that Western doctors believe are critically important. For example, some Hmong traditionally think that childhood diarrhea is "normal," not a symptom of illness. Non-Western and preliterate societies may have different explanations for some of the diseases known to medical science and may believe in diseases that have no known pathophysiology. These **folk illnesses** require specific treatments determined by symptoms, or by "folk diagnosis" methods, such as travel to the land of the spirits while the shaman is in a trance. The distinctions Western patients and physicians make between physical ill-

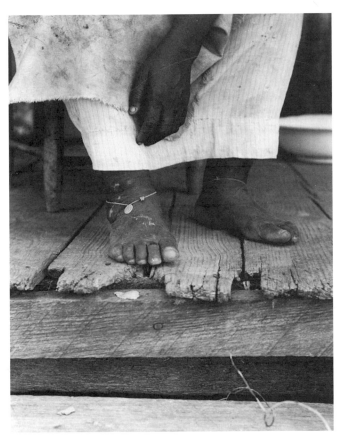

An amulet worn by a Mississippi sharecropper to ward off headaches Photograph by Dorothea Lange (1937). Courtesy of the Library of Congress, Washington, D.C., Prints and Photographs Division, FSA/OWI Collection, LC-USF34-017111-C. *Belief systems are powerful determinants of behavior, and patients can experience considerable relief from symptoms from their expectation that relief is forthcoming.*

ness and the spiritual world is often less clear or even absent in these cultures. The Hmong believe that many illnesses are caused by loss of one of several souls, and the diagnosis and treatment of such disorders requires that a **shaman** visit the spirit world to find the lost soul and convince it to return to the patient's body. Many cultures have a belief in an "evil eye" and the power of curses to cause disease. Latino ethnic groups have a number of folk illnesses including *mal ojo* (the evil eye), *empacho* (GI obstruction caused by food or other substances getting stuck to the wall of the stomach or intestines), *golpe de aire* (an illness caused by being struck by the wind), and *susto* (an illness caused by a frightening or other emotionally traumatic experience). Similar concepts are known by different names in many other cultures. *The history of the patient who believes he or she is suffering from what we label as a folk illness often clearly indicates that a particular belief system is present, but only if the physician is aware that belief in such illnesses exists in the patient's culture.*

Patients' behavior is impacted by their knowledge and beliefs regarding their symptoms and diagnoses. It is also impacted by the social meanings those symptoms and diagnoses have for them. The physician should be aware of the different social values attributed to specific symptoms and specific diseases by different groups. In most cultures today, the diagnosis of HIV/AIDS is heavily stigmatized and burdened with social values that may adversely impact a patient's seeking of needed medical diagnosis and life-saving treatment. In the past, leprosy was regarded as a shameful condition in Western societies, as it still is to some non-Western cultures such as the Hmong. The physician's ignorance of the patient's culture and its health beliefs will often lead to communication problems and mutual frustration.

> Some white man's hospitals don't cure the Navajos. They treat the illness, not the person. After an operation, a Navajo often goes to his medicine man to be purified, to be treated psychologically as well as physically.
>
> JOHN NOBLE WILFORD

Social Structure

The social structure of medicine is extremely complex and includes informal relationships among physicians and other health professionals, formal organizations such as hospital medical staffs, medical associations, and specialty societies. In addition, nonmedical organizations have tremendous impact on medical practice. These include groups representing other health professionals, governmental regulatory agencies, medical equipment and pharmaceutical manufacturers, and health insurance companies. Relationships between physicians and these organizations involve complex and dynamic issues of control over decision making and resource allocation. These complex power conflicts are tempered by equally complex mutual dependencies. Many patients, particularly those with different cultural origins, have little understanding of the constraints that health-care organizations place on physicians.

The physician's role within the health-care system has expanded greatly over the past 200 years, largely as a result of expanding scientific medical knowledge and technology. Antibiotics, vaccines, anesthesia, and surgical and obstetrical antisepsis have greatly increased the likelihood that a visit to the doctor will improve rather than worsen a patient's health status. In previous centuries, much more health care was provided within the family itself and by others such as midwives, apothecaries, barbers, or people with special knowledge of herbal remedies.

Advances in medical science have changed the scope of problems we regard as "illness." It was not that long ago that most mental illnesses were regarded as signs of possession by the devil or of moral rather than physical infirmity. The "medicalization" of an increasing number of conditions has not been without controversy—e.g., consider the

changes in how differences in sexual orientation have been regarded over the past 20 years.

There are numerous health professions and facilities in our society, each with its particular capabilities and relationships with the others. We attempt to make this complex system more rational and approachable through the concept of the "primary care physician." Ideally, **primary care** has three principal characteristics: It is *first contact care* —the source of care patients are supposed to seek first when feeling ill. It is also *comprehensive care*. The primary physician is supposed to meet most of the patient's health-care needs himself or herself and to be the one who advises the patient when other health-care services, e.g., a specialty consultation or a hospital stay, are necessary. Finally, it is *longitudinal care,* and the primary physician has a long-term relationship with the patient, which is not limited to a particular episode of illness. Unfortunately, the actual delivery of health care, especially for economically poor members of ethnic minorities, rarely reaches this ideal.

Societies with few scientifically trained medical personnel tend to rely on family, knowledgeable laypersons, and traditional healers as sources of health care and there is often little differentiation between healers and those concerned with spiritual well-being. In those cultures in which spiritual causes of illness are believed to be important, the authority of the healer may rest more on a "calling"—e.g., being "chosen" through supernatural means—than on education and training. In less highly differentiated societies, the healer's role may not be his or her primary occupation, but rather a secondary role.

Many cultures do have a degree of specialization among healers. They may have shamans who deal with illnesses caused by spiritual issues, herbalists who have expertise in treating illnesses amenable to herbal remedies, and others with expertise in treating traumatic injuries. Members of these cultural groups may be accustomed to seeking treatment from one or another of these healers according to their own best judgment or seeking treatment from more than one type of healer until one of them provides a coherent assessment and clear treatment plan. Paradoxically, even though our own health-care system is more complex than any other, with a wider array of specialists, *patients from other cultures with less highly differentiated medical systems may have a greater difficulty understanding the role of the primary care provider.* Their propensity to seek care from multiple providers may be perceived as "doctor shopping." They also may experience a primary physician's reluctance to refer to a specialist as a discriminatory decision to withhold optimal care.

> As it takes two to make a quarrel, so it takes two to make a disease, the microbe and its host.
>
> CHARLES V. CHAPIN

Language

*Medicine has a language of its own, and **medical jargon**, while essential for effective communication between colleagues, can be a substantial barrier to effective communication with patients.* Even when doctor and patient speak the same language, the quality of their communication depends on the patient's level of education and medical sophistication as well as the physician's ability to use terms known to the patient. When the physician and the patient do not share a language, Federal law as well as competent practice requires that an interpreter be utilized. Except in an emergent situation, when waiting for a medical interpreter would endanger the patient, it is not advisable to employ a family member, especially a child, as an interpreter. When communication with a patient requires translation, the potential for misunderstanding increases dramatically. Likewise, if a patient's native language does not even have its own words for common Western medical concepts, communication is even more challenging. (For example, some languages do not have words for illnesses we commonly diagnose, like cancer.) In addition, patients raised in less technologically advanced societies may not be at all familiar with common treatment modalities, e.g., radiation therapy. A skillful **medical interpreter** is of tremendous value in such circumstances, and *skill in working with medical interpreters is a core skill for physicians serving a culturally and linguistically diverse patient population.* In such settings, the interpreter must do much more than translate words from one language to another. He or she must also translate concepts regarding anatomy, disease causation, the diagnostic process, treatment modalities, prognosis, and the consequences of delayed treatment. The interpreter is not just a translation machine. The physician should consider the interpreter as an expert member of the team who can help in interpreting the patient's views of his or her illness and the patient's nonverbal as well as verbal responses to the physician's recommendations. The interpreter can also guide the physician with regard to the decision-making processes associated with seeking and accepting diagnosis and treatment. This will often require consultation between physician and interpreter both before and after the physician sees the patient.

Behavioral Expectations

The place of the health-care system within the larger society is influenced by that society's definition of illness. *Illness is generally defined by social scientists (as well as by most cultures) as pain and suffering associated with an inability to perform customary tasks and/or social role obligations.* The person who is sick is excused from these obligations until he

> Quit your pills and learn from Osteopathy the principle that governs you. Learn that you are a machine, your heart and engine, your lungs a fanning machine and a sieve, your brain with its two lobes an electric battery.
>
> ANDREW T. STILL
> Rural Missouri doctor and founder of osteopathy
> *The Autobiography of A.T. Still*

or she is again well. Simple refusal to perform one's duties is not illness and is not excusable. Voluntary nonperformance of social obligations may be defined as a crime (when laws are broken) or as a sin (when core values are rejected or taboos are violated). Cultures vary in how each of these forms of "deviant behavior"—illness, crime, and sin—is delineated, and an act that one society attributes to illness may be regarded as criminal in another cultural context. In fact, the differentiation of illness, crime, and sin is often difficult, even within a given society.

The sick individual is excused from the performance of customary obligations. A child with a fever does not have to go to school and he or she will be given an "excused absence." Likewise, an injured worker does not have to work, and he or she will be given "sick leave." However, these allowances are predicated on the person who has taken the sick role fulfilling the special obligations of that role. These include making appropriate efforts to regain health, usually by seeking medical care for the illness, and complying with the treatments prescribed by the health-care providers. In return, patients expect the doctor to take their complaints seriously, to treat them with respect, to take responsibility for their health care, to demonstrate competence in diagnosing and treating illness, and to provide them with information regarding their illness and its treatment. A doctor who is not competent or knowledgeable regarding the patient's illness is expected to admit his or her limitations and seek consultation from other physicians.

The relationship between healer and sick individual and the expectations each has for the other share many characteristics across cultures. The healer is expected to have expertise in determining the cause of the patient's illness and providing treatment for it. He or she is expected to act according to the best interest of the patient at all times. The patient is expected to answer the healer's questions honestly and provide the healer with pertinent information regarding current symptoms, past health problems, and other circumstances that might assist the diagnostic and treatment process.

In the United States, mature and mentally competent individuals are expected to decide for themselves if they are sick. Often, this basic decision is made after discussion with family members, and it is predicated on the recognition of symptoms as signs of illness. Symptoms that are believed to be the natural consequences of a recognized event and those that resolve spontaneously or with self-care and are not felt to threaten prolonged or permanent disability do not generally lead people to regard themselves as "sick."

In our culture, decisions about health care, including when to seek medical advice and whether or not to accept medical treatment, generally are made by the patient or, in the case of a child, by the parents. In many other cultures, such decisions are made only after consultation with the head of the family or another authority figure such as a community leader. This often results in a more prolonged decision-making process than physicians can readily accept, particularly when there is some urgency about initiating treatment. In addition, whom the family must consult before consenting to treatment may not be explicitly communicated to the physician who may not even know that the patient or family is delaying consent for treatment in order to consult others. Even if this *is* known, the physician may not have the opportunity to talk to the "real" decision makers. The decision makers may have the authority to make medical decisions for a patient, yet still be woefully ignorant of modern medical practice. *When a patient or family expresses a wish to delay consenting to diagnostic procedures or treatment, the physician should enquire whether there are others who should be consulted.* If there are, the physician should ideally offer to meet with those individuals to directly explain the medical issues and recommendations. Familiarity with the customs regarding medical decision-making in the groups residing in the physician's community is extremely important for all physicians and especially for primary care providers.

All cultures have cultural beliefs about avoiding illness and injury, but they do not necessarily share our belief in preventive medicine. On the other hand, they often have beliefs regarding illness prevention and health promotion that we do not share. For example, many Asian cultures have beliefs regarding what foods are appropriate for persons with specific health conditions, e.g., pregnancy or fever. Hospital diets in this country usually do not take these beliefs into account. Our practices such as periodic physical examinations for apparently healthy adults, prenatal care in medical settings, or well-child visits for healthy children have no counterpart in most non-Western cultures. In most cultures, and in our own until relatively recently, responsibility for health promotion resided entirely within the family.

Adherence to recommendations regarding health promotion and illness prevention is often challenging because of differences between patients' and physicians' understanding of disease processes and their respective behavioral expectations of each other. For example, there may be major differences in their values, e.g., regarding short- vs. long-term benefits and risks of various types of behavior. There are also likely to be differences in expectations regarding the responsibilities of the patient or of the patient's relatives for actions to retard the progression of chronic diseases such as diabetes. The culturally competent physician must be familiar with the family structure of the patient and the patterns of authority and responsibility within the family.

THE PRACTICE OF CULTURALLY COMPETENT HEALTH CARE

It is frequently useful to initiate a clinical encounter with some questions that establish the patient's expectations for the encounter. For example:
"Why are you seeking medical care at this time?"
"What do you think is the nature of your problem?"
"What do you think is the cause of your problem?"
"What do you expect of me?"
"How can I help you?"

Establishing these basic facts can facilitate any patient visit and enhance the likelihood that the encounter's outcome will be mutually satisfactory to both physician and patient regardless of cultural differences. It is important to realize, however, that the patient's feelings about the presenting problem may distort his or her responses. The patient may not easily reveal this fear that their symptoms are caused by a life-threatening disease.

A man from a culture that values stoicism in men may not readily admit to fear or pain. Many cultures have taboos against discussing sexual functioning, particularly with members of the other gender. Sensitivity to the emotional impact of specific symptoms or diagnoses is vitally important for the physician.

The importance of practicing culturally competent health care derives both from pragmatism and from the core values of our medical culture. Recognition that cultural factors influence our patients' health behavior, knowledge of health beliefs and practices within the groups to which we provide health care, and respect for these differences is absolutely necessary for the effective diagnosis and treatment of patients in a culturally diverse community.

Both physicians and their patients enter into encounters with patients with certain expectations regarding their behavior and our own. When these expectations are violated, we consciously or unconsciously seek to explain the discrepancy between what we expected and the observed behavior. If we are unaware of the role of cultural differences in shaping patient behavior, we tend to view the unanticipated behavior as deviant. We regard the patient who does not meet our expectations as uncooperative, difficult, or ignorant. If we are aware that cultural differences influence doctor-patient interactions, we can add "cultural differences" to our "differential diagnosis" of unexpected patient behaviors. The medical dictum, *"If you don't think of it, you won't look for it, and if you don't look for it, you may not see it,"* generally applies to the process of differential diagnosis; it also applies to the recognition of cultural factors in illness.

Knowledge of the patient's culture and the beliefs about illness and appropriate behavior for patients and healers held by the groups with which the patient is affiliated often

CASE EXAMPLE

A 7-year-old Hmong boy was referred to the orthopedics clinic with bilateral club feet. The surgeon recommended surgical correction, but, to his surprise, the parents refused treatment. This was seen as an irrational decision and contrary to the best interest of the child. In the face of the parents' adamant refusal to consider surgery, Child Protective Services was called, and a court order mandating surgery was sought. As part of the court's inquiry, a child psychiatrist was asked to evaluate the child and his parents. The psychiatrist determined that the Hmong believe that congenital deformities such as the patient's club feet represent retribution for some wrong doing by an ancestor, such as an unpaid debt. If the congenital deformity were repaired, the family would inevitably have another child with some equally serious handicap. The child whose deformity was repaired would suffer a greater social burden within his family than the burden that resulted from his untreated club feet. The court decided to permit the parents to refuse treatment, believing that within this particular cultural context the best interests of the child were served best by respecting the family's belief system.

CASE EXAMPLE

A 10-year-old Mexican-American boy was referred to a behavioral pediatrician for learning problems. Although the boy had been healthy throughout his life, his mother saw him as a vulnerable child and she had always been somewhat overprotective. Perinatal history was significant in that his mother had been in a motor vehicle accident during her pregnancy with the patient. While she had not been seriously injured, she appeared to connect the accident with the young man's subsequent learning difficulties. Being familiar with Mexican folk diseases, the doctor inquired whether the mother believed she had suffered from **"Susto."** She readily affirmed that she was convinced this was, indeed, the cause of her son's problem. The pediatrician recommended the child have psychological and language evaluations to determine how the boy's learning problem could be remediated most effectively, However, he also asked the mother whether she had consulted a **curandera** (a Mexican folk healer). He did not actually recommend she do so, but by asking the question, he "gave the mother permission" to seek traditional treatment for her folk disease at the same time more conventional diagnostic procedures were pursued.

can provide a shortcut to accurate assessment of unexpected behavior in clinical settings.

While knowledge of the common health beliefs and practices of an ethnic group can be of great value, it is important to realize that stereotyping the health beliefs and behaviors of ethnic or religious minorities can also lead one astray. To appreciate this, one need only reflect on the diversity of behavior in clinical situations seen among members of one's own cultural group.

ATTRIBUTES OF THE CULTURALLY COMPETENT PHYSICIAN

The practice of culturally competent health care requires that health-care providers and health-care organizations possess certain attitudes, knowledge, and skills. These are achieved through a developmental process that begins with the realization that cultural differences may influence patients' risks for illness and responses to illness and to health-care providers. The culturally competent physician is alert to the influences of culture on patient behavior and, rather than seeing these influences as an inconvenience, accepts them as an intrinsic part of the challenge of medical practice. Moving beyond acceptance, the culturally competent physician recognizes the importance of the patient's culture to his or her sense of identity and self-esteem and avoids actions and words that demean the patient's values and beliefs. The culturally competent physician values his or her ability to communicate well with patients of diverse backgrounds, recognizing this ability as a core element in overall clinical competence. *The culturally competent physician actively seeks knowledge about*

each patient's culture, believing such knowledge to be central to the practice of medicine.

Physicians who work well with culturally diverse patients are skillful in recognizing when their lack of knowledge of a patient's culture is compromising their ability to provide optimal care. Information about the health beliefs and practices of patients is actively sought and utilized by the culturally competent physician. Such information can be obtained from the medical and social science literature, from medical colleagues and other health professionals with experience in providing cross-cultural health care, and from patients themselves. **Community agencies** serving ethnic minority and immigrant groups are usually eager to assist physicians who wish to understand their patients better and to mediate the conflicts and misunderstandings that arise in health-care settings out of lack of cultural knowledge.

The attitudes, knowledge, and skills of the culturally competent physician are summarized in Boxes 22.1, 22.2 and 22.3.

BOX 22.1 Attitudes of the culturally competent physician

- Appreciates cultural diversity as a positive attribute of his or her community
- Is interested in and attempts to learn the contributions of cultural beliefs and practices to patient health and illness behavior
- Demonstrates respect for patients regardless of ethnicity, religion, language, educational level and economic status
- Values skill in providing culturally competent health care

BOX 22.2 Knowledge of the culturally competent physician

For each culture or population served:
- The genetics, epidemiology, physiology, prevention, diagnosis, and treatment of high incidence, culturally specific causes of morbidity and mortality

- Community and family social structures

- Cultural values of the patients he or she serves, with particular emphasis on values relevant to health, illness and care for the ill

- Patterns of health services use
  - Use of traditional healers
  - Use of medical services, beliefs, and patterns of adherence to recommended treatments
  - Traditional health beliefs
  - Recognition of illness
  - Classifications of disease
  - Knowledge of risk factors and preventability of disease

- Criteria for severity of illness and urgency of seeking treatment
  - When should help be sought
  - Who should be consulted for which type of illness
  - How to tell when a treatment is effective
  - Expectations for patient behavior
  - Expectations for practitioner behavior

- Family members' roles in caring for the ill and in making care decisions
  - Traditional health practices
  - Prevention
  - Diagnosis
  - Treatment
  - Rehabilitation
  - Traditional health practitioners
  - Categories of practitioners
  - Scope of practice

- Methods of diagnosis
  - Methods of treatment
  - Methods of prognostication
  - Patterns of referral and collaboration among practitioners
  - Practitioner/patient/family communication
  - Patterns of response to a diagnosis of a fatal disease or condition
  - Values related to "fates worse than death" that may affect acceptance of or adherence to recommended treatment
  - Patterns of belief related to stigmatization that are not similar to those of the culture of the physician and that may influence the patient's health-seeking and disclosure of symptoms for possible diagnoses to the physician or to the patient's relatives

BOX 22.3 Skills of the culturally competent physician

- Identify communication difficulties based on cultural differences between patient and provider
- Use cross-cultural knowledge in
  - determining the beliefs of the patient regarding his or her illness and teaching the patient about modern concepts of that illness
  - teaching patients about modern medical services and how to make best use of them
  - averting conflict
  - providing information that is comprehensible and acceptable
  - utilizing family and community social structures in decision making and patient care
  - utilizing traditional health practices and practitioners appropriately

- Use appropriate resources to enhance culturally appropriate care
  - Hospital social services
  - Medical staff expertise
  - Behavioral science faculty expertise
  - Medical interpreters

SUMMARY

Medical education tends to emphasize the statistically normal in the study of human anatomy, physiology, and behavior, and exceptions tend to be viewed as abnormal. However, the competent physician recognizes the difference between pathological conditions and normal variation in patients. Culture is a major source of variation in response to illness and to health-care interventions.

This chapter has discussed the role of culture in patients' efforts to maintain health and respond to illness. Awareness of our patients' culturally determined health beliefs and practices is essential for the competent practice of medicine in our culturally diverse society. Achieving culturally competence in medical practice is certainly a challenge, but it is necessary for the effective provision of health care to patients whose cultural background differs from our own.

CASE STUDY

Pluralistic Health Care and Kidney Failure

Mr. Yang is a 60-year-old Hmong man who has specialized knowledge as a Hmong spiritual healer. After the defeat of the U.S.-backed Hmong forces, he and his family fled to Thailand in 1987 and came to the U.S. a few years later.

Traditional Hmong religious services are often accompanied by consumption of alcohol, and Mr. Yang's services were in heavy demand in the refugee camp in Thailand. It was there, where he was drinking frequently, that he first noticed what the camp's Western medical doctor diagnosed as hives, attributed to an allergy to alcohol. The doctor told him he would die if he continued drinking, so after thinking about it Mr. Yang decided to stop.

When Mr. Yang came to the U.S. for the first 2 years he did not drink a lot of beer or wine, only Pepsi. At a feast in 1995, Mr. Yang said that he and some other people don't drink beer and wine now that they live in the U.S., but his host urged them to drink saying "that's why you guys have been 'female' since coming here, and now that I'm here all of us are 'male' and we will all drink beer." That started Mr. Yang drinking again. He participated in more ceremonies and drank and became ill again. Then he was invited by his in-laws to another town to perform a ceremony. "My in-laws bought wine and mixed it with *Krating Daeng* (Red Bull).* This made me feel like I was getting hives again and I thought that I was allergic to the *Krating Daeng*."

Mr. Yang was invited to a funeral ceremony, and he initially tried to refuse because his feet were swelling. However, Mr. Yang played the mouth organ and he was a gifted musician. He finally capitulated after his friends insisted that he attend the ceremony and perform. At Hmong funerals, the *geej* (gaeng or kheng in the Western alphabet) is played while dancing as part of a traditional ceremony, and the exercise seemed to help Mr. Yang. His swelling diminished and he felt much better after the funeral.

A relative came to see him one day and told Mr. Yang that he also had swelling that was helped by some medicine from Mexico. Mr. Yang took a shot and his swelling improved. He wanted another shot, but the medicine was all used up. One of his friends contacted someone in a town near the Mexican border who sent him five vials.

After the second shot Mr. Yang's swelling came back, and this time it went up past his knees and his face was peeling. He drove to Mexico and showed the medicine bottle to many pharmacists until he found the medicine. The pharmacist refused to sell it to him without a prescription from a doctor. Five other places told him the same thing. He then went to see a non-English-speaking Mexican doctor to get a prescription. She gave him a shot and charged him $61 and wrote him a prescription for oral medicine. The doctor said "Whoever gave you this medicine is your enemy, not your friend. It is not for your swelling, it is a steroid to help you make muscles." Mr. Yang said "It doesn't matter, I am adjusted to it, and it helps me. I came all this way just to buy this. I have plenty of oral medication, I am searching for just this medicine."

The Mexican doctor still refused, so Mr. Yang bought the medicine the physician prescribed.

The medicines the Mexican doctor prescribed had many side effects. Mr. Yang's ears were ringing, but he took the medicine for 7 days and the swelling got better.** Then his wife made an appointment for him at a local clinic. Mr. Yang got another kind of medicine and stopped taking the medicine from Mexico but he did not get better so he was referred to another doctor who specializes in kidneys. Mr. Yang took the new medicine and seemed to improve.

When asked why he thought he had his illness Mr. Yang said "I think it is not the food that caused this, I think it was the drinking ... I told my friends, my in-laws, we eat a lot of beef ... I don't think we would be ill like this naturally, there have to be people who were trying to get rid of us ... It is not so much the drinking. When we came to the departure camp in Thailand I was taking about 100 pills.*** I could feel my male strength weaken. After taking the pills I was always sleeping. I did not take the pills anymore. Whenever I watched someone do a shaman ceremony I would always be sleepy. Before, I was not like this. Wherever I sit, I would just fall asleep. After these pills, I feel my kidneys died. I feel I have become mentally disabled having taken so many medications. Now I'm waiting for a kidney."

When asked about his health care Mr. Yang replied "I think the U.S. health care really tries to help me. I have always been an easy person, so I never had any problem with any nurses or doctor. I use traditional healing. I have acquired knowledge of shamanism, but herbal medicine does not seem to help me."

Comments

This case illustrates more or less simultaneous acceptance and use of traditional medicine plus many sources of modern medicine. Despite the ideal of continuity of care there were great discontinuities (as well as pluralities) in Mr. Yang's care: use of herbal medicines and traditional spiritual treatments as first choices in a sequence of health-seeking, use of modern medicines obtained from friends and in Mexico, and medicines and other treatments obtained from several modern physicians in the U.S.

Cultural factors involved in this case include use of traditional medications and healing methods and traditional beliefs (e.g., Hmong believe that participation in traditional ceremonies, such as funerals, may help the performer of the ceremony; using a medication that was probably prescribed for continuous use for a period of several days, then evaluating and rejecting it).

---

*   A popular canned nonalcoholic tonic with high caffeine content that is now sold widely in the U.S., and is also sold in Thailand where it is sometimes mixed with alcoholic drinks.

** In traditional Hmong treatment it is common for a shaman to predict the cause and proper treatment (e.g., animal sacrifice to a specific spirit) and pledge to make the sacrifice if the patient improves after a certain number of days. If the patient does not improve after, say, 7 days, the diagnosis and prescription were incorrect and the shaman either repeats the ceremony or the patient may try another diagnostician.

***Apparently these were amoxicillin pills.

Hmong in Southeast Asia often report that peer pressure (applied to Mr. Yang to persuade him to drink alcohol) is the reason for starting or continuing to drink, smoke, or use narcotics. Shaming (accusing Mr. Yang of being "female"), and feelings of loss of maleness is another important theme in this case.

The case also illustrates doubts in Mr. Yang's mind as to the ultimate cause of the illness: food, alcoholic beverages, *Krating Daeng* tonic, modern medicine, poisoning, or sorcery. Even at the end of this case history, when Mr. Yang was waiting for a kidney transplant, it seems that he was not told, or did not understand, the modern medical etiology of his kidney failure.

- What would you do if you encountered a patient like Mr. Yang who is actively seeking health care for a potentially life-threatening situation from a variety of traditional and modern sources?
- How much difference would it make in your treatment of Mr. Yang if you knew this much background?

- How much of Mr. Yang's story do you think you would get from your usual medical history taking techniques?

SUGGESTED READINGS

Lipson, J.G., Dibble, S.L., & Minarik, P.A. (Eds.). (1996). *Culture & nursing care: A pocket guide.* San Francisco, CA: UCSF Nursing Press.
This is a handbook that addresses the health beliefs and practices of 24 ethnic minority groups. Each chapter includes practical information regarding group-specific considerations for diet, symptom management, diagnostic and therapeutic procedures, and many other topics. The handbook was written for nurses, but it is a valuable reference for all health professionals.

Pérez, M.A., & Luquis, R.R. (Eds.) (2008). *Cultural competence in health education and health promotion.* San Francisco, CA: Jossey-Bass.
This important book examines the relevance of culture to the health of communities. Each chapter is written by an expert, and the book addresses the relevance of race, ethnicity, and gender.

23 Complementary, Alternative, and Integrative Medicine

Mary L. Hardy, Margaret L. Stuber, & Ka-Kit Hui

> There is much that we can learn from complementary medicine to make our patients feel better while our science attempts to make them get better ... However, to encourage the terminally ill to spend the last few precious months of life chasing the false promise of a cure is as cruel as it is intellectually dishonest.
>
> MICHAEL BAUM
>
> If you are genuinely skeptical about a particular treatment, voice that skepticism during the period that the person is trying to decide whether or not to do the treatment. That's being honest and helpful. But if the person decides to do the treatment, then shelve your skepticism and get behind them 100%. At that point your skepticism is cruel and unfair and undermining.
>
> KEN WILBER
> *Grace and Grit*

INTRODUCTION

Over the last 25 years, growing numbers of patients have committed to the use of complementary, alternative and integrative therapies for conditions ranging from wellness/health maintenance to treatment of serious medical illnesses. Their interest has pushed the conventional medical community to address these modalities through increased research and the addition of information about complementary, alternative and integrative therapies to the curriculum of many medical, nursing and pharmacy schools. Demonstrating the importance of this trend, over forty medical schools have programs focusing on the use of complementary, alternative and integrative therapies at the time of publication of this book, and most medical schools have included lectures or courses about complementary, alternative and integrative therapies in their curriculum.

DEFINITIONS

Despite the growing interest and importance of complementary, alternative and integrative therapies, a great deal of confusion still exists about what are and aren't complementary, alternative and integrative therapies and even what to call this whole movement. Complementary and Alternative Medicine, or CAM, as defined by the National Center of Complementary and Alternative Medicine (NCCAM), is a "group of diverse medical and health care systems, practices and products that are not generally considered part of conventional medicine." This definition is limited, as some therapies usually provided by CAM providers, such as advice about diet and lifestyle change, are often included in conventional bio-medical treatment. Further, as CAM therapies are researched, found to be effective, and adopted by Western practitioners, this definition no longer accurately describes the field. An alternative definition proposed by Edzard Ernst notes that CAM therapies satisfy demands not met by conventional practice or diversify the conceptual framework of medicine. This way of defining CAM is especially useful for highlighting the differences between CAM and conventional bio-medicine in the conceptualization of health and illness as well as in the approach to the patient.

Reflecting these varied perspectives, a number of different terms have been used to describe this field. The first term used, **alternative medicine**, implies that patients use therapies instead of or separate from the Western system with very little interaction between the two systems. **Complementary medicine**, the next term to appear in common usage, describes "alternative" therapies acting as a complement to or in support of the dominant Western biomedical system. According to this definition, patients have access to both systems of care, with the CAM therapies employed to enhance the effects or reduce the toxicity of Western medicine. This evolution in nomenclature reflected a trend toward greater inclusion or at least consideration of CAM and/or it's modalities by mainstream medicine, as these approaches grew in popularity with the public.

Another commonly used term, **holistic or wholistic medicine**, as defined by the American Holistic Medical Association, places the patient at the center of care and consciously considers all aspects of the patient in providing care. Implicit in this system is the belief that the patient is more than just the sum of his or her component parts. Finally, **Integrative Medicine**, a term first coined by Andrew Weil, has been adopted by the academic community and many physicians practicing in this field. As defined by NCCAM, Integrative Medicine "combines mainstream medical therapies and CAM therapies for which there is some high-quality scientific evidence of safety and effectiveness." Integrative medicine physicians assist patients in choosing from a broad array of therapies ranging from the alternative to the conventional.

In order to indicate as broad a spectrum as possible, the term Complementary Alternative Integrative Medicine (CAIM) will be used when referring to this area for the remainder of this chapter.

> Similar diseases are cured by similar things.
>
> CHRISTIAN FRIEDRICH SAMUEL HAHNEMANN
> German physician and founder of homeopathy

Classification of Complementary Alternative and Integrative Medicine (CAIM)

NCCAM classifies CAIM therapies into five broad domains: alternative medical systems, biologically based therapies, mind-body interventions, manipulative and body-based therapies and energy therapies. **Alternative systems of medicine** are complete systems of care with a well-developed world-view. They typically include unique diagnostic strategies coupled with a variety of therapeutic modalities integrated into a comprehensive treatment plan. Examples include Traditional Chinese Medicine and Ayurvedic Medicine. When the individual components are not used as part of the complete alternative medical system, e.g., acupuncture only, they can be classified in one of the following categories.

Biologically based therapies emphasize substances derived from nature that are usually ingested or applied topically and include herbs, minerals, vitamins and other dietary supplements. **Mind-body interventions** modify the interaction between the mental and physical systems in the body and include yoga as well as all forms of meditation. **Manipulative and body based systems** involve movement of the physical body or its parts to enhance the structure of the body, correct posture or relieve strain. Examples include massage, Trager or Feldenkrais techniques, as well as chiropractic and osteopathic medicine. **Energetic therapies** posit the existence of an energetic field around the body or a flow of energy within the body that is modified by the practitioner. Examples include Therapeutic or Healing touch, acupuncture or Reiki.

EPIDEMIOLOGY AND PATTERNS OF USE

Utilization of CAIM has been increasing during the last two decades. In 2002 and 2007, the National Health Interview Survey (NHIS) reported on CAIM use in over twenty thousand adults and over nine thousand children. *In 2007, 38% of adults and almost 12% of children reported using some form of CAIM.* This was a slight increase for adults compared to the 2002 survey, when reported CAIM use was 36%. Data from the seminal surveys published by David Eisenberg in 1993 and 1998 also show an increase in use in the general adult population from 34% to 42%, with corresponding increases in number of visits to alternative providers and a 45% increase in the amount of money spent out of pocket for CAIM by users. Although this level of usage in the general population has been confirmed in a number of surveys, for certain medical conditions, such as osteoarthritis or cancer, utilization may be much higher and approaches 100% in some cases. In 2007, the 38 million users of CAIM made more than 350 million visits to CAIM providers.

The typical user of CAIM is usually described as female, white, well educated and of higher socioeconomic status. However, this common misperception underestimates use of CAIM by some ethnic populations, who may not consider their traditional therapies as alternative, and interest from socio-economically disadvantaged populations, who may not have the income to access certain types of CAIM therapy. In fact, in the NHIS survey, utilization of CAIM was highest (50%) in the Native American population with the lowest utilization reported in black (25.5%) and Hispanic (23.7%) subjects. Other surveys of inner city populations (lower socio-economic status) and a variety of ethnic groups have shown high interest in a variety of CAIM therapies.

Reasons For Use of CAIM

Reasons for use of CAIM vary greatly. Many patients use these therapies to treat chronic conditions as well as to maintain health and wellness. Poor health or perceived poor health may predict higher use of CAM. In some surveys, CAIM use was associated with more pain and greater emotional limitations in users. For female breast cancer patients, CAIM use has been associated with higher rates of psychosocial distress. Some users come to CAIM out of frustration with conventional medicine because of unmet needs, lack of effective therapy or dissatisfaction with Western care. Alternatively, others choose CAIM therapies because they are consonant with other lifestyle choices emphasizing natural or holistic values. For example, many people who use dietary supplements believe that they are supplementing a diet that is deficient in essential nutrients. Ironically, higher utilizers of CAIM often have better diets and healthier habits than nonusers. Overall, the majority of CAIM users do not reject biomedicine but combine conventional care with CAIM to enhance efficacy or reduce toxicity of Western therapy.

Members of the general public are most likely to use CAIM for painful conditions such as back pain, osteoarthritis, headache, or acute injury. Individual conditions will prompt use of specific therapies, such as fish oil for cardiovascular disease, St. John's Wort for depression or acupuncture for nausea associated with chemotherapy. Patients suffering from functional conditions poorly characterized and/or with limited conventional treatment options, such as chronic fatigue syndrome, fibromyalgia or irritable bowel syndrome, are particularly likely to use CAIM therapies.

> Did you ever see the customers in health-food stores? They are pale, skinny people who look half dead. In a steak house, you see robust, ruddy people. They're dying, of course, but they look terrific.
>
> BILL COSBY

There is no definitive list of therapies to be included or excluded in CAIM. For example, prayer intended to aid health is overwhelmingly the most popular CAIM intervention chosen by patients in surveys that offer this choice. However, not all experts count this as a CAIM therapy. Generally, the most commonly used modalities include natural products (vitamins, herbs, etc.) (17.7–35%) and deep breathing or meditation (9.4%). Manipulative therapies (chiropractic and osteopathic medicine) and other body based therapies accounted for the majority of visits made to CAIM providers in 2007. Dietary supplements (DS) may be used by up to 70% of the general adult population, especially if multiple vitamin use is included. Using a more conservation definition of a DS as a nonvitamin, nonmineral natural product (NVNM), utilization has still increased from 23% of the general population in 1999 to over 40% by 2007. Well-known CAIM therapies such as massage (8%), yoga (6%), or acupuncture (< 1%) were used much less often in NHIS and other surveys.

Consumers usually use more than one therapy at a time. For example, they often take several dietary supplements, and 50% of older dietary supplement users are also taking over the counter or prescription medications. Patients dealing with serious medical conditions such as cancer or heart disease will also use CAIM therapies. Use remains high, approximately 30%, even in patients immediately prior to surgery. Use by pregnant women and children is lower but still significant.

Expenditures On CAIM

One of the earliest estimates of CAIM expenditures, in 1997, was reported to total $27 billion, with approximately $12 billion spent on CAIM provider fees. According to the NHIS, *in 2007 consumers spent $33.9 billion in out of pocket expenses for CAIM goods and services.* Of the $22 billion in consumer self-care costs, almost half (43.7% or $14.8 billion) was spent on nonvitamin, nonmineral natural products. Consumers paid CAIM providers almost $12 billion directly while spending an additional four billion dollars for yoga, tai chi, chi gong and other classes. According to these two major surveys, the ways in which patients/consumers are accessing CAIM therapies may be changing. Visits to individual providers have dropped from a high of 628.8 million visits (3,176 visits per 1,000 adults) in 1997 to 354.2 million visits (1,592 visits per 1,000 adults) in NHIS in 2007. This reflects a re-distribution of services from provider-given to self-care for a number of modalities, such as relaxation therapy. However, other therapies have increased in utilization, such as acupuncture. Given the differences in the findings of these two large surveys, variations in the patterns of use cannot be conclusively asserted. What is clear is that overall utilization and the amount of money devoted to CAIM therapies have remained very high.

Patient Nondisclosure of CAIM Use

Before the publication of Eisenberg's landmark study in 1993, the extent of CAIM use was invisible to conventional medicine. For biomedical health practitioners, it was shocking to learn that 70% (a figure later confirmed in many other surveys) of their patients were using but not disclosing use of CAIM. Conversely, patients are very likely to disclose fully to the CAIM provider. Patients report that they are strongly reluctant to disclose CAIM use when they expect an overly negative response from their physician. Patients are especially reluctant to disclose if they are using CAIM and conventional medicine for the same condition and if they perceive that the doctor is only interested in scientific evidence. It has also been reported that patients may feel that Western physicians do not need to know about CAM use. Finally, and of concern to med-

BOX 23.1 Definition of integrative medicine

Integrative Medicine is the practice of medicine that reaffirms the importance of the relationship between practitioner and patient, focuses on the whole person, is informed by evidence, and makes use of all appropriate therapeutic approaches, health-care professionals, and disciplines to achieve optimal health and healing.

Developed and adopted by The Consortium of Academic Health Centers for Integrative Medicine, May 2004; Edited May 2005

ical education, many patients report they do not reveal CAIM use because they do not think that physicians are particularly knowledgeable about or interested in CAIM and thus do not have much to contribute to the discussion. In spite of this tendency toward nondisclosure, the majority of patients still would prefer to have their doctor involved in the oversight of their CAIM use. Increasing the knowledge base of physicians appears necessary if patients are to disclose their use of CAIM. Optimal care requires free and complete communication, not only between patient and physician, but among all providers.

INFORMATION SOURCES

Patients incorporate a wide variety of information into their medical decision-making, including advice from friends and family, anecdotes, popular literature, testimonials, personal intuition and advertising. Unfortunately, many patients do not identify Western medical practitioners as a major source for reliable information about CAIM. If patients are not generally getting information about CAIM from their physicians, where do they get it? Most patients report learning about these therapies from friends or family. Even though traditional print media (books, newspapers and magazines) are used by many patients, the internet has become an increasingly important source of information. However, information from this source may be difficult to assess and incorporate into decision-making. According to one study, both patients and physicians have difficulty distinguishing biased from higher quality information on the internet. At times, the sheer volume and inconsistency of information available is overwhelming. Unfortunately, despite the fact that patients have a strong preference to receive information about CAIM from their health center or physician, this rarely occurs—even when they are being treated for something as serious as cancer.

Patients report that they prefer that physicians initiate the discussion about CAIM, as this encourages patients to seek information from them. When physicians and other health practitioners do not counsel patients about dietary

supplements and CAIM use, patients will find other willing sources of information. Several studies have demonstrated that clerks in health food stores will almost always offer advice about product selection even when patients present with a serious diagnosis such as breast cancer. *Therefore, it is critical that providers always ask about CAIM use during their clinical encounters.* Developing an open-minded strategy of nonjudgmental inquiry will encourage the patient to disclose more fully. Having this discussion deepens the patient-physician relationship, improves treatment planning, and increases the safety of the patient. Without adequate information, the clinician cannot anticipate potential interactions between the CAIM therapy and conventional care.

RESEARCH AND CAIM

In response to growing consumer interest in CAIM, the United States Congress funded the Office of Alternative Medicine (OAM) in 1993, with an initial budget of several million dollars. This office became into a full center of the National Institutes of Health in 1998, with a budget of over $100 million dollars in 2008. The **National Center of Complementary and Alternative Medicine** (NCCAM) is responsible for training scientists and facilitating rigorous research into CAIM modalities, as well as educating the public about these therapies. Given the complex and heterogeneous nature of CAIM therapies, this has been a challenging endeavor.

Conventional medical research, originally designed to evaluate drug therapies, depends heavily on the randomized, double-blind, placebo controlled trial (RCT) to provide proof of efficacy. The purpose of the RCT is to eliminate bias and test standardized therapies in ways that are reproducible. Applying this same strategy to CAIM is problematic. For some therapies, development of an appropriate, indistinguishable, inert placebo to permit true blinding is difficult. For example, how would you blind an aromatherapy trial, especially for common scents like lavender or peppermint? It has been especially challenging to develop an appropriate inert placebo for acupuncture trials.

Beyond placebo issues, CAIM interventions are often complex and individualized for a particular patient, thus making standardized interventions difficult to achieve and comparisons between different trials challenging. Patients, when self-treating, often take multiple products, while those seeing CAIM providers usually receive several modalities concurrently. Further, two patients with the same medical condition may receive very different care from the same CAIM practitioner, unlike the usual Western practice.

Significant heterogeneity exists even when interventions seem comparable. For example, botanical products, even when extracted from the same plant, can vary greatly depending on the composition of the original starting material as well as on the methods used to prepare it. Rarely do two acupuncturists use exactly the same series of points and several hundred different styles of chiropractic adjustments exist. Despite these challenges, the number of research trials using CAIM modalities is growing. The NCCAM alone has funded over two thousand research projects in the last decade, and CAIM studies have been published in all of the major medical journals.

EVIDENCE-BASED MEDICINE AND DECISION-MAKING: PATIENT AND PRACTITIONER PERSPECTIVES

As it was first conceived, evidence-based medicine (EBM) was intended to use the best scientific evidence available to guide clinicians to make clinical decisions consonant with the patient's values and informed by their clinical experience. EBM was meant to help guide effective joint provider-patient decision-making, not provide a rigid algorithm dictating care. However, EBM also requires that practices proven to be ineffective or unsafe should be not be used. As applied to conventional medicine, the backbone of EBM is the randomized controlled trial. As discussed earlier, this is a relatively new invention in medicine. The first RCT was conducted 50 years ago, and the term "evidence-based medicine" first appeared in the medical literature a little over 10 years ago. Although high quality evidence is not currently available for the majority of medical decisions in conventional bio-medicine, there is a stated commitment by the medical community to use evidence to guide practice. However, despite this belief in EBM, when evidence would suggest a significant change in long-standing medical practice (such as starting screening mammograms at a later age), many practitioners and their patients are resistant to following this advice.

Applying EBM to CAIM practices can be even more problematic. For most therapies insufficient or contradictory evidence exists. Most therapies are generally safe (although this assertion may be controversial for a few therapies), but clear evidence for efficacy is frequently lacking. CAIM therapies are often applied in complex and individualized treatment plans that do not lend themselves to conventional biomedical testing paradigms designed to test more uniform interventions. In addition, patients and Western medical providers often disagree about the significance and meaning of the information used to make decisions.

Patient Perspective

As noted above, patients consider a wide variety of sources of information when making decisions about dietary supplements and CAIM use. They often utilize this information differently than physicians. Although scientific research information is considered useful, patients attach less importance to this kind of information than do clinicians. In fact, even when clinical trials report negative findings, as happened recently for glucosamine and chondroitin when used for osteoarthritis, committed users do not consider this data relevant. In the face of their own perceived benefit, they do not change their practice.

Consumers often rely on the advice of family and friends when choosing products or services and tend to be very interested in wellness or disease prevention as well as supplementing treatment of chronic disease. *Disease prevention or wellness was the reported reason for use of over half of the patients taking dietary supplements.* In addition, CAIM is often the first choice for self-limited illness (colds) or relatively minor chronic conditions (osteoarthritis). When combining CAIM with conventional medicine, especially for serious medical conditions, patients are usually interested in decreasing the perceived toxicity of Western therapies or enhancing their effect.

Consumers are generally well disposed to CAIM therapies. CAIM therapies are often perceived as efficacious—up to 98% of the time for some choices. Consumers report greater satisfaction with CAIM and dietary supplement use, noting the lower incidence of side effects and greater perceived safety of the alternative choices. This bias toward greater tolerability of dietary supplements and herbs can affect how often patients report adverse events. The more strongly their CAIM use is the outcome of their basic philosophical orientation, the less likely they are to report side effects. Thus, patients are choosing to use therapies because they have been personally recommended and are considered to be safe and well tolerated, rather than choosing therapies because of strong scientific evidence.

Provider Perspective

Conventional Western medical providers place a great deal of confidence in scientific evidence and generally want to follow EBM guidelines. Many times, rightly or wrongly, physicians will weigh scientific evidence more highly than patient preference, for example, when declining to use antibiotics to treat a viral cold. It has been suggested that there is no such thing as alternative and conventional medicine- there is only good medicine. According to this belief, as therapies and interventions become "proven," they would be assimilated into conventional practice. In fact, in some cases, this has happened. Many expert panels now include lifestyle interventions (diet, exercise, relaxation practice) in the early treatment of diseases like hypertension and hyperlipidemia. In addition, for low back pain, chiropractic care is considered an appropriate early intervention along with supportive care, and black cohosh is discussed as a treatment for vasomotor symptoms of menopause. However, many CAIM therapies continue to have incomplete or contradictory literature for efficacy and limited direct evidence for safety.

As the literature in CAIM continues to grow at a rapid rate, remaining knowledgeable of the range and nuances of this literature will become more difficult. Even though older, smaller trials showed consistent benefit, many large or more recent clinical trials of certain CAIM modalities/products have been negative, leading conventional providers to discount CAIM therapies. Clinicians need to be careful that their judgments are based on the totality of the evidence. For example, a large NIH sponsored trial of St. John's Wort (SJW) did not demonstrate effectiveness for depression. However, several subsequent meta-analyses, which included all of the rigorously conducted trials, concluded that *SJW is equally effective for mild to moderate depression as commonly used conventional drugs, often with fewer side effects.* Evidence of safety is usually based on case reports of adverse events that usually are rare, albeit very serious, reactions. This leads to a distorted view of the risk of most dietary supplements. In fact, physicians and pharmacists have often been shown in surveys to have incomplete knowledge about the risks of common dietary supplements. A good number of the studies conducted today on herbal medicines are small pharmacological studies on potential herb-drug interactions, with results that are not always confirmed in larger trials. To address this growing volume of heterogeneous data, many practitioners are depending on systematic reviews or meta-analysis as well as database sites that provide a synopsis of the available literature. Therefore, their analysis is bound by the limitations of their sources and the literature on which they are based.

CAIM providers, in contrast to bio-medical providers, do not feel very confident in their ability to interpret scientific trials and were largely not aware of recent large RCT's relevant to their area of practice. They often note that scientifically constructed trials do not measure their treatments as they are used clinically. Therefore, this type of evidence is generally not used in guiding practice of CAIM professional providers. They are more dependent on the empirical evidence collected over the long term of practice of many of these therapies (thousands of years for Traditional Chinese Medicine and Ayurveda). In practice, this usually consists of expert opinion which may vary considerably from practitioner to practitioner or from discipline to discipline.

COMMON CAM MODALITIES: SAFETY AND EFFICACY

Dietary Supplements

The definition of a dietary supplement (DS) is established by the law regulating these products. The Dietary Supplement Health and Education Act of 1994 (DSHEA) defines a DS as a product intended to supplement the diet that contains a vitamin, mineral, amino acid, herbs or other similar substances. These products are not intended to diagnose, prevent, treat or mitigate any illness and are to be taken orally. Manufacturing standards have been established by recent regulation subject to oversight by the FDA. The Office of Dietary Supplements (ODS) was established by the DSHEA act to "strengthen knowledge and understanding of dietary supplements by evaluating scientific information, stimulating and supporting research, disseminating research results, and educating the public to foster an enhanced quality of life and health for the U. S. population." The format and information contained on the DS label is regulated to display information about the composition of the product, the intended use and some limited safety data.

Dietary supplements are used by 70 to 90% of the United States population. The most popular supplements by far are multimineral multivitamins (MMV). After MMV, single vitamins such as vitamin C and E and minerals such as calcium or zinc are the most commonly used. Popular non-MMV include fish oil and glucosamine with and without chondroitin. These patterns of use are fairly stable from year to year. Vitamin D use is strongly increasing as new research reports positive findings and physicians begin prescribing this vitamin for their patients.

The safety of DS has raised concern in the medical community, although consumers generally consider these products safe. This assumption of safety is generally true for well-manufactured supplements. The law stipulates that products available before the passage of the DSHEA act are assumed to be safe unless specific information is available to the contrary. Regulatory authority is given to the Federal Drug Administration (FDA) to remove unsafe or improperly manufactured dietary supplements. The FDA has acted to remove unsafe products from the market

I believe that you can, by taking some simple and inexpensive measures, extend your life and your years of well-being. My most important recommendation is that you take vitamins every day in optimum amounts, to supplement the vitamins you receive in your food.

LINUS PAULING, PhD
Two-time Nobel Prize Laureate

including dietary supplements adulterated by drugs or toxic constituents. In order to improve the tracking of potential problems with DS, a recent law requires that dietary supplement manufacturing companies report all serious adverse events. Analysis of these reported cases, as they become available, should give a much clearer picture of the extent and severity of adverse events associated with dietary supplements in common usage in the United States.

The majority of the serious adverse events involving dietary supplements have occurred as a result of contamination with drugs or other toxic substances. For example, calcium carbonate has been contaminated with lead in the past and Chinese patent medicines have been found to contain a variety of pharmaceutical drugs. In the 1980's an outbreak of eosinophilic myalgia, a serious condition in which patients develop high eosinophil counts, muscle pain and neurological complaints, was traced to contaminated tryptophan, an amino acid used as a sleep aid. In the case of herbal supplements, misidentification of the species used or improper substitution of one species for another has resulted in serious adverse events.

Herbal Medicine

Botanical medicines, a subset of dietary supplements, are made from plants or plant parts that are considered therapeutic based on their constituents, taste or aroma. Botanicals, including herbs, represent the earliest medicine used in human history. Medicinal plants have been found in association with prehistoric remains that are more than 5000 years old. Traditional cultures such as China and India have historical evidence of continuous use of botanicals for over 3000 years. Until well into the 20th century, most conventional medicines were plant based. It is estimated that 25% or more of current drugs are still directly derived from plants. The World Health Organization estimates that for a large portion of the developing world, botanicals are still the principle medicines used. Herbal remedies are taken by approximately one third of the general population and may be used more frequently by certain ethnic groups in the United States.

Botanicals are often known by their common name (e.g., garlic), but their scientific name consists of the genus and species and is italicized *(Allium sativum)*. This Latin binomial is the most specific and exact way to refer to a plant because a single common name may belong to more than one plant. Botanical medicines are available in a number of different forms. They may be used in a fresh or dried form. Herbs are also commonly extracted either using water to make teas or decoctions as well as a water/alcohol mixture to make a tincture. Extracts can be standardized to one or more constituents in order to ensure potency and consistency. Products may also consist of isolated constit-

> The Lord hath created medicines out of the earth; and he that is wise will not abhor them.
>
> ECCLESIASTICS 38:4

uents such as soy isoflavones. Some of the most commonly used herbs include soy *(Glycine max)*, echinacea *(Echinacea angustifolia; Echinacea purpurea)*, gingko *(Gingko biloba)*, St. John's Wort *(Hypericum perforatum)*, black cohosh *(Actea racemosa)*, garlic *(Allium sativum)* and ginseng *(Panax ginseng or Panax quinquefolius)*.

Product variability provides a unique challenge in botanical medicine in several different ways. First, the huge array of products available can be overwhelming to patients and can complicate use. Attempts are made to reduce some of this variability by standardizing herbal products to one or more marker compounds. These compounds may or may not be the active ingredient in the herb and in many cases there isn't even a uniform technique used to measure these markers.

According to manufacturing regulations published by the FDA, the amount of marker compounds in all batches of the product should be the same with a 10% margin of error considered acceptable. The type of variation is called batch to batch variability. If variability is very high, this is usually considered a sign of a problem with the quality of the product. In addition, different manufactures can appropriately or inappropriately include different amounts or different compositions of these compounds in a given product. A study done at UCLA showed that marker compounds in a series of single herb products from different manufacturers can vary as much as 20 times from least to greatest concentration. Finally, herbs are often combined in unique formulas of multiple ingredients. For this reason, it is always advisable to see the actual bottles of the products patients are using and to counsel them not to change products without consultation with a health provider, as variations in the products can lead to differences in clinical response.

Adverse events with botanical supplements can result from several causes. Minor adverse events such as gastrointestinal upset are relatively common, although mild and self-limited. Allergic reactions have been reported, especially to plants in the Compositae family such as chamomile and echinacea. More serious reactions are very uncommon in well-manufactured products. Misidentification, adulteration and substitution with more toxic herbs have been reported occasionally with very serious results. Adulteration with drugs has been reported for Chinese patent formulas and by heavy metals for ethnic Ayurvedic formulas. Finally, herbs may have toxic constituents which can be harmful if the herb is not handled properly.

Medical providers often cite the potential for herbal products to interact with pharmaceuticals as a major safety concern. Rates of concurrent use drugs, over-the-counter and/or prescription, by botanical medicine users vary from 15 to 80% and in one survey over half of elderly DS users were concurrently taking prescription medication. Patients often believe that dietary supplements are safe and do not constitute a risk when combined with medication. In fact, one study reported that 40% of herbal product users felt that combining herbs with their drugs made each therapy more effective.

Despite patient beliefs, concern is justified for narrow therapeutic index drugs and caution should be used for certain herbs. Medications such as coumadin, digoxin, anti-retroviral drugs and cyclosporine have all had significant, adverse drug interactions reports. The most consistent herb-drug interactions have been reported for St. John's Wort, especially if the extract is high in the compound hyperforin.

However, the majority of interactions reported are either theoretical or of unclear clinical significance. Thus, the true incidence of herb-drug interactions is not clear and is probably lower than feared. In retrospective chart reviews and in evaluations at coagulation clinics, few interactions have actually been documented. Still, since the potential for interactions exists and the patient would therefore be at risk, it is important to encourage patients to disclose all natural product use to their physician and/or pharmacist to reduce the risk of adverse effects.

> The scope of herbal medicine ranges from mild-acting plant medicines such as chamomile and peppermint, to very potent ones such as foxglove (from which the drug digitalis is derived). In between these two poles lies a wide spectrum of plant medicine with significant medical applications. One need only go to the United States Pharmacopoeia to see the central role that plant medicine has played in American medicine.
>
> DONALD BROWN

Traditional Chinese Medicine/Acupuncture

Traditional Chinese Medicine (TCM), a system of medicine developed empirically over several thousand years, focuses on the flow of energy in the body. This energy, usually referred to as *Qi* or *Chi*, is not a concept familiar to Western medicine. In the TCM system, health is present when energy flows freely and the body is in balance. Characteristic patterns of imbalance are identified by assessing symptoms, looking at the tongue and palpating peripheral pulses. These patterns relate to particular energetic configurations of the body that may or may not correlate directly to Western medical conditions. TCM practitioners affect the flow of energy, either directly or indirectly, by using a number of techniques including acupuncture, *Tua Na* (abdominal massage), Traditional Chinese Herbal Medicine, diet and exercise such as *Tai Chi* or *Qi Gong*. Acupuncture, the technique most often used in the West, inserts thin needles into specific points located along pathways called meridians. These points can be stimulated by manual pressure (acupressure), by turning the inserted needles or by applying electrical current to the needles.

The typical practitioner of TCM is trained for 3 or more years to a masters or doctoral degree level and licensed by the individual states. Although Traditional Chinese Medicine is usually practiced by therapists trained in these techniques, certification for physician practitioners does exist. Physician training is much less extensive than that obtained by licensed practitioners of TCM and focuses on acupuncture only. Although TCM is a common practice in the cultures of origin for Asian Americans and a significant number of TCM providers are Asian, this approach to healing has become more widely available and is commonly used in the United States.

In 2007, approximately three million Americans used acupuncture to treat painful conditions, a three-fold increase in utilization over the previous 5 years. Evidence for the effectiveness of acupuncture exists for back pain, osteoarthritis of the knee, joint and neck pain, tendonitis and headaches. Acupuncture and acupressure have also been shown to be useful for relieving nausea and vomiting resulting from pregnancy and other causes.

In spite of the fact that TCM is conceived and practiced in a paradigm far removed from Western medicine, *the "map" of acupuncture points described classically is over 70% identical to the map of trigger points identified by a Western physician studying pain medicine.* Western theories regarding the mechanism of action of acupuncture for pain vary from increasing the production of endorphins at a central level in the brain to blocking painful sensory input at the spinal level. Recent scientific investigations are also beginning to reveal bio-physiological data regarding the underlying mechanisms of acupuncture that often correlate with traditionally described effects.

Acupuncture is generally considered safe, especially when properly performed by a skilled practitioner using sterile needles. Most adverse events are minor and self-limited. They include pain or bruising at the site of needle insertion, faintness or dizziness following treatment and initial exacerbation of symptoms. Very rarely serious adverse events related to trauma induced by needling have been reported including death, pneumothorax, hemopericardium and nerve damage. In a series of 229,230 patients with approximately 10 visits each (over 2 million visits total), mild adverse events were reported 9% of the time and only 2% of the patients experienced an adverse event that required treatment. Severe adverse events occurred in approximately 0.1% of this population. Infectious diseases such as hepatitis or HIV transmission have only been re-

> The results in Japan which I will relate surpass even miracles. For chronic pains of the head, for obstruction of liver and spleen, and also for pleurisy, they bore through [the flesh] with a stylus made of silver or bronze.
>
> JACOB DE BONDT
> describing acupuncture (1658)

ported when sterilization was inadequate. Most practitioners today employ single use, disposable needles.

Chiropractic Spinal Manipulation

Chiropractic medicine, developed in the 19th century, is based on the belief that proper alignment of the spine is essential to maintain the health of the body. When the spine is out of alignment (called **subluxation**), impedance of the function of the spinal nerves and peripheral neuromuscular system creates pain and ill health. Manual adjustment of the spine restores proper structure, thus relieving symptoms and restoring health. The most familiar style of chiropractic adjustment is a high velocity, high force adjustment of the spinal segments of the neck, thorax or low back. However, there are hundreds of styles of adjustment, many of which are more conservative and may use little or no force. In addition to adjustment, chiropractors often use modalities such as topical heat or ice, ultrasound, or electro-stimulation to relieve symptoms. Therapeutic exercises are given to strengthen the body as well.

Chiropractic treatment, as originally conceived, was intended to treat a wide variety of medical conditions but today is used principally to address musculoskeletal pain. Eighteen million adults received chiropractic care in 2007, mainly to treat chronic painful conditions such as headaches, back or neck pain. A course of treatment consists of repeated adjustments over time until the body is able to maintain the proper alignment. The strongest evidence for efficacy exists for low back pain, neck pain, headaches, and acute trauma such as whiplash, although chiropractic adjustments are used for a wide range of musculoskeletal disorders.

Chiropractic medicine is one of the most popular CAIM modalities, representing approximately a third of the practitioner visits in 2007 or almost 19 million visits annually. Despite the large number of adjustments performed yearly, serious complications are rarely seen. Adjustment is usually well tolerated with minor, self-limiting events occurring perhaps as often as 10% of the time. These include temporary exacerbation of the underlying symptoms, headaches, vertigo and nausea. Serious ad-

verse events, including death, stroke, peripheral nerve injury and the development of acute cauda equina syndrome, are rare. They have been estimated to occur as often as once in forty thousand adjustments or as infrequently as once in two million adjustments. Adjustments of the upper cervical spine have been associated with the most severe reactions such as strokes. Therefore, chiropractors are taught to identify patients at potentially higher risk and to modify their techniques accordingly. Absolute contra-indications to adjustment include fracture, infection or metastases of the area to be adjusted as well as rheumatoid arthritis, severe osteoporosis or carotid bruit (for cervical spine adjustment).

INTEGRATION WITH THE CONVENTIONAL MEDICAL MODEL

Given the differences between conventional medicine and most CAIM therapies, integration of these two services seems unlikely at first consideration. In fact, some CAIM providers are resistant to integration because they feel it will result in assimilation into conventional medicine and the unique features of their practice will be lost. Likewise, many conventional physicians are skeptical of including CAIM practices in their care. They have concerns that the CAIM practices will not be held to the same standard of safety and efficacy as conventional medicine. Despite these concerns, interest by a growing number of conventional and CAIM providers, as well as increasing patient utilization and strong patient preference to combine CAIM care with conventional care, is pushing both sides together.

Patients' are clearly interested in the joint use of CAIM with conventional medicine. When surveyed, more than 50% of current CAIM users wanted their CAIM care to be delivered at their primary care clinic. In addition, growing numbers of patients expect that their physicians will be knowledgeable about CAIM practices and be able to make referrals to appropriate products and/or providers. Patients generally want their conventional provider to supervise their CAIM use. A smaller number of patients will continue to seek care outside of the conventional setting. Even here, in order to optimize care, biomedical providers will still need to encourage these patients to disclose fully what they are using and be prepared to discuss their choices knowledgeably.

Response from conventional medicine to this increased patient interest has been varied. In order to develop the knowledge base regarding CAIM, increasing amounts of research money has been allocated and studies have been undertaken. Professional schools have generally acknowledged their need to teach their students at least the rudimentary issues involved in CAIM to prepare them for the inevitable patient questions. Now most medical, pharmacy, dental and nursing schools have information on CAIM included in their curriculum. In fact, growing numbers of physicians are electing to practice in this integrated model of care, called Integrative Medicine.

Integration may not be as impossible as it initially seems, for common ground does exist between these different models. For example, both systems are concerned with patient centered care. For CAIM, the individuality and uniqueness of the patient are at the heart of their practice. In conventional medicine, the current emphasis on individualized care reflects an awareness of genetic heterogeneity, as well as a return to values more prevalent in medicine before our increasing dependence on technological advances.

An interest in prevention is present in both systems of care, although their emphasis is different. Prevention represents a long-standing but somewhat neglected component of conventional medicine. In current practice, it is often defined in terms of disease surveillance to achieve early diagnosis such as use of mammograms and pap smears. Conventional medicine seems to be much less successful in motivating and supporting patients to make lifestyle choices that would prevent chronic diseases such as obesity, hypertension, some forms of cancer, hyperlipidemia and diabetes. Prevention in CAIM practices is considered a primary focus, with the goal often stated more positively as a restoration of wellness rather than simply the prevention of disease. Strong CAIM interest in components of treatment such as diet, exercise, stress reduction, all of which fit very well into conventional medical models of care, provide a large area of shared interest.

One model of integration which is used in some chronic pain clinics is a team-based approach. Teams consist of a variety of practitioners, including a medical provider. Groups sometimes practice in the same location but may meet for assessments and treatment planning, while practicing separately. The treatment plan for the patient is discussed with the team and includes those modalities with the best evidence for efficacy and the highest patient interest. The physician remains involved even as other modalities might be chosen as first line therapies, and make a conventional biomedical diagnosis and monitors the safety of the patient. Precedent for team approaches already exists in conventional bio-medicine, particularly in rehabilitation. However, there are still many factors which impede the development of this type of CAIM integrated practice.

One of the significant barriers to true integration of CAIM and biomedicine is the heterogeneity in the training and professionalism of CAIM providers. Some CAIM professionals already train at a level commensurate with physician training. For example, osteopathic training is identical to conventional medical care, with the addition of instruction in adjustment. The anatomy of the musculoskeletal system and the structural approach underlying diagnosis and treatment in Chiropractic medicine is very familiar to Western practitioners. Chiropractors and naturopathic medical physicians follow a basic science curriculum at the beginning of their training modeled on similar courses at conventional medical schools. One major difference between all CAIM professions and conventional medicine is that structured residencies in CAIM are not offered and practitioners can therefore practice independently immediately after graduation. Most CAIM professionals would strongly support and participate in these programs if they were available, but to date the economic support for them has not been present. Many CAIM professions are licensed at the state level (Traditional Chinese Medicine, Chiropractic, Naturopathic Medicine) and are regulated very similarly to conventional medicine. However, other common therapies are much less structured and regulated (massage therapy, herbal practitioners). Professional training is not standardized and is usually much shorter than the licensed professions listed above. In addition, some techniques, such as cranial sacral manipulation, may be taught to a wide variety of different CAIM providers. These differences lead to difficulties in creating smooth functioning teams that include conventional practitioners and biomedical facilities. With planning, appropriate credentialing and standards of practice can be established to address these issues.

Cost creates significant barriers to access. If CAIM treatments are not reimbursed by insurance, many people who want these therapies cannot access them. In response to consumer demand, a growing number of insurance providers have started to provide coverage using a number of different models. Some states have passed laws that mandate coverage of all licensed providers that compels parity in insurance coverage between CAIM providers and Western practitioners. CAIM providers are usually treated as primary care providers in such systems. Some people believe that utilization of covered CAIM services will greatly increase costs in medical systems, a major issue in times of severe economic stress on our existing health care system. Data on costs and cost effectiveness of CAIM when used within the Western system are scanty. Where coverage has been provided and costs have been evaluated, a substantial minority of patients did use CAIM services (approximately 14% in one study). They mainly used these services for pain management and the increase in expenditures was modest. Although CAIM providers believe that their low-tech patient centered style of care will provide equivalent or better results for chronic diseases, this assertion has not generally been tested scientifically, using good cost benefit outcome measures. So despite strong patient interest and growing willingness in the conventional and CIM communities, it is still not clear how CAIM and conventional medicine will integrate in the coming years.

CASE STUDY

Gail, an 18-year-old college student, has decided to start seeing an internist, rather than the pediatrician she had been seeing when she lived with her parents. Her initial concern is headache. She has had a mixture of migraine and muscle tension headaches since she was 14 years old, but these have become a more serious issue with the stresses of college life. Gail is otherwise very healthy. The only medication she is taking is an oral contraceptive, which she self-consciously says is to control her periods. Her migraines were initially linked to her menstrual cycle, and the oral contraceptive has fixed that problem. On careful investigation, it seems the headaches are primarily associated with socially or academically stressful episodes, which have been relatively common during her freshman year at a college that is far away for home.

Dr. Martin explains the interconnection of stress and tension headaches, and the approaches to prevent and to interrupt migraines. She gives Gail a list of vitamins and other dietary supplements that can be helpful in preventing or reducing the number of migraines, and tells her where she can get them. She also gives Gail a medication to take whenever a migraine first starts, and tells Gail to carry it with her. She encourages Gail to use the mouth guard that her dentist had given her to keep her from grinding her teeth at night. Dr. Martin gives Gail a link to an internet site that contains meditations and guided imagery she can download into her IPod. She encourages Gail to use those to relax before she goes to bed, or when she is tense. She also suggests the use of yoga and acupuncture. Dr. Martin makes a referral to the East West Medicine Clinic on campus, where there are licensed acupuncturists with whom she has worked. She sets up a follow up visit in 3 weeks.

SUMMARY

The CAIM movement has grown in scope and size in the last three decades so that now the majority of Americans have used some form of CAIM and billions of dollars are being spent annually. Patients have consistently chosen to use these therapies not only for self-limited and minor complaints but also for life threatening medical conditions. Patients have expressed a strong preference for their medical providers to be able to inform and guide them as they chose these therapies in order to maximize their positive outcomes while minimizing risk.

Given the wide array of therapies, products and practitioners available, medical students will need to take advantage of educational opportunities to broaden and deepen their knowledge of this field. It is important to understand the philosophy underlying the major CAIM therapies in order to facilitate communication with CAIM providers. Astute students will also familiarize themselves with information about the safety and the efficacy of CAIM interventions. To do so will improve communication with their patients, enhance the patient/physician bond and increase the patients' chances not only for optimal treatment but for real wellness!

SUGGESTED READINGS

Rakel, D. (Ed.) (2007). *Integrative medicine* (2nd ed.). New York: Elsevier.
   This textbook provides useful information on commonly used therapies, including what is known about mechanism of actions and effectiveness.

Institute of Medicine. (2009). *Integrative medicine and the health of the public: A summary of the February 2009 summit.* Washington, DC: Institute of Medicine.
   This is a very current overview of the use of a variety of modalities by the people of the Untied States, with recommendations from the leading medical experts in the country

WEBSITES

National Center for Complementary and Alternative Medicine (NCCAM)
   URL: http://nccam.nih.gov/
   The website for the Center with in the National Institutes of Health which funds research into complementary and alternative approaches to wellness and health care

Office of Dietary Supplements (ODS)
   URL: http://dietary-supplements.info.nih.gov/
   This website includes access to useful data bases, including the International Bibliographic Information on Dietary Supplements (IBIDS) Database: http://dietary-supplements.info.nih.gov/Health_Information/IBIDS.aspx and the Computer Access to Research on Dietary Supplements (CARDS): http://dietary-supplements.info.nih.gov/Research/CARDS_Database.aspx

The Impact of Social Inequalities on Healthcare

Russell F. Lim, Francis G. Lu, & Donald M. Hilty

Despite major steps forward in the fight against cardiovascular disease, there is compelling evidence in the United States that we have not been fully effective in translating, disseminating, and expediting the adoption of scientific advances to improve outcomes for our society. We have failed to develop public health infrastructures and health-care systems in parallel with the scientific progress to implement effective, evidence-based prevention and treatment strategies.

ROBERT BONOW et al.
Circulation, 2002;106:1602.

Disparities result in part from differences in income, wealth, employment and educational opportunities. These differences are large and unfavorable for African-Americans and other minorities.

JAMES S. JACKSON

There have been numerous reports over the last 15 years describing the impact of socio-cultural factors on healthcare disparities, but three reports are especially important.

The Institute of Medicine's (IOM) report, *Unequal Treatment: Confronting Racial and Ethnic Disparities in Health Care*, stated that after controlling for variations in insurance status, patient income, and other access-related factors, racial and ethnic minorities received poorer health care compared with majority patients with the same diagnoses. Likewise, a supplement to the *Surgeon General's Report on Mental Health*, entitled *Mental Health: Culture, Race, and Ethnicity*, stated that racial and ethnic minorities have reduced access to care when compared to the majority population, leading to mental health care disparities. Finally, the World Health Organization's *CSDH* (Commission on Social Determinants of Health) *Final Report: Closing the Gap in a Generation: Health Equity Through Action on the Social Determinants of Health*, showed that there were inequalities in health measures based on economic factors, stating as an example that the life expectancy in men in Washington, DC, is seventeen years greater than those in suburban Maryland. Furthermore, geography (e.g., rural settings) can lead to these and other disparities such as limited access to clinical care and role models.

Worse yet, other reports have documented that African Americans and Hispanic Americans are disproportionately diagnosed with schizophrenia, a diagnosis with a poor prognosis, when bipolar disorder, a more treatable illness with a better prognosis, would be a more appropriate diagnosis. Still other studies have shown that African Americans have been given "typical" oral and depot antipsychotics in higher doses, increasing the risk of serious long term side effects such as tardive dyskinesia, when standard of care is atypical antipsychotics and lower doses (although the CATIE study showed little difference in efficacy between the use of atypical antipsychotics versus typical antipsychotics). Other reports have shown that Latinos are more likely to be diagnosed with an affective disorder, despite the presence of psychotic symptoms that would suggest another psychiatric disorder is present.

Racial and ethnic health care disparities are important for many reasons. Ethically, physicians are obligated to provide high quality care, and they should be concerned if this level of care is not available to everyone. There are important public health implications as well. Disparities in healthcare are likely to result in a higher prevalence of infectious disease. Economically, disparities that cause higher morbidity, whether caused by an inability to pay for costly procedures or by misdiagnosis, result in higher overall health care expenditures. These affect all taxpayers because many ethnic minorities participate in Medicaid or other public insurance programs. Finally, the existence of racial and ethnic health care disparities is evidence of continued racial discrimination. It seems that, as a nation, we have far to go before we realize our founding fathers' assertion that all men were created equal and have equal rights.

Birth of a Sharecropper (1939) *James B. Turnbull (1909–1976). Transparent and opaque watercolor and graphite pencil on paper, sheet: 22 ½ × 31 ¾ in. (57.2 × 80.6 cm). Whitney Museum of American Art, New York; purchase 43.16. Lay midwives have delivered most of the world's babies.*

The **Liaison Committee on Medical Education (LCME)** has recognized the importance of diversity in health care, and has added the following objective to its list of standards and objectives for the accreditation of American medical schools: "Medical students must learn to recognize and appropriately address gender and cultural biases in themselves and others, and in the process of health care delivery."

In addition, the LCME added the following annotation to **Standard IS-16** effective July 2009:

> The LCME and CACMS (Committee on the Accreditation of Canadian Medical Schools) believe that aspiring future physicians will be best prepared for medical practice in a diverse society if they learn in an environment characterized by, and supportive of, diversity and inclusion. Such an environment will facilitate physician training in:

- Basic principles of culturally competent health care
- Recognition of health care disparities and the development of solutions to such burdens
- The importance of meeting the health care needs of medically underserved populations
- The development of core professional attributes, such as altruism and social accountability, needed to provide effective care in a multidimensionally diverse society

The objectives for clinical instruction should include student understanding of demographic influences on health care quality and effectiveness, such as racial and ethnic disparities in the diagnosis and treatment of diseases as well as developing solutions to overcome these disparities. The objectives should also address the need for self-awareness among students regarding any personal biases in their approach to health care delivery, and the development of altruism and social accountability. Direct experience in specialized programs in medical education that specifically train students to help the underserved (e.g., Latino, rural, urban) are underway at medical schools like those of the five University of California Schools of Medicine, where they have five-year PRIME programs for medical students interested in working with underserved populations.

In this chapter, we will present the evidence for health care disparities for racial and ethnic minorities, discuss some of the biases and barriers that create these disparities, and suggest individual, educational, and institutional strategies to reduce them.

HISTORICAL BACKGROUND

There have been health care disparities based on race, culture, and ethnicity, as well as for women, the poor, children, elderly, sexual minorities, religious groups, those living in rural areas, and persons with disabilities throughout American history. For example, Native Americans were almost wiped out by diseases brought from Europe, such as smallpox and tuberculosis, in the early 1600's through 1700's. The U. S. Government felt that Native-American health beliefs were odd, and the Office of Indian Affairs provided almost no medical services until the creation of the Indian Health Service in 1954. Many Native-American children sent to boarding schools became ill and died from tuberculosis. Others who became sick on the reservations were removed and treated in mainstream hospitals that were ill equipped to meet their needs. There was a widespread and systematic destruction of Indian culture: Native Americans were not allowed to speak their own languages, the elders (culture bearers) died prematurely from infectious diseases, and many Native Americans were driven from land their ancestors had lived on for centuries. Only more recently has the health of those in rural areas, including Native Americans, improved by telemedicine and culturally competent care.

African Americans experienced forced emigration and enslavement in the 1600–1800s, and they were denied basic rights such as suffrage and freedom. African Americans brought their own folk health system with them from Africa. However, these practices were not adequate to deal with the health challenges associated with poverty, slavery, and abuse. After the Union's victory in the Civil War, all slaves were emancipated; however, they were almost wiped out by disease. Former slaves had no formal health care until the **Freedman's Hospitals** were opened in the late nineteenth century.

It was not until the **Civil Rights Act of 1965** that the most blatant forms of segregation in health care were ended. Since that time, affirmative action programs have begun to increase the numbers of African-American physicians. However, African-American physicians are still dramatically underrepresented in the physician workforce. While African Americans represent about 12% of the U. S. population, only about 3% of physicians in the United States are African American.

Other immigrant groups came to this country more willingly, although these groups also suffered discrimination and marginalization. The Chinese came in the 1840–1850s, but were prohibited by U. S. law (the Chinese Exclusion Act) from becoming naturalized citizens from 1882 until 1943. It was illegal for Chinese workers to bring their wives to the United States until the War Brides Act in 1943. The Magnuson Act of the same year allowed Chinese immigrants for the first time to become naturalized citizens. Even then, their numbers were limited by strict immigration quotas until 1965, when the Immigration and Nationality Services was

passed. The "Model Minority" myth has led many people to think of Asian Americans as successful and high achieving, but the percentage of Asian Americans living in poverty is twice as high as the percentage of Caucasians living in poverty. Similarly, many Hispanic Americans have been exploited and marginalized, limited to menial labor or farm work, and denied health benefits or access to health care because of their undocumented status. Other White immigrant groups were discriminated against when they first arrived in this country, such as the Germans, Irish, Italians, Jews, and Poles, but have since joined mainstream American society.

Definitions

The National Institute of Health (NIH) defines **health disparities** as "differences in the incidence, prevalence, mortality, and burden of diseases and other adverse health conditions that exist among specific population groups in the United States." These health disparities include differences in overall life expectancy and higher rates of cardiovascular disease, cancer, infant mortality, birth defects, asthma, diabetes, stroke, sexually transmitted diseases, oral diseases and disorders, mental illness, and other disorders. Contributing factors include "reduced access to health care, increased risk of disease and disability due to occupation or exposure, [and] increased risk of illness due to underlying biological, socioeconomic, ethnic, or familial factors, cultural values, and education."

The IOM report, *Unequal Treatment: Confronting Racial and Ethnic Disparities in Health Care,* defined healthcare disparities as "racial or ethnic differences in the quality of health care that are not due to access-related factors or clinical needs, preferences, and appropriateness of intervention." The NIH definition is broader and includes both disease and health care, while the IOM definition is specifically targeted at health care delivery. If one compares the NIH definition to the IOM's, it becomes clear that there are other factors that influence access to health care, such as socioeconomic status (SES), the availability of health insurance, health literacy, geography, gender, sexual orientation, age, and immigrant status. The IOM report acknowledged these barriers, but its authors chose to focus on race and ethnicity and their effects on the quality and type of healthcare received. Indeed, the report states that "racial and ethnic minorities are less likely than whites to possess health insurance" as a result of larger numbers living in poverty. Even when poor members of minority groups have health insurance, it is often publicly funded. Other barriers to care are often present, such as high co-payments and inadequate access to transportation.

SES is related to health literacy, in that patients with low SES tend to have lower levels of education and know less about how to maintain health and prevent disease. In ad-

> The health status of all U.S. racial and ethnic groups has improved steadily over the last century. Disparities in major health indicators between White and non-White groups, however, are growing. In general, African-American, American-Indian, and Hispanic ethnic and racial groups are disadvantaged relative to Whites on most health indices, whereas Asian-Americans appear to be as healthy, if not healthier, than Whites on most indicators. These overall group comparisons, however, mask important differences in the health status of ethnic subgroups.
>
> NATIONAL INSTITUTE ON AGING

dition, according to the National Healthcare Disparities Report of 2008, persons of low SES are less likely to have insurance. Persons of low SES are screened less often for colorectal cancer, are less likely to get the recommended care for diabetes, are less likely to receive a flu shot, and are more likely to die after a myocardial infarction. Geography also plays an important role in the quality of healthcare. Because ethnic minorities tend to live in different areas than the Caucasian majority, they often do not have access to the same health care opportunities.

Health is also affected by gender. For example, Hispanic and African-American women have higher risks of developing cardiovascular disease than Caucasian women. One study showed that more than one in four women was uninsured at some time during the past year, and half of the uninsured women had no coverage for more than a year. However, women were more likely than men (32% vs. 24%) to have a health condition that needed ongoing medical treatment. Fifty percent of the women in the study regularly needed prescription drugs, but half of these women reported not filling a prescription in the past year because it was too expensive. Sixty percent of women without health insurance delayed getting medical care because they could not afford it. Sexual orientation is also associated with increased health risks; for example, lesbians report lower rates of preventative care than heterosexual women.

Geography (e.g., rural settings) can lead to these health disparities due to lack of access to care and other disadvantages (e.g., access to role models). For example, mental illness is common in rural areas of the U.S., but there is a shortage of specialty care in these areas. The lack of access to mental health care is a significant reason why rural depressed patients have three times more hospitalizations and a higher suicide rate.

First generation Mexican-American children have been shown to have worse health care outcomes than similar groups of Black and Caucasian children, and worse outcomes than second or third generation Mexican-American children. While foreign-born Blacks report higher health status, foreign-born Asian and Pacific Islanders and Hispanics are less likely to have routine cancer screening tests.

> One reason why medical history is not much taught in medical schools is that so much of it is an embarrassment.
>
> LEWIS THOMAS

American, Hispanic-American, and Asian-American patients were less likely than Caucasian patients to receive coronary angiography, coronary artery bypass grafts, and/or angioplasty. During the assessment of colorectal cancer, African Americans were less likely to have either a sigmoidoscopy or colonoscopy, and more likely to receive only a barium enema, despite the fact that they have a 20% higher incidence of colon cancer than Caucasians. African-American patients were half as likely to have carotid imaging after a transient ischemic attack, ischemic stroke, or amaurosis fugax (monocular loss of vision) than similar Caucasian patients. Caucasian patients waited half as long as African-American patients for a kidney transplant. Hispanic-American patients had twice the risk of dying from HIV related illness than White patients, even with the use of antiretroviral drugs prior to hospitalization. African-American patients were more likely than Caucasians to have their asthma attacks treated in the emergency room, and were more likely to be prescribed bronchodilators than corticosteroids. This suggests a management strategy for this population that was based on acute symptom treatment rather than the prevention of bronchospasms. Caucasian patients with diabetes were more likely to be tested for glycosylated hemoglobin and lipids, and to receive eye examinations and flu vaccinations than were diabetic African-American patients. Asian-American and Hispanic-American patients also received less analgesia postoperatively than Caucasian and African-American patients. In addition, non-White pregnant mothers were more likely to undergo Caesarian sections than White women. African-American and Hispanic-American children were less likely to receive medication after a physician visit than White children. These are a just a few examples that illustrate how racial and ethnic minority status can have a deleterious effect on health care.

EVIDENCE FOR HEALTH CARE DISPARITIES

Unequal Treatment: Confronting Racial and Ethnic Disparities in Health Care, cited numerous examples of disparities in health care for racial and ethnic minorities in cardiovascular diseases, cancer, cerebrovascular disease, renal transplantation, HIV/AIDS, asthma, diabetes, analgesia, rehabilitative services, maternal and child health, children's health services, and mental disorders. For example, African-

Mental Health Care Disparities, Diversity, and Cultural Competence

Unequal Treatment: Confronting Racial and Ethnic Disparities in Health Care also cited the Surgeon General's supplement to his landmark 1999 study, *Mental Health: A Report of the Surgeon General*, entitled *Mental Health: Culture, Race, and Ethnicity* (2001). This report documented striking disparities in mental health care for racial and ethnic minorities involving access to care, appropriateness of care,

Bud Fields and His Family at Home *Photograph by Walker Evans.* Courtesy of the Library of Congress, Washington, D.C., Prints and Photographs Division, FSA/OWI Collection, LC-USF342-008147-A. *Poverty is highly correlated with both morbidity and mortality.*

quality of care, and outcomes. Taken as a whole, these disparities impose a greater disability burden on racial and ethnic minorities.

BOX 24.1 Examples of mental health care disparities

- Disproportionate numbers of African-Americans are represented in the most vulnerable segments of the population—people who are homeless, incarcerated, in the child welfare system, and victims of trauma. Each of these populations has increased risk for mental disorders.
- As many as 40% of Hispanic-Americans report limited English-language proficiency. Because few mental health-care providers are Spanish-speaking, most Hispanic-Americans have limited access to ethnically or linguistically appropriate services.
- The suicide rate among American-Indians and Alaska Natives is 50% higher than the national rate; rates of co-occurring mental illness and substance abuse (especially alcohol) are also significantly higher among Native American youth and adults. Because few data have been collected, the full nature, extent, and sources of these disparities remain a matter of conjecture.
- Asian-Americans/Pacific Islanders who seek care for a mental illness often present with more severe illnesses than do members of other racial or ethnic groups. This, in part, suggests that stigma and shame are critical deterrents to service utilization. It is also possible that mental illness may be undiagnosed or treated later in the course of the illness in these patients because members of these ethnic groups are more likely to manifest physical symptoms as a result of their mental illness.

The Clinical Encounter

Almost all medical students will confront social inequalities and health care disparities when they begin their clinical work with patients. Patients come to a physician with needs, expectations, and preferences, all of which are culturally influenced. In addition, patients' help-seeking behaviors, the language they use to describe their symptoms, and their responses to medical recommendations are all profoundly influenced by culture. Physicians, likewise, bring to the medical encounter expectations and beliefs that are shaped by their own cultural identity and experience. Indeed, a physician's perception and assessment of clinical signs and symptoms can be incomplete and incorrect when the patient's cultural identity and norms are not taken into account. Clinicians have many diagnostic and therapeutic options available to them, and the choices they make will not necessarily depend on empirical evidence. Despite the modern emphasis on evidence-based medicine, many clinical decisions are still based on clinical judgment that is subject to possible bias and prejudice related to the physician's cultural identity.

It is an ironic fact that while half the world's population is dying as a result of diseases of poverty (largely starvation and infection) the other half is succumbing to diseases of affluence.

MALCOLM CARRUTHERS
The Western Way of Death

The clinical encounter will also be influenced by systems factors such as barriers to access, immigration status, and insurance status. The clinician will have to elicit a medical history, complete a physical exam, and order diagnostic tests, all of which have to be evaluated and interpreted with sensitivity to the patient's culture. Culturally competent physicians recognize that racial and ethnic biases and stereotypes can influence the diagnostic and therapeutic process.

Many patients distrust physicians. For example, African Americans are likely to be familiar with the infamous **Tuskegee syphilis experiment**, a clinical trial in which African Americans infected with syphilis were allowed to go untreated between 1932 and 1972—even though doctors knew antibiotics could cure the disease. Likewise, Native Americans have been misled and lied to by the U. S. Government many times. Some patients may expect that their physician will spend a great amount of time with them and give them a definitive diagnosis and cure. Others will fail to see the necessity for lab tests or physical contact. Many minority patients prefer to be seen by members of their own minority group. However, the limited number of minority physicians and medical students make it difficult for ethnic matching of physicians and patients to occur. This problem may be especially acute in subspecialties. For example, one study documented that African-American patients were less likely than average to have a cardiac catheterization within the first 60 days after a myocardial infarction. This initially appeared to be simply the result of racial bias. However, there was another explanation—demographic data showed that the African-American physicians in the study were internists, while the Caucasian physicians were cardiologists. At the time of the study, 1994–1995, there were only 316 African-American cardiologists out of almost 20,000 practicing cardiologists, or about 1.5%.

Convincing data documents that many minority patients experience racial discrimination in clinical encounters, which understandably results in mistrust of Caucasian doctors. For example, one study of African-American, Asian-American, and Hispanic-American patients in King County, Washington, showed that nearly one third of the African-American respondents experienced incidents of differential treatment, including rude behavior and racial slurs, during their lifetime, while 16% reported such incidents within the past year. These experiences resulted in patients delaying treatment or avoiding the individual or institution responsible, but less than half of the respondents had made a verbal complaint. Patients made comments like "I vowed never to take my child to [that] hospital," or "it was the last time my son would ever see [that] doctor." Such interactions obviously have a powerful impact upon the treatment (or lack thereof) that African Americans receive. The same study showed that one fifth of all Hispanic patients experienced discrimination at some time in their lives, and between 7% and 19% of Asian Americans did as well.

> In African-American communities, the word Katrina may take on the power of the term Tuskegee experiment.
>
> SANDRA L. GADSON, MD

Refusal of Treatment

Patients refuse treatment for any number of reasons, including fear of needles, distrust of physician, and differing health beliefs. These patients can be especially frustrating for physicians, but appreciating and understanding a patient's ethnic and cultural background may help the doctor understand the patient's reticence to do what the doctor believes is in the patient's best interest. The IOM report concluded that patient refusal was only part of the reason for the health care disparities experienced by racial and ethnic minorities.

Limited English Proficiency (LEP)

According to the 2000 census, there are over 11 million people in the United States who have Limited English Proficiency (LEP) and are linguistically isolated, which is an increase of 54% from the 1990 census. Without the ability to speak English, these individuals often cannot access health care without the help of a bilingual health care provider or an interpreter. In addition, the health care provider's inability to communicate in the primary language of a patient limits his or her ability to form an empathic connection with patients.

There are three less than optimal substitutes for a trained interpreter when a patient has LEP: (1) patients and providers themselves, who may possess partial communication skills; (2) family and friends; and (3) nonclinical personnel, such as housekeeping staff or bilingual bystanders. The last two methods compromise patient confidentiality, and are likely to result in less accurate translations. The use of children or adolescents to interpret for adult patients is extremely problematic due to the dynamics of the family relationships and is illegal in the state of California. The Office of Civil Rights (OCR) has issued guidelines for patients with LEP that has been released for implementation. These guidelines state:

> [E]very federal agency that provides financial assistance to nonfederal entities must publish guidance on how their recipients can provide meaningful access to LEP persons and, thus, comply with Title VI regulations forbidding funding recipients from "restrict[ing] an individual in any way in the enjoyment of any advantage or privilege enjoyed by others receiving any service, finan-

cial aid, or other benefit under the program" or from "utiliz[ing] criteria or methods of administration which have the effect of subjecting individuals to discrimination because of their race, color, or national origin, or have the effect of defeating or substantially impairing accomplishment of the objectives of the program as respects individuals of a particular race, color, or national origin."

In addition, the National Health Law Program (NHeLP), has published "Language Access in Health Care—Statement of Principles," which contains 11 principles: (1) effective communication is essential, (2) competent health care language services are essential, (3) funding of LEP services is essential, (4) all insurers should establish mechanisms to fund LEP services, (5) linguistic diversity in the healthcare workforce is essential, (6) LEP services are a responsibility of the entire healthcare community, (7) access to English as a second language classes should be supported, (8) quality improvement should address the adequacy of LEP services, (9) competency standards should be implemented, (10) data collection on primary language should be a research priority, and (11) language services should always be available. Over eighty professional organizations, advocacy groups, and insurance companies have endorsed these standards, including the American Medical Association, the American Psychiatric Association, the American Psychological Association, the American Medical Student Association, the American College of Physicians, the American College of Obstetricians and Gynecologists, the American Academy of Family Physicians, and the American Academy of Pediatrics.

LEP may be even more complicated in rural areas, as awareness and resources may be limited, and stigma may be more difficult to navigate around.

BOX 24.2 Examples of health and health care disparities

- Hispanic Americans were the least likely to have health insurance, least likely to receive flu or pneumonia vaccinations, and had the highest prevalence of poor or fair health.
- Cigarette smoking was common in Native American communities with a median of 42.2% for men and 36.7% for women. Black men without a high school diploma have the next highest smoking prevalence at 41.8%
- Blacks had the highest prevalence of hypertension, the highest self-reported prevalence of diagnosed diabetes, and the highest rate of hospitalizations for stroke.
- Ischemic heart disease and stroke were inversely related to education, income and poverty status.
- Among Medicare enrollees, congestive heart failure hospitalization was higher in Blacks, Hispanics and Native American/Alaska Natives than among Whites.

Prejudice and Bias

Prejudice is defined as "an antipathy, felt or expressed, based upon a faulty generalization and directed toward a group as a whole or toward individual members of a group," whereas bias is "a preference or an inclination, especially one that inhibits impartial judgment," or "an unfair act or policy stemming from prejudice." Thus, prejudice can result in bias, or bias can be less stereotypical, but still result in a nonimpartial judgment. While most physicians are quick to deny prejudice or bias in their work with patients, they may fail to recognize subtle or unintentional prejudicial attitudes that may be reflected in their behavior. Several studies have had clinicians evaluate vignettes showing simulated patients with the same sex and similar age suffering from pain, altering only their race. In one of these studies, male physicians gave the Caucasian patients twice as much hydrocodone (Vicodin) compared to African American patients, whereas the women physicians did the opposite. Other research has evaluated the influence of race and sex on medical students' perceptions of patients' symptoms to determine if subtle bias exists early in medical training. In one of these studies, 164 medical students were randomly assigned to view a video of a Black female or White male actor portraying patients presenting with identical symptoms of angina. The medical students felt that the Black woman had a less desirable health state than the White man with identical symptoms, and students were less likely to identify the Black female patient's symptoms as angina. Nonminority students reported higher health states for the White male patient, whereas minority students' assessments did not differ by patient. Male students assigned a slightly lower health status value to the Black female patient. The researchers concluded that there were significant differences in the ways the students evaluated patients based on their own ethnicity and gender and the patient's ethnicity and gender.

> They have no physicians, but when a man is ill they lay him in the public square, and the passersby come up to him, and if they have ever had his disease themselves or have known anyone who has suffered from it, they give him advice, recommending to do whatever they found good in their own case, or in the case known to them. And no-one is allowed to pass the sick man in silence without asking him what his ailment is.
>
> HERODOTUS

Stereotypes

Stereotypes are a way of using social categories, such as skin color, age, and gender, to simplify complex situations; stereotypes develop from our need to predict, understand,

and control situations. Unfortunately, they also tend to suppress an individual's personal characteristics that do not conform to the general profile created by the stereotype. In addition, there are "in" groups, for which we have positive feelings, and "out" groups, for which we have negative feelings. Stereotypes can also be implicit, and often the person who stereotypes others is not consciously aware of the influence of stereotyping. Stereotypes are profoundly important in health care; for example, stereotypes influence physicians' beliefs about whether or not patients will follow treatment recommendations. In one study, physicians were shown to believe that African-American patients were less likely to follow-through with treatment recommendations, and this belief clearly influenced the treatment decisions the physicians made.

Clinical Uncertainty

Most clinical decisions are made in the context of uncertainty, but diagnostic accuracy depends on reducing the amount of uncertainty as much as possible. Clinicians' beliefs about culture are sometimes used to reduce the amount of uncertainty in a clinical encounter; however, these beliefs have to be grounded in cultural competence that recognizes the individuality of a particular patient within his or her cultural context if they are going to be useful. For example, a physician may misinterpret the severity of the patient's symptoms because he or she is unaware of differing cultural norms for the expression of symptoms. Physicians are most familiar with their own cultural group, and they are likely to use their cultural background as a basis from which to understand the implicit messages being sent by body language, eye contact, tone of voice, or inflection. However, these nuances of communication may be expressed in different ways or mean different things in other cultural groups, and their meaning may be influenced by the patient's age, SES, gender, race or ethnicity.

INTERVENTIONS

Health care disparities can be addressed at many levels: (1) at the level of the individual provider, through education and recruitment of both minority physicians/medical students and those skilled and interested in working with minorities; (2) at the level of the office, clinic or hospital, by creating organizations that are more culturally competent, such as being more accessible to racial and ethnic minorities; and (3) at the level of legal and regulatory policy. Truly effective interventions will have to target all three—individuals, organizations, and systems. In addition, health care providers, administrators, and staff will all require more

training and sophistication in treating minority populations if we are ever going to successfully eliminate the profound health care disparities that currently exist in our society.

> The task of medicine is to promote health, to prevent disease, to treat the sick when prevention has broken down and to rehabilitate the people after they have been cured. These are highly social functions and we must look at medicine as basically a social science.
>
> HENRY E. SIGERIST
> *Civilisation and Disease*

CLINICAL INTERVENTIONS

The American Psychiatric Association (APA) focused on culture and its effects in developing the fourth edition of the *Diagnostic and Statistical Manual* (DSM-IV) in 1994, and its subsequent revision, DSM-IV-TR (Text Revision) in 2000. The DSM-IV and DSM-IV-TR included the Outline for Cultural Formulation (OCF) in Appendix I as well as a Glossary of Culture Bound Syndromes. The OCF provides a clinical tool for incorporating in the diagnostic assessment and treatment plan the effect of culture on four key areas: (1) cultural identity, (2) cultural explanatory models of illness, (3) cultural supports and stressors, and (4) cultural elements of the patient-clinician relationship. The last part of the OCF is the overall cultural formulation, incorporating 1–4 into a culturally appropriate assessment and treatment plan. The DSM-IV-TR also identifies culturally specific diagnoses such as acculturation problem and religious or spiritual problem in the section "Conditions that May be a Focus of Clinical Attention." Finally, there are sections in the narrative introductions to each of the major diagnostic categories for age, gender, and cultural considerations that will guide the reader to include these considerations in constructing the differential diagnosis. In addition to the DSM-IV-TR, there are many excellent books and articles on assessing the culturally diverse; several of these are described in the Suggested Readings at the end of this chapter, such as a recent book edited by Pedro Ruiz and Annelle Primm, entitled *Disparities in Psychiatric Care: Clinical and Cross-Cultural Perspectives*, which also includes many important chapters outlining disparities in most underrepresented groups and special populations, as well as strategies to address these disparities, including education, policy, parity, and access to care.

Many disciplines have developed **mnemonics** to help clinicians both remember and incorporate cultural issues when working with patients. The **BELIEF** mnemonic emphasizes exploring the patient's health Beliefs, eliciting an Explanation, helping the clinician to Learn from the patient, discovering the Impact on the patient, showing Empathy, and asking about Feelings. The **ETHNIC** mnemonic,

TABLE 24.1 The DSM-IV-TR outline for cultural formulation

1. Cultural identity of the individual

   An individual's cultural identity includes the individual's cultural reference group (s), languages spoken, cultural factors in development, etc.

2. Cultural explanations of the illness

   The cultural explanations of the illness refer to predominant idioms of distress and local illness categories. This includes meaning and severity of symptoms in relation to cultural norms, as well as perceived causes and explanatory models, and help-seeking experiences and plans.

3. Cultural factors related to psychosocial environment and levels of functioning

   These include social stressors and supports such as family or religious groups, as well as levels of functioning and disability.

4. Cultural elements of the clinician-patient relationship

   This includes ethnocultural transference and counter transference, as well as the use of an interpreter, and psychological testing.

5. Overall Cultural Assessment

   The overall cultural assessment is a summary of all of the above factors, and how they affect the differential diagnosis and treatment plan.

Adapted from Manson (1996).

TABLE 24.2 Mnemonics for incorporating cultural issues in patient care

BELIEF

Beliefs about health (What caused your illness/problem?)

Explanation (Why did it happen at this time?)

Learn (Help me to understand your belief/opinion.)

Impact (How is this illness/problem impacting your life?)

Empathy (This must be very difficult for you.)

Feelings (How are you feeling about it?)

ETHNIC

Explanation (How do you explain your illness?)

Treatment (What treatment have you tried?)

Healers (Have you sought any advice from folk healers?)

Negotiate (mutually acceptable options)

Intervention (agreed on)

Collaboration (with patient, family, and healers)

LEARN

Listen with sympathy and understanding to the patient's perception of the problem

Explain your perceptions of the problem

Acknowledge and discuss the differences and similarities

Recommend treatment

Negotiate treatment

Sources: Doobie et al. (2003); Levin, Like, and Gottlieb (2000); Berlin and Fowkes (1983).

---

designed for use by medical students during their clinical assessments, reminds students to ask patients to Explain their illness and Treatment, and to ask about whether they have sought help from folk Healers. They also have to Negotiate with the patient and plan an Intervention, Collaborating with the patient, family, and folk healers. The LEARN mnemonic is similar, as it encourages clinicians to Listen, but put emphasis on the clinician's role as a cultural broker in Explaining the problem, as well as Acknowledging cultural differences, and then Recommending and Negotiating treatment. Each mnemonic has its strengths and weaknesses, and the authors recommend combining parts from each one into daily clinical practice. These mnemonic devices are encapsulated in Table 24.2.

EDUCATIONAL INTERVENTIONS

All of the health sciences are now teaching students about cultural competence and diversity, so that students will develop the knowledge, attitudes, and skills necessary to facilitate the assessment and treatment of culturally diverse patients. Some of the most successful methods include cultural awareness exercises for attitudes, lectures to promote knowledge about particular cultural groups, and case-based learning to teach cultural case formulation skills. Other approaches have included teaching health care students how to work with an interpreter and various ways to elicit patient's cultural health beliefs. Specifically, *Unequal Treatment: Confronting Racial and Ethnic Disparities in Health Care* included two recommendations related to education:

Recommendation 5–3: Increase the proportion of underrepresented U. S. racial and ethnic minorities among health professionals. The benefits of diversity in health professions fields are significant, and illustrate that a continued commitment to affirmative action is necessary for graduate health professions education programs, residency recruitment, and other professional opportunities.

Recommendation 6–1: Integrate cross-cultural education into the training of all current and future health professionals.

POLICY INTERVENTIONS

Services-National Policies

Cultural and Linguistic Appropriate Services (CLAS) Standards

In 1998, the U. S. Department of Health and Human Services Office of Minority Health (OMH) requested a review and comparison of existing cultural and linguistic competence standards and measures on a national level, and proposed draft national standards language. An analytical review of key legislation, regulations, contracts, and standards currently in use by federal and state agencies and other national

organizations was conducted. Proposed standards were then developed with input from a national advisory committee of policy administrators, health care providers, and health services researchers. Fourteen standards at the health care organization level were created, defining culturally competent care, how to provide services in the appropriate languages for the client, and supporting cultural competence in the organization. These standards are presented in Table 24.3.

Healthy People 2010

Healthy People 2010 contains a comprehensive set of disease prevention and health promotion objectives for the nation issued by the U. S. Department of Health and Hu-

---

TABLE 24.3 National standards for culturally and linguistically appropriate services (CLAS) for culturally competent care

Culturally Competent Care

1. Health care organizations should ensure that patients/consumers receive from all staff members effective, understandable, and respectful care that is provided in a manner compatible with their cultural health beliefs and practices, and preferred language.

2. Health care organizations should implement strategies to recruit, retain, and promote at all levels of the organization a diverse staff and leadership that are representative of the demographic characteristics of the service area.

3. Health care organizations should ensure that staff at all levels and across all disciplines receive ongoing education and training in culturally and linguistically appropriate service delivery.

Language Access Services

4. Health care organizations must offer and provide language assistance services, including bilingual staff and interpreter services, at no cost to each patient/consumer with limited English proficiency at all points of contact, in a timely manner during all hours of operation.

5. Health care organizations must provide to patients/consumers in their preferred language both verbal offers and written notices informing them of their right to receive language assistance services.

6. Health care organizations must assure the competence of language assistance provided to limited English proficient patients/consumers by interpreters and bilingual staff. Family and friends should not be used to provide interpretation services (except on request by the patient/consumer).

7. Health care organizations must make available easily understood patient-related materials and post signage in the languages of the commonly encountered groups and/or groups represented in the service area.

Organizational Supports for Cultural Competence

8. Health care organizations should develop, implement, and promote a written strategic plan that outlines clear goals, policies, operational plans, and management accountability/oversight mechanisms to provide culturally and linguistically appropriate services.

9. Health care organizations should conduct initial and ongoing organizational self-assessments of CLAS-related activities and are encouraged to integrate cultural and linguistic competence-related measures into their internal audits, performance improvement programs, patient satisfaction assessments, and outcomes-based evaluations.

10. Health care organizations should ensure that data on the individual patient's/consumer's race, ethnicity, and spoken and written language are collected in health records, integrated into the organization's management information systems, and periodically updated.

11. Health care organizations should maintain a current demographic, cultural, and epidemiological profile of the community as well as a needs assessment to accurately plan for and implement services that respond to the cultural and linguistic characteristics of the service area.

12. Health care organizations should develop participatory, collaborative partnerships with communities and utilize a variety of formal and informal mechanisms to facilitate community and patient/consumer involvement in designing and implementing CLAS-related activities.

13. Health care organizations should ensure that conflict and grievance resolution processes are culturally and linguistically sensitive and capable of identifying, preventing, and resolving cross-cultural conflicts or complaints by patients/consumers.

14. Health care organizations are encouraged to regularly make available to the public information about their progress and successful innovations in implementing the CLAS standards and to provide public notice in their communities about the availability of this information.

The real public health problem, of course, is poverty.

WENDELL L. WILKIE
One World

man Services (USDHHS) to achieve over the first decade of the twenty-first century. Created by scientists both inside and outside of Government, it identifies a wide range of public health priorities in 28 focus areas and specific, measurable objectives. Its overarching goals are: (1) to increase quality and years of healthy life and (2) to eliminate health disparities. These 28 focus areas include access to quality health services, educational and community-based programs, environmental health, and improving the public health infrastructure. Also included is the Center for Disease Control's (CDC) Office of Minority Health and Health Disparities, whose mission is to "to eliminate health disparities for vulnerable populations as defined by race/ethnicity, socio-economic status, geography, gender, age, disability status, risk status related to sex and gender, and among other populations identified to be at-risk for health disparities."

World Health Organization's Commission on Social Determinants of Health

The Commission on Social Determinants of Health (CSDH) recommends that to improve health disparities, there are three principles of action: (1) improve daily living conditions, or the circumstances under which people are born, grow up, live, work and grow old, including improving access to health care by providing universal health insurance; (2) improve the inequitable distribution of money, resources, and power (the structural drivers of the conditions of daily life) which includes improving gender equity, and encourage political empowerment of underrepresented groups; and (3) measure the problem, evaluate actions, and continue to expand the knowledge base.

Professional Organizations, Accreditation Agencies, Foundations, and Advocacy Groups

The Commission to End Health Care Disparities (www.ama-ssn.org/go/healthdisparities) is a consortium of 50+ member organizations, including professional organizations such as the American Medical Association, the National Medical Association, other subspecialty organizations and state medical associations that was founded in 2004. This was a response to the IOM report, *Unequal Treatment,* with its mission to end health care disparities

by (1) increasing professional awareness, (2) improving education and training, (3) gathering data and information, and (4) improving workforce diversity.

The Joint Commission of the Accreditation of Health Care Organizations (JCAHO), which accredits hospitals, added new disparities and cultural competence accreditation standards in 2007, such as providing interpretation and translation, and proposed adding staff training on cultural sensitivity, accommodation of patients' cultural and personal beliefs and religious and spiritual practices in 2009. Private nonprofit agencies such as The National Committee for Quality Assurance (NCQA), which is dedicated to the improvement of health care quality, has also supported the development of culturally competent health care practices through the implementation of the CLAS standards, and by identifying effective programs through the Recognizing Innovation in Multicultural Health Care Award Program. Finally, the National Quality Forum, another organization devoted to improving the quality of health care by 1) setting national priorities and goals for performance improvement, 2) endorsing national consensus standards for measuring and publicly reporting on performance, and 3) promoting the attainment of national goals through education and outreach programs, has endorsed 45 practices to guide health care systems to provide culturally competent care. These practices are in seven domains: (1) **leadership** should reflect the diversity of the community served, (2) cultural competence should be **integrated** throughout the organization, (3) patient-provider **communication** should be clear and culturally appropriate, (4) **care delivery** should be culturally competent, (5) the **workforce** should reflect the diversity of the community and be trained to work with the diverse populations of the community, (6) the **community** should be engaged in the delivery of culturally competent care, and (7) **data** be collected to assess the cultural competence of services.

The Robert Wood Johnson Foundation funded the Commission to Build a Healthier America, and published a report entitled *Overcoming Obstacles to Health* in February of 2008 that stated that health is influenced by income and education, as seen in doubled infant mortality rates for mothers who are non-high-school graduates compared to mothers who were college graduates, self-reports of health status that decline as levels of education and income decline, and increased incidence of chronic illnesses such as diabetes and coronary heart disease in families with lower incomes. They also reported that people with higher incomes live up to six and a half years longer, that levels of income are linked with poor health regardless of ethnic group, and ethnic minorities have poorer health outcomes when incomes are matched. Their conclusion was that the burden of these lowered health outcomes resulted in increased health care costs of over one trillion dollars a year, and that improving the quality of primary and secondary education, as well as improving community safety, could reduce health disparities.

The most recent Robert Wood Johnson report, *Beyond Health Care: New Directions to a Healthier America*, published in April of 2009, outlined ten recommendations to improve children's health, including educational support (child care, special education), adequate nutrition for low-income families, healthy foods for school children, regular exercise programs, smoking prevention, improved housing, safe neighborhoods, and data for policy makers that will support these initiatives.

Research and Workforce: National Policies

National Center on Minority Health and Health Disparities (NCMHD)

The mission of the National Center on Minority Health and Health Disparities (NCMHD) is to promote and improve minority health and to lead, coordinate, support, and assess the NIH effort to reduce and ultimately eliminate health disparities. In this effort NCMHD conducts and supports basic, clinical, social, and behavioral research; promotes research infrastructure and training; fosters emerging programs; disseminates information; and reaches out to minority and other health disparity communities. The NCMHD hopes to increase the number of minority and ethnic populations that participate in clinical trials, as well as train minority researchers, and disseminate the results of such research. Their priorities include: (1) developing an integrated, cross-disciplinary national research agenda on health disparities, (2) promoting and supporting research capacity-building activities in the minority and medically underserved communities, (3) establishing broad aspects of two-way communication and outreach with the Center's many stakeholders, (4) collaborating with NIH research partners to sponsor activities involving minority health and health disparities, and (5) assessing, tracking, and monitoring the results of NIH minority health and health disparities research progress.

Workforce-Foundations and Advocacy Groups

The California Endowment supported the report, *Strategies for Improving the Diversity of the Health Professions* in 2003, which found that African American, Hispanic, and Native American students are extremely underrepresented in the health professions and health professional schools, and that this fact represents a public health crisis. The report states that there is a lack of educational opportunities for many minority groups, but that this issue can be addressed by better coordination between agencies that fund and implement programs to improve their educational opportunities. They recommend an evaluation of existing programs and additional data to support the effectiveness of such programs. Since many minority students come from low-income backgrounds, the high cost of a professional education is a significant barrier. They suggest funding not only scholarships for health professional students from low-income backgrounds, but also funding "upstream" programs in primary and secondary schools to increase the size of the applicant pool.

Similarly, the Sullivan Commission on Diversity in Higher Education, funded by the W. K. Kellogg Foundation, issued a report in 2004 called *Missing Persons: Minorities in the Health Professions*, which stated that the culture of health professional schools must change to adjust to changing demographics of the nation. New and nontraditional paths to the health professions should be explored, and there should be a high level of commitment from the administration to increase the diversity of students at health professional schools. Their report also suggests improvements in the pipeline of students going into the health professions, and improved funding for minority students in health professional schools.

Finally, the Greenlining Institute, a multiethnic research and advocacy institute, published a report on the diversity of the University of California's medical student body in 2008, entitled, *Representing the New Majority Part III, A Status Report on the Diversity of the University of California Medical Student Body*. The report states that although African Americans, Latinos, and Native Americans make up more than 40% of the population of California, they comprise less than 20% of UC medical students. The Greenlining report analyzes official enrollment data from the University of California Office of the President, which shows the number of applicants, accepted students, and enrollees at each of the five UC medical school campuses of each race, from 2001–2007. Their recommendation was to increase the size of the applicant pools of the minority students, as their rates of admission were proportional to their representation in the applicant pool.

Recruitment and Retention Policies

One approach to diversity is to recruit staff that have similarities to the patients they treat and the community they serve. However, this approach has met with only limited success, and increasingly clinicians are being trained to work with clients from many different cultures. Common interventions include training in cultural competence in residency/fellowship programs, subcontracting with minority providers to train majority staff, and tying executive promotion to demonstrations of success in providing culturally competent services.

Coordination with traditional healers and collaboration with community workers is becoming increasingly common in health care settings. Traditional healers are powerful symbols of their culture that can serve as partners in delivering culturally sensitive and appropriate services. Likewise, community workers have important links to the communities they serve and can guide patients who are baffled and confused by the complexities of contemporary bureaucracies associated with health care in the United States.

Administration or Organizational Accommodations

Common administrative interventions to reduce health care disparities include providing care in settings close to where patients live and work, provision of transportation, and, in some settings, home visits. The clinic milieu needs to mesh with patients' cultural values, and health care directives and instructions have to be available in the language of the patient. The problems associated with providing culturally competent services can be especially acute in rural areas, where few providers may possess the cultural competence necessary to provide appropriate services.

There are three types of program interventions that may be developed: Continuing Medical Education, administrative training, or innovative service models. We will provide examples of the first two. Continuing Medical Education (CME) programs for physicians in California must address cultural competence, as mandated by AB 1195. This means all programs should include: 1) relevant information on differences in prevalence, diagnosis, and treatment of medical conditions in diverse populations, 2) how to apply linguistic skills to communicate effectively with the target population, or the proper use of interpreters, 3) how to utilize cultural information to help establish therapeutic alliances with patients, 4) pertinent cultural data in diagnosis and treatment, 5) cultural and ethnic data in the process of clinical care, and 6) recommendations for appropriate cultural and linguistic resources (websites, handouts, reference cards, patient education, tapes/CDs/handbooks, local resources, etc.) in CME handout materials. Finally, the Office of Minority Health provides free CME credits online for learning about cultural competence at https://www.thinkculturalhealth.org/.

Providing Quality Health Care with CLAS is a curriculum that is aimed at helping health care organizations integrate the CLAS standards into their operating principles. It utilizes a strength-based approach that entails organizational self-assessment to help participants determine how best to implement these standards, building upon the system's existing infrastructure, mission and values. Participants will engage in small group, problem-based discussions that have been shown in many educational contexts to enhance creative problem solving and to more effectively develop higher-level understanding of topics discussed. Rather than having a "cookbook" approach that superimposes a model without attention to the unique challenges and strengths of a particular organization, the Center for Reducing Health Disparities at the UC Davis School of Medicine believes that this strength-based approach can more effectively develop leaders who can creatively implement these standards in complex organizations.

The curriculum is composed of three phases. The first phase, "Organizational Culture Assessment," involves interviewing the participants and other key personnel in the organization to assess the institutional culture, values, and history. This helps the facilitators to customize the curriculum to the participants. The second phase of the curriculum, the "Learning Workshops," is divided into four workshop sessions, each lasting 4 hours. In the last "Follow-up" phase, participants will also be asked to attend six monthly one-hour meetings to assist them in ongoing efforts to implement and maintain. Finally, the telecommunication revolution offers some solutions, such as telepsychiatry, and both patients and providers are turning to technology to ensure access to culturally competent care. Indeed, technology may offer better ways of "following" migrant workers (e.g., California Central Valley). Native American patients can be seen at any of a number of clinics in United States regions, when they travel or move—an option of continuity that is quite attractive.

Diversity in Health Care Professionals Increases Access to Care

Diversity among professionals will help reduce health care disparities. The IOM report, titled *In the Nation's Compelling Interest: Ensuring Diversity in the Health care Workforce*, released in 2004, summarized the evidence documenting that greater diversity among health professionals is associated with improved access to care for racial and ethnic minority patients, greater patient choice and satisfaction, better patient-provider communication, and better educational experiences for students while in training. The report made 25 recommendations addressing six specific areas: (1) improving admission policies and practices; (2) reducing financial barriers to health professions training; (3) encouraging diversity efforts through accreditation; (4) improving the institutional climate for diversity; (5) applying community benefit principles to diversity efforts; and (6) other mechanisms to encourage support for diversity efforts. The recommendations in Sections 1, 4, and 5 specifically addressed health professions educational institutions (HPEIs). They included the following:

- HPEIs should develop, disseminate, and utilize a clear statement of mission that recognizes the value of diversity.
- HPEIs should establish explicit policies regarding the value and importance of culturally competent care and the role of institutional diversity in achieving this goal.
- HPEIs should develop and regularly evaluate comprehensive strategies to improve the institutional climate for diversity.
- HPEIs should proactively and regularly engage and train students, house staff, and faculty regarding institutional diversity-related policies, expectations, and the importance of diversity.

Interventions For Improving Mental Health Care Disparities

The Surgeon General's Supplement to the Report on Mental Health, titled *Mental Health: Culture, Race and Ethnicity*, concluded with "A Vision for the Future" in which recommendations were grouped in areas according to six aspirational goals: (1) continue to expand the science base, (2) improve access to treatment, (3) reduce barriers to treatment, (4) improve quality of care, (5) support capacity development, and (6) promote mental health. The recommendation most relevant to education follows: "Minorities are underrepresented among mental health providers, researchers, administrators, policymakers, and consumer and family organizations. Furthermore, many providers and researchers of all backgrounds are not fully aware of the impact of culture on mental health, mental illness, and mental health services. All mental health professionals are encouraged to develop their understanding of the roles of age, gender, race, ethnicity, and culture in research and treatment. Therefore, mental health training programs and funding sources that work toward equitable representation and a culturally informed training curriculum will contribute to reducing disparities."

SUMMARY

It is clear that health care disparities are affected by expectations, beliefs, and attitudes that in turn are shaped by culture and influenced by gender, skin color, and age. Recent reports such as *Unequal Treatment: Confronting Racial and Ethnic Disparities in Health Care* has highlighted the health care disparities based on race and ethnicity that are still inherent in modern medical practice, and lead to inequitable care. These disparities result in poor health outcomes for racial, ethnic and cultural minorities, higher costs for all, and increased disease burden on society. They are therefore a major public health concern that should be of concern to all medical students. Unfortunately, the civil rights movement and the Civil Rights Act of 1965 have not been sufficient to provide adequate health care for all Americans. There is still much work to be done in the area of cultural competence and diversity that would help address these health care disparities in minority populations. We have discussed interventions for the problem of disparities that can occur on an individual, organizational, educational, or policy level. Perhaps a new generation of physicians—those reading this book—will be able to make a difference by working with the community, legislature, and professional organizations to help solve the vexing, intractable and clearly linked problems of social inequalities and health care disparities.

CASE STUDIES

M. V. is a 45-year-old Hmong woman with complaints of headaches, backaches, dizziness, and tiredness. She came to the United States from a refugee camp in Thailand 10 years ago. Ms. V. has 8 children, aged 15, 13, 11, 9, 8, 6, 4, and 2. The patient speaks no English, and lives in a poor part of town. She receives Medicaid, and is poorly educated. In order to get to her appointment at the Mental Health Clinic, she has to take several buses, and an interpreter has to be arranged for her. She believes her illness is caused by "bad spirits," and has already seen a shaman for treatment. She witnessed her father and mother being shot by the communists during their escape from Laos. Ms. V. is unemployed and has no job skills. She has nightmares and flashbacks, and hears the voices of her dead family calling to her. The patient has already tried to hang herself, and was hospitalized at the local mental hospital for 72 hours; however, she currently states that she would never attempt suicide again because of her children.

The case of M. V. is a common one in Sacramento, California. She has many barriers to accessing quality health care, including language, health beliefs, geography, low socioeconomic status, public insurance, and poor education. Patients such as these are often seen in the primary care setting, and their health beliefs and traumatic experiences are frequently ignored. Often it is difficult to get a trained interpreter for the Hmong language, and mental health issues are not often recognized when the presenting complaints are somatic. The patient needs a referral from the primary care provider to mental health services. The county's mental health system is required to provide services in the patient's language, including intake, assessment, treatment and access to patient's rights advocates. Providers are required to provide a culturally competent assessment and treatment plan that includes an assessment of the patient's health beliefs, as well as a collaborative approach that involves family and community members. In the refugee population, it is also very important to assess for traumatic events prior to coming to the United States, as the diagnosis of posttraumatic stress disorder could be missed. She also has come for mental health services at a late stage in her illness, typical of many non-Western patients.

H. G. is a 37-year-old monolingual Spanish-speaking woman from Mexico with diabetes. She works as a migrant farm worker in the Central Valley of California. She comes every harvesting season to help with the crops. Her blood sugar is never very well controlled, as she has no regular doctor in the United States, but she can get her medications in Mexico. She presents to the emergency room at the University Hospital with a foot ulcer that refuses to heal, and blood tests reveal that her blood sugar is alarmingly high.

This patient's situation presents some challenges, as H. G. is an undocumented worker who does not speak English, and does not live in the United States full-time. Important policy decisions will determine if she is seen, because of her undocumented status, and a culturally competent treatment plan would have to be created for her care here in the United States, as well as after her return to Mexico.

SUGGESTED READINGS

Agency for Healthcare Research and Quality. (2008). *Sixth National Healthcare Disparities Report (NHDR)*. http://www.ahrq.gov/QUAL/nhdr08/nhdr08.pdf
This report is an annual report commissioned by Congress to track relevant measures of healthcare disparities.

Commission on Social Determinants of Health. (2008). *CSDH Final Report: Closing the Gap in a Generation: Health Equity Through Action on the Social Determinants of Health*. Geneva, Switzerland: World Health Organization.
This is an important document with data comparing the health statuses of different nations and subpopulations of nations with recommendation for actions to reduce health disparities. http://www.who.int/social_determinants/thecommission/finalreport/en/index.html

Hays, P. A. (2008). *Addressing cultural complexities in practice* (2nd Ed.). Washington, DC: American Psychological Association.
This book is an excellent resource for learning how to do a culturally competent assessment in a mental health setting.

Institute of Medicine. (2004). *In the nation's compelling interest: Ensuring diversity in the health care workforce*. Washington, DC: National Academies Press.
A companion to *Unequal Treatment*, this report highlights the importance of a diverse workforce.

Lim, R. (2006). *Clinical manual of cultural psychiatry*. Washington, DC: American Psychiatric Press.
This book describes and illustrates the use of the DSM-IV-TR Outline for Cultural Formulation.

National Health Law Program (NHeLP). (2007). *Language access in healthcare statement of principles*. http://www.healthlaw.org/library/item.121215-language_access_in_health_car e_statement_of _principles_explanatory_guide_oc
Eleven principles on language access in healthcare, endorsed by almost ninety professional and advocacy associations, as well as insurance companies.

Ruiz, P., & Primm, A. (2009). *Disparities in psychiatric care: Clinical and cross-cultural perspectives*. Hagerstown, MD: Lippincott, Williams and Wilkens.
This book is a comprehensive review of health disparities in mental health in underrepresented groups that includes many strategies to reduce disparities, such as education, parity and policy approaches.

Smedly, B. D., Stith, A. Y., & Nelson, A. R. (Eds.). (2003). *Unequal treatment: Confronting racial and ethnic disparities in health care*. Washington, DC: National Academy Press.
This book is a ground-breaking study of the influence of race and ethnicity on medical treatment with controls for socioeconomic status. The accompanying CD-ROM contains important background articles, such as one by Byrd and Clayton on "Racial and Ethnic Disparities in Health Care: A Background and History," which is a brief history of ethnic disparities over the history of the United States.

25 Health Services in the United States

Arleen Leibowitz

> Once the formal teaching rounds were over, they talked only about the problems they faced. For some, the talk was about the malpractice crisis, the freeze on Medicare fees, the impact of diagnosis-related groups, and shrinking incomes. For others, it was the endless paperwork in applying for research funding ... Medicine, they said, was no fun anymore ... the faculty reminisced about the good old days, which neither they nor the students would ever see.
>
> CAROLA EISENBERG
> *It Is Still a Privilege to Be a Doctor*

The health reform legislation passed in 2010 ushers in a new era in health service delivery in the United States. However pioneering this legislation is in its commitment to provide universal access to medical care for all Americans, at the same time it preserves much of the structure of health care delivery in the United States. This chapter describes the existing health insurance arrangements upon which health reform builds and explores some of the deficiencies that health reform legislation is designed to redress.

The health system in the United States is actually a collection of systems that span the full range of organizational paradigms, ranging from a publicly funded, fully centralized system with salaried providers in the Veteran's Administration Health Care System to the shrinking segment of the private insurance system that still provides complete freedom to choose providers and services in a competitive marketplace. The federal Medicare program provides nearly universal coverage for persons over age 65, but coverage for persons under 65 is highly variable and depends on the individual's characteristics. Two-thirds of the nonelderly have private insurance coverage. For most of this group, an employer often takes on the role of both subsidizing the cost of insurance and choosing which options to make available to the employee. However, 5% of the nonelderly purchase insurance policies individually. Qualifying low income individuals can obtain insurance through **Medicaid**, a state and federal government program that provides insurance for about 14% of individuals under 65. Yet, in 2007, 17% of the population under 65 did not have health insurance.

In order to understand the various options facing individuals in different circumstances, it is important to examine the U. S. health care system through multiple lenses. Thus, this chapter examines the eligibility, financing, and structure of the multiple private and public insurance options. It first summarizes how the United States arrived at the myriad arrangements it currently uses. It then describes the eligibility and financing arrangements for the major eligibility groups: the elderly, the poor, and employed adults. The next section outlines how medical services are organized in different systems. Finally, it identifies a number of employer-based and government-run models of insurance markets.

THE LEGACY

The modern health care system in the United States has its roots in the early 20th century. In the early decades of the 20th century, physicians developed an increasing capacity to diagnose and treat acute medical conditions. These acute medical conditions were "insurable" because, while the population prevalence of acute conditions could be forecast, the likelihood that a particular individual would be afflicted was not easily predicted. Thus, by purchasing insurance, individuals could be protected against the risk of relatively low-probability, but costly, events. Although organized medicine was initially concerned about "third-party" intervention in their clinical and economic decisions—and in fact opposed the advent of insurance—health insurance emerged during this period as the mechanism for financing medical care in the private sector.

By the 1930s, medical care had become both more effective and more expensive, often well beyond the means of the average family, especially in the Great Depression. Although both state and national governments had taken on significant new responsibilities for a variety of other health-related issues (including workplace safety and workers' compensation, food and drug regulation, welfare, and Social Security), efforts to introduce government-sponsored health reform failed. The efforts of President Franklin D. Roosevelt, and later President Harry Truman, to enact comprehensive, government-sponsored health programs were defeated by organized medicine, the insurance industry, and conservative business leaders.

In the 1940s employer-sponsored health insurance began to fill the need left by the lack of government-funded social insurance. The growth in employer-sponsored insurance was spurred by collective bargaining as well as employers' use of health insurance benefits to circumvent wartime wage and price controls. The income tax exemption for employer-purchased insurance reinforced the incentive of workers to rely on employment group policies rather than on individually purchased policies for which there was no tax exclusion.

> The new medical-industrial complex is now a fact of American life. It is still growing and is likely to be with us for a long time. Any conclusions about its ultimate impact on our health-care system would be premature, but it is safe to say that the effect will be profound ... We should not allow the medical-industrial complex to distort our health-care system to its own entrepreneurial ends.
>
> ARNOLD S. RELMAN
> *New England Journal of Medicine*

The success of the medical care and public health systems in reducing mortality from acute conditions and infectious disease led to increases in life expectancy. As individuals lived longer, chronic degenerative illness supplanted acute and infectious disease as the major reasons for seeking medical care. Today, the United States spends 75% of its medical resources on the diagnosis, treatment, and rehabilitation of chronic diseases.

The unanticipated consequence of the new dominance of care for chronic disease was that medical costs became increasingly concentrated among a readily identified population. Thus, insurance, originally designed to protect individuals against unanticipated and stochastic health threats such as accidents or infectious disease, no longer proved a viable mechanism for financing care. Insurance companies sought to avoid enrolling those who could reliably be predicted to use high levels of medical services, i.e., those with chronic conditions, by engaging in "medical underwriting," that is, charging people with chronic conditions higher premiums. This spawned hundreds of com-

> Health care companies are not in business to heal people or save lives; they provide health care to make profits. In effect, in the necessary effort to control health care costs through the market mechanism, power has shifted from physicians and patients to insurance companies and other purchasers of services.
>
> GEORGE SOROS
> *The New York Times*

peting health plans that sought to keep premiums low by attracting low-cost subscribers and led to the shrinking of plans, such as Blue Cross, which offered community-rated premiums that did not vary according to the health status of the subscriber. At the same time, individuals with chronic conditions had the greatest incentives to purchase health plans with the most generous coverage. This situation, sometimes referred to as **moral hazard**, makes it almost impossible for insurance with community ratings to compete.

An employer group plan, which pools individuals with different health risks, can (if it is large enough) help overcome the problem of self-selection, and employer-based health insurance became the modal means of obtaining health insurance for working individuals and their families in the United States. However, many of those with the greatest chronic health care needs did not have access to employer-based insurance because they were either too old or too disabled to work. In the early 1960s, the group with the most consistent need for medical care, the aged, went almost completely uncovered.

Political forces were mobilized to address this classic situation of market failure, and in 1965 the United States passed legislation to establish the Medicare system, which provided insurance to all individuals over age 65. Currently **Medicare** provides health care coverage for 44 million beneficiaries, of whom 37 million are aged; the remaining 7 million are under 65 and disabled. More than 99% of persons over age 65 are now enrolled in Medicare.

The availability of funding to treat the medical conditions of the elderly helped fuel the rapid emergence of new technologies and procedures to address the disabilities associated with chronic conditions. This development was stimulated by the expansion of the country's chronic disease research infrastructure, including the creation and growth of the National Institutes of Health.

Medicaid was passed in the same year as Medicare to provide health care coverage for nonelderly individuals without access to employer group plans. Medicaid provides health insurance for the disabled, that is, persons who are unable to work due to their health conditions. It also covers recipients of the federal-state government-sponsored welfare program known as Aid to Families of Dependent Children (AFDC; an entitlement program replaced in the 1990s by Temporary Assistance for Needy Families, TANF). AFDC and TANF cover(ed) primarily families headed by unmarried women with dependent children and were (are) designed to allow mothers to remain out of the labor force to care for their young children. Any substantial employment tends to raise family income above the eligibility thresholds for AFDC (TANF), and thus Medicaid. Thus Medicaid follows in the tradition of welfare assistance rather than social insurance.

In the late 1980s Medicaid was expanded to require the provision of health insurance for children of low-income parents, whether or not their families received welfare income support. This decoupling of insurance eligibility from welfare eligibility secured comprehensive health coverage for poor children. Medicaid does not provide health insurance to all low-income individuals, however—only 46% of the nonelderly with incomes under the poverty level are covered. Some groups, such as young men with low incomes and no children, are not eligible for Medicaid coverage unless they are disabled. Depending on state law, poor married couples, even with children, may be ineligible. Moreover, the income eligibility requirements often restrict coverage to only the poorest individuals. These requirements vary enormously across the states.

Numerous attempts prior to 2010 to increase the government's role in assuring that all Americans—not just the elderly, disabled, and some of the poor—are insured have been unsuccessful. Efforts to build on the existing employer-based system by requiring all employers to finance health insurance were advanced by President Nixon in 1974 and by President Clinton in 1993. Despite considerable public support, these proposals were defeated largely through the efforts of the conservatives and business and insurance communities with vested interests in the existing system. Some have argued that the development of Medicare and Medicaid, which addressed the needs of two vulnerable populations, had the paradoxical effect of undermining claims for a publicly organized health plan for the general population.

Failing to gain support for universal, government-sponsored coverage, policy advocates argued for, and won, incremental expansions of public programs. Some of these additions are disease-specific, such as targeted programs for end-stage renal failure (through Medicare) and HIV/AIDS. Others represented expansions of insurance to whole populations, such as the children of low-income parents, through the State Children's Health Insurance Program (SCHIP). These incremental actions have tended to exacerbate rather than ameliorate fragmentation of the health care system.

In the United States, insurance is framed as coverage for "an individual," and each insurer provides coverage for only a small part of the population, with a changing mix of enrollees from year to year. This fragmentation impedes population-based prevention and health promotion efforts and undermines the ability of citizens to organize for reform.

In addition, the fragmentation fostered the growth of vested interests that opposed any change to the status quo. These stakeholders profited from the existing system and had substantial incentives to thwart a comprehensive, unified health insurance system. Countering the health reform initiative proposed by President Clinton in 1993, commercial insurers and small employers were successful in framing comprehensive public-sector initiatives as "big government," "anti-individual," and "antichoice." Clinton's health plan was labeled an "NHS-like" system (referring to the British National Health Service), despite the fact that it built on the existing employer-based system and private medical practice and allowed for a choice of insurance plans as well as a choice of providers.

The recession of 2008 accelerated the decline in employer-based health insurance. The loss of coverage, the growth in the numbers of uninsured Americans, and the escalating costs of health care led President Obama to identify health reform as one of the highest priorities for his administration. A comprehensive health reform bill, building on existing institutions to extend health insurance coverage, was passed in 2010. The next section describes the financing and eligibility requirements of health insurance as they existed prior to the passage of the 2010 health reform legislation.

> The steeply rising health-care costs remind me of what Jack Kent Cooke, the owner of the Washington Redskins, supposedly said when he was asked why he fired George Allen as his football coach: Cooke is quoted as saying, "I gave Allen an unlimited budget and he exceeded it."
>
> MARK SIEGLER

FINANCING AND ELIGIBILITY

As a result of this checkered history, a variety of health insurance financing arrangements coexists in the United States. The federal **Medicare** system pays for health insurance for virtually all persons over 65 as well as the long-term disabled. **Medicaid**, a federal/state program for low-income and disabled persons, provides coverage for 14% of the nonelderly population. Employer-based coverage underwrites health insurance for 61% of the working-age population and their dependents. About 5% of nonelderly individuals, who do not qualify for either Medicare or Medicaid coverage and are not offered insurance by their employer, purchase individual health insurance policies. The federal government also pays for the care for individuals in certain categories, e.g., veterans or those affected by particular diseases, such as HIV/AIDS. However, many people (about 46 million in 2008) had no health insurance at all. There is enormous variation in the financing arrangements for these different groups; thus, the arrangements for each group are described separately below.

Medicare for the Elderly

Medicare is a national insurance system, not a national health-care provision system. That is, the federal government either pays bills for care received by beneficiaries from private physicians and hospitals or pays to enroll a beneficiary in a prepaid managed health-care plan. In an insurance-based system, the benefits covered reflect an orientation to infections and acute illness that prevailed at the time Medicare was enacted in 1965. Thus, Medicare benefits did not initially cover medication and, until recently, had very poor coverage for preventive health care, such as mammograms or immunizations. Medications have been covered since 2006, but long-term care coverage is not included as a Medicare benefit.

Established in 1965 under Title XVIII of the Social Security Act, Medicare provides hospital insurance, known as Part A coverage, and supplementary medical insurance, known as Part B coverage, and since 2006, Part D for Drug coverage. Each component is financed differently.

Hospital insurance, through Part A, is financed through the Hospital Insurance Trust Fund, which is funded by a Medicare tax of 1.45% on the total annual earnings of all workers. An equal amount is assessed on employers. Health reform legislation is likely to increase these payroll tax rates. Most beneficiaries qualify for Medicare Part A with no individual premium contribution because they or a spouse have worked 40 or more quarters in Medicare-covered employment. People with fewer than 40 quarters of Medicare-covered employment pay a monthly premium for hospital coverage.

Supplemental Medical Insurance, through Part B, is financed by the Supplementary Medical Insurance Trust Fund, which by law derives three-quarters of its support from general revenues and one-quarter from the beneficiary. Although Part B is voluntary, 93% of those eligible take advantage of the substantial federal government subsidy of the premiums and enroll in Part B.

Part D is another voluntary component of Medicare. The federal government provides a defined contribution to the private drug plans for each Medicare enrollee (beneficiaries can also gain drug coverage by joining a managed care plan or other kind of private plan offered under the Medicare Advantage feature of the program). Enrollees pay a monthly premium that makes up the difference between the federal government contribution and the plan's cost of providing drugs. Thus, from the point of view of the federal government, Part D is a **defined contribution** plan, where the government's financial liability is capped. In contrast, Medicare Parts A and B are **defined benefit** plans in which

> The increasing ability of physicians to disentangle specific disease entities ... was an intellectual achievement of the first magnitude and not unrelated to the increasingly scientific and prestigious public image of the medical profession. Yet, we have seen a complex and inexorably bureaucratic reimbursement system grow up around these diagnostic entities; disease does not exist if it cannot be coded.
>
> CHARLES E. ROSENBERG
> *The Care of Strangers: The Rise of America's Hospital System*

the scope of covered services is set and the federal government commits to pay the costs of providing those services.

Since the 1980s Medicare has paid hospitals prospectively, based on **Diagnostic Related Groups** (DRGs). The hospital receives the same amount of payment for each patient in a DRG, independent of the patient's actual length of hospital stay (an adjustment is made for "outlier" cases). DRGs have been credited with giving hospitals a strong financial incentive to deliver care efficiently, and have resulted in an overall shortening of the length of hospital inpatient stays.

Medicare Part B covers eligible physicians' services and outpatient hospital services, medically necessary services of physical and occupational therapists, some home health care, as well as most medical services (e.g., laboratory tests, imaging). Some services important to older patients, such as eyeglasses and hearing aids, are not covered. Additionally, a limited number of preventive services such as mammograms have only recently been covered. Theoretically, there is some control on the use of high-technology services, but it is not clear that Medicare strictly audits appropriate use of expensive technologies such as positron emission tomography (PET) scans or implantable cardiac defibrillators.

Beginning in the early 1990s, Medicare reimbursed physicians for the services they deliver based on a **resource-based relative value scale** (RBRVS), or the Medicare Physician Fee Schedule. This administered price schedule is the product of the relative values determined as a function of the amount of skill and time involved in each procedure and prices per relative value unit that reflect the variation in practice costs from area to area.

Reimbursements for Part B services are subject to an annual deductible, $131 in 2009, and coinsurance of 20% of the Medicare-approved fee for services after meeting the annual deductible (with the exception of mental health services for which the coinsurance rate is 50%). Some low-income elderly covered by Medicare are also eligible for the Qualified Medicare Beneficiary (QMB) program, under which Medicaid pays out-of-pocket medical expenses, such as Part B premiums, deductible, and coinsurance amounts. Medicaid also pays for services for these "dual eligibles" that are not included in Medicare coverage, but are available under the state Medicaid program such as nursing facility care beyond the 100-day limit covered by Medicare, eyeglasses, and hearing aids.

Many Medicare beneficiaries obtain supplemental private insurance that covers 80% of the patient's cost-sharing obligation, which means that the patient pays only 4% of the bill at the time of service (.2 × .2). The availability of supplemental **Medigap** insurance lowers the cost of medical care and stimulates additional use (both useful and inappropriate) that adds to Medicare's costs, because it pays 80% of the total bill.

Enrolling in a Medicare health maintenance organization (HMO) is another way to lower cost sharing for outpatient services, without generating moral hazard (although favorable selection and substantial federal subsidies to managed care plans have meant that Medicare pays more on average for these beneficiaries than if this population had stayed in traditional Medicare). HMO enrollees also typically have wider coverage of preventive and other needed services such as eyeglasses and hearing aids.

Since January 1, 2006, all Medicare beneficiaries have been able to select a private company to provide insurance to cover the costs of medication under Medicare Part D.

Medicaid for Low Income and Disabled Persons

Medicaid is jointly financed by federal and state governments, but is administered by the states. Federal law requires that Medicaid cover families that qualify for the state's cash welfare programs for families with dependent children, as well as low-income pregnant women and children. Low-income Medicare recipients and disabled persons receiving Supplemental Security Income (SSI) are also eligible for Medicaid. These requirements reflect the origins of Medicaid as a mechanism for providing health insurance to certain categories of nonelderly individuals who could not be covered by employer-based insurance because they were not in the labor force. The health reform legislation expands Medicaid eligibility to include persons with income up to 133% of the federal poverty level.

The **State Children's Health Insurance Program** (SCHIP) provides insurance to children of low-income parents whose earnings exceed the Medicaid ceilings. By June 2008 monthly enrollment in SCHIP had reached 4.8 million children, compared to Medicaid's enrollment of 29.9 million children. Together, Medicaid and SCHIP cover half of low-income children and one-fourth of all U. S. children.

Although Medicaid and SCHIP provide health insurance for the poor, they do not provide medical assistance for all low-income persons. To be eligible for Medicaid, a recipient must be a U. S. citizen or a legally admitted immigrant who has been a lawful permanent resident for at least 5 years. *The federal government pays for at least half the cost of Medicaid expenditures in every state.* Medicaid is a matching grant program with a formula that ensures that the federal share is greater in low-income states. The federal government finances 70% of SCHIP costs, considerably greater than its share of Medicaid costs in most states. Unlike Medicaid, for which the Federal government matches state funding for all the individuals who meet the state eligibility criteria, the federal SCHIP funding is capped annually for each state.

The reliance on state funding for Medicaid has proved problematic, particularly during economic downturns, when states' tax revenues decline. Even in times of economic expansion the inexorable increase in the cost of medical care has created fiscal problems for most states. *Medicaid is the second largest program in most states' general fund budgets,* accounting for about 21% of state spending, and it was the most rapidly growing component of state expenditures in the early 2000's. To avert having Medicaid spending crowd out other important expenditures, states have implemented a variety of policies to reduce Medicaid costs: cutting or freezing provider payments, trimming benefits, restricting program eligibility or making enrollment more difficult.

Families with dependent children who qualified for cash welfare programs made up about two-thirds of Medicaid recipients prior to 2010, but accounted for just 27% of the program's expenditures. Disabled individuals who receive Supplemental Security Income (SSI) also receive Medicaid coverage, and they have much higher per capita costs than those eligible via income-support programs. SSI is a federal program that provides monthly cash payments to aged, blind, and disabled people who have little or no other sources of income. Disabled people who have not contributed to Social Security for a sufficient number of quarters to be eligible for SSDI receive SSI and are also entitled to Medicaid. The Medically Needy program, available at state option, permits individuals who would be categorically eligible, but whose assets or income exceed the state criteria, to become eligible for Medicaid because of extremely high medical expenses.

Historically, Medicaid eligibility criteria have varied across the states because the eligibility criteria for AFDC (now TANF), SSI, and Medically Needy programs are set by the states. Although the federal government mandated that states cover pregnant women and preschool children with family incomes under 133% of the federal poverty level and school-age children in families with parental income under the poverty level, states could receive federal matching funds for covering children and pregnant women with incomes up to 200% of the federal poverty level. Similarly, the federal government mandated that states provide Medicaid to disabled persons receiving SSI income support, but states, at their option, could provide Medicaid to the disabled whose incomes exceed the federal payment. Spending for these nonmandated beneficiaries accounts for one-third of all Medicaid expenditures.

Since Medicaid is targeted to a low-income population, cost-sharing requirements are minimal. Patients pay nothing or a very nominal amount for each service, whether the patient is enrolled in an HMO or traditional Medicaid. In some states, enrollees may also be required to pay a nominal co-payment to receive services. Families in 32 states must pay a small monthly premium to enroll their child in the SCHIP program. Historically, most Medicaid enrollees were not asked to pay a premium. Recently, state Medicaid plans have been allowed to charge premiums for some individuals. Evidence from the states that have instituted premium payments suggests that *charging even modest premiums for Medicaid leads to disenrollment and increased numbers of uninsured*. For instance, Oregon instituted an income-related premium of $6 to $20 in 2003, and recent evidence suggests that Medicaid enrollment in Oregon dropped by nearly two-thirds as a direct result of the increased premiums and cost-sharing. Enrollment in Rhode Island's Medicaid program fell by 20% when premiums were instituted, and only half of those who dropped out of the program became insured by other means.

Employer-Based Insurance

Employer-based insurance remains the predominant insurance mechanism for most employees and their families. Prior to the implementation of health reform, employers were not legally required to provide insurance to their workers, except in Hawaii and Massachusetts. As of 2009, 158 million individuals (61% of the population under age 65) held employer sponsored insurance coverage. About half were insured through their own employer, while the other half were covered as the dependent of a worker. As described above, employer-based insurance is a historical legacy, which has the value of creating insurance "groups" that are less subject to risk selection than the insurance markets for individuals.

Ninety-nine percent of large firms of 200 or more workers offered health insurance in 2008. The situation is different in smaller firms with fewer than 200 workers: In these companies, the percentage of employers offering insurance is lower and has dropped from 68% in 2000 to 62% in 2008. Small firms not only face higher premiums due to the small size of their risk pool and administrative costs for small groups, but they are also more likely to have low-wage workers and part-time employees. As a result, only 43% of employees of small firms with fewer than 25 workers were covered by employer-sponsored insurance (provided either by their own or a family member's employer), in contrast to 67% of employees of large firms with 200 or more workers.

Employers that offer health insurance select the offerings from which the employee may choose and subsidize the premium costs. From the worker's point of view, employer-sponsored health insurance provides two major financial advantages. First, employers appear to underwrite the majority of the costs, although most economists would argue that the true costs are shifted to the employees in the form of lower wages and salaries. Employers "pay" on average, 85% of the premium for covering the worker and 74% of the costs of family coverage.

The second advantage is that neither the employer's nor the employee's contribution is counted as taxable income to the employee. If we consider the loss of revenue to the government as a "tax expenditure," the United States has the perverse policy of spending much more for the health insurance of higher income individuals than for lower income individuals. This policy is the opposite of the more progressive financing that prevails in other developed countries.

Despite the long history of employers providing insurance and the income tax advantages for their continuing to do so, many employers decided to drop this employment benefit in the face of escalating health insurance premiums from 2000 on. The high costs of medical care reflected in the annual premium rates for employer-sponsored insurance have affected employers in many ways. In 2008, the average premium across all employer sponsored plan types was $4704 for single coverage and $12,680 for family coverage. Equally worrisome to employers is the fact that health insurance premiums have been rising at rates at least twice those of the Consumer Price Index since the year 2000, and premium inflation has limited employers' ability to grant wage increases. Indeed, workers' earnings grew about 3% per year from 2000 to 2006, while health insurance premiums grew at a rate of 8% a year. Workers' contributions to premium costs have remained relatively stable in percentage terms, but the underlying growth in premium costs translates into increased dollar contributions to premiums made by employees.

The rise in premiums, along with a decline in union activity and the growth in employment in small firms, which are less likely to offer insurance, contributed to an increase in the number of uninsured individuals prior to 2010.

Individual Insurance Policies

A large number of health insurance companies sell nongroup policies to individuals who pay the premiums themselves. About 5% of the under 65 population obtained private, nongroup insurance in 2005. The premiums for these policies tend to be higher than those for employer group policies, partly because there are no economies of scale in marketing. A second reason for the high premiums is the **adverse selection** that such individual plans experience. To protect themselves against this adverse selection, individual insurance plans often impose **medical underwriting**, which restricts the coverage of preexisting conditions such as chronic diseases or may lead the insurer to refuse to sell insurance at any price to persons with chronic conditions. Some individual insurance plans also adjust their covered benefits so that the policy will be attractive only to healthy and risk-averse subscribers.

Individual plans can be both restrictive and expensive. Nearly 60% of those who sought nongroup health coverage found it difficult to identify an affordable plan, and 20% were denied coverage, charged a higher price, or faced the exclusion of an existing medical condition from coverage. Some states, such as Massachusetts, have passed "guaranteed issue" laws that require all companies licensed in the state to sell health insurance to accept all applicants at community-rated premiums or within a rate band of a community rate. Other states have established high-risk pools to provide insurance policies to persons with medical conditions that have caused private insurers to refuse to insure them.

Veterans

Veterans of the U. S. armed forces are eligible for care at a Veterans Health Administration (VA) facility. The VA covers a full range of services, including long-term care. The Federal government uses a global budget to fund a network of federally run hospitals, and to employ salaried providers. There is no fee to patients who meet a means-test or who experienced a "service-connected" injury. Veterans who do not meet one of these eligibility criteria are required to make co-payments and may be required to find care outside the VA.

Individuals with Particular Diseases

Some individuals with particular diseases are eligible for care under federal or state arrangements. For example, the federally- and state-funded **Ryan White Care Act** pays for medical treatment and pharmaceuticals for low- and moderate-income people living with HIV/AIDS. The income-eligibility criteria for the program are considerably more generous than those that apply to Medicaid. Some states have historically had separate pharmacy coverage for those who were above income cutoffs for Medicaid (e.g., New Jersey had a Pharmacy Assistance for the Aged and Disabled benefit.)

> The problem of the uninsured continues to grow quietly; in the long run, its effects will be so pervasive that it is bound to re-emerge as a major national issue. If it does not, then we will find ourselves living in a much meaner America than many of us who entered the healing professions ever imagined.
>
> STEVEN A. SCHROEDER
> *New England Journal of Medicine*

The Uninsured

In 2008, 46 million Americans were uninsured because they did not meet any of the above criteria—they were not over 65, they did not meet the categorical eligibility requirements for Medicaid, they were not veterans, neither they nor their family members were employed in a firm that offered health insurance or they could not afford to purchase either employer-linked or individual insurance policies. Individuals who did not have health insurance and did not qualify to receive services because of their status as veterans or their medical conditions received medical care in a variety of settings—county hospitals, community health centers, migrant health centers, sexually transmitted disease (STD) clinics, and free clinics.

This care is episodic and primarily addresses acute conditions. It is more difficult to obtain care for chronic diseases, for which care often involves long waits at hospital outpatient departments, where choice of providers is limited. Consequently, the uninsured tend to get less care than those with health insurance. When they do receive services, the uninsured are often billed the full charges, while insured patients are billed at lower rates negotiated by their health plans. Ultimately, the services are often paid for by county or state government, although the federal government contributes to the care of the uninsured through the Disproportionate Share Hospital (DSH) grants. Much of the outpatient care for the uninsured is delivered by nonprofit organizations such as Planned Parenthood or free clinics that depend on charitable donations.

ORGANIZATION AND MANAGEMENT OF MEDICAL CARE

When health insurance was becoming more widespread in the United States in the 1930s and 1940s, individuals made their own choices about health-care providers with little outside guidance, while insurers performed primarily a financial function—collecting premiums and dispensing reimbursements. So-called **indemnity insurance** made little attempt either to manage the care or to negotiate with phy-

Spurred by the need both to control costs and to improve quality, there has been a slow evolution in the United States toward medical care delivery systems that are more vertically integrated. The years since 1990 have witnessed a rapid growth in HMOs and other types of managed care. The various forms of managed care now dominate the private health insurance market (only 4% of enrollees in employer-sponsored health insurance had conventional, indemnity insurance in 2009).

This section describes four broad mechanisms under which health care costs are reimbursed: indemnity insurance, health maintenance organizations, preferred provider organizations, and integrated health systems such as the Veterans Administration and military treatment facilities. These differ in the degree to which they are vertically integrated, the amount of cost control they provide, and the degree of choice available to subscribers to select their own medical providers and decide on the amount and type of care they receive. These canonical forms represent the major elements in the choice set available in the United States.

Indemnity Insurance (Non-PPO)

Indemnity insurance is the traditional type of reimbursement insurance in which insurance companies bear the risk for medical care expenditures, reimburse a fixed percentage of billed charges, and impose no restrictions on the patient's choice of provider or services used. This was the dominant form of health insurance in the 20th century and accounted for 73% of the employer-sponsored market as late as 1988. Medicare was also organized as indemnity insurance at its inception, reflecting the prevalent employer-

sicians and hospitals about their charges. However, this was also the period of development of group model **health maintenance organizations** (HMOs), which attempted to both manage care and control costs in order to provide both insurance and medical care under a fixed, capitated payment.

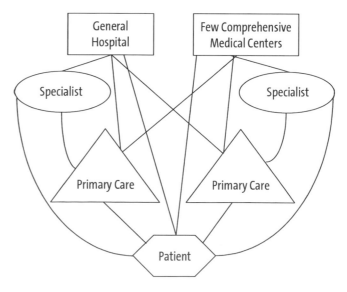

FIGURE 25.1 Indemnity insurance system

based models in 1965, when Medicare became law. By 2009, this form of conventional insurance had shrunk to 4% of the private, employer-based market. In contrast, indemnity insurance remained the dominant form within Medicare for persons over 65.

Indemnity health insurance itself imposes little structure on enrollees' medical care choices, as illustrated in Figure 25.1. Although this figure shows a hierarchy of relationships among providers, with primary-care providers referring to specialists and hospitals, the patient's choice of services is not channeled to particular providers, and the hierarchy is not well integrated. The medical sector dominates and functions independently of other sectors, such as public health or population health. Financing for this system was largely out of pocket prior to the 1940s, and became dependent on employer-sponsored insurance or government payment after that time.

Reimbursement health insurance lowers the price of care to patients, and results in incentives for individuals to overuse personal, individual medical care (**moral hazard**), leading to increased demand for services. Because of its orientation to insurable events, preventive or health promotion services tend to be poorly covered. Thus, patients are led to focus on episodic (insurable) medical services and to slight preventive care and treatment for chronic diseases.

Physician incentives in this early health system structure were well aligned with those of the patient. Both sought to obtain as much care as possible for the patient, which also has the effect of increasing the income of the physician. Some physicians also owned or operated facilities, raising questions of conflict of interest.

Patients select their own providers, although they have few sources of data to inform the choices they make. The lack of structured relationships among providers makes it difficult for physicians to coordinate care for an individual patient. In the indemnity insurance model, the primary role of insurance companies is to collect premiums and distribute payments to providers on the basis of billed charges. Thus, insurance companies have little ability or incentive to monitor the appropriateness of the medical services provided or the procedures used. We may characterize these arrangements as the "unmanaged care" system.

Is there no hope? the sick Man said.
The silent doctor shook his head,
And took his leave, with signs of sorrow,
Despairing of his fee tomorrow.

JOHN GAY
The Sick Man and the Angel

Health Maintenance Organizations

The initial model of managed care was the group-or staff-model HMO, which combines the roles of insurer and provider of medical care. Today, newer HMO models called **Independent Practice Associations** (IPAs) contract for, rather than directly provide, medical care. Either type of prepaid insurance plan receives a fixed capitation payment to provide all needed medical care for a patient in a given time period. The patient pays low or no copayment as long as care is obtained from the HMO's affiliated physicians and hospitals.

The HMO providers form a closed system—there is generally no coverage for medical services obtained from providers not associated with the HMO. HMOs usually require subscribers to choose a physician or medical group as a primary care physician (PCP), who is then responsible for providing general medical care. The PCP acts as a "gatekeeper" who must authorize treatment from a specialist or other provider or admission to the hospital. The HMO itself may also have an administrative or coordinating role in managing high-cost services through a process of utilization review and management. Medical care received without authorization or from a provider or facility not in the HMO's network is not generally covered, except in an emergency situation.

The HMO system of care is fully vertically integrated, as illustrated in Figure 25.2, providing the HMO the opportunity to monitor the appropriateness of all the medical

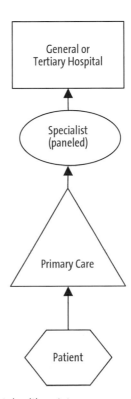

FIGURE 25.2 Prototypic health maintenance organization

care that the patient receives. The HMO serves a defined population and is, therefore, able to monitor health care at a population level. However, because insurance status is usually tied to employment, individuals may remain with the same HMO for only a short period of time before switching to a different HMO or a different form of insurance, potentially undermining the downstream benefits to the HMO of monitoring its enrollees.

The fact that the HMO is a provider of care and is also financially responsible for the services the patient receives means that HMO providers have an incentive to limit services—and some charge to withhold necessary care. Despite these concerns, health outcomes appear to be comparable between HMO enrollees and individuals insured by indemnity insurance.

It is important to distinguish between the two major types of HMO—the **group/staff model**, in which providers practice in a location owned and managed by the HMO, and the **individual practice association** (IPA) model, in which services are provided by physicians practicing in their private offices or in medical groups. IPA physicians do not have an exclusive relationship with the prepaid plan, and may treat patients with different HMO, PPO, or indemnity insurance coverage. Although both types of HMO receive a fixed payment per patient per month, the way in which providers are compensated differs. In the group/staff model, HMO physicians are paid largely on a salary basis, although they may also receive annual bonuses if costs are below the expected target. In the IPA model HMO, all or part of the capitation is given to the primary care physician or medical group, which then has the responsibility to provide all needed primary care within a fixed budget. The IPA physicians and medical groups thus share directly in the insurance risk. In this system, individual physicians may face stronger financial incentives to limit the amount of services delivered in order to stay within the budget than is the case in the group/staff models. This reverses the incentives physicians face in the indemnity system, where the incentives are for physicians to deliver more care. HMOs, however, have incentives to provide preventive care that will control chronic disease, since the HMO is responsible for *total* health care costs. HMOs use a variety of methods to pay for services from specialty physicians and hospitals.

Despite the vertical integration within the medical sector, the HMO is not well integrated with population or public health sectors. The fact that HMOs have a known population of subscribers, however, allows them to engage in some population health efforts, including reminders about preventive health services, and disease promotion programs such as smoking cessation or weight-control clinics. These are activities that benefit from economies of scale and appear to be more common among group or staff model HMOs than among IPAs. HMOs increased in popularity in the early 1990s, covering 31% of insured workers at their peak of popularity in 1996. However, the percent-

> Behind false claims of efficiency lies a much uglier truth. Investor-owned care embodies a new value system that severs the community roots and Samaritan traditions of hospitals, makes physicians and nurses into instruments of investors, and views patients as commodities. Investor ownership marks the triumph of greed.
>
> STEFFIE WOOLHANDLER and DAVID HIMMELSTEIN
> *Canadian Medical Association Journal* (2004)

age of workers insured by HMOs fell to 20% in 2008, largely because of the development of less restrictive models of managed care. The Point of Service (POS) arrangement allows the subscriber to choose an HMO provider or a non-HMO provider for any particular service. Patient cost-sharing is higher, however, if the patient chooses to go outside the HMO panel of contracted providers. POS plan enrollment grew from 7% of insured workers in 1993 to 24% in 1999 and then fell to 12% in 2008.

Preferred Provider Organizations

A Preferred Provider Organization (PPO) resembles an HMO in that it has a hierarchy of providers and may require authorizations for costly services. Similar to IPA pro-

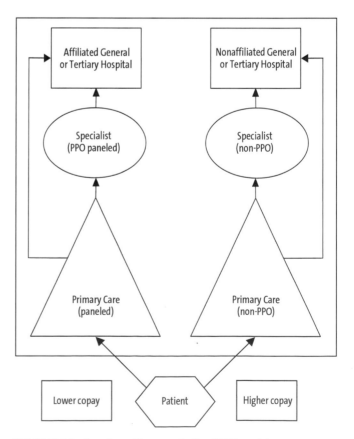

FIGURE 25.3 Preferred provider organization (PPO) model

viders, PPO physicians practice in their own offices and many physicians serve both IPA and PPO patients. PPO network physicians and hospitals accept lower levels of reimbursement than nonpreferred providers in exchange for the promise of greater numbers of patients. The PPO presents financial incentives for its enrollees to seek care within the PPO network of physicians and hospitals, but these incentives are not as strong as those facing HMO enrollees, because services provided by a nonpreferred provider are still partially covered.

Unlike HMO providers, PPO providers do not bear risk for medical use, since they are not capitated as HMO providers are. PPO plans may charge lower premiums than indemnity plans because they have negotiated lower rates with physicians and hospitals, and also because they require preauthorization for costly services. Thus, PPOs use some of the utilization controls employed by HMOs, but allow patients the option of a wider choice of providers, albeit at a higher price. The greater provider choice and the less stringent utilization review allowed by PPOs have led to increasing PPO enrollment over time. Whereas only 11% of workers were covered by a PPO insurance plan in 1988, fully 58% were enrolled in PPOs in 2008.

One variant of the PPO plan is the **consumer-driven plan** (CDP). A CDP typically has a high deductible, with insurance that begins to cover costs after an enrollee pays a minimum deductible of at least $1,100 for an individual or $2,200 for family coverage. Often no deductible is applied to preventive care and higher cost sharing is required for services received from out-of-network providers. The CDP plan is structured like a traditional insurance plan—providing protection against the small probability of large losses. CDPs are often combined with pretax spending accounts to provide limited coverage for the small losses as well. In 2008, 8% of workers enrolled in these high deductible plans.

Direct Service Provision

Some individuals do not carry insurance, but receive their medical care directly from a fully integrated health system, like the VA or a military treatment facility. These financial arrangements are similar to a staff model HMO in that providers are salaried and hospitals are financed by a fixed annual budget. The VA differs from an HMO, however, in not being the exclusive provider for a defined population. Thus, veterans can opt in and out of the VA system and, if there are supply constraints, the VA can prioritize which veterans receive care. Thus, it is more difficult for the VA than for an HMO to implement population health assessments or interventions because the population covered is not uniquely defined. However, the VA has been a leader in implementing clinical information systems that facilitate patient receipt of greater amounts of recommended preventive care and care for chronic diseases than a comparison group of non-VA patients.

MARKETS FOR HEALTH INSURANCE

Although prior to 2010 there was no single health insurance market that all Americans could access, there were a number of localized efforts by employers, public programs, and states to bring consumer choice into health insurance markets in the United States. This arrangement, initially called "managed competition," has been adapted by many large employers, including the federal government. Recently, some states have established "insurance connectors" or "insurance exchanges," which are marketplaces for insurance policies open to all residents of a state.

The managed competition market or insurance exchange provides a structured marketplace for health insurance that individuals can use to select the health plan that meets their needs in terms of provider choice, cost, convenience, or coverage of benefits. The ability of individuals to switch plans at designated times allows for flexibility over time.

This section describes the efforts of state and federal governments and other purchasers of health insurance to use markets to structure the choices available to their workers or clients into a managed competition framework in order delegate the organizing and provision of medical care to other entities.

Employer-Sponsored Plans with Internal Markets

During the period when indemnity insurance was the predominant form of insurance, employers typically offered a single health insurance plan. If sponsors gave employees a choice of insurance plans, they provided generous subsidies to all plans offered, making little effort to direct employees to select lower cost plans.

Currently, employees of large firms (with 200 or more workers) are commonly presented with a choice of health insurance plan options. On average, 64% of large firm employees are offered a choice of two or more plans, while 36% are presented with only one plan option. In contrast, workers in the small firms that offer health insurance are more likely to have only a single option. Only 28% of employees whose firms have fewer than 200 workers are able to choose among two or more health plans.

Among the larger employers offering multiple plans, many firms have switched from defined-benefit support, where the employer pays a fixed proportion of the premium (sometimes 100%), to a defined-contribution arrangement, where the employer pays a fixed amount toward the premium, and the employee pays the difference. Under defined contribution, the employee bears the marginal cost of choosing a more costly plan with a wider range of services covered, lower cost-sharing requirements, less restricted choice of providers or greater quality and convenience of services delivered. This section discusses some of the prominent examples of managed competition frameworks.

The Federal Employees Health Benefit Program (FEHBP)

The Federal Government offers over 350 health plans under the FEHB Program to employees in locations across the country. Although not all plans are available at all locations, at least seven non-HMO plans and several HMOs are available nationally.

When they are first hired, federal employees are presented with a choice of plans for themselves and their dependents. They may switch plans without penalty once a year during the Open Enrollment period. To aid in choosing among plans, FEHBP disseminates information on premiums and plan quality. The on-line plan comparison site includes information on premium rates and patient cost-sharing, consumer satisfaction, and links to quality scorecards and plan brochures.

The health plans offered are very heterogeneous in terms of coverage because they design their own benefit structure, with minimum guidance from the federal personnel office. Price, rather than coverage, seems to be an overwhelming element in employees' choice of plan. Over half of the federal employees in 1996 chose a plan in the lowest third of the premium distribution and another 38% chose a plan in the middle third.

The premium levels of the different health plans vary, but the Federal government provides a defined payment of 75% of the plan's premium or 72% of the weighted average premium across all plans, whichever is less. The federal personnel office negotiates premiums with the plans, but it is not constrained by a global cap on spending. The consumer's contribution to premium can come out of pretax income, and is therefore less burdensome to the employee. There is neither geographic nor risk adjustment of premiums in FEHBP, but there is little evidence of risk selection.

Medicaid

Like many employers, *states have been attempting to shift their Medicaid costs from a defined benefit arrangement to a defined contribution arrangement by enrolling Medicaid recipients into managed care.* By requiring Medicaid recipients to enroll in managed care, the state delegates the responsibility for managing medical care and reduces uncertainty about the state's Medicaid expenditure per enrollee. By 2004, 61% of Medicaid recipients nationally were enrolled in HMOs.

Although a number of states mandate that certain groups of Medicaid beneficiaries enroll in managed care, the states offer a choice among managed care plans to the beneficiaries. Medicaid recipients do not face financial incentives to choose a cost-efficient plan, since they are not required to share in the premium costs and all plans cover the same benefits. Rather, recipients choose primarily on the basis of perceived quality or convenience. Evaluations to date show that, on the whole, *managed care plans provide quality that is equivalent to that in Medicaid nonmanaged care, although levels of patient satisfaction tend to be lower.*

Medicare

Originally, the Medicare program provided government-funded indemnity insurance, and its primary function was to reimburse providers, with little management of medical care. However, the option to select an HMO to provide their care has been open to Medicare enrollees since the beginning of the program. The Balanced Budget Act of 1997 attempted to stimulate this option by creating the "Medicare + Choice" plan. Medicare HMOs were aggressively marketed in the 1990s by health plans that found them quite profitable because they were reimbursed at a rate of 95% of the average cost of non-HMO beneficiaries in their area, while they enrolled seniors with lower than average health care needs. HMOs were required to add services until their average costs equaled the capitation rate. Many beneficiaries were attracted by these additional benefits, such as coverage for prescription drugs, eyeglasses or hearing aids, and enrollment in Medicare HMO plans grew from 1.8 million in 1990 to 6.6 million in 2000. The number of enrollees fell to 4.9 million in 2004, as increasing numbers of HMOs withdrew from the Medicare + Choice market following the introduction in 2003 of risk-adjusted premiums, which apparently made the Medicare market less profitable.

The Medicare Prescription Drug Improvement and Modernization Act of 2003 (MMA) introduced more of a managed competition market by changing the mechanism for setting premiums for Medicare HMO plans. Starting in 2006, premium rates were set by a bidding process. If a plan's bid exceeds the average fee-for-service (FFS, i.e., traditional indemnity) Medicare costs in its area, the enrollee must pay the difference. If the plan's bid is lower, the enrollee gets a rebate of 75% of the difference.

> Like many other observers, I look at the U.S. health care system and see an administrative monstrosity, a truly bizarre mélange of thousands of payers with payment systems that differ for no socially beneficial reason, as well as staggeringly complex public systems with mind-boggling administered prices and other rules expressing distinctions that can only be regarded as weird.
>
> HENRY AARON

State Plans for Individuals and/or Small Businesses

Massachusetts and California have attempted to set up insurance "connectors" that create a kind of managed competition market to provide a choice of health insurance products to small firms or individuals—two groups that have difficulty obtaining insurance in the private, individual market at affordable prices. This section will review these as well as the efforts of Tennessee to leverage its Medicaid plan through a competitive market in order to provide health insurance coverage to uninsured residents who were not Medicaid eligible.

Massachusetts

A 2006 Massachusetts law mandated that all state residents be covered by health insurance. To help individuals who are not insured by their employers or public programs find insurance plans, the state set up a Health Insurance Connector, which organizes a market to offer quality-certified insurance products that are affordable by small businesses and individuals.

Affordability is a major issue for the uninsured, so the state provides subsidies to persons with income less than 300% of the Federal Poverty Level to help them purchase managed care products from organizations that participate in the state's Medicaid program. State funding previously directed to the Free Care Pool, new state funding and federal Disproportionate Share payments support the subsidies. In addition, employers with 10 employees or more who do not provide health insurance pay a "fair share" payment that is used to subsidize premiums.

Tennessee

In 1994 the State of Tennessee replaced its Medicaid program with a managed care system called **TennCare**. Individuals who were previously covered by the State's Medicaid program, residents who were uninsurable due to current or past medical conditions, and those not eligible for employer- or government- sponsored health care coverage selected one of the competing, state-chartered nonprofit managed care organizations (MCOs) offered by TennCare. The MCOs were paid on a capitated basis with funds drawn from a global state health budget comprised mostly of state and federal dollars originally earmarked for the Medicaid program, supplemented by revenue from co-pays, deductibles and means-tested premiums required of beneficiaries with income above the federal poverty level.

At its height, TennCare provided health coverage to 1.5 million people. However, over time, TennCare was besieged by demands from hospitals and physicians for higher capitation rates to stave off insolvency. At the same time, patients' groups lobbied for increased services and benefits, which Tennessee attempted to fund by cutting reimbursement rates to hospitals and physicians. In January of 2002, a federal judge ruled that TennCare had failed to provide adequate screening, diagnosis and treatment for children and ordered the state to place over 500,000 enrollees into a separate program to be overseen by someone appointed by the court. Subsequently, Tennessee dropped its reliance on capitation and reverted to more traditional Medicaid funding.

California

California's Pacific Health Advantage program (PacAdvantage) was a not-for-profit health insurance purchasing pool established in 1992 to provide a marketplace where small businesses with 2 to 50 employees could purchase affordable insurance products. It offered businesses a choice among more than a dozen health plans, including HMOs, PPO, and POS. However, because individuals and firms were not mandated to have health insurance, the plans were subject to adverse selection, which resulted in the eventual pullout of most of the health insurance insurers, PacAdvantage ceased operations at the end of 2006.

SUMMARY OF THE U. S. HEALTH CARE SYSTEM

The United States has a fragmented and convoluted medical care system with overlapping responsibilities across programs and serious gaps in coverage. Most nonelderly Americans receive health insurance through an employer plan. As detailed above, employer-sponsored health-care plans vary widely in terms of the organization of care (traditional indemnity, HMO, PPO, or POS arrangements) and the amount of choice among plans. Some individuals are insured through both their own and their spouses' employer-based plan. Employers' contributions to this coverage are increasingly structured as defined contributions, with the employee paying the marginal cost of more expensive plans.

The federal government sponsors insurance for some

groups not easily covered through employer arrangements—the elderly, the disabled, and the poor. The federal Medicare system provides (nearly) universal insurance for the elderly and covers a standardized set of benefits. However, these benefits are not comprehensive. Consequently, many seniors have either obtained supplemental coverage through their previous employers or have purchased "Medigap" policies in an individual insurance market to cover these additional expenses and must coordinate their supplemental insurance with Medicare reimbursements. Low-income seniors depend on their state-run Medicaid program to pay for items that are not covered under the standard Medicare plan, such as eyeglasses, hearing aids, or long term care. Medicaid eligibility and the effectiveness of coverage for the poor varies across the states. Although there is a federal requirement to cover a core set of benefits, enormous variation in provider reimbursement rates affects the fulfillment of benefits.

Persons who are not offered employer-based insurance and who do not meet the eligibility criteria for government plans remain uninsured unless they purchase a private individual policy at a high premium. The cost of "uncompensated care" for the uninsured in emergency situations is either passed on to insured patients or is financed by local, state, or federal governments or charitable contributions.

As specific coverage issues have gained attention and political appeal, the United States has made incremental changes to patch gaps in the coverage system—such as the SCHIP program for children and the Ryan White program for HIV/AIDS. Such adhoc adjustments serve to complicate the system—creating substantial inconsistencies in eligibility, benefit packages, and administrative requirements—and result in wasteful attempts to shift costs across programs. It is little wonder that the United States is estimated to spend 24% of its health care expenditures on administration!

In the past, the American public has shown a preference for maintaining a health insurance system that depends on the private market, rather than the government, to provide health care and has rejected several attempts to institute a national health care system. With the passage of health reform legislation in 2010, the U. S. has joined all other advanced developed nations in making a commitment to provide access to health care for all its citizens. However, the reform legislation builds on the fundamental features of the prior U. S. system, relying on a patchwork of private and public programs to achieve universal coverage.

Although all citizens will be mandated to have health insurance, health reform will not institute a single-payer system like those operating in other advanced, developed nations. The U. S. will continue to rely on a fragmented set of health care financing arrangements. Medicare will continue to serve the elderly; Medicaid will be expanded to cover a greater share of low-income individuals; however, most of the nonelderly will continue to receive employment-sponsored health insurance. Indeed, larger employers will be required to either provide insurance or pay a fee for covering their workers. Individuals who are not covered through these channels will be able to purchase individual insurance policies through health insurance exchanges, similar to the Massachusetts prototype. Unlike prior individual insurance policies, the plans offered through the exchanges must provide guaranteed issue and guaranteed renewal. They may not charge rates that depend on medical history or health conditions. Government subsidies will help to make the policies affordable to low-income families and individuals.

The 2010 health reform legislation represents a major advance in providing for universal health insurance coverage, yet it retains substantial continuity with the health financing system developed over decades in the United States. By building on existing arrangements, the plan minimizes disruption, allows for consumer choice and addresses some of the most egregious problems in the prior system, such as medical underwriting. However, it does not completely address the organizational incoherence of the prior arrangements. Several European countries (e.g., The Netherlands, Germany, and Switzerland) built their national insurance plans on the framework of existing employer-paid arrangements. The United States can learn from their experiences to construct a more organizationally coherent system that maintains consumer choice and promotes competition among plans in order to deliver high quality health care to all Americans at an affordable price.

SUGGESTED READINGS

This is a constantly evolving area. Many of the numbers cited are from the following sites, which can be used for updates and further details.

http://www.kff.org/
  This is a nonpartisan source of facts, information, and analysis for policymakers, the media, the health care community, and the public. Information is always provided free of charge, and includes the most sophisticated policy research, as well as basic facts and numbers. The Kaiser Family Foundation is not associated with Kaiser Permanente or Kaiser Industries.

http://www.cms.hhs.gov/MedicareEnRpts/
  This website provides the latest information on Medicare coverage including Hospital Insurance (HI) or Part A and Supplementary Medical Insurance (SMI) or Part B. This site also contains various Medicare enrollment tables. There are national and state enrollment trends, state enrollment by aged, disabled and all, as well as county level enrollment.

http://www.cms.hhs.gov/MedicareMedicaidStatSupp/

The Medicare and Medicaid Statistical Supplement CD offers approximately 300 pages of statistical information about Medicare, Medicaid, and other Centers for Medicare & Medicaid Services (CMS) programs. The Supplement includes charts and tables showing health expenditures for the entire U. S. population, characteristics of the covered populations, use of services, and expenditures under these programs. It is one of the most comprehensive sources of information available on health care finance in the U. S.

http://www.cdc.gov/nchs/data/hus/hus09.pdf

Annual volumes produced by the National Center for Health Statistics provide a wealth of data on Health Status and Determinants, Use of Health Resources and Health Care Expenditures and Insurance. The volumes are entitled, e.g., Health, United States, 2009.

http://content.healthaffairs.org/

Health Affairs provides up to date information on current health care policy and health care economics.

Part 6

Appendices

Appendix A
USMLE Type Questions

Chapter 1: Brain, Mind, and Behavior

1. A young woman has just been told that there is a mass in one of her breasts that may be malignant. Which of the following brain processes is most likely to be impaired as she listens to the explanation of the physician?
   A. Implicit memory
   B. Encoding and storage of memory
   C. Retrieval of memory
   D. Short-term memory
   E. Long-term memory

2. The presence of mirror neurons in the brain enables people to do which of the following?
   A. Conceptualize spatial images as they would be in reverse
   B. Create empathy by feeling what another person is feeling
   C. Make maps of the internal intentional state of another person's mind
   D. Reflect back to someone else how they appear to others
   E. Connect across the two hemispheres of the brain

3. Which of the following is true about implicit memory?
   A. It does not require conscious, focal attention to be encoded
   B. It requires the hippocampus to be activated
   C. It includes autobiographical memory
   D. It becomes available in the second year of life
   E. It is remembered in narrative form

Chapter 2: Families, Relationships, and Health

1. A young man who is a cancer survivor states that the cancer experience has given him a better sense of what is important in life. This is an example of

A. posttraumatic stress
B. denial
C. posttraumatic growth
D. identification with the aggressor
E. projection

2. A young woman with schizophrenia lives with her parents, who are deeply emotionally involved in her life and are very critical of her appearance, behavior, and friends. Which of the following is the best statement about the impact of this type of relationship on the course of her illness?
   A. It will result in a need for more medication
   B. It will mean she has fewer relapses
   C. It will result in a need for less medication
   D. She is more likely to be paranoid
   E. She is more likely to be withdrawn

3. The two distinct components of emotional support for patients which have been found to be related to religion or spirituality are best described as which of the following?
   A. Inner peace and meditation
   B. Social support and personal faith
   C. Denial and rationalization
   D. Ritual and dogma
   E. Charismatic leader and social norms

Chapter 3: Birth, Childhood, and Adolescence

1. A 3-year-old child is brought in for a screening physical examination prior to starting preschool. Which of the following would be considered developmentally *inappropriate* for a child of this age?
   A. The child throws a temper tantrum when she cannot get a toy she wants

B. The child is afraid of sitting on the toilet, as she fears she will get flushed away

C. She sometimes has "accidents" with her urine and feces

D. Her articulation makes her speech sometimes difficult to understand

E. She has a vocabulary of about 10 words

2. A 14-month-old child is hospitalized with "failure to thrive." Which of the following is best describes what this diagnosis means?

A. The child is unhappy although the family situation is good

B. The child is small for age without any major medical diagnosis

C. The child has multiple organ failure

D. The child is being abused and is withdrawn

E. The child is anxious and cries when separated from the mother

3. Which of the following is the best statement about the concept of temperament?

A. It is a set of inborn traits that organize the child's approach to the world

B. It is the environmentally determined way a child responds to the world

C. It is the term used to describe how a child manages aggression and anger

D. It is the term used to describe personality in children

E. It is the term used to describe how anxious or depressed a child is

Chapter 4: Early Adulthood and the Middle Years

1. Triangulation in a family relationship is best explained by which of the following descriptions?

A. A child pitting his or her parents against each other to get his own way

B. Use of a third person to avoid direct confrontation between two people

C. Use of the family to avoid dealing with issues at work

D. Use of work to avoid being with a spouse or children

E. Struggle between two parents over who is closest to a child

2. Which of the following is true about women working outside the home compared to homemakers?

A. Divorce rates have decreased as more women have entered the work force.

B. Career-oriented women are more likely to marry

C. Working women report worse mental and emotional health

D. The risk of divorce increases with the amount of the woman's income

E. The risk of divorce decreases with the amount of the woman's income

3. According to Erickson, a key developmental issue of young adulthood is best characterized by which of the following?

A. Making a contribution to the world

B. Making an impression on the next generation

C. Achieving the capacity for intimacy

D. Becoming close to one's family of origin

E. Dealing with financial concerns

Chapter 5: Old Age

1. Which of the following is a true statement about changes in brain function and structure associated with "normal" aging?

A. Decrease in cerebral spinal fluid

B. Decrease in communication skills

C. Decrease in brain volume

D. Decrease in ventricular size

E. Decrease in primary and tertiary memory

2. Living situations for older people in which housing and meals are provided as well as limited help with everyday living activities and transportation are called which of the following?

A. Board and care

B. Assisted living

C. Elder hostels

D. Skilled nursing facilities

E. Retirement homes

3. Which of the following best describes the responsibility of the physician regarding driving by elderly patients?

A. Identify those persons who may be unsafe to drive

B. Tell patients to stop driving when they are over 85

C. Determine driving competency

D. Keep patients independently driving as long as possible

E. Tell patients to stop driving when they are over 75

Chapter 6: Death, Dying, and Grief

1. A 34-year-old woman recently diagnosed with an astrocytoma appears quite cheerful despite the poor prognosis of her tumor. When told the location of the tumor

makes surgical resection impossible, she appears unaffected. Using the typology of Kubler-Ross's stages of dying, which of the following is the most likely stage of this patient?

A. Anger
B. Denial
C. Bargaining
D. Depression
E. Acceptance

2. A young woman is concerned about her 68-year-old father who recently lost his wife to lung cancer. Based on the literature on bereavement, which of the following is the most accurate statement about the implications of this stress on the father's health?

A. He is at greater risk for psychiatric problems, but not for medical illness
B. He is at greater risk for death of all causes
C. He is greater risk for lung cancer, given the exposure to his wife's illness
D. He is likely to become noncompliant with treatment of his own illnesses
E. He is at no greater risk of illness on the basis of his loss

3. A 58-year-old man with end-stage liver disease states that he is not interested in pursuing a liver transplant, saying "I have lived long enough, and others need the transplant more than me." Which of the following is the best clinical response to this statement?

A. Treat him for depression as he is clearly suicidal
B. Tell him he owes it to his family to have the liver transplant
C. Have him psychiatrically evaluated for suicidality
D. Assess whether he understand the options and consequences
E. Document that he has made a decision, and take him off the list

Chapter 7: Chronic Pain

1. Which of the following is the appropriate term for contingent withdrawal of an aversive stimulus when and only when the behavior occurs?

A. Negative reinforcement
B. Positive reinforcement
C. Punishment
D. Extinction
E. Classical conditioning

2. Which of the following is the most accurate statement about factors contributing to chronic pain behavior?

A. Dramatic pain behavior indicates influence of operant factors
B. Observed behavior is consistent with self-report of behavior
C. Behavior is influenced by both positive and negative reinforcement
D. Functional disability is directly related to pain intensity
E. Behavior is consistent with conscious motivation and goals

3. Which of the following is a therapeutic approach to chronic pain which addresses how patients perceive and understood their pain and their expectations and hopes for treatment?

A. Biofeedback
B. Cognitive-behavioral therapy
C. Physical therapy
D. Mindfulness meditation
E. Trigger point injections

Chapter 8: Stress and Illness

1. Homeostasis is best defined as which of the following?

A. A state of activation in response to stress
B. The tendency for the body to maintain an optimal state
C. The ability of the body to convert food into energy
D. A developmental stage in males
E. A state of relaxation following intense exertion

2. The chronic sympathetic nervous system activation that characterizes a stress response triggers the release of glucocorticoids into the blood, resulting in which of the following?

A. Decreased angiogenesis
B. An autoimmune condition
C. Suppression of the immune system
D. Proliferation of killer T cells
E. Increased peripheral blood glucose levels

3. A 35-year-old man has decided to quit his pack-a-day cigarette smoking to help resolve his chronic bronchial distress. Despite a nicotine patch, he finds he has cravings after each meal, during coffee breaks, and at social gatherings. Which of the following best explains these episodic cravings?

A. A genetic predisposition to nicotine addiction
B. Avoidance of nicotine withdrawal symptoms reinforces smoking
C. Nicotine cravings conditioned to cue situations
D. Culturally reinforced smoking behavior
E. Modeling of smoking behavior by his parents when he was young

Chapter 9: Addictions

1. An 18-year-old man presents in the clinic requesting treatment for cocaine abuse. Which of the following is the best evidence-based treatment for cocaine abuse?
   A. Modafinil
   B. Cognitive behavioral therapy
   C. Naltrexone
   D. Insight-oriented psychotherapy
   E. Bupropion

2. Which of the following is an FDA-approved treatment for opioid dependence, including treatment of withdrawal?
   A. Buprenorphine
   B. Naltrexone
   C. Acamprosate
   D. Disulfiram
   E. Varenicline

3. Different drugs of abuse exert actions on many different transmitter systems. On the other hand, they have some attributes in common. What do they commonly facilitate?
   A. Dopamine metabolism in the striatum
   B. Dopamine release in the nucleus accumbens
   C. Dopamine reuptake in the substantia nigra
   D. Mesolimbic serotonin release
   E. Serotonin release in the amygdala

Chapter 10: Psychodynamic Approaches to Human Behavior

1. A physician has just told a patient that he has liver cancer. In response to a question from the patient concerning his prognosis and treatment, the physician launches into a lengthy and highly technical discussion of age-corrected mortality rates and double-blind studies of chemotherapy. Which of the following is the defense mechanism this physician appears to be using?
   A. Intellectualization
   B. Displacement
   C. Projection
   D. Repression
   E. Regression

2. A medical student makes a conscious effort to temporarily set aside his marital difficulties to study for the next examination. This is an example of which of the following?
   A. Undoing
   B. Denial

C. Sublimation
D. Turning against self
E. Suppression

3. A patient is angry at his physician for being late for an appointment, but is not comfortable confronting her directly. Instead, he tells the physician how angry he was with a colleague earlier in the day while the colleague kept him waiting while he met with another employee. This is an example of which of the following defense mechanisms?
   A. Reaction formation
   B. Repression
   C. Identification
   D. Displacement
   E. Fixation

Chapter 11: Facilitating Health Behavior Change

1. Which of the following best describes the role of physicians in relation to facilitating health behavior change in patients?
   A. Physicians diagnose and treat illness, not behavior
   B. Physicians provide information about the impact of health behavior
   C. Physicians require compliance with health behavior plans
   D. Physicians help patients to find motivation to change
   E. Physicians tell patients what they need to do

2. Which of the following is the best description of the response to proposed behavior change of patients in the *preparation stage* according to the Transtheoretical Model?
   A. Tend to resist any proposed behavior change
   B. Require the most commitment to change in terms of time and energy
   C. Do not plan to change their behavior in the next 6 months
   D. Have not yet resolved their ambivalence toward changing
   E. Need the physician to tell them what to do next

3. The health care provider's role in Motivation Interviewing is best described as which of the following?
   A. Invite the patient to consider new information and offer new perspectives
   B. Inform the patient of the best course of action
   C. Refrain from discussing health behavior change with the patient

D. Make sure the patient knows how dangerous their current behavior is

E. Bring in others to confront the patient with the need to change

Chapter 12: Human Sexuality

1. A 35-year-old man has come to the outpatient medicine clinic for an "executive physical" for his new job in management at a large advertising company. He was married 6 months ago. As part of the thorough history, he states that he has been having ejaculation problems almost immediately after vaginal penetration. His wife has been very frustrated by this and has pleaded with him to get some help. Which of the following is a true statement to use in advising this man about his problem?

A. Psychological issues are the primary cause in the majority of such cases

B. This is a rare problem, occurring in less than 5% of men

C. One useful approach to this problem is the "squeeze" technique

D. This is normal at this stage of the marriage and needs no treatment

E. There is nothing that can be done, so his wife needs to learn to live with it

2. A 22-year-old woman comes to her gynecologist at her husband's urging. She has recently admitted to him that she finds intercourse painful, and he thinks there must be something wrong with her. Which of the following is the best first response to this young woman?

A. Reassure her that intercourse should not be painful, and that there are things that can be done to help her

B. Tell her that this kind of problem is almost never anatomical, and recommend that she seek marital counseling

C. Advise her that this is usually the result of a current or past vaginal infections, and start asking about the number of past sexual partners

D. Counsel her that pain on intercourse usually reflects experience with sexual abuse, and ask her if her father molested her as a child

E. Assure her that intercourse should not be painful, that her husband must not be doing it right, and suggest sex therapy

3. You see a 45-year-old man who is a long-time patient of yours for a check-up. You know that he was widowed 5 years ago and recently remarried, and so you ask him about it. He comments that he is more active and happy now, with a companion who shares his interests in camping and hiking. However, he admits with a little embarrassment that he is concerned about one thing. "My first wife always liked sex, and we could really satisfy each other, if you know what I mean. With Dora, I don't seem to be enough." Using gentle questions, you learn that his new wife does not have an orgasm during sexual intercourse, but rather requires additional clitoral stimulation. Which of the following is your best response to this situation?

A. Recommend marital counseling, as there is clearly something wrong in the relationship

B. Reassure him that most women do not have orgasms with sexual intercourse alone

C. Prescribe something to allow him to maintain an erection longer, so he can satisfy his wife

D. Suggest he use a condom, to allow him to delay ejaculation

E. Tell him that at his age sex is not as important as it was in his 20s

Chapter 13: Medical Student and Physician Well-Being

1. A third-year medical student is holding a retractor in the operating room during surgery. She observes that one of the surgical residents is repeatedly making sexual comments to a fourth-year student who is also in the OR. The other student appears very uncomfortable, but is not saying anything. Which of the following is the most useful approach to this situation?

A. Speak with the other student afterward and offer to help speak with the attending about the resident

B. Speak with the other student afterward and commiserate about the sexualized culture of surgery

C. Join in the sexual joking with the resident, to distract attention from the other student

D. Speak up immediately, and angrily tell the resident that this is inappropriate behavior

E. Immediately report the resident to the Chairman of Surgery

2. While on his Obstetrics and Gynecology clerkship, a third-year medical student is told to help the attending with a procedure. Once in the room, the student realizes that the procedure is a second trimester surgical abortion. He is a deeply religious Catholic and is horrified that he is expected to participate in something he views as murder. Which of the following is the best approach to this situation?

A. Participate and then report the attending for power abuse

B. Ask to observe rather than participate

C. Ask to be excused and briefly explain why

D. Participate and make arrangements so it does not happen again

E. Reconsider the choice to become a physician

3. A first-year medical student finds himself struggling as he prepares for his first examination in medical school. He has always had trouble with multiple-choice question exams, but was able to do well in college because he spent a lot of time studying—and it was always clear what the teachers wanted you to know. Now he feels that the amount of material is overwhelming, and the sample exam questions take too long for him to read to complete a test in the time allotted. Which of the following is the best approach for this student?

A. Do the best he can and be ready to drop out if he fails the exam

B. Do the best he can on the exam and seek help if he fails

C. Contact the Dean's office or Office of Disabilities for help

D. Find out from the professors exactly what will be on the exam

E. Reconsider the choice to become a physician

4. Two second-year medical students who are in a small learning group together notice alcohol on the breath of another student in the group. Talking about the student together, they realize she has been late to class a lot recently, appears irritable, and has lost a lot of weight. Which of the following is the best interpretation and next step for these two students to take regarding their observations?

A. Assume she is stressed, but it is her business, and leave her alone

B. Assume she is stressed and needs support, and invite her to some social events

C. Assume she is stressed and impaired, and report her to the Dean's office

D. Assume she is stressed and ill, and start asking others if she has HIV

E. Assume she is stressed and depressed, and encourage her to seek help

Chapter 14: Medical Ethics

1. Which of the following is considered one of the four basic principles of medical ethics?

A. Maleficence

B. Confidentiality

C. Informed consent

D. Respect for autonomy

E. Trust

2. In which of the following situations do the principles of beneficence and nonmaleficence come into conflict for the physician treating a pregnant woman?

A. The fetus is diagnosed with a heart condition that must be treated with surgery immediately after birth

B. The mother is diagnosed with leukemia during the second trimester, which should be treated with chemotherapy

C. The mother requests help in stopping smoking

D. The father asks for the medical records of his wife

E. The mother asks not to be told the gender of the baby after the ultrasound

3. A 52-year-old woman is diagnosed with breast cancer. The prognosis is good with mastectomy, but she says she is not going to pursue any further treatment as she "cannot face that surgery." What two principles of medical ethics are in conflict in this case?

A. Respect for autonomy versus justice

B. Nonmaleficence versus justice

C. Confidentiality versus nonmaleficence

D. Beneficence versus respect for autonomy

E. Justice versus confidentiality

Chapters 15: The Physician-Patient Relationship

1. Which of the following statements about the placebo effect is true?

A. Certain personality types predictably respond to placebos

B. Once a patient knows it is a placebo, it loses all effectiveness it had

C. Placebos work for pain, but not for objectively measurable problems

D. Placebo responses can be long-lasting

E. Placebos do not cause side effects

2. Which of the following is the factor that has been shown to best predict a patient's self-report of symptom improvement?

A. The physician's choice of the most effective drug

B. The patient's sense of being fully listened to at the visit

C. How long the physician has known the patient

D. How thorough a physical exam was conducted

E. The patient's education and income level

3. Which of the following is the best statement of why the patient's story of the illness is important for healing?

A. Patients like to feel they are the center of attention during office visits

B. Patients believe in anecdotal evidence, not scientific fact

C. The story conveys the meaning of the illness, and meaning is essential to healing

D. The story may include diagnostic clues the physician missed while taking the history

E. Telling the story is a helpful emotional catharsis for the patient

Chapter 16: Communicating with Patients

Which of the following is the best approach if there is a discrepancy between a patient's description of his or her mood and what the physician observes in the patient's body language?

A. Confrontation

B.

Silence

C. Facilitation

D. Direct questions

E. Transition statement

2. A young physician is interviewing an elderly woman who asks him how old he is. Which of the following would be the best response to her question?

A. I am sorry but I do not answer personal questions

B. I am 28 years old but I'm very well trained

C. You seem concerned about my youth. Don't worry. You're in good hands

D. Perhaps you're concerned as to whether I can be of help to you

E. I just look young. I know what I am doing

3. A patient informs the physician during an initial interview that he is having mood swings. Which of the following would be the most useful response for the physician to make?

A. You don't seem unusually depressed to me

B. What do you mean by mood swings?

C. We have some very effective treatments for bipolar disorder

D. What else is troubling you?

E. Have you been abusing alcohol or drugs?

Chapter 17: Diagnostic Reasoning

1. The proportion of all patients with the condition who are correctly identified with a positive test result is best described as which of the following?

A. The test's specificity

B. The test's sensitivity

C. The test's predictive value

D. The test's likelihood ratio

E. The test's probability

2. Expert clinicians generally hold that a correct diagnosis is identified in the vast majority of undifferentiated patients using which of the following?

A. A skillfully elicited history

B. A careful and complete physical examination

C. Judiciously chosen blood tests

D. Appropriate imaging studies

E. Consultation with an expert team

3. When a test has fairly high sensitivity and specificity, which of the following results when it is applied in a population with a very low prevalence of the target condition?

A. Most of the positive test results will be true positives

B. Most of the positive test results will be false positives

C. Most of the negative test results will be false negatives

D. Few of the negative test results will be true positives

E. Few of the positive test results will be false positives

Chapter 18: Patient Assessment

1. Which of the following is the best description of the unique feature of projective tests of personality?

A. Use of ambiguous test stimuli to which the person responds

B. Use of objective norms against which to evaluate the person

C. Use of large numbers of true/false questions

D. Use of the results to predict behavior in the future

E. Use of different versions for different ages

2. A 48-year-old man with chronic alcohol abuse presents for evaluation of forgetfulness. A previous note in his chart states that he has exhibited confabulation. Which of the following best describes what has been observed?

A. The patient deliberating feigned impairment in memory

B. The patient had no short-term memory impairment

C. The patient denied impairment in memory despite obvious failures

D. The patient made a variety of implausible excuses for the memory failures

E. The patient reported events and experiences which never actually occurred

3. Which of the following best describes the meaning of an IQ score?

A. A person's genetically determined capabilities
B. How a person's mental age compares to his chronological age
C. How a person compares to others in his age group
D. A person's maximum capabilities
E. A person's educational performance level

Chapter 19: Recognizing and Treating Psychopathology in Primary Care

1. Approximately 80% of deaths in which of the following age groups are from accidents, homicide, or suicide?
   A. 15 to 19 years
   B. 20 to 29 years
   C. 30 to 39 years
   D. 40 to 49 years
   E. Over 50 years

2. Many children experience difficulties with emotional regulation, the ability to direct and modify intense feelings, and impulse control. Which of the following is an example of an "externalizing problem" due to poor emotional regulation?
   A. Worrying a lot
   B. Feeling hopeless
   C. Feeling sad and unhappy
   D. Taking unnecessary risks
   E. Fear of new situations

3. Fetal alcohol spectrum disorder (FASD) typically results in which of the following?
   A. Widened palpebral fissures
   B. An accentuated philtrum
   C. A thick upper lip
   D. Growth deficiencies
   E. An enlarged head

Chapter 20: Managing Difficult Patients

1. A 32-year-old man presents to the Emergency Department requesting pain medication. The man has a swollen left knee and gives a history consistent with an ACL tear. However, the amount of pain the patient reports is more that is usual for this type of injury. Which of the following is the best approach to this patient?
   A. Give the patient as much pain medication as he wants in the ED, but nothing to take home
   B. Give the patient the usual amount of pain medication given for that type of injury, to take as needed
   C. Don't give any pain medication, as the patient is clearly seeking drugs
   D. Titrate the pain medication and instruct the patient about a regular schedule of pain medication with a taper
   E. Give the patient mild medication but tell him it is very strong

2. A 25-year-old woman with cystic breast disease has been calling the outpatient clinic almost daily, with questions about diet, herbs, acupuncture, massage, and different types of mammograms. Her grandmother died of breast cancer at age 40, so her concern is understandable, but overwhelming. Which of the following is the best approach to this patient?
   A. Tell her she is only allowed to call once a week
   B. Give her the nurses' pager number, so she can feel there is always someone who can answer her questions
   C. Set up frequent and regular visits with the doctor and/or nurse
   D. Recommend she see a surgeon about a prophylactic mastectomy
   E. Tell her she clearly is psychiatrically ill and give her benzodiazepines

3. A 48-year-old woman with a 20-year history of diabetes mellitus is seen in the outpatient diabetes clinic for her regular visit. One of the staff cringes as she sees the patient walk in, saying that the patient never follows her diet or exercise plans. Which of the following would be the best recommendation to the staff for approaching this patient?
   A. Have the patient meet another patient who is blind and has lost her leg to diabetes, to impress upon her the risks
   B. Assess what it is about the plan that seems too difficult to do, and how the patient could be helped to feel able to do it
   C. Tell the patient that she is letting everyone in the clinic down by not taking care of herself when they are all trying to help her
   D. Set up the appointments so that the patient does not come on the day that staff person works in the clinic
   E. Suggest to the patient that she may be happier with another doctor

Chapter 21: The Humanities and the Practice of Medicine

No questions

Chapter 22: Culturally Competent Health Care

1. Illnesses like "the evil eye" *(mal ojo)* and *susto* are best understood as which of the following?
   A. Primitive conceptualizations of psychiatric illness
   B. A culturally defined health belief
   C. Religious explanations of psychiatric illness
   D. Superstitions that keep people from getting health care
   E. Uneducated versions of hysterical illness

2. Which is the most appropriate response to parents who are refusing surgical correction of a child's deformity because they see the deformity as a punishment from God?
   A. Call social services, as this is child neglect
   B. Tell the parents that this is not how we do things in the United States
   C. Consult the family's religious leader, to see if this is the general belief
   D. Do the surgery anyway, as the parents are clearly psychotic
   E. Discharge the child and family from care, as uncooperative

3. A 60-year-old man presents with liver disease. He has failed to stop drinking alcohol despite several warnings of how dangerous this is for him. He states that drinking is a part of the healing ceremonies his culture requires, and it would be shameful for him to refuse. Which of the following is the best approach to this situation?
   A. Refuse to treat him unless he stops drinking
   B. Ask if there is any way for him to drink less, or to use a substitute
   C. Tell him the alcohol does more harm than the ceremonies are doing good
   D. Ask him to help you understand about the role of alcohol in his culture
   E. Ask his wife to come in, and tell her he is killing himself

Chapter 23: Complementary, Alternative, and Integrative Medicine

1. A 24-year-old woman comes to the internal medicine clinic requesting acupuncture for her cocaine cravings. She has recently completed a drug rehabilitation program and has not used cocaine in over a month. However, she is experiencing severe cravings, which make it difficult for her to concentrate in graduate school, and has heard from others that acupuncture can help. Which of the following is the best approach to her question?
   A. Tell her there is no real evidence of the effectiveness of acupuncture
   B. Refer her to a psychiatrist, as she clearly needs more help
   C. Tell her it is better to stay with one modality of approach
   D. Discuss acupuncture as one of the options in a full care plan
   E. Reluctantly refer her to an acupuncturist, while telling her it won't work

2. A 72-year-old man is in the intensive care unit with congestive heart failure. The nursing staff is upset when the family asks to bring a "healer" to visit in the ICU. Which of the following is the best response to this request?
   A. Tell the family that this is not permitted and try to make alternative arrangements
   B. Tell the nurses that the patient is dying anyway, so they should let the family do what they want
   C. Find out what type of intervention is proposed and whether this would be safe in an ICU setting
   D. Ask the social worker to educate the family about hospitals in the United States
   E. Make arrangements to discharge the patient to a hospice setting, where these things can be set up

3. Which of the following is true about the use of complementary and alternative medicine (CAM) in the United States?
   A. Over 60% of the population reports using some CAM in the past 12 months
   B. CAM is most often used for acute pain
   C. Most of the evidence supporting use of CAM is from randomized, controlled trials
   D. CAM is most often used by people who are not well educated
   E. Most people who use CAM in the Unites States are not citizens

4. Which of the following best describes the quality control mechanism in the United States for herbal medications and dietary supplements?
   A. The Food and Drug Administration evaluates them like any other medications
   B. The Federal Trade Commission monitors them for truth in advertising
   C. There is no federal regulation of herbal supplements because they are considered food
   D. There is no need for federal regulation, as they have no medical effect
   E. There is no need for federal regulation, as they are natural and thus safe

Chapter 24: The Impact of Social Inequalities on Health Care

1. According to the Surgeon General's *Supplement to the Report on Mental Health*, entitled *Mental Health: Culture, Race, and Ethnicity*, which of the following specific ethnic groups living in the United States is most overrepresented in the homeless and incarcerated populations as well as child welfare system?
   A. African Americans
   B. Hispanics
   C. American Indians
   D. Asian Americans

2. According to the Surgeon General's *Supplement to the Report on Mental Health*, entitled *Mental Health: Culture, Race, and Ethnicity*, which of the following specific ethnic groups living in the United States has the highest suicide rate?
   A. African Americans
   B. Hispanics
   C. American Indians
   D. Asian Americans

3. Which is of the following is relatively equally represented across all ethnic groups in the United States?
   A. Cardiovascular disease
   B. Liver transplantation
   C. Diabetes
   D. Stroke
   E. Mental illness

Chapter 25: Health Services in the United States

1. Which of the following is the term used for the traditional type of reimbursement insurance in which insurance companies bear the risk for medical care expenditures, reimburse a fixed percentage of billed charges, and impose no restrictions on the patient's choice of provider or services used?
   A. Preferred provider organization
   B. Health maintenance organization
   C. Indemnity health insurance
   D. Individual practice association
   E. Defined contribution plans

2. The current standard Medicare plan covers which of the following?
   A. Hearing aids
   B. Eyeglasses
   C. Long-term care
   D. Dialysis
   E. Transportation to appointments

3. As of 1/1/2010, which of the following groups do not automatically have access to federal health insurance in the United States?
   A. Veterans
   B. People over 65 years old
   C. People on welfare who have HIV/AIDS
   D. People with disabilities
   E. Healthy young adults

Appendix B
Answers to USMLE Type Questions

Chapter 1: Brain, Mind, and Behavior

1. B is correct. High emotional stress impairs the immediate tasks of learning, encoding, and storage of memory, but not retrieval. Implicit memory is nonverbal memory, which is likely to be enhanced, not impaired, under these high stress circumstances.
2. C is correct. Mirror neurons make maps of the internal intentional state of another person's mind by creating in the viewer the sense that they are doing it as well. Although this has implications for empathy, it is less about emotion than about intentionality.
3. A is correct. Implicit memory is among the earliest forms of memory and does not require focused attention or activation of the hippocampus to be encoded. It is not in narrative, nor is it a part of autobiographical memory.

Chapter 2: Families, Relationships, and Health

1. C is correct. Posttraumatic growth is reported by many cancer survivors, who say that the traumatic event caused them to re-evaluate their priorities. They report finding more meaning in life and not worrying so much about things that now appear trivial to them.
2. A is correct. Emotional overinvolvement and criticalness by family members exacerbate psychotic conditions, leading to more relapse and a need for more medications. No specific type of symptoms is related to this type of family interaction.
3. B is correct. The social (instrumental) support of a community of believers is a separate component of support from the support of an implicit sense of meaning or faith. Inner peace and meditation are both more private components of spiritual support, while the charismatic leader and social norms as well as ritual and dogma are all more extrinsic components of religious support. Denial and rationalization are classic psychodynamic de-

fense mechanisms—not valuable aspects of spirituality for support.

Chapter 3: Birth, Childhood, and Adolescence

1. E is correct. A child of 4 years should be able to speak in simple sentences, so this child's language is quite delayed. She will not yet have complete control of bowel and bladder, and articulation may be still difficult. Cognitive development is such that magical thinking is quite normal.
2. B is correct. Failure to thrive refers to growth failure in a young child without obvious medical reasons. It is a description of the problem, but does not indicate the etiology. The child is often not eating properly, which may or may not be the result of anxiety, depression, or abuse.
3. A is correct. Temperament is genetically determined and helps to shape the way that a child interacts with the environment. It thus has an impact on aggression, anger, anxiety, and depression, but it is not any of these. It contributes to, but is not equivalent to, the development of personality.

Chapter 4: Early Adulthood and the Middle Years

1. B is correct. Triangulation is the use of a third person to avoid direct confrontation between two people. This is most classically done by having a child serve as a distraction from marital problems between the parents, or by having an outside sexual partner rather than confronting sexual problems in a marriage.
2. D is correct. Although it remains true that the increase in women in the work force has correlated with in-

creased divorce rates, working women report better mental and emotional health than homemakers. Career-oriented women are still less likely to marry than those who are working in other types of jobs, and those who make more money are more likely to divorce. However, one must be careful about all of these correlates, as they do not reveal the directionality of the relationship. It may well be that women who have their own incomes are more able to leave unhappy marriages than those without adequate incomes, rather than that working makes women less happy in marriages. It also may be that women who are less healthy emotionally are less able to get employment, rather than that their being at home leads to emotional distress. This will undoubtedly continue to be researched!

4. C is correct. Erickson saw each phase of life as having a major developmental task. For young adulthood, he described it as achieving the capacity for intimacy. This often involves some distancing from the family of origin. Dealing with financial concerns is a major task of middle adulthood. Generativity, which includes making a contribution and an impression on the next generation, would be situated in late adult life.

Chapter 5: Old Age

1. C is correct. The total brain volume decreases over time, which in turn increases ventricular size and may increase or leave cerebral spinal fluid volume the same. Communication skills do not decrease with normal aging. Although some aspects of memory do decrease with aging, these do not include primary or tertiary memory.

2. B is correct. An assisted-living setting provides help for those who have difficulties with instrumental activities of daily living such as shopping, cooking, laundry, cleaning, and driving by providing services similar to what would be found in a hotel: meals served in a dining room, shuttles, and housekeeping services. A board and care facility provides somewhat similar services, but in addition does some monitoring of the people, as they are usually there because of psychiatric rather than medical problems. Retirement communities are apartments or condominiums for older people, which have other amenities, such as shuttles and exercise facilities.

3. A is correct. Although physicians do have an obligation to determine whether it a patient is safe to drive (such as reporting those with seizure disorders), they need not try to stop people from driving at a certain age nor to determine competency.

Chapter 6: Death, Dying, and Grief

1. B is correct. This is denial—which in this system of thinking is a phase of adjustment and not a pathological response to dying.

2. B is correct. He is at increased risk of death from all causes. This does not appear to be due solely to nonadherence to treatment nor to psychiatric consequences of the loss, and it is clearly not due to contagion or toxic exposure. Rather, it appears to be the result of an interaction between grief and the body, probably mediated through the immune system, leaving one more vulnerable to a variety of illnesses.

3. D is correct. Any adult who refuses treatment must be assessed for truly informed consent. This means they need to understand that they have a problem, that there are options for treatment, and that they understand the possible consequences of those options. His decision can be neither automatically overruled nor accepted without such assessment. Psychiatric assessment might be indicated, but he is not clearly suicidal, simply based on this statement. Nor would it be appropriate to impose one's own views about transplantation on a patient.

Chapter 7: Chronic Pain

1. A is correct. Positive reinforcement works by *providing a reward* when (and only when) a particular behavior occurs; negative reinforcement works by contingently *withdrawing an aversive stimulus* when and only when the behavior occurs; punishment works by contingently *administering a negative stimulus* when and only when a behavior occurs; and extinction *decreases the frequency* of a behavior by discontinuing whatever was reinforcing it. All of these are principles of operant conditioning, not classical conditioning.

2. C is correct. Pain behavior is influenced by both positive and negative reinforcement, meaning it is influenced both by the positive outcomes related to the pain and the avoidance of negative things due to the pain. Functional disability is not closely related to the paint intensity, nor is the conscious motivation related to the pain behavior. Dramatic behavior rarely is actually associated with operant factors, which are intrinsic rewards of the behavior such as attention.

3. B is correct. Cognitive behavior therapy emerged from behaviorally oriented programs. Rather than focusing solely on changing overt behaviors, these programs address how patients perceive and understand their pain and what expectations and hopes they hold for treatment, control of pain, and for the future. They also address the personal losses that so often co-occur with

chronic pain as well as patients' emotional responses to pain and loss. Physical therapy is designed to improve strength, flexibility, and endurance without exacerbating pain. It helps patients to distinguish "good pain," i.e., harmless pain associated with building muscle, from "bad pain" or exercise that seriously exacerbates the underlying painful condition. Biofeedback monitors physiological responses (muscle tension, peripheral skin temperature, heart rate, and/or electrodermal responses) and then feeds this information back to the patient via an auditory or visual modality. Trigger point injections are acute interventions for a specific area of pain, and mindfulness meditation is a technique for relaxation and letting go of recurrent disturbing thoughts.

Chapter 8: Stress and Illness

1. B is correct. Homeostasis is the tendency for a body to maintain an optimal state of balance. It applies to many aspects of body function, such as the tendency of heart and lungs to become more active with physical exertion.
2. C is correct. Chronic stress leads to depression of the immune system. This would be the opposite of increasing killer T cells or causing an autoimmune reaction.
3. C is correct. Although cigarettes do lead to a nicotine addiction, which sustains smoking behavior, even with nicotine replacement the behavioral cues for smoking can set off episodic cravings, as anyone who has tried to quit smoking knows. This has to do with habitual behavioral and the environmental reminders of smoking, which lead to the craving.

Chapter 9: Addictions

1. B is correct. Cognitive-behavioral approaches have more of an evidence base than any other modality, including insight-oriented therapy and medications. Modafinil can help with excessive daytime sleepiness, which may be related to use of cocaine. Naloxone blocks the opiate receptors and is used for treatment of some other drugs of abuse. Bupropion is helpful in the treatment of nicotine cravings, and some new data suggests it may helpful for methamphetamine addiction, but it has not been shown to have much utility for cocaine abuse.
2. A is correct. Buprenorphine is a partial mu-agonist that binds tightly to the opioid receptor. By definition, partial agonists have a ceiling effect beyond which additional medication does not increase the effect. The implications for this are to limit the number of overdoses and the fatalities that would come from a full opioid agonist. Naltrexone is an opioid antagonist used for alcohol ad-

diction; it is thought to target the positive reinforcement properties of alcohol and would not be helpful in treating the symptoms of withdrawal from opioids. Acamprosate is a taurine-derived compound that targets NMDA receptors and glutamate tone in alcohol-dependent individuals. Disulfiram is used to treat alcohol addiction by blocking the second step in alcohol metabolism, resulting in the accumulation of acetaldehyde if a person consumes alcohol. Varenicline is a partial nicotinic agonist that binds to the alpha-4, beta-2 nicotine receptor located within the nucleus accumbens, and is used for smoking cessation.
3. B is correct. Evidence is accumulating to show that addictions affect similar brain regions. These fibers and centers associated with the ventral tegmental region of the brain stem and ending in the nucleus accumbens of the striatum and prefrontal cortex are known as the mesolimbic and mesocortical pathways. Lesions in these pathways have been shown to block the rewarding behavioral effects of addictive drugs. The primary neurotransmitter associated with these pathways is dopamine. This area, sometimes called the "pleasure center" of the brain, has been shown to be responsible for a wide variety of behaviors, including attention, pleasure, euphoria, reinforcements and salience (incentive), motivation.

Chapter 10: Psychodynamic Approaches to Human Behavior

1. A is correct. Intellectualization is a common defense used by physicians and researchers. It uses conceptual thinking to distance one from the emotional aspects of an emotionally charged event. Displacement would mean reacting to something else with the emotions appropriate to the charged event. Repression means unconsciously avoiding thinking or feeling about the charged event at all, and regression is reacting as though one were in an earlier developmental level. Projection is acting as though someone else is feeling what you are feeling.
2. E is correct. Suppression is a conscious attempt to keep an emotional response out of current awareness. Denial requires trying to say it was not true, and turning against self implies blaming. Undoing requires a symbolic way of making a reality feel untrue, and sublimation is burying the resulting feelings in something more acceptable to the individual.
3. D is correct. This is displacement of the current feeling to another circumstance. Reaction formation would mean that the anger was avoided by acting very happy with and being friendly to the doctor. Identification would have the patient taking on the same behavior as

the doctor. Fixation would be perseveration about that incident in future relationships with the doctor or in other similar relationships. Repression means unconsciously avoiding thinking or feeling about the incident, so the patient would not be aware of feeling any anger at all.

Chapter 11: Facilitating Health Behavior Change

1. D is correct. Although physicians do provide information on the impact of health behavior, this lies with the goal of helping patients find the motivation to change. They provide guidance, but ideally do not tell patients what to do nor require compliance.
2. D is correct. In the preparation stage, patients are still resolving their ambivalence to making changes. At all stages there is resistance to change, but this is not the most difficult stage, nor is it a stage in which no behavior change is anticipated in the next 6 months.
3. A is correct. The interaction between physician and patient is one of open discussion and sharing of information, with the patient being the decision-maker.

Chapter 12: Human Sexuality

1. C is correct. Premature ejaculation is quite treatable, and the "squeeze" technique is one useful approach. This condition should not be accepted as something one just has to live with, nor as a phase that will be "outgrown"—although the latter may well be true in some cases. It is a relatively common problem and is not entirely psychological, although excitement contributes to it.
2. A is correct. Dyspareunia, or pain during intercourse, is often due to problems that are relatively easily addressed, such as inadequate lubrication, vaginal infections, or abrasions. Marital counseling, sexual counseling, or further sexual history may be useful, but would not be the first response to this presenting statement.
3. B is correct. It is actually unusual for woman to consistently experience orgasm through the stimulation of sexual intercourse alone. Only 30% of women regularly achieve orgasm from sexual intercourse, 30% are unable to reach orgasm through sexual intercourse, and 40% have difficulty achieving orgasm from sexual intercourse alone. Helping him feel comfortable with other types of stimulation is all that appears necessary in this situation.

Chapter 13: Medical Student and Physician Well-Being

1. A is correct. The first step with someone you don't know is to speak with the other student and supportively see if something can be done jointly to address the situation. It might then be appropriate to report the resident, but it is best to make sure the other student is agreed to this approach. Joining in the banter or creating an angry confrontation might serve to distract attention from the other student, but does not actually resolve the problem. Simply accepting this as a cultural problem may be the easy way, but will not lead to changes.
2. C is correct. It is appropriate for a student or a physician to ask to be excused from participation in an activity that is inconsistent with that person's values and beliefs—within the boundaries of not abandoning the patient. A physician must be able to retain the integrity of his or her beliefs while dealing with people of many differing beliefs. This should not be a reason to drop out of medical school, but it is also not a power abuse situation—unless the attending forced the student to participate even after becoming aware of the problem.
3. C is correct. Medical schools truly want all of their students to graduate and will offer support for students who are able to do the work but need some accommodation or help with study skills. Not seeking or using help until after one has had multiple failures is a surprisingly common response for medical students, who are accustomed to being quite self-reliant. Finding out what is on the exam is probably an approach that worked in college, but it will be less effective in medical school and beyond.
4. E is correct. The first step with a colleague who may be impaired is to let them know that you have noticed, be supportive, and encourage them to get help. Ignoring it is not a good option, nor is just offering your social support if the person is truly impaired. Starting rumors is obviously wrong, but reporting it to the Dean's office may be the right thing to do—but only if they do not follow through after receiving encouragement to seek help themselves.

Chapter 14: Medical Ethics

1. D is correct. Nonmaleficence, beneficence, justice, and autonomy are the four basic principles.
2. B is correct. This is the conflict between doing good and not doing harm. Treating the mother for leukemia would result in damage to the fetus or in a premature birth. The others may have ethical issues, but not this conflict.
3. D is correct. Although you want to respect this woman's autonomy to make her own medical decisions, the prin-

ciple of beneficence, or doing good, is in conflict in this case, given her need for possibly life-saving treatment.

Chapters 15: The Physician-Patient Relationship

1. D is correct. The effect of a placebo can be long-lasting, as they create physiological changes in the body. This can happen even when patients find out it was a placebo. Because there are physiological changes, there can indeed be side effects of placebos. There is no specific personality that predicts response to placebos, and placebos can cause objectively measurable changes.
2. B is correct. The perception by a patient that they were really heard is not only one of the best predictors of the patient's satisfaction with the visit and treatment, but also predicts relief of symptoms. This is more important than the medication, how long the physician has known the patient, the education of the patient, and how complete a physical examination was done.
3. C is correct. Although the story may include information that is helpful, the key aspect of the story is the conveying of the meaning of the illness.

Chapter 16: Communicating with Patients

1. A is correct. Confrontation in this case means stating that one's observation is different from what has been said. It can be a very simple statement such as "you look sad." Facilitations refer to words or sounds that encourage the patient to keep talking, and transition statements help the physician to change to a new area of discussion or exploration. Both are useful, but not in this particular situation.
2. D is correct. Speaking to the concern behind the question is the best approach, and this can be in the form of a hypothesis, rather than a defense about one's competence.
3. B is correct. It is essential to know what the patient means by this term before any assumptions are made, be they about depression, alcohol, or bipolar disease. Changing the topic is not useful at this juncture.

Chapter 17: Diagnostic Reasoning

1. B is correct. A test's "sensitivity" states how well it performs in patients who have the target condition (accord-

ing to the gold standard). In other words, the sensitivity of a test is the proportion of all patients *with* the condition who have been correctly identified (positive test result, in our table, a/a + c). Specificity makes an analogous statement about how well the test performs in patients *without* the target condition, i.e., the proportion of all patients without the disease who have been correctly identified (negative test result, in our table d/b + d).
2. A. is correct. Expert clinicians generally hold that a correct diagnosis is identified through a skillfully elicited history in about 90% of all undifferentiated patients. However, this has not received objective confirmation. Regardless, following the history and the physical examination, the clinician makes one of two decisions: Either sufficient diagnostic certainty exists to allow treatment without further testing, or the clinician desires additional diagnostic tests to confirm the suspected diagnosis or to differentiate between multiple remaining possibilities. The need for additional testing, as well as the number and complexity of tests requested, differs dramatically between expert and novice.
3. B is correct. The proportion of patients in the population who have the target condition (also-called disease prevalence) has a dramatic impact on the information the test provides the clinician. For example, even when a test has fairly high sensitivity and specificity, when it is applied in a population with a very low prevalence, most of the positive test results will be false positives.

Chapter 18: Patient Assessment

1. A is correct. Projective tests use vague or ambiguous stimuli to encourage people to speak about their own thoughts. They have been validated to tell some things about the testtaker's personality. Although there are different versions for different ages, this is not unique to this type of psychological test. These tests do not have yes/no questions, are not objective, and are not predictive of future behavior any more than most other psychological tests are.
2. E is correct. Confabulation is an invention of events to cover for lapses of memory. It can sometimes be quite convincing and at other times is quite fantastic, but the goal is to fill in the missing pieces of history.
3. C is correct. The intelligence quotient gives an estimate of how a person's intellectual capability compares to the mean of others of that general age range (child, adolescent, or adult). The IQ is affected by environment, so it is not an indication of the maximum capability or the genetically determined capabilities. It is not a comparison of mental age to chronological age, although this is a common misunderstanding of it.

Chapter 19: Recognizing and Treating Psychopathology in Primary Care

1. A is correct. Over the past 60 years, the leading cause of death for adolescents has changed from natural causes to injury and violence. Overall mortality rates for young people rise by 239% when they reach ages 15 to 19, with violence responsible for this dramatic increase.

2. D is correct. *Externalizing* problems are described as failures of emotional regulation in which emotions are displayed in impulsive anger and attacks on other people or things. Examples of externalizing behaviors include fighting with others, taking unnecessary risks, and not understanding other's feelings. The other symptoms are examples of *internalizing* problems, in which inhibition or fear is the primary manifestation of failure of emotional regulation.

3. D is correct. Fetal alcohol spectrum disorder (FASD) refers to a range of mental and physical defects that develop in an unborn fetus when the mother drinks alcohol during pregnancy. The alcohol in the bloodstream crosses the placenta and interferes with normal development of the fetus. Some babies born with FASD have distinctive facial characteristics including short palpebral fissures, an indistinct philtrum, a thin upper lip, and small head. With or without these facial characteristics, children with FASD are often seriously handicapped with symptoms that include growth deficiencies, skeletal deformities, facial abnormalities, organ deformities, and central nervous system handicaps.

Chapter 20: Managing Difficult Patients

1. D is correct. Pain medication must be adjusted and titrated for each patient individually, with the understanding that anxiety increases the perception of pain. The physician has to be careful not to punish patients whom they view as drug-seeking, and to treat the pain without overreacting to requests for medication, which may speak to anxiety as much as pain.

2. C is correct. Patients who are anxious often communicate this with frequent requests for reassurance. Strict limits on office visits may backfire with increased emergency department visits. It is usually far better to set up regular ways to provide this reassurance, such as groups of regular visits, than to try to avoid them altogether or to violate regular boundaries by giving out private numbers.

3. B is correct. When a patient does not adhere to treatment recommendations, the temptation is to try to frighten, avoid, or shame the patient into doing what is "good for them." If the problem is seen as the patient feeling un-

able to do what is necessary, a different and more effective approach can be taken to help the patient feel more able to do what is needed.

Chapter 21: The Humanities and the Practice of Medicine

No questions

Chapter 22: Culturally Competent Health Care

1. B is correct. These "folk illnesses" are connected with a particular cultural set of beliefs, which are not necessarily religious. This does not necessarily reflect a primitive, hysterical, or superstitious approach in the pejorative sense in which these words are generally used. The illnesses are not all what would be considered psychiatric, although they could arguably be seen as due to mind-body interactions.

2. C is correct. Working with a religious leader is the best first approach. In this way, the physician can see if this is a usual belief of this group, or whether it is aberrant and represents a decision the religious leader may be able to change, or one that warrants one of the other approaches.

3. D is correct. By gaining more information and by conveying that the physician understands that this is important and is not easily set aside, one if more likely to learn what the issues really are and how best to approach them sensitively. All of the other options fail to communicate that this is a dilemma for this man, by presenting only one "correct" option.

Chapter 23: Complementary, Alterative, and Integrative Medicine

1. D is correct. The idea of acupuncture should be discussed as a part of the overall plan, with appropriate evaluation of the potential utility. Acupuncture has some evidence of utility in some situations, and a request for an exploration of this option should not trigger a psychiatric referral. However, simply making a referral is not adequate, particularly reluctantly, if you want the patient to continue to inform you about all of the options they are exploring for care in the future.

2. C is correct. Further exploration is the appropriate next step. It is not necessary to forbid all healing efforts that

are not part of Western medicine, even in the hospital. Nor is it necessary to use them only when a patient is dying. However, one must be aware that common rituals, such as those involving a lighted candle would not be safe in most hospital rooms.

3. A is correct. CAM is used by the majority of the population in the United States, most of whom are citizens. Well-educated people are more likely to use CAM, as are people with chronic rather than acute conditions. Most of the evidence regarding CAM at this point is descriptive, although studies are now being done to increase the evidence base.

4. B is correct. Herbal medications and dietary supplements are considered food, meaning that they are monitored by the Federal Trade Commission for truth in adverting and not by the Federal Drug Administration.

Chapter 24: The Impact of Social Inequalities on Health Care

1. A is correct. African Americans are overrepresented among the homeless and incarcerated populations as well as among those in the child welfare system.

2. C is correct. American Indians have a much higher rate of suicide than that of the dominant or Caucasian culture.

3. B is correct. Of this list, only liver transplantation has not been found to cause significant health disparities, possibly due to a national monitoring process.

Chapter 25: Health Services in the United States

1. C is correct. Indemnity health insurance was the most common type of insurance in the United States prior to 1988 and is still the model used for Medicare. All of the others listed either let others bear the risk for medical care expenditures or impose restrictions on the patient's choice of provider or services used.

2. D is correct. Dialysis is covered by Medicare even for people under the age of 65. "Medigap" policies are currently necessary to cover the costs of hearing aids, long-term care, and eyeglasses for people with the current standard Medicare plan. Transportation costs must be covered separately.

3. E is correct. At this point, unless healthy young adults are employed by the federal government, they must purchase health insurance on their own or through an employer.

Index